D0463167

973.92
A 1

DISCARDED

PASADENA CITY COLLEGE
LIBRARY
PASADENA, CALIFORNIA

AMERICA WANTS TO KNOW

AMERICA WANTS TO KNOW

THE ISSUES & THE ANSWERS OF THE EIGHTIES

Compiled by
Dr. George Gallup

A NORBACK BOOK

A&W PUBLISHERS, INC. • **New York**

Copyright © 1983 by George Gallup, Sr. and Norback & Company, Inc.

All rights reserved. No part of this work
may be reproduced or transmitted in any form
or by any means, electronic or mechanical,
including photocopying, recording, or any
information storage and retrieval system,
without permission in writing from the publisher.

Published in 1983 by
A & W Publishers, Inc.
95 Madison Avenue
New York, NY 10016

Manufactured in the United States of America
Designed by Diane Saxe

10 9 8 7 6 5 4 3 2 1

Library of Congress Cataloging in Publication Data
Main entry under title:

America wants to know.

   Includes index.
1. United States—Economic conditions—1971-
2. United States—Social conditions—1960-
3. Public opinion polls—United States. ʟI. Gallup,
George Horace, 1901-
III. Title.
HC106.8.A43   1983   973.927   82-13885

ISBN 0-89479-109-5

CONTENTS

OCT   1983

PREFACE

I S THERE ANY SCIENTIFIC EVIDENCE that God exists? How can we reduce crime? How many hours must a person work to pay his or her taxes?

Has anyone found a cure for heart attacks or cancer? Is anyone even close? Why can't the United States auto industry compete with the German and Japanese? Who actually governs the United States?

Why are families breaking up? What special advantages would a woman have as President?

These and other provocative questions are at the core of *America Wants to Know*, which explores concerns vital to Americans and provides insight into them from a wide variety of authoritative sources. In researching and writing *America Wants to Know*, we discovered a spirit of optimism pervading the nation. Americans are deeply concerned about a wide variety of serious issues and problems. But unlike the late 1970s, when individuals were pessimistic about their own futures and that of the American Dream, the mood is now upbeat, reflecting the belief that problems will be solved and times will get better. Because it focuses on contemporary issues of major consequence, *America Wants to Know* also provides an historical record of America's concerns in the 1980s, and offers clues to the nation's direction in the years ahead.

In collecting the material for this book, we departed significantly from conventional polling techniques. By soliciting the public's own questions, we turned the tables on the traditional polling practice of asking the public to respond to our questions. The questions were selected in two stages. First, members of our staff submitted questions they thought Americans wanted answered about the problems they face in their daily lives. In the second stage, we asked small groups of people what topics concerned them most. These two efforts produced hundreds of questions. The next step was to submit the questions most often asked to a panel of 526 ordinary citizens in all parts of the country. These individuals rated each question on a scale of one to ten, based on personal interests. Finally, the 100 questions given the highest ratings were presented to a wide variety of distinguished experts. Among those consulted were Isaac Asimov, Dr. Mary S. Calderone, Leon Jaworski, Rollo May, Dr. Michael E. DeBakey, Norman Cousins, Shirley M. Hufstedler, Dr. Linus Pauling, B. F. Skinner, Robert L. Heilbroner, Jean Mayer, and Julia Child.

The survey is organized by subject, each introduced by essays that are intended to provide a framework for a better understanding of contemporary issues.

America Wants to Know reflects broad areas of interest from economics and social issues to general and mental health, from industry and technology to the environment, politics, and foreign affairs. The questions and replies take a probing look at American life in general, often debunking myths and, in many instances, challenging widely accepted premises.

What emerges from this survey are the chief areas of concern today, among them the future course of the American economy. Questions about inflation, the budget, mounting federal deficits, and taxes are prominent. Social issues are highlighted in concern about crime, race relations, prisons, drugs, addiction, and the changing nature of the population. The survey identifies some significant shifts in our goals and expectations, in our views on education, and our perceptions of the role the media take in shaping political processes and social change. Other questions deal with important personal commitments such as religion and its place in the individual's life, as well as its effects on a person's day-to-day decision-making.

Perhaps no subject touches every life as directly as health. What we eat, how we exercise, how we can avoid illness, how we can continue to function effectively as we get older, and how we should select proper medical care and pay a fair fee for it are concerns which occupy more and more of our time. We can see this by glancing at the best-seller lists where books on diet, health, and self-improvement predominate, or by looking out the window at the joggers and physical fitness enthusiasts. Part of this interest can be interpreted as an emphasis on the self and self-improvement. But in a larger sense, such interest represents a desire to improve the quality of one's life and enhance one's life-style both from a physical and mental standpoint. Indeed, our survey shows that the concept of health proceeds on the assumption that mental health is as important an ingredient for well-being as physical health. This idea is widely endorsed by mental-health experts, although Americans have not yet universally accepted it. The experts say that to enjoy life we need a balanced, positive attitude in dealing with problems.

Not surprisingly, sex is a major topic of interest. Americans seem to believe that enjoyment of sex is a desirable goal, one within the reach of healthy adults that is eminently pleasurable. How to enhance that pleasure—for oneself and for a partner—is something worth pursuing. How that goal can be achieved is what many people would like to know.

American society is undergoing a second revolution in health care. The first was the elimination of dread diseases. Now there seems to be an emphasis on preventive health care and an interest in dealing with every affliction. Are there any cures for allergies? Is there a successful cure for headaches? Effecting a cure may be as simple as taking a single treatment or as complex as altering a lifetime of habits. What is the best way to stop smoking? No one answer suffices, although it is interesting to note the implication in the question—that smoking is inherently harmful and that most smokers would like to stop. There is no simple vaccine for many of the health threats that now face Americans. Nor is it easy to change lifelong patterns. Half the battle, the experts say, is persuading people to assume responsibility for their own health. This can be seen quite clearly in the area of nutrition. What we tend to forget, the experts remind us, is that good food and good nutrition often are one and the same.

The answers about food and health concern not only those who love good food but everyone who wants to enjoy good health. What kinds of food will we be eating in the future? Julia Child, the famous cookbook author and TV personality, says, "I am concerned with fresh raw produce, which I think will continue to improve. Public demand will increasingly force an upgrading in quality all along the line. Once the public gets used to good food, it is not going to accept inferior substitutes." But Dr. Jean Mayer, president of Tufts University in Medford, Massachusetts, and for twenty-five years a professor of nutrition at Harvard, says, "It would be pleasant to be able to say that we will be eating more fresh, farm-grown foods. However, it is likely that the American diet will contain as many, if not more, processed foods." The questions also reflect serious concern over cancer, the second leading cause of death in the United States after heart disease. Linus Pauling, the Nobel Prize winner, uses this occasion to reiterate his belief in the values of vitamin C: "Several epidemiological studies have shown that a high concentration of vitamin C and vitamin A or other vegetables and fruits rich in these substances decreases the incidence of cancer significantly." The experts also point out that cancer is an all-inclusive term for a variety of diseases and that significant progress is being made toward understanding their complexity.

Offering evidence that inner belief is vital to the healing process, the experts explain how the brain functions in relation to the body. They also explain the interplay between psychology and physical functioning, par-

ticularly in the area of sexual dysfunction. Medical problems rarely
underlie cases of sexual dysfunction, the experts say, pointing to psychological causes that can be managed easily. This type of treatment and
the promise of biofeedback—the monitoring and use of blood pressure,
heart rate, muscle tension, and body surface temperatures to deal with
various anxieties—are rated highly by the experts for the treatment of
certain kinds of ailments.

For serious physical ills, the experts provide guidance to help the public
choose a "good" hospital. One recommendation is to investigate all local
hospitals while you are well in order to pick the one that best suits your
needs should you become ill. The experts note, however, that the choice
of a hospital may not be the patient's decision. "Patients select doctors;
doctors select hospitals," says Scott Fleming, senior vice-president of
Kaiser-Permanente Medical Care Program in Oakland, California.

After health, probably no other subject directly affects Americans as
much as the economy—particularly the state of their own pocketbooks.
In the late 1970s and early 1980s, recessions, high unemployment,
mounting federal budget deficits, and double-digit inflation encouraged a
gloomy attitude. Many Americans are anxious to know if inflation can
ever be brought under control or eliminated. Murray Weidenbaum,
chairman of President Reagan's Council of Economic Advisors, is one of
the experts addressing this question. Other questions in this section are
designed to find out how Americans can pay lower taxes, or whether a
better system can be devised to pay for government and social services.
The future of the Social Security system is another serious concern:
When those who are now thirty reach retirement age, will social security
be available? Robert Barr is among those responding to this question.

Looking ahead, people want to know how new technological developments will affect America's economy and future growth. Can the United
States, which once led the world in automobile production, computers
and electronics, but has since been supplanted, lead the world into a new
phase of post-industrial society? The experts suggest that America is,
indeed, in the forefront of a new phase—the production of information
as a commodity. They also see the United States as the leader in new uses
of space and biotechnology. Computer technology, for example, is beginning to influence every aspect of our lives, from video games to
advanced microchips that process information in microseconds. The
future in these fields is intriguing. In space, the experts say, we are
entering a new era—exploitation rather than exploration. "We are just
beginning to emerge as galactic citizens," says former astronaut Dr.
Brian O'Leary.

To accomplish these tasks we will need to use our energy resources
prudently and concern ourselves with our environment. How will the
nation satisfy its energy appetite? Will coal or nuclear power become the
energy source of the future? Most experts agree that any successful
domestic energy policy will depend, in part, on Americans' willingness to

curb their energy use and to find alternatives to petroleum. So long as the national policy is committed to making America energy-independent, the experts assert, then federal funds will continue to support the nuclear industry. Will there be sufficient energy, food, and natural resources in the immediate future? The forecasts for the year 2000 vary enormously. The answer depends on how different nations view the problems of the future and thereby set their priorities.

Americans are increasingly concerned about crime, and a number of questions in the section on social issues reveal their apprehension. Crime threatens society at its most basic level—on the street, at work, and at home. Violent crimes—murders, aggravated assaults, rapes, and robberies—occur in all parts of the country. No longer is violent crime considered an urban phenomenon. Who commits these crimes? About 90 percent are the acts of males, and half of the perpetrators are under twenty-one. Criminologists are reassessing the complex causes of violent crime and are finding that the activity may be linked with the changing character of American society. Frank Scarpitti of the University of Delaware, for example, provides statistics to show that crime soars with the unemployment rate. A number of the experts consulted on this question are professionally involved in devising imaginative solutions to these pressing problems. Scarpitti suggests the decriminalization of victimless crimes as one step in dealing with the problem. Gary Gottfredson feels that the schools can help provide a deterrent by broadening the scope of the curriculum to give students more vocational work.

How has society tried to deal with the increase in serious crime? Incarceration is the prime and time-tested remedy, but it is obvious that the American public is fed up with the current prison system and has serious doubts about its effectiveness. In any case, Americans have widely recognized the need for prison reform. As the crime rate has risen, judges have responded to the public outcry by putting more criminals away for longer periods of time. As a result, the facilities are badly overcrowded and have a high prisoner-to-guard ratio. Recidivism is extraordinarily high, testifying to the failure of rehabilitation efforts. The racial composition of the inmates is out of proportion to the general population, fueling the belief that minority Americans continue to have difficulty coping with society. Moreover, unrest, beatings, and homosexual rapes are all too commonplace in prisons.

How can the country manage such a cauldron? Experts on the criminal justice system offer some probing explanations, propose alternatives, and give reasons why reforms will be slow in coming. "Rehabilitation must take place in the community," says Jim Hackler, professor of sociology at the University of Alberta, "and even though this involves risks, these risks are not greater than the ones created when inmates learn to adapt to the prison environment. Unfortunately, the United States is constantly being guided by political opportunities in this area rather than by evidence." Dr. Lee H. Bowker, associate dean of the School of Social Welfare at the University of Wisconsin, asserts, "In the final analysis, no prison program can hope to be 100 percent successful when prisoners are returned to the same community conditions that contribute to the criminal behavior for which they were incarcerated."

Drug abuse and alcoholism are becoming a serious concern. Dan Anderson, president-director of the Hazelden Foundation in Center City, Minnesota, argues that prevention is the best solution to these problems. But Jerome F. X. Carroll, director of psychological services at the Eagleville Hospital and Rehabilitation Center in Eagleville, Pennsylvania, points out that our primary prevention programs have not been very successful. He suggests a variety of individual approaches, such as teaching young people how to make good decisions, how to assert themselves, how to form intimate relationships with others, and how to relate constructively to their feelings and needs.

A series of questions on pregnancy and abortion reveals deep-seated worries. What should be done about unwanted pregnancy? Why is the problem of unwanted pregnancy so widespread? Dr. Mary S. Calderone, the noted sex educator, blames parents who refuse to learn how sexuality develops in the young child and what their role in that development is. By the time a child reaches adolescence, she thinks, it's too late to establish a trust relationship. However, Rosemary Diamond, president and cofounder of Birthright of Chicago, pins the blame on "acceptance," particularly since the 1973 Supreme Court decision creating easier access to abortion. She feels the decision encouraged sexual activity at earlier and earlier ages. "One family's acceptance," says Mrs. Diamond, "can influence a neighborhood, a school group, business and social acquaintances, an extended family, eventually the society at large, which is happening today." As for what can be done, Mrs. Diamond maintains: "An emphasis on abstinence for the unmarried is a *must*."

Birth control remains one of the central social dilemmas, cutting across religious, social, and scientific lines. There is no ideal method of controlled contraception currently, but the experts predict that in five to ten years a contraceptive device with minimal side effects will be available.

A look at some of the major political issues today—abortion, school prayer, and capital punishment—forcefully illustrates that religious feelings still run strong in the country. A key question deals with where the line should be drawn between private beliefs and public morality. Do scientific beliefs support or contradict faith in religious teaching? And are Americans, on the whole, really "one nation under God"? All this leads to the question posed previously: Is there scientific evidence that God exists? Isaac Asimov, the author of more than 200 fiction and nonfiction books, explains that "the existence (or nonexistence) of God may well be among scientifically unknowable phenomena." As for the evidence, he is quite emphatic: "No! None!"—a view disputed by those who insist that the laws of probability rule out completely the chance or random explanation of life.

The media have become the most significant influence in political affairs, supplanting the diminishing influence of political parties. The media define issues, identify certain citizens they consider worthy of public attention, and give them visibility. This recent development has not escaped the attention of the questioners, who are quite concerned about what the economic concentration of media ownership implies in a democracy. A. H. Raskin, former deputy editor of the editorial page of *The New York Times*, notes that with the ownership of the media concentrated in the hands of a few large corporations, the need for making a profit could replace a sense of responsibility in providing the best possible coverage of the news. (After he supplied his answer, such major American newspapers as *The Washington Star, The Minneapolis Star*, and the *Philadelphia Bulletin* went out of business. And, the owners of *The Daily News* in New York City, with the largest circulation of any newspaper in the country, put their paper on the block, threatening to close if a suitable buyer could not conclude a deal.) Nevertheless, Raskin asserts that the press remains virtually unhampered in its pursuit of the news. Serge Denisoff, a professor at Bowling Green State University, is concerned about the symbiotic relationship between journalists and the entertainment and political figures they cover. The essays in this section reflect a fundamental concern about the responsibility of the media.

When only half of all eligible citizens cast their ballots, as they did in 1980, it makes one wonder who is actually governing the nation. According to C. Joe Carter, professor of government at Adams State College in Alamosa, Colorado, "The United States is actually governed by a large number of special interest groups—farmers, ranchers, teachers, laborers, skilled workers, professionals, environmentalists, organized religions, and businesses." The special organizations, he says, help office seekers become office holders.

A steady impetus for change has always stood out in our national character. But social changes have been particularly turbulent over the last twenty years. These are identified in *America Wants to Know*, and the contributors attempt to make sense of the many different changes our country is experiencing. In a discussion on the future of the family, for example, Robert Francoeur, professor of human sexuality at Fairleigh Dickinson University, writes that we are undergoing a shift from a male-dominated society to an egalitarian society. The way we were, the way we are, and the way we will be are explored in a section on attitudes and expectations. Does the "average" American exist? The "average" American is not a suburban or city-dwelling white, Protestant mother of two who holds a job and watches television more often than she goes jogging. In fact, there are millions of divorced fathers, married farmers, unemployed youths, homemakers with large families, elderly widows and widowers, young singles, and so on. While it is difficult to account for every individual, the specialists can evaluate changes, see patterns, and note trends.

In real life, no one is "average," and the American way of life is being pursued by 220 million individuals, each in his own way. Their major concerns about the present and the future are articulated in *America Wants to Know*.

George Gallup, Sr.

ACKNOWLEDGMENTS

Grateful acknowledgment is made to the following persons for their invaluable participation in this book:

Dr. John W. Aberle
Dr. Jack E. Adams
Freda Adler, Ph.D.
Dr. Gilbert H. Ahlgren
Prof. George W. Albee
John H. Aldrich
H. Alexander, Ph.D.
Prof. Chadwick F. Alger
Kenneth N. Anchor, Ph.D.
Dan Anderson, Ph.D.
David E. Anderson, Ph.D.
James A. Anderson
M. H. Anderson, M.D.
Richard W. Anderson, M.D.
Tetsuo Arakawa
Stephen H. Archer
Charles J. Armstrong, Ph.D.
Isaac Asimov
Ralph E. Bailey
Albert W. Baisler, Ph.D., LL.D.
Robert M. Ball
Dr. Jack Baranson
Prof. James David Barber
Dr. Sharon N. Barnartt
William J. Baroody, Jr.
James W. Bartlett, M.D.
John V. Basmajian, M.D.
Edward J. Beattie, Jr., M.D.
Fred L. Behling, M.D.

Folkert O. Belzer, M.D.
Douglas J. Bennet Jr.
Larry Berg, Ph.D.
Prof. Robert E. Berney
Larry E. Beutler, Ph.D.
R. Bruce Billings, Ph.D.
Donald D. Black
Francis L. Black, Ph.D.
Prof. James L. Blawie
Dr. Max R. Bloom
Prof. Lincoln P. Bloomfield
Larry Bogart
Prof. Edna Bonacich
John F. Bookout
Kenneth R. Bordner
Helen Bottel
Prof. Jack Botwinick
Dr. Lee H. Bowker
Jack Bowman
James Boyle
Edward S. Brady, M.S.
Prof. Donald Brandon
Prof. Curtis Braschler
George A. Bray, M.D.
Paul A. Brinker
Prof. Daniel W. Bromley
Prof. Harvey Brooks
Melvin S. Brooks
Dr. Joyce Brothers

Prof. F. G. Brown
Prof. Clifford E. Bryan
Prof. William Buchanan
Randolph Bufano
William P. Bundy
Gene Burd
C. Emory Burton
Thomas G. Burish, Ph.D.
Mary S. Calderone, M.D.
Prof. James D. Calderwood
Bettye M. Caldwell, Ph.D.
Daniel Callahan
Prof. Rondo Cameron
Bruce A. Campbell
Dr. Doris K. Campbell
Dr. Wray O. Candilis
Prof. Arthur Canter
Prof. E. Ray Canterbery
Paul P. Carbone, M.D.
Dr. D. H. Carley
David Carliner
John G. Carlson, Ph.D.
Prof. Leonard A. Carlson
Jerome F. X. Carroll, Ph.D.
C. Joe Carter, Ph.D.
Wilmoth A. Carter, Ph.D.
Walter S. Cartwright, Ph.D.
Dr. Ben Cashman
Emery N. Castle
Prof. H. Paul Castleberry
Louis Cenci
Dr. Edward C. Chang
Dr. Mark R. Chartrand
Dr. Samuel B. Chase, Jr.
Julia Child
Prof. John R. Christiansen
Prof. Laurits R. Christensen
Prof. Reo M. Christenson
Prof. Albert M. Church III
Victor G. Cicirelli, Ph.D.
William G. Clancy, M.D.
Prof. Kenneth E. Clark
Prof. Kenneth W. Clarkson
Todd R. Clear, Ph.D.
Prof. Alan Clem
Prof. Walter C. Clemens, Jr.
Prof. William B. Clifford II
Dr. Bernard Clyman
Stephen M. Cobaugh
Dr. J. I. Coffey
David Cohen
Dr. Gerson D. Cohen
Harold A. Cohen
Dr. Lawrence S. Cohen
Prof. Steven G. Cole
A. Lee Coleman
Ellen C. Collier
Roger Conner
John E. Corbally
Prof. Richard C. Cortner
Pauline E. Council, Ph.D.

Frances R. Cousens, Ph.D.
Norman Cousins
Dr. Donald O. Cowgill
Albert H. Cox, Jr.
Herbert J. Cross, Ph.D.
Michael L. Culbert
Robert G. Culbertson
Dr. W. David Cummings
Donald J. Dalessio, M.D.
Prof. Anthony D'Amato
Prof. Arlene Kaplan Daniels
T. S. Danowski, M.D.
E. E. David, Jr.
Dr. Michael E. DeBakey
R. Serge Denisoff
Prof. Joseph S. DeSalvo
Roman W. DeSanctis, M.D.
Prof. Marian C. Diamond
Rosemary Diamond
Prof. Manuel Diaz
Prof. Carl Djerassi
William E. Donoghue
Joseph T. Doyle, M.D.
K. W. Dumars, M.D.
William S. Dunkin
William H. Dutton
Donald B. Effler, M.D.
E. J. Eichwald, M.D.
Stuart E. Eizenstat
Albert Ellis, Ph.D.
Roger Enloe
Alfred S. Evans, M.D.
Richard S. Farr, M.D.
Dan H. Fenn, Jr.
Sybil Ferguson
Edwin J. Feulner, Jr.
M. Finland, M.D.
Carmen J. Finley, Ph.D.
Prof. David D. Finley
E. B. Fisher, Jr., Ph.D.
Gerald S. Fisher
Dr. Hans Fisher
Stephen Fleck, M.D.
Scott Fleming
James R. Flynn
Prof. John P. Fox
Muriel Fox
Robert T. Francoeur, Ph.D., A.C.S.
Prof. Ronald E. Frank
Howard Frazier
Carlton Fredericks
Prof. Victor R. Fuchs
H. Laurance Fuller
Dr. Charles Furst
Curtis B. Gans
Sol. L. Garfield, Ph.D.
Lawrence Garfinkel
Partricia A. Gavett
Larry Gibbons, M.D.
Barbara Gilchrest, M.D.
Prof. Norval D. Glenn

Victor M. Goode
Gary D. Gottfredson
Prof. Leo Grebler
David G. Greene, M.D.
Prof. William T. Greenough
Prof. Eugene Gressman
Dr. Jerry Grey
Milton Gwirtzman
Dr. Pierre C. Haber
Sylvia S. Hacker, Ph.D.
Prof. Jim Hackler
Walter F. Hahn
Prof. Walter W. Haines
Michel T. Halbouty
Dr. Roger Hamburg
Dr. Robert W. Hammel
M. Gene Handelsman
Dr. Clifford M. Hardin
Oscar Harkavy, Ph.D.
Dr. Neil E. Harl
Kenneth Harms
Robert A. Harper
Prof. C. Lowell Harriss
Dr. Lafayette G. Harter, Jr.
Dr. Craig Bond Hatfield
Leonard J. Hausman
J. Ray Hays, Ph.D., J.D.
Alexander Heard
Frederick Hecht, M.D.
Prof. Robert L. Heilbroner
Prof. A. James Heins
Joseph M. Hendrie
Victor Herbert, M.D., J.D.
Robert M. Heyssel, M.D.
Leonard J. Hippchen, Ph.D.
Walter E. Hoadley
John C. Hobbins, M.D.
Walter Hoffman
Arthur I. Holleb, M.D.
Dorothy R. Hollingsworth, M.D.
Prof. Robert R. Holt
Ralph W. Hood, Jr., Ph.D.
Prof. Rollin D. Hotchkiss
Prof. Jerry F. Hough
Jane T. Howard
Hon. Shirley M. Hufstedler
Marion Hayes Hull
Prof. J. McVicker Hunt
J. Willis Hurst, M.D.
Janet Shibley Hyde, Ph.D.
Maurice Jackson, Ph.D.
David W. Jacobs, Ph.D.
Leon Jaworski
Burtell M. Jefferson
Prof. Arthur R. Jensen
Prof. Malcolm E. Jewell
James Hervey Johnson
Dr. Robert C. Johnson
Vernon E. Jordan, Jr.
Prof. Lawrence M. Kahn
Martin Katahn, Ph.D.

Ken Kelly
Prof. Lyman B. Kirkpatrick, Jr.
Edmund Klein, M.D.
Walter G. Klopfer, Ph.D.
Klaus Knorr
Alfred G. Knudson, Jr. M.D., Ph.D.
Richard A. Kunin, M.D.
John R. Kupferer
Steven M.S. Kurtz
Goldie Kweller
Prof. Sylvia Lane
Arnold A. Lazarus, Ph.D.
H. M. Lee, M.D.
Daniel M. Lentz
Prof. Larry L. Leslie
Prof. Edward M. Levine
Harry Levinson
Jerre Levy, Ph.D.
John C. Lilly, M.D.
Prof. C. Eric Lincoln, Ph.D.
Prof. Richard W. Lindholm
Peter G. Lindner, M.D.
Henry Cabot Lodge
E. W. Lovrien, M.D.
David Loye
Joel F. Lubar, Ph.D.
Dr. David R. Mace
Prof. Fritz Machlup
Paul D. MacLean, M.D.
H. G. MacPherson
James W. Maddock, Ph.D.
Robert M. Magnuson
Prof. Brendan Maher
Rev. C. J. Malloy, Jr.
John A. Maloney
Dr. Karl Maramorosch
Thomas L. Marchioro, M.D.
Judd Marmor, M.D.
Leon C. Martel, Ph.D.
Douglas S. Massey, Ph.D.
Kenneth P. Mathews, M.D.
Reginald F. Mattison
Rollo May, Ph.D.
Dr. Jean Mayer
Dr. John F. McCarthy, Jr.
R. Paul McCauley, Ph.D.
Michael McCloskey
John F. McDermott, Jr., M.D.
F. James McDonald
Donald W. McEvoy
Dwight C. McGoon, M.D.
Dr. Pat McGowan
J. Alexander McMahon
Patricia McMahon
John McVernon
Margaret McWilliams, Ph.D.
John W. Megown
Doris M. Meissner
Joseph J. Melone
Dr. Ronald I. Meltzer
Rodger E. Mendenhall

Alan S. Meyer, Ph.D.
E. Joe Middlebrooks
Rufus E. Miles, Jr.
Ernest C. Miller, Ph.D.
Dr. Glenn W. Miller
Prof. Lynn H. Miller
Dr. Perry Miller
Prof. Aubrey Milunsky
Sylvester R. Mlott, Ph.D.
Charles G. Moertel, M.D.
Anthony P. Monaco, M.D.
Marabel Morgan
Woodrow W. Morris, Ph.D.
Prof. G.O.W. Mueller
Karen Mulhauser
Thomas B. Mulholland, Ph.D.
Prof. J. Carter Murphy
Prof. George C. Myers
John S. Najarian, M.D.
W. Russell Neuman
Prof. Theodore M. Newcomb
Guy R. Newell, M.D.
James A. Nicholas, M.D.
Prof. William Nordhaus
Philip S. Norman, M.D.
Charles M. O'Brien, Jr.
John F. O'Connor, M.D.
M. K. Ohlson, Ph.D.
Dr. Brian O'Leary
Erdman B. Palmore, Ph.D.
Richard T. Pascale
Richard A. Passwater, Ph.D.
Linus Pauling
F. Paul Pearsall, Ph.D.
James Peirce
John Pekkanen
Michael J. Pelczar, Jr.
James A. Perkins
Florence Z. Perman
Gilbert A. Peters
Rev. Ted Peters
Donald E. Petersen
Martin Peterson
Russell W. Peterson
Dr. Ferinez Phelps
Letty Cottin Pogrebin
Dr. David Poling
Richard Pollock
Ithiel de Sola Pool
Gail L. Potter
Lawrence Power, M.D.
Robert J. Powitzky, Ph.D.
Nathan Pritikin
Raymond D. Pruitt, M.D.
Louis T. Rader
A. H. Raskin
Arif Stephen Rechtschaffen, M.D.
Milton G. Rector
John A. Reinecke, Ph.D.
Richard J. Regan, S.J.
Richard Restak, M.D.

Frank H. T. Rhodes
Dr. Robert M. Rice
Richard A. Rifkind, M.D.
J. William Rioux
Eli Robins, M.D.
Jacquelyn Rogers
Paul J. Rosch, M.D.
Roger N. Rosenberg, M.D.
Ian M. Ross
Isadore Rossman, M.D., Ph.D.
Lillian B. Rubin, Ph.D.
Melvin H. Rudov, Ph.D.
Dr. Richard O. Russell, Jr.
David C. Sabiston, Jr., M.D.
Dr. Franklin C. Salisbury, J.D.
Harrison E. Salisbury
Prof. Barbara G. Salmore
Triloki N. Saraf
John C. Sawhill
Prof. Frank R. Scarpitti
Dr. Patricia Schiller
Phyllis Schlafly
Senator Harrison "Jack" Schmitt
Maxine Schnall
Prof. James H. Schulz
James K. Selkirk
Rudy Ray Seward, Ph.D.
Peggy Shaker
William H. Shaker
C. Norman Shealy, M.D., Ph.D.
Gail Sheehy
Albert L. Sheffer, M.D.
Edwin F. Shelley
Richard E. Shepherd
Prof. Donald W. Shriver, Jr.
Hugh S. Sidey
Arthur Simon
William E. Simon
B. F. Skinner
Solomon S. Steiner, Ph.D.
Theodor D. Sterling
Dr. Michael G. Stevenson
Howard R. Swearer
Prof. D. Szabo
Dr. Albert Szent-Györgyi
Tad Szulc
John A. Talbott, M.D.
Earl C. Tanner
Edward Taub, Ph.D.
Dr. Charles W. Thomas
David D. Thompson, M.D.
Prof. W. Scott Thompson
Prof. Lester C. Thurow
Prof. E. Paul Torrance
Prof. S. Sidney Ulmer
U.S. Dept. of Labor,
Bureau of Statistics
Prof. Elliot S. Valenstein
Paul VanArsdel, Jr., M.D.
Betty M. Vetter
Paul C. Warnke

Dr. Carol I. Waslien
Prof. Harold W. Watts
Prof. Charles N. Weaver
Murray L. Weidenbaum
Prof. Roman L. Weil
Arthur M. Weimer
Alvin M. Weinberg
Prof. Susan Welch
Henry Wendt
Dr. Clifton R. Wharton, Jr.
Prof. Urban Whitaker
Jack E. White, M.D., F.A.C.S.
Francis O. Wilcox

Prof. Aaron Wildavksy
Prof. Leslie T. Wilkins
John C. Willke, M.D.
Dr. Peter A. Wish
Robert K. Woetzel, Ph.D., J.S.D.
Dr. Seymour L. Wolfbein
Prof. Marvin E. Wolfgang
Dr. Diana S. Woodruff
Richard G. Woods
Prof. Richard A. Wright
Joanne Yurman
George Zeidenstein
Dewey K. Ziegler, M.D.

AMERICA
WANTS
TO KNOW

ECONOMICS

INFLATION HAS WREAKED such havoc on our society that the economy has replaced sports as the number one subject of discussion in America's living rooms. While few offer identical solutions for the problem of inflation, most experts agree on its fundamental causes.

The United States emerged from World War II in a unique and enviable position. Germany was divided and its productive facilities had largely been bombed out of existence. England was continuing its steady economic decline. Russia was reeling under the ravages of Stalinism. Japan was entering a period of reevaluation and healing. Buttressed by our military and political dominance, American corporations entered a period of extraordinary international growth. Raw materials—obtained cheaply from whatever part of the globe they were available—were processed and turned into manufactured goods by our technologically advanced plants at home, and then sold back to those same countries at a profit. The world became one vast market for American goods, and our country amassed an extraordinary amount of wealth.

By the 1960s, our tremendous wealth had started to bring about some fundamental changes in our society. One no longer had to produce rubber tires or sheets of steel in order to accumulate wealth. The service industries—including such professionals as lawyers, accountants and media people—began to seize control of the economy, and it soon became easier to make a comfortable living in a profession aimed at redistributing our country's wealth than it was in a job creating that wealth.

With the advent of television as an advertising medium, the shift in emphasis from production to consumption became complete. Instead of investing millions in keeping up with the latest in steel technology, it became more lucrative to "invent" twenty or thirty different brands of soap and to create a market for each with a carefully crafted advertising campaign. If Henry Ford's technologically advanced assembly line, that turned a couple of dollars of steel and bolts into an automobile worth quite a bit more, was the paradigm of America's first industrial age, then Ray Kroc's McDonald's fast-food outlets, promoted by Madison Avenue's most sophisticated techniques, were typical of the money to be made in our postindustrial society.

The availability of easy money also had a great effect on our social structure. Our country, built on an ethic that stressed thrift and hard work, gradually became a leisure society. Another effect was the creation of a class of students, professors and journalists who recognized the need for some segments of society to contemplate justice and the way things ought to be. Social justice programs—such as welfare, food stamps and affirmative action—became widespread methods for redistributing our nation's wealth. Money seemed to abound, so no one really cared that these programs were funded by the United States Treasury printing presses.

By the 1970s, however, the deluge of Japanese television sets, stereo equipment and cars had become indicative of a new trend: foreign countries, which had placed their capital in developing technologically sophisticated factories rather than in deodorants, began to produce products that were superior to our own. American manufacturers were no longer able to compete successfully in our own markets. The twenty-fold increase in the price of oil began to drain away huge amounts of our capital to OPEC. And these mounting federal deficits resulted in a level of inflation that encouraged an attitude of gloom and doom.

As we enter the 1980s, American financial and social institutions are beginning to change in response to the new economic challenge our country faces. Sears, Roebuck will now be selling stocks and bonds and real estate alongside their lawnmowers and vacuum cleaners. Women have entered the work force in ever greater numbers, at least partially to make up for the ravages of inflation on the family budget. And worker-controlled companies—an idea that would have been labeled "creeping socialism" a mere ten or twenty years ago—is a growing trend, because it seems to increase the productivity and output of workers.

In the following section on economics, a group of experts offer their insights into the new shapes the American economy is likely to take.

THE ECONOMY
AND INFLATION

NOT SO LONG AGO, parents could confidently tell their children that a penny saved was a penny earned. Saving was smart—so smart in fact that a sure thing was "like money in the bank."

In the current state of the economy, however, money saved does not necessarily equal money earned, especially if the saving is done in a standard savings-bank account. Assuming 10 percent annual inflation, a dollar put into a savings account earning 5¾ percent annual interest actually loses value each year. Thus a dollar saved in the beginning of the year amounts to only about ninety-six cents after twelve months in savings, and even less if income taxes take their toll. In fact, if inflation and interest rates continue at their current levels, parents may tell future generations that a dollar saved is cents less—as well as senseless.

A large number of Americans already appear to have lost interest in savings. Currently, we save less than a nickel of every dollar we earn. Compared with the approximately thirteen cents per dollar saved by West Germans and the almost twenty cents per dollar saved by Japanese, meager savings make us appear to be a nation of spendthrifts.

Yet for most of us, inflation has meant anything but happy-go-lucky spending. As consumer prices rose during the last decade, many families have been buying less: less meat, since the cost of many varieties more than tripled in the 1970s; less fuel, since retail gasoline prices almost quadrupled between 1971 and 1981; and less real estate as mortgages soared above the means of many would-be homeowners.

Inflation has affected everyone, but particularly those in such occupations as teaching where pay hikes have not generally kept pace with the rising cost of living. For people in these jobs, as well as for the growing numbers of unemployed and retired or disabled living on fixed incomes, inflation has meant a lowered standard of living and deflated hopes for the future.

However, not everyone wants an immediate end to inflation. In general, borrowers have benefited from the inflationary climate. Many have piled up debts at relatively low interest rates, and gambled that they will be able to pay off their creditors in the future with devalued dollars. So far, the gamble has usually paid off.

On the whole, though, inflation works against the average wage earner. The economic situation has taken such a toll on the nation that some economists call our period the "Great Inflation," equating it to the Great Depression of the 1930s in terms of national importance. Not only is the inflation of the last decade more severe than in the past, but it does not conform to the nation's usual pattern of economic dips and rises. Inflationary periods of the past usually came at the end of wars; for example, the cost of living rose after the War of 1812, the Civil War, and world wars I and II. Postwar declines later helped to reduce the cost of living again, although generally not to prewar levels.

Many economists trace the beginning of the Great Inflation not to the *end* of a war but to 1965, in the *midst* of the Vietnam War. At that time, consumer prices, one measure of inflation, were rising at the relatively tame rate of 2 percent a year. As President Johnson escalated the war in Vietnam, and the war against poverty at home, the cost of living began to escalate as well. By the time President Nixon took office in 1968, the rate of consumer-price increases had more than doubled to over 4 percent a year. To make what was then considered high inflation even worse, by 1971 the nation faced an unusually bleak combination: inflation accompanied by high unemployment.

Both presidents Nixon and Ford committed themselves to reducing inflation, but when President Carter came to office in 1976, consumer prices were climbing at the rate of 5.8 percent per year. Four years later, when President Reagan assumed office with a mandate to mend the economy, consumer prices were rising at the rate of about 13 percent a year.

Although the rate of inflation has lessened somewhat, the Great Inflation continues to exact a great price. People have found that their week's grocery money no longer buys a week's worth of food; former savers have begun to wonder if they should plan for the future or just spend while they can. The following experts' answers discuss the outlook for one of America's major providers for the future—the Social Security Administration—and examine the causes of inflation as well as the possible cures.

CONTRIBUTORS

Dr. Jack E. Adams, Professor of Economics, University of Arkansas at Little Rock, Arkansas

Robert M. Ball, U.S. Commissioner of Social Security 1962–73

Dr. Max R. Bloom, Professor of Real Estate and Urban Land Economics, School of Management, Syracuse University, Syracuse, New York

Paul A. Brinker, Professor of Economics, University of Oklahoma, Norman, Oklahoma

James D. Calderwood, Joseph A. DeBell Professor of Business Economics and International Trade, School of Business Administration, University of Southern California, Los Angeles

Dr. Wray O. Candilis, Bureau of Industrial Economics, U.S. Department of Commerce, Washington, D.C.

E. Ray Canterbery, Professor of Economics, Florida State University, author of *The Making of Economics* and articles in the *Journal of Political Economy* and *The New York Times Magazine*

Dr. Samuel B. Chase, Jr., Managing Associate, Golembe Associates, Inc., Washington, D.C.

Laurits R. Christensen, Professor of Economics, University of Wisconsin, Madison, Wisconsin

Dr. Bernard Clyman, Vice President (retired), Office of Social Security Affairs, Equitable Life Assurance Society of the United States, New York, New York

Joseph S. DeSalvo, Professor of Economics, University of Wisconsin, Milwaukee, Wisconsin

Milton Gwirtzman, Attorney; Chairman of the Bipartisan National Commission on Social Security

Dr. Lafayette G. Harter, Jr., Professor of Economics, Oregon State University, Corvallis, Oregon

Robert L. Heilbroner, Norman Thomas Professor of Economics, New School for Social Research, New York, New York

John R. Kupferer, Executive Vice-President, National Association of Home Manufacturers, Washington, D.C.

Fritz Machlup, Professor of Economics, New York University, New York, New York

Joseph J. Melone, CLU, CPCU, Senior Vice-President, District Agencies Department, The Prudential Insurance Company of America, Newark, New Jersey

Ernest C. Miller, Ph.D., Professor of Human Resources Management, Management Department, School of Business, California Polytechnic State University, San Luis Obispo, California

Dr. Glenn W. Miller, Professor of Economics, Wichita State University, Wichita, Kansas; Professor of Economics, Emeritus, Ohio State University, Columbus, Ohio

Richard E. Shepherd, Executive Secretary, National Association of
    Mature People, Oklahoma City, Oklahoma
William E. Simon, former Secretary of the Treasury
Roman L. Weil, Professor of Accounting and Director of the Institute of
    Professional Accounting, Graduate School of Business, University
    of Chicago, Chicago, Illinois
Arthur M. Weimer, President, Weimer Business Advisory Service, Inc.,
    Bloomington, Indiana
Aaron Wildavsky, Professor of Political Science, University of California,
    Berkeley, California

WHAT EXACTLY IS INFLATION AND WHY
DO WE HAVE IT? CAN IT EVER BE BROUGHT
UNDER CONTROL—OR ELIMINATED?

Paul A. Brinker. Inflation may be defined as rapidly rising prices. There
are several causes of inflation. One is demand-pull inflation where there
is too much spending, possibly by the government. A second type is
cost-push inflation caused by business monopolies or labor unions
pushing up prices and wages. Problems in certain industries such as
food, oil, housing and medical care may push up prices although the
money supply will have to increase, or other prices will drop.

Inflation can be controlled. Too much spending can be eradicated,
and business and labor monopolies can be prosecuted. Dislocations in
industry tend to be corrected by the "invisible hand." Increased prices
tend to attract firms into an industry and increase supply and thus
lower prices.

James D. Calderwood. Inflation is said to exist when the general price
level is rising in excess of 1½–2 percent a year. A rise in prices of less
than 1½–2 percent a year is mostly offset by improvement in the quality
of goods and services. A rise in the general price level can embrace some
rapidly rising prices, some stable ones and even some falling ones (mini-
calculators and digital watches in recent years); we are talking averages.
The most comprehensive measure of inflation is the "Gross National
Product (GNP) deflator"; the most publicized one is the Consumer Price
Index (CPI) although it has many technical deficiencies.

Historically, inflation has been caused by too much money chasing
too few goods, as happened during the Revolutionary and the Civil
War. Today the causes are more complex but an excessive growth of
the money supply is still the starting point for understanding inflation
in the U.S. since 1966.

The main elements in this inflation have been:

1. An excessive growth of the money supply.
2. A succession of large federal budget deficits which have been largely financed by the creation of new money.
3. A fiscal policy which has emphasized the redistribution of existing wealth rather than the creation of new wealth—taxing heavily those sectors of society whose job it is to save, invest and produce, and passing the money on to those who consume (social programs, etc.).
4. Growing cost-push pressure on business which have forced prices up. These have been of two kinds: (a) Labor costs rising faster than productivity. The basic rate of inflation is approximately the percentage increase in labor costs minus the percentage increase in productivity. The gap has been widening as productivity has lagged. (b) Costs related to legislation and programs designed to improve the quality of life, including environmental and safety legislation, delays in licensing of nuclear power plants and new drugs, and general government red tape which absorbs corporate money and time in unproductive activity.
5. International factors, especially the escalation of oil prices since 1973. Others have included the decline in the international value of the dollar during most of the 1970s, which made imports more expensive, and periodic jumps in food prices when poor foreign harvests caused a surge of buying of U.S. farm products.
6. The psychology of expectations. Increasingly, the public (business, labor, consumers, investors, etc.) has become convinced that the government has neither the will nor the ability to fight inflation and that it will therefore continue. This led the public to act in ways which made inflation worse—unions pushing up wages in anticipation of price increases, business pushing up prices in anticipation of cost increases, and so forth.

From an economic point of view inflation can definitely be controlled and even eliminated. The real question is whether we have the political will and ability to take the necessary measures and pay the necessary price.

In 1955, the CPI actually fell. During the decade 1955-1965, we had no inflation (the conventional price indices rose at an average annual rate of 1-2 percent). During the first half of the 1960s, we enjoyed growth, falling unemployment, diminishing budget deficits, a series of tax cuts, a foreign trade surplus—and no inflation! To return to this the following are necessary:

1. Gradually reduce the rate of monetary growth until it approximates the growth rate of the GNP—and keep it there.
2. Reduce—and eventually eliminate—the federal budget deficits.

3. Restructure the tax system to place more emphasis on the stimulation of saving, investment, productivity and growth, and less on increasing consumption.
4. Take steps to spur productivity.
5. Strike a reasonable balance in legislation and policy between our desire for a better quality of life and our need for growth.
6. Remove or scale down such obstacles to lower prices as farm price supports, import restrictions and excessive regulation of industry.
7. Pursue a vigorous policy to develop alternative energy sources.

From an economic viewpoint, these measures could reduce and eventually eliminate inflation. The real problem is getting people to understand what needs to be done and to accept some painful readjustments in the short run and getting Congress to pursue the right policies.

E. Ray Canterbery. Inflation occurs when the prices of all or most goods and services rise at the same time. For example, a higher price for coffee may simply lead the household to substitute tea. But if the prices of both tea and coffee or all beverages go up, there is no escape from paying more for the same quantities as before and the household's standard of living will fall unless its money income rises enough to cover these higher costs. A family at the poverty margin may starve if its money income cannot cover the rising cost of its basic necessities.

There are many causes of a one-shot inflation, but only a few vital forces can keep inflation going. Bulges in total demand in excess of the economy's productive capacity can start prices upward but only a sustained excess demand or other elements can keep prices moving heavenward. Increases in the prices of various inputs in the productive process can lead to inflation if such prices or cost surges are in excess of improvements in output per worker or productivity. Unit costs of production otherwise rise and these higher costs are passed on to the consumer. The indexing of various government payments to the CPI also quickens the inflationary process.

As the competitive structure of the American economy has changed to one of gigantic enterprises, such as GM, Westinghouse, ITT and Exxon, confronted by powerful labor unions, such as the UAW, the temptation of entire industries to use price increases to cover rising costs has been irresistible. Once inflation begins to smolder, these institutional arrangements can cause it to flame. A large share of union wages is tied directly to inflation in escalator clauses that provide cost of living increments for members. Understandably, workers resist the erosion in their living standards, and the balance of union workers demands wage increments to slow the slide in their purchasing power. This sets the pace for wages throughout the economy.

The attempts of labor to maintain its old standard of living, once a demand-pull inflation was ignited by the Vietnam War escalation of the

Johnson Administration in the late 1960s, led to wage increases, and cost increases that "pushed" the inflation along and fanned its flames. Then, the massive jump in oil prices (and thus production costs) beginning in 1973 negatively affected the transportation, utility and chemical industries, adding further fuel to the cost-push inflationary fire.

If inflation is sufficiently severe and long lasting, people begin to expect it. Americans do today. We buy more goods faster in the expectation that they will cost even more tomorrow. These preemptive purchases create relative shortages (a special kind of demand-pull) that can create an inflationary firestorm such as that experienced by the U.S. in 1978 and 1980. Expectational inflation is a self-fulfilling prophecy. Yet people are not stupid. Expectations are grounded in reality and thus the structural bases of inflation must be altered in order to reverse expectations.

Inflation can be controlled. As its causes are social, however, only political or social solutions are feasible. Competition used to keep prices in check. Consumers would face down a higher price by switching suppliers. However, confronted with a higher price for both Exxon *and* Mobil, the consumer has no effective power. Our economy is no longer structured on a competitive model, therefore the consumer is no longer king (despite the margarine commercial). Only a new social contract in which the consumer is brought together as an equal partner with labor and management in wage and investment decisions will make inflation manageable. The conventional devices—tight money to reduce demand or marginal tax rate changes directed at supply—create problems of unemployment and income redistribution without cutting off the supplies of inflationary fuel.

Dr. Samuel B. Chase, Jr. Inflation is an increase in the general price level, as measured by a price index with no bias (a theoretical dream that can be approximated rather well using existing techniques).

Inflation can be brought under control through the following steps: (1) eliminate federal budget deficits (over business cycle); (2) reduce the collective bargaining power of unions; (3) redirect antitrust law enforcement to horizontal mergers that have resulted in anticompetitive consequences; and (4) reform tax laws to encourage people to work and to invest their money in productive enterprises.

In the long run, under the above circumstances, the policies of the Federal Reserve would be of little consequence, unless it were to lose its independent status and come under the direct and immediate control of the administration or Congress. That is, the fundamental cure for inflation is not to be found in the policies of the Federal Reserve.

Laurits R. Christensen. Inflation is a sustained upward movement in the general level of prices. Inflation will always occur if the volume of money and credit increases more rapidly over time than the volume of goods and services available to be purchased. There is no disagreement among economists that inflation *can* be controlled or eliminated. The solution is simply for the federal government to exert sufficient control over the volume of money and credit—a task clearly within its powers.

The controversy among economists over inflation arises not over whether inflation can be eliminated, but how rapidly to pursue this goal. The problem is that it is costly to eliminate inflation because the actions taken to suppress growth in the money supply also result in the dampening of economic activity, leading to unemployment of labor and capital. Virtually all economists would like to see inflation eliminated at the smallest overall cost, but there is great disagreement as to which approach will, in fact, be the least costly. At one extreme are those who argue that the cost will be smallest if there is a very gradual slowing down in the growth of the money supply. They believe that this approach will cause less shock to the economy and thereby entail less waste in terms of goods and services not produced. At the other extreme are those who argue precisely the opposite. They claim that the gradualist approach will cause the greatest waste, and they advocate a shock treatment as the least costly cure. They argue that if the government can convince the people that it intends to take whatever action is necessary to control inflation over a short period of time, then people will quickly adjust their behavior, and economic activity will be depressed for only a short period of time rather than for the prolonged period proposed by the gradualists.

In addition to the extreme position, there are of course many intermediate points of view. All observers are able to point to some episode in the past to support their position. But none of the claims is completely convincing or conclusive. The result is that we are some distance from a consensus on the best way to eliminate the current inflation, even though there is unanimity that we can and should do so.

Robert L. Heilbroner. There is more than one kind of inflation. Inflations sometimes occur because nations lose control over their money-issuing mechanisms, as in the runaway inflation of post–World War I Germany. Inflations regularly accompany the waging of wars, as governments create money to buy military goods and supplies, thus flooding the economy with excess purchasing power.

The inflation of the last two decades is different. It is not a runaway. It is not the direct consequence of war finance. It is best viewed as an aspect of the malfunctioning of modern day, power-bloc, welfare-oriented, government-underpinned capitalism. In modern capitalist systems, many forces push the cost structure upward—strong unions, monopolistic enterprises and public cartels (such as OPEC). A welfare orientation that seeks to protect the well-being of weaker groups leads to insurance provisions such as the indexing of Social Security, cost of living adjustments and other provisions that match increases in costs with increases in money incomes. And a powerful government underpinning of spending assures that recessions will be relatively limited in scope.

These changes remove the historic tendency of capitalism to manifest its instability through depressions. Instead, downward price movements are blocked and stifled, whereas upward movements are encouraged and stimulated. The consequence is an economic system that becomes increasingly inflation-prone. This general susceptibility is worsened by the growth of a general expectation of inflation—an expectation that becomes self-fulfilling.

Inflation is, therefore, the consequence of deep-seated changes in the structure of capitalism—namely, the emergence of large unions, corporations and state enterprises; the acceptance of an insurance-minded state policy with respect to the general well-being; and the emplacement of government floors under the workings of the system. Unless one believes that these institutions can be substantially altered, there seems no chance that inflation will be brought under control by such mild measures as monetary restraint, balanced budgets and the like.

In my opinion, only institutional changes capable of limiting the upward-tending instability of the system will remove the inflationary threat. These changes are the counterpart of the floors that have effectively eliminated the downward cumulative movements of the past. They would include permanent (or stand-by) wage and price controls, a tax structure designed to restrain unwanted increases in demand, and probably the dismantling of indexing and other "pass-through" arrangements. Such changes are not likely to be achieved until a consensus has been achieved as to the importance of bringing the inflationary propensity under control, and the inadequacy of less far-reaching measures to achieve this end.

Fritz Machlup. Inflating means blowing in or blowing up, and inflation is the process of being blown up or the state of having been blown up. It can refer to many things, such as the inflation of a tire or a balloon, or an inflated ego. In economics, it also refers to many things. A good writer should therefore always specify whether it is price inflation (consumer-price inflation or wholesale-price inflation), wage inflation, profit inflation, income inflation, demand inflation, currency inflation, credit inflation, budget inflation and so forth. In discussions between the two world wars, economists agreed that it would be confusing to use the word inflation to denote price inflation; and for at least two decades the word inflation, without a modifier, was used to refer to the overexpansion of credit and effective demand. Only after the Second World War did economists join journalists in using the word inflation, without a modifier, to refer to rising price levels.

The question of the causes of price inflation is so confusing and controversial because people often forget that nothing has only *one* cause. A clearheaded writer would not speak of causes but rather of necessary and sufficient conditions. If any condition is sufficient to bring about a result in all possible circumstances, then it might be promoted to the rank of cause. In economics, however, there is almost nothing that would deserve to be regarded as a *sufficient* condition. On the other hand, there are things in economics that might be recognized as *necessary* conditions for the achievement of specified results. If we are asking what can be named as a necessary condition for the process of price inflation, we can indeed give an unqualified answer: a continuing increase in the quantity of money.

Some people confuse a price increase from one year to the next with price inflation. Price inflation is a process that continues for a period of several years. Since prices are not only matters of negotiation and agreement but also require eventual payment, a larger quantity of means of payment will be necessary to sustain an uplift of prices month after month through several years. To be sure, for half a year, or perhaps a whole year, rising prices might be financed by a faster turnover of an unchanged quantity of money, a condition usually explained as a reduction in the demand for cash balances. An enduring price inflation, however, cannot be financed without an increase in the quantity of money and, hence, credit inflation and/or currency inflation is a necessary condition of price inflation.

It would be wrong to conclude from this statement that it is easy to stop price inflation—easy because all you have to do is to stop further creation of money. The point is that control of the money supply is impossible in some countries because laws and institutions do not give the government the power to control the credit expansion of commercial banks. In other countries control over the money supply may be impossible because the lawmakers are unwilling to have the control mechanisms exercised. Most often, control of the money supply is simply not wanted, because people realize that the "turning off of the faucet" would induce heavy unemployment. These people favor continuation of the inflation of credit and prices because they fear the consequences of the monetary tightness that would be necessary to stop the spiral.

Attempts to reduce the annual rate of price inflation gradually over several years will usually be associated with protracted unemployment; attempts to reduce price inflation to zero within a few months are likely to increase unemployment to an especially high level—for a year or two. Attempts to reduce unemployment by means of monetary expansion will probably accelerate price inflation without keeping unemployment down for more than a few months. Monetary expansion and the price inflation that it supports will not increase employment in the long run. Yet, the hope that more spending will lead to more employment seems to survive all contrary experiences. If one political party eventually learns that inflation of credit and prices is never a cure for unemployment, the opposition party will quickly insist that it is or, at least, that inflation is the smaller evil. As long as governments, legislatures or the masses believe that creating and spending more money will create more jobs, monetary expansion and price inflation cannot be eliminated.

William E. Simon. Inflation is a monetary phenomenon. It occurs when a nation's supply of money increases significantly more quickly than the rate of goods and services produced. This definition is widely accepted by economists, liberal and conservative alike.

The debate occurs over the causes of inflation. It is clear to me, however, that if inflation depends on money supply, then only government can cause inflation because only government has the authority to print money. It therefore follows that, contrary to popular opinion, inflation is *not* caused by OPEC, oil companies, labor unions, greedy businessmen or foreign exporters. No, the culprit is government deficit financing, whether in answer to the demands of special interest groups, as a result of a full employment program, or simply as part and parcel of the liberal ideology that demands womb to tomb government care for all citizens.

When the government spends beyond its means, it must finance its deficit in one of three ways. It can raise taxes, but this is very unpopular in peacetime. It can borrow from the public, but this has the effect of raising interest rates and diverting capital from productive purposes. Or, it can print more money. This route has the most disastrous consequence of all—rampant inflation—but it's not harmful in such an obvious way and this "solution" therefore tends to be the most politically expedient.

The cure for inflation is very simple on paper, but terribly difficult to implement politically. Obviously, the government must stop printing so much money, and this, in turn, requires it to cut spending. But politicians don't get elected by promising less, by telling constituents their programs are going to be dropped or reduced. Even if the politicians summoned the courage to keep spending down, the cure for inflation is bitter medicine at first; stemming the growth of money supply initially involves lower economic growth and higher unemployment. So it takes a tremendous amount of political staying power to pursue an anti-inflationary program.

Ultimately, the American people are responsible for holding down inflation. If we continue in the current vein of economic myopia and go on demanding extravagant programs from the government, our elected politicians are likely to provide them, and the inflation rate will continue to soar. In the end, we get the government we deserve.

Roman L. Weil. Inflation is rising *general* prices. It is not rising oil prices, not rising food prices, not rising housing prices, and not increasing specific prices of any kind. Food prices, for example, can rise while the average of general prices is stable or declining. Such an event is not inflation, although many writers would imprecisely use the phrase "food-price inflation."

Inflation results from the supply of money increasing faster than the supply of goods. Average prices must rise when the amount of money increases relative to the amount of goods and services to be acquired with those funds. If the money supply does not increase, then rising prices for a specific commodity such as food must be offset by decreasing prices for some other goods and services. Inflation does not, and cannot, result from the behavior—greedy or otherwise—of participants in the economy who attempt individually or in cartels to increase the prices they receive for their own goods and services. Even if such participants succeed in increasing the prices they receive, in the absence of an increase in money, some other prices will have to decline, so that general prices do not change.

To say that inflation results from the supply of money increasing relative to the supply of goods and services is somewhat like saying a flu results from a virus. Until one knows what causes the virus, one is not necessarily able to cope with the resulting problem. The policy question about inflation is, "What causes the money supply to increase relative to the supply of goods and services?"

The federal government controls the money supply. Our government has found increasing the money supply a more convenient way than raising taxes to pay for the goods and services it wishes to acquire for itself (or to transfer to others).

I suspect the government preference for indirect fund raising through inflation, rather than directly through taxes, results from politicians' finding reelection easier after increasing inflation than after increasing taxes. Inflation can be brought under control (and eliminated), but doing so requires a disciplined government elected by an educated and disciplined public which prefers fewer government services (or higher taxes) to inflation.

WITH THE RISING PRICE OF HOUSES, WILL MANY AMERICAN FAMILIES CONTINUE TO BE ABLE TO BUY THEIR OWN HOMES? IF NOT, WHAT WILL BE THE ALTERNATIVES? WHAT WILL THE HOUSES OF THE FUTURE BE LIKE?

Dr. Jack E. Adams. Housing must be viewed as a commodity which expends service through time. Thus, the household bundle of goods and services will, of course, be adjusted for rising housing prices which exceed real personal income gains. An increase in housing prices to the typical consumer must include higher market interest rates as the consumer competes with corporate grants and developers in the money market. The market interest rate becomes $i_m = i_r + (\Delta P^e/P)$, where i_m is the market rate of interest, i_r becomes the real rate of interest, and $(\Delta P^e/P)$ amounts to the inflationary expectation. In essence, an acceleration of rising housing prices which are larger than real personal income growth perhaps will induce a more intensive added worker effect (i.e., spouse enters labor market) in order to increase the flow of household income. Also, adjustments in the family collection of goods and services will perhaps be adjusted downward. The outcome will be a smaller bundle of housing service (i.e., fewer square feet) and perhaps fewer boats, cars, lengthy vacation trips and so forth.

The efficient household decision making unit will always be faced with the basic economic problem of how to allocate a scarce household personal income flow to meet unlimited human wants (i.e., adequate housing service). Therefore, American families should be able to purchase their own homes, provided other sacrifices are forthcoming. For example, creative financing (low-interest mortgages via bond money subsidies or seller financing) and mortgage flexibility, although lagging, will be induced by rising housing demand. Nevertheless, some financing schemes, such as low-interest bond money, can eventually have at least a limited price increase effect on the resale of such housing. Why? Because in the event of extraordinarily high mortgage interest rates, the below-market-interest rate (i.e., low-interest bond money) can become quite a selling attribute to the contemporary American household.

Future housing will obviously be smaller and will be provided in a land-saving manner whereby perhaps the zero-lot-line concept (housing is constructed on one property line with a yard on the remaining sides of the housing unit) is utilized. Furthermore, even though the energy efficient smaller dwelling place has a higher price tag, a significant portion of the increased price reflects an attempt to offset rising energy prices. Thus, since energy and housing service must be viewed as joint consumption, one must not overreact to rising housing prices, provided energy usage is constrained as an integral part of the "bundle of housing service."

In the final analysis, the condominium will be a permanent fixture on the future housing scene. Of course, one must not forget the refurbishing of blighted residential areas as many Americans continue to exemplify nostalgia about the "good ole days." A policy that should never be widely utilized in the future event of geographic housing shortages is the rent control device. The outcome is a shortfall of rental housing and an induced crowded living environment as landlord dollars flow to more profitable investment streams.

During the 1980s, the housing dilemma should be somewhat reconciled as the postwar population succeeds in at least partially reaching an overall satisfactory housing dream in middle-class America. There will, of course, always be public housing and other subsidized housing programs in the lower range of the household spectrum. Perhaps not all of these programs will be viewed as a "continuous graveyard of good intentions."

Max R. Bloom. Since the mid-1900s, there has been an enormous increase in the supply of new housing and in the condition of the housing supply. The most recent trends appear to show a divergence between prices of new and existing housing, with the latter showing signs of weakening in some areas.

The inflation experienced during the past decade, including increases in the prices and costs of housing has brought rising concern to the "affordability" of housing, both for owner-occupancy and rental. While there is disagreement as to whether housing has become less affordable, it is clear that it is a very real problem for many families.

The concept of affordability or ability to pay is ambiguous and complex, and presents difficult measurement problems. In the past, affordability tended to be measured by inexact rules of thumb such as 20–25 percent of current income for housing or a house price-income ratio of 2½ percent. This ignored the evidence of the wealth position of consumers, as well as the impact of different financial terms on the ability to pay. In a period of stable or slowly rising prices it caused no particular concern for most American families as fixed rate long-term mortgages were generally available.

However, with the onset of a more severe inflation, the financial difficulties of mortgage lending institutions, as well as the diminished investment desirability of relatively low fixed-rate mortgages in the face of increasing interest rates, the fixed-rate mortgage appears to be an anachronism. It is rapidly being supplanted by a variety of alternative mortgage loan instruments such as variable rate mortgages (VRM), graduated payment mortgages (GPM), adjustable rate mortgages and reverse annuity mortgages, which confound borrower and lender alike. As of September 1981, a single-family mortgage interest rate exceeded 17 percent in some areas and house sales and new residential construction are continuing their decline.

The rise of mortgage interest rates, coupled with an increasing size of mortgage loans, has increased the level of monthly mortgage payments to such an extent that many would-be purchasers are unable to qualify for mortgage loans on the basis of a conventional 20–25 percent eligibility factor. Consequently, this factor has been relaxed and many would-be borrowers may now qualify even if the ratio exceeds 30 percent. This represents pressure on current first year income; with increasing incomes, this ratio declines over time where fixed rate mortgages are used. In the case of GPMs, it is hoped that income may keep pace or exceed the later increase in mortgage payments. For VRMs, it depends on the relation between increases (or decreases) in incomes and mortgage interest rates. Although the use of new types of mortgage instruments is increasing, much uncertainty remains as to how they might fare in a different economic environment.

There is little doubt that for many families of moderate and low incomes, especially racial and ethnic minorities who also may lack minimum down payments, home ownership continues to be an elusive goal. Newer mortgage instruments may prove to be helpful for some families in this category.

However, it is important to appreciate that the reliance on cash-flow approaches to affordability masks the important role which has been played by the home as an inflation hedge and its impact on net housing costs over a period of years. For many families in the past decade, real interest rates, after adjustment for inflation and income tax advantages, have been negative and their economic return on housing investment has been substantial. Of course, this varies widely as it is affected by tax and age status (especially in relation to taxation of capital gains), duration of occupancy, financial liquidity and income and wealth status, as well as the condition of local housing markets and inflationary expectations. Approximately two-thirds of American households own their homes, including many who have paid off mortgages. However, some families have remortgaged their homes to obtain funds for investment and/or consumption. The economic advantages of homeownership are generally greater for upper income families. It is understandable that moderate income families (who also can benefit) are more concerned with the high present cash-flow obligations of homeownership. These families are interested in housing as an inflation hedge, thus the trade-off with nonhousing consumption can cause financial pressures.

In considering the issue of affordability it is also important to understand that the single family home is both a consumers' good and an investment good. As an investment, it assumes considerable importance in an inflationary environment. While there is widespread expectation that inflation will continue at a high rate, any significant economic downturn would adversely affect house prices.

Home purchase includes not only single family units, but, also, condominiums which may be either detached structures, or, more typically, are in high-rise and garden type complexes, physically indistinguishable from rental housing. The condominium unit is an ownership unit, and, therefore, the above comments relative to homeownership advantages are equally applicable. In part, increasing costs of single family homes during the 1970s resulted from an increase in the size of homes with more amenities.

Rental housing presents a special problem, both in terms of financing and cost-revenue relationships. During the 1970s, the proportion of rental housing, including subsidized housing, tended to decline. Rental housing costs, especially operating and maintenance expenses, have increased placing upward pressure on rents which still lag behind the

CPI; however, during these years the proportion of income spent for rent has increased. Renters generally have lower incomes than home-owners and do not share in the income tax benefits available to home-owners.

Current trends in mortgage finance are not favorable for high-volume rental housing construction (except, possibly, for higher rent projects) considered affordable by moderate and low-income families, some of whom may be assisted by various federal and state subsidy programs.

Currently a presidential commission is preparing its recommendations for a new approach to housing. Since urban initiatives have a relatively low priority in this period of fiscal restraint, it is uncertain that this commission will recommend a shift in priorities which would entail an increase in federal support for housing for moderate and low-income groups. Indeed, the economic outlook appears uncertain. If the adminis-tration's anti-inflation program is unsuccessful, the economic conse-quences could be severe and further adversely affect the already seri-ously weakened housing market and housing opportunities for many families. Paradoxically, if the program succeeds in reducing inflation at the cost of increased unemployment and diminished economic activity without a significant decline in mortgage interest rates, the housing market would also be weakened.

Homes of the future will continue to reflect design and technological innovation, particularly in the area of energy efficiency. In many metro-politan areas, there may be a tendency towards smaller lot sizes and smaller homes, depending on local market forces. As a means of reduc-ing sales prices, some homes may be offered in a less than completed state so that the prospective purchasers may complete the home with their own labor. An increase in attached-type homes (now called town-houses) will help reduce costs of building and land.

Dr. Wray O. Candilis. With problems such as energy self-sufficiency, declining productivity, reindustrialization, capital adequacy and per-sonal savings capturing the attention of government policy makers, housing as a national priority is being de-emphasized, at least in the short term. This fact, plus persistent inflationary pressures, lackluster business activity and interest rate volatility have combined to diminish the vigor of the housing and mortgage markets during the past few years.

In the long term, however, a number of factors will evolve, producing an economic environment conducive to the realization of the potential home buyer's dream. Inflation will be less formidable in the 1980s than it was in the 1970s, while the two-wage earner family and strong household formation will provide a healthy backdrop to future housing demand. Cost and energy considerations will, of course, result in reduc-tions in the size of the average new house but no revolutionary building processes are expected to emanate in the years ahead.

Depository institutions, especially savings and loan associations and mutual savings banks, have not been able lately to provide the needed capital to the housing markets but thanks to recent reforms that broadened both the deposit-liability and the investment-asset powers of the thrifts, their capability to compete and to adjust will be considerably enhanced. Furthermore, the secondary mortgage market will be needed more than ever before, with the attention being focused on pension funds and private mortgage-backed securities.

With much more capital needed in the near future for an ever expanding housing market, buyers and sellers will be utilizing creative financing techniques to finance home purchases. Such devices are already being used in the form of mortgage assumptions, wraparound mortgages, land contracts, owner takeback of first or second mortgages, and other variations of the sales transaction. In addition, to enhance the ability of additional homeowners to participate in the market in an inflationary economy, alternative mortgage instruments, such as variable rate mortgages, graduated payment mortgages, rollover mortgages, indexed mortgage financing, equity participation mortgages, will become increasingly popular at the expense of the fixed-rate mortgage.

To summarize, the housing and mortgage industries are undergoing substantial changes that will have a strong influence on buyers and sellers of homes in the present decade. Although change entails both opportunities and potential disruptions, there is no doubt that after a short period of adjustment, the long-term outlook holds great promise for the economy as a whole and for housing in particular.

Joseph S. DeSalvo. During the 1970s, housing prices rose 133 percent, while after-tax incomes rose only 103 percent. A commonly used housing affordability criterion is that the cost of owning a home should not exceed 25 percent of a family's total yearly income. By this criterion, housing became less affordable during the 1970s. One study found that from 1970 to 1976 the proportion of families that could afford homeownership fell from 46.2 percent to 27 percent. If a similar study were performed today, it would probably show that an even smaller percentage of families could afford homes.

In view of these facts, it is not surprising that the press has devoted considerable space to the issue of housing affordability, dwelling at length on the dire circumstances facing the prospective home buyer. However, a strange thing was going on in the housing market. More new housing was built in the 1970s than ever before, and its quality was rising. Families purchased houses with more amenities—bathrooms, fireplaces, basements, garages—and with more living area. Perhaps strangest of all, in light of the traditional affordability criterion, was that the proportion of the housing stock that was owner-occupied *rose*.

The solution to this puzzle lies in an understanding of the costs of homeownership. Housing affordability studies, such as the one mentioned earlier, usually count as homeownership costs, mortgage payments, property taxes, and maintenance and operating expenses. These are certainly costs, but they are not all of the costs facing homeowners nor, more importantly, do they include the financial benefits to homeownership which act as offsets to the costs usually measured. A more complete accounting of costs would include, in addition to mortgage interest, the interest foregone on the homeowner's money tied up in home equity as well as the costs of transferring ownership (brokerage fees, closing costs, etc.). While these additional costs may not be insignificant, it is the benefits to homeownership that are really important. These are, first, the expectation of capital gains and, second, various tax advantages.

When housing prices rise faster than the general price level, opportunities for real capital gains are available to homeowners. The expectation of such gains acts to offset the expected costs of homeownership, thereby making home purchase more attractive than otherwise. In addition to this benefit of homeownership are the tax advantages. Mortgage interest and property taxes are deductible in calculating taxable income for federal income tax purposes. Perhaps less appreciated is the exemption of the implicit rental income on owner-occupied housing. (This is counted as income, as it should be, in the National Income Accounts from which we get the GNP figures, but it is not so counted for federal income tax purposes.) Finally, there is the favorable treatment of capital gains, which for housing, like other assets, are taxed at rates lower than those applicable to ordinary income and which for housing, unlike other assets, may be deferred for many years and are subject to a substantial exemption.

When all of the costs and benefits of homeownership are taken into account, as was done in a recent study by Professor Douglas Diamond, it is found that real homeowning costs *fell* by about 18 percent during the 1970s. What happened was that the expectation of higher real housing prices and thus of real capital gains almost exactly matched the actual rise in real housing prices, so that homeownership became an almost perfect inflation hedge as well as a good investment. Furthermore, there was a decline in real mortgage interest costs and in property tax rates. These last two factors accounted for about 10 percentage points of the total decline. The remaining 8 percent was due to the tax advantages of homeownership. So we see that people were simply responding rationally to decreasing costs of homeownership during the 1970s and that there wasn't an affordability crises after all.

Does this mean we don't have to worry about housing affordability in the 1980s? No, it just means that we must be careful in drawing inferences from narrowly defined housing prices and costs rising faster than incomes. In fact, there appears to be some cause for concern, at least over the early years of this decade.

Because of the substantial rise in mortgage interest rates, starting in the second half of the 1970s and lately reaching levels higher than those since the Civil War, the cost of homeownership, accounting for all the benefits discussed earlier, *rose* in 1979 after falling almost without interruption during the rest of the 1970s. That rise is undoubtedly continuing today. In response, prospective homeowners are looking at smaller houses on smaller lots and with fewer of the amenities. Many are turning to condominiums and, in certain states, cooperative apartments which permit some of the benefits of homeownership but at usually lower prices than comparable single-family detached houses. Sellers are participating more in the financing of their homes by prospective buyers than was formerly the custom, and they are beginning to lower their prices, too. Government has lessened many restrictions on lending agencies, and the recent tax legislation should aid prospective home buyers.

Whether the cost of homeownership will continue to rise through the 1980s is unknown. As the experience of the 1970s shows, however, the housing market is surprisingly resilient. We thought costs were rising when in fact they were falling. Maybe the same will be true of this decade.

John R. Kupferer. Two-thirds of the nation's families live in homes they own. But in today's high-priced market it is questionable whether many of them would be able to afford to buy the homes they now live in, were they coming into the market for the first time.

Housing affordability is the crucial issue for a new generation of 41 million Americans who will reach the prime home-buying age of thirty sometime during the 1980s. By shifting into manufactured housing and innovative building techniques and configurations, home builders have recently made significant progress on the housing cost front. The affordability of homeownership in the future, however, is an issue that ultimately will be decided in the public sector, where government has traditionally set policies favoring the goal of homeownership.

In the past, renting was the answer for families not able to afford homeownership. However, high housing costs have diminished opportunities in the rental as well as for-sale segment of the market. Most renters would be unable to pay the fair market rent of a unit in an apartment building under construction today.

A breakthrough in housing costs is possible in two areas. First, record high mortgage interest rates have priced the majority of the nation's families out of the market. While mortgage financing is expected to remain a relatively more expensive proposition than it has been in the past, a decline in interest rates of only a few points can reduce typical monthly mortgage payments by a hundred dollars or more. Lower mortgage rates are well within the realm of possibilities if the national government adopts more balanced fiscal and monetary policies—reduced spending and faster growth in the money supply.

Second, local government can have a major impact on land and development costs by reversing restrictive land-use requirements: no-growth zoning laws, and unwarranted "hidden taxes" in the form of excessive utility connection fees, building permit fees, inspection fees and often unrealistic building codes. Local government officials may reconsider their approach to new development once they realize that they are standing in the way of housing opportunity for their constituents and economic growth in the community. Various studies have reported that government red tape can increase the cost of a new home by 20 percent or more.

What will the house of the future be like? It probably won't be much different from the house of today. The steady evolution of housing to meet the needs of the first-time home buyer with a smaller family will continue. Houses are generally becoming smaller, with greater emphasis on more efficient use of space and more liveable traffic patterns and design. New homes are more energy efficient and better insulated. As it becomes more cost-effective, passive-solar energy will gain wider use. Today, almost 85 percent of all homes are built with one or more prefabricated components, and the trend is accelerating. Where land costs are high, there is a rising demand for attached townhouses and zero-lot-line homes, which are built on narrow lots in which one side of the home, without windows or doors, is built on the lot line, while the other side of the house contains windows and doors overlooking a comfortable side yard offering privacy and security for children.

Arthur M. Weimer. American families will continue to buy their own houses provided financing is available. This will depend on the volume of savings which will depend on the rate of inflation which also influences interest rate levels. New types of mortgage instruments probably will play an important role.

Inflationary expectations have stimulated an artificially high demand for houses. Investor rather than consumer considerations have governed many decisions to buy houses in recent years. A speculative aspect has developed with many buyers purchasing two, three or more houses in the hope of price appreciation.

If inflationary expectations subsided, the speculative element would be removed from house prices and the consumer considerations would gain in importance relative to investment and speculative factors. Interest rates would then come down and permit the financing of houses in more affordable terms than in a highly inflationary period. New types of mortgage financing or other types of mortgages would serve to protect lenders against interest rates and purchasing power risks.

During the recent inflationary period people demanded somewhat bigger houses than earlier. If inflation subsides, family needs rather than investment and speculative considerations are likely to control decisions and somewhat smaller houses may grow in popularity. This tendency will be accelerated by energy costs and related factors. Town-house and condominium arrangements may grow in importance relative to single-family detached houses.

WHEN THOSE WHO ARE NOW THIRTY YEARS OLD REACH RETIREMENT AGE, WILL THERE BE SOCIAL SECURITY MONEY FOR THEM?

Robert M. Ball. There will undoubtedly be changes in Social Security by the time the present thirty-year-olds reach age sixty-five, but I am sure that having contributed to the program over a lifetime of work will guarantee that the United States government will recognize its obligation to make payments on retirement.

The government has an obligation based on the payment of social security taxes. The right to Social Security benefits is a government promise that will not be broken because voters will insist on that obligation being met. Social Security is the best way to provide the economic security that people need. It provides protection not only against the loss of income and retirement, but also in the case of total disability and the case of the death of the wage earner in the family. The benefits are kept automatically up to date with average wages prior to the time the worker applies for benefits and after that it is both inflation-proof and tax-free. Administrative costs are only 1.3 cents out of every dollar and the protection follows the worker from job to job. It is a deservedly popular program.

Doubt has been cast on the ability of the Social Security system to make payments in the distant future by people who do not understand the way in which Social Security is financed. They express concern that the trust funds do not have enough money in them to cover future benefit payments. This is true. The Social Security trust funds are not designed as large interest-earning funds as is the case with private insurance annuities sold to individuals. The Social Security trust funds are contingency funds designed to see the program through the ups and downs of unexpected economic developments. This pay-as-you-go approach has the advantage of making it possible for Social Security benefits to be kept up to date automatically with rising prices, whereas relying on interest earnings on accumulated funds makes it impossible for private insurance to guarantee an inflation-proof system. The money to pay for Social Security benefits in the period from 2015 on, when people now aged thirty will be drawing benefits, will come very largely from Social Security taxes paid at that time just as Social Security benefits today are paid by Social Security taxes today.

Because of the aging of the population, Social Security taxes in the next century (or a contribution from general revenue to the system) may need to be somewhat higher than today to provide the level of benefits now promised. Under present law, the current rate covering old-age and survivors insurance and disability insurance of 5.35 percent of earnings (the rest of the Social Security tax of 6.65 percent is for hospital insurance under Medicare) is scheduled to go to 6.2 percent in 1990. Under some sets of demographic and economic assumptions, these rates will be sufficient to carry the program more or less indefinitely, while under more pessimistic assumptions, it might be necessary to increase the Social Security rates again around the year 2015. In any event, increases would not be so large as to constitute an increased burden on workers in 2015 than present rates are for workers today. Workers in the year 2015 and beyond will have higher real wages than those today and there will be many fewer young people below the age of twenty to support. Somewhat higher costs for caring for the elderly in the future may be part of the cost of maintaining relatively low population growth. A big increase in the birth rate would decrease relatively Social Security costs but it would greatly increase pressure on the environment and on the level of living of the whole community.

Certainly there is no reason to expect that a future generation of wage earners will want the retired elderly of that time to live at a lower relative level of living than those today, and that is what the issue is.

Paul A. Brinker. Yes, there will be Social Security money for today's thirty-year-olds at retirement. The problem in the future will be difficult, because today there are three workers for every retiree. In the future there will only be two. Benefits may have to be reduced somewhat, and taxes increased. Only the first $29,700 is taxed in 1981, and this base could be raised much higher to reach the middle-income group more.

E. Ray Canterbery. There will be Social Security benefits upon retirement for those now thirty years old, but the benefits will be more in line with payments into the system (Social Security payroll taxes). In 1979 the average retiree got back in just one year 72 percent of all he or she had put in during a lifetime and the retiree who had been a low wage earner got back 118 percent of all he or she had put in. However, during the next half century the system will be viewed more as it was originally conceived, as a minimum retirement program supplemented by private pensions and personal savings. The present social welfare aspects of Social Security will be replaced by a negative income tax or some other means of making welfare grants directly to the poor.

The immediate future for Social Security is not nearly as bleak as commonly believed. The high inflation and unemployment of recent years have been the major causes of more money going out of the system than is coming in. As in so many situations, a sick economy is contagious. Social Security benefits are tied to the consumer price index so that payments automatically increase with the rapidly rising prices of the goods in that index. Moreover, fewer people working means fewer people contributing payroll taxes to the system. A program that effectively solves the problems of inflation and unemployment will aid social security.

The projected long-run imbalance between income and outgo stems from a declining birth rate and rising longevity that will cause the ratio of retirees to workers to soar when the World War II babies begin to retire around 2012. However, with a falling birth rate, workers will have fewer dependents and can better afford to make larger payments into the system. These demographic characteristics should carry us safely into 2035 when we shall panic about other things. Meanwhile, tying benefit increases to the slower-moving average wage rate or to the GNP price index, eliminating the minimum monthly benefit and dropping college student benefits will suffice to make Social Security secure.

Dr. Samuel B. Chase, Jr. Yes, but Social Security benefits are likely to grow much more slowly in future years, and the Social Security system will require assistance from the general fund of the Treasury rather than continuing to be—or appearing to be—self-financing.

Dr. Bernard Clyman. It is inconceivable that the federal government would even allow the Social Security system to be in default in its benefit payments.

It will meet those payments by doing one or more of the following:

1. Raise the minimal retirement age from sixty-five to sixty-eight, with probably increased financial discouragement of retirement at earlier ages.
2. Use the general revenues of the U.S. Treasury to meet its financial payout requirements.
3. Liberalize its immigration policies to permit more workers to join the employed labor force and thereby increase Social Security contributions.
4. Slow down (and possibly cut back) the increase in benefit payout.

Milton Gwirtzman. Yes, today's thirty-year-olds will receive Social Security as long as the American people are willing to support Social Security in the future as they have up to now.

Most people realize that the taxes they pay for Social Security do not accumulate in an account waiting for them to retire. The money is used to pay the benefits for their parents' generation, just as their children's taxes will be used to pay their benefits. This pact between generations, begun by President Franklin Roosevelt, has worked so far, keeping old people out of the poorhouse and making it far less necessary for children to have to worry about the economic security of their parents as they grow old.

The doubts about Social Security's ability to pay benefits when people now in their thirties retire arise from declining birth rates. There will be fewer working people left to pay the taxes thirty to forty years from now; and it is questionable just how high payroll taxes can be raised for Social Security. One way to solve this problem is to start about twenty years from now, to gradually raise the retirement age to sixty-eight instead of sixty-five. People retiring at sixty-eight then will still receive as good a deal from Social Security as people do now. Why? Because, according to the best medical estimates, they will be living (and collecting benefits) several years longer than at present.

The Social Security system, with its tax-free, inflation-proof monthly checks, available to all workers, has served the nation well so far, and deserves the public support it will need in the future.

Dr. Lafayette G. Harter, Jr. No, thirty-year-olds will not receive Social Security in the future. It is not practical for a nation to lay aside money (take it out of circulation) and then later release it to be spent in large quantities. While the deflationary effects of saving the money might not be too serious (it might be invested in increasing production), the rapid release could be inflationary when these people retire, unless offset by reductions in purchasing power somewhere else in the nation.

The problem is that when the thirty-year-olds of today retire, there will be so many of them in comparison with people who will be working. Whether individuals save up for their own retirement, receive retirement funds from their employers, or simply draw Social Security benefits, their consumption will be a strain on the economy.

If our economy should grow enough in the next thirty-five years, the strain may not be too great. At historical growth rates we should be two to three times as wealthy as we are now. However, if our economy should fail to grow, we may be talking about what may be called the "heartbreak generation."

Joseph J. Melone. Social Security is a vital and integral part of the economic structure of our society, and it will continue to serve as a basic floor of protection for individual economic security. There will be changes in the system. Rates of increases in benefits will be limited when wages do not rise as rapidly as the CPI. In recent years, Social Security benefits have kept pace with inflation to a greater degree than the incomes of the working population. The working population (the Social Security taxpayers) will not tolerate that degree of income transfer over any extended period of time.

A second and related change will be an increase in the normal retirement age provision under Social Security—increasing gradually from age sixty-five to sixty-eight starting soon after the turn of the century. The ratio of persons age sixty-five and over to our labor force population will increase for many years to come, putting a significant Social Security tax burden on the working population. Increases in retirement ages help at both ends of the equation—more people in the labor force paying Social Security taxes, while shortening the benefit period. Improvements in health and longevity since the start of the program in 1935 suggest the need for serious consideration of this proposal.

Lastly, my optimism regarding the future of Social Security is based on a belief that the U.S. economy will experience major improvements in productivity in the next two decades. Economic security in money terms is meaningless. The only real economic security is availability and affordability of goods and services and that is a function of the level of productivity of the economic system.

Ernest C. Miller, Ph.D. The entire Social Security system is a subject of intense controversy at various levels of government and among the public in general. This act allocates payment of designated monies to a group of individuals, termed retirees, who meet two basic criteria for eligibility: (1) have paid a given amount of money (premiums) into the system for a given period of time, and (2) have reached the designated retirement age in order to qualify for monthly annuity payments for the balance of their lives . . . and their spouses' lives.

Inherent in the Social Security system is an implied promise by the federal government that individuals who meet these criteria will, as a matter of national commitment, receive a return from the system. In order to meet his commitment, and remain fiscally solvent, it now appears that a series of legislative changes to the system will be forthcoming. Such changes might well include increases in premium levels; extending the qualification age from sixty-five to sixty-eight, sixty-nine, or even seventy; elimination of the age sixty-two early retirement provision; and changes in the scales method of computing annuities. Inherent in all of these, and possibly more changes, is the need for a new method for the perpetual funding of the system, and a method for insuring the continuous availability of annuity funds for payment.

If we assume that Congress will take the necessary action to achieve these goals (a foregone conclusion), then we must likewise assume that the Old Age, Survivors, and Disability Insurance Act will continue to remain in force for generations to come. Thus, it can be assumed that every person currently enrolled in the Social Security system, or soon to be enrolled, can be assured with reasonable certainty that when he or she reaches the designated age of retirement, sufficient funds will be available in the form of a continuous monthly annuity.

Dr. Glenn W. Miller. Persons born in the early 1950s will be able to receive Social Security benefits when they reach retirement age. Social Security, by far the most significant economic security program enacted in the United States, in place for more than forty years, built into the late-life economic assumptions of almost all of our population, and a necessity in a society as complex and interdependent as ours, will not be abandoned. Retirement benefits, based on a public program, will be paid to older persons when they leave the labor market.

This is not to say that Social Security, exactly as we know it in 1981, will be available. The program today is quite different from the program we envisaged in the original enactment of 1935. Various congresses and administrations have expanded the coverage (of persons and risks) enormously, and simultaneously have raised the level of protection against economic risks. Thus the costs of the Social Security program have risen sharply while, in recent years, a sluggish economy with an unacceptably high level of unemployment has cut into the revenues derived from payroll taxes. A day of reckoning and some modification, but not the dawn of bankruptcy or abandonment, is facing the nation.

As to needed modifications, every person in the labor force can be blanketed into the Social Security program—essentially most federal and many state and local government employees can be covered. The age at which persons qualify for full or reduced (early retirement) benefits can be raised gradually in view of increasing life expectancy and demographic trends, especially the ratio of Social Security beneficiaries to persons paying payroll taxes. Some of the protections provided under Social Security, while needed and defensible social protection, are not work-related, as is retirement. We lose wage or salary income through retirement, and a payroll tax to finance retirement insurance is defensible. Ill health in our later years and severe disability at any age are likely to develop from causes that are not work-related. Payroll taxes are not the most defensible source of funds to finance such benefits. Further, financing through payroll taxes suggests greater costs of Social Security than really are a part of the expense of ensuring income to the retired and their dependents in old age. General revenue funds can be utilized in financing some of the social insurance now financed by payroll taxes. Inter-fund borrowing between the four Social Security trust funds can be permitted. Further, the Social Security Administration can be allowed, under carefully stipulated circumstances, to borrow, at interest, from general revenue funds.

Congressional actions, as outlined above, should be prompt but not unduly hurried; modest inter-fund transfers can give a few years in which to improve an ailing, but not markedly unsound, program. In the early 1980s the Old Age and Survivors Insurance trust fund received about nineteen dollars for every twenty dollars paid out. Obviously this can't go on indefinitely, but there can be time to deliberate and act thoughtfully, since other, admittedly smaller, trust funds, such as Medicare and Disability, are in better condition.

Despite the growing criticisms and fears expressed in the early 1980s about Social Security, it is here to stay. Major developed nations of the world have economic security systems more extensive and more costly than ours. In this nation nearly 36 million persons receive monthly benefit checks, 90 percent or more of those over age sixty-five as well as younger early retirees, survivors and disabled. More than 90 percent of all workers are paying taxes that are the foundation of their right to economic security benefits for them and their dependents, in cases of retirement, death or disability. The patterns of other developed nations, the moral, economic and political forces in our nation, and expectations of almost all workers of their entitlement to Social Security make it highly likely that Social Security is with us to stay—probably modified, but not eviscerated.

Richard E. Shepherd. Currently, with the Social Security Trust Funds having just enough money to pay four months' benefits if income were to completely cease, the Social Security board of trustees concludes that there will be enough income to pay benefits beyond the turn of the century.

This statement is especially encouraging because it was made during a period when recent unemployment reduced income, and double-digit inflation increased expenditures from the funds.

But changes will be needed, and these changes will have to include increasing the amount of income to the trust fund and restraining expenditures from the fund.

The quality and stability of Social Security after the turn of the century will reflect directly the nation's economic picture . . . which means that unless we achieve a low unemployment rate and control inflation, today's thirty-year-olds will have to live on reduced benefits.

Aaron Wildavsky. There will be Social Security benefits for today's thirty-year-olds because government will not go back on its obligation. The questions will be where the money comes from and how much and at what retirement date.

PERSONAL FINANCES AND INVESTMENTS

*I*F YOU ARE LIKE most Americans, you are looking for ways to make what you earn stretch as far as possible. You need to carefully budget the money you work for, and you want your money to work for you. In recent years, Americans have found that, though they have been earning more, inflation has been taking more of what they earn. The following table, based on figures from the Bureau of Labor Statistics, illustrates how the spending powers of many American workers have actually declined during periods when wages were rising.

AVERAGE EARNINGS FOR PRODUCTION OR NONSUPERVISORY MANUFACTURING WORKERS IN THE U.S.

| | Gross Average Weekly Earnings | | Married Worker with Three Dependents | |
	YEARLY DOLLARS	1967 DOLLARS*	YEARLY DOLLARS	1967 DOLLARS*
1960	89.72	101.15	80.11	90.32
1965	107.53	113.79	96.78	102.41
1970	119.83	103.04	115.58	93.38
1975	163.53	101.45	166.29	103.16
1980	234.39	94.51	242.63	97.83

*The earnings in 1967 dollars were adjusted according to changes in the CPI for Urban Wage Earners and Clerical Workers.

What do you do when your take-home pay does not take you as far as you need—or want—to go? A solution for some is to retain the same spending habits, charging items they cannot pay cash for, and then borrowing money to pay bills. Consciously or unconsciously, many families choose this route and, as a result, end up deeply in debt or even bankrupt.

An alternative is to carefully tailor the family budget, stretching dollars here, cutting away excess there, and, perhaps most important, discovering the actual limits to the family's income and planning to spend only within those limits. One universal recommendation from money experts is that a family should plan not to spend all of its disposable income (that is, the money left over after paying for housing, food, and other necessities). At the very least, they advise, families should reserve some money and keep it readily accessible in case of emergencies.

Once families achieve some financial security through insurance and savings, they can contemplate the more risky but potentially more lucrative field of investments. Currently, there are hundreds of financial publications, investment advisory services, and personal advisors eager to counsel would-be investors. There is so much information available, in fact, that the mountains of statistics can be as confusing as the terminology used in the investment world.

During the last decade, some of the most profitable investments were not found on Wall Street but in more tangible items, such as real estate, jewelry and collectibles that survived the blight of inflation. Currently, however, some experts are prophesying upturns in the stock market as well as in other intangible investments, such as bonds. Many people, especially small investors, hedge their bets by buying shares in mutual funds managed by professionals who invest the money in diverse stocks, bonds, and other income-producing sources. By spreading the shareholders' funds over a wide variety of investments, mutual-fund managers relieve the shareholders of some of the risk and much of the day-to-day worry of investing. Yet many investors—both small and large —thrive on the risk and excitement of financial speculation. While others are having financial nightmares, they are dreaming about the big kill.

The following section offers advice to middle-income Americans battling their budgets, as well as to those who are preparing to invest. It gives advice on investments for the 1980s and tells what to look for in investment advisors.

CONTRIBUTORS

Dr. John W. Aberle, Professor of Marketing, San Jose State University, San Jose, California

Stephen H. Archer, Professor, Department of Economics, Williamette University, Salem, Oregon

Albert H. Cox, Jr., President, Merrill Lynch Economics, Inc.; Chief Economist, Merrill Lynch and Co., Inc., New York, New York

William E. Donoghue, author, *Complete Money Market Guide*, and publisher of Donoghue's *Moneyletter*, Holliston, Massachusetts

Gerald S. Fisher, attorney, financial consultant and publisher

A. James Heins, Professor of Economics, University of Illinois, Urbana, Illinois

Walter E. Hoadley, Executive Vice-President, Bank of America, San Francisco, California

William Nordhaus, John Musser Professor of Economics, Yale University, New Haven, Connecticut

M. K. Ohlson, Ph.D., Professor of Economics, Metropolitan State College, Denver, Colorado

Harold W. Watts, Professor of Economics, Columbia University, New York, New York; Senior Fellow, Mathematics Policy Research, Princeton, New Jersey

WHAT IS THE MOST PRACTICAL BUDGET FOR THE AVERAGE AMERICAN FAMILY EARNING FROM $10,000 TO $25,000 A YEAR?

Stephen H. Archer. The most practical budget for the average American family in the $10,000 to $25,000 income category varies considerably depending mostly upon: income; family size; ages; region of the country; employer-provided benefits; city or rural living; personal tastes.

But representative of that is the annual budget for a four-person family at two budget levels for *urban* United States as computed by the U.S. Department of Labor, Bureau of Labor Statistics for 1980 in *News* released April 22, 1981.

TOTAL BUDGET	$14,044	$23,134
A. Total Consumption	11,243	16,969
1. Food	4,321	5,571
2. Housing	2,608	5,106
3. Transportation	1,160	2,116
4. Clothing	907	1,292
5. Personal Care	352	471
6. Medical Care	1,298	1,303
7. Other Consumption	597	1,109
B. Other Items	583	957
C. Social Security and Disability	881	1,427
D. Personal Income Taxes	1,337	3,781

This family consists of an employed husband, age thirty-eight, a wife not employed outside the home, an eight year-old girl and a boy of thirteen.

Housing (A2) includes household operations (utilities) as well as home furnishings. Personal Care (A5) includes such items as cleaning, laundry, cosmetics, haircuts, etc. Other consumption (A7) includes recreation, reading, tobacco, alcohol and education. Other items (B) include life insurance, occupational expenses, contributions and gifts.

For the lower budget category, the total budget varies from $20,987 in Anchorage, $18,480 in Honolulu, $15,735 San Francisco–Oakland to $13,082 in Atlanta, Georgia, nonmetropolitan areas (populations of cities of size 2500 to 50,000). Costs were 6 percent lower than for metropolitan areas.

A. James Heins. One of the great aspects of being an American is the ability to spend money in accordance with the dictates of taste. Most people tend to think of this principle as applying to the rich; but it is the most important principle in determining the practical budget for all income groups, one that makes the most of any dollar income.

The family that earns an income in the range of $10,000 to $25,000 a year is considered a lower middle income family. Most families in this situation spend about 30 percent of their income on housing and utilities, but that percent will tend to be smaller as income increases. Food, depending crucially on family size, takes up about 25 percent of income. Again, this percent tends to decline as income increases. Transportation averages about 20 percent of income.

Totaling these percentages leaves the typical family with only 25 percent for other purchases: clothing, medical care, entertainment, and education. At an annual income of $10,000, the residual amounts to $2,500, hardly a king's ransom. These numbers should serve only as guides. The practical family deviates from them as their tastes and circumstances dictate. In many cases, families having incomes in the $10,000 range can avail themselves of public programs—medical aid for example—to supplement their income.

More important than the precise division of dollars among uses is the capacity to make dollar expenditures actually improve family well-being. Understandably, expenditures for frills may appear to improve the low income family's image among its peers. The family that resists this practice however, and uses its money for education or travel, soon comes out ahead. Nothing can be more revealing about this aspect of the American family than observing the brands they buy. All too often the relatively poor family purchases name brands while the wealthier family buys generic goods. These decisions have more to do with making a "practical budget" than the precise percent to be spent on the various budgetary components in the first place.

Walter E. Hoadley. The nature of budgetary decisions and the amount of budgetary flexibility for dealing with emergencies vary greatly for the family with an income of $10,000 and a family with an income of $25,000. The $10,000-a-year family (assuming a four-person family) is operating around the poverty level in 1981. The family with the $25,000-a-year income is the typical middle-class family, for the median income of all families in 1981 is around $25,000.

Generally the marginally poor family must allocate a larger portion of income to such fixed consumption expenses as food, housing, transportation, clothing and medical care. As shown in the table below, about 75 percent of income goes to these essential types of living expenses. After paying taxes the family is left with little more than 10 percent of their income for other expenditures such as personal care, savings, emergency expenses, education, leisure, travel, etc. The middle income family allocates less than 65 percent of income to fixed consumption expenses and has roughly 13 percent of its budget left for other needs. Note that such a family pays about 25 percent of income for taxes.

EXPENDITURES AS PERCENT OF TOTAL INCOME*

	Marginally Poor Family	*Middle Income Family*
A. Fixed consumption expenses	74.2	62.3
1. Food	31.0	21.2
2. Housing	19.3	23.1
3. Transportation	7.4	7.5
4. Clothing	7.3	6.4
5. Medical care	9.2	4.1
B. Taxes	14.3	24.9
1. Social security & disability	6.2	4.0
2. Personal income taxes	8.1	20.9
C. Flexible portion of budget	11.5	12.8

*Source: Calculated from data contained in "Urban Family Budgets and Comparative Indexes for Selected Urban Areas, Autumn, 1978," Bureau of Labor Statistics, U. S. Department of Labor.

The marginally poor family has substantially fewer options, for the bulk of the income must go for food and other necessities of living. With limited funds, the most practical budget dimension is to find more ways to spend on the best value of food, housing, medical care and transportation that is available at current prices. No doubt some of these families could make more effective use of their income, but this involves their individual information-decision process. At present most of these poorer families are found: (1) to rent living space because they cannot afford to purchase their own home. That is why a smaller portion of their total income goes for housing than is the case for the middle income family. (Home-owners normally allocate a greater portion of their budget to housing than do those who rent. Part of this reflects the high cost of buying a home and also that housing represents a major investment as well as providing shelter); (2) to spend about 40 percent of total income for such fixed costs as food and medical care, as compared with 25 percent for the middle income family; (3) to be hit particularly hard by social security taxes while the middle income family is affected more by personal income taxes.

In general, the most practical budget for the broad average spectrum of American families would probably fall within the following guide-lines: (1) one-quarter of the budget for housing; (2) nearly one-quarter of the budget for food; (3) no more than one-quarter of total income for taxes; (4) about one-fifth of the budget for other consumer expenses; (5) save around one-twentieth of total income. These guidelines must be flexible to allow for important differences in income, family re-sponsibility, age and life-style. The young family just buying a new home or condominium will, and should, allocate a greater portion of income to housing costs. The middle-aged couple whose children have left home should save more for their retirement years.

M. K. Ohlson. A budget is one of the luxuries that a family in the $10,000–$25,000 income range probably cannot afford unless it owns a home purchased before the use of short-term variable interest rate mortgages. The reason for this is that the major components of the family's expenditure, e.g., rent or house payments, heat, light, gasoline, etc., are out of its control.

Rather than to attempt a budget I would advise a family to make a list of priorities. If items high on the list increase in price, expenditure on those things ranking lower may be reduced.

Harold W. Watts. The average American family of four is more likely to be spending in the range from $13,000 to $30,000 at the present time. About one out of five will be worse off and one out of five better off.

At around $20,000, some 25 percent is typically spent on food, about 30 percent on housing and 20 percent on transportation. Clothing, medical care and all other items make up the remaining 25 percent. At the higher expenditure levels, a little more is spent on transportation and a little less on food as a proportion of total spending. Young families, especially couples, usually spend a larger share on durable goods until they have built up a working inventory of such items. Older couples are usually stocked up with various kinds of inventories and spend more on food and medical care. The older ones also do more saving if they are still actively employed.

But all of these are based on *averages* of the budgets of sensible people pursuing their own best interests. Most people deviate in some ways from these patterns and many follow very different rules, yet they seem sensible within particular circumstances. Different people have different priorities and life patterns. Some save by making clothes so they can travel more. Others will have different economizing strategies and different indulgences. So it is probably not sensible to imitate an average budget or any other single pattern. Family budgets should reflect the interests and abilities of family members, even when the budget is as low as $13,000. The higher levels naturally allow more indulgences, but still require serious management efforts—many things can be afforded one-at-a-time, but they can't be afforded all at once.

The most practical budget must always be one that stays within one's means, which includes the choices of more earning efforts versus more free time. But in this as in every other respect, practical and satisfying budgets must reflect individual interests and priorities. Rigidly pre-scribed budgets are like rigid reducing diets. They take most of the fun out of living and expressing one's individuality.

WHAT IS THE BEST INVESTMENT TODAY AND WHY?

Dr. John W. Aberle. Money market funds appear to be the best invest-ment for the average person at the moment. They offer interest that exceeds the rate of inflation and provide the liquidity that most investors need.

The reasoning cited is based upon the notion that the stock market currently is undervalued. Yields presently are below those of money market funds. There is uncertainty about the workability of the supply economics advocated by the Reagan administration. Consequently, this doesn't seem to be the time to invest in common stocks.

At the moment the odds appear to favor the point of view advanced by the advocates of the new economics. Inflation seems to be easing which in turn should cause interest rates to decline. In response, the equity market, now undervalued, should increase in value. When and if this occasion appears cash can be taken from the money market fund and placed in equities. The easiest and safest way for the average person to do this is to place cash in a money market fund supervised by an investment management firm that also manages a number of equity funds. Funds can be transferred from the money market fund to one of the equity funds by a mere phone call.

Albert H. Cox, Jr. The best investment for the 1980s, in my judgment, will be American industry. By and large, our industries did poorly in the 1970s. Many were victims of excessive government regulation and taxation, high inflation and interest rates, weak domestic markets (for the same reasons), and superior foreign competition. Now, there is great political pressure to reduce the burden of government on our industries, and on individuals as well. The result will be lower taxation, inflation and interest rates, stronger domestic markets for our companies, and a sharp revival of America's ability to compete in world trade. In the 1970s, the best investments were those which reflected a highly inflationary economy (e.g., real estate) and a malfunctioning economy (e.g., gold). In the 1980s, the best investments should be those which benefit the most from a more stable and prosperous economy (e.g., common stocks in American companies).

William E. Donoghue. No-load mutual funds are easily the best investment today. They solve two of the thorniest problems individual investors encounter when they begin to invest; lack of diversification and transaction costs (commissions). Mutual funds investing means you can diversify two ways: first, the fund itself will be diversified in that it is invested in many different securities; and second, that with no loads or commissions to pay for most mutual funds, you can easily invest in several types of mutual funds—money market mutual funds, bond funds, equity (stock) funds, gold funds, etc.

After the bad experience many investors had with "load" mutual funds during the early 1970s (falling values and high—8 percent—commissions paid to get into the funds, which restricted your exit from the funds) two major developments have made the mutual funds attractive to individual investors; the growth of the no-load or no-commission mutual funds and the emergence of money market mutual funds which provide investors a safe parking lot in which to wait out stock or bond market declines.

These improvements in mutual fund investing, combined with the ready availability of telephone switching services which permit easy transfer of investments between funds with differing objectives have put the individual investor back in the driver's seat when it comes to managing his investments.

Gerald S. Fisher. There is no best investment today. Each investor's needs, financial condition, short- and long-term goals must be considered. However, if one were to say—all things being equal—the answer would be residential housing to be leased or rented. The reason is that the tax deductions allowed and the appreciation will combine to give one a better return than anything currently available, with very little downside risk.

A. James Heins. For the investor with risk capital the best investment in the years ahead, based on 1981 prices, is common stock. During the 1970s we survived a period in which a combination of inflation and high progressive taxes on dollar income diverted risk capital from plant and equipment to real estate, gold, art and other specialty investments. The result was reduced savings rates and an aging industrial plant. Prices of art, real estate and gold soared; stock prices stagnated.

This behavior has led to lagging economic growth, further inflation and idle resources. As a result, the American public elected a new regime that promised to cut government spending for social programs that diminished work effort and also cut tax rates across the board by 25 percent over a three-year period. This program was substantially enacted by the United States Congress in 1981.

The substantial reduction in marginal tax rates included in this program—plus diminished inflation—will lower the cost of capital to American business and lead to renewed industrial growth. The revamping and scaling down of social programs will reinforce these effects. A main beneficiary of reindustrialization will be holders of common stock in American enterprise.

It is necessary to caution the reader that these remarks were made when the Dow-Jones Industrial average stood at about 1000. Substantial increases in stock prices will diminish the potential gains to new investors. Note also that investment results depend on stock selection as well as market performance. For typical investors, a diversified portfolio of stocks—or mutual funds—that reflects their tax situation would serve them well. For aggressive investors, options and specific stock selection remain alternatives.

William Nordhaus. There is no single best investment for people who are not gamblers. Rather, individuals or families should put their eggs in half a dozen baskets.

To be concrete:

1. Buy a home or apartment, but do not put more than 50 percent of your net worth in it.
2. Don't forget that for most people a major part of retirement funds are in Social Security.
3. Put 75 percent of remaining funds in no-load neutral funds of different varieties (growth, foreign, index funds).
4. Put the rest in money market mutual funds.

Above all, don't get suckered into commodities, gold, art, tax shelters or real estate unless you are very wealthy or have first-rate advice.

Harold W. Watts. Productive assets that have alternate uses are always good investments. The assets need not be tangible; in fact, for the young there is no better investment than development of mental and physical capacities—what is called human capital—that allow for a wide variety of employments or further specializations. Even parents who want to endow their children with special advantages should consider whether more education and training is not a better bet than accumulations and bequests of more tangible assets.

Land and property have always been popular, and have the advantage of multiple uses. But the most likely case for such property investment being safe depends on the alternative of using the property directly for a residence, farm or business. This is a real advantage and is a valid reason for investments in real estate. The myth that real estate always goes up is not a good reason as many disappointed investors could testify.

In other areas, the most promising investments are usually spotted and exploited by those who have some special knowledge or contacts or experience. A wise would-be investor will always seek to use his or her knowledge and experience to gain similar edge.

WHAT SHOULD A PERSON LOOK FOR IN AN INVESTMENT ADVISER?

Albert H. Cox, Jr. No single individual or institution can provide *the* best investment advice for you. It is a matter of the proper fit between your own personal investment leanings and preferences and the wide variety of advisers who specialize in, or put major emphasis on, certain kinds of investments. Look for an adviser who can demonstrate reasonable success over a period of at least ten years. Avoid those who boast of fantastic success, and who guarantee the same in the future. Chances are very great that this type will be just as wrong in some future period as they were right in some past, and probably fairly short, period. The best investment professionals can help you. They *can* do better than you could. But don't count on miracles. The political, economic and investment environment is too turbulent for that.

William E. Donoghue. I recommend subscribing to a few good investment newsletters rather than using an investment adviser. These newsletters will teach you how to make investment decisions yourself. And a subscription to an investment newsletter or two totals less than $200.

A good investment newsletter, not simply a tout sheet, but a publication that teaches you as you go along, can be a very good investment. After all, no one knows you and your specific needs better than yourself. So no one can manage your money as well as you can.

Gerald S. Fisher. Aside from the technical qualifications of education, training and experience, your investment adviser should be a person of patience. Your adviser must take the time to truly understand your financial picture in detail, determine with you your needs, short-term and long-term and suggest a comprehensive plan that will help you achieve your goals. Lastly, he must be willing to work closely with your accountant and attorney.

Harold W. Watts. An investment adviser should be a person who inspires your trust as an objective and thorough analyst of one or several markets in which you might want to invest. His or her advice should be sensitive to the nature of your accumulation goals, and the kinds of risks you are prepared to undertake. It should also be based on a complete understanding of your existing portfolio. Such a person is almost impossible to hire unless one has several hundred thousand dollars to invest, and it is unwise to substitute the biased views of a broker or salesman. Consequently, the small investor is best advised to limit his ventures to the areas that he or she knows well or is prepared to study and learn about.

Next best, one should look for an adviser whose motivations for the growth and preservation of your wealth are close to your own. Sometimes a family member may be helpful but the main principle is that the adviser's honor and prestige be as much at stake as his continued retention as a paid adviser.

TAXES

MORE THAN 200 YEARS AGO the citizens of Boston risked economic ruin in order to protest the financial burden England had placed upon them: a tax on imported teas. Throughout the colonies, merchants and consumers cried out against "taxation without representation." In Boston, an irate group rebelled by adding the taxed tea not to boiling water but to the churning waters of Boston Harbor.

In the last two centuries Bostonians, like taxpayers throughout the country, have both gained government representation and taken on a host of new taxes. Whereas they once were asked to pay only an import tax on teas, in 1980 the citizens of Boston were required to pay city taxes, Massachusetts state income and sales taxes, federal income taxes, and other miscellaneous taxes, such as Social Security and estate taxes. Bostonians, however, are by no means the highest taxed Americans. A 1977–78 study by the Census Bureau found that New Yorkers had that dubious honor; they paid community taxes more than four times higher than the national per capita average.

How have taxes accumulated so rapidly? Not without a struggle. Believing with Justice John Marshall that "the power to tax is the power to destroy," early Americans resisted taxation in general. State governments imposed sales taxes and tariffs, but the nation evaded federal income taxes until the Civil War.

In 1862, Congress instituted a type of income tax labeled "progressive" because it takes greater amounts as the taxpayers' income progresses up the scale. The Civil War also brought additional sales taxes. This type of tax is considered "regressive" because it exacts equal sums from the poor and rich; it takes greater proportions of income as the taxpayers' incomes decline. Congress dropped the progressive income tax in 1872 and then tried to revive it in the 1890s. The Supreme Court, however, ruled the income tax unconstitutional because its burden was not fairly distributed among the states.

The average taxpayer might yearn for a return to the days of universal tax shelters. The above-average taxpayer would have even greater reasons for nostalgia: some of America's greatest fortunes were amassed around the turn of the century when business tycoons could pocket virtually all of their profits. Those golden days ended in 1913 when the Sixteenth Amendment gave Congress the right to collect taxes on the incomes of both individuals and corporations. Wisconsin had already begun collecting state income taxes from its residents in 1911; as of 1980, 42 other states also imposed income taxes. In 1939, Philadelphia became the first city to charge its residents income taxes; since then about 4,000 other communities have followed suit.

State and local taxes can take a considerable bite out of American incomes, but it is the federal income tax that takes the single largest share. In 1979, more than 90 million people filed federal income tax returns. These taxpayers brought the government over $250 billion, paying for the largest share (44.7 percent in 1978) of the federal budget.

Of course, not all of the 90 million or so taxpayers who send in their tax forms contribute willingly to Uncle Sam's upkeep. To find would-be evaders, the Internal Revenue Service (IRS) audits about 2 percent of all returns. A computer chooses most of the returns to be audited, basing its decision on numerous factors, such as the taxpayer's profession and income. Those with incomes over $50,000, for example, make up less than 6 percent of the population, but that small minority accounts for a sizable proportion of those that the IRS reviews: about 1 in 6 people in this group can expect to be audited. Although time-consuming, audits pay off for the IRS. In the past few years, about 1,500 people a year have been found guilty of tax fraud, and many more are asked to pay back-taxes due to errors in their returns.

The Reagan administration's new tax bill may make it somewhat easier for taxpayers to be honest. The bill's relief measures include the following provisions: married couples will no longer need to get "tax divorces" to avoid the marriage penalty of two-income couples; Americans can accumulate greater amounts of untaxed savings and pay lower tax rates on unearned income; and, perhaps most significant, federal withholding taxes will be cut by 5 percent in 1981 and by 10 percent each year in 1982 and 1983.

Many of the tax cuts, however, will affect primarily the more affluent Americans, and some may be offset by inflation or hikes in other taxes. For all taxpayers who seek more tax relief, who wonder how much of their working lives they will devote just to paying taxes, and who want to know how they can reduce their private tax burdens, the following section offers some answers.

CONTRIBUTORS

Robert E. Berney, Professor of Economics, Washington State University, Pullman, Washington

R. Bruce Billings, Ph.D., Lecturer in Economics, University of Arizona, Tucson, Arizona

Curtis Braschler, Professor of Agricultural Economics, University of Missouri, Columbia, Missouri

Willard T. Carleton, Professor of Business Administration, University of North Carolina, Chapel Hill, North Carolina

Albert M. Church III, Professor of Economics, University of New Mexico, Albuquerque, New Mexico

Dr. Neil E. Harl, Charles F. Curtiss Distinguished Professor in Agriculture and Professor of Economics, Iowa State University, Ames, Iowa; Member of the Iowa Bar

C. Lowell Harriss, Professor Emeritus of Economics, Columbia University, New York, New York; Executive Director, Academy of Political Science

Walter E. Hoadley, Executive Vice-President, Bank of America, San Francisco, California

Richard W. Lindholm, Professor and Dean Emeritus of Business, University of Oregon, Eugene, Oregon

Dr. Glenn W. Miller, Professor of Economics, Wichita State University, Wichita, Kansas; Professor of Economics, Emeritus, The Ohio State University, Columbus, Ohio

J. Carter Murphy, Professor of Economics, Southern Methodist University, Dallas, Texas

M. K. Ohlson, Ph.D., Professor of Economics, Metropolitan State College, Denver, Colorado

William H. Shaker, Executive Vice-President, National Tax Limitation Committee, Washington, D.C.

Lester C. Thurow, Professor of Economics and Management, Massachusetts Institute of Technology, Cambridge, Massachusetts

Murray L. Weidenbaum, Director, Center for the Study of American Business, Washington University, St. Louis, Missouri

HAS ANYONE EVER COME UP WITH A BETTER SYSTEM OF FINANCING GOVERNMENT OTHER THAN TAXATION?

Robert E. Berney. The basic ways of transferring resources from the private sector to the public sector are the following: (a) commandeering resources; (b) expansion of noninterest-bearing debt or the money supply; (c) selling interest-bearing debt; (d) license fees, fines, special charges; (e) taxation.

People who prefer the draft to an all-volunteer military force are saying that they prefer the government's commandeering of labor services to the purchasing of this service in the open market. Proponents of the all-volunteer military generally feel that the draft is an inequitable form of taxation. Rather than falling progressively or proportionally on all members of our society, the burden of the draft falls on a very small subset of our society, the draftee. There is no reason why all government services could not be provided this way but it would be both inequitable and probably very inefficient.

Paying for government services by expanding the money supply is likely to be inflationary unless the economy is faced with a serious depression. Inflation is normally considered a most inequitable tax, falling most heavily on those with fixed incomes or incomes which grow at rates slower than inflation; and with lenders who have not correctly anticipated the rate of inflation. Inflation is also thought to discourage savings and cause other serious inefficiencies in our economy.

Paying for government services by expansion of government debt caused serious problems for the cities of New York and Cleveland. While the federal government is unlikely to be faced with similar bankruptcy problems, many feel that postponing the payment for current services leads to excessive and unwise government spending. Debt sales are also inefficient in that a growing proportion of the budget must be used to cover interest charges. In the past, growth of the federal debt has caused the Federal Reserve to monetize more of the debt and this is inflationary.

With the passage of Proposition 13-like measures in many states, more and more state and local government services are being financed by increased fees, fines and other charges. If we can assume a reasonable distribution of income, the pricing and sales of government services may improve the operation of government. But this only works with a limited amount of government goods and services: those where people who do not pay for them can be excluded from their benefits. For truly public good, where no one can be excluded from the benefits, other revenue raising devices must be used.

Over the longer run, taxes are the best way of financing public goods provided by government. But clearly some tax structures are better than others. A good tax structure is: (a) one which will ensure that the costs of government will fall on those who benefit from government in roughly the same proportion; (b) one which taxes people with the same amount of income and wealth equally; (c) one which taxes those with relatively more ability-to-pay-taxes more. Thus, the answer to the question is that taxes are probably the best way to finance more public services, but our present tax structure is far from ideal. Better tax systems have been devised than the one we presently have.

R. Bruce Billings, Ph.D. Taxes can be thought of as the price we pay for goods and services provided by the federal, state and local governments.

In the private sector, each of us is free to spend as much or as little of our income as we choose on each available good or service, such as cars, houses and haircuts. Each person's expenditures reflect his individual desires and the freedom to choose the use of his income. For goods provided by the government, however, the decision on how much of each good and service to provide and how it will be paid for are made through the political process rather than in the market place. Thus individuals can not adjust their payments for government goods, or the amount of those goods provided, to reflect individual preferences. Each must abide by the will of the majority as expressed through the political process.

The only practical way to finance most governmentally provided goods and services is through taxes that are compulsory payments equal to some percent of a person's income, property, purchases, sales, shipments or other economic activities. Historically, taxes have also been imposed on individuals just for living in the community, independent of economic ability, in what is known as a "head tax." Taxes have also been imposed at times upon the occasion of a coming of age, marriage, death or for the right to leave the community (to compensate those remaining for their economic loss of a productive laborer).

Although taxes are necessarily the primary source of government funds, some government services are at least partially financed by user fees which are only paid by those using the specific service. The U.S. Postal Service is a good example, as are entrance and camping fees at national parks. Some cities also impose fees for sewage treatment, trash pickup and other services, and these fees may be either voluntary (if you don't want the service you don't have to pay) or compulsory, in which case you pay even if you don't want that particular service. In the latter case, the fee is a tax. The imposition of specific fees or user charges is possible but undesirable for services such as interstate highways, elementary education and fire protection. Fire protection was provided in some areas by private, unregulated companies which provided service to subscribers for an annual fee. They would also respond to fires at the property of nonsubscribers, offering to put out the fire for a very large fee (which the owner could accept, or let his house burn to the ground) or to buy the burning house for a very low price. User charges are impractical or impossible for governmental services such as national defense, police protection, city streets and public health services. The only practical way to obtain enough revenue to finance the production of all of the goods and services that people want from the government and for which it is undesirable or impossible to impose user charges is through compulsory tax payments.

Since there is no way to finance most governmentally provided services other than compulsory taxation, the serious challenge is to develop an equitable and efficient tax system which raises enough revenue to pay for the desired services without seriously damaging individual freedom and private economic incentives.

Curtis Braschler. With a system of social organization built around private ownership of the means of production (land, labor, capital and management) the government has no other means of raising revenue than taxation. Thus, for provision of those services that must be accomplished collectively (national defense, education, maintenance of order and rule of law) the very existence of government and thus society itself depends upon the ability of the government to tax the privately owned means of production.

Real public issues regarding the rate of government taxation center on the question of the use of government taxation powers for income and wealth redistribution. Less critical are the concerns about the level of taxation to support activities which must be done by collective decision.

Willard T. Carleton. No one has ever come up with a better system of financing government other than taxation.

Albert M. Church III. Government supplied goods and services which are divisible can be sold at their true opportunity cost to those willing to pay for them. This use of user charges is more functional at the local government level for such services as trash pickup, water, electric and sewer utilities and to a lesser extent police and fire protection. These include fees for harm done to others from pollution, dangerous driving and other socially destructive activities. Taxes levied on transactions and corporations are ultimately paid by persons, but they are less aware of the tax burden because the tax is reflected in higher product prices and lower income. The tax burden should be shifted to those who benefit, and user charges are the first step. The second is to levy taxes on people, their incomes and their expenditures.

There are alternatives to taxation but they are not desirable ones. Expropriation of wealth by means other than taxation such as regulation and ownership redefinition is one. Another is to finance government via printing money and inflation. The result would be more disastrous than the dabbling with this technique has been thus far in this country.

Dr. Neil E. Harl. The question is what is meant by better. User fees can be used to fund some governmental services. For those truly public goods such as national defense, for which user charges would be impossible to administer, direct taxation is necessary. Another drawback of user fees is that the burden falls totally on the user; as a matter of public policy, others perhaps should share in that particular burden.

C. Lowell Harriss. Changing terminology will not alter the reality that governmental exactions are compulsory. Government must be paid for. We can do a little through conscription and other forced actions—not generally to be recommended. Government can itself own property and charge for its use, e.g., lease of offshore oil-drilling instead of sale or gift of the public domain.

Some tax systems are better than others, but that is not the import of the question. Fees and charges have their place, not only as sources of revenue but also as allocating devices and methods of reducing the quantity of some services demanded. The proper role of pricing, fees, etc., is larger than generally used in this country. But at the largest such a source would not go far to meet the costs of government today.

Tribute from captured enemies has been used.

Borrowing does have its place as a temporary means. Money creation can serve to some slight extent over the years, but doing so involves complex matters of monetary policy and is likely to lead to inflation.

Richard W. Lindholm. The use of taxes can be decreased by reducing government responsibilities or by using the price system. Procedures utilizing direct labor or cooperative arrangements are utilized in communist areas. The problems appear to be at least as great as those encountered by the tax system.

J. Carter Murphy. No better system has been found. Governments do often sell some services to users in circumstances in which the users may opt for or against a service and its price. On the other hand, many government services are, by their nature, consumed collectively—such as national defense—so that the degree to which any individual is a user or beneficiary of the service cannot be ascertained. In these latter cases there is no alternative to taxes based on some standard of equity.

Lester C. Thurow. In a communist society such as the Soviet Union, no taxes are collected. The state controls prices, and prices are simply set at the level that leaves the state with enough revenue to do what it needs to do. But the basic tax problem does not disappear and cannot disappear as long as the government needs to spend money. Thus, it must have some technique for raising money. One way or another, that means taking income away from its citizens.

Murray L. Weidenbaum. The answer is yes, but for limited purposes. In contrast to taxation—which is based on the general notion that government activities benefit all citizens and thus that all should contribute to its support—we also have the notion of user charges. This concept flows from the idea that not all government activities are like the military establishment, which protects the security of all members of the society and therefore should be paid for by all citizens.

Admission fees to public parks are a good example of this other approach. Charges for personal copies of public records are another. It is the users of the government's recreational facilities who derive benefit from them—as it is the recipients of government publications—and those specific groups should pay for their costs.

The post office may be the largest example of the user charge or specific benefit approach to financing government. In general, the postage we buy covers the cost of the items we mail. But in practice, this system is more complicated than that. For example, schools can mail educational materials at especially low rates. In turn, the post office receives an annual subsidy from the Treasury to cover these and other public service activities. Thus, the balance between equity and efficiency is struck in such a way as to attempt to provide for national interests (e.g., education) and also provide the incentive for individuals to economize in the use of government services.

Some government programs which benefit specific groups are financed by taxation as a matter of deliberate public policy. A notable example is welfare, where it is the intention of the society to transfer income from one group to another. All this may make for an untidy state of government financing, but it reflects the great variety of views that are held by the members of a democratic society and the need to accommodate them.

HOW CAN AMERICANS PAY LESS TAXES?

Robert E. Berney. As an individual, if you hire a better tax lawyer, tax accountant or study the tax code more diligently you can probably shift part of your tax burden onto those who are spending less time or money on preparing their tax returns. Income from capital gains, from state and local bonds, is treated preferentially. Fringe benefits are generally nontaxable. Buying housing and other durables with credit will lower your taxes if you itemize. The list could go on for pages. In addition, there is a growing "underground" cash economy—10 to 20 percent of GNP by some estimates—where people pay less taxes because they are not reporting their cash income. But this is tax evasion and you can end up in jail.

But since taxes are the primary way we pay for government services over the longer run, if Americans, on the average, want to pay less taxes, they must demand fewer services from government. Certain individuals can take advantage of various tax exclusions, deduction, exemptions and credits—the tax loopholes—to shift their tax burden to others in society. But there is no free lunch. If we all take more advantage of the tax loopholes, tax rates will go up or the amount of government services will go down.

An exception to the above rule has been developed by Arthur Laffer of the University of California at Los Angeles. He says that at high rates of taxation a lot of resources (e.g., investing in tax shelters, getting income into capital gains) are locked into unproductive programs simply to avoid taxation. If tax rates are reduced these resources will be released and can be used for producing an increase in real income and at the same time, increasing real tax revenue.

Albert M. Church III. From an individual standpoint the way to accomplish this goal is to exercise maximum tax avoidance techniques and for those willing to take chances, evade taxes. For the aggregate, the only way to reduce taxes is to reduce government expenditures and to ensure that the economy is operating at full employment and growing. Reaganomics and local tax limitations are only partial steps. The structure of government institutions and the legislative process requires change so that each expenditure decision is linked more closely to a revenue raising decision. The present set up of different legislative committees responsible for spending and others for revenue thwarts this linkage and encourages fiscal irresponsibility.

Neil E. Harl. Americans can pay less taxes by simply expecting less in services and transfer payments from government. However, government services contribute greatly to the quality of life for all. The great myth is that middle and high income taxpayers do not benefit from government services. Indeed they do. Some governmental services are so much a part of reality and have been around so long that it is not generally realized that tax reserves are utilized to support those particular services; such as airports, airline subsidies, subsidies to shipping companies, postal service, the road system, public schools, parks and flood control projects.

C. Lowell Harriss. The cost of government—taxes—can go down only if government spending declines (rises less rapidly). An individual, of course, can try to arrange his/her affairs to take advantage of avoidance opportunities. We hear that many people operate in an "underground" economy and do not report income; disobeying the law is clearly reprehensible. One can reduce effort and save less, sacrificing pre-tax income and ending with less after taxes. For the public as a whole, however, the cost of government is the crucial issue. Vital decisions rest in the choices about expenditure.

Walter E. Hoadley. There are numerous ways in which Americans can pay less taxes, and many changes are already underway across America and more are being recommended by the Reagan administration and members of Congress.
They include:

1. Reducing inflation and interest rates which could have a tremendous impact on lowering taxes, for the interest costs on the federal debt, the indexing of social security, and the normal in-

flationary costs of buying goods and services are the major source of rising government expenses.

2. Greatly improving the productivity of the economy will reduce the tax burden by leading to lower inflation as well as generating an "economic growth benefit" which can be used to pay for additional government services without raising taxes in the future.
3. Eliminating wasteful and ineffective government spending programs.
4. Reducing the burden of government regulations which has been estimated to save from $50 to $100 billion a year in taxes.
5. Streamlining overlapping and duplicating government programs and combine funding sources into block grants to state and local governments. This is being proposed in many social areas by the federal government.

Americans of course can reduce their individual tax burdens by increasing their legal tax deductions. This is most readily accomplished now by purchasing a home since the interest costs and property taxes are deductible items. Taxpayers can also seek to protect their incomes by investing in tax exempt bonds, tax sheltered real estate investments, etc. However, these are not really solutions to the problem, but mainly avoidance. Housing is an exception, for the owner-occupied house is a major social as well as individual investment, and has long been supported as part of our national policy.

It is obviously far better for taxpayers and the nation to attack the root of the tax problem directly—i.e., cut excess government—than to look for more legal ways to escape the burden of high taxes. As taxes climb the temptation to evade taxes also rises which can undermine our system. Consequently taxes must not rise further except in publicly understood and accepted emergencies.

R. Bruce Billings, Ph.D. Since taxes are the payment for government provided goods and services, the obvious way for Americans as a group to pay less in taxes is to reduce the quantity and/or quality of goods and services (such as national defense, highways, schools and police protection) provided by the government, or to reduce the amount used for transfer payments to recipients of programs such as Social Security, government retirement, unemployment compensation, welfare and food stamps. The other way to reduce taxes is to increase the efficiency of the government; that is, produce the same goods and services with less labor and other resources. This is very difficult to do, however, since what appears to be an increase in efficiency to one person may be regarded as a reduction in the quality of public services by another. Both employees who may lose their jobs and department heads who may suffer a reduction in prestige with a reduction in the number of employees under their supervision will strongly oppose labor-saving innovations.

The lack of competition also reduces the incentives toward cost-saving innovation which is one of the most important sources of our high living standard. Reducing government tax revenue may force great attention to efficient production by government officials, although it will also reduce the services provided by government. Americans can only pay less in taxes overall by requiring fewer governmental services or by having such services provided at a lower cost.

M. K. Ohlson. Taxes may be reduced irrationally by the voters (as in California) or by the appropriate legislative body. If we assume there is to be a rational change, there must be some consideration of the relationship between the taxes saved and the services foregone. This varies according to the level of government.

State and local governments collect and spend about half of the taxes. The bulk of their expenditures provide education, streets and highways, police and fire protection, and commonly amount to 80 or 90 percent of the state and local budgets. If these taxes are to be reduced it becomes a matter of deciding which services are to be cut and by how much. This seems to be the major difficulty; everyone wants to reduce the service preferred by someone else.

At the national level, the greater portion of the expenditure is used to pay for past, present and future wars, next largest are pensions and other human services. Unless the intention is to increase the misery of those who benefit from the human services, any reduction in federal taxes must be based upon a reduction in military expenditure.

William H. Shaker. The way to pay less taxes is to increase productivity and to constrain the growth of government.

This can be brought about by imposing an external rule on government. Without such a rule, many are fearful that government's share of people's incomes will continue to increase. Several states have amended their constitutions in a way that limits the growth of taxation and government spending to the growth of the state's economy. A similar constitutional amendment has been proposed for the U.S. Constitution.

Under such a rule, the government take of the economic pie may only increase when the people's income can bake a bigger pie. Proponents believe that such an external rule will result in a healthier and revitalized economy. It then should be possible for people's incomes to increase more rapidly than the cost of government, with the result of a lower tax burden for all Americans.

Lester C. Thurow. Americans can pay less taxes if they are willing to get fewer public goods and services.

W MANY HOURS IN A FORTY-HOUR WEEK MUST AVERAGE PERSON WORK TO PAY ALL OF HIS OR HER TAXES (LOCAL, STATE AND FEDERAL)?

t E. Berney. According to the Tax Foundation, the average worker United States in 1981 had to work until May 10 until his or her total tax bill to federal, state and local governments was paid in full. In 1970, he or she had to work till April 28; in 1940, March 9; and in 1930, February 14. Assuming the accuracy of their data, in 1981 the first 14.4 hours in the average worker's forty-hour week were required to pay for his or her federal, state and local taxes.

One should also note that we pay a smaller share of our weekly wage in taxes than most industrialized countries. We pay more, however, than Sweden, the Netherlands, Norway, Denmark, Belgium, France, West Germany and Great Britain.

Albert M. Church III. The average is highly misleading because the federal tax structure is progressive and the personal and corporate tax code is so complex that using nominal tax rates to compute tax liabilities is misleading. Furthermore, tax evasion (illegal) as well as avoidance (legal) is growing. These tax reduction techniques have been stimulated by: (1) inflation which means that nominal incomes and tax liabilities increase faster than real incomes (purchasing power); (2) well publicized examples of politicians and others in the private and public sectors who have violated tax laws and other ethical standards without receiving commensurate punishment; (3) a realization that many government programs and subsidies are wasteful and inefficient which makes people less willing to pay taxes. It should be recalled that the U.S. tax system is almost entirely self-assessed. This gives wide latitude to taxpayers in interpreting what their "fair share" is.

These factors mean that the average nominal tax burden means little. It would be worthwhile to observe the effective tax rate for various income classes and by occupation, geographical region, etc.

Dr. Neil E. Harl. About fourteen to fifteen hours per week for a year, on the average. That figure varies by income level, deductions and credits against income tax, the amount and type of property owned and special circumstances relative to imposition of excise and other taxes. The pattern of consumption is also a relevant variable, including consumption of tobacco products, alcoholic beverages and certain imported goods.

R. Bruce Billings, Ph.D. The average person must work about twelve hours out of every forty-hour work week to pay all of his or her federal, state and local taxes. This includes personal income and Social Security taxes, retail sales and excise taxes, property taxes on home values and in some states a tax on the value of personal property such as automobiles. In addition, taxes imposed on business firms are passed on to consumers in higher prices, passed back to employees as lower wages, or reduce the income of business owners. Each tax reduces someone's income, although it is not always obvious whose income is being reduced. If there were no taxes (and therefore no governmentally provided goods and services), the average person would work only twenty-eight hours per week to have the same spendable income as is now obtained by working forty hours per week.

Tax burdens vary substantially by region of the country due to cost differences and to variations in the level of services provided by state and local government. Tax burdens also vary widely due to individual circumstances so that some people would spend much more than twelve of every forty hours working to pay taxes while others would spend less.

What should be obvious is that the benefits derived from that twelve hours of taxpayer labor to pay the government each week may well be a bargain. None of his income would have much value without an effective national defense and a local police and court system which preserve our economic system and the right to life, liberty and the pursuit of happiness. Additionally, many valued private goods would be worthless without complementary public goods: automobiles require highways and streets; recreation vehicles, camping equipment, etc. require National Parks; home plumbing requires city sewer service; and the use of a multitide of products requires the city trash collection and disposal service. To think of the taxes paid only as a burden to be avoided would miss the whole purpose of the federal, state and local governments' existence, which is to provide goods and services which people want and need but cannot otherwise obtain efficiently.

C. Lowell Harriss. The national average of hours worked to pay one's taxes would be around fifteen. In some states and localities, of course, the figure would be lower. In some it would be higher. I am not able to judge the median but would expect rather little difference. This estimate makes certain assumptions about the shifting of corporate earnings, property and payroll taxes.

Richard W. Lindholm. About one-third or about thirteen hours of a forty-hour week will pay for local, state and federal taxes.

Really what a person, plus capital, plus natural resources, produce for the public sector is all of the transfer payments plus production of government and government purchases from the private sector and that is about one-third of the GNP.

Dr. Glenn W. Miller. In the early 1980s the average person will lose a quarter to a third of all income to financing all levels of government which translates into perhaps a dozen hours per week. Variations in the level of sacrifice are great; some persons receive more from government than they pay while others pay amounts well above the norm. On the whole as time passes, we all are paying more, both in dollars and as a percent of income, to support government. The amount and proportion of all taxes which go to the federal government has grown enormously in the past half century. It is doubtful if the present national administration can slow or reverse the trend permanently.

The amount of our work-time that goes to support government must be examined in the light of the functions of late-twentieth-century government. International tensions cause more of our resources to go into military preparedness. Internal problems from "law and order" to education, roads and streets, and the "social safety net," so widely discussed in 1981, are resulting in "more hours of work" going into efforts to address these problems effectively. Internal and international interdependence, along with unbelievable power to destroy (as well as to produce) suggest that the long-run trend of government expenditure will not turn downward, despite the early 1980s expectations, or hopes, of many. The percentage of gross national product required to finance government activity in many of the more developed nations of the world now stands well above that of the United States.

Payments made by individuals to government are not necessarily made to pay for benefits which we or our families enjoy. Some do; some do not. The gasoline tax which we pay on the fuel which we put in our cars, sales taxes on consumption goods, or the excise tax we pay on a bottle of wine are related to satisfactions we derive from consumption. On the other hand, property taxes for the support of schools relate to the assessment of our property, not the number of children we have in school. We may pay for many years into social security taxes and early death and/or no dependents may result in little or no return. Many of us may never call for police or fire or ambulance protection. Members of society pay directly or indirectly for government services that may benefit others—or ourselves—with little or no relationship to our level of tax payments. This fact, unlikely to change, does much to explain the rise in the cost of government.

Citizens of the United States, especially in the last half century, have evidenced the growth of a philosophy of increasing expectations—indeed rising entitlement. This attitude is probably more widespread than the growing opposition to high taxes, which, in the early 1980s, is arousing much interest. While there are numerous interest groups, often competing, as a nation we are likely to see very large public expenditures continue for military preparedness, social protection of economic risks (from social security to farm price supports), public schools, subsidized transportation and many other services. The day of government as basically the provider of military protection and the ensurer of "law and order" is long past.

William H. Shaker. In 1980, government, at all levels, expended the equivalent of approximately 44 percent of the U.S. personal income. This equates to 17.6 hours or a little over two days per week that the average American must work to pay his taxes. Government imposed regulation is also a form of taxation. Adding the cost of regulation, the average American begins working for himself after putting in 22.4 hours per week to pay for costs imposed by government.

Americans pay taxes both directly (property taxes, sales taxes, personal income taxes, etc.) and indirectly (corporate income taxes, government deficits, and the like). It is important to recognize that business and corporations do not pay taxes—they merely collect taxes in the form of high prices for goods and services. The individual American is the one who ultimately bears the burden of all taxation. Forty-four percent of personal income equates to 17.6 hours per week.

There is still another form of hidden taxation; and that is the cost of government regulation which is estimated to consume an additional 12 percent of personal income. Adding this 12 percent to the previous 44 percent amounts to 56 percent; and this equates to 22.4 hours per week that the average American must work to pay his taxes.

SOCIAL ISSUES

*T*HIS SECTION OF *America Wants to Know* is dedicated to social issues. Here we find the experts lamenting the current state of affairs in the United States and devising imaginative solutions to the problems that beset our society.

Crime is a subject that appears often in the newspapers. It is well known that crime—particularly violent crime—has increased dramatically in the last two decades. According to FBI statistics, murder, rape and aggravated assault increased an average of more than 100 percent between 1965 and 1978. The question, of course, is what causes all this crime—and what can be done to stop it?

Ken Kelly, a member of the board of directors of the Prisoners Union in San Francisco, places the blame on societal models. As a result of scores of interviews with inmates, he deduces that it is common knowledge that police, judges, politicians and doctors all break the law quite regularly; therefore, it is not uncommon to find the attitude that there is nothing wrong with committing a crime—the only thing wrong is to get caught at it.

Frank Scarpitti of the University of Delaware presents statistical evidence that the crime rate soars in tandem with the unemployment rate; suggesting that fuller employment in the economy might reduce crime. Dr. Scarpitti also suggests that decriminalizing victimless crimes (such as drug abuse, gambling and prostitution) would allow our nation's law enforcement officials to focus their attention on crimes that do have victims, and would have the side effect of decreasing crime in some cases.

Perhaps the most imaginative approach to crime prevention is voiced by Gary Gottfredson in his essay on the role of schools in crime prevention. Mr. Gottfredson asserts that schools are the prime ground for socialization of children. If children become involved in school activities—and have an emotional stake in them—the chances are reduced for their acting in an antisocial manner. He suggests that schools broaden their scope, moving away from strictly academic studies to include vocational programs and other areas of competence. Schools should also provide jobs in community-related activities so that students have a broad range of activities to choose from in receiving their training. He deems it crucial that students find an area in which they can excel and receive positive reinforcement.

Going hand in hand with the problem of crime is the problem of prisons. Several of our experts feel the United States has a lot to learn from Northern European countries, particularly Sweden, in running an effective prison system that rehabilitates inmates. Prof. Clifford E. Bryan describes Sweden's prisons as quite small, located in home communities where inmates can often keep their jobs, maintain close family contacts and, as a result, maintain a sense of identity and responsibility. In the United States, Professor Bryan says, the prisons are large, the guards contemptuous, leaving little time or room for rehabilitation.

Dr. Leonard J. Hippchen, however, feels that valid approaches to rehabilitation already exist and need only to be applied. These include nutritional therapy and moral rehabilitation, the latter based on the assumption that most criminals are retarded in the development of their moral conscience. Dr. Lee H. Bowker also believes that social science has identified many rehabilitative techniques that show promise. Unfortunately, the legislatures have been slow to appropriate money for such things and, Dr. Bowker concludes, no prison can be effective when prisoners go back to the same community conditions that contributed to their criminal behavior.

Capital punishment is another aspect of our criminal justice system that troubles our experts as well as Americans in general. Dr. Freda Adler notes that the presence or absence of the death penalty has not seemed to bear a relationship to the murder rate, nor has evidence that it will deter crime proved conclusive. In actuality, she continues, murder appears to be one of the least deterrable crimes, occurring most often in the heat of passion or excitement. Robert G. Culbertson concludes that the death penalty cannot be a deterrent since its application is uncertain. He points out that the number of executions annually is minuscule compared with the numbers of persons convicted of murder.

Illegal drugs certainly play a role in increasing the nation's crime rate and, along with the more socially accepted alcohol and nicotine, play havoc with health and safety. Preventing addiction to these drugs is a concern addressed by our contributors. Dr. F. X. Carroll feels that our programs to educate young people have not been very successful and that we must examine both the individual and environmental causes of addiction. John McVernon urges that presentations of dramatic exaggerations of the dangers of drugs be replaced with programs and an environment to help young people develop a clear concept of what is important to them in life.

In examining another facet of addiction, William S. Dunkin describes a union-management approach to dealing with alcoholism in the work place, while Joanne Yurman discusses identification of those who have a higher than average risk of developing drinking problems. An example of such a group, she says, are children of alcoholics, 50 percent of whom may become addicted themselves.

Want to stop smoking? Several experts tell you how, stressing psychology, will power and simple alteration of certain kinds of behavior.

Why "Johnny can't read" has been bothering Americans for a long time. In our section on education, Frank H. T. Rhodes finds the answer in several places. He cites the pervasiveness of television, lack of communication between adults and children, lack of interest in education by many older people who are voting down school budgets, lack of teacher competency and lax standards on the part of public schools. Mr. Rhodes offers several solutions to the situation.

The changes in education that our experts predict for the future include increasing use of the computer, cable television, video discs and other innovations as teaching tools. Post-industrial society will be increasingly information-loaded, science-driven and technologically complex, according to Alexander Heard, who sees the liberal education becoming even less a part of the future than it is now. Dr. Larry L. Leslie foresees a trend toward reducing the size of school operational units, especially in urban areas; the decline of school busing; and smaller schools on all levels, with new physical plants being built on a smaller scale. Unlike Mr. Heard, he even sees a resurgence in popularity of the small liberal arts or moderate-sized comprehensive college. Espousing an unusual view of our educational system, Dr. Melvin H. Rudov discusses why he feels that compulsory education is "sentencing our children to institutions for crimes they did not commit."

Another crucial area discussed by the experts is the subject of the media. Serge Denisoff of Bowling Green State University sees the ratings war as the biggest threat to American media. Because of the tremendous importance of attracting viewers for television and readers for newspapers and magazines, news is often recast in the form of entertainment.

Professor Denisoff is also concerned with the symbiotic relationship between journalists and the entertainment and political figures whom they cover. Since journalists need access to these prominent personalities in order to get information for their stories, and since these prominent personalities often owe their positions of influence to the exposure they receive in the media, the media is often turned into nothing more than a public-relations vehicle for famous people.

Other media experts give summaries of what we may expect in the future for television and home entertainment centers. A fundamental concern about the responsibility of the media seems present in all of the essays.

Perhaps the most eloquent essay in the following section was written by A. H. Raskin, a former editor of *The New York Times*. Mr. Raskin begins by saying, "One can believe, as I do, that America's news media are the freest in the world and still worry whether that is free enough." The ownership of large publishing houses, newspapers, radio and television stations, and cable systems is now being increasingly concentrated in the hands of a few large corporations.

Mr. Raskin worries that the distinction between "communications" and "entertainment" is now being blurred. Large corporations with little interest in the free flow of information and ideas now control many media of communication, and the bottom line—the necessity of making a profit—is threatening to replace a sense of responsibility in providing the best possible coverage of the news. But Mr. Raskin ends his essay on a note of optimism. He says that the senior managers of the large television news departments and national newspapers continue to emerge from the editorial end (rather than the business end) of the operation, and he hopes that they will continue their dedication to presenting high quality news.

One issue we hear about often in the media is illegal immigration. David Carliner sees the number of illegal aliens in this country as insignificant when one realizes that the United States has a population of 230 million. He feels that there is no definitive evidence that we need to stop the flow of immigrants and that we should tolerate, even welcome them. Roger Conner, on the other hand, feels that these immigrants, who often come to the U.S. with the simple motivation of bettering their lives, compete with American workers at the entry level and therefore should be barred. He advocates expanding the Border Patrol, particularly along the Mexican border.

Probably the most emotionally charged subject in this section is that of pregnancy and abortion. Teenage pregnancies are on the increase. The reasons, according to Prof. William B. Clifford, are inadequate knowledge and use of contraceptives and the rise in the number of sexually active teenagers. Education stressing the risks of pregnancy, venereal disease, and the use of contraceptives before sexual activity begins would help alleviate the problem, he continues. Herbert J. Cross says that use of contraception is inhibited by the fact that adolescents must admit they are about to do something that will incur disapproval of parents, teachers and possibly of peers. Often, he continues, each sex expects the other to take care of contraception, or both are too embarrassed to mention it. Society must change its attitude before these inhibitions are able to disappear, Dr. Cross concludes. Stressing traditional values, Rosemary Diamond expounds the view that abstinence, not sex education programs, is the answer to teenage pregnancies. We should not balk, she says, at setting restrictions on young teens in the matter of sexual behavior. Mrs. Diamond adds that the legalization of abortion has encouraged sexual activity at an earlier age.

Is abortion a right or an abomination? Daniel Callahan explains that there is no easy answer since both sides of the abortion debate see potential symbols of the way we live together as a community in the moral and legal issues involved. Abortion, he says, is a question that few societies in history have been able to deal with, much less resolve. While some of our contributors see a pro-life amendment to the Constitution as imposing the religious dogma of a few on the majority, Dr. John C. Willke considers it a protection of the civil rights of the fetus. Some religious leaders do condone abortion under certain circumstances, as evidenced in the view of the Rev. C. J. Malloy, Jr., who feels that "to deny [women] the privilege of choice is but to reduce them to chattel."

The question of whether religion is gaining or losing ground as an influence in the lives of Americans elicits positive answers from most of the contributors to this section. Yet, some have reservations. Donald W. McEvoy deplores the growing lack of sensitivity to the oppressed in our society, even though more people are attending religious services than ever before in our history. Ted Peters cites the growth of enthusiasm for ancient pagan religion outside the church, while Dr. Gerson D. Cohen calls the emergence of some movements to the theological right in Christianity, Judaism and Islam "a sign of theological vacuum in many quarters and of panic in others."

CRIME

*F*ROM THE FIRST Indian raids to the most recent front page horror stories, violence and crime have been woven into the fabric of American society. The nation's violent-crime rate has exploded within the last two decades, leading some experts to wonder if crime—and citizens' fear of crime—will tear our society apart.

Figures from the Federal Bureau of Investigation's Uniform Crime Reports illustrate what Chief Justice Warren Burger has described as the criminals' current "reign of terror" in the United States. In the thirteen-year period between 1965 and 1978, the crime rate per 100,000 people in the United States increased across the board. The most frightening increases, however, were those in violent crimes: 80 percent more murders, 147 percent more aggravated assaults, and 166 percent more forcible rapes.

Criminologists criticize the FBI's crime reports as incomplete and often inaccurate. Experts estimate that only about a quarter of all robberies and less than half of all rapes and burglaries are reported to the police. The cases that are reported, however, clearly show that violent crimes, defined by the FBI as murders, aggravated assaults, forcible rapes and robberies, are occurring in all parts of the country. Quiet rural and suburban areas are now facing some of the same problems that have long afflicted the inner cities. Last year, some crime—anything from a tire slashing to a fatal knifing—hit almost a third of all American households.

City dwellers, however, remain the hardest hit. In 1972, for example, the population of Houston had a murder rate estimated at 22.5 per

100,000, almost twice that of San Francisco (11.4), but well behind that of Detroit (46.1). The violent-crime rate in Houston soared in the 1970s, as reflected in the figures reported to the FBI:

CRIME RATE IN HOUSTON PER 100,000 POPULATION

	Murder	Forcible rape	Robbery
1972	22.5	36.9	390.8
1975	25.6	43.3	473.3
1980	41.0	68.6	717.7

Houston is by no means unusually dangerous; it is similar to many other American cities, especially in the south. During the first half of 1980, New Orleans led the nation in rate of murders, Dallas in rapes, New York City in robberies, and St. Louis in aggravated assaults, according to the Citizen's Crime Commission of New York. Meanwhile, one nationwide study found 41 percent of all Americans "highly fearful" of crimes.

Who commits these violent crimes? Almost 90 percent of those arrested for violent crimes are male and most are young: more than half are under 25 years of age. Some criminologists had hoped that as the post–World War II baby-boom generation grew up the crime rate would go down. The anticipated slowdown seemed to occur in 1977, when the nation's overall crime rate fell 7 percent. In 1978, however, the overall crime rate rose 1.3 percent, with violent crimes gaining even more: murders climbed 2.3 percent and rapes soared 6.5 percent. As rates continue to climb, criminologists are reassessing the complex causes of violent crime. The current high level of crime, they predict, may not be just a youthful phase, but a part of the changing character of American society.

Both concerned citizens and law enforcement officials are searching for ways to reverse the trend toward more and increasingly violent crimes. This search, they say, is urgent because crime is threatening our society at its most basic level—on the street, at work and in the home. As Chief Justice Burger argued, funds to fight crime "should be as much a part of our national defense as the budget of the Pentagon."

CONTRIBUTORS

Freda Adler, Ph.D., Professor of Criminal Justice, Rutgers, the State University of New Jersey, New Brunswick, New Jersey

Donald D. Black, Director of Education, Father Flanagan's Boys' Home, Boys Town, Nebraska

Dr. Lee H. Bowker, Associate Dean, School of Social Welfare, University of Wisconsin, Milwaukee, Wisconsin

Prof. Clifford E. Bryan, Department of Sociology, Idaho State University, Pocatello, Idaho

Robert G. Culbertson, President, Academy of Criminal Justice Sciences, Illinois State University, Normal, Illinois

Gary D. Gottfredson, Research Scientist, Center for Social Organization of Schools, The Johns Hopkins University, Baltimore, Maryland

Kenneth Harms, Chief of Police, Miami, Florida

Hon. Shirley M. Hufstedler, former Secretary, U.S. Department of Education; now in private practice in Los Angeles, California

Burtell M. Jefferson, Chief of Police, Metropolitan Police Department, Washington, D.C.

Ken Kelly, Board of Directors, Prisoners Union, San Francisco, California

R. Paul McCauley, Ph.D., Professor of Justice Administration, University of Louisville, Louisville, Kentucky

Donald W. McEvoy, Senior Vice President for Program Development, National Conference of Christians and Jews, New York, New York

Prof. G. O. W. Mueller, Chief, United Nations Crime Prevention and Criminal Justice Branch, New York, New York

Robert J. Powitzky, Ph.D., President, American Association of Correctional Psychologists, Washington, D.C.

Milton G. Rector, President, National Council on Crime and Delinquency, Hackensack, New Jersey

Frank R. Scarpitti, Professor of Sociology, University of Delaware, Newark, Delaware; President, American Society of Criminology, 1980–81

Prof. D. Szabo, Director, International Center for Comparative Criminology, University of Montreal, Canada; President, International Society for Criminology, Paris, France

Leslie T. Wilkins, Research Professor, State University of New York, Albany, New York; Senior Research Fellow, Department of Sociology, University of Bristol, England

Marvin E. Wolfgang, Professor of Sociology and Law, Center for Studies in Criminology and Criminal Law, University of Pennsylvania, Philadelphia, Pennsylvania

Richard A. Wright, Assistant Professor of Sociology, McPherson College, McPherson, Kansas

WHY IS VIOLENCE ON THE INCREASE IN POPULATED, INDUSTRIAL AND URBAN AREAS? WHAT CAN BE DONE ABOUT IT?

Kenneth Harms. To address the issue of violence is to address human behavior. Many people engage in violence during a crime. However, this activity is not a simple problem that can be eliminated by the police, the criminal justice system or the government. The solutions to violent crime problems are as complex as human behavior.

Human behavior is the result of social factors and change. Law, science, education, social service, industry, labor and religion must be enlisted as effective instruments of social change. These factors create a climate in which the family unit can prosper and grow. Too often, however, family violence desensitizes and brutalizes a young, impressionable child. The single parent—or no parent—home seldom offers proper guidance and control for the child. The intrusion of drugs into the child's life not only dulls and incapacitates his emotional growth but its availability and traffic creates disrespect for law itself.

Inadequate housing, unemployment and poverty have long been cited as causes of crime and violent behavior. These are not causes at all but merely the breeding grounds of antisocial behavior. Though this community might be small in size, compared to the city within which it exists, the level of fear not only permeates this community but affects the life style of those in adjacent areas.

This fear exists because violence is condoned as a means for achieving a desired result. Though violence may be successful in achieving this result, the outcome is usually of criminal nature or, at best, of no social benefit.

This increased violence is a reflection of many things. It indicates a failure of the family, a failure of the schools and a failure of other social institutions that are responsible for generating character.

To create an atmosphere in which persons not only refute violent behavior but encourage passive coexistence will require a change in thinking and a change of heart. We all must share common goals which will allow us to live a peaceful life. But we must also share the responsibility of providing a judicial system in which to deal with those who not only do not share the common goals of peace and harmony but in fact disrupt society to the extent of causing injury and even death to some of its members.

The criminal justice system must carry out its duties in an expeditious manner. Punishment must be consistent and effective. The police, criminal courts, prisons and probation system are integrally linked in one fundamental sense. What happens in one has a profound effect on what happens in the others. Each part must not restrict its responsibility or support to its own area of specificity, but rather should collectively offer to the community the assistance needed in establishing a safe and secure environment. If some individuals resist this way of life and consistently inflict injury and fear upon the other members of our peaceful society, the criminal justice system should be supported wholeheartedly in its apprehension, adjudication, rehabilitation and punishment duties.

When viewed as an extension of society's needs for these safeguard functions, the criminal justice system can, together with all members of society, begin to reduce the causes of violence and the acts of those who engage in violent behavior.

Burtell M. Jefferson. Numerous socioeconomic factors have been consistently mentioned by law enforcement officials, criminologists, sociologists and the like, to explain why violence is on the increase in highly populated, industrial and urban areas. The Uniform Crime Reports, maintained by the FBI, define violent crimes as murder and nonnegligent manslaughter, forcible rape, robbery and aggravated assault. A general survey of the social, cultural and economic conditions of our cities provides a basic foundation on which to analyze violence.

The various demographic characteristics of a given area may help to explain this growth phenomena. In describing the demographic profile of most urban areas, we must mention crowded cities which have a high resident density; thus providing more opportunities for crime, a greater number of potential offenders, and more stress that could contribute to criminal activity. In addition, the inner cities are bulging with a populace that is from fifteen to twenty-four years of age, minority, and male— the grouping which is most likely to commit a violent crime. This grouping has other distinct characteristics often mentioned in any discussion of violence—high unemployment and low income. A job can make all the difference to a potential criminal. Yet, how can we explain why crime, for instance, increased in Detroit during the boom of the go-go years of the 1960s only to fall in the late 1970s, just as the auto industry began to tumble? Poverty may well tip people into crime, but no one can yet say how it happens or explain why most people even in the worst conditions remain basically honest.

Another oft cited reason for the increase in violence is the growing anonymity in American society: people don't stay in one place long enough to know their neighbors, much less look out for them. Chief Justice Burger in his 1981 speech before the American Bar Association offered additional explanations for increased violence. The schools, said Burger, ". . . have virtually eliminated any effort to teach values of integrity, truth, personal accountability and respect for others' rights." The effectiveness of current police practices, coupled with policies built into the legal system which permit convicted criminals to repeatedly return to the streets, are all contributory factors. Likewise, mention must be made of crowded prisons and the effectiveness of a system which confines offenders behind walls, yet because of overcrowded conditions is unable to provide a decent setting for constructive educational and vocational rehabilitative programs. Offenders are generally released having developed a worse attitude than they had when they were first incarcerated.

What can be done about this deadly phenomenon? There is no one approach, no quick answer. Indeed, the criminal justice system is just one part of the total picture. The family, community, neighborhood and other social controls are all vitally important. The police and the courts cannot do it alone. Citizens have to ask more of themselves and be willing to get involved. Emphasis must also be placed on the deterrent effect of swift and certain consequences: swift arrest, prompt trial, certain penalty and at some point finality of judgment which is free of legal loopholes. Attention should also be directed at the relationship of crime to factors that are directly amenable to manipulation through modifications in policy or the use of available resources (e.g., the deployment of police resources, drug treatment programs, the availability of youth recreation facilities). In addition, it is necessary to determine the relation of crime to factors that are not subject to control through government policy (e.g., summer heat) and to those that are modified with great difficulty (e.g., unemployment, availability of drugs). By examining simultaneously the associations of a large number of variables with crime, it would be possible to determine whether or not a change in official policies for certain factors would be expected to produce a significant change in the level of crime.

Decent jobs, better housing, health care and education are among the most fundamental steps we can take in the long run to deal with the question of violence. Most officials, however, realize that we cannot wait for social progress to make significant gains in the "war against crime." Current plans for improvement, therefore, will hopefully include zeroing in on each stage of the criminal justice system—police, courts and corrections. While remaining optimistic, I believe the unified, combined efforts of various facets of our community will eventually produce a needed change. Yet, if crime can't be controlled until America's sense of community is made whole, then a pessimistic view would hold that it isn't likely to happen in our lifetime.

Milton G. Rector. Recognizing that there is much that is not known about the sources of violence—even its prevalence is in dispute—one nevertheless can attempt some generalizations. (Violence reported to police indicates dramatic increases. Victim reports to the U.S. Census Bureau indicate little increase for the past seven years.)

We must distinguish between violence per se and stranger-to-stranger violence. Most violent assaults are between friends or family members. The best known means of family violence and potential homicide reduction is to train police and family counselors to respond in teams when called to intervene in family disputes. Violence between friends and strangers frequently results from drug or alcohol influence and addiction. Changes in public policy and strategy for drug and alcohol control and treatment of addiction should be studied and debated.

Violent crimes are at all socioeconomic levels in the country, but those who commit the preponderance of violent crime are apt to be among the poorest in the population and living in the most densely populated industrial urban areas. For any substantial drop in violence, steps must be taken which allow large numbers of the poor to rise to the level of the middle class. This would probably be the single most significant ameliorative action that could be undertaken.

There are other factors which have to be dealt with including the availability of handguns, obtainable with ease in most parts of the nation. Even if one state bans guns or requires regulations and licensing they can be obtained without difficulty in another. Fear of a potential handgun in every home or apartment must be acknowledged as a factor in police shooting of civilians.

Another factor in violent crime is that violent behavior has an organic and physiological basis. Individual thresholds for aggression and violence vary widely. Thus, individuals respond differently to different stimuli. One person will withdraw in anger where another will attack. The withdrawing person may attack under drug or alcohol influence. While scientific research into the physiological mechanisms which may determine or predetermine individual violence is in its infancy, increased understanding of the physiology of human behavior promises new and profound means of reducing violence.

Violence is also part of the American cultural scene: on television or in movie entertainment violence is absorbed by impressionable children; reporting of violence receives high priority from the news media; gratuitous violence in sports enlivens hockey games and football games. As one critic has put it, violence is as American as cherry pie.

Merely getting tough with offenders in the hope that this will deter them and others is a costly and ineffective way of controlling violence. Such measures have already been tried and found wanting. Confinement for violent offenders may be essential, but the larger problem relates to the quality of society rather than to individual offenders. Programs designed to encourage and nurture the willingness to abide by the law are needed. Public reactions to violent crimes based on a policy of vengeance and increased retribution as expressed by increasingly severe sanctions deny the presence of external forces which contribute to violence and can only diminish the quality of life in America.

Professor D. Szabo. Ever since Plato we have been told that a community of more than 5,000 persons cannot be controlled by ordinary mechanisms of social control and conflict resolution. In complex, rootless, mobile, urban mass societies there is no known device for designing a model of social control that really works.

There is no way to solve the problem with "more of the same," e.g., the traditional criminal justice system approach. Only community reorganization, general drafting of the citizenry, will do it. This can be done by recreating small social units with decentralized social and administrative responsibilities where every citizen can be called to account for his role in social control. Professional law enforcement and judicial personnel should serve as resource persons; people should be offered tax deductions to compensate for community crime prevention services: crime watching—street patrolling—refuge and foster homes for youngsters in troubled or disorderly premises, among other things.

As a corollary to social disorganization and fragmentation, the shared value and norm system of the community has shrunk to a very low level. The presence of large cultural, moral and ethnic minorities unable to integrate, does not allow the recreation of this needed common denominator in the large urban communities. The sense of community is gone forever! Conflicting value systems are maintaining a quasi-civil war atmosphere.

Only the reinstatement of family responsibility can solve any problem of this kind; restoring the obligations and authority of the family and the school system by keeping them accountable for the law-abiding behavior of their members. The authority and legitimacy of all the other social institutions, including the criminal justice system, are based on these two primary institutions.

Swift, certain and fair law enforcement and sentencing procedures—all of which are lacking in present day U.S. practice—are needed. I endorse Chief Justice Burger's 1981 primary diagnostic, at the American Bar Association meeting in Houston. Without this sweeping reform and efficient gun control, we are fighting windmills.

Diagnostic facilities for the psycho-physiological setup should be dramatically improved. The persistent violent offender is a high risk "patient": very little real effort has been made to effectively translate scientific (biological as well as psychological and social) observations into programs which result in the concrete protection of society.

The bio-psychological and genetic psychology of behavior control has known dramatic progress in the last fifteen years or so. The research and pilot projects already carried out should be systematically replicated on a large scale.

There are a host of variables—social, cultural, judicial, administrative and personality-related—accounting for criminal behavior. All of them should be tackled at once.

We know much more than we use in the everyday administration of criminal justice and crime prevention programs. It is not science that is deficient: it is that our use of it is catastrophic! By inducing social change, we need to destroy or suppress practices, attitudes, even sometimes institutions, and then to construct new ones.

HOW CAN WE BEST REDUCE JUVENILE CRIME? ADULT CRIME?

Freda Adler, Ph.D. Worldwide comparative studies (e.g., by the United Nations) indicate that nations with intact and tight social control systems, including families, villages, caravans and religious units, have the least amount of crime and delinquency and that nations in which these so-called indigenous social control systems have disintegrated in the wake of urbanization, have increasing crime rates, especially property crime rates. This criminality can only partially be controlled through the criminal justice system, with its police, courts and penal mechanisms. To some extent crime prevention through environmental engineering (design of houses, open spaces, lighting, safety devices, etc.) is possible. But sure and long-lasting reduction of both adult crime and juvenile delinquency is possible only by combination of professional crime prevention, through both the criminal justice system and environmental design, with the creation of substitute control systems which approximate in their capacity to guide and support, the once powerful indigenous social control systems.

Such surrogate systems can be found in divergent modern societies with low crime rates, as Japan, in which the industrial and work community exert a powerful influence of social control, or in the Soviet Union, in which the political cell, the neighborhood and the school system exert social control functions. Western societies have rejected these surrogate social control systems and pay a correspondingly higher price through crime and delinquency. Nevertheless, even without going to the extremes of Japan or the Soviet Union, crime reduction is possible in Western society, albeit more slowly, if extant community resources could be strengthened, including families, kindergartens and public schools, resurrected neighborhoods and community organizations, linked with an improved criminal justice system, which, indeed, is only now emerging as an integrated system geared toward crime control.

Robert G. Culbertson. We can best reduce juvenile crime by upgrading our educational system at the elementary level and developing mechanisms whereby we better respond to learning disabilities. Many children find schools to be frustrating and to do little more than enhance feelings of failure. Center city schools have little chance to contribute to a child's potential because of density factors, unemployment and a general lack of motivation. As a nation we have not come to grips with this critical problem.

Adult crime will be reduced only when we concentrate our efforts on the repeat offender. At the same time there is a need to develop a large number of punishments which are middle range. Often courts are faced with only a choice of probation or incarceration, although there are a large variety of punishments which can be imposed that involve more than probation and less than incarceration.

Ken Kelly. This is a very complex question that has been asked by millions of people over the centuries. The answers given by various experts fill countless volumes in libraries throughout the world.

Over the past twenty years I have talked with thousands of prisoners, ex-prisoners and professional people within the criminal justice system in seeking an answer to this question. There may be hundreds of things we could try to reduce crime by juveniles as well as adults, some might work and some might not. However, the two things that I think are absolutely essential will probably never come to pass.

First, our societal role models would have to undergo some drastic changes. In order to persuade juveniles or adults that crime is not acceptable in any society, the role models for that society must be untainted and free from lawlessness and corruption. This is certainly not true in any society that I'm aware of and least of all in ours. One has only to pick up a newspaper or turn on the television to see that police, judges, politicians, doctors, lawyers, etc., are constantly being found guilty of violating the laws we have enacted. This is interpreted by many people to mean that it's acceptable to break society's rules and that it's only a "crime" if you happen to get caught.

Second, if one studies any of the many statistical reports that have been prepared by various agencies, we find that it's an undisputed fact that the crime rate rises very significantly with the unemployment rate. In my opinion, if we could ever manage full employment, crimes involving theft would be almost negligible and even crimes of violence would be greatly reduced.

Milton G. Rector. To reduce delinquency requires an ability to change or control the forces which produce the problem. Both crime and delinquency are acts of individuals whose rationale for such acts is linked to personal attitudes, values and problems. So infinite are the number of variables within society and within each individual that they defy solution by one crime reduction strategy.

Nearly all teen-agers participate in activities which could result in criminal arrest and conviction. Few are arrested. For the middle class, toleration and informal forces for positive social controls enable maturation and a developing sense of self-esteem to reduce the desire or need to commit crimes. The lack of such toleration, neighborhood controls and esteem-building options converge to bring a disproportionate number of young people from minority and low socioeconomic levels into the justice system.

One cannot say that delinquency is caused by broken homes, being poor or black, being subjected to neglect and abuse, having learning disabilities, little education attainment or few skills for employment, or suffering from drug or alcohol abuse. Many law-abiding adults experienced combinations of some or most of these problems in their youth. However, it is also a fact that a high percentage of young people arrested as repeated delinquents have suffered from one or more of those problems, and were unable to cope. Persons who have average levels of education and employable skills are seldom arrested for street crimes and stranger-to-stranger assault.

Therefore, reduction of juvenile delinquency or adult stranger-to-stranger crime requires a long-term public strategy addressing such broad socioeconomic needs as family unity, quality education, housing and employment and health services for those sectors of our society (poor and minorities) which are disproportionately represented in the juvenile and adult clientele of the justice system.

For the short term, every effort should be made to direct costly criminal justice resources and priorities to the serious, repeat offenders and to keep delinquents, not prone to the use of violence, out of the justice system through a variety of other interventions. These include services to strengthen family capability: local dispute settlement; youth restitution programs; volunteer programs to supplement supervision and family control; placement in substitute homes; health services for drug and alcohol addiction; remedial education; employment skill training; and activities to aid in developing a sense of individual worth and esteem.

Where confinement is required for the small number of persistently violent delinquents, it will not reduce subsequent delinquency unless it is short-term, diagnostic in terms of individual causation and capable of helping the offender overcome educational, employment and social disabilities.

In developing policies and strategies to reduce delinquency, it is imperative to acknowledge that while crimes are individual acts, the forces which shape the attitudes and values behind such acts are many and in most cases have a bearing on the culpability of the individual.

Adult crime, like juvenile delinquency, pervades all sectors of society. The Internal Revenue Service estimates at least $50 billion unpaid annually on about $210 billion of unreported income. A like amount is embezzled, stolen or damaged annually through white-collar, corporate and employee crimes. A multibillion dollar toll is taken by illegal activities or organized crime, most of which require the collusion of public officials. The number of robberies, assaults, burglaries, thefts, rapes and murders reported to police and subsequently listed in FBI Uniform Crime Reports actually has the smallest economic impact and, undoubtedly, the fewest numbers of all crimes committed. Still these latter crimes account for the high level of public fear and for most public expenditures for crime reduction.

Since 1968 massive efforts at crime reduction have been made by strengthening law enforcement and criminal justice systems through a 600 percent increase in annual fiscal support. They have not produced the results anticipated. More police and different strategies in police deployment, court-imposed mandatory and longer sentences, greater reliance on jail and prison sentences, and the restoration of the death penalty have dramatically increased the costs of the justice system's response to crime. It has had little or no effect on reduction of the categories of crimes reported to police.

Few personnel in the criminal justice system are trained or equipped to deal with the more costly and pervasive categories of white-collar, business and organized crimes. Most crimes are still not reported to the police. Of those reported, few are cleared by arrest. A small percent of the police make most of the quality arrests. Most police time is still spent on activities unrelated to crime. Delays in the court process blunt the deterrent effect of adjudication soon after apprehension. Stranger-to-stranger crimes are not reduced by getting tougher because leniency is not the problem. The American criminal justice system is one of the toughest in the world on offenders who are convicted—especially those at the lower economic level. We incarcerate more people for longer terms than do most nations.

Proactive strategies to reduce crime by adults must address the moral standards and value systems of millions of Americans who violate the criminal laws daily to satisfy a need or greed of the moment or as a calculated risk or method of doing business. As with juvenile delinquency, adult crimes which receive greatest attention from the criminal justice system and the public are those committed disproportionately by the poor and minorities. Unemployment per se cannot be viewed as a cause of crime. However, forty years of correlations consistently show every increase in unemployment is accompanied by increases in robbery, homicides and prison population. This confirms that unemployment is a factor that must be considered for crime reduction. Likewise, lack of education cannot be blamed and indeed the consequence of a better educated minority population may result in reduced robberies and burglaries but more embezzlement, tax cheating and employee theft, unless the general issues of society's value systems are simultaneously addressed.

Strategy to Reduce Crime in America (stranger-to-stranger crime) published by the National Advisory Commission on Criminal Justice Standards and Goals (U.S. Government Printing Office, 1973) lists the following priorities in dealing with stranger-to-stranger crime:

1. The highest attention must be given to preventing delinquency, to minimizing the involvement of young offenders in the juvenile and criminal justice system and to reintegrating juvenile offenders into the community.
2. Public and private service agencies should direct their actions to improve the delivery of all social services to citizens, particularly to groups that contribute higher than average proportions of their numbers to crime statistics.
3. Delays in the adjudication of criminal cases must be greatly reduced. Implicit here is that certainty of punishment is a greater deterrent than severity of punishment.
4. Increased citizen action in activities to control crime in their community must be generated, with active encouragement and support by criminal justice agencies. The implication is that the criminal justice system is a reactive system and is about as effective as it will become. Citizens must do more for themselves and for each other

at the neighborhood level—not just to reduce opportunities for criminal acts but to increase the informal forces for positive and social control which can help prevent crime.

Frank R. Scarpitti. Crime is a convenient way of referring to a wide range of behavior that happens to violate the law. Thus, it is behavior which cannot be linked to one class, sex, race, age or even set of psychological motivations. Since there are apparently many things which serve to motivate people to commit illegal behavior, crime prevention programs, for both juveniles and adults, have been quite unsuccessful.

Some substantial amount of both juvenile and adult crime is committed by persons of lower socioeconomic status, however. There are street crimes, involving various kinds of lower level property offenses as well as assaults. There is no doubt in my mind that a large proportion of these crimes is linked directly to the offender's status, and represents an adaptation to poverty, unemployment, frustration, racism and other types of physical and emotional deprivation. This type of offense could be reduced if all people were brought into the mainstream of American economic, political and social life. Providing jobs, raising living conditions, giving people hope, would serve to reduce much of the juvenile and adult crime about which our nation is so concerned.

Another way to reduce both juvenile and adult crime is simply to decriminalize a number of behaviors now defined as illegal. A number of states have already removed juvenile status offenses (e.g., truancy, running away, incorrigibility) from the jurisdiction of the juvenile justice system. Although these actions have not solved the child's problems, they have redefined the behavior so that the youth is not defined or treated as a delinquent. Decriminalizing the so called victimless offenses—drug use, gambling, prostitution, etc.—would also reduce the adult crime rate, allow the police and courts to concentrate on more serious offenses, and even reduce many secondary criminal offenses (e.g., the drug user who must steal to buy drugs on a highly inflated illegal market).

There are no simple ways to reduce either juvenile or adult crime. Since crime is complex social behavior, committed by large numbers of people with highly diverse social and emotional characteristics, any measures taken to reduce crime will affect only a portion of the targeted population. In my opinion, we can best reduce *some* crime by decriminalizing a number of behaviors now defined as criminal and by allowing all members of our society to share in the nation's abundance.

Marvin E. Wolfgang. There is substantially no difference between juveniles and adults in the measures needed to reduce crime. Better education, better housing, improved employment, reduced alienation—all of these are desirable projects for society in general, not for purposes only of reducing crime but for the promotion of social justice. Since the disadvantages of poor education, inadequate income and disrupted family structure are closely related to crime, the federal and state governments should do all they can do to rectify these conditions. But these major social changes transcend the criminal justice system.

When I was introduced to President Johnson, and he was told that I am a criminologist, he asked me the journalist's question: "Well, professor, after all your studies on delinquency and crime, what would you recommend as the single most important suggestion to reduce the crime rate?" To his apparent consternation, I replied, "Reduce the fertility rate." This was not facetious.

I am still serious. Demographically, the great rise in violent crimes between 1963 and 1975 was caused by the swelling fifteen to twenty-four age group which resulted from the post–World War II baby boom. Little we do to try to prevent crime or to rehabilitate offenders has much effect on crime rates or recidivism. But by reducing the birth rate, especially among the poor who could economically benefit from fewer children, the proportion of crime, and particularly the crimes of violence-prone persons in the fifteen to twenty-four age group, would also be considerably reduced.

Finally, only a small number of males in their late adolescent–early adult years are responsible for most of the serious violent crimes. Identify them, incapacitate them, suggest treatment for them, use society's resources of time, talent and money to work on them, and we will be able, I think, to reduce much crime. Most offenders, whether juvenile or adult, are only one-time offenders. We can forget and forgive them. The chronic offender we need to restrain, restrict and control. Make no division between juvenile and adult offenders, for most serious offenders begin as juveniles.

WHAT CAN THE SCHOOLS DO TO HELP IN REDUCING THE OVERALL PROBLEM OF CRIME IN AMERICA?

Donald D. Black. Unfortunately, a great deal of the burden for this problem rests with the existent school programs. I would suggest that the following items be considered by the school system.

Each student should have a set of goals and a set of short-range objectives. This practice has been required in the education of all handicapped students, according to public law 94–142, but it is also totally necessary for all students. Each student should have input into his/her educational program.

Exploratory education should be provided for all students, keeping in mind that many students will change their minds during their school tenure. The college-bound student may decide to be a mechanic; some of the mechanics may decide to become college-bound students. All students should be prepared with viable alternatives and a marketable skill.

A social skills curriculum should be implemented for all students. Ex-commissioner of education, Sidney Marlin, has been quoted as saying, "Most people in the real world don't lose their jobs because of incompetence, they lose their jobs because of the inability to get along with their fellow man." The fact is, most employers will take the time to train an employee who will cooperate, be pleasant and is reliable. It is possible to insert a strong core of needed social skills into the educational curriculum.

Each student should know, on a daily basis, if he or she is actually accumulating the necessary skills, the same way a stockbroker keeps track of the stocks and bonds that he has purchased. Then the student and teacher can make decisions regarding the relevancy of the educational program for that individual student.

Dr. Lee H. Bowker. The schools have only a tangential relationship to American crime. They contribute to juvenile delinquency (and through it, to adult crime) to the extent that they label youngsters who have special learning problems or unusual behavior patterns as failures and give them the impression that they cannot live successful and productive lives in a law-abiding society. To help in reducing crime, the schools need to make every effort to offer a wide range of programs that are attractive, effective and appropriate to the needs of students from diverse social backgrounds (including income, race and ethnicity), with different ability levels and having a wide assortment of life goals.

Professor Clifford E. Bryan. Schools should attempt to become smaller and to eliminate age segregation. Many schools are now so large that students and teachers do not know each others' names, interests, abilities, life styles and potentials. In larger schools, only those students with exceptional talents and skills in one or two areas of activity are recognized and rewarded for their contributions; the majority of students are perpetually relegated to the side lines and are taught that they have little, if anything, to offer to their schools and their communities. In smaller schools, it is often essential that all students participate in a variety of activities, sometimes with the same teachers; plays, sports, music and related efforts need the participation of most students in order to be conducted. With participation comes a sense of "belonging-ness" and a sense of shared goals which require cooperation. This could do much to reduce the alienation and hostility currently found directed toward the larger schools and the outside community by young people.

Age segregation, which has come about in attempts to accommodate population increases with a minimum of new school construction, has produced high schools, junior high schools, middle schools and early elementary schools in which children never have the chance to meet others who are more than a couple of years younger or older than themselves. Behavioral and attitudinal fads, desirable and undesirable, quickly flourish and are rapidly disseminated when massive groups of same-aged peers are unable to encounter the diluting and mitigating influences of students who are older and more experienced or those who are younger and need to be protected. Such school-related situations have been accused of promoting hardened and calloused attitudes among same-aged students toward all other age groups.

Gary D. Gottfredson. Most crime is committed by school-aged youth. Over half of the arrests for property crimes and over a third of the arrests for violent crimes are arrests of males between the ages of thirteen and twenty, but these youths compose less than one-tenth of our population.

In the last century the involvement of youth in gainful employment has declined dramatically while their participation in formal secondary education has soared. Today, unprecedented proportions of youth are enrolled in school. They spend large amounts of time in school rather than being directly involved in work or even (to some degree) in the preparation for work.[1]

Secondary schools now serve many persons who in the past would not have continued their schooling through high school. Traditional academic schooling may be expected to be difficult and uncomfortable for some of these youths. Indeed, there is good evidence that the more a young person has difficulty with academic course work, the more likely the person is to get into trouble with the law and to be disruptive in school.[2] Therefore, the development of appropriate forms of education for the large group of students for whom traditional schooling is ill-suited could help reduce crime.

We need ways to change schooling to prevent delinquency. The following four basic ideas help to explain why schools are important in crime prevention:

1. Everyone learns and develops characteristic ways of approaching life and its challenges as a result of his or her experiences. We learn by observing how others behave and noting the consequences of their behavior, and we learn from the rewarding, or punishing experiences of our everyday lives.

---

1. Gary D. Gottfredson, "Schooling and Delinquency," in L. Sechrest and S. Martin (eds.), *The Rehabilitation of Criminal Offenders: New Directions for Research* (Washington, D.C.: National Academy Press, 1979), President's Science Advisory Committee on Youth, *Youth: Transition to Adulthood* (Washington, D.C.: U.S. Government Printing Office, 1973).
2. Jerald G. Bachman, et al., *Adolescence to Adulthood: Change and Stability in the Lives of Young Men* (Ann Arbor, Mich.: Institute for Survey Research, 1978).

2. All of us would behave in self-gratifying and socialized ways were
    we free to do so, but socially generated constraints hold our
    impulses in check. We conform not only because of formal
    mechanisms of social control such as laws, police, the courts, and
    so on, but also because of more personal social bonds that create
    for us stakes in conformity. According to Travis Hirschi, these
    social bonds include attachment to parents, peers and teachers;
    commitment to conventional social goals; involvement in con-
    ventional social activities; and belief in conventional social rules.[3]

    Attachment to parents, teachers and nondelinquent peers con-
    strains us from delinquent behavior because most people value
    adherence to central social norms. Commitment to conventional
    social goals—educational attainment, a good job, a steady income
    —also creates stakes in conformity. Misconduct can jeopardize a
    person's educational or career prospects. A person committed to
    success in education has something to lose by misconduct. A
    person not committed to such conventional social goals has little
    to lose. For example, a person who perceives little realistic prospect
    of doing well in school may have little commitment to education
    and thus have little to lose. These perceptions and commitments
    develop through the social learning process.

    Involvement in rewarding conventional activities such as school
    work, athletics, community service clubs, church or artistic groups
    also constrains a person from engaging in delinquent behavior. It
    does so, not only because it takes up time, but also because
    misconduct can jeopardize a person's opportunity to participate in
    rewarding activities. An involved youth has something to lose by
    misconduct. An uninvolved youth does not. If only "good" stu-
    dents can participate in athletics, a poor student learns that he or
    she has little reason to be involved in schoolwork, and thus may
    have little to lose by delinquent behavior.

3. People differ in the resources they bring into a social situation.
    These resources are determined in part by a host of socioeconomic
    influences, and differences in the background characteristics or
    resources among people result in individual differences in the
    scholastic ability and social skills youths can call upon in school. A
    person who lacks scholastic or interpersonal resources will have
    difficulty gaining rewards in school.

4. School is a major social institution in the life of an adolescent—a
    place where the social learning process is played out. Youth can
    find ways to be rewarded for their schoolwork, become attached
    to teachers and nondelinquent peers, become involved in con-
    ventional activities, and have experiences that strengthen their
    belief in conventional social rules, and thus strengthen their

3. T. Hirschi, *Causes of Delinquency* (University of California Press, Berkeley, 1969).

restraints against misconduct. Alternatively, and too often, youth with low academic and interpersonal skills will find schools "rigged" against them.[4] Because they have difficulty with school-work, because they do not behave as model youth, they experience failure in school. This failure weakens the bonds of social control. Attachment fails to develop because the social interaction in school is unrewarding, and commitment to educational goals is perceived as unrealistic. Involvement is undermined because only the good student can participate, and belief in the validity of rules and the law is undermined because the youth cannot make the system work for himself or herself.

So, school rewards can restrain youth from delinquency. The bonds of social control are strengthened for youths who find school rewarding, and they are weakened for youths who do not. Weakened restraints produce a cycle of continuing school failure and delinquent or disruptive behavior. On the other hand, experiences of school success result in a cycle of continuing academic achievement and vocational or career success. If the schools provide few opportunities for many students to experience academic success or be rewarded for their educational experiences—if they are "rigged" against poor students because they reward only the top students—then many students have little reason to be attached to the school or to be committed to educational goals. If the school fails to provide clear, firm and consistent responses to behavior or if school personnel are unclear about appropriate responses, then it is difficult for students to learn to cope with the environment, and belief in conventional social rules may erode.

Schools can act to break this cycle. Naturally, the range of options and the realistic scope of organizational change is limited. But many strategies are within the scope of a school's action. Schools can: (a) avoid a narrow focus on academic performance and foster and reward a broad range of demonstrable competencies; (b) increase student involvement and attachment to the community by giving students rewarding roles in helping community members and other students, and by providing work-related experiences; (c) give students access to success by rewarding weekly progress; (d) involve parents in concrete tasks to improve student performance by providing them with reports on student progress and teaching them how to reinforce gains;[5] (e) make school rules fair, firm and consistent, and make sure that students understand them and participate in setting them up; (f) exercise administrative

4. Eugene R. Howard, *School Discipline Desk Book* (West Nyack, N.Y.: Parker, 1978).

5. For reviews of successful experiments along these lines see Beverly M. Atkeson and Rex Forehand, "Home-Based Reinforcement Programs Designed to Modify Classroom Behavior: A Review and Methodological Evaluation," *Psychological Bulletin*, November 1979, pp. 1298–1308; and Richard Barth, "Home-Based Reinforcement of School Behavior: A Review and Analysis," *Review of Educational Research*, Summer 1979, pp. 436–458.

leadership in developing explicit plans for school improvement, and in executing those plans; and (g) assess the extent to which strategies are being implemented and to which they are working, and use this information to revise strategies or objectives in a continuing cycle of improvement.

Hon. Shirley M. Hufstedler. Schools can do nothing in isolation from the communities in which they exist. If the communities tolerate crime and violence, and in many ways escalate it, the schools are helpless to control crime. With the dedicated support of parents and other citizens, however, the schools can do a great deal. Schools cannot teach values that do not exist in the society around them. We would have very little crime in the United States if the "straight society" did not support many of the criminal elements in the community. If the larger community continues to buy goods that are known to be stolen, we cannot stop burglaries, because burglars require fences, and fences require buyers. We cannot teach nonviolence, when the larger society commends violence, as long as it is directed at someone else. We cannot tell poor youngsters to avoid crime, when the larger society itself indulges in crime. To be sure, the poor primarily indulge in the very crime that is the most appalling to all of us.

The key to crime prevention in the schools is to teach, by example as well as by precept, the essential dignity of all human beings. That means valuing youngsters who are not like the rest of us. As long as we preach one set of values, and follow another, the youngsters are not going to learn to be law-abiding. The schools cannot be a substitute for the community values that are not spoken, but are very much in evidence. In short, schools cannot make up for all the failures of our society. All of society must start to make up for its own.

We should not complain when youngsters follow what we do, and not what we say. We should not be surprised that teachers cannot solve what the parents have not. Crime, violence and ignorance would not survive if we were willing as a country to support our teachers, our school administrators and our children. Our criminal problems are not those of someone else, they are problems of each of us. When we understand that, we will at last have a reason to believe that all of us can help in solving the problems of crime in this country.

R. Paul McCauley, Ph.D. Education at many religious institutions lacks or at best fails to present a philosophy of reason. People must be judged by what they think as well as by what they do. Students, who are people, need to be able to think! They need to consider alternative courses of action before acting.

As a professor, I am saddened by the number of students who receive degrees and have not been educated. Simply, the schools have not made the student think, and value then is derived from impulse rather than conscious thought. It appears to me and others that this impulse action is central to crime at all ages but especially for the fourteen to twenty-one age group.

Education must measure student performance on more than memory and technique. Reason must transcend all else if we are to act beyond this moment.

Before the student is asked to reason we must ask, "Who is going to have the teacher teach reasoning?" The quality of our teachers is therefore suspect and that is precisely the central issue in crime in America: our society has devalued reason and education, and lacking a philosophy, reason has been raped—a devastating crime.

Professor G.O.W. Mueller. At one time the belief existed that crime is, in large measure, attributable to ignorance and lack of education. Indeed, prison populations consisted mostly of under-educated persons. Later, studies on hidden (unreported) crime, research on white-collar crime (criminality in high places and often committed by abuse of economic or political power by persons in high places), as well as self-report studies, made it fairly clear that the phenomenon of crime is not confined to the poorly educated, but exists among the population at all educational levels. Simply, the nature of crime depends largely on educational attainment. Academic education, however, does create opportunity for employment with greater job satisfaction and greater capacity to fulfill normal economic needs.

To be effective in curtailing crime rates, an educational system must do more than merely impart academic knowledge. Where an educational system assists other social control systems, like the family, religious groups and other voluntary organizations, in character building of young people, in assisting youngsters in finding their ways into adulthood, in citizenship and the economic life of the community and the nation, there is demonstrably a wholesome influence on the crime rate, as demonstrated by a number of United Nations studies and reports. Yet, it has also been pointed out that the potential of the public school system in this regard remains, as yet, largely unfulfilled. Therefore, United Nations resolutions call on all governments to include character building and the dissemination of knowledge of law and justice in the programs of public education. This becomes all the more important with the unfortunate decline of the capacity of families to fulfill this role which once was exclusively theirs.

Robert J. Powitzky, Ph.D. Probably the one social agency that has the greatest impact on every American is the educational institution. In considering what schools can do to help in reducing the overall problem of crime in America, one must place neither all the blame nor all the responsibility on this agency. However, the unique relationship of the schools to the average American citizen and community can be maximized more fully in preventing and facing crime.

The simplest and probably most prevelant anticrime programs implemented by schools are educational courses on substance abuse and the criminal justice system. More innovative programs include field trips and rap sessions with addicts or offenders. Although research has not adequately addressed the issue of which is the most effective program, for what age group, it is safe to say that many successful programs do exist and should be duplicated. Furthermore, this author believes that the ninth grade is the most effective target group with "refresher" courses given the senior year.

Other important programs include those alternatives for students who do not respond to the traditional school setting. These programs provide an option to students being expelled or dropped from schools, factors closely related to criminal behavior. Every effort should be made to keep young persons motivated and exposed to some kind of supportive educational environment, specifically designed for the subculture involved.

A more complex program concept—one which requires much more space than available here—has been attempted by a few progressive school systems. This concept focuses on understanding the processes involved in the assimilation of values and moral development. Various didactic and experiential techniques should be further developed to help students to learn the importance and nature of responsible behavior. Some didactic materials have been developed in the study of laws, moral development and values clarification. These transcend the content of values to focus on their origins. Experiential programs include student government, student involvement in community decision-making positions, problem-solving groups, due process disciplinary hearings, etc. Again, the underlying objective of these programs is to go beyond dogma to an understanding of the nature of and necessity for responsible behavior.

Schools must expand beyond their traditional objective of acquisition of information, and should help alleviate the crime problem by reaching into the community, even into the family. Schools could address crime-related problems of anonymity and family disorganization by helping develop volunteer, self-help groups that may serve as needed "extended families" and by forming neighborhood self-study, problem-solving groups composed of heterogeneous ages.

Although schools cannot shoulder all the responsibility of the frustrating problems of crime, their impact must be recognized and their role expanded to address a wide range of problems in living, including unlawful behavior.

Leslie T. Wilkins. In any consideration of the relationship between education and crime, I am very concerned as to the definition of crime which is to be inferred. If one is not particularly careful, ideas as to restrictions of activities can be extended to restrictions on the diversity of thought and speech. No educational institution should be associated with processes which restrict thought or speech. However, the concept of crime relates to the idea of intent, and the idea of intent is no more than the idea of thought. This can be very dangerous ground for any regulatory attempts in a democratic society. Educational institutions should discuss these dangerous issues and other ideas without advocacy of any particular viewpoint. In schools, the methods of education which would probably help with crime are the same as those which would also help to increase rational participation in political processes of the country. Crime, in this regard, cannot be separated from politics. This fact should be faced and openly discussed.

In short, I do not think that schools should concern themselves with crime as a category, but rather should consider issues which fall under the heading of the quality of life. (Crime, of course, is a subset of dysfunctional behaviors within this area which are so classified in the law.) Calling an act a crime does not, however, tell us very much about the nature of that act, except that it is disapproved, but it does tell us precisely what action will be taken by authority with regard to that act. Crimes are acts which are dealt with through the machinery of government called the criminal justice process. Thus, posing questions as to crime is, to a degree, posing questions in the language of answers. This is a poor strategy for problem solving.

We have yet to find valid and useful ways for describing crime as a problem; that is, as a problem to which we may seek a solution. One does not solve a problem merely by identifying the appropriate person to blame. Blame allocation is not identical with problem-solving behavior.

Richard A. Wright. A majority of criminologists agree that America's schools could potentially be a very effective force in preventing criminal behavior. Sociological research has repeatedly demonstrated that delinquency is most prevalent among students who perform poorly in academics and athletics—when youngsters fail to achieve success legitimately, they often strive to regain their lost self-esteem by participating in illegitimate activities. Unfortunately, many of the same delinquents will be arrested a few years later for committing criminal offenses.

Too frequently, schools only cater to the needs of academically and athletically talented students. Recently, the National Advisory Commission on Criminal Justice Standards and Goals and the Senate Subcommittee on Delinquency offered numerous recommendations that if implemented would make educators more responsive to the needs of all youth. For example, it was recommended that schools should: (1) guarantee the literacy of youngsters; (2) provide special language services to non-English speaking students; (3) develop job training programs; (4) emphasize the values of justice and democracy when conducting school policy; (5) establish nontraditional educational programs for delinquents; (6) improve guidance and counseling programs; (7) encourage teachers to become more sensitive to the needs of delinquents; (8) develop strategies for disciplining troublesome students without resorting to suspension; (9) strive to reduce the number of students in classrooms and the size of school buildings; and (10) seek student and parental involvement in delinquency prevention programs. Until most of these policies are implemented, less privileged youth will benefit from far too few legitimate opportunities to succeed in American society.

WHAT CAN RELIGIOUS INSTITUTIONS DO TO HELP IN REDUCING THE OVERALL PROBLEMS OF CRIME IN AMERICA?

Dr. Lee H. Bowker. In general, religious institutions neither cause crime nor are likely to significantly contribute to its decline. Crime is defined by political institutions and dealt with, insofar as it is dealt with at all, by the criminal justice system. However, religious institutions can make an important contribution to the fairness of the criminal justice system by highlighting the moral dimensions of proposed laws and administrative regulations.

Professor Clifford E. Bryan. With more than 370 religious denominations in our nation, nearly any person can find a religious justification for any kind of behavior. Some religious factions are now working quite strenuously to outlaw various behaviors that are currently legal—abortion is an example. To the extent that this particular effort is successful, it is estimated that 600,000 women each year will have to be imprisoned; this estimate is based on the number of women obtaining abortions who claimed that they would have done so even if such procedures were illegal. This is unlikely to reduce the crime rate in our nation.

Some of the reportedly more successful approaches that have been developed by religious authorities have been in the area of working with prisoners. One church, using its collective resources, sponsored an "Adopt-A-Con" program to find jobs, housing and funding to aid the adjustment of those just released from prison.

One critical area for prisoners revolves around family relationships. Married men, when sent to prison, often find that their wives obtain divorces. Several reasons account for this: prisons are often so far away that the wives are unable to visit and maintain desirable contacts; wives' friends and relatives may encourage divorces, as might be true for social welfare officials; visits in prison may be so uncomfortable and disconcerting that the wives might curtail them (especially when women and children might be subjected to body searches on such occasions);

and prisoners' families might just not be able to afford very many visits. As a result, parolees frequently find that, when they are released, they have no homes nor families to help them reenter community life. Religious institutions, in times of such crucial need, could do much to maintain and enhance the quality of prisoners' family relationships by providing funds, transportation, visitation rooms and related projects.

Research suggests that many, if not the majority, of female prisoners have children; little is known about what happens to such children. Religious institutions could provide quite valuable support in those cases in which mothers are convicted of crimes.

Religious institutions can probably be most effective in focusing efforts on individual cases. An attack on the "overall problems of crime" is likely to be prohibitively expensive, energy-consuming, and met and rebuffed by competing religious ideologies which, in turn, can only produce doubt and confusion within the larger population.

R. Paul McCauley. Religious institutions need to develop a philosophy of "religion in practice." For example, helping is a fundamental principle in most religions. Helping one another is the essence of crime prevention. Therefore religious institutions being altruistic by doctrine need to translate this into action. Such institutions can be a dynamic force in certain sectors of a community even if no more than the limits of a parish.

Also, many of those convicted of crimes and on probation, parole or in confinement need and often seek spiritual leadership or guidance. These people, although already law violators, need the resources that can be provided best by religious institutions. Recidivism is of primary concern in criminological and judicial circles. Religious institutions may play a significant role in repeat offenders.

Finally, religion in institutions is often viewed as another program, another big con. Religious institutions must meet the needs of diverse clientele and therefore must themselves be diverse, even attractive— especially to those who hold little respect for themselves or religion.

Donald W. McEvoy. First, the churches can sensitize their own memberships to the moral responsibilities for personal honesty in their dealings with others. Most of the white-collar crime in America—which is far more costly to the society than street crime, burglary, even murder and rape—is committed by persons who are affiliated with churches. So, that looks like a good place to begin.

Second, the churches must be led by their leadership to see crime within its societal context. The crimes that terrify people, and make them hostage to their homes when night falls, are inextricably inter-related to poverty, unemployment, deficient education, lack of adequate community support systems, family disintegration and the alienation and resultant rage which grows out of dependency and despair. And all of these are related to racism. Unless the religious institutions take it upon themselves to correct the societal inequities which breed crime there is little that can be done. Making full employment a religious agenda item would probably be the churches' best hope to become relevant to the problems of crime.

Third, the churches could motivate their membership to work for a significant reform of the entire criminal justice system. This would include the demand for equal treatment of all citizens by local police regardless of age, race or economic condition. It would also include the development of a new corrections system which would be humane and reflective of religious ethics. It would demand a review of the system which frequently limits the job opportunities of convicted felons and perpetuates the cycle of criminal involvement.

Fourth, the churches should elevate the concept of reverence for life in such a way that they would lead the fight to ban handguns in America. As long as church people support a system that results in the country being an armed camp, violence and death will continue.

Fifth, I suggest that the religious institutions become more deeply involved (as is inherent in both Judaism and Christianity) in constructive concern for the victims of crime. The man whom the good Samaritan helped (the New Testament's primary illustration of love) was a victim of crime, after all.

Professor G. O. W. Mueller. While there is little research to demonstrate the impact of religious institutions on crime rates, there is a widespread belief among criminologists and policy makers within government and religion that religious institutions can and do have a significant impact on crime rates.

The United Nations 1977 World Crime Survey tends to support this belief by showing that countries in which there is a pervasive impact of religious institutions on daily life have relatively low crime rates. But there are also low crime rates in some countries in which religion as such plays a very small role but where, perhaps, religion has been replaced by other ideologies. Religious institutions can have a direct, indirect or extended impact on crime rates. The direct impact results if, as in some Islamic countries, religion becomes a closely supervised daily practice with direct control over individuals. The theory of this direct impact of religion on criminality was exemplified by one of the unanimously adopted resolutions of the Sixth United Nations Congress on the Prevention of Crime and the Treatment of Offenders (Caracas 1980), which requested the secretary-general of the United Nations to focus the world crime efforts on "reinforcing Man's faith in his ability to follow the path of good." Religious institutions can have a perhaps even greater impact on crime rates—especially in Western countries like the United States—by impacting family and social life in an effort to maintain family cohesiveness and to supplement it by providing an additional supportive system for the maintenance of social harmony.

Unfortunately, organized religion can normally reach only its own members, while perhaps the greater need for the provision of social support exists with respect to nonmembers. Fortunately, many religious groups are providing extended support to juveniles and adults in trouble with the law, whether on an individual or group basis, by an outreach in the community and in correctional facilities. While there are no reliable statistics to prove the effectiveness of this extended outreach, the multitude of success stories would support the belief in its effectiveness.

There is one additional service which religious institutions have been providing increasingly and effectively in recent years, especially in America: since crime control systems, to be popularly accepted and effective, must also be equitable and humane, the moral power of organized religion has become a wholesome influence on the way criminal justice systems operate in practice.

Robert J. Powitzky, Ph.D. Although no one group of institutions and no one area of social problems can be identified as the focal point of crime prevention, religious institutions must consider what they can do to help reduce the overall problem of crime in America.

Possibly the most unpopular and therefore most overlooked area of interaction with crime is the tendency for religious institutions to support the legislation of morality. Many persons are thrown into the criminal justice system because of their problems with alcohol, drugs, sex, etc. Research has shown that once in that system, for whatever reasons, it is extremely difficult to separate from it. Being identified as a criminal has a devastating effect on a person's self-image and his or her view of society, especially for younger persons. Religious institutions must reconsider which "sins" should be handled by the secular criminal justice system and which problems in living should remain in the domain of the church.

A second major area of needs that religious institutions can help meet involves the concept of extended family. Two factors that strongly correlate with criminal behaviors are: (1) family disorganization and (2) a lack of significant others (i.e., anonymity). Most religious organizations are aware of specific successful outreach programs; these should be duplicated and expanded. Where these programs typically fail to reach those that need them most is in the tendency for religious institutions to establish and reinforce subtle or overt requirements for acceptance into the "fold." Outreach programs must be aware of and guard against exclusive expectations regarding race, social class, family composition, lifestyles, etc. Institutions should focus on programs for children and teen-agers, since they are most susceptible to social influence.

Religious institutions need to help educate people to understand the processes of moral development and values assimilation, in addition to simple rote learning of dogma. It is more important for purposes of reducing criminal behavior that a person understands the nature and purposes of responsible law-abiding behavior, than to try to memorize codes of conduct. Religious institutions also can serve a very useful function in ministering to juvenile and adult jail inmates, prison inmates, probationers and parolees. Such ministry includes crisis intervention, family support services, role modeling and postrelease support systems.

Religious institutions cannot shoulder all the blame for problems of crime in America, nor can they be expected to provide all the answers. However, if they do accomplish some of the above, the impact of crime in America may be alleviated somewhat.

Leslie T. Wilkins. Perhaps the best strategy is to regard religion as an irrelevant classification for crime analysis. In any general terms there is either a positive or an uncertain correlation. Some religions clearly and directly stimulate crime (although not, of course, defined by them as such). Among these we might quote the community murders of the Jones Church and the crimes committed by either extreme in Northern Ireland. It is far more difficult to find examples in the opposite direction.

What can religious organizations do? They could be less dogmatic and make far fewer claims to know the truth. They could seek to inculcate tolerance of variety in opinions. But in this case, most religions would cease to exist. In so far as religious organizations attempt to discuss ethical concerns, they might be helpful. However, more or less by definition, religions cannot be tolerant of the views of other faiths and of nonbelievers. Hence, the very nature of religion is to stimulate (or provide a basis for) conflict. Uncertainty of truth is more likely to lead to tolerance and tolerance to lesser levels of conflict and, hence, to lesser levels of crime. Agnosticism (not atheism) is perhaps the best antidote for criminogenic factors in society.

The alliance between religious organizations and power (money or political) should be rejected. Religions become a grave danger for humanity when there is a close association between the faith and the state. In many types of religions (not only "christian"), the Church is the State, is the Law. Most outsiders regard the killings in Iran as crimes, but because of the dominance of the religious order, these are excused or praised as representing the "will of God." Which "God" does not matter—he will provide an equally useful excuse so long as the people believe in Him. In religious thought, the whole of humanity can be divided into "them" and "us," and "crime" is what "we" say it is! Perhaps it is not possible for religions to concern themselves with those actions which would improve the quality of life for all mankind. If this were possible, it would help. But would the organizations so concerned be "religious"? Not according to my definition.

Richard A. Wright. The role of religion in reducing crime is one of the more enigmatic issues in criminology. Interestingly enough, sociological research reveals that there is no link between religiosity and criminal behavior (i.e., persons who attend church regularly are almost as likely to engage in unlawful activities as persons who rarely attend). This research finding probably reflects the diminished influence of religion in inculcating persons with morally appropriate attitudes and values in our technological and secularized society.

Religious institutions, however, do perform an important role in the rehabilitation of juvenile and criminal offenders. In this way, religion has helped to reduce the extremely serious problem of recidivism in American society. Various religious groups have been instrumental in organizing community-based youth centers, counseling services, and halfway houses (which are useful alternatives to the segregation of juvenile delinquents in state correctional schools). Likewise, the clergy has historically provided essential advisory and counseling services to inmates in penal institutions. Considering the recent decision by the federal government to dismantle the Law Enforcement Assistance Administration (an agency which during the past decade has spent millions of dollars to help state governments devise innovative criminal prevention and rehabilitation programs), the support that religious organizations provide for rehabilitative services will become increasingly crucial in the future.

PRISONS

*I*S THE KEY to prison reform a return to capital punishment and stiffer sentences or a move toward better rehabilitation and educational programs? Are most of the criminals in America's prisons willful wrongdoers or just social failures?

No matter what stand the experts take on these questions, there is one point on which almost everyone agrees: there is a desperate need for some type of prison reform.

As the nation's crime rate has worsened in recent years, so has the situation within prisons. The court system, responding to demands that it "get tough" with crime, has been putting more criminals away for longer periods of time. In the last decade, the inmate population of American state and federal prisons leaped more than 60 percent, reaching a record high of 329,122 in 1980. Moreover, on the average, the convicts being crowded into the prisons are staying there longer. Since 1965, the length of the average prison term has stretched from eighteen months to almost three years.

In comparison to the citizens of other wealthy, industrialized nations, Americans use prisons excessively. In 1977, for example, Denmark's rate of imprisonment was 28 people per 100,000, and only 19 percent of those imprisoned were serving sentences of a year or more. In contrast, the United States had an imprisonment rate of 215 people per 100,000, with an overwhelming 98 percent of the inmates serving sentences of a year or more.

The American judicial system now faces the problem of where to put all the criminals who have been sentenced. The recent Supreme Court decision permitting prison officials to double convicts up in single cells provides some additional spaces—at least temporarily. For more long-term needs, sixty-two new prisons are now being built nationwide to house the growing criminal population, and still more are proposed for the future. Since prisons tend to rank low on taxpayers' lists of priorities, however, it is not known how many new institutions will ever make it from the drawing board to the prison board.

Finding enough beds behind bars is just part of the problem. The prisons are also plagued by poor facilities, racial unrest (although blacks make up only 12 percent of the general population they comprise 48 percent of the prison population), high prisoner-to-guard ratios, and a high incidence of such crimes as beatings and homosexual rapes.

Dirty, dangerous and overcrowded with criminals serving long sentences, the nation's prisons are ripe for violent riots like the one that ripped apart the New Mexico State Prison at Santa Fe. The 1980 Santa Fe riot left thirty-three dead and many more slashed, beaten, and sexually assaulted. Correction officials say that more riots like this are inevitable if deteriorating prison conditions are not brought under control.

How can the country change its prison system? Recently the courts have been experimenting with alternatives to prisons. Some judges sentence offenders, especially those who have committed property crimes, to compensate their victims and pay heavy fines instead of serving jail terms. In other communities, judges permit nonviolent offenders to serve their sentences by working at community service under the supervision of a parole board. In the case of one woman who was convicted of manslaughter, the judge took into account her prior good record and extenuating circumstances of the case; instead of being sent to prison, she was sentenced to a term of house arrest during which she was required to stay in her own home under parole board supervision.

But perhaps the best cure for the problem-ridden prison system is a healthy dose of crime prevention. That is the tactic taken by inmates in the Juvenile Awareness Project Help at New Jersey's Rahway State Prison. Lifers at the prison meet with youthful offenders to discourage them from continuing in crime. The lifers' method: they give the teenagers a close-up view of just how horrible prison really is.

CONTRIBUTORS

Freda Adler, Ph.D., Professor of Criminal Justice, Rutgers, the State University of New Jersey, New Brunswick, New Jersey

Dr. Lee H. Bowker, Associate Dean, School of Social Welfare, University of Wisconsin, Milwaukee, Wisconsin

Prof. Clifford E. Bryan, Department of Sociology, Idaho State University, Pocatello, Idaho

Todd R. Clear, Ph.D., School of Criminal Justice, Rutgers, the State University of New Jersey, New Brunswick, New Jersey

Robert G. Culbertson, President, Academy of Criminal Justice Services, Illinois State University, Normal, Illinois

Dr. Pierre C. Haber, Director, The Psychology Society, New York, New York

Jim Hackler, Professor of Sociology, University of Alberta, Edmonton, Alberta, Canada

J. Ray Hays, Ph.D., J.D., Psychologist and Attorney, Houston, Texas

Leonard J. Hippchen, Ph.D., formerly of the Department of Administrative Justice and Public Safety, Virginia Commonwealth University, Richmond, Virginia

Ken Kelly, Board of Directors, Prisoners Union, San Francisco, California

Frank R. Scarpitti, Professor of Sociology, University of Delaware, Newark, Delaware; President, American Society of Criminology, 1980–81

Prof. D. Szabo, Director, International Center for Comparative Criminology, University of Montreal, Canada; President, International Society for Criminology, Paris, France

SOME PENOLOGISTS CLAIM THE DEATH PENALTY DOES NOT STOP PEOPLE FROM COMMITTING MURDER. WHAT IS THE EVIDENCE ON WHICH THEY BASE THIS CLAIM?

Freda Adler, Ph.D. Probably no criminologist would claim that the death penalty does not stop some people from committing some murders. Rather, the claim most frequently made is that the threat or application of the death penalty does not have any greater impact on the murder rate than does the threat or application of lesser sanctions, such as long-term imprisonment. Comparative studies, *Capital Punishment* by Thorsten Sellin (Harper and Row 1967), indicate that the availability of capital punishment in one neighboring state, and its absence in another, seems to have no bearing on the murder rate of the two states. Nor does it seem to make much difference on the murder rate when a state abolishes the death penalty, or reintroduces it. Worldwide comparative studies by the United Nations led to the same conclusion: the presence or absence of capital punishment bears little relationship to the murder rate. Indeed, the argument has been made that the existence of capital punishment teaches people that taking life is an acceptable means of solving social problems. But the evidence on this issue is likewise inconclusive.

Murder appears to be one of the least deterrable crimes, in as much as most murders are committed in a state of relative excitement (frequently among friends and relatives) and thus the threat of the death penalty is psychologically too remote to have any impact on the perpetrator's action. Some homicides are committed by fanatical perpetrators (e.g., terrorists) who likewise are beyond the reach of the threat of death, or are motivated by the excitement of potential death. However, some potential perpetrators undoubtedly are deterred by a potential death sentence. Most people do not kill because to do so is revolting and immoral. The surest way of reducing the homicide rate is to strengthen these moral convictions.

Robert G. Culbertson. Any punishment must be certain. Severity of punishment will not serve as a deterrent if the punishment is not certain. When one considers the number of murders in this country each year and the number executed, the death penalty is obviously not certain. The recent studies focusing on homicide show some new trends. For example, it was previously assumed that all homicides were the result of some kind of defective interaction between persons who knew each other. Family conflicts and marital conflicts are two examples. In these cases, homicide was clearly an act of passion and we have not found a deterrent for passion; there is none. More recent studies show a randomness to some homicides and again we have a situation which has no deterrent. The random homicide in which the assailant does not know his or her victim is classified by some as barbaric. There is no deterrent to barbarism.

Some estimates indicate that the cost to bring a person to execution now exceeds $1,000,000.00. The lengthy appeal process in our judicial system further undermines the certainty of the death penalty. Recent examples of the death wish, national attention to one's execution, also raise some serious questions regarding the effectiveness of capital punishment.

Finally, there are a number of instances where juries are reluctant to render a verdict which will result in death. It is the legislator who "barks" in passing the death penalty, but it is the private citizen who must "bite" so to speak. He or she is often reluctant to do so.

Frank R. Scarpitti. The belief that capital punishment deters men and women from capital offenses has long been advanced by its proponents. The "deterrent effect of the death penalty" argument is considered the strongest defense for continuing executions as a means of punishment for deliberate murder. Yet, close social scientific examinations of the long-term and short-term effects on United States citizens of executions by the state yield four basic arguments in opposition to the deterrent effect that is assumed of capital punishment. First, as recently as 1978, studies indicated that murder rates remained constant despite trends away from capital punishment. Second, where one state has abolished capital punishment and another contiguous state has not, the murder rate is no higher in the abolition state than in the retention state. Third,

given the special circumstances of most homicides, possible consequences are usually not considered by most murderers at the time of the
offense. Fourth, recent studies have discovered short-term brutalization and demoralization effects of capital punishment; that is, an *increase*
in homicides is found in the month or so following state executions. The
last two of these assertions will be elaborated upon.

The deterrence argument assumes that rational judgment operates in
the decision to kill someone. It is assumed that the murderer has full
knowledge of the ranges of certainty and severity of legal punishment,
that he is aware of the potential for the state to use lethal violence
against him for his offenses. There are reasons to doubt these assumptions. Most murders are acts of passion between people who are angry
and frustrated, and who know one another. Many murders are the
result of assaults occurring under the influence of alcohol, clouding
rational thought processes. Many murderers have previously and repeatedly assaulted the victim, who is often intoxicated and unarmed.
Most murderers, and particularly those sentenced to death, do not fit
the model of the calculating killer. This is one reason why the deterrence argument is not seen as a particularly good justification for capital
punishment.

Very recently, two researchers have published an article assessing the
impact of executions. They concluded that far from deterring murder,
capital punishment actually stimulates it. Their research uncovered that
"In New York State (a state that has conducted more executions than
any other) there were, on the average, two additional homicides in the
month after an execution." This brutalization effect is consistent with
social science research on other violent events; publicized suicides, mass
murders and political assassinations or attempted assassinations. It is
possible that by executing offenders we are acknowledging that people
"deserve to die," and are therefore devaluing life. This argument is
proposed by a researcher who, in a historical study of 12,000 American
executions, found a demoralizing effect far outweighing any conceivable
deterrent value.

We must conclude from available studies that the deterrent effect of
capital punishment is based on highly questionable research or on
speculation. A more likely deterrent will probably be found among a
number of social, structural and economic factors that are consequential
for rates of homicide.

WHY HAVE WE NEVER FOUND A WAY TO REHABILITATE PRISONERS OR TO KEEP THOSE WHO HAVE SERVED PRISON TERMS FROM CONTINUING A LIFE OF CRIME?

Dr. Lee H. Bowker. In the first place, the majority of America's prisoners are not recidivists, so it is not correct to assume that prisoners
usually return to a life of cime. In the second place, it is not accurate to

suggest that we have never found a way to rehabilitate prisoners. Social science has identified many rehabilitative techniques that show promise; but legislative bodies are unwilling to appropriate the funds to fully implement programs incorporating these techniques. In the final analysis, no prison program can hope to be 100 percent successful when prisoners are returned to the same community conditions that contributed to the criminal behavior for which they were incarcerated.

Professor Clifford E. Bryan. While there is no single way in which we can rehabilitate all prisoners, research studies do suggest various approaches which could be more effective. Officials could pay more attention to efforts being made in Sweden. In that nation, prisons are quite small, often located in home communities so that inmates can keep their jobs and maintain close family contacts. Ex-inmates find that the police officers who arrested them are often the same people who work to help them become reestablished in the communities.

Our prisons, by comparison, have become much too large. Guards, who have the most contact with inmates, cannot or do not bother to become acquainted with them; all inmates, no matter their backgrounds and problems, are treated alike, usually with contempt. With smaller prisons, guards could become true "correctional officers" by teaching reading, writing, mathematics and other subjects that so many inmates need so badly.

A recent study concluded that family relationships are one of the better predictors of postrelease adjustment. At present, most prisoners are sent so far from their homes that family visits are quite difficult. One result of this for married prisoners is a divorce rate as high as 90 percent. Such men, when released, have no families nor homes to which they can return.

When male prisoners are asked why they first committed a major crime, the answer is frequently, "Because of some woman." If female inmates are asked, the reply is often, "Because of some man." Many crimes are committed because of actions occurring with, for or against a member of the opposite sex. While this suggests that programs should be developed which might promote healthier heterosexual relationships, prisoners are typically sent to single-sex institutions. Prison authorities sometimes claim that "only about 20 percent" of the inmates "ought to be there" since the remainder are not considered to be particularly dangerous. The hardened sociopaths, who cannot or will not change, set the stage for hatred, homosexual rapes, and the continual threat of violence. Others in the prison population must adjust to these conditions, hardly a suitable manner for becoming reintegrated in the larger society.

Part of the reason that ex-prisoners continue in a life of crime is that many have little choice as a matter of survival. In some states, a parolee is given as little as fifteen dollars to begin a new life. With small amounts of money to aid until the first pay check arrives on a new job, which can be from two to four weeks, parolees are expected to find a residence, suitable transportation, and take care of their daily personal needs. Many find that they are nearly compelled to resort to petty crimes while waiting for their first pay check. Finding good jobs is exceptionally difficult; ex-inmates, who have to fill out a job history section of an application form, are not encouraged when they discover that they are competing with applicants who have college degrees.

The above problems strongly suggest that increased consideration should be given to small, community-based correctional centers which emphasize inmate employment, the maintenance of family relationships, the development of healthier heterosexual attitudes, the upgrading of skills for correctional officers and, perhaps just as important, efforts to provide some kind of appreciation for or reparation to the victims.

Todd R. Clear, Ph.D. There is no single treatment method available that is consistently effective at preventing new criminal involvement of released prisoners. There are believed to be two primary reasons for this failure of treatment. First, offenders vary widely in their motives for criminal involvement, their potential for pursuing legitimate behavior and their amenability to treatment—in short, they have a wide variety of needs. No single treatment program, no matter how broad or flexible, can respond to all or even most of these needs. Increasingly, evaluations of narrowly focused treatment programs for selected subgroups of offenders (for example, behavior therapies for nonmanipulative, multiple offenders under eighteen years of age) show some successes, and the trend is toward targeting treatments for certain types of offenders.

Second, prisons are simply a poor setting for any type of rehabilitative program, regardless of its proven value for changing offender behaviors. This is particularly true for the crowded, ancient facilities commonly used across the country, but it is necessarily true for any total institution that is based on regimentation and dehumanization. If we wish to emphasize methods that prepare offenders for noncriminal life-styles, we should minimize the length of incarceration and only use it as a last resort. Prisons reinforce antisocial values for most who are placed there.

Dr. Pierre C. Haber. The rehabilitation of prisoners is difficult because they do their time in institutions whose dual function is a paradox—the inmates are to be punished and at the same time reformed. Under these circumstances, inmates are rebellious and do not cooperate. After all, it is the individual convict who must initiate or assist in the process of personality change.

Recidivism, a penological term for rearrest *and* conviction after an initial sentence, is high because the offenders sentenced to imprisonment are generally the young, violent repeaters of predatory acts. The less aggressive criminals who may be rehabilitated through the criminal justice process are diverted to programs involving probation, community service, monetary fines and suspended sentences.

For some defendants, crime is a "rite of passage" and they will find an alternative way of making a living. The trauma of imprisonment and the aging (maturing) process act to reduce criminal behavior; crime rates drop markedly after the ages of thirty-five to forty. They accept the fact that they are not successful criminally and that incarceration robs them of freedom and pleasure.

Jim Hackler. Many still suffer under the delusion that criminal behavior is solely a characteristic of the individual and that some sort of exorcism will remove criminal tendencies. Human beings operate in a social environment that not only influences the behavior but also defines the behavior as criminal.

Prison experience rarely changes those social settings and social networks for the better. Occasionally, a program helps an individual inmate, or a probation officer may open up a job opportunity that may change a criminal career. More frequently, an inmate is socialized into an inmate subculture, learns new opportunities for crime and becomes aware of his new limitations for doing well in the outside world because of his prison experience. In addition, the inmate subculture often teaches that the world is unjust—those in more influential positions gain wealth through unethical means but are not punished.

Several northern European countries have paid attention to the evidence that prisons *remove* individuals from those social controls in a society that are most meaningful. Those social controls that keep most of us in line operate because we are integrated into social institutions. Such social integration cannot be achieved in prison.

Prisons are for punishment and short periods of incarceration will achieve that goal. Rehabilitation must take place in the community, and even though this involves risks, the risks are not greater than the ones created when inmates learn to adapt to the prison environment.

Unfortunately, the United States is constantly being guided by political opportunism in this area rather than by evidence.

J. Ray Hays, Ph.D., J.D. In every society there are individuals who do not conform to the rules of society. These individuals break the law for a variety of reasons. One reason is because the person lacks the skills necessary to make a living. Rehabilitation programs geared to provide basic vocational skills have proven successful, yet such a "cure" is not possible for all individuals who engage in criminal and delinquent behavior because the motivation for criminal behavior is not always amenable to change.

The role of the prison system in the United States, in some instances, is simply to protect the public by isolating the deviant individual. Sometimes the nature of the personality of the person precludes any consideration of rehabilitation. There are some individuals, then, that the prison system can never hope to rehabilitate.

Society should not consider the prison system to be a failure when such individuals are discharged, paroled or released and then reengage in criminal acts. Such individuals should simply be retried, convicted and resentenced with the understanding that the passage of time alone can change some individuals.

As long as crime pays more for some people than does a law-abiding life, we can expect some repeated criminal activity. Only through understanding that the goals of our criminal justice system must be suited not just to the needs of society but also to the needs of the defendants can we hope to get a better record against recidivism from our prison systems.

Leonard J. Hippchen, Ph.D. The answer is that we have! In essence, two major approaches have shown themselves to be most effective, even with the most serious types of delinquents and criminals: nutritional therapy and moral rehabilitation.

Nutritional therapy stems from a large bulk of recent scientific research which shows that behavioral problems related to antisocial behavior can result from such biochemical imbalances as: (1) vitamin-mineral deficiencies-dependencies; (2) environmental toxicity, i.e., lead, copper, mercury, aluminum, cadmium; (3) hypoglycemia, a genetic or dietary imbalance of sugar metabolism; (4) imbalances of the brain neurotransmitters; (5) minimal brain dysfunction (damaged brain lesions); or (6) cerebral allergies, especially allergies to certain foods.

Moral rehabilitation is based upon the assumption that criminals were retarded in their moral conscience development, and that the primary rehabilitation need is to educate the antisocial person to understand the laws of personal and social moral functioning. A method known as emotional maturity instruction, developed and tested in several settings with delinquents and criminals in the state of Georgia, has proved very effective in changing even the most recalcitrant and hardened criminals.

Other adjunctive rehabilitation methods also can prove useful, such as meditation therapy, physiological reconditioning and intellectual development, but nutritional therapy and moral rehabilitation appear to be the building blocks out of which a new, more socialized personality can be built.

Research in each of these areas is continuing and, hopefully, more demonstration projects soon will be undertaken to illustrate more fully and convincingly that prisoners can be successfully rehabilitated while under confinement, whether in a community or institutional setting, and that recidivism rates can be as low as 2–3 percent.

Ken Kelly. For some inexplicable reason our sense of pioneerism or willingness to try new methods when we fail at something does not seem to apply when we are dealing with criminals or social misfits. We persist in using strict and harsh punishment which only serves to punish, it does not rehabilitate or resocialize.

Programs that might rehabilitate prisoners are not instituted because too many people feel that these programs would amount to coddling the prisoners.

A contributing factor to the glaring lack of rehabilitative programs in our prisons and jails is that guard and law enforcement unions are constantly putting pressure on lawmakers and public officials to keep professional or treatment oriented personnel out of "their" institutions for security reasons. In the few institutions throughout the country where treatment programs have been introduced, the effectiveness of these programs has been negated by the fact that custody-oriented guards and administrators will not permit psychologists, psychiatrists, therapists and other treatment professionals to operate effectively.

In view of these facts, I would state unequivocally that the criminal justice or penal system has never seriously intended to rehabilitate or resocialize prisoners.

Professor D. Szabo. Why have we not cured the common cold? Because it is a simple name for a very heterogeneous, complex phenomenon! The same is true for the so-called rehabilitation of prisoners. We know, however, more about what does not work than what really does work. Purely repressive legislation, punitive law enforcement and extensive use of prison simply do not work. A whole library demonstrates the truth of this statement, as well as the everyday experience of all those who are working with criminals.

We have to deal with traditional methods. As nobody has the solution, why not experiment? It cannot be worse. For example, why not make more systematic use of community work programs? Why not sentence people to compensate or reimburse victims by sentencing them to $100,000 fines instead of five years of costly imprisonment. And the fine should be collected through forced labor under some sort of surveillance. We have to do away with retributive vengeance. Utilitarian patterns should be reinforced by the restitution mechanism.

The American way to deal with criminals (the true ones, the persistent violent offenders) is similar to the Soviet way of dealing with agriculture: the basic assumptions on the nature of facts being false, they lead to inconsistent and contradictory conclusions. Thus, the actions based on these conclusions can only be inefficient.

DRUGS AND ADDICTION

*F*ASHIONS IN DRUGS change. In the 1940s, nicotine was "in," and film heroes such as Humphrey Bogart were rarely seen without cigarettes dangling suggestively from their lips. Thanks to the surgeon general's warning and a strong, insistent antismoking campaign, tobacco's popularity began a very slow decline in the 1960s. Instead of puffing on cigarettes, everyone from rock musicians to middle-aged middle Americans started lighting up "joints," or marijuana cigarettes. The use of other drugs, such as LSD, barbiturates and heroin, also increased, but for most young people marijuana became the illicit drug of choice.

Marijuana is still the most widely used illicit drug in the United States, but it is no longer quite so chic. Experimenters of the 1980s have developed a more expensive taste: cocaine. Touted for the exhilarating, seemingly harmless high it offers, cocaine's popularity has grown quickly around the country in recent years. Surveys by the National Institute on Drug Abuse estimate that among Americans aged eighteen to twenty-five, cocaine use doubled between 1977 and 1979 alone.

While new drugs become in along with new hemlines and hairstyles, older drugs are not necessarily abandoned. Alcohol, for example, has never lost its appeal for many. In 1971, the Department of Health, Education and Welfare estimated that 7 percent of all Americans were addicted to alcohol. Today's teen-agers may be trying cocaine for the first time on a large scale, but studies show they are also still using marijuana—although in somewhat decreased numbers—as well as smoking and drinking. In fact, alcohol may be becoming more popular among youths. One government study of youths aged sixteen to seventeen found that in 1972, 35 percent of those surveyed said they had used alcohol within the previous month; by 1977, the number was up to 52 percent. Increasingly, drug-abuse agencies face the problem of patients who are simultaneously using several drugs. These addicts combine drugs by, for example, drinking to relax, sniffing cocaine to get high, and taking barbiturates to come down.

No matter what the drugs, though, addictions of all kinds share certain basic similarities. According to one medical definition, drug addiction is "characterized by an overwhelming desire or need to continue use of a drug and to obtain it by any means, with a tendency to increase the dosage, a psychological and usually a physical dependence on its effects, and a detrimental effect on the individual and on society."[*]

CONTRIBUTORS

Dan Anderson, Ph.D., President-Director, Hazelden Foundation, Center City, Minnesota

Jerome F. X. Carroll, Ph.D., Director of Psychological Services, Eagleville Hospital and Rehabilitation Center, Eagleville, Pennsylvania

Louis Cenci, Executive Director, National Interagency Council on Smoking and Health, New York, New York

Prof. Steven G. Cole, Department of Psychology, Texas Christian University, Fort Worth, Texas

William S. Dunkin, Director, Labor-Management Services, National Council on Alcoholism, Inc., New York, New York

E. B. Fisher, Jr., Ph.D., Associate Professor of Psychology; Director of the Behavior Therapy Clinic; and Associate Director of the Diabetes Research and Training Center, Washington University, St. Louis, Missouri

Steven M. S. Kurtz, M.A., Doctoral Candidate in clinical psychology at Washington University, St. Louis, Missouri

Reginald F. Mattison, Associate Director, Health and Temperance Department, General Conference of Seventh-day Adventists, Washington, D.C.

John McVernon, Director of Community Projects, National Association on Drug Abuse Problems, Inc., New York, New York

Alan S. Meyer, Ph.D., Formerly Director, Drug Education Center, Public Education Association; currently with the U.S. Government

Sylvester R. Mlott, Ph.D., Associate Professor, Department of Psychiatry and Behavioral Sciences, Medical University of South Carolina, Charleston, South Carolina

---

[*]From *Dorland's Illustrated Medical Dictionary*, 24th edition. Philadelphia: (W. B. Saunders, 1965).

J. William Rioux, Senior Associate, National Committee for Citizens in
    Education, Columbia, Maryland
Jacquelyn Rogers, Founder, Smokenders, an international smoking-
    cessation organization
Joanne Yurman, Director, Prevention and Education Department, Na-
    tional Council on Alcoholism, Inc., New York, New York

IS THERE ANY WAY, THROUGH EDUCATION OR OTHER MEANS, TO PREVENT PEOPLE FROM BECOMING ADDICTED (TO ALCOHOL, DRUGS, ETC.)?

Dan Anderson, Ph.D. Almost everyone agrees that the best solution
to alcoholism and drug addiction would be primary prevention; that is,
to prevent or minimize alcohol and drug-related problems before late-
stage treatment or rehabilitation becomes necessary. However, effective prevention strategies are still in their infancy.

Current prevention programs are usually special projects, such as
early education about drinking and drug use. Other projects convey
public information through the mass media and large communication
organizations. Still other projects involve voluntary organizations and
various community groups.

Various studies having to do with regulating or controlling the consumption of alcohol are also being examined. Since the relationship
between per capita alcohol consumption and alcohol-related problems
continues to be a reliable relationship—the more alcohol consumed in a
given area, the more alcohol-related problems—studies having to do
with controlling the level of availability of alcoholic beverages are also
being considered, especially for young people.

Without question, specialized education about alcohol and drugs is
useful. Helping people to learn to be more responsible for their own
behavior in an alcohol- and drug-using and abusing culture is not
impossible—but difficult.

Jerome F. X. Carroll, Ph.D. First, we must directly and honestly acknowledge that our primary prevention programs have not been very
successful. Drug and alcohol use and abuse by youth have increased, not
decreased, in recent years. For the most part, prevention efforts have
revolved around school-based programs designed to convey basic information and "facts" about drugs and alcohol. Typically such programs
were intended to prevent substance abuse by evoking fear and intimidation among students and their parents.

The reasons these programs have not been more successful are twofold. One, ignorance concerning drugs is not the major cause of substance abuse. To build preventive programs primarily around cognitive
interventions, therefore, is a mistake. Second, fear and intimidation, at
best, have only temporary suppressive power.

We must recognize that substance abuse and substance dependence are the result of not only destructive individual dynamics (fear, frustration, inadequacies, deficits, etc.) but also negative social forces (child abuse and neglect, parental and peer modeling of substance abuse, inescapable and oppressive poverty, etc.). Alcoholism and drug dependence, in other words, are forms of ecological dysfunction.

Prevention of any form of ecological dysfunction must examine all of the individual causes *and* environmental causes (and their interactions) that together dispirit and deprive people of their opportunities and potentials to be the best they can be. To prevent substance abuse, therefore, we must undertake a variety of individual interventions, such as teaching young people how to make good decisions, how to assert themselves, how to form close, intimate relationships with others and how to relate constructively to their feelings and needs. Simultaneously, we must also seek to enrich our environment through such means as reducing racism, sexism, poverty, child and spouse abuse, senseless and merciless competition, and ignorance.

Having the local juvenile police officer speak to the seventh and eighth grade classes about the "evils of smoking marijuana" or having a well known television star "work" a student assembly or meeting of the PTA on the same topic is a meaningless and futile gesture which can only sow the seeds of distrust and cynicism among our youth. Rather than prevent substance abuse, this would contribute to its occurrence.

William S. Dunkin. The most effective method discovered to date for preventing alcoholism is to be found in the joint union-management approach to dealing with this problem in the work place. Briefly, an employer organization adopts a policy announcing that alcoholism will be treated exactly as any other disease, and then sets up a program which deals with all employees whose job performance falls below minimum acceptable standards.

The employee is given a firm, fair choice between accepting confidential help (for whatever problem may be causing the poor job performance) or accepting the disciplinary consequences of that poor performance.

In effective programs of this type, large numbers of "problem drinkers" are identified and eventually motivated to do something about the problem, often five to ten years before the addictive phase of the disease is reached.

Furthermore, most of these programs report recovery rates ranging between 65 percent and 85 percent and some even higher.

Reginald F. Mattison. Successful prevention is accomplished by aiding individuals to make a personal choice and dependency on a power outside of themselves, which is God. We help by teaching about addiction through literature, lectures, audio visuals of every type, and personal sharing by individuals.

Prevention can be enforced but it will not guarantee compliance. If at any given moment the enforcement is relaxed and the individual makes a choice to experiment, there is the risk of addiction. Only as they are motivated, instructed and led to make a personal choice not to participate (on their own) can prevention be said to be successful. The power from God is available awaiting our sincere request, to keep us from addiction.

John McVernon. There is a way to prevent people from becoming addicted.

The prevention of the destructive use of drugs begins with providing good information on how chemicals act on our bodies and what their helpful and harmful effects can be. Most experts agree that dramatic exaggerations of the dangers of drugs are counterproductive. Those scare tactics stimulate curiosity and encourage experimentation. The truth is powerful enough, but providing those important facts is only the beginning of prevention.

People do not become addicts just because they are ignorant of the harm which may come their way. The best efforts at prevention have less to do with drugs and more to do with life. To prevent dangerous drug use, men and women, young and old, must have a clear concept of what is important to them in life. They must have some notion too of how to make decisions that will lead them toward the goals they seek. Those lessons are learned best by seeing models of that kind of goal orientation within one's family.

If we look closely at how to make effective decisions, we see the process has a number of stages. First, we need to know what our goal is. Then we can sort out the possible paths to solutions, seek advice from others, project what possible difficulties we may meet and finally commit ourselves to a realistic path of action. Does that sound complicated? Examine your experience and you will see you do it many times each day.

Poor decisions about drug use lead to drug problems and for some, addiction. To be addicted does not mean that one is a dangerous character any more than not being addicted means one is an outstanding citizen. Addiction is simply a physical state. After repeated doses of a mind-influencing drug, the body chemistry changes so that the organs do not function normally unless that substance is in the system. Addiction is a condition which often does trap people and isolates them from the human family. Deciding to use drugs does not automatically mean that an individual is an addict or even in trouble. Sometimes the way others react to drug use influences the direction that drug use takes. Over-reaction suggests that the person is lost already. Underreaction gives the message "drug use is OK."

Damaging drug use is averted by caring for the person and helping him to sort out just what his drug use means to him and how his drug use may be changing him.

At the same time, listening to your children, making reasonable demands, respecting their individuality, showing your love, encouraging constructive activities, providing them with a sense of their roots and exploring with them their goals in life . . . all are preventive activities since they promote responsible living. We have to appreciate the accomplishments of the young and be patient with their failures.

If we really care, we provide a good example of wise drug use and acknowledge always that our children, like ourselves, given the right circumstances and making the wrong decisions might become addicted to drugs. It is important to realize that peer pressure may lead to experimentation with drugs but never explains the making of an addict.

Honest law enforcement efforts, schools which provide a good curriculum well taught, houses of worship that are open to the young, and caring families combine to make a highly effective prevention plan.

J. William Rioux. Yes, addiction can be prevented but a lot will have to change. The problem is societal at its core. So many young people feel life is a bore, that there is little reason to struggle, to attain, to arrive at a place, that life becomes a search for thrills—even ones which can become highly destructive. Drug education programs, more sophisticated, trained school personnel whom young people can talk to, and parents decidedly with more resolve to stand fast against drug use will help. But probably most crucial of all will be the American culture sorting itself out—standards, rigor, goals and the value of living life with a purpose.

Joanne Yurman. Alcoholism has three recognized levels of prevention activity: primary, secondary and tertiary prevention. Primary prevention is concerned with keeping a problem from developing before it even starts. Secondary prevention attempts to control the worsening of an incipient problem after it has begun. Tertiary prevention involves the treatment of alcoholics or problem drinkers to prevent future recurrences of the problem.

There is evidence that all levels of prevention activities are successful. Primary prevention is seen as a cumulative and ongoing process which depends on a number of strategies including public and school education, passage of laws to regulate the manufacture and sale of alcohol, and the promotion of group sanctions or norms which are conducive to moderate use of alcohol. Because of the number of types of primary prevention approaches and because its goals are long-term, the immediate impact of activities is hard to measure. However, we do not know that the results from a number of educational programs show positive signs. While it is difficult to measure a nonevent—that is, forestalling or preventing the disease alcoholism in individuals—it is possible to measure knowledge, attitude and behavior changes regarding alcohol use. Indeed many programs show the cultivation of responsible attitudes and drinking behaviors among young people.

Secondary prevention, or intervention, aims to identify alcohol consumers who have a higher than average risk of developing problems and to assist them in obtaining early treatment or in modifying their behavior to eliminate or minimize the risk. An example of such a group is children of alcoholics, 50 percent of whom it is estimated may become alcoholics or drug abusers themselves. Research has only begun to identify these children, but the programs dealing with them report substantial progress.

Another successful secondary prevention approach takes place in the occupational programming sphere. These programs identify problem drinking employees and provide intervention techniques for referral and treatment to enable them to return to health and regain adequate job performance levels. As Mr. Dunkin reported (page 107), these programs report recovery rates ranging between 65 percent and 85 percent, often five to ten years before the addictive phase of the disease is reached.

Recent studies on tertiary prevention or treatment suggest that alcoholism treatment is effective. Sustained abstinence and improved psycho-social adjustment have been shown for populations where social instability and low socioeconomic class were not factors.

To sum up, I would answer that alcohol prevention is possible and happening at all three levels. While more long-term research is necessary to follow up on results of prevention programs, current evidence shows that there are a variety of strategies to prevent addiction to alcohol.

WHAT IS THE BEST WAY TO STOP SMOKING?

Alan S. Meyer, Ph.D. It is easy to stop smoking—a fact to which millions of smokers since Mark Twain can attest. The trick is to stay stopped, to quit. The use of nicotine, like the use of heroin, alcohol and other addictive substances, is easier to stop before it becomes entrenched in the physiological, psychological and social pathways of an individual's life style. If one wants to quit, it is therefore better to stop early in the course of one's smoking career. Since most young people experiment with cigarettes but don't become regular smokers, this is the time to quit. Unfortunately, the easy capability of quitting before the habit is firmly established is often wasted on those who don't want to quit.

Regular smokers who have passed this point of early quitting still have a better statistical chance of staying off cigarettes if they happen to be male, or have some college education, or smoke less than forty cigarettes a day, or better yet, happen to be a doctor. Not all of these characteristics, however, are subject to choice. If discontinuing smoking were a matter of simple choice, the best way for anyone to quit would be to decide to give up smoking. Indeed, for some regular and even heavy smokers, this is the best way. An individual's experience may motivate him or her sufficiently to cease smoking. But for many, the decision to cease is part of a complex process. The strength of the internal motivation is only one of several factors at work: it may be outweighed by the psycho-physiological strength of the habit, undermined by visual cues and social pressures for continued smoking, or weakened by the lack of social and other supports for continued abstinence.

Most quitters cure themselves. Heavy smokers may be more successful if they cut back before stopping "cold turkey." Some smokers are able to taper off. No one method is best for all. For those who feel the need for outside help, they can choose from a variety of programs and approaches. These include medical clinics, group and individual psychotherapy, chemotherapy, suggestion, and other positive or negative reinforcement techniques—singly or in combination. Since we don't yet know what the best approach is for each type of smoker, potential quitters should learn about different approaches and decide which approach sounds and feels best to them. Local health organizations can help provide such information. Smokers should guard against using previous failure as a reason not to try again.

Many quitters fail on their first try. If one approach doesn't work, try it again or try another. Help is often needed to allay the fears which precede stopping and to deal with subsequent anxieties. It may help to have an ego-enhancing reason to quit based on strongly held values (e.g., resolving not to be controlled by clever commercials). Those who stop must avoid the many easy rationalizations always available to justify giving up the effort.

Smoking is an addictive behavior and it takes grit and determination, and sometimes more, to really stop. The support of loved and respected persons can be important. Friends who have successfully quit can provide special understanding. For some smokers it is helpful to perceive the degree to which their habit is socially disapproved. For others it may help to recognize how much their smoking lowers the quality of life for others as well as the growing evidence of the unhealthy effects it has on their spouses and their children, both before and after birth. Of course, such perceptions may increase the anxiety of some who want to quit or cause others to assert more than ever their right to smoke. Many women who have asserted this right have found it particularly difficult to quit. They should take some hope from the notion that a completely liberated woman should be able to turn to safer cigars or pipes or to just plain quit, as easily as a man.

Louis Cenci. According to the experts the best way to quit smoking is to make the commitment and then to quit cold. All the evidence points to the quit cold method as the most effective especially for complete and long-term cessation. For those persons who find the quit cold method too difficult it is recommended that they consult their physicians.

Persons who need other support are often able to quit when they join groups in stop smoking programs. They should communicate with local chapters or affiliates of the American Cancer Society and the American Lung Association for information and help in choosing cessation programs. In addition, their physicians may be able to guide them to other cessation clinics.

E. B. Fisher, Jr., with Steven M. S. Kurtz. For most people, the best way to stop smoking is by planning ahead for several weeks and then quitting totally on a chosen "quit date." Some people also quit by cutting down gradually. This may be helpful, but if one procrastinates too long in having that last cigarette, and smokes just a few cigarettes a day for an extended period of time, making a final quit may become increasingly difficult.

For those who are extremely heavy smokers, it may be helpful first to cut down to about one pack a day. After adjusting to this level, one can choose a quit date, plan ahead for it and quit totally on that date.

Some people can continue smoking only a few cigarettes a day for an extended period of time. Such a smoking pattern is probably not a serious medical risk. However, many seem to find it hard to maintain such a modest smoking pattern without eventually increasing the number of cigarettes smoked. Thus, smoking a few cigarettes a day may constitute a risk of more extended smoking in the future.

What is the best method to quit smoking may be a very individual thing. And after considering the alternatives, individuals are often most able to decide what is best for themselves.

Before attempting to quit, the reasons should be carefully considered. It is important that people quit for reasons of their own. Being pushed into it by a health professional or a family member is not a good reason. Without clear, personally significant reasons for quitting, success is unlikely. Better to mull over the issue, thinking about whether or not to quit than to make a series of half-hearted attempts which lead to failures and only make the task seem increasingly difficult.

It is helpful to record all the cigarettes one smokes for a few days to a week. This will point up the situations which are likely to be troublesome after quitting. By identifying these, one may be able to make effective plans for dealing with them. Many people think they already know their smoking habits. However, most find new and useful information by recording all their cigarettes for a period of time prior to quitting. This should include recording the place, time, and reason or motive for each cigarette. It may be also helpful to record how much each cigarette was desired at the time it was smoked.

Planning in advance for situations likely to be difficult will help. Consider changing routines to make smoking unavailable (e.g., go to movies) or to avoid cues which might provoke urges to smoke. It may be useful to avoid parties or some social gatherings for a period of time after quitting. Switching flavors associated with smoking may help. For instance, switching from coffee to tea, from scotch to beer, from white to red wine, etc., all may help.

The support of other people can be a big help. Discuss with a spouse, family members, friends or coworkers the situations likely to produce trouble. Warning them of expected difficulties may make them a bit more sympathetic and more willing to tolerate the problems of the ex-smoker. They may also identify things they can do to help. For instance, a cooperative spouse or coworker who is still smoking may be willing to forgo cigarettes at times when they most surely might tempt the quitter. For instance, a spouse may be willing to delay the after-dinner cigarette for a half-hour, making it easier for the quitter to resist it altogether.

Most ex-smokers are worried about becoming a bore to those around them. Nevertheless, it is worthwhile telling friends about progress, problems encountered and feelings of satisfaction or accomplishment. This may put off some friends who smoke, but nonsmoking friends will probably be good natured about giving encouragement and support and offering help if they are able. Creating a supportive social network may be a real help in staying off cigarettes.

After about three months, urges for cigarettes become quite infrequent. Thus, life after this period is not as difficult as the initial few weeks. Surveys of ex-smokers we have conducted at Washington University in St. Louis indicate that most who have quit for over six months rarely feel strong urges to have a cigarette. Rather, they report having *thoughts* about cigarettes. At times, these are indeed fond thoughts. But they are not strong urges which are difficult to combat. The occasional strong urge to have a cigarette may well be combatted by the very knowledge that it is infrequent and by the good feelings about not smoking which begin to develop after several months without cigarettes.

In the event of a relapse or setback, many people give up. It's almost as if the relapse were an excuse for concluding that the task is impossible. It's not. In fact, our surveys show that many who quit smoking have failed more than twice before being successful. A relapse should be a signal to renew one's efforts. Understanding what went wrong and brought on a relapse or setback may lead to plans which will smooth the path to eventual success.

Quitting smoking is hard. Don't try it without planning carefully how to do it. Don't be hard on yourself by trying to do it as if it were easy. Choose a period when you can give it the time and attention it needs. Be easy on yourself in other areas while you are trying to quit. Think and work hard at it but be good to yourself. You deserve it because quitting smoking is one of the wisest and most beneficial things you can do for your health.

Jacquelyn Rogers. For the majority of smokers, the best way to stop smoking is to recognize that smoking isn't just a nasty little habit that can be dealt with by a single treatment or simplistic methods; smoking is probably the most complex excess behavior in our society. The complexity of smoking resides in the fact that it is: (1) a physiological addiction (nicotine); (2) a well-practiced habituation (conditioning); (3) habitual in regard to continuing and repetitive practice; (4) an oral manifestation whereby the mouth becomes accustomed to a great deal of attention and gratification if smoking is stopped without proper preparation; (5) an energy booster; (6) a psychological dependency (the crutch); (7) a stress and anxiety regulator; and (8) a social form.

The amalgam of these conditions forms a compulsion. Therefore, unless the smoker deals with both the addiction and the compulsion, his or her efforts largely lead to failure. Compounding the problem, each failure proscribes additional failures.

For a small minority of smokers who are not compulsive but rather social smokers, successful quitting (abstinence) can be achieved much more simply. Often a physician's strongly stated advice to stop smoking can be sufficient motivation.

For the majority of smokers, however, the best program is a multi-modality type, such as Smokenders, which teaches people to break the habit *before* they stop smoking so that they gain control of the total problem and are completely prepared to make the break.

The most important aspect of quitting smoking is motivation: first, to enter a treatment program; second, to comply with the instructions; and third, to have developed an intense desire to be free of the smoking habit. Control programs are successful only if they are able, through sophisticated techniques, to increase a smoker's motivation to quit.

There are two very important measures to effective smoking cessation: the first is immediate success, and the second is long-term success. Unless the smoker has developed a changed attitude and views quitting smoking as desirable and pleasurable, the chances of relapse are great. Obviously, successful control programs must have an element which deals with changing the smoker's attitude about cigarettes—from a beloved old friend to perhaps a friend who has betrayed him.

While there are no hard statistics on cold-turkey quitting, it is believed that 90 percent of all smokers over the age of eighteen have tried cold turkey at least once. (My educated guess is an average of at least five times per smoker.) There are some smokers that have never been able to bring themselves to actively try to quit. Informal surveys indicate that there are very few cold-turkey quitters who remain abstinent for more than a year.

Wrong ways to quit smoking are:

1. To please someone else.
2. To view quitting as a tragic loss and to feel deprived of a great pleasure and therefore, feel sorry for oneself.

3. To tell everyone you are quitting. The chances are, as you go cold turkey, you will soon resume smoking and the guilt and embarrassment are unfair to you.

4. Fear. While fear may cause you to stop momentarily—because a relative or neighbor has developed lung cancer or had a sudden heart attack in the prime of life—the problem is that fear doesn't last. The mind is designed to forget the ugly and the painful, and the strength of the habit returns in force.

5. Substituting pipes, cigars, chewing gum, food, fingernails, etc. The root of the problem has not been eliminated and the smoker will most likely resume smoking at the first stressful experience.

6. To be so discouraged that failure becomes a self-fulfilling prophesy. Unfortunately, the majority of smokers have come to believe that their problem is unique and that they cannot hope to quit smoking. They persuade themselves to accept the consequences.

7. After evidence of cancer, cardiovascular or pulmonary diseases. Motivation to quit, although reasonable, becomes harder since the victim feels "the damage has already been done." Indeed, anxiety creates the intense need to smoke. Therefore, enforced abstinence under these circumstances creates intense psychological anguish.

8. Expecting your doctor to have an instant remedy—a pill!

The first thing that a smoker must do is to recognize that although smokers universally say "I enjoy smoking," it is more likely a well-developed rationalization created by a combination of persuasive advertising and the relief of discomfort when one has been deprived of a nicotine fix beyond the body's comfort level.

Smoking knows no social, educational or economic barrier. Abstinence is as elusive for Supreme Court justices and top-ranking government and industrial executives as it is for youngsters and ordinary workers.

The best way to stop smoking is to reach out for expert guidance and support. Until then, the next best thing to do is to begin to "sell" yourself on reasons why it might be nice to be free of the smoking habit like—I will be able to run/play/swim more easily or, I won't be worried about my bad breath.

Sylvester R. Mlott, Ph.D. Before a person can actually stop any habit, he must know what made him start it in the first place. This is the first step on the tumultuous road to breaking the smoking habit. Probably the most important reason for starting to smoke is the desire to conform to social and cultural factors. Once the habit is started, the physiological addiction to nicotine perpetuates it. The act of smoking allows one to cover up social anxiety by providing an object to "fidget with." All the motions involved in taking the cigarette from the package to that first puff help to reduce tension, and provide a rewarding reason for having a cigarette. Since anxiety is decreased by smoking, it then becomes a compulsive act, and like all compulsive behavior, is a device for increasing feelings of safety and serves as a kind of magic spell to protect one from threat. Smoking allows the individual to feel grown-up and mature while at the same time serving as an oral pacifier. Just as a child enjoys the nipple or pleasure associated with the lips, the grown-up enjoys his cigarette. We have also been psychologically conditioned to believe smoking is a sign of masculinity, or a sign of femininity. Lastly, we have been conditioned to believe a cigarette helps us relax, yet investigations have revealed that smoking increases muscular unsteadiness. It's not the cigarette itself, but the break in routine that is relaxing.

We all tend to smoke more when tense, fatigued or uncomfortable. Unfortunately, vacations don't always coincide with the time one decides to kick the habit; but an effort should be made to get more rest, avoid conflicts, arguments and turmoil, and to condition oneself to relax throughout the day without the prop of a cigarette. Since support and reassurance are needed by all of us in any difficult endeavor, the would-be nonsmoker should inform those around him, family, coworkers, and friends, of his intention to stop smoking.

Once the person has decided that he definitely will terminate the smoking habit and has accepted the fact that temptation will always threaten, he is ready to begin breaking the environmental cues that previously elicited smoking. The old routine and its environmental cues must be extinguished and replaced by new noncigarette-associated cues. The idea is to change completely the routine followed in setting where he previously smoked. To give a specific illustration, a man who customarily smokes a cigarette with his first cup of morning coffee should attempt to try one or another means of not smoking in that context. If his usual routine involves arising from bed, putting on a robe and slippers, plugging in the coffee pot, going outside for the morning paper, then sitting down at the kitchen table with a lighted cigarette and cup of coffee, he should break up this routine thereby changing the environmental cues associated with that cigarette with his morning coffee. Perhaps he could forgo reading the paper in the mornings or take his coffee to a different room to be enjoyed. The important objective is to break up the routine of having the cigarette, at a certain time, at a certain place, while doing certain things.

Of course, there are some situations where the cigarette urge is actually not in our repertoire of conscious acknowledgment. Such situations come as somewhat of a surprise when we begin a program of nonsmoking and need a modified approach. An example would be Mr. X who usually cuts his grass in a somewhat predetermined manner, starting on the front lawn and slowly working to the back. He was surprised to find that as he approached the rear gate, he had the urge to smoke a cigarette. Realizing that, changing his route, and thereby changing environmental cues, he did not give in to the cigarette urge but continued to cut the grass for several more minutes. When he did stop, he found himself wanting his usual glass of iced tea and, once again, changed his routine, and decided not to have anything to drink. He then found himself headed for the picnic bench where he always enjoyed his "breaks" involving a cold drink and cigarettes. Again, realizing the importance of breaking the sequence of stimulus-response cues, he chose the patio steps as his resting place rather than the usual picnic bench, thereby assuring the nonreinforcement of the cues associated with smoking.

In the final analysis, this approach, like any other approach, depends upon the individual's sincere desire to terminate the habit.

WHAT IS THE MOST SUCCESSFUL CURE FOR DRUG DEPENDENCE?

Dan Anderson, Ph.D. Most people in the field of alcohol and drug dependency treatment agree that there is no *cure* for harmful dependency on chemicals. The illness can be *arrested* but not cured. Once an individual has been detoxified (dried out) and treated in an alcohol or drug program, there is a good chance that the person can, with ongoing support, maintain total abstinence. We refer to such people as recovered or recovering since recovery seems to be a lifelong process.

Recovery means more than just not drinking or using drugs. It includes, but is not limited to: developing and maintaining self-control in order to avoid drinking or using drugs; adopting a new life style of coping with life rather than simply avoiding problems; living one day at a time with the help of a higher power greater than one's self.

There are numerous treatment programs available for alcoholism and drug abuse or addiction. These include Alcoholics Anonymous or Narcotics Anonymous, specialized alcohol and/or drug rehabilitation programs, therapeutic communities, detoxification programs, outpatient clinics and aftercare programs. Each program is designed for certain clients in need of certain services. The most appropriate program will be the one that helps the client to gain sobriety and learn a new life style without chemical use.

Jerome F. X. Carroll, Ph.D. The use of the word "cure" in the question complicates my answer. The vast majority of experienced workers in the field would argue that an addict/alcoholic is never cured of his or her addiction, since he or she can never again use the substance(s) of abuse without becoming addicted again. Only a very small minority of experts believe *some* addicted people, once successfully treated, could use a substance formerly abused without again becoming addicted.

Another difficulty posed by the question is that no one can now answer the question with any degree of scientific confidence, since insufficient research exists on this important question.

My answer, based on ten years of clinical experience working with both drug dependent and/or alcohol dependent men and women, is that there is no one "most successful cure." The varied forms of addiction—most addicted people below the age of forty are multiple substance abusers, that is, they have abused both drugs and alcohol—and the varied causes of addiction (both personal and environmental) rule out a universally effective, single treatment approach.

Substance abusers, moreover, typically have many collateral problems in addition to their abuse of drugs and/or alcohol. What is needed, therefore, is a comprehensive human services delivery system which can address these problems (serious educational deficits, no marketable job skills or work experiences, legal problems, severe loneliness and guilt, uncontrollable anger and rage).

Also needed is a network of human services that can provide continuity of care over an extended period of time as the substance abuser moves through the various phases of treatment, be it detoxification, intensive inpatient, outpatient, halfway houses, Alcoholics Anonymous and/or Narcotics Anonymous. Typically, an addicted person may require one and one-half to two years of intensive treatment, followed by many years of participation in Alcoholics Anonymous and/or Narcotics Anonymous in order to remain sober and be able to lead a full and satisfying life.

A successful cure, therefore, requires access to and involvement with a multi-modality, multi-disciplinary human services delivery system capable of serving all forms of chemical dependence. This system must also be capable of coping with the multiplicity of interrelated psychological, biological and social problems which are part of the addictive lifestyle. Such systems must also be capable of providing continuity of care over an extended period of time.

Professor Steven G. Cole. There is no most successful "cure" for drug dependence. Factors that contribute to a successful cure for drug dependence are numerous. First, drug-dependent persons who sincerely desire to be free from any dependence on drugs are more likely to be cured than those who are not sincere. Second, treatment staff who sincerely desire to effect a cure and who have a strong belief in the effectiveness of the treatment they are using are more likely to cure a drug-dependent person than are less sincere treatment staff. A third factor that contributes to a cure for drug dependence is the length and frequency of exposure to treatment. Drug-dependent persons who have been exposed to numerous treatment episodes are more likely to be cured than are those who are being treated for the first time.

My examination of the literature has suggested to me that none of the "cures" for drug dependence reach a desirable level of effectiveness. In my opinion, the best approach to building an effective cure for drug dependence centers around offering a combination of inpatient and outpatient treatment that is flexible enough to allow entry at various stages of treatment based on an assessment of each individual's needs.

Reginald F. Mattison. The most successful cure for drug dependence I know of and have witnessed is a miracle of God through conversion. It involves a number of factors:

1. A desire and a decision on the part of the individual to accept Jesus as his personal savior and obey His instructions as revealed through the Bible.
2. Daily renew this relation with God through prayer. This means to ask God for help to accomplish His will in our lives for that day.
3. Help others with needs by sharing how God has helped solve our problems.
4. Daily study of God's Word for constant growth in knowledge and inspiration for continuing the experience.
5. Associate with others who have similar aims and experience for group strength.

Because Alcoholics Anonymous incorporates some of these principles if not all, it has had the success with alcoholics thus far.

The most important factor in all of this is the individual choice and surrender to a power outside our own strength, God.

John McVernon. The proverb "once an addict always an addict" is pure myth. Most people who become intensively, compulsively and destructively involved with drugs sooner or later free themselves of the habit.

Any experience that helps addicts see how bad off they are and also shows them that things could be better is the best cure for addiction. Awareness and hope are the keys to recovery. The realization that they are in trouble provides the motivation. The strategy for treatment moves one through the steps to full functioning. There are a whole variety of approaches and programs which accomplish this. I am inclined to think any technique works for the motivated addict and no program works without the motivation.

Certainly the drug-free therapeutic community does the job by creating a substitute family which challenges negative behavior and rewards positive living. Methadone treatment programs use medication to stabilize the physical addiction while encouraging return to the community through education, employment and better functioning in the home. Community programs appeal to racial pride, ethnic heritage or religious convictions to condemn wasteful drug use while enhancing the individual's sense of self. Twelve-step programs, like Narcotics Anonymous or Pillanon, use the lessons learned in Alcoholics Anonymous to illustrate the damage heavy drug use inflicts on oneself and others, and then involve the person in helping others by passing on the message.

The vast majority of people with drug problems leave the drugs behind on their own. This liberating awareness of how bad off they are comes from some event in life—an accident or the loss of a job; or through the loving but concerned words of a parent or friend; or out of the depths of their own being where the pain and the loneliness finally break through. Given that new insight, they then can grasp hold of that part of their life which still remains intact and struggle toward their recovery.

There are many, many paths into addiction and just as many ways out. The essence of any "cure" is to stop the destructive process by creating awareness of where this course of drug-taking has brought the individual. Then, when that addict wants out, to assure him that recovery is possible and walk with him the first few steps back into the mainstream of life.

EDUCATION

T HE CHALLENGE TO EDUCATORS has never been greater. Communities are tightening their school budgets; demoralized teachers are complaining of "burn-out"; and social critics are giving failing grades to the nation's school systems. Meanwhile, the body of knowledge to be taught grows with every scientific development and every historical event.

While the body of knowledge is fast increasing, the student body is decreasing. According to *The Condition of Education, 1980 Statistical Report* by the National Center for Education Statistics, "the character of education in the 1980s will be shaped to a large extent by the size of the population it serves." The baby boom of the 1950s has grown up to be the adult boom of the 1980s, and the school-age population has shrunk accordingly. In 1956, 36 percent of the American population was under eighteen; by 1975, the percentage had dropped to 31. According to Census Bureau estimates, the youth population fell to 28 percent in 1980 and will continue to decline to reach a projected low of 24 percent in 1990. For the school systems, this demographic downturn means a halt to almost twenty years of rapid growth. In most states, that translates into widespread school closings and reduced teacher employment.

Although the numbers of students are declining, the percentages of kids going—or not going—to school have remained fairly stable. In 1978–79, for example, an overwhelming 97 percent of all five- to seventeen-year-olds were enrolled in school. How often did they actually make it to classes? Nationwide, about 8 percent were absent on any given school day in the 1970s. The absentee rate in large-city schools tended to be much higher; for example, almost 25 percent of the public-school students in Boston and New York City were absent each school day.

What about the students who do sit at their desks each day, how much do they learn? A 1977 study of the subjects taught in elementary schools asked teachers how much time they spent each day on various subjects. The average number of minutes devoted to each subject were: reading, eighty-six; math, forty-four; social studies, twenty-five; and science, twenty. In comparison, it is estimated that the average child spends a whopping three hours in front of the television set each day. Not surprisingly, educators worry about the literacy of generations that grow up more accustomed to flipping a channel than turning a page.

Concerns about the nation's "numeracy" rival worries about declining literacy. Educators contend that the math and science abilities of today's students will determine whether the United States will continue to be a leader in technology. So far, studies of students' "numeracy" are not encouraging. For example, a comparison of mathematical assessment scores of nine-, thirteen-, and seventeen-year-olds between 1972–73 and 1977–78 show that the only students with appreciable improvement were nine-year-old blacks; their scores rose from 15 percent below the national average to 10 percent below. Performance declined significantly among thirteen-year-old whites (3.4 percent) and among all seventeen-year-olds (3.8 percent).

Overall, progress in the sciences has declined more than progress in reading, according to statistics from a 1976 study:

NATIONAL ASSESSMENT OF EDUCATIONAL PROGRESS TESTS: PERCENTAGES OF CORRECT SCORES

Year	Reading			Science		
	9 YR.	13 YR.	17 YR.	9 YR.	13 YR.	17 YR.
1970–71	64.0	60.6	72.1	61.1	60.2	45.6
1974–75	65.2	60.7	72.0	59.4	58.3	42.3
Change	+ 1.2	+ 0.1	− 0.1	− 1.7	− 1.9	− 3.3

To ensure that students attain at least the reading and math abilities necessary for basic survival skills—filling out a job application, reading directions, understanding bank statements, etc.—more and more states are requiring that would-be high school graduates pass minimum competency tests. These tests, the products of widespread concern about the quality of education in the nation's schools, require students to have anywhere from eighth- to eleventh-grade skill levels.

The minimum competency tests are designed to identify those students who have somehow managed to earn passing grades without really learning basic course material. But while a few students just barely pass, a large percentage are eager to *surpass*—both in school and in future professions. In a 1978 survey, half of all high school seniors said they definitely planned to continue their education after graduation. It is encouraging to note that more than 30 percent planned to graduate from four-year colleges; 9 percent were determined to go on to graduate and professional schools after college.

CONTRIBUTORS

Charles J. Armstrong, Ph.D., Educational Consultant; retired college professor and university president

Albert W. Baisler, Ph.D., LL.D., Educational Consultant; former president

Alexander Heard, Chancellor, Vanderbilt University, Nashville, Tennessee

Hon. Shirley M. Hufstedler, former Secretary, U.S. Department of Education; now in private law practice in Los Angeles, California

Dr. Larry L. Leslie, Director and Professor, Center for the Study of Higher Education, University of Arizona, Tucson, Arizona

Dr. Jean Mayer, President, Tufts University, Medford, Massachusetts; former Professor of Nutrition, Harvard University, Cambridge, Massachusetts

James A. Perkins, Chairman, International Council for Educational Development, New York, New York

Gilbert A. Peters, President Association for Higher Education of North Texas, Richardson, Texas

Frank H. T. Rhodes, President, Cornell University, Ithaca, New York

J. William Rioux, Senior Associate, National Committee for Citizens in Education, Columbia, Maryland

Melvin H. Rudov, Ph.D., President, Affiliated Risk Control Administrators of Pennsylvania, Inc., Pittsburgh, Pennsylvania

Howard R. Swearer, President, Brown University, Providence, Rhode Island

Dr. Clifton R. Wharton, Jr., Chancellor, State University of New York

WHY IS LITERACY DECLINING AMONG CHILDREN AND YOUNG ADULTS IN THE UNITED STATES? WHAT CAN BE DONE TO IMPROVE IT?

Hon. Shirley M. Hufstedler. We shall be as literate a people as we care to be. If adults believe that literacy is important for themselves and for their children, and if we also believe that it is important for other people's children, we shall become a literate nation.

We cannot expect children to believe that literacy is important when no one in their families reads anything. Television is a fascinating and important medium. But television does not teach the value of literacy.

Schools, acting all by themselves, cannot create a literate population. Schools in our nation must have the support from the whole country. That means that persons who do not have children in school must appreciate the need to help schools teach children. Senior citizens can assist youngsters and themselves by entering into voluntary programs with their local schools. Children must be valued in our society before children are willing to go through the struggle to learn. We cannot tell the nation's children to do things that we are unwilling to do ourselves. When we can give of ourselves to the nation's youngsters, those children will learn to value literacy and to value the society in which we live.

Frank H. T. Rhodes. Blame for the declining literacy among America's young people must be shared by society as a whole. Part of the problem is certainly the pervasiveness of television in the American home and its usurpation of more traditional means of communication—reading and even talking. The average person will have watched some 22,000 hours of television by the time he or she graduates from high school—far more time than will have been spent in the classroom. Moreover, several studies have indicated that parents and their children spend, on the average, only 14 minutes a day talking to each other—and much of that time is consumed by orders ("Take out the garbage.") rather than by meaningful discussion. The problem is compounded by the rapid rise in the number of working mothers (about 35 percent now work full-time) whose children are left to their own devices after school.

With families dispersed across the nation rather than across town, many older people (and they are a growing sector of our population) are voting down school budgets from which neither their children nor their grandchildren will receive direct benefit. Rising costs and lower achievements on the part of many students are creating widespread distrust of public education and, ironically, they are making the public less willing to support the enterprise.

A major concern is teacher competency. From throughout the country have come reports of teachers, some with advanced degrees, who are functionally illiterate. As many as 20 percent of those now employed in teaching may not have the basic skills in writing, reading and arithmetic that they are supposed to teach. Part of the problem, certainly, is the kind of student that chooses education as a major. Traditionally these have included less able students than those entering other professional programs. Moreover, the field of education has become the playground of the theorist—with concepts of questionable utility in the classroom.

The schools, too, are suffering from lax standards and the push for "relevance" that was so strong in the 1960s. Easy electives have replaced many rigorous academic courses and today only about 4 percent of all students take the most academically challenging courses, despite much talk about the need to get back to basics.

Certainly competence in reading, writing and computation is necessary for the development of higher learning, but there are dangers in the back to basics movement, too. It can be used too easily to remove all "frills"—art, music, literature, computing (but certainly not athletics)—from the curriculum on the ground that these are interfering with the student's concentration on the three R's and costing the system too much money. It can also lead to narrow vocationalism, in which the student is taught the intricacies of accounting or auto mechanics rather than those skills of analysis, synthesis and appreciation of the aesthetic so essential to a full and productive life.

Compounding the problem are a host of new regulations and legislative fiats that have diverted both the resources and energies of teachers and administrators from their basic tasks of teaching students.

If the blame for this sorry state of public education must be shared, so must the solution. Some 85 percent of the adult population (including many teachers) favor some sort of competency testing for teachers. But we also need parents who are concerned about their schools and their children and willing to devote time to both. It is no coincidence that in schools with active Parent-Teacher Associations, all other things being equal, students are more likely to excel.

We need school boards dedicated to maintaining both the quality and the efficiency of their schools and willing to allow competent, dedicated teachers and administrators to do the jobs for which they were hired. Boards must also work to convince the public that a strong, adequately supported school system is in the best interest of everyone—whether or not they have children in school. But too often local boards have found themselves ruling on the appropriateness of certain textbooks or curricula, areas in which they may have little expertise.

Colleges and universities have two principal roles to play in the improvement of public education. First, those that offer teacher training programs should carefully examine their requirements to ensure that their graduates have the skills needed to do their jobs effectively. Increased emphasis on learning subject matter may be needed along with less on "education" courses. It has long been true at the college level, and it may well be true at the lower levels, that the most effective teachers are those who are truly interested in and dedicated to their disciplines. Yet most of those now teaching at lower levels are more closely allied to the profession of "teaching" than to the disciplines they teach.

Second, colleges and universities have a responsibility to work with the lower schools so that students receive the preparation that will enable them to succeed in postsecondary education. Renewed emphasis on college entrance requirements may be needed. While some have argued that the return to requirements may exclude disadvantaged students from higher education, it can also be argued, more convincingly I believe, that the lower schools should equip all students, regardless of race or economic status, with the skills necessary to meet the established requirements. It is, after all, a failure to impose high enough standards that has led, in part, to the current failures of public education.

It also may be necessary for schools and colleges to work together to develop new curricula and new ways of teaching, as has been done successfully with the teaching of writing in the San Francisco Bay area.

For too long American education has been a "layer cake," to borrow a phrase coined some fifty years ago by Henry Clinton. Primary, secondary and postsecondary programs have been piled on top of each other and held together at best by a thin layer of frosting. If colleges and universities are to help the leaders of the next generation realize their full potential for productivity, they must work with their counterparts at lower levels to devise an integrated system focused on that common goal.

J. William Rioux. I think we are coming out of a period (1960–1980) when the entire country went through a trauma of successive blows to its equilibrium—Vietnam, Watergate, the drug culture, the young rebellion. There was no way schools could be effectively insulated from those blows. The result was an uncertainty about priorities, an uncertainty about how much parents and the public would support the profession with regard to standards. Indeed, some of the counterculture people later became teachers and in dress and outlook perpetuated a laissez-faire attitude; if it feels good, do it—creativity as opposed to rules. The rude awakening has been upon us for the last several years and I think a tightening-up process is under way. I am optimistic that the literacy rate will reflect this change.

WHAT DO YOU SEE AS THE EDUCATIONAL SYSTEM OF TOMORROW?

Charles J. Armstrong. The educational system of tomorrow will become increasingly diversified in form, method and content. There will be less emphasis on formal classroom instruction, more on individual, personal learning—in the home, on the job, during leisure time.

The single most important change-producing factor in education is the changed and changing nature of the family. Very few families today fit the traditional pattern of working husband, housekeeping wife and one or two children at home. Instead, the vast majority of marriages (or nonmarriages) are those in which both spouses work. Also, an increasing number of children are being supported by a single working parent. Such patterns are particularly characteristic of people in their twenties, thirties and early forties.

As a consequence the number of young children being placed in day care, nursery and other preschool centers is growing at a staggering rate, and a tremendous expansion of such facilities will be necessary.

Much more will be expected of these preschool systems than at present. They cannot be merely custodial institutions. They must provide a diversity of educational and socializing experiences for children from the age of two to six or so: much of the parenting—the inculcation of basic skills, attitudes and values formerly done in the home; instruction in the fundamental skills of reading, writing and calculating; and the awakening in the child of the desire to learn and to create.

As a result, these children (and they will be the large majority) will enter public school at age six or so already knowing the three R's, and the schools must adapt to this fact. The child's instinct to learn must not be stifled and stultified by boring repetition of things already learned.

This will pose a tremendous challenge and opportunity to the public schools. Parents have become increasingly disillusioned with the public school system, and if the schools fail to adapt, parents will find ways to force adaptation, or else send their children to private schools, as we see happening more and more often today.

If the schools take full advantage of what such children already know, they can move them along much more rapidly. The time thus saved can be put to the child's advantage by using it to stimulate the joy of learning as well as the acquisition of values and insights which will enable him to make a much more intelligent choice of future career paths. At the same time, the child at a relatively early age should be given, under general school supervision, actual working experience in a variety of jobs, so that he may find out for himself what it means to work and to produce.

All of this can help greatly to reduce or eliminate the child's all-too-frequent alienation, hostility and disaffection which lead to juvenile delinquency and crime, and generally disrupt the life pattern.

The choice of later patterns of education, whether for a trade, clerical, managerial, paraprofessional, professional or other career will thus become more intelligent, helping to avoid the waste of time and money otherwise spent in programs unsuited to the individual.

There will be much more emphasis on individual learning in the home for people of all ages. Even a young child can learn to use a computer and tie into large computer banks or libraries for information retrieval. We shall see much wider and more sophisticated use of learning cassettes, video tapes, computer displays, cable television and other forms of telecommunications. Learning will become a lifelong process, especially for the growing number of people who change careers several times, often necessitating a return to school or other instruction. Others will want to increase their appreciation of the humanities and fine arts.

Colleges and universities, many of which, in a desperate attempt to survive, have diluted standards to absurdity, will find a new and larger role in meeting the educational needs of people of all ages. There will be increased interest in the cultural aspects of our heritage, as people with more leisure time seek to use that time enjoyably and creatively.

Finally, business and industry will become more and more involved in education. Even now many imaginative and forward-looking companies are providing day care centers for employees' children, where parents can spend coffee and lunch breaks with their children and thus strengthen the family bond.

Education of tomorrow will fit the pattern of tomorrow, which will demand rapid change, great diversification, and above all, creative imagination.

Albert W. Baisler, Ph.D., LL.D. Tomorrow's educational system will be a reflection of America's numerous cultures. It is important to design this education system to meet these challenges. Respect for the languages of our foreign neighbors, many of whom attend school and college with us, needs to be developed. Appreciation and interpretation of their cultures will benefit business relationships and political understanding.

For three centuries our nation has enjoyed a rich heritage of respect for education throughout the world. Rewards have been manifest in our commerce, industry and social institutions. Respect for the democratic values of freedom and mutual respect must be reflected in the historic character of the "educated person."

Emergence of computer technology will demand changes which incur moral and social responsibility so that this does not become an age of electronic nightmare. Youth and adults must be taught as never before the hazards of drugs, misuse of power, observance of law and order with education and action for the greatest good for all—a control so that freedom and privacy of the individual is not violated.

There should be a greater emphasis on career planning as computer languages appear and employers plead for competent associates with practical "hands-on" experience, so that students will be prepared for immediate employment.

An emergence of respect for occupational education will occur in the future paralleling a renewal of the emphasis on the liberal arts. A radical change in attitudes among traditionalists must occur. This change will be characterized by a new acceptance of the technical assistant working shoulder to shoulder with the professional.

There will be a need to revive privately sponsored schools. Citizens want exposure to worthy values and are willing to spend money to maintain such schools. Teachers also may express a desire to teach in such schools. And money management will place greater emphasis on accountability. Administrators will be required to limit curriculum to community and professional needs.

Our latent strength, power, spirit, intellect and imagination must be activated to renew and strengthen our great American heritage. So we must search for, discover, support and then benefit from education's intricate design.

Alexander Heard. Tomorrow's education will be universal in two new senses. Formal instruction will be required for almost all vocations and avocations. Five centuries of invention have assured that. Education will also be sought in all age groups. In virtually all activities, recurring education will be needed to stay productive and competitive.

Education will be increasingly dynamic technologically. Cable television, computer aids, video discs and a wide range of other innovations will alter modes of instruction more rapidly and radically than in the past. Many new forms of classroom will appear and more demands will be made on community facilities to offer learning opportunities.

Tomorrow's "system" will see a more widely disparate set of institutions and formal processes than we now have, many of them unconnected with each other, by which information is transferred, skills developed, intellects trained, insights stimulated, habits disciplined, knowledge acquired, curiosities satisfied, pleasures derived and values shaped. Education is acquired in the United States now through well over 100,000 elementary and secondary schools and more than 3,000 colleges and universities of diverse size, purpose, quality and sponsorship. Millions of people now study in educational programs offered by financial, business and industrial concerns, by the armed services, by civic centers, churches, art galleries, museums, publicly financed institutes, private proprietary institutions and a variety of other organizations. The vehicles for delivery of educational services in the future will be even more numerous and diverse and the need for their better integration and articulation will mount.

Postindustrial society will be more than now an information-loaded, science-driven, technologically complex set of systems. As Henry Adams might note, such a society is likely to be increasingly one of fractured traditions, disrupted social institutions and disturbed individual psyches. Educational institutions will be asked to respond. Scarce resources will create pressures for cooperation among all types of social services, private and public, intended to provide opportunities for learning, healing and personal growth.

The liberal education we have traditionally celebrated in the United States will be a small part of the educational future, smaller than in the past. The market for competence is more immediate than for wisdom. And it is easier to produce specialized technical comprehension than to produce political inventiveness and integrated personalities. The future will test whether educational systems can truly help individuals separately, and societies collectively, to learn new intellectual processes and to remodel old emotional reflexes fast enough, while retaining a sense of the whole firmly enough, to protect and generate values by which people can prosper safely together.

Dr. Larry L. Leslie. In asking a question such as this, there is an implicit expectation that dramatic changes are ahead. In some important ways education most certainly will change, but I strongly suspect that the central core of education will remain essentially the same.

One can go back in time to at least Plato's academy and identify the common features of education that persist today. Perhaps most persistent is the role of teacher. Substitutes have come and gone, mediators have been introduced, the teaching role has been subdivided many times, assistants have been appointed, and all sorts of styles and methods have been tried, but the teacher remains as the central character in the educational process. Further, the form of instruction is essentially the same. Notwithstanding many exceptions, the overwhelming instructional mode is still heavily verbal, is still made to a single class usually of from fifteen to forty students and is still presented in person. So the core of education will remain the same. What of the changes?

Around this central core, noticeable and sometimes dramatic innovations will be observed. Almost all will be in areas that could be viewed as supplemental to, or enrichments of, the historical educational process involving teacher and students. Substitutes for this historical process will be for selective groups, or persons physically located in isolated areas.

One example will be instruction at home through cable television with linkups to home computers. With its large channel capability, cable television will offer not only many more traditional courses but will greatly expand the opportunities for cultural enrichment and personal growth—opportunities that will be presented on a noncredit basis. Home computers will greatly expand the nature of courses that can be offered through video, home modes and alternatives for self-instructional, self-motivational experiences. But again, these approaches will substitute for traditional instruction only for such groups as the physically handicapped and the nontraditional college or high school age groups. For others, cable television and home computers will be supplemental learning devices, particularly in areas of personal, often avocational, interest.

Another change will be in decentralization and reduction in size of the organizational unit. Although large high schools and giant universities will remain, there will be a general trend toward size reduction. At the elementary and secondary level, the very large urban school districts increasingly will be broken down into operating subunits so that parents can once again feel close to and exercise control over their schools. This trend will be enhanced by a decline in school busing to achieve racial integration and by greatly increased competition from private schools which will offer precisely the kind of responsiveness to parental wishes that is so much desired. Partly as a response to these forces and simple changes in demographics, the size of junior and senior high schools will diminish too, with new physical plants being built on a scaled-down basis. Even at the college level, the value of the small liberal arts or moderate-sized comprehensive college will realize a resurgence as the liabilities of enormous size become better known.

Another change will be in curriculum. For some time to come, there will be increased emphasis upon basic education and less attention to what has come to be called the educational frills and fads. At the collegiate level there will be, by 1985, a noticeable return to general and liberal education with a concomitant reduction in technical/vocational and professional education. Eventually, American education will settle into a more balanced curriculum approach, somewhere between the wild swings of the past.

Dr. Jean Mayer. What I hope to see is an educational system that provides equal access for every individual and the opportunity to continue learning throughout life. I would like to see young people graduate from college with some understanding of our civilization and their place in it; some perception of how society works and their role as citizens of the world's greatest democracy; training in a discipline that is deep and broad enough so that they may contribute something in their field and grow with it; an experience of the arts that will enrich their private lives; and a knowledge of the basics of health care that will help them to maintain their bodies in good physical condition.

James A. Perkins. Educational systems for the rest of this century will maintain many, if not most, of today's forms, structures and purposes. The kindergarten, elementary and secondary schools, colleges and universities, and adult and further education institutions will still be with us. The proper balance between liberal and professional education, domestic and international orientations, selective and open admissions, academic and vocational tracks, and the imperatives of equal opportunity and the manpower requirements of industrial societies—all these educational problems will be on the agenda of faculty and association meetings.

But changes in national and international environments will exercise their torque on the evolution of educational systems. A few of the most powerful can be identified.

The scientific-industrial revolution will still be in full swing. This means an increasing emphasis on basic and applied science (both natural and biological), engineering and the administrative talents required to manage a complicated economic and social system. Business administration is an example.

The revolution of rising expectations is already changing to a revolution of rising demands. Equity and justice will be the banners demanding educational opportunity for all levels of competence. Talents, sexes, racial and ethnic minorities will still be high concerns. To accommodate these demands, there will be an increase in two-year nondegree colleges, adult education programs by correspondence, television, as well as increasing options for local out-of-school opportunities.

The need for central policy-making with an increasing demand for decentralized administration: The need for trained manpower and research on the one hand with the demand for equality of opportunity on the other will continue to lead to increased centralization of policies and the initiation of national programs. But the very machinery required to manage such central activity will continue to lead to a countervailing effort to meet local needs and individual aspirations. We can expect many institutional experiments designed to achieve these twin objectives.

There will be increased involvement of the arts in the university—from arts appreciation to arts performances. Artistic talent will take its place alongside cognitive ability as a proper concern of the educational system.

Throughout all these developments, there will be a gradual shift of emphasis from the classroom to the home and factory and the learning center. Technology makes it possible but the demand for learning options makes it necessary.

Gilbert A. Peters. The component of "the system" with which I might offer some measure of insight is the part dealing with the future delivery of higher education to the learner. The traditional lecture method by a single teacher in a room with dozens or hundreds of students must give way to a more efficient and effective system of teaching and learning, such as computers and television. While the effectiveness of these two methods of delivering instruction has consistently been shown to be equal to or better than traditional methods, there has been no broad move toward their adoption because the costs per unit taught have not been shown to be dramatically more favorable . . . until now.

New pressures on institutions, including inflation, declining enrollments, requirements for better productivity and competition, are causing educators to review delivery options. This, together with the plummeting costs of broadband communications systems locally (cable television), regionally (microwave) and nationally (satellite), has caused a significant new investment in the design and trial of alternative, distance-reducing learning systems. Learners, themselves, are adding their voices to more efficient ways of getting instruction, given their new time constraints and increasing costs for transportation.

The system of tomorrow will be well-laced with in-home delivery of upper division, graduate and continuing professional education materials via television (cable, DBS satellite, videotape, videodisc) and microcomputer. Regional and statewide educational telecommunications systems are now emerging to lead the way. Higher education will become, to a significant extent, a cottage industry by A.D. 2000.

Frank H. T. Rhodes. From the earliest colonists, who, as one historian remarked, built themselves a college almost before they had built themselves a privy, Americans have recognized the singular importance of an educated citizenry. Originally rooted in the study of the classics; then gradually including, with the advent of the land-grant movement, practical instruction in agriculture and the mechanic arts; adding research as a major emphasis at the turn of the century; and becoming more accessible to students of all social classes and levels of ability, the American system of higher education is now as diverse as the 3,000 institutions of which it is composed.

That diversity will continue through the closing years of this century and beyond. Comprehensive universities and particularly community colleges, which have emphasized professionalism and vocationalism in recent years, will continue to exist side by side with colleges of liberal arts, which attempt to train sensitive and informed citizens capable of creative thought and analysis. The liberal arts, in fact, may reassert their place in many of the more "professional" institutions. Many postsecondary institutions are defining a core of basic knowledge which they believe all students, regardless of professional aspirations, should be familiar with. Recent studies have indicated, moreover, that even in professional fields, liberally educated men and women tend to rise to the upper echelons faster than their professionally trained counterparts.

Yet there is a growing concern that the love of learning and the breadth of interest so vital to liberal education is being neglected in the primary and secondary schools by "no-frills" education which ostensibly aims to get back to basics. While it is true that without a firm grounding in the three R's, appreciation of the arts and humanities is difficult, it is equally true that without exposure to the arts and humanities at an early age, students can become so immersed in the mechanics of learning that they never experience its joys. It will be a challenge for our schools in the years ahead not only to improve basic skills, something they have done rather poorly during the past two decades, but also to use those basic skills as the starting point for a fuller and more rewarding education—an education that will provide the basis for lifelong learning, both through structured academic programs and through individual study.

The explosion of knowledge that has characterized the world since the turn of the century will continue, and a host of electronic information storage and retrieval systems will replace the augmenting and more traditional media. Computer literacy will take its place as a vital component of a liberal education. In the typical library, the scholar will pore over microfilms and search for information via computer more often than he or she will rummage through dusty stacks of paper books.

The information explosion, and the technological revolution of which it is a part, will necessitate refresher courses for professionals throughout their working lives. Already recent graduates in high technology fields such as engineering, computer science and medicine, are finding that many of the specifics they learned have been made obsolete by new discoveries and new inventions.

The technical revolution will also change the character of the work we do. The provision of services is already displacing the production of goods as the country's major economic activity and in such an economic environment, an educated work force will replace machinery as the key to increased productivity.

Our educational system must respond not only by updating the information it imparts to the student but also by focusing on the underlying concepts and paradigms that will enable students to assimilate new information throughout their lifetimes.

Melvin H. Rudov, Ph.D. I am answering this question in terms of what I think the educational system of tomorrow ought to be rather than what I think it will be. I do not think the educational system of our country is going to change unless drastic steps are undertaken to change it, and I do not know who the change agents might be. Some preliminary comments will underscore my feelings in this matter.

A number of years back, I returned to Pittsburgh, the city of my birth and rearing. I had come from upstate New York, which had one of the better educational systems in the country, only to find out that my children were ensconced in the same educational system that I had left some three decades earlier. When I mean the same educational system, I do not mean that the name of the educational system was the same, nor do I mean that the names of the schools in that system were the same. I mean that nothing in the system had changed. Nothing.

In that three-decade period, we must as a nation have gone through at least four or five different philosophies of education; we had done a tremendous amount of educational research, and had developed a tremendous amount of educational technology, yet there was no sign of the results of any of these efforts having penetrated this urban school system. So when I make the distinction of what ought to be rather than what is going to be, I am pointing to the fact that unless we wrest our educational system from those people who call themselves educators and who have had it cast in concrete that they will be the dictators of the education of our teachers, dictators of the licensing of our teachers, and to some extent the dictators of the philosophy and curricula of our educational system, we are going to continue to have the same abominable mess in our educational system that we have today.

I think that another way of answering this question is to look at the philosophical underpinnings of our educational system. We seem to forget why we decided we were going to have free public education in the first place. We certainly were not interested in education, and at the time we were less interested in children. We were only interested in the fact that children were working in mines and factories, taking jobs that adults could have had. In fact, the problem that we faced as a nation at that time is no different from the one we are currently facing with illegal aliens supposedly scalping jobs in the border states. Our solution to this problem was compulsory education. That is, we required our children to attend schools through their mid-teens under the penalty of law. Whenever you go into the drug-, crime- and violence-infested urban schools that we have today, we find out that this compulsory education is in fact sentencing our children to institutions for crimes that they did not commit.

A third way of looking at the problem is in terms of what we are creating through our school systems. The answer is nothing, other than a segment of our society which is being given custodial care for some period of time. Our high-school graduates are totally incapable of filling meaningful jobs within our economic sector. Somewhere back in time, we decided that vocational education was for the misfits that had to be maintained in a custodial manner. So the dropouts, the mentally retarded, and those with behavioral problems ended up in vocational schools, and a pejorative taint was attached to this type of education. Meanwhile, the students that remained in the mainstream (i.e., the regular school programs) were graduating, and although they had possibly had a bit of shop or home economics appreciation, they had no vocational skills. Our country needs carpenters, electricians, plumbers, masonry workers, electronics repair personnel, etc., and we are unable to use a high-school graduate for any of these trades. If our high-school graduates want to enter those trades, they have to start their training from scratch as if they had not had twelve years of education.

We might be enthralled with the romantic idea of how much a person's life is improved by having been exposed to Shakespeare, but it is when we try to expose disinterested students to Shakespeare that we end up having the disciplinary, educational apathy and vandalism problems that characterize our school systems. Therefore, I think it is necessary for us to throw out all existing philosophies of education. Let's forget the aphorisms that we are educating the whole child, that we are educating them for their maximal appreciation of life, etc., etc., and start with the notion that we are educating them for only one thing, and that is to take their place in the job market. When we do so, we get an entirely different structure to our school system.

What changes should be made? First of all, those students that are on an academic track become quite few. Perhaps only 20 to 30 percent of our students ought to be in schools getting the type of didactic education that we are giving today to most students. Letting the numbers of students who are in such a program dwindle will save money and increase the quality of their education. Many schools could be closed. Only the best teachers need be retained. The distractions caused by the behavioral problems and those students whose interest in academic training is nonexistent or marginal will disappear totally.

The remainder of the students would start out with an efficient form of today's elementary education. They need only be in this type of environment until they have achieved some reasonable performance level in reading, writing and arithmetic. Usually, this should be mastered by the sixth grade by the majority of students (there is no reason why students who cannot master the basic skills within six years cannot continue for a year or two until they do master them). We would then have every student who is trained at a level required for a wide variety of lower level jobs. It would also be necessary to require that employers maintain job requirements consistent with the actual educational level required. There is no reason why someone with a sixth grade education, for example, cannot stock or clerk in a department store. There is also no reason why such employers should be allowed to require a high school or college education for such jobs.

The rest of the educational system should be conducted outside of what we now call schools. This is where some tremendous amount of creativity, additional to what I present here, is necessary. I am not going to pretend that I have either developed the ideas fully enough myself, or that I am capable of developing them to the extent that is necessary to make this a momentous improvement in the educational system we currently have. I am only trying to lay down some initial concepts. The rest of the educational and training system should be divided up into sectors. One of the sectors should be government. There is a tremendous number of services that our government can be doing for us that it is currently not doing for want of labor. I think that people would be amazed at what a twelve- to fourteen-year-old child could do in the way of job performance if he were motivated to do so.

The motivation can come from many avenues. First of all, we should stop treating twelve- and fourteen-year-old children as infants. They can work and they can learn. They can do both at the same time. They are capable of being trusted, but first of all they have to be treated like young adults. Part of such treatment could come from giving them some jobs with a reasonable amount of responsibility.

A second form of motivation is going to be the necessity of following through with this type of an educational track long enough for the student to make a reasonable dent in the job market. A third one is going to come from the very nature of the educational process; that is, it should be made so interesting that the students are going to want to be involved in this type of an educational program. Maybe part of the time would be spent helping meter maids write tickets, and learning the laws under which the citations are made. Maybe part of the time would be spent in the courts doing clerical and fetch-it work, but after years of some exposure in the various departments and bureaus of the governmental system, my guess is that you are going to produce much better citizens who are more aware of the functions of the government. Certainly, they will learn more than they would ever learn in a civics, history or political science course.

Obviously, some exposure to the building trades for some of the upper-year students is necessary. Exposure to the transportation and communications industries also is of some necessity. Agriculture, food processing and food service might be another, depending on the geographical area. The healthcare field is another field to which exposure should be included. When students graduate from this program, they should be able to indicate to themselves, to a counselor, or to a post-graduate educational institution what it is that they would like to do for a living. Most high-school graduates today do not know what careers they would like for they do not have much of an idea what people do in the work world.

What I am talking about is not just exposure (Dewey's old notion of learning by doing) but a graded series of activities in which the earliest activities consist of exposure, the next group is the mastering of simple skills, and the final one is the acquisition of journeyman level skills in any of the trades. I am thinking of something along the lines of Project Able, which was designed for the Quincy Vocational High School, Quincy, Massachusetts. Project Able was a masterful curriculum development project. It was one in which the students could drop out at any time and have marketable skills. As long as they remained in the program at least twelve weeks, they had marketable skills. The longer they stayed in the program, the higher the level of skills they acquired.

The training need not be all teacher oriented. The bulk of the learning can be done with advanced technology. Films, film strips, video cassettes, on-line computers should become most of the teachers of tomorrow.

The place to acquire these skills is not in the school systems of today. What we need is a program which coordinates the students' activities within companies, firms and institutions that are specifically structured to accept some number of these students. An additional by-product of this type of an educational process would be exposure to potential employers. I am convinced that if this type of training is put into place with the proper amount of administrative control, that we will produce students who are ready for the market place upon their graduation, who will know where to go to get the jobs, and will be able to perform at a reasonably high level. Meanwhile, we will watch our unemployment rate tumble, we will watch the apathy, drug abuse and vandalism that the students would be otherwise exhibiting decrease drastically. We will use fewer school buildings and save money and we will see a decrease in violence. We will also see a drastic improvement in the education of that 20 to 30 percent of students who remain in the current type of educational program. This will occur because they will have much higher-qualified teachers and also because they will not have the drag that is afforded by the other 70 to 80 percent who do not want to learn the types of things which are taught to those pursuing an academic track.

Howard R. Swearer. The higher education system in America has always been reflective of, and responsive to, the needs of society. From

the colonial period, when the need was for a cadre of educated clergy-
men, to the post-World War II era, when the need was for great
numbers of engineers, scientists and educators of both sexes and all
races, the educational system has responded amazingly well. To extrapolate from past successes is risky, but it seems likely that the American
educational system will continue to respond. The question educators
ask, therefore, is: What will be the needs of society tomorrow to which
the educational system must respond today?

Perhaps the fundamental need of American society is for a more fully
developed sense of community. We must encourage a stronger sense
that as family members, as workers, and as citizens, we are inseparably
and gladly linked by bonds of responsibility to one another. Tomorrow's
solutions to many of the major problems of our society—from unemployment and pollution to drug addiction and crime—will require that the
bonds of community be strengthened. It is uncertain whether the
America of tomorrow will be more or less wealthy, whether it will be
more or less centralized and complex. In any event, the need for a more
developed sense of our connectedness and responsibility to one another
will be crucial.

Given the uncertainty even among experts about the shape of American society tomorrow, the best education will continue to be a good,
demanding, broad-based liberal education. A liberal education prepares
people to be flexible, to continue learning over a lifetime and, most
important, to take responsibility for themselves as free persons in an
uncertain world.

Given the need under any circumstances for a strengthened sense of
community, the educational system of tomorrow will have to place
increased emphasis in several areas. Most certainly the study of communications, from speech and writing to mass media and computers,
will be central. The art and science of communication will be at the heart
of community building. Central also will be international studies and
what might be called community studies—internships with government
and industry during which students come to understand the bonds
which unite people within a company or agency and which tie companies
and agencies to the larger world. With regard to research, it seems
possible that the emphasis will shift somewhat toward applied rather
than basic research although the distinction between the two is becoming blurred.

The system of higher education to meet the needs of tomorrow will
not be drastically different from today's system, but it will be more lean
and, perhaps, even more diverse. Some private and public colleges and
university campuses will close despite a growing demand for continuing
education. Community colleges will continue to prosper and will become even more responsive to the needs of the immediate community.
They will constantly innovate new courses and vary the mix of liberal
and vocational education as the needs of the community change. At the

other end of the spectrum, a relatively small number of major universities will be encouraged to see their mission even more than in the past as responding to the need for national and world community. Such universities will be expected to bring together outstanding students from a variety of backgrounds, from across the nation and the world. Finally, it would not be very surprising if access to the postsecondary educational system became linked in some way—perhaps through financial aid—to performance of a period of service (civilian or military) to the community.

The pronounced trend of the last decade toward older students and continuing and continuous education will accelerate. The "for profit," specialized schools will play an important role in this spectrum of higher education. Enrollment in medical and law schools will level off or decline while those in engineering and allied fields, such as computer science, will increase.

In the final analysis, the educational system of tomorrow will be shaped by the students we educated yesterday. If we have done our jobs well, the American educational system will continue to be the envy of the world.

Dr. Clifton R. Wharton, Jr. The explosion of knowledge in science and elsewhere means we need to rethink college's traditional time frames more urgently than ever. A moment's reflection makes it clear you simply cannot cram into an arbitrary four-year period the same fraction of today's available knowledge in a given field that you could acquire twenty, thirty or forty years ago. Moreover, the range and depth of knowledge needed by today's educated citizen and productive employee is far, far greater than that which can be assimilated in four years. Thus, the self-evident question: How realistic is the four-year baccalaureate? Why not a five-year degree—or a three-year one? Is the baccalaureate meaningful at all any more? You could argue persuasively, I think, that today's LL.B. or M.B.A. is actually the equivalent of yesterday's B.A.— at least in terms of comparative employability, prestige, etc.

Given the almost dizzying increase and turnover in knowledge in so many fields, many of the historical and social bases for the four-year bachelor's program no longer exist. At least in the immediate future, however, cultural inertia and personal economic situations will probably work against full-scale restructuring. What that means is that educators are going to have to think more and more in terms of an undergraduate curriculum that prepares the individual for a lifetime of learning: a curriculum that will serve as the foundation for lifelong education including both formal, degree-oriented learning and a whole range of complementary activities in updating, revision, and (if you will) knowledge-servicing or educational maintenance. Like your automobile, your personal word processor or your videodisc player, your college education is going to need periodic overhauls to keep it viable.

What will be demanded, therefore, is a basic college curriculum that a computer hardware specialist might call highly compatible with future developments. To use that jargon a little further, the graduate's intellectual situation henceforth will be one of an ever-advancing interface between past, present and emerging knowledge. So long as higher education clings to the four-year bachelor's degree, the least we can do is make adjusting to that perpetual advance as smooth and efficient as possible.

IMMIGRATION

*F*OR MANY PEOPLE, immigration to America is still symbolized by the now-defunct immigration offices at Ellis Island. Working at peak efficiency, officers at Ellis Island at the turn of the century could process up to 5,000 immigrants daily. Sometimes, however, more than 15,000 immigrants would arrive in a single day.

The immigration officers briskly checked masses of bewildered foreigners, many of whom spoke no English. Doctors quickly examined the would-be Americans, looking for communicable diseases or disabling afflictions. Most of all, officials looked for anyone they suspected would become a criminal or welfare burden on the state. Because of the country's rising prostitution rates, young unmarried women were watched with particular care. If a young woman immigrant claimed she was engaged to an American, officials might search for her fiancé and require that the couple marry before the woman was accepted into her new country.

Despite such protective measures, Ellis Island had an open-door policy by modern standards. At the turn of the century, there were no quotas for European immigrants. So of the approximately 12 million immigrants who came to the tiny island off New York City, only about 2 percent were turned away. Today, in contrast, the United States limits legal immigration to a total of 270,000 a year, but illegal immigration is a growing problem.

Eighty years ago, the whole process of immigration was dramatically different. Immigrants flooded into Boston, Baltimore and New Orleans as well as New York. The East Coast received a far greater share of immigrants than the West due to restrictive legislation concerning immigrants from Asia. The Chinese Exclusion Law of 1882 did just what its name suggests until it was repealed in 1943. The Automatic Exclusion Act of 1917 barred entry of Asians and Pacific Islanders until it was superseded by legislation in 1952.

If racist legislation denied entry to many Asians, other immigrants flocked to the land of opportunity. The greatest tide of immigration began around 1840. During the previous decade, only about 600,000 newcomers had entered the United States. The 1840s saw settlers sailing to America in record numbers, including thousands of German political refugees and Irish victims of the potato famine. Almost three times as many immigrants entered the United States in the 1840s as had come in the 1830s and the numbers continued to rise dramatically throughout the century. In the 1860s and 1870s, about 2.5 million immigrants arrived each decade; during the 1880s more than 5 million settled here. By 1890, a third of the population of Boston and Chicago had been born in foreign countries, and New York, which had twice as many Irish as Dublin, housed more citizens of foreign extraction than natives.

Waves of Catholic and Jewish immigrants from southern and eastern Europe gave rise to fears that "foreigners" would overwhelm the predominantly Protestant, Anglo-Saxon United States. In 1921, Congress passed (over President Wilson's veto) the first law restricting the number of European immigrants. This law, like the later National Origins Act, limited the total annual immigration. It also cut off the entry of many "new" immigrants by setting quotas on annual immigration from different countries. This system determined how many immigrants could come from any given country as a percentage of how many citizens from that country were already in the United States as of an earlier census. The Displaced Persons Act of 1948 made special provisions for immigrants who come to this country as political refugees or as victims of national calamities.

In 1980 more than 530,000 Cuban and Haitian refugees joined the 270,000 legal immigrants to bring the total authorized immigration to more than 800,000. Immigration officials estimate that anywhere from 500,000 to one million more people enter the country each year illegally, most coming across the Mexican border.

Today's immigrants usually come from Asia or Latin America rather than Europe. Southern and western states receive most of the influx—willingly or unwillingly. Unknown numbers of Latin Americans come across the Texas border each year; 150,000 to 200,000 legal and illegal immigrants arrived in California last year, many of them coming from Southeast Asia.

Immigration is a problem for many areas. As in the past, officials worry whether the newcomers will become burdens on the state or criminals; natives resent the immigrants who compete with them for jobs and housing. One sign of a state's concern is Florida governor Robert Graham's recent suit against the federal government for its failure to restrict the flow of more than 150,000 refugees into his state.

Can illegal immigration be stopped? Should it be? Experts offer their opinions.

CONTRIBUTORS

David Carliner, Attorney, specializing in Immigration and Nationality Law, Washington, D.C.; Chairman, International Human Rights Law Group; Chairman, Immigration and Nationality Committee, Administrative Law Section, American Bar Association

Roger Conner, Executive Director, Federation for American Immigration Reform (FAIR)

Leo Grebler, Graduate School of Management, University of California, Los Angeles, California

Douglas S. Massey, Ph.D., Population Studies Center, Department of Sociology, University of Pennsylvania, Philadelphia, Pennsylvania

Doris M. Meissner, Acting Commissioner, Immigration and Naturalization Service, U.S. Department of Justice, Washington, D.C.

THE NUMBER OF ILLEGAL ALIENS WHO COME INTO THE UNITED STATES EACH YEAR IS REPORTED TO BE IN THE HUNDREDS OF THOUSANDS. WHY IS THIS THE CASE AND WHAT CAN BE DONE ABOUT IT? SHOULD ANYTHING BE DONE ABOUT IT?

David Carliner. The major reason for the large number of aliens who enter the United States illegally each year is the current restrictive policy by the United States government limiting the number of Mexican citizens who are able to come to this country either for permanent residence or to work here temporarily. Historically the United States/Mexican border was open. Intermittently during recent history, large scale entries of Mexicans to the United States for the purpose of employment were encouraged, if not facilitated, by the United States government. Since 1965, severe restrictions have been imposed upon persons who previously had entered this country legally. As a result, those who had previously entered legally continued to enter unlawfully.

Since economic factors appear to justify the continued admission of Mexican nationals to the United States, the law should be modified to adjust to the demographic reality.

Although there are a substantial number of persons, other than Mexicans, who are in the United States unlawfully, the number of such persons in a population of 230 million is so insubstantial that it does not present a major social, economic, legal or even political problem. Unless we are to cut off the flow of visitors to the United States and make our country a walled fortress, the problem of persons who enter this country and decide to remain either permanently or for prolonged periods of time will persist.

The lack of definitive evidence that the population in the United States needs to be capped indicates that our society can tolerate, even welcome, the flow of people who have enriched not only our economy but our culture.

Roger Conner. Legal immigration in 1980 was over 808,000. In addition, although hard figures are impossible to find, several hundred thousand illegal immigrants are estimated to enter the United States each year. In the late 1970s, over a million apprehensions of illegal immigrants were made each year, over 800,000 of them on the southern border. The Border Patrol estimates that, for each apprehension they make, two or three illegal border crossings are successful. In addition, several million people each year, who enter the United States legally as visitors, students or temporary workers, are not recorded as leaving—and some portion of them stay on as illegal immigrants.

Of these illegal immigrants who either enter the United States illegally or overstay legal visas, a modest, conservative estimate would be that in the late 1970s about a half-million people a year became permanent illegal residents of the United States. It is generally accepted, though without very good studies or evidence, that about half of illegal immigrants come from Mexico; the other half come from dozens of countries, particularly the Philippines, South Korea and Central American and Caribbean nations.

Most illegal immigrants come to the United States for economic reasons: to get a job, to earn more money than they could in their home countries, and to better themselves. While these are commendable motivations, illegal immigrants compete with American workers who are looking for entry-level jobs. As of 1981, the United States had the highest unemployment rate of any western industrialized democracy, 7.6 percent, and half of all new jobs that are created in the United States go to new legal and illegal immigrants.

As illegal immigrants become institutionalized in the United States, and as they become more familiar with American ways, they more and more seek access to governmental services and welfare programs such as education, Aid for Dependent Children, subsidized housing, and nonemergency medical care. In several recent court cases, they have been granted the right to such services, and governmental agencies have been forbidden to question the legal status of those who seek aid. This dilutes the amount of aid available for citizens and legal residents of the United States, and burdens taxpayers. In addition, those who are concerned about population pressures on America's resources and environment generally desire to reach a stable, nonexpanding United States population: legal and illegal immigration together contribute about half of current United States population growth, and at their current levels ensure that the United States will never reach a stable population level.

Illegal immigration is so high for two reasons. First, United States laws against it are not being enforced. During any work shift, fewer than 350 Border Patrol officers patrol the 2,000-mile border with Mexico—fewer people than are patrolling the grounds of the United States Capitol. While the magnitude of illegal immigration has grown in the past twenty years (apprehensions were ten times greater in the late 1970s than they were in the early 1960s), the Border Patrol and the investigations force of the Immigration and Naturalization Service are no larger now than they were then.

Second, it is not illegal for an American employer to hire an illegal immigrant. Therefore, it is not difficult for an illegal immigrant to find work in the United States, particularly since many illegal immigrants will work for less pay and in worse working conditions than American workers should have to accept.

Although it is sometimes said that immigration laws are impossible to enforce, the truth is that we have not made any effort to enforce them. A modest increase in the number of Border Patrol officers and Immigration and Naturalization Service investigators and a law prohibiting the hiring of illegal immigrants should be sufficient to discourage most people from attempting to come to the United States illegally, and should enable us to apprehend the great majority of those who do come.

Leo Grebler. The reason why is persistent large-scale unemployment and underemployment in Latin-American countries and enormous difference in earnings potentials for job holders. On the United States side, it is the employers' interest in cheap labor; for the Mexicans, it is the proximity to the United States.

Illegal immigration could and should be more effectively controlled. Quite apart from the contested question whether it generates net benefits or net costs to the United States, one of the prerogatives of a sovereign nation is to regulate entry. We do for immigrants from most countries. That we don't for Mexicans and other Spanish-speaking represents a legally unsanctioned double-standard and a policy of hypocrisy. Further, the constant addition of illegals keeps the reported average socioeconomic status of Spanish-speaking low when those with permanent residence in the United States are making considerable progress.

One remedial step would be a sharp increase in appropriations for the Immigration and Naturalization Service including the Border Patrol. Another would be a compulsory identification card for all United States residents that would be required for all job applications, so employers could no longer plead ignorance about the status of illegal workers. The argument that such a card would interfere with civil rights cannot be taken seriously. Finally, the interest of Mexico in an outlet for its unemployed and the legitimate demand of United States employers for seasonal workers can be met by introducing an improved version of the Bracero program that was terminated in 1964. The new United States–Mexico agreement should assure more adequate supervision by our government of decent job and housing conditions.

Douglas S. Massey, Ph.D. Illegal migration to the United States is a result of inequality in the distribution of economic opportunity throughout the world. It is tied to conditions that prevail in both developed countries, such as the United States, and less developed countries, such as Mexico.

Within less developed countries, the rate of population growth typically exceeds the rate of job creation. This imbalance produces widespread underemployment and severely restricts the chances for economic advancement in less developed societies. This gap between population and economic growth has widened in the recent past and will no doubt persist for some time. Thus developing countries now contain, and will continue to house, a large and growing pool of potential migrants.

Within developed countries, a persistent demand for unskilled labor continues to attract migrants, both legal and illegal. The reasons for such demand—even in the face of high domestic unemployment—are complex, and have been the subject of much debate among scholars. In some cases, native workers may be reluctant to take jobs at wages employers are able to offer and still remain in business; or natives may refuse work considered to be of demeaning social status. In other instances, employers may deliberately bypass native workers in favor of illegal immigrants willing to work longer hours for lower wages, and under less favorable conditions. Finally, entirely new industries may arise to take advantage of large and growing supplies of cheap, undocumented labor that have accumulated in certain locations. Whatever the reason (probably all have some truth), illegal migrants generally experience little trouble securing employment in this country. The key consideration is that while wages and working conditions may be poor by United States standards, the opportunities they afford seem generous compared to those migrants could have expected had they remained in the home countries.

In the past, imbalances in the degree of economic opportunity between the United States and less developed regions have not inevitably led to migration. More often migration has been initiated by active recruitment on the part of employers, and in some instances, the government. The large flow of undocumented migrants from Mexico, for example, is only the latest phase in a long-standing tradition spurred by periodic recruitment that began in the 1880s. However, with the rise in literacy and the spread of mass media throughout the developing world, migration may originate increasingly in the spontaneous actions of individuals seeking the better life they know to exist in the United States.

No matter how a migrant flow is started, once begun it tends to grow and become self-perpetuating. The money migrants send to their family members at home provides tangible evidence of opportunities in the United States; and word of success spreads rapidly. As migration increases over time, networks of personal and familial ties develop between sending and receiving areas, which serve to facilitate further migration. In many countries of Latin America and the Caribbean, these ties and networks are now being created. Given the self-feeding nature of migration and the increasing number of potential migrants in the developing world, illegal migration to the United States can be expected to increase in the coming years, unless there are marked changes in current United States policies.

By most accounts, the United States possesses the technical ability to stop, or at least significantly deter, illegal migration. What it lacks is the political ability to do so. In spite of repeated tries, it has not been possible to achieve a workable political consensus on this issue.

Since illegal migration benefits and hurts different segments of our society, any change in the status quo ultimately entails a redistribution of wealth. As other observers have noted, our system of government is ill-equipped to deal with such issues. Any meaningful change in policy is bound to affect some well-organized interest group adversely (labor, business, blacks, Hispanics, consumers, etc.) and this group will use political and legal means at their disposal to stop it. When ideological biases and emotional attitudes surrounding the immigration issue are also considered, it is obvious that broad-based agreement on this divisive issue will be difficult to secure.

Before a solution to the immigration dilemma can be achieved, Americans must develop a consensus as to the kind of economic and social structure they envision for this country, and on the number of immigrants that can reasonably be assimilated into it each year. They must then articulate a policy based on that consensus and be able to implement it over the inevitable objections of special interest groups. Until this occurs, illegal migration to the United States will continue and probably grow.

Doris M. Meissner. The reason why so many people enter the United States illegally each year is simply to get a job that pays a decent wage, something unavailable to them in their native countries. It is certainly in the national interest that the United States immigration laws be enforced to protect the collective interest of United States citizens, which is why such laws were enacted. Effective enforcement of a national law making it illegal to knowingly hire an undocumented alien is generally considered essential in the effort to slow down the current high rate of illegal entry into the United States.

THE MEDIA

*F*OR THE LAST TWO DECADES, the trend in America's mass media has been the ever-increasing control by several large corporations over the production and distribution of information and entertainment. It is a trend that has affected television, music, film, and book and newspaper publishing, but it is most apparent in the newspaper industry.

By 1979, over half of the nation's newspapers were owned by chains, and the top five—Knight-Ridder, Gannett, Newhouse, The Tribune Company and Times-Mirror—controlled 25 percent of the nation's daily newspaper circulation.

In major cities, the concentration of news sources has been severe. New York City, which once boasted fourteen competing daily newspapers, now has only three. In 1980, there were only thirty-five American cities with two independent competing daily papers. One of the latest casualties was the afternoon *Washington Star*, which folded late in 1981, leaving the nation's capital with only one newspaper, the *Washington Post*. The *Washington Post* itself owns *Newsweek*, two other dailies and four television stations.

The film, book and music industries are dominated by conglomerates such as Warner Communications, Gulf & Western and MCA, Inc. Time, Inc., the huge magazine publisher, also owns Book-of-the-Month-Club; Little, Brown; and Home Box Office, a cable television network.

CBS, perhaps the original communications company, was a struggling radio network when William S. Paley purchased it in 1928. In 1980 it had nearly $4 billion in sales. It owns five television stations, fourteen radio stations, the country's largest record company, four publishing houses and is moving into cable television production. All this in addition to the CBS Television Network.

The broadcast industry—television—remains in the control of the three major commercial networks, ABC, NBC and CBS. Public television offers an attractive alternative but little competition. The rapid spread of cable television and smaller UHF systems may eventually lead to greater competition but even the most optimistic observers put that several years in the future.

This economic concentration has given certain corporations an enormous and lopsided influence over what is read and seen in the entire country. The power and resources of papers like *The New York Times* and *The Washington Post*, the Associated Press, and television news divisions like CBS News have led to an overall conformity of *what* news is covered and *how* it is covered.

Because of the impact of the Watergate investigation and television news, reporters have become celebrities, mythologized in films like *All the President's Men* and entertainment shows like "Lou Grant." The news itself, particularly local television news, has taken on all the trappings of entertainment.

What has not happened, however, is the restriction to any great degree of the press's freedom to report the news. By virtue of the First Amendment, the media are virtually hampered by government control.

The rights of a free press date from 1735 when Andrew Hamilton, a Philadelphia lawyer, argued the case of John Peter Zenger, a publisher jailed for attacking the colonial government and charged with libel. In his defense, Hamilton went beyond the libel charges and argued that freedom of the press was a basic right and one that should not be abridged.

In 1971, the Supreme Court ruled 6–3 in favor of *The New York Times* in the "Pentagon Papers" case, stating that only in rare and compelling circumstances—not demonstrated by the government at that time—should the government be allowed to infringe on the press' First Amendment rights.

Despite recent court rulings, such as a 1978 New Jersey Supreme Court ruling that neither the Constitution nor state law gives reporters absolute privilege in refusing to divulge their sources of information, the press in America remains free from government interference.

The broadcast industry *is* regulated by the government—the Federal Communications Commission (FCC). But the power of the regulators has rarely been exercised: only once in its history has the FCC ever revoked a broadcaster's license.

Under the Communications Act, broadcasters must adhere to the "equal time" provision, which guarantees all political candidates access to the airwaves. They must also follow the Fairness Doctrine, a vague guideline which stresses the viewer's right to hear all sides of any controversial issue.

The press, and especially television, has come under severe criticism in recent years for everything from excessive sex and violence in its programming to its allegea ability to control both the public life of the country and the personal lives of its citizens.

The intrusion of television into the American lifestyle has been both rapid and spectacularly complete. In 1949, there were only four million homes with television sets. By 1963, almost everybody had one. It has been estimated that the average American has the television on for more than seven hours a day, and spends only fourteen minutes of that same day talking to the other people in the house.

The media has helped to reshape the political process, and the majority of political advertising now goes to television. It is widely accepted that John Kennedy won the 1960 election largely because he projected a better image during the televised debates than Richard Nixon.

When Walter Cronkite reported from Vietnam in 1968 that the war could not be won, Lyndon Johnson remarked to an aide that he knew he had lost the confidence of the average American. The credibility of an American president was finally surpassed by that of a network anchorman.

The dominance of the three networks (as well as the other major communications conglomerates) will remain, although the television industry may expand dramatically with the advent of cable television. One experimental system, Qube, pioneered by Warner Communications in Columbus, Ohio, now provides 60 channels and a two-way communications system, allowing viewers to vote on local political issues from the comfort of their living rooms.

All three major networks are involved in producing programming for the emerging cable industry as are several other corporations that have the financial resources. ABC and Westinghouse Broadcasting are producing a cable news service that will cost $40 million the first year alone.

The viewer may eventually have a variety of channels to choose from, but the channels may all be broadcast by the same few networks.

CONTRIBUTORS

James A. Anderson, Professor of Communication, University of Utah, Salt Lake City, Utah

Gene Burd, Ph.D., Associate Professor of Journalism, University of Texas, Austin, Texas

Norman Cousins, Adjunct Professor, School of Medicine, University of California; former editor, the *Saturday Review*, Los Angeles, California

R. Serge Denisoff, Professor of Sociology, Bowling Green State University, Bowling Green, Ohio

Ronald E. Frank, Associate Dean and Professor of Marketing, The Wharton School, University of Pennsylvania, Philadelphia, Pennsylvania

David Loye, Co-Director, Institute for Futures Forecasting, Carmel, California; author, *The Spinx and the Rainbow: An Exploration of the Brain and the Future*

W. Russell Neuman and Ithiel de Sola Pool, Research Program on Communications Policy and Department of Political Science, Massachusetts Institute of Technology, Cambridge, Massachusetts

A. H. Raskin, Associate Director, the National News Council; former Assistant Editor, the Editorial page, and labor columnist, *The New York Times*

HOW FREE ARE THE NATION'S NEWS MEDIA, INCLUDING NEWSPAPERS, MAGAZINES, RADIO AND TELEVISION?

Gene Burd, Ph.D. The amount of freedom for the United States news media is related to the economic, political and technological forces and pressures in society. News media are dependent on the economic support of audiences (readers, viewers, listeners) through subscriptions or purchase of goods through advertising. Thus, high television ratings and large newspaper circulations help deliver news to both inform and entertain large numbers of people with majority or mass tastes and interests. Those who object to content may boycott advertised products, cancel subscriptions, turn off televisions or radios, or seek smaller, alternative media which may have greater freedom as audiences often pay directly or subsidize the costs of news rather than depend on advertisements. Also, news media freedom may be affected economically by capital expenses, chain ownership, labor strikes, increasing costs of newsprint, ink and equipment, and high postal rates reducing size and frequency of publication.

Freedom of the news media may be restricted by external and internal social values. News may be withheld for local and national security (e.g., kidnap searches and troop movements). Journalists may also reflect or reject community standards of morality and the public interest through decisions such as use of four-letter words, publication of names of juvenile offenders, and news on sex and violence. News media may also have conflicts of interest as newspeople identify with and share ideas with those in power, participate themselves in public decisions on civic projects, or are offered freebies, junkets and other favors.

There are also the internal, organizational pressures in newsrooms, where different versions of the truth pass through different hands before printing or broadcasting. Externally, pressures on the newspeople come from those seeking access to the public through news releases, press agents, meetings and events, and pickets and demonstrations competing for media space and time. News may also be evaluated by letters to editors, journalism reviews, ombudsmen and press councils.

Although news media are free to be "watchdogs" of the government and fight for the citizen's "right to know," there are legal restraints through laws on libel, slander and obscenity, statutes on treason and sedition, and constitutional qualifications of First Amendment rights guaranteeing both a free press and fair trial in regard to pretrial publicity. Reporters who depend on authorities for information and who seek to protect confidential sources may face contempt of court and/or jail. In some cases, journalists have been killed for seeking or revealing the truth in their communities. Reporters face the technological realities of deadlines, headlines and air time, amidst difficulties of verification and attribution. The news media face hoaxes and cover-ups, constant source denials and refusals to confirm what reporters may already know but cannot prove, "off the record" comments, lack of shield laws to protect sources and reporters, and lack of open meetings and open records despite freedom of information laws.

Finally, news media freedom to criticize comes under the rules of fair comment based on facts and lack of malice. The press is free to probe, but may be restrained by rules against invasion of personal privacy. The electronic media must operate in the public interest to retain licenses, and the news media themselves have self-imposed codes of ethical restraint and conduct.

Norman Cousins. It seems to me that the question is not whether the nation's news media are free, but whether that freedom is being properly exercised.

R. Serge Denisoff. The news media in the United States, due in part to the guarantees of the First Amendment, enjoy a degree of freedom without parallel in most of the world. Its freedom, however, is far from absolute. There exist numerous external and internal factors which impinge upon the functioning of the media.

The Burger-led Supreme Court has affected the news-gathering abilities of the news media. Decisions dealing with search and seizure in newsrooms by law enforcement personnel and the debate over coverage of court proceedings, while not devastating, have raised legal questions about freedom of the press.

A more potentially dangerous threat, especially in the electronic media, is the almighty ratings and circulation numbers sought by members of the media. Sixty-four percent of Americans receive their daily information from television. There is a severe struggle between the networks and local broadcasters for a commanding portion of this audience. In this competition, as Walter Cronkite has warned, there exists a tendency to sensationalize and even glamourize news. The news *qua* entertainment syndrome is a growing threat to the freedom of reporters.

Newspapers and weekly national magazines, in order to attract more readers and raise advertising revenues, have turned more to entertainment formats focusing on lifestyle and gossip sections. It is true that coverage, especially in major markets such as New York, Washington, Baltimore, and Los Angeles, is far superior to the twenty-two-minute television news reporting which is characterized by little in-depth footage. The popularity of CBS's "60 Minutes" and ABC's "Nightline" is an encouraging sign amidst rumors that the national evening news shows may be expanded an hour—if the affiliates agree. The internal structure of the media, both electronic and print, imposes greater restraints in some instances than external socioeconomic and political forces.

Agenda setting in the news media is controlled by a handful of organizations. Due to factors of prestige and economics *The New York Times, Washington Post,* and the wire services determine what is newsworthy. As numerous studies have indicated a feature story in the *Times* generally reappears on the networks, and in the pages of national weekly news magazines. The wire services, particularly the Associated Press with its international network of bureau offices, enjoy a similar influence. The *Post,* United Press International and Reuters are not far behind. Critics have charged that the current state of journalism is leading to a greater homogenization and standardization of what is read and seen. The decline in the number of daily newspapers and the growth of news syndicates such as Knight-Ridder have only fueled this criticism. The cost of paper, union demands, urban flight and falling readership have closed the doors of many papers and magazines. The afternoon edition in many cities is now a historical artifact.

Another internal problem for freedom of the press is the gatekeeping function exercised in all media. Gatekeeping decisions, as David Manning White and others have suggested, are colored by a host of factors such as time and space and the personalities of reporters and editors. *Washington Post* editor Ben Bradlee's faith in Woodward and Bernstein contributed to the breaking of the Watergate saga. Ironically that same trust when applied to Janet Cooke's series on a nonexistent eight-year-old drug addict produced one of the more embarrassing episodes in American journalistic history.

The relationship of news gatherers or reporters also distorts the flow of information. Despite the rise in investigative reporting in all segments of the media, reporters are still dependent on their subjects. This relationship varies from medium to medium and the status of the subject. Politicians and entertainment personalities are dependent upon media for that all-important commodity, public exposure. Consequently, in these instances, news gathering is transformed to an exchange process.

The reporter wants a good story. The public personality desires air time or press space. This process creates an almost symbiotic relationship . . . as long as the rules of the game are followed. The more important a journalist or medium the better the cooperation. Unfortunately, not all reporters or media outlets enjoy the power of exposure afforded *The New York Times* or CBS News. Less powerful media organizations frequently become public-relations adjuncts or outlets. A majority of sports writers and broadcasters are classic illustrations of this type of reporting. Friendships can equally skew the news. John F. Kennedy was a master of wining and dining important journalists. Public-relations people in the entertainment and corporation fields frequently use this ploy with considerable success. Major news organizations do discourage fraternization. However, it is not always possible given the competition between news gatherers. "Exclusives" and "inside" reports are still highly desirable and prestigious.

The American news media is not free in the ideal sense, but to paraphrase Winston Churchill, it is freer than all the rest.

A. H. Raskin. One can believe, as I do, that America's news media are the freest in the world and still worry whether that is free enough. What concerns me is danger from within, much more than from without. Mass communications is an expensive business and getting more so all the time. That makes for a steadily increasing concentration of ownership in both print and electronic journalism and for a growing intrusion into the communications field of conglomerates with no primary interest in, much less commitment to, the free flow of information and ideas.

This trend toward centralization and homogenization has been accelerated by the advent of cable television and the attendant war among corporate giants for control over franchises. There has been very little evidence that this scramble has anything to do with rivalry in trying to devise more effective or imaginative ways to utilize cable's almost limitless potentialities for broadening the scope of human knowledge. Rather, its focus is obsessively on opportunities for expanding profits.

The end result, I fear, may well be a public perception of journalism as indistinguishable from any other big business, with bottom-line considerations paramount. That is an insecure foundation for freedom of the press, which must rest on confidence by the citizens that the agencies of information on which they rely are independent and diverse enough to equip them with the knowledge required for intelligent participation in a fast-changing society. I am happy to note, by way of antidote to these apprehensions of mine, that up to this time most of the people in command of the great newspaper chains and the news departments of the television and radio networks have come out of the editorial side and been given a firm charter to maintain the integrity of news operations to which they personally have always been dedicated.

To the extent that the conglomerate overlords of the future recognize the need for keeping that precept dominant, both in fact and in public perception, my fears would diminish.

HOW MUCH TELEVISION
DOES THE AVERAGE AMERICAN WATCH?
HOW WILL TELEVISION BE USED IN THE FUTURE?

James A. Anderson. The problem in answering the question, how much television does the average American watch, lies in the definition of two words: "average" and "watch." For the past several years a consortium of university scholars has been observing television usage in the homes of families throughout the United States. We have been continually struck by the diversity in the way people use television. There are people who use television as their major leisure-time activity, viewing every night for hours at a time. But there seems to be a larger number who are indifferent to the set. They view haphazardly and appear to have little commitment to the activity. There are a fair number of people who are highly selective in their viewing, picking particular programs perhaps once or twice a week. Finally, a very common form of viewing is not viewing at all, but listening while going about some other activity or task.

Viewing patterns change through the years. Child and adult vary markedly in the free time they have at different times according to the schedule of competing activities. The statistics that we read—the average household has the television set on over seven hours per day; the average child watches over twenty hours per week—probably have little meaning in the face of the differences we observe between people. Rather like saying the average color of the American car is black because when you add all the colors up that's what you get.

In the homes that made regular use of television, most viewing was of a low priority, shared-attention type. How much viewing was intent, attentive and sought out? Less than an hour per day.

Making a prediction about a regulated industry is full of traps. Regulation, its presence or absence, controls the future of television. And regulation is dependent on the mix of individuals appointed to the task. Presuming that the current deregulatory impetus continues, the marketplace will force television service into greater and greater diversity. As more of the United States is wired for cable, more and more services will become economically feasible and the mass audience economically less attractive. As an example, Warner Cable has just instituted a twenty-four-hour music service on television with continuous rock concerts; background listening with an occasional stop and look at the stars. This pattern copies that which the magazine industry followed some thirty years previously with the demise of the large-circulation, general-interest magazines and the rise of a myriad of specialty sheets. Network television viewing during prime time has begun a slight decline—the first ever—in response to competition from independent stations, cable and home video recorders. I would expect that decline to continue. The consumer will find more special interest programming in entertainment, education and information.

We might also look forward to a major communication system incorporating television and hard copy (paper) delivery. Should personal transportation continue to increase in cost and effort, telecommunication usage will also increase. We have the technology to work, shop, go to school, converse and visit via telecommunication now. Whether the application will become widespread depends on the cost structure of our present methods.

Ronald E. Frank. Estimates from different sources vary as to the number of hours per week the average person watches television. It is my judgment, short of a detailed review of various sources of viewing behavior data, that it is at least eighteen to twenty hours per week and most likely closer to twenty-five hours per week.

I would expect the number of hours of television set usage to continue to increase in the future as it has in the last decade; however, I am considerably less certain as to how much of an increase there will be in program viewing as opposed to the use of the set for nonprogram applications such as for playing video games, shopping and/or phone directory type look-ups. These applications could lead to an increase in set on-time but not program viewing time.

Cable television is still in its infancy. It is my guess that in the long run it will have a relatively modest effect on average program viewing time. Its principle effect will be to increase the number of different programs viewed. I will go out on the proverbial limb, and predict that its long-term impact will be primarily to reduce the average audience size of television programs and hence its effect will be primarily to redistribute viewing across a wider range of alternatives. I would expect as average audience size declines that more of the American public's idiosyncratic special interests (across different segments in the population) will be reflected in the nature of program content than is currently the case.

David Loye. The amount of television the average American watches is a matter of record in various widely used texts. How television will be used in the future is also the subject of many projections—e.g., to do our shopping, voting, banking, accounting, computing, game playing, in addition to its use for multi-channeled entertainment. I would focus, however, on two contrasting scenarios of critical underlying importance.

One is George Orwell's projection of television as the device used within a totalitarian state whereby Big Brother watches everyone through sets that broadcast both to and from every home and gathering place. The other is the scenario outlined in sources such as the ending chapter of my book *The Healing of a Nation* or Alvin Toffler's *Future Shock* and explored by studies incorporating Gallup organization research. Here, by contrast, television in the future would be used to strengthen democracy by providing citizens with the means to directly receive the best possible visual-verbal presentation on an issue, to directly register their vote by pressing buttons on their sets, and to thereafter receive the thrilling feedback of seeing how the vote goes, town by town, region by region, across the country.

This contrast poses the fundamental choice for us. Television can be used to make us a group of narrow-minded and shallow followers of the authoritarians, as trends in present religious broadcasting of the Moral Majority ilk could foreshadow. Or it can be used to enlarge our minds and give us the courage to think for ourselves while acting responsibly toward all humankind, as one glimpses in the rare best of its present commercial and public programs—e.g., Bronowski's *The Ascent of Man* as well as programs like "M*A*S*H" and "Barney Miller" of a regularly prosocial nature. In this sense, television in the future can be servant or master—and this is a much more important consideration than anything else about it.

I would project this dilemma will continue, with television acting as both servant and master as far into the future as one may guess at this time.

W. Russell Neuman and Ithiel de Sola Pool. Americans watch a great deal of television. According to the A. C. Nielsen viewer-diary estimates it comes to four hours and twenty-eight minutes a day for the average American over two years of age. Special electronic meters attached directly to the television in a representative sample of households reveal that the set is actually on an average of six hours and twenty-six minutes a day. From eight to eleven in the evening one can expect roughly 50 percent of the nation's households to be viewing for a total audience of about 90 million people. It is no wonder that television is frequently dubbed America's favorite pastime.

Women watch more than men (about an hour more a day on the average) and older men and women watch more than their younger counterparts. Teens watch the least of all age groups with an average of three hours, twenty-seven minutes a day.

Viewing has been going up fairly steadily since the introduction of television in the late 1940s. Viewing in the average television household from 1960 to 1980 increased by a little more than an hour a day. Although many have argued that there must certainly be a limit to the growth in daily viewing, it seems likely to continue for a while with the expansion of viewing alternatives on cable television and especially the subscription channels which offer uncut and uninterrupted recent motion pictures.

Predictions for television viewing's future years depend on one's definition of television. Video games, special cable and broadcast channels providing news, stock reports and a variety of information resources in a text format, as well as videodisc and videotape represent new video technologies already being marketed. As a result of this new competition, the level of viewing of traditional network programming has declined slightly and that trend may continue to a degree, but the involvement of the average citizen with video, broadly defined, may continue to grow.

PREGNANCY AND ABORTION

*T*WO OF THE most controversial issues of our time are linked together in the following section: abortion and teen-age pregnancy. It is not that most abortions are performed on teen-agers, although women under twenty years of age account for 30 percent of all abortions and only 16 percent of all live births. Nor is it that teen-age pregnancies usually end in abortion; an estimated half end in live births. What joins the two issues is a single basic problem: What should be done about unwanted pregnancies?

In 1980 legal abortions ended an estimated 1.5 million pregnancies. Not only is abortion the most frequently performed operation in the country, but it is also the most frequently and fiercely debated. People on either side of the abortion debate contend they are trying to preserve rights that the other side would destroy. "Pro-choice" advocates claim that legal, safe abortions must remain available to women who want them. To deny a woman the right to abortion, they argue, is to deny her the right to decide what she should do with her body. Members of the "pro-life" movement denounce abortion as murder and argue that it denies an innocent human being's right to life.

Historically, much of the debate around abortion has centered on the question of when human life begins. Until the early 1800s, the United States generally followed English common law concerning abortions. Under this tradition, women could obtain abortions until the time the fetus was judged to "quicken" or come to life, generally at about the eighteenth or twentieth week of pregnancy. Individual states began to regulate abortions more strictly in the 1800s, however, and by the end of the century, there were antiabortion laws throughout the country.

Yet laws did not prevent women from obtaining illegal and often unsafe abortions. Illegal abortions and abortion debates continued in the United States while each state adopted its own policy regarding abortions. In 1973, however, the Supreme Court ruled in *Roe* v. *Wade* that women have a constitutional right to abortions during the first six months of pregnancy. As to the question of when life begins, the court decided that the judiciary is "not in a position to speculate on the answer."

Backed by the Supreme Court, legalized abortions spread throughout the country, and the annual rate of abortions doubled between 1973 and 1980. Abortions have been made safer and easier by medical advances, but medical advances have also enabled doctors to save premature infants carried as short a time as five months. As the point at which fetal life is viable outside the womb is pushed back with developing technology, the question of when life begins becomes even more complicated. Pro-life advocates in Congress have proposed a human life statute that would define human life as beginning at the moment of conception and thus would make any abortion legally equivalent to murder. Pro-choice advocates, however, argue that such a ruling is arbitrary and would deny abortions to the millions of women and young girls who need them.

Pregnant young girls are a particular concern to both pro-choice and pro-life groups. Not only do teen-agers have a high rate of unplanned pregnancy and abortion, but the social consequences of unwanted pregnancies are usually much greater for young girls than for mature women. Pregnancy often interrupts a teen-ager's schooling, presents a health risk for both the mother and the infant, and limits the mother's future earning capabilities.

Of course, the catchall term *teen-age pregnancies* includes many young women who have carefully planned their babies: teen-agers who graduate from high school at seventeen, marry at eighteen, and are eager for their first child to arrive before they turn twenty. The picture for most teen-age mothers, however, is considerably more troubled. One problem is that relatively few teen-age mothers have husbands to help them rear their children. According to statistics from a 1980 report by the Department of Health, Education and Welfare, in 1969, 24 percent of all white teen-age mothers were single; by 1978, the proportion had grown to 40 percent. Teen-age mothers have even greater problems in the black community. In general, black teen-agers have much higher rates of pregnancy than white teen-agers, and the vast majority of black teen-age mothers are single. In 1969, 72 percent of black teen-age mothers were unmarried; by 1978, the proportion had reached 90 percent.

The birthrate among teen-agers has decreased somewhat in recent years in line with the general decline in the birthrate. But the number of teen-age pregnancies—although not necessarily teen-age births—is expected to increase dramatically in future years as more teen-agers experiment with sex. Meanwhile, the rate of abortions for all women continues to rise. Why is the problem of unwanted pregnancy so widespread among both adult women and teen-age girls? What are the major issues involved? The following answers to questions on teen-age pregnancy and abortion offer a spectrum of opinions.

CONTRIBUTORS

Mary S. Calderone, M.D., Co-founder and President, Sex Information and Education Council of the U.S. (SIECUS), New York, New York; co-author, *Family Books About Sexuality*

Daniel Callahan, Director, The Hastings Center, Hastings-on-Hudson, New York

William B. Clifford II, Professor, Department of Sociology and Anthropology, North Carolina State University, Raleigh, North Carolina

Herbert J. Cross, Ph.D., Professor of Psychology and Director, Human Relations Center, Washington State University, Pullman, Washington

Mrs. Rosemary Diamond, President and Co-founder, Birthright, Chicago, Illinois

Patricia A. Gavett, Executive Director, Religious Coalition for Abortion Rights, Washington, D.C.

Sylvia S. Hacker, Ph.D., Assistant Professor of Community Health, Schools of Nursing and Public Health, University of Michigan, Ann Arbor, Michigan

Robert A. Harper, Clinical Psychologist in private practice, Washington, D.C.

Goldie Kweller, National President, Women's League for Conservative Judaism, New York, New York

Rev. C. J. Malloy, Jr., General Secretary, Progressive National Baptist Convention, Inc., Washington, D.C.

Patricia McMahon, Executive Director, Catholics for a Free Choice, Washington, D.C.

Karen Mulhauser, Executive Director, National Abortion Rights Action League, Washington, D.C.

John C. Willke, M.D., President National Right to Life Committee, Washington, D.C.

WHY ARE SO MANY TEEN-AGERS BECOMING PREGNANT OUT OF WEDLOCK? WHAT CAN BE DONE ABOUT THIS PROBLEM?

Mary S. Calderone, M.D. So many teen-agers become pregnant out of wedlock because parents refuse to acquire the knowledge science now has about how sexuality develops in the young child, and their role in that development. It's too late by adolescence to establish a trust relationship that would have helped the adolescent develop a knowledge and value system adequate for making rational decisions about sex after puberty.

We can help by accepting the scientific fact that normal infants are all born with the capacity for sexual pleasure (reproductive capacity does not develop until puberty) and by socializing the sexuality of infants and young children. This can be done by: (a) accepting the validity of the child's self-pleasuring as a part of sexual development; (b) teaching it correct names for all sexual parts and how to identify them; (c) teaching the child privacy for its sexual pleasuring; (d) linking present sexual pleasuring with future reproductive capacity for procreation by choice; and (e) establishing a home value system that applies to all one's actions, not just to sexual actions.

William B. Clifford II. So many teen-agers are becoming pregnant out of wedlock because of the following reasons.

1. Improved health conditions have increased the chances that out of wedlock conceptions will be carried to term and have also increased the capacity for conception.
2. Lack of effective contraceptive use: inadequate knowledge and availability of contraceptives, and teens discount likelihood of conception.
3. There is a delay between initiating sexual activity and seeking any kind of birth control assistance.
4. Continuing rise in number of sexually active teen-agers.
5. Increase in frequency of intercourse.
6. Tendency to adopt less effective methods of contraception due to misinformation about safety and effectiveness.
7. Abortion and marriage no longer seen as appropriate response to premarital pregnancy by many teens.
8. The nature of teen sexual activity is spontaneous, a value conflict is created when one "plans for it" by establishing regular contraceptive use.

The problem can be combatted by:

1. Improving the levels of use of effective contraception as well as the timing and quality of use.
2. Improving knowledge (educating) about risks of pregnancy before sexual activity is initiated.
3. Improving accessibility to effective contraceptive methods.
4. Improving contraceptive technology.
5. A comprehensive family planning program sensitive to the needs of teens.

6. Strengthening the motivation of teens to seek and use contraception.

Herbert J. Cross, Ph.D. It seems that more adolescents are reproducing at a greater rate than ever because there are more of them than there ever have been. Also, the rate of reproduction is greater than ever and seems to be on the increase. Overpopulation creates more overpopulation. In a highly technical society such as the United States, many of the adolescent offspring are unable to contribute to the labor force because they are poorly educated, stemming from the inability of their parents to offer good parenting. Civilization has become so complex that vital parenting skills are hard to obtain without education or economic self-sufficiency. Adolescents do not have that parenting skill because they are economically dependent themselves. In societies where adolescents can make an economic contribution, mating at an early age is more likely to be socially acceptable.

The recent strong liberalization of sexual attitudes and intense public interest in sex have been spurred by the profit motive and freedom of the press. This liberalization, combined with social changes which have contributed to increasingly hedonistic, sensation-seeking values have in turn stimulated liberalized sexual standards among adolescents. Furthermore, as more households are headed by single people, and singles are allowed more socially acceptable sexual freedom, adolescents will surely emulate their older siblings. They are even more likely to emulate their own cultural heroes, most of whom seem to be rock stars.

These factors, along with the decreasing influence of traditional religion as well as morality, have allowed a natural phenomenon to assert itself as a great social problem.

There is clear research evidence that the age of initial sexual experience has dropped discontinuously with previous decades. Recently, there has been a sharper increase in youthful sexuality than ever before. The evidence is not as strong that the age of puberty has declined, but the prevalent scientific opinion is that young people are pubertal at an age earlier than ever before.

It is most unfortunate that when these nubile, healthy, young teens begin to mate, they do not use contraception until, on the average, one year after becoming sexually active. In order for contraception to be practiced by young lovers (mates is perhaps a more appropriate term), they must exercise some planning ability. Such planning ability comes with emotional and cognitive maturity which most young teens do not possess. Furthermore, contraception is not easily available, and even the mention of contraception is discouraged by many parents for fear that it will stimulate their children's interest in sex.

Adolescent contraceptive use is further complicated by the necessity to plan for sexual behavior. Adolescent females must admit, at least to themselves and to whoever supplies the pills or devices, that they plan to do something of which their parents disapprove and which may be stigmatized by most of their teachers and even by some peers. Contraception is further inhibited by the attributing of responsibility to the opposite sex. Girls have frequently expected the boys to take care of it, and vice versa. Some teen-agers have admitted to being too embarrassed to mention contraception for fear that they would anger their partner, or lose him or her. Adolescent ignorance is a frustrating reason for lack of contraception. Some teens have stated that they thought you must have sex for a year before fertility, or that an orgasm (female or male) was necessary, or that the laws of reproduction did not apply to them. Unfortunately, only a small minority of adolescents understand that bearing a child will have a profound effect on their lives.

Another factor in poor adolescent contraception is the chauvinism expressed by males who expect females to take care of it because condoms decrease their pleasure ("showering in a raincoat"). While the pill does not affect female pleasure, many adolescent females know of the health hazard and are afraid to use it.

Unfortunately, traditional sex education has not affected birthrates among teen-agers, even among one group of primipara females in a special program who bore their second child at a rate faster than their peers.

It seems impossible to completely stem the tide of adolescent fertility in a relatively free society. No government in the western hemisphere is ready for the policing necessary to enforce adolescent celibacy.

Many social problems would be somewhat alleviated, however, if an antireproductive ethic were adopted by society at large. Such is not likely to happen soon, however, nor is there likely to be any government discouragement of family size, even though research evidence shows that smaller families produce healthier children.

A partial answer to the adolescent fertility problem would come through promotion of contraception through easier access, perhaps through family planning clinics and youth centers. Sex education should be taught from a family life and psychology-of-adjustment perspective in the upper elementary grades, and peer counseling could be more effectively used by adolescents and preadolescents. Sex information centers and pregnancy counseling services are available on many college campuses now, and they are performing a useful service. If such services could be offered in a modified form in high schools, and even in elementary schools, they would be useful.

Contraceptive information could also be disseminated from women's centers as it is now on many college campuses. Women's centers in high school would be helpful, as well as store-front women's centers in inner cities.

Obviously, not many of these reforms will be currently instituted in the United States in the 1980s. Current political leadership does not even recognize the necessity of abortion as a means of population control.

Overpopulation in America will eventually precipitate enough social chaos to override political conservatism and allow a policy of population control.

REFERENCES

Chilman, C. W., "Adolescent Sexuality in a Changing American Society." Department of Health, Education and Welfare; National Institute of Health Publication #79-1426.

Hopkins, J. R., "Sexual Behavior in Adolescence." *Journal of Social Issues,* 1977, pp. 33, 67-85.

Terhune, K. W., "A Review of the Actual and Expected Consequences of Family Size." Calspan Report No. DP-5333-G-1, Department of Health, Education and Welfare; National Institute of Health Publication #76-779.

Mrs. Rosemary Diamond. In a single word the reason so many teens are becoming pregnant out of wedlock is "acceptance." Margaret Mead in her writings about the family has said that no society, no matter how primitive or prehistoric its culture, has ever totally accepted a child born out of wedlock. Since the 1973 Supreme Court decision created the easy accessibility of abortion, sexual activity has been encouraged at earlier and earlier ages. Out of wedlock sexual activity is the bottom line when discussing out of wedlock pregnancy.

Sexual education classes have been expected to serve as a panacea for avoidance of pregnancy and sexually transmitted diseases and thus have been encouraged by parents, teachers, sociologists, counselors and medical personnel. These programs have become more of a cause of sexual activity in the young than a cure. Most sex education programs are based on the premise that knowledge about the pitfalls of sexual activity will act as a deterrent and thus only those who are "appropriately protected" will engage in such activity. By the same token those who take drivers' education while being educated to drive safely are also expected to use this education behind the wheel of an automobile at the conclusion of the course, assuming, of course, that they are properly licensed. Although it is not specifically mentioned in the curriculum, there seems to be an assumption that sexual activity will be engaged in and that the purpose of the program is to arm students with knowledge about appropriate preventatives so that no unwanted pregnancy results. Abstinence or chastity are not stressed.

We adults have uncanny expectations of our children in that we assume that they will act maturely in regard to sexual activity. We do not expect our young teens to drive until they have been licensed or to vote or serve in the military until they are of age but we balk at imposing restrictions on their sexual behavior. Perhaps, we are saying more about ourselves than about the young in this failure to set limits. Perhaps, we are saying we don't want anyone to place restrictions on us in this area and therefore we shrink from setting up guidelines for others.

Sexual activity and resultant pregnancy have become a puberty rite. Parents in another era would have exerted their authority over such activity but in today's milieu they are usually the last to know about their children's sexual liaisons. Adolescents today enjoy great freedom. If a young person has not responded to parental authority from early childhood, it is unlikely that he or she will suddenly realize the wisdom of parental advice. Thus, the parents who may have relied on the sex education taught by the school may now have to cope with an unwed pregnant daughter or a son who is responsible for fathering a child—a problem which they had so fervently hoped to avoid. Most families have concern and love for their daughter, especially during her most vulnerable time of pregnancy. They stand behind her in her wish to keep her baby and allow her to bring their grandchild home to be reared jointly by the two generations. This sets a pattern of acceptance among their daughter's peers and among the parents' peer group. One family's reluctant acceptance can influence a neighborhood, a school group, business and social acquaintances, an extended family, and eventually the society at large; which is what is happening today.

Sex education programs which dispense information about pregnancy prevention and sexually transmitted diseases which accompany promiscuity are a colossal mistake. These programs which have increased in numbers have a high failure rate if you consider the number of pregnancies, abortions and cases of venereal disease now prevalent. The loss of self-esteem which accompanies any of the above, along with an alarming increase in adolescent psychiatric problems and in teen suicide are cause for concern. Early childhood sex education programs should be eliminated and courses for parents should be instituted which will prepare the parents with enough current scientific information to enable them to educate their children, and at the same time instill their own moral values. An emphasis on abstinence for the unmarried is a must.

Sylvia S. Hacker, Ph.D. Teen-agers are becoming pregnant because they have been caught in the middle of enormous and unprecedented cultural changes in this country. In a short period of time, our society, which anthropologists had at one time labeled as sexually restrictive, has seen an erosion of once strongly supported norms regarding sexual behavior. A restrictive society is one in which adults conspire to prevent young people from learning about or engaging in sexual activities. This norm worked because all adult and peer institutions reinforced it. This was undermined by our relative freedom from survival concerns following our post–World War II economic prosperity. We began to pay attention to self-fulfillment, and by the 1960s there existed the so-called me generation, determined to do their own thing. Such a phenomenon greatly contributed to the decline in influence of authorities such as the church and parents. With no substitute norm for sexual behavior to replace the old one, the previous, strongly reinforced pressure not to have sex before marriage succumbed to defiance of adults and to a greater peer pressure to "try it" at younger and younger ages.

The problem is that old norms die hard and their influence is still very much alive. Thus, in this rapid period of change, we are experiencing two moralities side by side, the old one clashing with the new. The result has been that although young people are engaging in sexual activity beginning at age ten and up, they have been given little or no knowledge and training on how to handle it responsibly. Because the parental generation was not prepared to teach their offspring anything about sexuality, the young are caught in the dilemma of "doing it" but essentially in an atmosphere of denial that they are sexual beings—they can't admit such activity to parents who still see it all as highly taboo. The dissonance between knowledge and behavior has resulted in over one million teenage pregnancies each year with over two-thirds accidental. In addition, venereal disease is at epidemic levels.

What is needed is rejection of the outmoded philosophy that knowledge is harmful. Informed individuals tend to be more responsible individuals. However, we cannot stop at merely teaching the "plumbing." We must surround the facts about reproduction with decision making and problem solving—about choices, about the concept of readiness, and above all about taking responsibility for one's behavior. The fundamental principle in educating young people must be nonexploitation of self and of others. Examining this principle can constitute an entire curriculum, and must include the concept that sexuality exists on a broad continuum. It must emphasize the fact that we are sexual from birth, and that our sexuality is an inextricable part of our identity, but that we must handle it with care. It involves everything from exploring one's own body and masturbation, hand holding with another person, reciting poetry to each other, kissing, necking and petting (with all their variations), and intercourse. But, one must learn, along with the pleasures of these activities, the risks entailed. In fact, one of the leading health hazards for young people is sexual intercourse. They risk all types of sexually transmitted diseases, too-early pregnancy with its dangers to the mother and fetus, underdeveloped offspring, psychological trauma, anxieties of teen parenting, etc. Statistics on these phenomena abound, and must be introduced to our young. If they object, consider you old-fashioned, call you preachy, then they must be challenged (as part of education) to debate you and defend their objections with data. Only on the basis of such careful examination can decisions be made with greater safety and responsibility than is presently being done. Teaching must be about how to communicate with each other, ways of enjoying each other sexually without necessarily including intercourse, knowing when one is ready for a serious relationship, the precautions necessary when engaging in intercourse, the enormous responsibilities in rearing a child, etc. This is the crucial training which our young people need, similar to the kind they must receive in learning driving or camping skills. Mistakes made in any of these areas are too often irrevocable.

Robert A. Harper. A high portion of teen-agers are becoming pregnant out of wedlock because of the inadequacy of sex education in general and of instruction in the use and the desirability of contraception in particular. Moreover, abortion continues to be propagandized in our society as a heinous crime rather than a desirable alternative (for both the teen-ager and society) to an unwanted pregnancy. Prevention of pregnancy is preferable to its early termination, but abortion (when factually presented as a healthy medical choice rather than a violation of supernatural superstitions) has considerably fewer undesirable consequences than teen-age pregnancies carried to term.

To suggest that the solution to the problem of teen-age pregnancies is either (1) to keep teen-agers away from sex or (2) to have them get married so that the children will be born in wedlock is to indicate that such propagandists (such as right-to-lifers) are wholly out of touch with a teen-ager's human nature and with the evils that are likely to result for both parents and children by forced marriage. The actual solution, not easy but possible, is to provide tremendous financial support and expert educational counsel for such existing groups as the Planned Parenthood Association and the National Abortion Rights Action League and for such additional groups needed to effect widespread reeducation of the American people on sex and related phenomena.

ACCORDING TO RELIGIOUS LEADERS AND LEGAL AND MEDICAL EXPERTS, WHAT ARE THE MOST IMPORTANT ISSUES IN THE CURRENT ABORTION DEBATE?

Mary S. Calderone, M.D. Abortion and contraception relate solely to reproduction. I am interested only in the totality of human sexuality— which only occasionally (even if inopportunely or too often) ties in with reproduction.

Daniel Callahan. The current debate about abortion manifests itself in the two most important issues that have dominated earlier debates, in this country and in others as well. The first is that of the moral status of the fetus—its right to life. The second is how, in the face of moral conflict, laws and policies ought to be devised—in particular, how ought they to reflect and respect the views of those who believe that individual women should have the final right to make abortion decisions. While there have been furious debates in recent years about the extent to which, if at all, the government should pay for abortions for the indigent, the fundamental moral and political issues have remained essentially the same.

It is the persistence of those issues that has been the special mark of the abortion debate. They are issues that are not amenable to a major shift because of new scientific information (on, say, the biological development of a fetus), nor do changing patterns of marriage and the family seem to alter the essence of the problem.

The abortion debate has also been marked by a strong tendency by both sides to see potential symbols of the way we live together as a community in the resolution of these moral and legal issues. For those on the pro-life side, the larger symbolic question is whether our society will have the moral courage to protect the most innocent and defenseless among us, the fetus. For those on the pro-choice side, the larger symbolic issue is whether women are to be allowed to manage their own biological destiny without the interference of the state. The pro-life side does not believe that the way the moral issue of abortion is decided can be separated from some fundamental values about marriage and the family, our attitudes toward children and the role of law as a moral educator. The pro-choice side is equally prone to see abortion in a larger context, that of women's rights, support of the poor and the advancement of civil liberties in general.

For all of these reasons, abortion is rarely seen as an isolated issue, removed from many other moral and political issues. The fact that so few societies have found what even they would consider an ideal solution suggests that no quick resolution is in store for ours.

Patricia A. Gavett. The religious denominations and organizations which support a woman's right to choose view the efforts to ban abortion as a serious threat to the First Amendment guarantees of church/state separation and free exercise of religion. Although these groups hold widely varying viewpoints on when abortion is morally justified, all agree that there are instances when it is an acceptable alternative to a problem pregnancy. The proposed antiabortion constitutional amendments attempt to define the fertilized egg as a "person," entitled to protection under the Fifth and Fourteenth Amendments. While no one disputes that physical, potential human life begins with conception, the question of when "personhood" occurs has always been in the realm of the theological. While some religions believe that the conceptus becomes a person at fertilization, most do not share that view. To place one particular religious doctrine into the Constitution or civil law forces all citizens to comply with it even if it is contrary to their own faiths. Legislation designed to restrict access to abortion prohibits individuals, whose religions teach that abortion may be a moral alternative, from the free exercise of their own beliefs. Since there is no general public consensus on the morality of abortion, the pro-choice religious community believes it must remain a matter of individual decision, based on one's own conscience and religious beliefs and free from governmental interference.

Goldie Kweller. Not being a medical expert nor a legal authority, I can relate to this question only as a religious leader, who represents the largest women's synagogue organization in the world, with over 200,000 members.

We firmly believe that Judaism teaches certain constraints regarding abortion. However, we believe that these belong in the private sector and that the separation of church and state are the best guarantee of religious liberty and civil rights for all. We continue to teach sensitivity to potential life, and it is taught in the synagogue and in the home, where it belongs, but we are also aware that women have the right to make a choice, especially where the life of the mother is threatened. Although, as Jewish women, concerned about the low population increase among our brethren, we passed a resolution at our biennial convention in 1976 and reaffirmed it in 1978 and 1980, which reads:

> Women's League for Conservative Judaism believes that freedom of choice is inherent in the civil rights of women. We also believe that the welfare of the mother must always be of primary concern. We therefore urge our Sisterhoods to oppose any legislative attempts through constitutional amendments, deprivation of Medicaid, family services, and other current welfare services, to weaken the force of the Supreme Court's decision permitting abortion.

Rev. C. J. Malloy, Jr. Some of the vital issues regarding abortion are: When does life begin? After conception, what rights do women have to deliberately abort? What are the circumstances involved? Who makes the choices?

Matters which enter into debate are: rape, incest, life or death for the mother or child, and the age of the mother.

Women should be the ones who make the determinations and choices regarding their bodies, health and mental conditions. To deny them the privilege of choice is but to reduce them to chattel.

Patricia McMahon. Abortion is a fact in our society and a need. Whether or not it is legal or publicly funded, abortion will continue to be performed because women will find themselves in need of the procedure. The major issues then which are born of the fact of abortion are two:

First, given that abortion for the present, at least, is legal, how will legislatures, courts and the health care system separate religious views held by some groups of citizens from the public need for policies which provide access to abortion for those who need it? Thus, what is the appropriate balance between private morality and public policy?

Second, if abortion is legal, but available only to women with economic resources above a certain level, does this constitute an unconscionable form of class, and possibly racial discrimination? Therefore, is our society committed to adequate health care for all citizens?

The decision to have an abortion can be one based on economic, health or social need. The weighing of the morality of the decision is an essentially private and often religiously oriented process. Consequently, a pluralistic society must seek fairly to balance private morality and public policy; interests of church and state; individual health concerns and societal resources. We believe the balance must be found in favor of privacy, self-determination, equal access for all to medical care, and separation of church and state.

Karen Mulhauser. Because of conflicting moralities and disagreement within the medical, legal and religious communities, the paramount issue in the public debate on abortion is that some women who are unwillingly pregnant will have abortions irrespective of any legal restrictions. Women will risk, and indeed they have risked throughout history, their lives and criminal sanctions to end unwanted pregnancies, with the full understanding that under their particular circumstances it is the moral thing to do. No amount of wishing it were otherwise will change that fact.

There are secondary issues of great importance but none is as important as this. An abortion prohibition amendment to the Constitution, or other restrictive legislation, is an attempt to place the religious dogma of some denominations into secular law that would govern the lives of all who have different religious beliefs. Such a prohibition would be no more successful in changing behavior than the previous religiously motivated prohibition movement in this country. It would, however, be as successful as its historical precedent in driving the practice underground. The issue is not whether abortions will be performed but where they will be performed and by whom. Religious dogma simply cannot be enforced on this country by laws.

Other issues involved in the debate include public health concerns and critical aspects of enforcement and criminal penalties if abortion were illegal again. It is much safer to have a legal abortion than to carry a pregnancy to term. It is estimated that there were 40 deaths per 100,000 illegal abortions. Two hundred to four hundred women died each year from illegal abortions prior to 1970 when abortion became legal in New York State. Opponents of legal abortion would like to reverse the 1973 Supreme Court decision which legalized abortion by amending the U.S. Constitution to say that the word "person" applies from the moment of fertilization. Before the Congress and the states do something as drastic as this, some very tough questions should be asked—and answered. Such a constitutional amendment would do far more than recriminalize abortion. It would affect every law which currently applies to people after birth. First, how would the states attempt to enforce such a total ban on all abortions? Through which law enforcement agencies would the program of enforcement be carried out? The FBI? State and local police departments? Or will a new bureau of pregnancy investigation be necessary to monitor all pregnancies and pregnancy terminations to ensure that no fetus is deprived of rights accorded to persons? Will the total ban apply to birth control methods as well when they work after fertilization? IUD's and some birth control pills do just that, as do morning-after treatments for rape victims.

How will the "criminals" who have and who perform abortions be prosecuted? What are the charges against premeditated abortion? Murder? Manslaughter? What is the punishment? Imprisonment, with a life sentence? Five months? Two years? Who will decide? And what will happen to the families these criminals leave behind?

With particular relevance to the budget-cutting 1980s, a critical question is: where will the millions of dollars required to enforce this law, track down "criminals," and prosecute and imprison them, come from? From the federal government? From beleaguered local and state governments?

The final issue in the abortion debate is one of government interference in the private lives of citizens. Abortion is a decision which should remain an individual and family choice. Matters so intimate as fertility must never be given over to government control. To allow today's government to pass laws prohobiting abortion in the interest of encouraging childbirth gives a future generation's government a precedent to selectively prohibit childbirth among certain segments of the population, or to otherwise extend this intrusive restriction.

Abortion or birth: the decision should be a personal and family matter and not a government decision.

John C. Willke, M.D. The central question is: when does human life begin? The only other question is: will you protect all human life equally or will you allow or legislate discrimination against an entire class of living humans in this case on the basis of place of residence (living in the womb)?

The first question must be answered as the biologic-scientific question that it is (the answer is "from fertilization") not by religious or philosophic beliefs or theories as they should not be used as the basis for making law. The other question is clearly a civil rights issue and must be answered in that context.

RELIGION

"IN GOD WE TRUST," our currency proclaims. According to the Declaration of Independence, the "Creator" endowed us with "certain inalienable rights," and our Pledge of Allegiance proclaims us to be "one nation under God." Yet do most Americans actually believe in God and practice their beliefs? Or do they just pay lip service to older religious values and view religious institutions as quaint, but outmoded?

A look at some of the major political issues today—abortion, capital punishment, school prayer—forcefully illustrates that religious feelings still run strong in the country. The First Amendment guarantees freedom of worship, but where do citizens draw the line between private beliefs and public morality?

In the past, there have been periods when religious fervor took hold of most of the nation. In the 1740s, Americans experienced the Great Awakening, a mass religious revival that shook the country. Traveling preachers raved about the agonies of hell until their audiences groaned and shrieked in despair. Converts roamed the streets singing joyfully about their salvation. Many more orthodox Christians thought that it was hell on earth.

Eventually, the awakened converts tired, but the nation continued to worship enthusiastically. Men learned to read so they could understand the Gospel; they founded universities to train ministers. Not everyone was uniformly pious, but freethinkers, such as Benjamin Franklin and Thomas Jefferson, kept most of their doubts to themselves. When the famous French statesman Alexis de Tocqueville surveyed the United States in the 1830s he declared there was "no country in the world where the Christian religion retains a greater influence over the souls of men than in America."

Christians were not the only ones who welcomed the freedom to worship in the United States; Jews began coming to the colonies in the 1600s. At first only a very small minority of the immigrants were Jewish, but their numbers increased rapidly in the late 1800s. By one estimate, the number of Jewish congregations rose from about 75 in 1850 to more than 600 by 1900.

Immigrants from Ireland, Germany, Italy, France and eastern Europe brought new vigor to the Roman Catholic church. It is estimated that the number of Catholics in the United States climbed from about 700,000 in 1840 to more than 12,000,000 by the turn of the century— more than all of the Methodists, Presbyterians and southern Baptists combined.

The Roman Catholic religion is today the largest single faith in the United States, yet there are more Protestants than Catholics because there are so many different Protestant denominations. Several of the largest Protestant sects originated in the United States: Mormonism, Seventh-Day Adventism, Christian Science, Pentecostalism and Jehovah's Witnesses.

In recent years, the United States has seen the rapid growth of religious groups that do not conform to the traditional Judeo-Christian heritage. Muslims and Buddhists, along with small, sometimes highly controversial cult groups, such as the followers of Reverend Sun Yung Moon, have attracted many new believers.

In the 1960s and early 1970s, small new churches and cults based on teachings of Eastern religions caught the public's attention. Socialites consulted gurus and rock groups sang the praises of Eastern faiths. Protestant Fundamentalists remained relatively silent during this period, but they never lost their following among a large segment of the population. Sunday morning radio continued to broadcast Fundamentalist religious services, and throughout the Bible Belt, Billy Graham continued to draw huge crowds.

In recent years, Fundamentalist groups have resurfaced and begun to play a prominent part in American politics. Some groups claim the Fundamentalists are now too prominent and too political. They point to the 1980 elections in which candidates supported by conservative churches won dozens of seats in Congress, and Ronald Reagan, the Moral Majority's candidate, won by a landslide. More liberal groups also worry about the influence that Fundamentalists have had on determining such issues as school curriculum, the right to abortion, media censorship and capital punishment. On the issue of teaching evolution in the schools, for example, Fundamentalists have come out strongly against Darwin's theory and for the biblical "creationist" theory of Genesis. As a result, in about 30 states, conservative churches have won the right to teach the biblical theory as an accepted alternative to the scientific theory.

On the following pages, experts in the field of religion discuss how scientific beliefs support or contradict faith in religious teaching and whether Americans, on the whole, really are "one nation under God."

CONTRIBUTORS

Isaac Asimov, biochemist; writer of science and science fiction, New York, New York

Dr. Gerson D. Cohen, Chancellor, The Jewish Theological Seminary of America, New York, New York

James Hervey Johnson, President, The Atheist Association, San Diego, California

Rev. C. J. Malloy, Jr., General Secretary, Progressive National Baptist Convention, Inc., Washington, D.C.

Donald W. McEvoy, Senior Vice President for Program Development, National Conference of Christians and Jews, New York, New York

Ted Peters, Associate Professor of Systematic Theology, Pacific Lutheran Seminary and Graduate Theological Union, Berkeley, California

Dr. David Poling, Senior Pastor, First United Presbyterian Church, Albuquerque, New Mexico

Donald W. Shriver, Jr., President of the Faculty and William E. Dodge Professor of Applied Christianity, Union Theological Seminary, New York, New York

IS RELIGION GAINING OR LOSING STRENGTH IN THE UNITED STATES?

Dr. Gerson D. Cohen. The emergence of the Moral Majority and the many evangelistic movements of the theological right has been interpreted in some quarters as a sign of religious revival. To the contrary, it seems to me that this phenomenon, observable today in Christianity, Judaism and Islam, is rather a sign of theological vacuum in many quarters and of panic in others. Instead of providing genuinely creative religious responses to problems that reflect radical change on the social, philosophical and aesthetic levels, the theologians of these movements seem to be engaged in a desperate effort to formulate their responses to new conditions only within received, traditional categories. In fairness to them, it should be said that they are at least not permitting religion to be governed by political considerations alone. Rather, they demand that society make some effort to shape itself according to religious norms.

That they go to the other extreme, and refuse to meet contemporary quests on any level other than their own, is what makes them religious extremists.

History provides many precedents for this situation. Innovative theological response is extremely difficult, in part because it appears to conflict with one of the normative values of religion—to introduce at least a semblance of stability and theological continuity in a changing world.

When people lose their faith in progress and redemption, when indeed they have no hope for eschatological fulfillment, their perplexity and confusion cry out for courageous religious leaders who, recognizing the challenge of rapid social change, will invoke the legacies of the various religious traditions in a new way. In so doing, they will restore hope to their constituencies and congregations, conveying to them a new sense of the meaning and purpose of life.

Believing, as I do, that we stand on the threshold of such a breakthrough, I conclude that religion in the United States will soon emerge from its present semistatic state and resume its position of strength and moral leadership in this nation.

James Hervey Johnson. Religion is growing enormously in financial strength with its tax exemptions, and with this strength it is gaining much political strength.

Religion is losing strength among college graduates, intellectuals and scientists, but atheists generally are reluctant to openly criticize religion.

The sexual restraints inherent in religion have been largely discarded by the younger generation.

Rev. C. J. Malloy, Jr. Man is incurably religious, according to sages of past years, and it is apparent that religion is still a dominant force in the lives of people in America, as well as in many other parts of the world.

In spite of the prevailing conditions in society, religion appears to be gaining in popularity with all age groups. There are numerous religious sects and persons who seek to show men and women how to live, publicly and personally.

In conclusion, I would say that religion is gaining strength in the United States.

Donald W. McEvoy. As a social phenomenon it is apparent that religion is gaining strength in America. More people are attending religious services than ever in our history, more religious books are being bought and published, religious personalities and organizations are having more impact on political decisions both local and national than ever. If you choose to define religion by the self-identification of those who designate themselves religious, then you would have to say that religion is gaining strength.

On the other hand, if the essence of true religion is (as I believe it to be) "to do justice, to love mercy, and to walk humbly with God" then I would have to conclude that religion is definitely on the wane in American life.

Mainstream churches, which a decade ago were showing signs of sensitivity to the oppressed of our society, now appear to have retreated back into concern for institutional survival and personal comfort. Conservative churches are experiencing significant growth by preaching a "gospel" comprised of about equal parts of three elements. These are (a) an antiintellectual authoritarianism which provides absolute answers in a time of social uncertainty, (b) civil religion which attempts to tie religious truth to American triumphalism, and (c) an appeal to fundamental selfishness to preserve the status and benefits of the white middle class at the expense of minorities and the poor.

Black churches, which for a quarter of a century were the prime motivators of social concern and the sensitizing agent in the church-at-large, have themselves withdrawn and become more reactionary. Even Judaism, which has always been in the forefront of all the battles for justice and benevolence to the dispossessed of our society, has largely retreated back into primary concern for survival and personal defense.

The strength of religion is growing. The power of religion is diminishing. This situation, however, is not a unique development. Genuine religion has always been practiced and nurtured by the creative minority within, or on the fringes of, "institutional religion."

Ted Peters. Religion is gaining strength in the United States both within the churches and outside of it. During the 1960s, it was said that "God is dead." People generally believed that the secular and scientific mentality—which believes religion to be a primitive or premodern and hence outdated state in human development—would soon win the day. A surprise overtook us during the 1970s, when there occurred a tremendous outburst of spiritual fervor. The most salient example was the charismatic movement within Protestantism and Roman Catholicism. It was God's way of reminding the human race that it is not alone. To some extent this religious fervor will continue into the 1980s.

Outside the church there has been a rebirth of enthusiasm for ancient pagan religion. I call this neo-gnosticism. There is growing belief in such things as cosmic monism, the separation of spirit from matter, the idea that a divine spark exists within each person, reincarnation, Jesus viewed as a gnostic teacher, and all of this combined with a new reverence for the theory of evolution. This set of beliefs, reminiscent of the gnostic cults of ancient Rome, is finding its way into our culture through oriental mystical cults, and the human potential movement.

This growing religious fervor is not necessarily Christian. The Christian religion was born in a cultural atmosphere highly charged with the religions of the ancient Roman Empire. Until just recently, our Christian leaders have been struggling against the irreligion or nonreligion of modern secular society. As our society becomes more religious, many Christians will mistake this for progress. From the Christian point of view, paganism is not progress.

Dr. David Poling. The religious concerns and interests and aspirations of people have always been strong and vital. There may be wide fluctuations in the weakness or strength of particular denominations—some have declined numerically and others, such as southern Baptists and Mormons, have soared in numbers. But the religious focus and concern of men and women seem universally powerful.

Presently, a conservative trend within the Christian community represents a need on the part of thousands for a dependable, supportive fellowship. The uncertainty of world affairs, the era of rapid social change, the stress in business and employment, have brought many a deeper awareness of their spiritual needs—perhaps the best and most lasting foundation in dealing with the perplexities of life. In my own ministry, I see an increase of singles seeking out the Christian fellowship. A rising number of men and women want a church wedding to anchor their views and feelings toward life and one another. Also, parents of children are more and more seeking out the ethical, moral, spiritual value system of organized religion to offset the weakness of the public school arena in these matters.

Donald W. Shriver, Jr. Currently I believe that religion is gaining strength, chiefly in its influence through television. I see little sign of its influence, however, in the shaping of the complexities of contemporary political policy, where its adherents have often publicized very simplistic answers in recent years.

IS THERE ANY SCIENTIFIC EVIDENCE TO PROVE THE EXISTENCE OF GOD?

Isaac Asimov. No! There is no scientific evidence to prove the existence of God.

Science deals with those phenomena capable of being observed and measured objectively. Ideally, those phenomena with which science deals should yield the same observations and measurements when different people using different instruments are involved.

There may well be an infinite number of phenomena which, for one reason or another, cannot be observed and measured at all; or, if they can be observed and measured, are available only to some observers and not others, or affect different observers very differently. Such phenomena are either intrinsically unknowable, or depend on so many subjective variables that no satisfactory agreement can ever be reached about them.

The existence (or nonexistence) of God may well be among these scientifically unknowable phenomena. If so, God can become "known" in various nonscientific manners—through revelation, insight, intuition, dreams, visions, etc., etc., etc.

The trouble with these nonscientific methods is that they do not seem to carry conviction. At least there are innumerable versions of God among human beings and no general consensus has ever been reached. Indeed, there have been hatreds carried to the point of wars, massacres and individual tortures based on disagreements over even minor aspects of the existence, nature and actions of God.

But as for scientific evidence for the existence of God? No! None!

Ted Peters. This is the kind of question which perpetuates the misunderstanding between the scientific community and those who have religious sensibilities.

First of all, the word "science" refers more to a method of doing research than it does to a body of knowledge. The scientific method assumes from the beginning that God cannot be a factor in research. Belief in God, angels, demons or any supernatural phenomenon is precluded. Scientific research operates with the presupposition that only natural explanations can be used for natural phenomena. And God is not a natural, but rather a supranatural person. Therefore, to ask if science can prove the existence of God produces only a confusing answer, because science assumes at the outset that it can say nothing about God. To ask a scientist to prove the existence of God is like asking a German to speak French, or like asking an auto mechanic to fix a broken violin.

There is a God, to be sure. He draws us toward himself through the drama and beauty and power of life. In addition, he has himself revealed something essential about his personality through the death and resurrection of Jesus Christ. To find out what God has revealed, we should go not to modern science but rather to the biblical scholar.

Donald W. Shriver, Jr. No, there is no scientific evidence that either proves or disproves the existence of God. There is much evidence, however, that is compatible with a belief in God. Proof is something else. Furthermore, there are many assumptions and current theories of science itself that are not proven, either. And some parts of scientific assumption, like theology, are inherently unprovable.

GENERAL
HEALTH

AMERICANS ARE PREOCCUPIED with diet and health. Books on the latest fad diet or exercise plan for weight control are best-sellers. In fact, social commentators maintain that health and diet worries have replaced sex as the primary basis for feelings of guilt in our society.

Many experts assert that the United States has entered the second revolution in health care. The first revolution was characterized by the elimination of such dread diseases as smallpox, influenza and tuberculosis. The second revolution is marked by the widespread interest in "preventive" health care—the prevention of disease by control of one's diet, exercise, and life style.

This concern with preventive health care is lauded by many. A report issued by the Senate Select Committee on Nutrition and Human Needs condemned the standard American diet of meat, potatoes and "junk food," and stated that Americans should start to change their diets to include more fresh fruit and vegetables, whole-grain breads, and fish and poultry.

On the other hand, the increasing concern with health has spawned entirely new areas of consumer fraud. People who are normally intelligent and critical in making daily decisions can suddenly seem to lose all sense when it comes to losing weight. They espouse scores of fad diets that may result in the temporary loss of excess pounds—but at the cost of a threat to their general health, and of no benefit whatever to the long-term control of their weight. Our nation's concern about health has also given rise to dependence on vitamins and other dietary supplements, and an interest in a host of exotic medical techniques, such as shiatsu and acupuncture.

Health care in America involves more than preventive medicine. One disease—cancer—has caught the national interest far more than any other in recent years. The word *cancer* is actually a catchall term to describe more than a hundred specific diseases that are all characterized by abnormal cell growth.

James K. Selkirk, of the Oak Ridge National Laboratory, distinguishes between two different approaches to cancer therapy: the first seeks to discover the root causes of cancer and to develop a therapy based on these root causes; the second is characterized by trial and error, in which physicians experiment with various chemical and physical agents to see which have an effect on stemming cancerous growth. Most of the successful treatments now available are the result of the latter approach. Dr. Selkirk and others look for dramatic breakthroughs in the understanding and treatment of cancer as a result of new scientific methods based on discoveries in the area of DNA reproduction.

Harold A. Cohen, of the Maryland Health Services Cost Review Commission, comes up with some particularly interesting answers to another question that concerns all of us: the high cost of hospital care. Mr. Cohen sees four general reasons for high hospital costs. First, hospital costs are very different from other consumer expenses. Largely because of the nature of payment (92 percent of hospital bills are covered by outside agents, particularly insurance companies), few people shop around for the best price when selecting a hospital as consumers might do when looking for other services. Because hospitals are reimbursed by the insurance companies, there are few constraints on their costs and no competitive pressure to keep the prices down.

Mr. Cohen asserts, second, that doctors, as "managers" of hospitals, tend to encourage hospitalization because it increases their incomes and the income of their corporate employer, the hospital. Third, because of the high emotional stress that is associated with disease, people do not question costs and treatments the way they might question other expenditures. And, fourth, because of the general separation of health from hospitalization, people can abuse their health, thereby incurring higher hospital costs, without realizing the relationship between the two, and without feeling the serious economic consequences because of insurance coverage.

Health has become a subject of great interest to Americans. Because of the nature of our consumer-oriented marketplace, many valid—as well as invalid—notions about health care have taken hold in the past decade. In the following section, the experts debunk some popular misconceptions about health and give sound, down-to-earth advice about a variety of related subjects.

MEDICINE AND GENERAL HEALTH

Wᴇ ᴀʀᴇ ᴋɪʟʟɪɴɢ ᴏᴜʀsᴇʟᴠᴇs by our own careless habits.
We are killing ourselves by carelessly polluting the environment.
We are killing ourselves by permitting harmful social conditions to persist—conditions like poverty, hunger and ignorance—which destroy health, especially for infants and children.

Thus begins the 1979 surgeon general's report, *Healthy People.* As its title suggests, the report emphasizes health more than illness, preventions more than cures.

The following section on medicine and general health deals with all phases of the current health revolution: surgery to repair the body and vitamins to strengthen its natural resistance, drugs to treat diseases and techniques to prevent the body from succumbing to sickness. Two questions concern specific cures: Are there any cures for allergies? and What is the most successful cure for headaches? But as the experts' answers illustrate, effecting a cure may be as simple as taking a single treatment or as complex as altering a lifetime of health habits.

There is no simple vaccine for many of the health threats that now face Americans, the surgeon general's report stresses. Rather, the cures will stem, at least in part, from an increased awareness of our bodies and a willingness to lead healthier lives.

There is no doubt that medical breakthroughs such as successful organ transplants save lives, and it is these breakthroughs that offer hope to the seriously ill. Yet while high technology makes headlines, it generally affects only a very small proportion of the population. On the other hand, an everyday routine such as toothbrushing or jogging may improve the health of many.

The idea that good health does not begin at the doctor's office is not new. Decades of research have shown that factors such as obesity, smoking, drug and alcohol abuse, high blood pressure, poor diet and sedentary living are all related to high rates of chronic disease. Moreover, public opinion polls show that most Americans believe that preventive measures, such as reducing smoking and maintaining proper weight, can do more to ensure good health than any wonder drug or new treatment.

How has the country translated knowledge into action? There are some healthy signs of change. Physical fitness programs have boomed, especially among the middle and upper classes. Throughout the country, people's increased awareness of nutrition and the danger of high fat, sugar and salt intake is reflected both in the new "health food" products appearing on supermarket shelves and in the reduced per capita consumption of high cholesterol foods such as butter, cream and eggs. Despite these energetic measures, however, Americans still tip the scales toward obesity. The problem is especially pronounced among women: approximately a quarter of all women twenty to seventy-four years of age weigh at least 20 percent more than the optimal weight for their height. About 14 percent of the men in the same age group are also substantially overweight, and almost half of all American adults believe they have a weight problem.

Smoking, too, takes its toll. There has been a considerable decline in smoking for all groups except teen-age girls, but in 1979 about one-third of the adult population still smoked regularly. There has been little change in the nation's per capita alcohol consumption in recent years, and an estimated 10 percent of the adult population has a drinking problem.

As anyone who has ever tried to diet or quit smoking knows, it is not easy to change lifelong habits. Nor is there any guarantee that even the most Spartan way of life will safeguard good health. Some of the factors that predispose people toward disease, such as aging or genetic makeup, are beyond human control, and some diseases seem to strike at random. Moreover, even the healthiest person can fall down a flight of stairs or be hit by a truck.

By the same token, however, some factors are indisputably within our control, and experts contend that half of the battle is convincing people to assume the responsibility for their own health.

CONTRIBUTORS

Folkert O. Belzer, M.D., Professor and Chairman, Department of Surgery, University of Wisconsin Hospital and Clinics, Madison, Wisconsin

Francis L. Black, Ph.D., Professor of Epidemiology and Microbiology, Department of Epidemiology and Public Health, Yale University School of Medicine, New Haven, Connecticut

Jack Bowman, President, Lederle Laboratories, Wayne, New Jersey

Edward S. Brady, M.S., Emeritus Professor of Pharmacy, University of Southern California, Los Angeles, California

Randolph Bufano, Nutritional Consultant

Donald J. Dalessio, M.D., Chairman, Department of Medicine, Scripps Clinic, La Jolla, California

Michael E. DeBakey, M.D., Baylor College of Medicine, Houston, Texas

K. W. Dumars, M.D., College of Medicine, University of California, Irvine, California

E. J. Eichwald, M.D., Professor of Pathology, Department of Pathology, College of Medicine, University of Utah, Salt Lake City, Utah

Alfred S. Evans, M.D., M.P.H., Professor of Epidemiology and Public Health, Yale University School of Medicine, New Haven, Connecticut

Richard S. Farr, M.D., Senior Staff Physician, National Jewish Hospital and Research Center, Denver, Colorado; Professor of Medicine, University of Colorado Health Sciences Center, Denver, Colorado

M. Finland, M.D., George Richards Minot Professor of Medicine, Emeritus, Harvard University, Cambridge, Massachusetts

John P. Fox, Professor Emeritus, Department of Epidemiology, University of Washington, Seattle, Washington

Carlton Fredericks, Ph.D., lecturer, consultant and media commentator on nutrition

Dr. Robert W. Hammel, Professor of Pharmacy Administration, University of Wisconsin, Madison, Wisconson

Frederick Hecht, M.D., Tempe, Arizona

Victor Herbert, M.D., J.D., Chief, Hematology and Nutrition Laboratory, Veterans Administration Medical Center, New York; Professor of Medicine, State University of New York, Downstate Medical Center, Brooklyn, New York

John C. Hobbins, M.D., Professor, Departments of Obstetrics and Gynecology and Diagnostic Radiology, Yale University School of Medicine, New Haven, Connecticut

Dorothy Reycroft Hollingsworth, M.D., Professor of Reproductive Medicine, University of California, San Diego, California

Rollin D. Hotchkiss, Professor of Genetics, Rockefeller University, New York, New York

H. M. Lee, M.D., Medical College of Virginia, Richmond, Virginia

E. W. Lovrien, M.D., Professor, Medical Genetics and Pediatrics, University of Oregon, Health Sciences Center, Portland, Oregon

Dr. Karl Maramorosch, Professor of Microbiology, Waksman Institute of Microbiology, Rutgers, The State University, New Brunswick, New Jersey

Thomas L. Marchioro, M.D., Professor of Surgery, Department of Surgery and Head, Division of Transplant Surgery, University of Washington School of Medicine, Seattle, Washington

Kenneth P. Mathews, M.D., Professor of Internal Medicine and Head, Division of Allergy, University of Michigan Medical School, Ann Arbor, Michigan

Aubrey Milunsky, MB.B.Ch., D.Sc., F.R.C.P., D.C.H., Professor of Pediatrics and Obstetrics and Gynecology; Director, Center for Human Genetics, Department of Pediatrics, Boston University School of Medicine, Boston, Massachusetts

Anthony P. Monaco, M.D., Harvard Medical School; Chief, Harvard Deaconess Transplantation Service, New England Deaconess Hospital, Boston Massachusetts

John S. Najarian, M.D., Professor and Chairman, Department of Surgery, University of Minnesota Hospitals, Minneapolis, Minnesota

Philip S. Norman, M.D., Professor of Medicine, Johns Hopkins University School of Medicine, Baltimore, Maryland

Roger N. Rosenberg, M.D., Professor and Chairman, Department of Neurology, University of Texas Health Science Center at Dallas, Southwestern Medical School, Dallas, Texas

Albert L. Sheffer, M.D., Associate Clinical Professor, Harvard Medical School; Director, Allergy Clinics, Beth Israel Hospital, Brigham and Women's Hospital; Chief, Allergy Section, New England Deaconess Hospital, Boston, Massachusetts

Paul P. VanArsdel, Jr., M.D., Professor of Medicine and Head, Section on Allergy, University of Washington, Seattle, Washington

Henry Wendt, President, Smith Kline Corporation, Philadelphia, Pennsylvania

Dewey K. Ziegler, M.D., Head, Department of Neurology, The University of Kansas College of Health Sciences and Hospital, Kansas City, Kansas

IS THERE ANY DIFFERENCE BETWEEN BRAND NAME AND GENERIC DRUGS?

Jack Bowman. The question does not involve differences between brand name and generic name drugs as much as it does differences in the reliability of drug manufacturers. Companies that maintain extensive research and quality control facilities and those with only marginal facilities may market both brand and generic name products. A manufacturer with minimal standards is probably more likely to market substandard products, whether these are sold under generic or brand names. While the standards set by government agencies help to assure acceptable quality in drug products, it is not possible for these agencies to monitor the quality of more than a small proportion of all those produced.

The other difference in pharmaceutical manufacturers involves their commitment to research. The research-oriented drug companies discover and develop new drugs; others do not invest in research. Research and development for a new chemical entity drug is estimated to cost more than $50 million and usually requires more than ten years to complete. Yet only a small proportion of discoveries ever develop into successful products. Such expenses and investment risks must be reflected in the prices of the resulting products (usually marketed under brand names). Furthermore, the supply of advanced new drugs is highly dependent upon the ability of these companies to pay for past, present and future research and development. Obviously, this also affects the supply of new generic drugs. Drugs that are marketed as generics exist because the companies that first discovered and developed them made the necessary investment in scientific resources.

Edward S. Brady, M.S. There are always some differences between one manufactured product and another. This is true for drugs, whether marketed under one or more brand names, or under their generic names by a number of suppliers. Both patient and physician should focus their concern on the important therapeutic differences that might affect the outcome of treatment.

Variations in some critically important medicines have been reported; digoxin and thyroxin are two examples. The U.S. Food and Drug Administration has taken steps to correct variations in product efficacy, and insists that drug product failure is unlikely. However, patients on long-term therapy for chronic conditions (heart, epilepsy) should be cautious about any change in drugs (brand to second brand or brand to generic). It is also important to consider the following points:

1. Only about 10 percent of the 200 most frequently prescribed drugs are available from more than one manufacturer, because of patent restrictions.
2. Drug product selection is usually a matter of choosing from several brands, e.g., ampicillin capsules are available under nine brand names, no generic.
3. Hospitals usually purchase their drugs from reputable manufacturers, with price as the sole consideration.
4. A brand name does not make a drug any more effective.
5. The integrity and reputation of the manufacturer is the best assurance of the product quality

Randolph Bufano. There are two differences between brand name and generic drugs: First, the difference in price and second, the mystique surrounding brand names.

Carlton Fredericks, Ph.D. Not only are there differences between some generic drugs and their brand name counterparts, but there may be differences in the efficacy of the same drug when marketed by different companies as a generic, as well as when it is marketed under several trademarks.

There are generic drug manufacturers who produce drugs that are as satisfactory as those from the large manufacturers of brand name medications. This means careful control of tableting, to make sure that the tablet will actually dissolve and be utilized in the intestinal tract; that it will not deteriorate significantly within its anticipated shelf life, and that no contaminants are present. There are also, undoubtedly, manufacturers of generic drugs whose quality control is less efficient, and whose products will therefore compare less favorably with the brand name equivalents.

When it is critical that a given blood level of a drug be achieved and maintained, as with digitalis, for instance, it is my opinion that the physician must protect the patient by stipulating that there should be no substitution of the prescription; however, that precaution might well apply to substitution of another brand name drug, as well as to a generic type alone.

Where such critical criteria are not applicable, it appears to me that there is no valid reason to subject the public to the much higher costs of brand name drugs. This would be true in a large majority of the medications for which prescriptions are issued.

Dr. Robert W. Hammel. There usually are differences, which may or may not be therapeutically significant, between directly competing drug products. There may even be significant differences in safety or effectiveness between a brand and a generic, between brands and between generic versions of a drug. However, whether a firm markets a product under its generic name or under a brand name (trademark), in itself has no medical significance. What is important is that the firm consistently market a uniform, high quality, effective product.

The lack of therapeutic equivalence among competing products could be due to any number of factors. These include: formulation differences; differences in the manufacturing process; differences in product stability; variation in quality control and testing, before and after production of a drug; differences in particle size; lack of sterility or the presence of contaminants.

The innovator of a new drug typically markets its product under a trademark or brand name. It is this firm that has had the most experience in manufacturing the drug, and it is this firm's product that has been used in full clinical trials to meet the Food and Drug Administration's most demanding requirements for safety and effectiveness.

Different bioavailability (a drug's ability to be absorbed or used by the body) among directly competing drug products produces varying patient response to different versions of the same drug. Thus, once a patient has responded favorably to a specific drug product, it is prudent to continue using that same product, and avoid switching to another manufacturer's version. This desirable practice is facilitated by the use of brand names.

Victor Herbert, M.D., J.D. No—there is no difference between brand name and generic drugs. By federal law both must be biochemically identical as well as of equivalent bioavailability. That is, there must be nothing added to or subtracted from the pill that adversely affects how it is absorbed or used by the body.

Henry Wendt. The debate over the question of brand versus generic drugs is complex, and the complexity begins with the terminology used. Asking whether there is a difference between brand name and generic drugs is like asking if there is a difference between Chevrolets and automobiles. Obviously, "Chevrolet" is a trademark describing a very specific product manufactured by a specific company that makes machines for use in transportation. The word "automobile" by contrast, is a nonspecific, generic name. It applies, anonymously, to any one of a large number of vehicles used for personal or business transportation. Some of these vehicles may be comparable to a Chevrolet; many, for a variety of reasons, will not be. The most important thing to remember is that the purchaser of a Chevrolet is certain of the source of that product. However, if a product labeled "automobile" is purchased, the buyer would not know the product's source nor the manufacturer's reputation for quality products.

The same is true when it comes to drugs. Many are sold under brand names, names that clearly identify their source. Most, without question, are of high quality—most, but not all. Other drugs are sold only under their generic names, and when the prescription is written or filled that way, the source may be unknown, or may change each time the prescription is filled. By prescribing a specific brand name, your physician designates a specific drug produced by a specific manufacturer—a drug that, in his or her experience, has performed consistently and well in clinical practice. On the other hand, use of the generic name simply identifies a class of products, without identifying the source of any one product within that classification; that is, the name of the manufacturer and its reputation for excellence and quality products.

One would like to believe that all manufacturers of drugs respect and meet the legal and scientific standards set for their products. However, a glance at the recall reports of the Food and Drug Administration proves that this assumption is naive.

The debate on this issue often centers on price, and there is good evidence that drugs sold under nonproprietary names often cost less. There is no magic about this of course. The manufacturer who markets a drug many years after that product was first synthesized, tested, proven safe and effective, introduced to medicine and pharmacy on a worldwide basis—the manufacturer who undergoes none of those efforts and expenses—can offer the product for less. It is important to bear in mind, however, that the innovator of that product is probably conducting additional research on the drug even twenty years or more after its introduction. Moreover, some of the income from that product is probably paying for new research to develop improved compounds, perhaps in an entirely different field of medicine. Again, the follow-on manufacturer may shoulder none of those burdens.

This does not mean, of course, that consumers should never trust generic drugs, nor does it suggest that a brand name *per se* can be regarded as an assurance of superior quality. But it is meant to demonstrate that there is no simplistic answer to the question of generics versus brand name drugs. Interested consumers should, I suggest, discuss it with the family doctor or pharmacist, who has the experience and the personal interest required to make an intelligent and economical choice of the most appropriate individualized therapy that best suits the patient's needs.

CAN BIRTH DEFECTS BE AVOIDED? IF SO, HOW?

K.W. Dumars, M.D. Perhaps this question should be paraphrased to read: Can parents minimize the risks of delivering an atypical infant? Although birth defects cannot be prevented totally, the risks faced by all parents for delivering an infant with a birth defect can be minimized.

What is a birth defect? We all recognize an obvious birth defect, such as absence of fingers or toes, a cleft lip/cleft palate, or a congenital heart disease. But what about juvenile diabetes, severe anemias, or late-onset diseases, even cancer? These are also birth defects.

Some factors bearing upon the birth of our children are not under our control, particularly the genetic endowment provided by the newborn's parents or grandparents or by even more remote ancestors. There are, however, a number of specific actions that we as parents can take to reduce the risks, and those are outlined below.

   A. Actions That Reduce Environmental Risks
      1. *Immunization*
        Prior to pregnancy women should be aware of their history of childhood disease and immunizations. German measles (rubella) and, to a lesser extent, regular measles (rubeola), if acquired by the mother during pregnancy, can have a devastating effect upon the fetus. Venereal diseases, such as syphilis, can also devastate infants; thus routine screening

for these is done during pregnancy. A rare yet troublesome acquired maternal infection that can affect the fetus is toxoplasmosis, a disease carried by the domestic cat. Therefore, during pregnancy, the mother should particularly avoid handling of cat litter.

2. *Prenatal Care*

There is a correlation between prenatal care for the mother and reduced risk for birth defects. Possibly the seeking of prenatal care is a decision which, in itself, identifies a lower-risk family. Indeed, this decision may be the important factor rather than the prenatal care itself. In either case, prenatal care is related to reduced risk.

3. *Nutrition*

Attention to optimum weight gain during pregnancy is important. With rare exceptions, nutritional excesses or deficiencies cannot be cited as a cause of a specific birth defect. However, it is known that severe maternal malnutrition is associated with small birthweight and an increased rate of spontaneous abortion. Also, mothers who have a metabolic problem—diabetes, hypothyroidism, or phenylketonuria (PKU)—have a significantly higher risk for the delivery of a handicapped child.

4. *Drugs and Environmental Chemicals*

There is a correlation between either prescribed or illicit drug usage and the occurrence of birth defects. Any drug may statistically increase the risks. It is not known whether this increased risk is due to the specific effect of the drug or to the reasons for which the drug is taken. A number of books have been written on the topic of drug effects in pregnancy. Certain drugs are teratogenic; that is, they produce structural abnormalities in the fetus or infant. An incomplete list of teratogenic agents and associated problems includes thalidomide (congenital amputations); steroid hormones with androgenic activity, e.g., allylestrenol, chlormadinone, ethisterone, medroxyprogesterone, norethindrone, and the prototype progesterone (virilization of the female fetus and testicular abnormalities in the male); stilbestrol (adenoma of the vagina and postpubertal clear cell cancer of the vagina); folic acid antagonists and methotrexate, used primarily in treatment of cancer, and warfarin, used to reduce blood coagulation (growth retardation); phenytoin (dilatin) and tridione, used for treatment of convulsions (growth retardation and congenital malformations).

Other drugs, although not teratogens, affect the fetus, e.g., antithyroid drugs and sedatives. The sedatives to be avoided include: barbiturates, valium, narcotics, including methadone; and heroin. (The fetus becomes addicted to heroin if the mother uses heroin during pregnancy.)

The use of alcohol during pregnancy is inadvisable. There is very real risk to the fetus if the mother uses large amounts of alcohol during pregnancy. The effects of an occasional cocktail or glass of wine during pregnancy are not known; so any use of alcohol is best avoided.

Maternal smoking very definitely interferes with normal fetal growth so that the liveborn is often smaller than average.

There are also hazards to reproduction in the workplace. It is suspected that prolonged and/or frequent maternal exposure to volatile gases in operating rooms, to ethylene oxide (a gas used in the plastics industry), to manufacturing of methotroxate, and even to lead fumes (found in gasoline) may, at the least, affect fertility and may also produce birth defects. Paternal exposure to lead and di-bromo-chloropropane (DBCP) interferes with fertility.

5. *Radiation*

The only absolutely safe X ray is no X ray. Maternal exposure during pregnancy to diagnostic X-ray studies of the chest, long bones or head carries very little risk. If X rays of the abdomen and pelvic area must be taken, the fetus should be shielded. In general, the risks from diagnostic X ray of the abdomen are minimal, but such X rays should be postponed, if possible, until after pregnancy.

The risk from therapeutic X ray is an entirely different matter. A mother who must be treated with X ray during pregnancy must be aware that a significant risk for miscarriage, and risk to the infant, exists. The results of exposure to low-level radiation, which occurs in industry and mining, for instance, and even naturally occurring radiation from outcroppings of radioactive ore or from the stratosphere are controversial. However, to rephrase the first statement; the only safe radiation is no radiation.

6. *Childbearing Age*

There is an optimum age for child bearing. Child bearing during the teen-age years and after thirty-five increases the risk for birth defects. The older mother faces a higher incidence of chromosome abnormalities in the child. The older father may stand an increased risk of having a mutant in the sperm which, if transmitted to the fetus, causes a birth defect (achondroplasia). In teenagers, the risk is not genetic, but related to the smallness of the pelvic structure.

B. Genetic Influences

Parents should be aware of the availability of genetic counseling and of amniocentesis, a test that makes prenatal diagnosis possible. Both are particularly important for individuals at increased risk—families with a history of genetic disease, chromosome abnormality or certain developmental disorders such as spina bifida, and mothers over thirty-five years of age.

Through newborn screening, early detection of PKU, galactosemia or hypothyroidism allows for early treatment which effectively modifies any handicap.

In summary, the health of the unborn can be enhanced by the following:

1. Childbearing between the ages of nineteen to thirty-five
2. Delaying conception for at least six months after a pregnancy or abortion or after discontinuing birth control pills
3. Consistent prenatal care
4. Immunization against infectious disease
5. Avoidance of *any* unnecessary drugs or X rays
6. Avoidance of alcohol and tobacco
7. Use of available genetics services

Following these steps will not avoid birth defects, but it will minimize the risk of their occurrence in your offspring.

Frederick Hecht, M.D. Yes—there is no question that birth defects can, in many cases, be avoided. The primary safeguards are:

1. For women to avoid the following, during pregnancy: teratogenic agents (such as X-irradiation), dangerous chemicals (such as alcohol) and hazardous drugs (such as dilantin and antimetabolites) during pregnancy
2. For women to be immunized prior to pregnancy against rubella (German measles)
3. For couples to be screened for genetic carrier states (e.g., for the Tay-Sachs gene and sickle-cell trait)
4. For couples to receive genetic counseling
5. For women, when appropriate, to be offered prenatal genetic diagnosis (ultrasound and usually with amniocentesis)

The avoidance of birth defects depends on the degree of commitment by physicians, government and, especially, by parents-to-be.

John C. Hobbins, M.D. It is impossible to prevent all birth defects because today's knowledge of the causes of various defects is incomplete and prenatal diagnosis is not possible in all types of fetal abnormalities.

Basically, birth defects are either acquired or inherited. The ideal way to avoid them is to prevent their formation.

An acquired defect results when a fetus is exposed to an agent, such as a chemical or virus, during the first three months of pregnancy when the organs are at a critical stage of development. A few agents—the infamous thalidomide, for instance—can directly cause birth defects. Others, such as alcohol may or may not result in fetal abnormalities, depending in part upon the dosage and duration of exposure. Still others have been suspected of being associated with higher rates of birth defects, but there is not sufficient data to indicate a direct cause and effect relationship. In general, however, it makes sense to avoid exposure to any drug (unless indicated), food additives, fumes of any kind, X rays and even to avoid potentially beneficial substances, such as vitamins, in megadosage.

A birth defect is inherited when one or both members of a couple pass on defective genes to an offspring, resulting in an abnormality of structure or function. Geneticists will investigate the family history in order to estimate the probabilities for a couple at risk of having a baby with a birth defect. Many inherited conditions can spring up spontaneously as a result of mutations and, therefore, rarely recur, while others have invariable inheritance patterns resulting in 25 percent to 50 percent recurrence rates. In addition, some birth defects are maternal-age dependent. For example, some chromosomal abnormalities such as Down's syndrome more frequently occur in the children of mothers who are over thirty-five years of age, and/or fathers who are over fifty-five.

One way to avoid birth defects is for people who are at increased risk of fetal abnormalities to avoid having children. An alternative, however, is prenatal diagnosis. The aim of prenatal diagnostic techniques is to identify those fetuses doomed to death or disability. In these cases, the patient in her second trimester has the option to terminate pregnancy. Happily, in the majority of cases, prenatal diagnosis provides the couple at risk with the knowledge that their fetus is apparently normal. The psychological "lift" for these couples is appreciable.

With present technology, many birth defects also can be characterized in utero with regard to life sustaining potential or quality of life. In yet other situations genetic screening programs identify fetuses with potentially lethal conditions and, by timely delivery or in utero treatment, they can be saved.

Prenatal diagnosis is accomplished through various techniques, some of which are invasive. Amniocentesis involves the withdrawal of fluid from the amniotic sac through a very thin needle. The cells contained in the fluid are cultured and the chromosomes within are microscopically evaluated. The fluid itself can be analyzed for enzymes, fetal protein and genetic material. Each of these can be altered in certain fetal abnormalities.

Today, with high frequency sound waves (ultrasound), it is possible to visualize the fetal outline and individual organs. Therefore many conditions that result in fetal deformities of heart, cranium, spine, abdomen and limbs can now be diagnosed. A recently developed technique, fetoscopy, allows fetal viewing and direct sampling of fetal tissue and blood. Since the method has an inherited 5 percent risk of fetal mortality, it is reserved for conditions with high recurrence rates.

Fetoscopy creates another exciting potential—treating certain fetal conditions with clones of cells or substances in which the fetus is deficient, and administering these through the umbilical cord. This represents an exciting step forward in the attempt to remedy some fetal abnormalities now labeled as "hopeless."

Dorothy R. Hollingsworth, M.D. Many birth defects can be avoided by taking the following precautions:

1. Emphasis on good health, normal weight and nutrition before conception
2. Good control of chronic medical problems before conception (i.e., diabetes, epilepsy, etc.)
3. Avoidance of *all* drugs (prescription, over the counter, street drugs, nicotine, alcohol) during the critical first seven to nine weeks of gestation
4. Rubella immunization before conception

At the present time, however, there are some birth defects that *cannot* be avoided. These are defects caused by:

1. Chromosomal abnormalities
2. Autosomal dominant and recessive genes for birth defects
3. Sporadic problems (i.e., cretinism)
4. Exposure to illnesses during pregnancy (i.e., Herpes virus, cytomegalic inclusion cell virus, toxoplasmosis, etc.)

Rollin D. Hotchkiss. Birth disorders are divided into two broad categories: physical or physiological injuries occurring during the birth process, and inheritable defects present in the body at birth and noticeable in varying degrees at birth or during subsequent growth of the individual. Both types of defect include so many different disorders that only some in each group can be avoided or offset.

Injuries occurring during the birth process ("congenital" disorders) can result from unfavorable orientation or mishandling of the fetus, poor nutrition or infectious diseases acquired from the mother's own body or the birth environment. In general, these are individual accidents that can be anticipated, largely avoided, and that can be offset or corrected when they do occur. The "Rh factor" blood disease, for example, can often be avoided by taking care that a mother of a certain vulnerable type does not develop the opportunity to react against the blood cells of her own child. Attentive, experienced physicians and medical personnel can do much to prevent most such fundamentally avoidable mischances.

Every human being carries inheritable traits and tendencies; some of them are harmful enough to be recognizable at birth or soon after. The tendency for a "defect" to be taken as a sign of inferiority is unfortunate and should be discouraged. However, it is important to screen for the early signs of some of the common heritable disorders. The most significant factor is the stage of development at which the disorder affects the individual. If the disorder acts on the individual during pregnancy, some degree of malformation (anatomical or functional) will be found at birth. Usually, this malformation can only be alleviated, not prevented—except by the extreme course of terminating the pregnancy, after some kind of early recognition. If the disorder acts mainly during infancy, there is some chance of alleviating it, as more knowledge of such childhood disorders is acquired. (For example, there is one metabolic deficiency that is less disastrous if it is offset by careful diet control during infancy. Otherwise, it produces distressing effects, particularly on mental development.) Various other heritable disorders, fairly widespread in the population, develop later, or even very late in life. Increasingly, modern medical knowledge can help to offset them, and can recognize, at earlier and earlier stages, that they existed as "birth defects."

One approach to alleviating genetic deficiencies has been much speculated about and discussed: altering an individual's genetic constitution by genetic and chemical means. This does not, at present, offer a practical route for treatment of embryos or individuals. Instead, genetic engineering is directed toward a more promising area—supplying the products or substances that make up for the inborn genetic imbalances.

E. W. Lovrien, M.D. Yes, birth defects can be avoided, but not completely prevented. The incidence, that is the frequency at birth, can be reduced in the following ways:

1. Avoiding marrying a relative
2. Receiving optimal prenatal care
3. Limiting childbearing to the ages between twenty and thirty five
4. Not smoking during pregnancy
5. Not using alcohol during pregnancy
6. Avoiding all medications that are unnecessary including aspirin, tranquilizers and perhaps anticonvulsants

In addition to these precautions, couples, prior to child bearing, could explore their own families to seek clues that might better prepare them for any risks to their offspring. High risk couples could seek alternatives when planning their families—adopting foster children, for instance. Such high risk couples would include mothers who are juvenile diabetics and parents who transmit single-gene disorders (such as PKU or osteogenesis imperfects).

Prof. Aubrey Milunsky. There are over 3,000 recognized birth defects or genetic disorders. Indeed each of us carries a handful of harmful genes. Since the causes of birth defects can be environmental or genetic, those couples planning to have children should be sensitive to both these dimensions.

Environmental causes include viruses (such as German measles), medications (such as hormonal preparations), alcohol, lead and many other noxious agents. Simple avoidance of the many known harmful environmental factors will help diminish the risk of having a child with birth defects due to environmental causes.

Genetic counseling is an important consideration for those who might be at risk for having a child with an hereditary defect. It is important for all couples to know their family history, especially if they have family members with mental retardation, birth defects or genetic disease. Genetic counseling should be sought if either of the partners has a genetic disease or might be a carrier. (While we are all carriers, the risks of carrying certain harmful genes are greater within specific ethnic groups. For example, Ashkenazi Jews are at greater risk for having a child with Tay-Sachs disease; blacks are at a greater risk for having a child with sickle-cell anemia; those of Mediterranean extraction—Italians, Greeks, Turks, etc.—are at greater risk of having a child with a serious hemolytic anemia called thalassemia. Genetic counseling should also be sought if the couple has already had a child with birth defects. Such counseling will apprise them of the options available, which would include carrier detection tests, prenatal diagnosis with selective abortion, artificial insemination by donor, tubal ligation, vasectomy or adoption.

In order to avoid birth defects in their offspring, couples are advised to seek genetic counseling before or at the time of marriage, but certainly before conception of their first child.

ARE THERE ANY CURES FOR ALLERGIES?

Richard S. Farr, M.D. It is impossible to answer this question without first defining the term allergy as "a broad spectrum of untoward physiologic events mediated by any of the known immunologic mechanisms." With this definition in mind, allergic conditions range all the way from the patient who sneezes in the fall due to ragweed pollen, through patients who develop a rash following an exposure to poison ivy, patients who develop anemias following allergic reactions to medications such as penicillin, to patients who develop aching, hot swollen joints following injections of such things as horse serum. Notice that I have not included asthma here because the fundamental problem for an asthmatic is not an allergy. Instead, the asthmatic's condition is due to hyperreactive airways or "twitchy lungs." These "twitchy lungs" can be stimulated to wheeze or cause asthma by a variety of different stimuli including temperature changes, exercise and even allergies.

Now, to answer the question: "Are there any cures for allergies?" If one accepts the idea that avoidance of an offending substance constitutes a cure, then indeed, there are cures for such conditions as poison ivy, and for allergic reactions to certain medicines. On the other hand, despite some remissions that occur in certain cases of asthma and hay fever, and the causes of these remissions are not clearly understood, patients should not be looking for cures. Realistically, they should expect to be placed on a medical management program that will stabilize their hyperreactive airways or prevent the hay fever symptoms. Antigen injections (allergy shots) may help reduce the amount of allergic stimulation required to induce asthma or hay fever. However, it is highly unusual for such injections to cure the problem.

Kenneth P. Mathews, M.D. In attempting to answer this question, it seems desirable first to clarify what type of "allergies" are being discussed. In common nonprofessional parlance, the term is used most often to denote certain types of immediate hypersensitivity states: hay fever, allergic asthma, allergic hives or severe reactions (anaphylaxis) from insect stings or drugs. However, the original definition of the term, and the scope of interest of many physicians specializing in this area, is much broader than this. It encompasses so-called delayed-type hypersensitivity reactions; examples of these include tuberculin-type hypersensitivity to transplanted organs, autoimmune diseases and tumor rejection. This discussion will be limited to immediate-type hypersensitivity reactions.

There are three general principles involved in trying to treat these types of allergic problems: first, determination of and avoidance of the offending allergen(s). When possible, this is the preferred form of treatment and comes close to providing a cure for the disease. An example: when a patient is diagnosed as being allergic to horses and guinea pigs, the patient simply avoids exposure to these animals. However, in some instances the cause of apparent allergic reactions cannot be determined. In many other cases the offending allergen cannot readily be avoided—allergenes such as various pollens in the air or house dust. Another problem is that patients often are sensitive to multiple allergens, only some of which can readily be avoided.

The second therapeutic approach to allergies is to suppress allergic symptoms by various medications. This is necessary when the cause cannot be avoided, and often such treatment is quite effective. Nevertheless, symptoms will return when the medicines are stopped, if exposure to allergens continues. Therefore, this type of treatment hardly constitutes a "cure."

A third general therapeutic approach is "hyposensitization," "desensitization" or "immunotherapy." The patient is given a series of injections of the offending allergens, starting with very minute dosages and gradually increasing to relatively large doses over a period of time. This usually increases the patient's tolerance to allergens that he cannot avoid. However, in most cases, this mode of treatment alone provides less than 100 percent relief, and there is a tendency for symptoms to return some period of time after the injections are discontinued. (The period of time varies with each patient.) In summary, therefore, it could be said that allergies frequently can be controlled but rarely are cured because the capacity to react to offending allergens may remain latent and may manifest itself again upon reexposure to offending allergens under adverse circumstances.

Philip S. Norman, M.D. There are no real cures for allergies. Modern treatments help symptoms, may even control them entirely, but there is considerable risk of relapse when treatment is stopped.

Albert L. Sheffer, M.D. An allergy is an altered response to an ingested, inhaled or injected substance to which most people are tolerant. Patients who are allergic appear to have a genetic capacity to develop asthma, hay fever, eczema and certain types of urticaria as well as life-threatening anaphylactic reactions to one or more of these substances. These patients may be relieved of their allergic symptoms by avoiding the allergen. Where this is not effectively practiced the symptoms may be controlled by pharmacologic agents and/or immunotherapy. The latter is a treatment program in which increasing concentrations of allergenic extracts are administered at regular intervals in an effort to reduce the allergic symptoms. Such a program is effective in diminishing inhalant allergen (hay fever) symptoms.

These treatments have been designed to circumvent the patient's inability to avoid the allergic reaction. Although some patients appear to "outgrow" their symptoms—they seem to develop a spontaneous improvement and may never experience allergic symptoms again—current immunologic data suggest that once sensitized always allergic, and only by omitting the allergen can one be certain of avoiding an allergic reaction in the future.

Paul P. VanArsdel, Jr., M.D. First of all, what are we talking about when we discuss allergies? People use the word "allergy" in one of three ways. The first and most scientific way is to use the word to describe an acquired sensitivity to animal, plant and chemical substances in the environment. These substances remain innocuous for most people throughout their lives. The substances are also innocuous for allergy-afflicted people until the sensitivity develops. This sensitivity is usually associated with the appearance of an antibody (a blood protein of a unique type) that interacts with the foreign substance in a very specific manner, in the way that a key fits a lock. Allergy may develop to pollens, dust, animals (including insects), mold spores, foods, drugs and chemicals. It may occur from breathing, eating, injection of the offending substance, or from skin contact.

The second way people talk about allergy is in terms of the ailment itself. When exposed to the things they are allergic to, patients will get allergic diseases, such as asthma, hayfever, skin rashes, digestive disturbances, fever, shock, or, less often, disturbances to internal organs such as the liver or kidney.

The third and obviously unscientific use of the word allergy is to indicate a strong aversion to something, as in "allergic to work." This kind of allergy is incurable, and I will not discuss it further.

The word "cure" can be defined as "restoration to health or a sound condition." If a person with asthma that is due only to cat allergy avoids cats, the asthma goes away. Another person may break out with a skin rash during penicillin treatment because of allergy. The rash will go away in a short time if treatment with that drug is stopped. In a practical sense, both these people were cured; that is, their asthma and skin rash, respectively, were cured. The latent allergy to cat and penicillin, however, may remain indefinitely.

Allergic people who cannot avoid things they are allergic to may also be cured, though not so predictably. Some people are cured by immunotherapy (or desensitization) injections. The injections build up tolerance through gradually increasing doses of the substance to which the patient is allergic. This is particularly effective in restoring complete tolerance to people who have had allergic reactions to bee, wasp or hornet stings.

Some allergic people are cured by time alone. Asthma in a child sometimes goes away, especially during adolescence. Latent penicillin allergy may also go away—in due time, in some people—after they have suffered a reaction.

Although many people will not be cured completely, and although we are not yet able to eradicate the sensitizing antibody with any reliability, most people, with proper treatment, can have their health restored sufficiently so that they are "as good as cured."

WHAT IS THE MOST SUCCESSFUL CURE FOR HEADACHES?

Donald J. Dalessio, M.D. Most benign headaches are caused by muscle contraction. Therefore, the most successful cure for headaches is to learn to relax the great muscles of the head and neck and to achieve a certain degree of contentment and tranquility. They can also be relieved by a rest and sleep. If none of this can be achieved, the most useful medication is aspirin (acetylsalicylic acid): two five gram tablets, repeated in two hours if necessary. Aspirin has multiple therapeutic effects including pain relief and inhibition of inflammation. Its effects on prostaglandin synthesis, a potent blood vessel dilator, may also make it useful in mild migraine.

A migraine headache is generally assumed to be a more severe episode, in which the blood vessels, in particular, are involved and with associated brain irritability. If the migraine attack becomes sustained, ordinary pain relievers, such as aspirin, are not likely to be useful. Then one resorts to drugs that reduce the size of the blood vessels, most often ergotamine tartrate, in one of its various forms. If migraine headaches occur repeatedly and begin to interfere significantly with one's productivity and lifestyle, headache prophylaxis should be considered. This involves daily medications. For example, propranolol might be given. This interferes with the nervous and vascular reactions that produce migraine. The attempt here is to prevent headache, rather than aborting a headache that has already started.

Certain behavioral methods, such as biofeedback training and relaxation techniques, are used when trying to change the responses of the nervous system through will training and conditioning. These procedures are usually employed to avoid medications, and if the headaches are severe and recurrent. To be successful, such training, though not difficult to learn, requires constant practice and diligence.

Since headache may be the first sign of brain disease, it should not be ignored, especially if severe and persistent. For example, headache may be the primary sign of brain tumor, stroke or cranial arteritis, among other disease conditions. Here the headache is secondary and the primary aim of treatment should be to cure the disease producing the headache.

Roger N. Rosenberg, M.D. Headache is a symptom and not a disease. It can be caused by many neurological disorders. Some of these are quite minor but a limited number can be serious and require urgent neurological care. Therefore, there is no single cure for headache. Instead, each patient's headache problem must be thoroughly and accurately analyzed and a careful evaluation made.

Most headaches are due to depression or stress. The patient has periodic headaches that are clearly related to tension, stress or to some personal problem with which he is dealing. Headaches increase as a bandlike constriction around the head and with rest or analgesics the headache is resolved. Psychiatric care may be necessary in order to help the patient resolve the depression or cope with the chronic stress.

In some cases, headache can be a symptom of high blood pressure, a brain tumor, an infection within the nervous system and other metabolic diseases such as kidney failure, chronic lung disease and abnormalities in the regulation of blood sugar. The patient must have a careful general physical examination and a neurological examination followed by a thorough clinical laboratory evaluation that looks for metabolic, infectious or other systemic diseases. The headache will resolve when the identified disease is specifically and effectively treated. Aspirin or other analgesics must only be used for benign headaches or when no major disease process has been identified.

Dewey K. Ziegler, M.D. There is no cure for headache. The susceptibility to headache is common to a large percentage of the population, probably throughout the world, although it has only been studied in certain nations.

Many drugs function more or less effectively as pain relievers. These include aspirin, acetoaminophen and others. Very strong analgesic medication such as opiates should probably be avoided in the treatment of headache. There are several medications which are now effective in preventing onset of headache in varying degrees, including propranolol, amitriptyline and methysergide maleate. In addition, headache is markedly affected by the psychological state and many maneuvers directed toward muscle relaxation and mental relaxation have been effective in preventing headache and also in effecting some relief at the time of severe pain. For those who are subject to headache, certain hygienic measures must be kept in mind: excess use of alcohol intensifies the susceptibility to headache as do prolonged periods of fasting.

WHAT HUMAN ORGANS CAN BE TRANSPLANTED? WHAT RESEARCH IS TAKING PLACE IN THIS FIELD?

Folkert O. Belzer, M.D. Transplantation is the transfer of an organ or tissue from one individual, the donor, to another individual, the recipient (allotransplantation) or, from one place to another place in the same individual (autotransplantation), for the purpose of replacing one or more lost functions of the grafted part. Because autotransplantation does not involve genetic differences between donor and recipient, immune responses to the transplant do not develop and immunosuppression is not necessary. Autotransplantation will not be considered further here, except to say that it includes many common surgical procedures, such as hair transplants, skin grafting, nerve and tendon grafts, and a variety of plastic surgical procedures called tissue flaps. Several kinds of allotransplants will also not be considered further here because they are presently in an experimental stage of clinical development (transplantation of the lung and pancreas); or, because they are useful only as a research tool in experimental animals (thyroid transplants); or, because they have very limited clinical application for some reason (transplantation of bone, thymus, blood vessel and parathyroid gland).

The most commonly performed tissue transplant, although it is not usually thought of as such, is the blood transfusion. The lost function in this case may be the transport capacity for oxygen, nutrients, and wastes, or the hemostatic functions of blood components. Trauma and blood loss, and diseases of the bone marrow, liver and blood are the usual indications for blood transfusions.

Probably the second most commonly transplanted organ is the cornea of the eye. Currently, these are being done in about 300 American medical centers, with a total of about 12,000 transplants each year. There are approximately a dozen ophthalmological conditions, occurring in patients of all ages and resulting in destruction of the cornea, that can be treated by corneal replacement. For reasons that are not well understood, tissue rejection is much less of a problem with corneas than with other tissues. Because of this, the long-term success rate is excellent, about 80 percent overall, but depends somewhat on the original eye disease. Rejection, when it does occur, is usually treated locally rather than with systemically administered (and consequently systemically toxic) drugs.

Next to blood transfusions and corneas, kidney transplants lead the list of most frequently transplanted organs. Since the first successful human kidney transplants were done in 1954, this method of treatment for kidney failure has continued at an annually increasing rate; currently about 4,500 per year are done in the United States, in approximately 100 medical centers. The realization that organ transplantation is therapeutic and most of the lessons in clinical immunology have come from this large experience.

Transplantation of the human heart was first accomplished in 1967. Although it has been repeated several hundred times in about sixty medical centers since then, it is still being done regularly as a therapeutic modality in only one American medical center. Heart transplantation when done in a small minority of highly selected patients with heart disease is definitely therapeutic. However, it is clearly not applicable to most patients, a significant difference when compared to kidney transplantation. Despite this limitation, successful transplantation of the human heart was a significant accomplishment. Apart from its biological function, the emotional importance of the heart is evident from other uses of the word in our language (heart of the matter, heartfelt thanks, hardhearted).

Hepatic (liver) transplantation in humans was first attempted in 1963. The world's experience with hepatic transplant comes mostly from two medical centers, one in Denver, Colorado, and one at Cambridge, England. About 300 patients have received liver transplants, nearly all of them from one of these two centers. Most patients have had liver tumors, cirrhosis of the liver, or congenital biliary atresia, a condition where the bile ducts fail to develop. Of the organs discussed here, the technical aspects of liver transplants have been the most difficult, partly because of the dual venous blood supply to the liver, and partly because of the numerous possible ways of reestablishing bile flow. Livers for transplantation, like hearts, must come from cadaver donors. Liver transplant recipients, like heart transplant recipients but unlike kidney transplant patients, have no alternative means of sustaining life other than successful transplantation.

Bone marrow transplantation, like blood transfusion, does not require that the donor or the recipient undergo major surgery. Instead, the marrow is removed from the bone (sternum or pelvis) through a special needle, specially prepared, and injected into the veins of the recipient. The marrow donor is always a living, close relative of the recipient. One unique aspect of bone marrow transplantation is that the tissue being transplanted is itself capable of producing an immune response. Success therefore depends not only on controlling the immune response of the recipient against the transplanted bone marrow, but also the response of the transplanted marrow against the recipient. About 400 bone marrow transplants are being done annually in approximately twenty American medical centers. Most patients requiring bone marrow transplants have leukemia or some other disease that causes failure of the bone marrow.

Most kinds of organ and tissue transplantation share several common problems. First, there is an inadequate supply of donor organs which, usually, must come from cadavers. Second, organs that are available for transplantation can be preserved for a limited time only. Third, rejection is a natural biological phenomenon arising from the genetic differences between donor and recipient. If not prevented, this results in the immunological destruction of the graft. Attempts to solve these four problems form the basis of most research efforts today.

Regarding the first problem: medical research is unlikely to provide a solution for the inadequate supply of donor organs. There are potentially enough people dying under conditions that would make them eligible organ donors to supply all of our needs. However, only a fraction of these eligible donor organs are retrieved for transplantation. Great progress has been made within the last decade, but continued efforts at public and professional education, as well as social and legal reform, are necessary.

Once they are outside the human body, deprived of a nutrient blood supply, tissues will inevitably die, usually beginning within minutes. They will become unusable for transplantation unless some method of preservation is employed. All successful preservation techniques to date involve two processes: perfusion of the organs with special fluids to remove blood and change the cellular environment; cooling to retard cellular metabolism and delay the onset of cell death. A machine was developed in 1968 to accomplish this for the kidney. This machine is still in use and allows preservation of this organ for up to seventy-two hours. This gives adequate time for compatibility testing, for the preparation of recipients for surgery, and for relocating organs and recipients from one transplant center to another, to minimize organ wastage. Unfortunately, this technique does not allow preservation of whole organs other than the kidney beyond a few hours. There is also insufficient time for more sophisticated compatibility tests that are becoming available or will become available in the future. More elaborate preparation of recipients for surgery would also be possible if preservation time could be extended. One obvious and currently active area of medical research is the attempt to freeze and "bank" transplantable organs, as is now possible with blood products.

The most active and fruitful research being done today is in the area of prevention and treatment of rejection. Testing for histocompatibility prior to transplantation and immunosuppression after transplantation with steroids and other pharmacologic agents (imuran, cytoxan, Antilymphocyte globulin) have been the mainstays of therapy for over a decade. However, they are not effective enough or specific enough, and are excessively toxic for many patients. Long-term success rates with kidney, heart and liver organs continue to approximate only 50 percent and the overwhelming majority of patients suffer at least some undesirable drug-related side effects. A simultaneous, three-pronged effort to eliminate the problem of graft rejection is necessary and encompasses the bulk of today's research efforts in transplantation. First, better methods of compatibility testing must be found so that there is less tendency for rejection to occur. Second, more effective, more specific and safer drugs and techniques must be found to suppress immune responses that do occur. Third, most recently, and perhaps most importantly, the ability of recipients to respond immunologically against specific grafted tissues must either be attenuated or at least quantified prior to transplantation so that transplantable organs, a scarce natural resource, can be given to individuals least likely to reject them.

Continued progress in organ transplantation will undoubtedly occur in the years ahead because: experts are confident that the obstacles to successful organ replacement can be overcome through medical research; and there is a growing realization that death and disability due to diseases of vital organs can be prevented by organ replacement.

Michael E. DeBakey, M.D. Among the human organs and tissues that can be transplanted are blood, selected blood cells, bone marrow, bone chips, the cornea, the kidney, the heart and the liver. The lungs and pancreas have been transplanted, but the results have not been encouraging.

Considerable research is taking place in this field, and much progress has been made in a better understanding of the rejection phenomenon and its control. There remains much to be learned, however.

E. J. Eichwald, M.D. The urge to provide substitutes for lost or failing portions of the human anatomy goes far back in time. Replacement by man-made devices—prostheses—has come a long way; from the peg legs and arm hooks of amputees depicted on medieval paintings, to contact lenses and hearing aids, to pacemakers and "iron lungs," to artificial kidneys and the possibility of a totally artificial human heart. Further progress may be slow in coming, and very expensive in view of the complexity of artificial devices. Also, prostheses cannot handle tasks of growth and differentiation, of procreation, and of central nervous system regulation.

Nature-made substitutes—transplants—lack some of these limitations. The history of transplant attempts goes back into antiquity, and is replete with blatantly false claims—from Indian legends on the transfer of heads or souls, to Baron von Munchhausen's spectacular feats in horse surgery, to present-day televised horror stories on the transfer of the brains from criminals.

In the early years of this century, the genetic relationship between the donor of a transplant and its recipient was recognized as the decisive factor determining success or failure. It was not until World War II that rejection of transplants, while genetically determined, was recognized to be an immune phenomenon. Since that time, progress has been substantial, as evidenced by the presence of thousands in our midst kept alive by transplanted kidneys; by the mushrooming of transplantation laboratories and societies; by the numbers of transplant services and registries; and by the presence of transplant journals, books, symposia, and conventions on a worldwide scale. New light has been cast and new directions given to areas as diverse as surgical technology, physiology and pharmacology, immunology and endocrinology, genetics and embryology, and even ethics, medical law and social psychology.

Nature provides an excess of ready-made substitutes but to locate and utilize them has proven difficult. Many of these difficulties—locating transplants, and of their maintenance, transfer, and survival—came into focus as kidney transplantations advanced from the experimental laboratory to the bedside.

Live or deceased humans are the best source of potential transplants —kidneys, hearts, livers, corneas, skin, hemopoietic (liver), and endocrine tissues, to name a few. (The process of procuring transplants is called "harvesting.") Cadavers are an obvious source but have distinct disadvantages. As the interval between time of death and transfer to a recipient increases, the chances of success diminish. Tests aimed at determining the suitability of a transplant for a given recipient (compatibility tests) lengthen this time interval. This applies particularly to the victims of accidental death, who are the most desirable sources, often being young and in good health. Live donors present other problems. For one, they cannot donate unpaired organs (heart, liver) and the donation of corneas is not proposed. The donation of some other tissues (e.g., bone marrow, kidney) may cause disease and harvesting them may put physicians in violation of the Hippocratic Oath not to hurt their fellow man. Formidable legal, social and psychological obstacles are still in the way of full utilization of both cadavers and live donors. Simians, goats and pigs have also been used as donors (xenogeneic transplants) but are too incompatible to be used extensively.

The interval between harvesting and placement (ischemia time) needs to be kept at a minimum. Oxygen lack, clogging of blood vessels and retention of waste products result in liberation of autolytic enzymes that endanger survival of renal tubules, liver cells and heart muscle cells. Successful perfusion techniques and maintenance at low temperatures have extended permissible ischemia time. This, in turn, has facilitated the airmailing of kidneys to recipients of optimal compatibility, as determined by sophisticated computer systems. This does not apply to transplants of heart or liver for which permissible ischemia time is much shorter. Other tissues are less dependent on an immediate oxygen supply (e.g., skin, endocrine tissues). They have been maintained in tissue or organ culture for considerable periods of time; suspensions of lymphoid or tumor cells are stored at the temperature of liquid nitrogen ($-79°C$) for unlimited time periods.

Transplants are expected to survive and function in their new environment. Certain transplants (endocrine tissue) function until their cells are rejected, while others (bone, dura, heart valves) function even though their cells have succumbed to rejection, because their function is merely mechanical. Actually, they are prostheses, not transplants.

Transplants of large viscera require the speedy establishment of anastomoses with the recipients' blood vessels. This requires much surgical skill and is undertaken only in some "tertiary" centers. The fate of transplants is distinctly influenced by the skill and experience of the transplant teams.

Surgical anastomoses are not required for transplants of skin, cornea or hemopoietic cells. They are smaller and less dependent on a complex blood supply, although able to establish vascular anastomoses of their own. They exist closer to nutrient fluid, and therefore manage to fend for themselves.

Organs or tissues that have been properly harvested, maintained, and transferred tend to fare surprisingly well for several days, weeks, or even months. Occasionally, immediate (hyperacute) rejection is observed; this is in effect, nonacceptance. However, unless the donor and the patient are one and the same person (autologous), an identical twin, or in the case of inbred laboratory animals, of the same strain and line as the recipient (syngeneic), a rejection reaction (homograft response) occurs. The purpose of this reaction is to kill off the transplant. It is an immune response to substances (histocompatibility antigens) on the surface membranes of the foreign cells. Each specie, each strain (in man, each individual) and, in part, each style of tissue has its own specific histocompatibility antigens. These can be measured by the strength of the immune response they evoke, and can then be coded as having a "strong" or a "weak" effect. Appropriate donor selection consists of avoiding "strong" differences, through tissue-typing. Total compatibility is not achievable except with autologous or syngeneic donors. After a transplantation has been done one faces the task of preventing and suppressing rejection reactions against remaining histo-compatibility antigens (host vs. graft), and also, mainly in the case of bone marrow transplants, reactions of the transplant against the recipient (graft vs. host or GvH reactions). Suppression implies inter-ference with the recipient immune responses. This is accomplished in a number of ways: physical (irradiation); chemical (e.g., azathioprine, cyclosporin A); hormonal (corticoids); serologic (antilymphocyte serum called ALS). Most commonly a combination of methods is used— whatever combination works best. Immunosuppression, particularly when prolonged, carries a double danger for the patient: lower resistance to infections, and a significant increase of cancer. Interestingly, pre-operative blood transfusions, particularly if donor-blood, tend to im-prove the fate of the transplant.

A. Kidney transplantation is widely practiced the world over in "tertiary" care centers. Well over 40,000 kidneys have been transplanted, with an increasing proportion being harvested from cadavers. In most transplant centers technical failures and hyperacute rejection are rare. The one-year survival rate of cadaver transplants is between 60 percent and 75 percent, with most failures occurring during the first few months. Transplant failures beyond one year are relatively rare. Repeat trans-plants, if rejection of the first occurs, are frequently undertaken. Hemodialysis of recipients is usually practiced prior to transplantation and subsequent to transplant rejection. The most formidable road block to wider application of kidney transplantation is lack of available organs. A continuous and devoted effort is needed to assure an adequate supply.

B. Human heart transplantation, first undertaken in late 1967, and accompanied by much publicity, has had a stormy course. It is technically more difficult than kidney transplantation, and depends entirely on having accident cadavers available and on a minimal ischemia time. In the absence of an experienced, devoted, highly skilled team of sub-stantial size (implying high cost), significant success is unlikely. Under optimal circumstances, a five-year survival of 50 percent of recipients has been achieved, with occasional survival of ten years or more. The total number of human heart transplants, in one center alone, counting both failures and successes, is above 200. An interesting new develop-ment is the transplantation of heart and lungs together. Although more formidable on first glance, the surgical procedure is actually simpler, due to the need for fewer vascular anastomoses and a more spacious operative field. However, the tracheas of transplant and recipient have to be joined securely which at times is difficult.

C. Suspensions of bone marrow cells are transplanted to patients with immune deficiencies, with bone marrow failure (aplastic anemia) with acute leukemia and, recently, with congenital bone marrow disorders, e.g., sickle-cell disease. Immune deficient patients benefit from the presence of immunologically responsive cells in the transferred bone marrow—and have the added advantage of requiring little or no immunosuppression since rejection reactions will be absent or minimal. Patients with aplastic anemia or leukemia require severe immunosuppression, except when the bone marrow to be transplanted is the patient's own—harvested during a period of remission, and stored. Immunosuppression is accomplished by either irradiation or chemical means (e.g., cytoxan) which in leukemia has the added purpose of destroying leukemic cells. Prognosis is less favorable with leukemics since nests of leukemic cells tend to escape destruction.

The presence of immunoresponsive cells in bone marrow transplants is highly desirable and even necessary to immunosuppression, but poses the danger of GvH disease. These cells tend to react against the tissues of the recipient (liver, bowel, skin, etc.), and fatal GvH disease can occur. Attempts to reduce this danger consist of pretreating the marrow with specific antisera directed against potentially aggressive cells.

Prognosis is most unfavorable in leukemias, unfortunately the most common of these disease groups. Still, up to 13 percent of acute leukemics treated with marrow transplants have survived up to ten years. A successful program requires a highly skilled and experienced multidisciplinary medical team.

D. Transplantation of a liver, which can only be taken from a cadaver, is accomplished after removal of the patient's own diseased liver. It requires a degree of surgical skill only a few surgeons possess. It is therefore unlikely to become a widely accepted form of treatment of bile duct malformation, cancer, or cirrhosis. Posttransplant immunosuppressive management appears to be particularly difficult. Still, in one of the few centers in which this procedure is undertaken, almost 200 livers have been transplanted, with 30 percent to 40 percent of the patients surviving for over one year, and in at least one case, more than ten years.

E. Corneas are probably the most commonly transplanted tissue. It is a fair guess that more good has been accomplished in this way than by all other human transplants, in terms of alleviating human suffering. Paradoxically, establishment of a blood supply to the transplant must be avoided, as it will bring on rejection. The metabolic needs of corneal tissue can be satisfied by simple diffusion of nutrients, supplied at the transplant's periphery, where the recipient's residual avascular corneal tissue is joined to the transplant.

F. Attempts to relieve diabetics of the need for daily insulin injections, and to avoid late vascular complications, have involved transplanting isolated insulin-secreting islets. These are taken from cadaveric pancreases, or from pancreatic tissue in which the noninsulin-secreting components have been obliterated. These procedures are still in an experimental stage, and have not yet found significant clinical application.

H. M. Lee, M.D. Currently, kidney, liver, heart, pancreas and lung have been transplanted with clinical success as an integral organ unit with blood vessels pedicle. Theoretically, any organ with blood vessels pedicle can be transplanted.

Experimentally, intestine has been transplanted in the human without functional success. Other organs such as brain, female reproductive organs and testes have been transplanted experimentally in animals; there are no known human trials so far.

Research involves how to prevent and/or treat the rejection phenomena: how to match better; understanding the rejection mechanism better and more precisely; finding better and more precise ways to prevent and/or treat rejection including newer and better drugs.

Thomas L. Marchioro, M.D. With current surgical techniques virtually any organ of the body can be transplanted. However, there are certain organs which, although they can be transplanted, will not manifest complete function. These are organs in which the function depends upon an intact nerve supply. The most notable of these would be the brain, which has been transplanted in monkeys. In these experiments, the brain has survived but is nonfunctional because its nervous connections had to be severed. Similar problems occur with transplantation of limbs. These problems are not quite so severe with replantation but they still exist. The principle limitation is that of nerve regeneration.

The practical facts as of June 1981 are that kidneys are transplanted with great frequency, hearts and livers with reasonable frequency, bone marrow quite commonly and other organs, such as the pancreas, lung, intestines and various endocrine glands with lesser frequency. The principle problem with those organs that are being transplanted with lesser frequency is failure due to rejection, although technical factors may be important in any given case.

There is extensive research being done in the field of organ transplantation, at various levels. An enormous effort is being expended in the field of immunology trying to understand the basic mechanisms of rejection and their control. Significant advances have been made in our understanding of the immune system and the various subsets of lymphocyte populations. The various interactions of these lymphocytes and their specific role in modulating the immune response has been elucidated in recent years. Further work along this line promises to give us much more control over manipulating the immune response. Similarly, research into human HLA (human leukocyte antigen) inheritance patterns has given considerable insight into the mechanisms of the inheritance of disease as well as the immune response of one individual to another's tissues. Continuing efforts in this direction promise to give us clues as to which combinations of transfers would be most advantageous.

Other research is concerned largely with discovering agents that will permit us to manipulate the immune system without serious toxicity to the patient. Recent efforts in this direction have focused on such manipulations as thoracic duct drainage in which the lymphocytes are depleted from the body, the use of cyclosporin A, an immunosuppressive drug which is quite powerful and promises to replace currently used immunosuppressive agents, and preliminary use of monoclonal antibodies as a means of immunosuppression. Total lymphoid irradiation is another modality of immunosuppression that is undergoing trials. Here, the lymph nodes of the body are irradiated, similar to the techniques used for patients with Hodgkin's disease.

Anthony P. Monaco, M.D. Currently, the human organs that can be transplanted are the kidney, heart, pancreas, bone marrow, skin and cornea. The human lung has also been transplanted on several occasions. Experimentally, almost every organ of the mammalian system has been transplanted in one way or another.

At the present time, the technical aspects of organ transplantation have been more or less solved. Almost any organ can be surgically transplanted. The major problem continues to be the tendency of the body to reject the foreign organ or tissue.

Extensive research is taking place to prevent or subvert the normal immunological response of the body to foreign organs, causing their immunological rejection. This research has taken many forms. There are many new drugs or chemical agents that are constantly being investigated for possible use as immunosuppressive drugs which will prevent immunological rejection. The newest drug is called cyclosporin. Both experimentally, and in early clinical trials, this drug seems to be extremely effective in preventing rejection.

Another major area of research is an attempt to induce a specific type of unresponsiveness or nonreactivity on the part of the organ recipient, so that he would not reject the organ transplant. This specific unreactivity or unresponsiveness, if induced, would prevent the necessity of taking immunosuppressive drugs to prevent the immunological rejection reaction. Since these drugs frequently cause severe side effects or induce a high degree of susceptibility to infections, the investigations into achieving specific unresponsiveness are extremely important. Hopefully, when methods are produced to induce this unresponsiveness, organs will be transplanted without any difficulty and many diseases will be cured by organ replacement.

John S. Najarian, M.D. The list of organs that can be transplanted, in the order of those most frequently used, would be: skin, cornea, kidney, heart, liver, pancreas, bone marrow, lung and small intestine.

As to the second question regarding research: most of the research in organ transplantation is now directed at getting a better match between donor and recipient, to avoid rejection. The studies in matching involve a better definition of serological determinants of genetic markers. This is called HLA typing. More recently, a new method of matching under another gene locus, called DR matching, is being investigated. It seems to be even more predictable of success than the other method. Finally, in living, related organ transplants, another test that can be used is the MLR (mixed lymphocyte reaction). This is a method in which the lymphocyte (white blood cells) are put together in a test tube; the reaction between the donor and the recipient lymphocytes is determined by the degree of radioactive material that is taken up by the lymphocytes during this reaction. With these three methods of matching, a good match between donor and recipient can be achieved, thus allowing us to use smaller doses of immunosuppression.

The next most active area of research in the organ transplant field involves better drugs to suppress the immune response of the recipient. The first immunosuppressive drug to be used was Imuran; the second was Prednisone. Both of these drugs are still used in preventing rejection. In 1967 antilymphocyte globulin (a serum raised in horses to react against the lymphocytes of man) was developed and this also has been added to the immunosuppressive regimen.

The new areas being investigated include a drug called cyclosporin A which seems to be more effective than Imuran, Prednisone and antilymphocyte globulin combined. Prospective randomized trials on that particular drug are now being done.

In addition, a very powerful immunosuppressive modality, total lymphoid irradiation, is currently being investigated. This involves the x-radiation of the lymphoid areas of the body, namely the lymphnodes and the spleen, before transplantation. This technique is quite cumbersome and involves approximately four to six weeks of irradiation to the recipient before transplantation. However, in circumstances where all other immunosuppression has failed, this method appears to be very effective. This would be used in recipients who have rejected at least two previous grafts on standard immunosuppressive therapy.

A better method of preserving organs is another area in research that continues to be pursued. Currently, we can preserve kidneys for seventy-two hours; but most of the other organs, except the cornea and the skin, can only be preserved for approximately eight to twelve hours, and occasionally for twenty-four hours. We are working on techniques that would enable us to freeze tissues and this would give us indefinite storage. The only organ that we now freeze and preserve in this way is bone marrow and this is only being done experimentally.

Finally, another area of research in organ transplantation concerns technical improvements in the specific organ transplant itself. This involves better ways of connecting blood vessels, biliary ducts, etc. This type of surgical alteration and improvement goes on continually.

IS IT POSSIBLE THAT A PLAGUE FROM AN UNUSUAL STRAIN OF SOME DISEASE COULD WIPE OUT A LARGE PROPORTION OF THE UNITED STATES POPULATION?

Francis L. Black, Ph.D. Yes, this is possible, but a key word in this question is "unusual." New germs appear with some frequency but it would be an unusual germ that spread sufficiently easily and was also sufficiently lethal to cause the death of a large proportion of the U.S. population. There is no evidence that any of these new germs have come from any source off the earth; they all seem to have been the result of mutation in, or recombinations between, previously existing germs.

If the new germ were a virus, the only effective way we would have to fight it would be with a specifically designed vaccine; and it has always taken at least a year to prepare a vaccine against a new virus. Bacteria have the ability to swap and collect genes which give them resistance to antibiotics and it is not impossible that one would appear which had acquired resistance to all the antibiotics we have available at present. A larger parasite, perhaps one presently living in some animal species, might acquire the ability to infect man and be responsible for a new plague. These larger organisms can be very difficult to control. Fortunately, however, their complexity makes it more difficult for them to change their genetic constitutions.

The last time a new plague killed a significant proportion of the U.S. population was in 1918–1920, when a new form of influenza killed nearly one out of a hundred Americans. The effect of this epidemic was especially severe because those who died were mostly young adults, in the prime of life and with families to raise. Eventually, nearly everyone was infected. Those who did not die became immune, and the virus disappeared. More recently a new lethal virus, called Rift Valley fever, has appeared in Egypt and killed many people. Also, a new and extremely infectious virus is now causing severe conjunctivitus, but fortunately almost no deaths, in the tropical parts of the world.

One other circumstance, that would combine high infectiousness and lethality in a widely dispersed disease, might occur by deliberate action in warfare. If any of several currently known disease agents could be delivered to a large part of the U.S. population, many would die before we could learn the cause and bring defense measures into effect. Such a germ might be introduced either into the air or into the water supply, but to kill a substantial proportion of the U.S. population it would have to be introduced at many points at approximately the same time. I believe this would be difficult for an enemy to achieve.

Alfred S. Evans, M.D., M.P.H. The great plagues of history that wiped out millions of people have been brought under control, or even eradicated, in the United States and most developed countries. This has been accomplished through improved personal hygiene and standards of living, public sanitation, environmental control, and immunization. These plagues include pneumonic plague (the Black Death), epidemic (louse borne) typhus, cholera, yellow fever and smallpox. In some instances, (e.g., smallpox), it is believed the disease has actually been eradicated through the efforts of the immunization program of the World Health Organization: the last natural cases occurred in Somalia on 26 October 1977 and on 9 December 1979. The Global Commission for the Certification of Smallpox Eradication certified that, indeed, smallpox had been eradicated from the world. Vaccination is now only required in four countries of the world—Kampuchea, Madagascar, Djibouti and Chad. Only six laboratories, working under stringent World Health Organization safety requirements, still hold the virus in their deep freezers.

The other diseases that caused the great epidemics are still around but are usually kept under control by eternal vigilance and surveillance. However, the threat is still there. For example, a new strain of cholera, the El Tor strain, spread out from Borneo in 1961 to involve thousands in Asia, Africa and some parts of Europe. About eleven cases have even occurred in Louisiana, spread by improperly steamed oysters harvested from infected waters; no epidemic has occurred. The pneumonic plague bacillus exists in rodents in the United States' West and Southwest. Malaria has been introduced into this country by Vietnam veterans and refugees but good mosquito control and active surveillance of cases have limited its spread. Similarly, yellow fever, another mosquito-borne disease, has reemerged in South America and Africa and has the potential of spreading here, given inadequate mosquito control. There is an effective vaccination available.

In the United States, these epidemic diseases are under good control. Influenza remains the last great unconquered and uncontrolled plague. Every ten years or so, a new strain emerges. Often, this appears first in China and then spreads to involve the U.S. and the world in great pandemics like the 1957 and 1968 outbreaks. (A pandemic is defined as a worldwide epidemic.) Fortunately, the death rates of these more recent outbreaks have never approached that of the 1918 pandemic, but the threat of such severe outbreaks exists; witness the swine flu affair of 1976.

Can any of these diseases arise again in the U.S. as our population becomes susceptible again or a new variant arises, producing widespread disease and mortality? The answer is "probably not," under *natural* conditions of spread and if our excellent surveillance and control systems—the National Center for Disease Control in Atlanta and various state health departments—are efficiently working and properly funded. But, under *unnatural* conditions of transmission—i.e., intentional spread or biologic warfare—we are at risk to widespread infection and disease from those infections to which we have no immunity. This lack of immunity could result from discontinuance of our vaccination programs (smallpox), or of our environmental control measures. Another possibility is the effective introduction and deliberate spread of diseases, like Lassa fever or Marburg fevers from Africa; diseases previously unknown in the United States. Even man-made virulent mutants or recombinants of certain organisms could be prepared. Microbiological forms released into the air by airplanes or organisms or toxins seeded in the water supply of major cities could produce disability and death in most of the exposed population. Thus it is highly important that eternal vigilance and surveillance be maintained against natural spread, and that national and international agreements against biological, chemical and nuclear warfare be maintained and strongly enforced.

M. Finland, M.D.   My answer to this question, whether it is possible for a "new plague" to wipe out large numbers of our population, can be summed up as follows: possible—yes; probable—no.

John P. Fox.   Natural occurrence of "a plague from an unusual strain of some disease that could wipe out a large proportion of the U.S. population" is an extremely remote possibility. Such "Andromeda" strains would not arise *de novo* but by mutation of some existing agent.

The one agent known to be capable of such mutation is type A influenza virus and historically the 1918–1919 pandemic of "Spanish" influenza is an example of the phenomenon in question. Indeed, the 1976 swine flu affair illustrates the great concern that this possibility arouses. (The 1918–19 pandemic is believed to have been caused by a type A "swine" influenza virus.) While pandemics due to new type A influenza viruses do occur with some regularity, they are not associated with the high mortality seen in 1918–19. The latter is believed to have been due largely to complicating bacterial pneumonias which, at the present time, can be treated successfully with antibiotics.

The other possibility, based on historical precedent, is that agents, existing in lower vertebrates, will adapt to other lifecycles, including man's. Particular examples: the viruses of equine encephalomyelitis (eastern, western and St. Louis) which emerged in the United States in the 1930s. The most widespread of these, the St. Louis virus, remains a significant health problem but never threatened to "wipe out a large proportion of the population."

Probably the more realistic concern relates to unnatural occurrence—

that is, biologic warfare. Fortunately, there are few, if any, serious candidate agents for such use against man. (Anthrax is one rather tenuous possibility.)

Dr. Karl Maramorosch. It is unlikely that diseases caused by unusual strains of *bacteria* or *rickettsiae*, would wipe out many people, because there are adequate amounts of broad spectrum antibiotics that could prevent death and contain an epidemic. When it comes to *viruses*, the answer is YES!

A new, virulent strain of influenza could evolve. This could occur by virus hybridization in nature in strains carried by birds. Dense populations of birds with flu viruses accumulate in summer in the Arctic and return to temperate and tropical areas of the western and eastern hemispheres. A new strain could become adapted from birds to humans in densely populated areas (Hong Kong, Southeast Asia, China) and spread all over the world (Asian flu's hypothetical origin). Fortunately we have the know-how to attenuate influenza virus and to manufacture a vaccine for a new strain, but this would require several months and in the meantime people would not be protected.

There are several exotic viruses that are much more dangerous and that, if introduced accidentally or deliberately, actually *could* wipe out numerous people. No cure or preventive vaccine is known for such viruses as Lassa, Marburg or Eboli. (Some of these diseases exist in rodents, others in as yet unknown reservoirs.) They could be brought to the United States, accidentally, by travelers from the parts of Africa where they occur.

DIET AND NUTRITION

*F*OR MOST OF US, food is fun. It may be succulent seafood fresh from the water, steaming spaghetti topped with savory tomato sauce and grated cheese, bread still warm from the oven or simply ripe fruit served with icy sherbet. At worst, food just fills our stomachs. At best, it is one of life's great pleasures.

But *nutrition* is another thing. Nutrition tends to be associated with less tempting tidbits, such as lima beans and liver, vitamin pills and wheat germ. We may know that seafood, well-made pasta with cheese, whole-wheat bread and fresh fruit are all nutritious. We may even know that studies in nutrition, such as the Senate's Select Committee on Nutrition and Human Needs report in 1976, advise that Americans turn from the traditional diet of meat, potatoes and apple pie to meals with more poultry and fish, vegetarian entrées, whole-grain breads and fresh fruit and vegetables. What we tend to forget is that good food and good nutrition often are one and the same thing.

The price of this forgetfulness runs high. People have always suffered from hunger, especially in underdeveloped countries. Even in the United States, a country known for its high food consumption, many people are undernourished, particularly those with low incomes and special nutritional needs, such as young children, pregnant women and the elderly. Yet the hungry are only part of the nation's food problem. Instead of the classic malnutrition caused by too little food, much of the malnutrition in America today stems from too much poor-quality food. Americans may grow fat on soft drinks, hamburgers and ice cream, but they will miss out on vital nutrients as they are putting on unwanted pounds.

A look around the typical supermarket illustrates some of the food-related problems Americans face. First, there are the shoppers themselves, many of whom are overweight. Some experts estimate that as much as 30 percent of the American population is overweight, and the percentages run even higher for those over sixty-five years of age.

Clues to some of the causes of this weight problem can be found in the thousands of items neatly and appealingly displayed on supermarket shelves. Whole rows of candy and snacks lure hungry shoppers. Cooks in a hurry can take their pick from enticing selections of prepared frozen and canned entrées, highly processed baked goods, and imitation foods such as "cheese food" made with little or no dairy products and "fruit-flavored" drinks made without fruits. Not all convenience and processed foods are nutritionally deficient, however, some foods are nutritionally *enhanced* by the manufacturers. But often highly processed foods gain commercial value while losing nutritive value, so consumers end up eating so-called empty calories.

Bread, the staff of life, offers a prime example of the problems caused by overprocessing. For centuries, people in Western countries depended on bread as a staple of their diets. White bread was prized for its delicacy, but only the wealthy could afford it. The rest of the people had to be content with dark or whole-grain breads. In the late 1800s, however, technological advances in the milling of flour made it possible to extract the germ of the wheat from the flour economically, thus producing white flour that was cheap enough for the masses. Millers found that white flour kept longer than whole wheat, and people preferred the more prestigious white bread, so production shifted away from the traditional whole-grain breads. Later, however, nutritionists found that this "advance" was actually a nutritional setback. The poor in particular suffered because the white bread they depended upon offered them less iron, less vitamin B_1 and less of other vital nutrients than the whole-grain breads they had traditionally eaten.

In recent years, there has been a move back to whole-grain flours and other foods that retain their natural nutritional values. The 1976 senate report advocated further changes. "We find that at the same time a significant minority at home and perhaps a majority overseas are going hungry, many Americans are consuming too many calories. . . . Obesity is a major health problem, and the food industry, stimulating consumption, produces foods with 'empty' calories and artificially differentiated foods, relying for their appeal on salt, fat, sugar and artificial colorings and flavorings."

The following section on diet and nutrition deals with questions about the American diet—present and future—and about the nutritional benefits of the foods we eat. The answers concern not only those who love good food, but everyone who wants to enjoy good health.

CONTRIBUTORS

Jack Bowman, President, Lederle Laboratories, Wayne, New Jersey

Edward S. Brady, M.S., Emeritus Professor of Pharmacy, University of Southern California, Los Angeles, California

George A. Bray, M.D., Professor of Medicine, University of Southern California, Los Angeles, California

Dr. D. H. Carley, Professor of Agricultural Economics, University of Georgia, Athens, Georgia

Julia Child, food expert, chef, author, television personality

T. S. Danowski, M.D., Clinical Professor of Medicine, University of Pittsburgh Shadyside Hospital, Pittsburgh, Pennsylvania

Sybil Ferguson, Founder, Diet Center, Inc.

Dr. Hans Fisher, Professor and Chairman, Department of Nutrition, Rutgers, the State University, New Brunswick, New Jersey

Carlton Fredericks, Ph.D., lecturer, consultant and media commentator on nutrition

Dr. Robert W. Hammel, Professor of Pharmacy Administration, University of Wisconsin, Madison, Wisconsin

Victor Herbert, M.D., J.D., Chief, Hematology and Nutrition Laboratory, Veterans Administration Medical Center, Bronx, New York; Professor of Medicine, State University of New York Downstate Medical Center, Brooklyn, New York

Richard A. Kunin, M.D., Nutrition-oriented physician and psychiatrist; President, Orthomolecular Medical Society; author of *Mega-Nutrition*

Peter G. Lindner, M.D., Director, The Lindner Clinic, South Gate, California; Chairman of the Board, The American Society of Bariatric Physicians

Dr. Jean Mayer, President, Tufts University, Medford, Massachusetts; former Professor of Nutrition at Harvard University, Cambridge, Massachusetts

Margaret McWilliams, Ph.D., R.D., Professor of Food and Nutrition, California State University, Los Angeles, California

Nathan Pritikin, nutritional scientist and author

Dr. Carol I. Waslien, Executive Officer, League for International Food Education

WHAT IS THE BEST DIET PLAN FOR HEALTHY PEOPLE OF PROPER WEIGHT? FOR HEALTHY BUT OVERWEIGHT PEOPLE?

George A. Bray, M.D. The best diet for healthy people who do not have a problem with weight can be summed up under three phrases: *balanced diet; moderation of intake for all foods; variety in the diet*. These basic ideas have been spelled out in more detail by the Dietary Guidelines for Americans entitled "Nutrition and Your Health" and issued jointly by the Department of Agriculture, and the Department of Health, Education and Welfare (Health and Human Services). The seven principles they suggest, are:

1. Eat a variety of foods.
2. Maintain ideal weight.
3. Avoid too much fat, saturated fat and cholesterol.
4. Eat food with adequate starch and fiber.
5. Avoid too much sugar.
6. Avoid too much salt.
7. "If you drink alcohol, do so in moderation."

If you are overweight, and it is appropriate to lose weight, you should consult with your physician first to make sure that the approach you want to use is appropriate for you. The basic principles for weight loss are simple, but putting them into practice is often difficult. Basically, to lose weight you have to reverse your energy balance. That is, you have to take in fewer calories, or burn more calories, than you did before. A number of methods have been suggested to accomplish this, including such approaches as: nutritional education, behavioral changes, increasing energy expenditure and amount of exercise taken, and special purpose diets. During the past few years, I have evaluated a number of different programs to help people lose weight and believe that the most effective ones bring together elements from all of these approaches.

T.S. Danowski, M.D. The logical method of coping with obesity, and especially in children, is to avoid it entirely. In other words, the most effective therapy is prevention. The danger signal is a body weight just barely above normal. At that point, treatment should be most intense because there is a maximum likelihood of success: by watching the intake of carbohydrate, fat and protein; and by converting excess calories to work and heat.

The goal is lifelong normal weight, achieved by avoiding any significant weight gain. For most people this means staying within +20 percent of the so-called ideal weight for their height at age twenty-five. This precept is based on the fact that, for most people, exceeding the +20 percent (by reaching +35 percent to +50 percent above the ideal) presages a lifetime of obesity interrupted by only transient weight losses.

Prevention or correction of excess weight should be achieved by eating less of all that makes up a normal American diet, and by increasing physical activity on a daily basis. It should not be attempted through intermittent diet plans.

Sybil Ferguson. Diet plans for healthy individuals at proper weight and people who are healthy but overweight are basically the same.

The best diet plan for every person is a nutritionally balanced diet that can be followed for the rest of a person's life. Top nutrition cannot be "hit and miss" if people are to function at peak efficiency and maintain lifelong health.

Obesity is a national concern, with more than 80 million frustrated, overweight Americans counting calories, eating poorly, skipping meals, feeling moody, deprived and yet constantly hungry. These people are looking for immediate, miraculous results. Yet they invariably return to their old eating habits. As a result, over 200 million dollars are spent, annually, on diet foods, pills and gadgets with only 2 percent of these dieters keeping their weight off.

I have been fifty pounds overweight, and I have tried every diet in existence. I lost the weight numerous times but always gained it back until I put my nutrition knowledge to work and discovered the secrets of permanent weight control.

For lifelong results, stop counting calories and start counting the life sustaining nutrients: proteins, fats, carbohydrates and water. In my search for permanent weight loss, I found it was imperative to eat a balance of nutritious foods, not only to lose unwanted pounds but also to maintain ideal weight. Nutritious foods actually help keep you thin. Lean meats, fresh fruits and vegetables and whole-grain foods are not fattening. Refined carbohydrates (white sugar and flour), saturated fats, too much salt, caffeinated beverages, alcohol and drugs are the culprits—not only in creating obesity, but also in destroying the health of Americans.

American consumption of foods rich in fiber, such as fresh fruits, vegetables and whole grains, has dropped considerably (40 percent) in the last fifty years. These fibrous foods play a significant role in satisfying hunger and controlling weight. These foods require more chewing and more saliva than most foods, and that extra chewing sends a signal to the brain that "the body is satisfied." Chewing bulky foods not only gives more of a feeling of being full and satisfied, but it also helps alleviate indigestion.

Refined sugars (also caffeine) play havoc with the system, sending the blood sugar skyrocketing, then dropping it just as quickly, resulting in fluctuating blood sugar. When blood sugar is low, it leaves a person hungry, irritable, moody and depressed. Refined foods (white sugars, flours and processed foods), again, require almost no chewing, have no "staying power" (the "I'm satisfied" feeling), quickly leave the stomach and provide little nutrition. So a continuous diet of these foods keeps a person on a vicious eating cycle. The natural sugars in fruits and vegetables work in just the opposite way, because they are encased in rich fibers. As a result, they are digested more slowly and become excellent sources of energy—the blood sugar climbs steadily and stays constant. A stable blood sugar is the key to maintaining weight goal and feeling great!

Fibrous foods also reduce calorie-absorption-efficiency in the small intestine. Thus, only about 92 percent of the calories in high-fiber foods are available, compared to 97 percent in refined foods. The average American woman could lose ten pounds a year (men, eighteen pounds a year) just by avoiding refined foods and by eating the same amount of calories of foods rich in fiber.

To balance nutritional intake, fat consumption should not exceed 30 percent of your daily food allowance. However, fat is necessary in the diet, because it adds satiety value to a meal, helps keep your skin soft and supple and acts as a carrier for fat-soluble vitamins A, D, E and K.

Water is the most important nutrient we consume. Some experts recommend that dieters drink eight, eight-ounce glasses every day. Water carries nutrients to the cells, alleviates premature wrinkling, and aids in eliminating waste from the body.

Since most Americans have a constant struggle with fluctuating weight, here are some simple suggestions to keep your weight and health intact:

1. Lose unwanted pounds and maintain ideal weight by eating a balance of nutritious foods every day.
2. Be aware of calories; but count nutrients, making certain that a balance of proteins, fats and carbohydrates are eaten. Choose foods in each of these categories that are rich in vitamins, minerals and fiber. Proper nutrients alleviate craving for more.
3. A healthy diet should consist of 10 to 14 percent protein—forty-six grams, daily, for women; fifty-five grams for men. (Two 3½-ounce servings of meat equal forty-nine grams). Be aware that when too much protein is eaten, (a ten-ounce steak, for instance) only three to four ounces are utilized as protein. Some of the additional is utilized as nitrogen; the rest is stored as fat.
4. Over half of your diet (55 to 61 percent) should consist of natural carbohydrates and "naturally occurring sugars" (fruits, vegetables and whole grains). America's diet of refined and processed foods is the culprit in Americans being habitually constipated and is a suspect in contributing to many degenerative diseases, including cancer of the colon, which alone kills over 50,000 Americans annually.
5. Reduce consumption of fat in the diet. Your diet should have no more than fifty to sixty grams of fat a day. For health reasons, saturated fats (fats in meats, eggs, butter, etc.) should be reduced to about fifteen to twenty grams; and unsaturated and poly-unsaturated fats (mainly peanut, corn, safflower, and cottonseed oils) should constitute about thirty-five to forty grams a day. For

example, in a given day, the following foods total fifty-six grams of fat: two large eggs, one chicken breast, two tablespoons of oil, two teaspoons of butter, two cups low-fat milk, three fruits, two slices of bread. (The tiny amounts of fat in vegetables are insignificant.)

6. Avoid excessive food additives, such as salt, seasonings, chemicals and preservatives. Too much salt is a suspect in contributing to hypertension, strokes and heart disease. (Be aware that one-fourth teaspoon of salt will cause a dieter to retain one-half pound of water.) Chemical food additives are not food and are foreign substances to the body. Some additives are noted carcinogens (cancer-causing agents) and others (especially artificial colors) create hypertension in children as well as adults.

7. Drink eight, eight-ounce glasses of water every day. Reduce intake of caffeinated beverages and alcohol. Alcohol causes an increase in body weight and depending on the strictness of the diet and the amount of alcohol consumed, can prevent weight loss for up to three days. Caffeine creates a "yo-yo" syndrome with the blood sugar.

As you can see, a nutritionally balanced diet is imperative for permanent weight control and total health; and there are no nutritional short-cuts. No fads, gimmicks, pills or shots will help change the poor eating habits acquired by most people. Americans must modify their eating behavior by returning to basics and eating foods in their natural state—foods that provide nutritional fuel for optimum health. These basic principles, if applied, create stamina, a sense of well-being, and enable each person to really "look and feel like a million."

Peter G. Lindner, M.D. There is obviously no universal diet suited for peoples of all ages, different cultural and ethnic backgrounds, and differing levels of activity. Nevertheless, one can construct a model based on the Recommended Daily Allowances (RDA) which, themselves, are based on the best available nutritional knowledge at any point in time. The RDA are updated every five years and thus represent the most useful, concise and sound nutrition information, based on current research in the science of nutrition. They are published by the Food and Nutrition Board, National Academy of Sciences-National Research Council, in booklet form, and I strongly urge anyone concerned about a proper diet plan to obtain a copy. The most current revision is the ninth edition, 1980.

Based on these RDA, the diet should be adequate in calories to support normal weight and contain the recommended amounts of protein, carbohydrate and fat (as listed in the RDA for differing ages, sex, pregnancy, lactation, etc.). It should also contain the other twenty-eight micronutrients (vitamins and minerals) that are considered adequate and safe daily dietary intakes, and that contribute to the maintenance of good nutrition for practically all healthy people in the United States. Specific details on all this are accurately described in the publication mentioned above.

As a general guideline, it is best to choose from a large variety of foods. This assures a better chance of getting adequate nutrients. The amount of fat in the diet should also be kept at or below recommended levels.

For overweight healthy people, the same basic nutritional rules apply, but the *caloric* intake should be deficient. In this case, the extra calories to support life will have to come from the energy that has been stored, mainly in the form of fat. While the weight loss is occurring the individual should, however, maintain normal nutrition with respect to all the other nutrients as listed in the RDA.

It should also be pointed out that our word diet comes from the Greek word *diaita* which refers to a "manner of living." Thus, the best diet plan involves more than just the foods one eats. It literally includes a way of life. Adequate activity and moderation in food intake are general guidelines for a good lifestyle.

Eating can provide a number of secondary gains. (Often one eats for reasons other than hunger.) Therefore, a good diet plan includes finding alternate ways to satisfy the needs formerly assuaged by eating. This involves taking some positive steps to become interested in many of the other rewards, satisfactions, and pleasures that life offers.

Margaret McWilliams, Ph.D., R.D. The Basic Four Food Plan is the best diet guide for people of proper weight, and also for overweight people. Those who are overweight need to select the low fat or nonfat alternatives in the various food categories to reduce their caloric intake. They should also avoid consumption of servings larger than those suggested in the plan. Additionally, they need to be aware of the food they are eating so that excessive food is not eaten unintentionally. For healthy persons, a regular program of exercise and physical activity helps maintain health and proper weight. This is true whether a person is of proper weight, or is overweight.

The elements of the Basic Four Food Plan are:

> Milk and dairy products—two or more servings (eight ounces each) daily for adults and up to four servings for children and teenagers
>
> Meat and meat substitutes—two or more three-ounce servings daily, with emphasis being given to the consumption of chicken, turkey, fish and also legumes
>
> Fruits and vegetables—a total of four or more servings (one-half cup each) to be distributed as follows:

one citrus or other good source of vitamin C, one dark
green leafy or yellow vegetable on alternate days to provide
a source of vitamin A, two or three additional servings of
fruits or vegetables to total four servings in this group
Breads and cereals—four or more slices or servings daily (emphasis
should be on whole grain and enriched products)

For help in weight control and generally healthful eating, the regular
inclusion of soups and use of nonfat milk are recommended.

Nathan Pritikin. The best diet plan for healthy people is one consisting
mainly of whole grains and whole-grain products, vegetables, fruits and
dried beans and peas. These foods should be unprocessed or only lightly
processed, and should be prepared with herbs and spices instead of fats,
oils, sweeteners and salt. Such a diet is high in bulk and low in calories,
and is very similar to the diet eaten by many people in undeveloped
areas of the world where degenerative diseases—heart disease, diabetes,
hypertension and breast, prostrate, and colon cancers—are rare. This
diet contains only 1/5 the fat and 1/10 the cholesterol of the average
American diet.

For overweight people, the diet prescribed above will result in a
moderate rate of weight loss and will also prevent their regaining
weight after the ideal weight is attained. People who wish to lose weight
more rapidly can temporarily limit calories even more by restricting the
amount of grains and dried beans and peas in the diet while emphasizing
salads, soups and vegetarian entrées.

WHICH ARE THE MOST NUTRITIOUS FOODS (PER SERVING) AND WHICH ARE THE LEAST NUTRITIOUS?

Dr. Hans Fisher. Unfortunately, there is no single food that provides
all nutrients at just the right levels required by our bodies. Foods that
come close, milk and eggs, contain relatively high amounts of cholesterol
and saturated fat which can be harmful to some people during certain
stages of the life cycle. The most nutritious foods, therefore, are a
combination of fresh fruit, vegetables, whole-grain cereals, lean meats,
poultry and fish. All of the above to be eaten in variety and moderation.

The least nutritious foods are those foods that are too rich in saturated
fat and cholesterol, such as very fatty cuts of meat, and also, foods that
are exceedingly high in added sugar. The latter create the danger that
the person eating them will be satiated before ingesting a balanced diet.

Richard A. Kunin, M.D. The single most nutritious food is sardines,
eaten whole. For vegetarians, combined servings of whole grains with

beans or peas offer a complete spectrum of nutrients. Indeed, this is the staple diet for most humans on the planet.

The least nutritious food is—lettuce.

Peter G. Lindner, M.D. I presume that this question refers to nutrients other than calories. By definition, calories are nutritious, especially in an underweight person. Thus, all foods have nutritious value. If one eliminates the need for extra calories, since the average American ordinarily gets an adequate amount, and often an excessive amount, then the most nutritious serving would be one that contains the most nutrients per calories in a serving. The least nutritious food would contain only calories and very little other nutrients.

Generally, foods that are low in fat content are more nutritious, since fat contains more calories per unit than the other three food categories (carbohydrates, proteins, alcohol). However, alcohol, with the exception of some wines, also contains mostly calories and little else. It contains slightly less energy than fat (seven calories per gram versus nine calories per gram for fat). Sugar and highly refined carbohydrate products also offer few nutrients other than calories. Of course, some of these products have been enriched artificially to make up for this deficiency.

Using the above definition of nutritious (i.e., eliminating calories from that definition), one could classify lean meat, fish or fowl, fresh fruits and vegetables and milk as the most nutritious foods. Sweets, candy, some highly refined flour products, soft drinks and alcohol would thus be included in the least nutritious group.

It is important to recognize that food serves many functions in our society other than satisfying nutritional needs. Thus, it is not necessarily recommended that one limit oneself only to nutritious foods, and never ingest nonnutritious ones. The deprivation one feels from prolonged periods of such self-imposed limitations, especially in our culture where we are surrounded by an abundant and extremely palatable food environment, is bound to lead to an overreaction at some point in time. Usually, this results in a binge on nonnutritious foods. Therefore, the diet should emphasize the nutritious group, and be rounded out with limited and reasonable amounts of "least nutritious" foods to maintain the emotional health of the individual. The total concept of good health includes mental as well as physical health. The diet should allow for an optimal level of both.

Dr. Jean Mayer. The least nutritious foods are those that provide calories but that have no other nutritional value: saturated fats (polyunsaturated fats supply the essential fatty acids), sugar and alcohol.

It is more difficult to designate the most nutritious foods because the key to a good diet is variety. No one food supplies all the forty-odd essential nutrients in the right amounts needed by the human body for growth and maintenance.

A nutritious diet provides sufficient (but not too many) calories in menus made up of fresh or lightly processed foods: leafy green and deep yellow vegetables; citrus fruits, tomatoes, raw cabbage, salad greens, and other sources of vitamin C; potatoes and other vegetables and fruits; milk and milk products; meat, poultry, fish, eggs, dried beans and peas; whole-grain or enriched breads, flours, and pastas and cereal grains, like rice and buckwheat; and butter and fortified polyunsaturated margarine.

Margaret McWilliams, Ph.D., R.D. The most nutritious foods are: nonfat milk, milk-based soups, fish, poultry, eggs, vegetables (including potatoes), most fruits, and whole-grain breads and cereals (without high caloric additions).

The least nutritious foods are soft drinks, virtually all candies and alcoholic beverages.

Nathan Pritikin. It is impossible to answer this question in an absolute manner. To do so would necessitate assigning arbitrary values to the various nutrients—protein, vitamins, minerals, fiber, etc. Does "nutritious" mean only that a food is a rich source of *certain* nutrients? If so, which ones? Is cantaloupe, for example, nutritious because it is a rich source of vitamins A and C, or is it nonnutritious because it contains virtually no protein? Does milk deserve a high rating because it contains protein and calcium, or a low rating because it contains no vitamin C, iron, or fiber? Furthermore, is a food nutritious if it contains large amounts of many nutrients but also contains large amounts of cholesterol, the main constituent of arterial plaques that cut off the blood supply to the heart?

In reality, every nutrient has an important role to play, and poor health will result if a diet is deficient in any of the nutrients. We are on the wrong track when we lose sight of the principles of variety and balance in our diets. There is no "superfood" that contains all the nutrients we need. Eating a wide variety of fruits, vegetables, and whole grains will provide us with the necessary nutrients in the proper amounts. Simple as these foods are, they are our "superfoods."

IS THERE PROOF THAT VITAMIN PILLS ARE EFFECTIVE?

Jack Bowman. There is scientific and medical evidence that the use of supplementary vitamins is nutritionally and medically useful where diets are inadequate or in cases of certain illnesses.

Along with proteins, fats, carbohydrates and minerals, vitamins are needed in the body's process of converting food into energy and in promoting the growth and maintenance of body tissues. They participate in the formation of blood cells, hormones, nervous system chemicals and genetic materials. Without vitamins, chemical processes essential to life could not occur.

Because the body cannot make vitamins in the amounts necessary for adequate nutrition, they must be obtained from a variety of foods that, together, make up a sound diet. In spite of the abundance and variety of foods available, many Americans do not eat well-balanced diets according to studies by several government agencies.

Inadequate nutrition can decrease a patient's ability to combat illness or injury. Since an increased requirement for vitamins occurs under a variety of conditions, nutritional deficiencies can develop on diets that had previously been adequate. As examples: restrictive dieting, excessive alcohol consumption, excessive physical stress such as pregnancy and nursing, and certain disease conditions. Infants and children may require vitamin supplementation due to growth patterns, and some elderly people may need them due to reduced absorption of the B-complex vitamins and the tendency to eat less nutritious food.

While appropriate vitamin supplementation has proven effective in handling conditions like those mentioned above, it is important to recognize that overdosage with certain vitamins, such as vitamins A and D, can be harmful.

Edward S. Brady, M.S. Science has proved, beyond any doubt, that vitamins are effective in the prevention and cure of many disease states that are caused by vitamin deficiencies. Some of these diseases and the specific vitamins involved are: scurvy (vitamin C), rickets (vitamin D), pellagra (niacin), beriberi (vitamin B_1), and pernicious anemia (vitamin B_{12}).

However, vitamins are not effective in many conditions for which they are popularly recommended and used. Examples are: colds (vitamin C), failing sex drive (vitamin E), graying hair (Paba), failing eyesight (vitamin A). While multi-vitamin pills are used on a daily basis by millions, there is no evidence that they are needed. Daily supplementation of the diet with a single vitamin is probably even less rational. As long as the many myths about vitamins persist and are believed, it is likely that most vitamin pills will not be effective for the treatment of the self-diagnosed conditions for which they are self-prescribed.

Carlton Fredericks, Ph.D. Studies that I conducted for a Ph.D. dissertation revealed a significant difference in the adequacy of the vitamin intakes of my students, as compared with those of a demographically-equated control group. That difference, which was accompanied by a significantly higher level of health in the experimental group, was not due to their more careful selection of foods, which they did exhibit, but was clearly attributable to their more general and competent use of vitamins as dietary insurance.

Published papers in reputable journals have verified both the prophylactic and the therapeutic effectiveness of vitamin (and mineral) supplements. Therapeutic responses have been reported in such indications as autism, schizophrenia, mental retardation (including Down's syndrome), arthritis, myopia, types of cancer, types of dermatitis, vitreous floaters, a type of senile dementia, myoneuropathies, infertility, allergies and innumerable other disorders. My own observations indicate that uterine fibroid tumors, cystic breast disease and the disturbances common in the menstrual cycle of American women yield to dietary procedures as simple as the use of supplements of the vitamin B complex.

Both dietary surveys and biochemical examinations have confirmed the presence of multiple vitamin deficiencies in many segments of the American population. Assuming normal absorption and utilization of vitamin supplements, it is obvious that routine supplementing of the American diet would provide millions of Americans with an adequacy of vitamin intake that they are not now achieving.

I find it illogical to question the effectiveness and the usefulness of vitamin supplements, while not addressing the deficits of vitamins created by American dietary habits and modern food technology. One need only consider that the refined carbohydrates that supply 50 percent of the calories in the average American diet have suffered processing losses of pyridoxine, selenium, choline, inositol, fiber, and other important substances that are frequently employed by medical nutritionists in the prevention and the treatment of numerous disorders that tax our medical and hospital resources. Is it really logical to examine the effectiveness of restoring these factors—by whatever means—to our nutrition?

Dr. Robert W. Hammel. Vitamins are organic substances that are provided in small quantities in the diet. They are essential for good health and growth. People who consume smaller amounts of vitamins than are needed to maintain essential body functions develop deficiency diseases such as night blindness, beriberi, scurvy, rickets or pellagra. Early proof of the effectiveness of ascorbic acid, or water soluble vitamin C, is attributed to Lind, a physician in the British Royal Navy. In 1747, he conducted a clinical trial on patients suffering from scurvy. Six groups of patients received different prescribed regimens, one of which was oranges and lemons. Those who received the citrus fruits, rich in ascorbic acid, recovered rapidly.

Later studies by others have demonstrated the need for what we now call the water soluble vitamin B complex: thiamine, riboflavin, nicotinic acid, pyridoxine, pantothenic acid, biotin, folic acid, cycanocobalamin, choline and inositol. The need for the fat soluble vitamins A, D and K has also been proven. While fat soluble vitamin E may facilitate the absorption, storage and utilization of vitamin A, its necessity for man has not been proven. Many signs and symptoms of vitamin E deficiency seen in animals seem to resemble disease states in humans. However, there is little evidence that vitamin E is of nutritional significance in man or is of any value in human therapy.

Some vitamins are produced in our bodies while others are provided in an adequate amount by a well-balanced diet. Nevertheless, vitamin deficiencies may be caused by such factors as unbalanced diets, reducing diets, alcoholism, prolonged diarrhea, diseases of the liver and biliary tract, pernicious anemia, or increased tissue requirements due to such items as stress, injury, or the use of certain drugs such as oral contraceptives.

However, taking excessive quantities, especially of fat soluble vitamins, may be harmful and should be avoided. Before taking a single vitamin, such as vitamin A, or a multiple vitamin, one should consult one's physician or pharmacist. They are familiar with the health factors associated with the need to supplement the diet with one or more vitamins, as well as with the RDA of the essential vitamins. The RDA were recently updated by the Food and Nutrition Board of the National Research Council.

Some health claims for vitamins have not been proven. For example, large scale tests using vitamin C, even in high daily doses, did not show it to be effective either in treating or in preventing the common cold. Additionally, there is no evidence to support the superiority of so-called natural vitamins. An example: ascorbic acid, whether it is extracted from rose hips or synthesized in the laboratory, has the same nutritional and therapeutic value.

Victor Herbert, M.D., J.D. The only proof of effectiveness of vitamin pills sold directly to the public is in the treatment of vitamin B_{12} deficiency. This deficiency is rarely present in the purchasers of such pills. The public has been led to believe that vitamin pills provide "nutritional insurance." In fact, the scientifically sound way to provide "nutritional insurance" is to be sure that when one looks back at the end of the week, one has had the equivalent of four portions of food each day from the grain groups, four from the fruit and vegetable and fruit juice group (including at least one fresh and uncooked), two from the meat group (which includes fish and poultry), and two from the milk group (which includes cheese, yogurt and ice cream). Such a diet provides all the needed vitamins in adequate quantity to sustain normal health. When we measure the tissue levels of vitamins in people on such diets, regardless of how much they smoke or how much stress they are under, they are normal.

WHAT KINDS OF FOODS WILL WE BE EATING IN THE FUTURE?

George A. Bray, M.D. The answer to this question—what kinds of foods will we be eating in the future?—depends in part on how far into the future you want to look. During the coming decade several current trends are likely to continue. First; as the number of working women continues to rise there will be a continuing growth in processed foods and complete packaged meals, and a tendency to eat outside of the home more often. A second trend that will run counter to the first, and that may well be important, is the desire to improve the nutritional quality of the average diet by obtaining more fresh fruits and vegetables, and more grains and cereals. Meat consumption, always a mark of affluence, may well be modified as the price of meat increases.

In the somewhat more distant future, food patterns are likely to be influenced by economic patterns and world population. As the number of people in the world increases, the price of food will rise more rapidly because the extra amounts of land available for extra food production will be marginal. These rising costs for foods, particularly meat which requires a large consumption of grain, may increase the move toward an increase in use of foods that have been less intensely processed.

Dr. Dale H. Carley. The kinds of foods that we will be eating in the future will not be a whole lot different than what we currently are eating. However, the form of the foods may change substantially. The emphasis will be on foods with long shelf life, easily prepared in the home, highly nutritious, not very bulky, and energy efficient. For example, milk may be ultra high temperature processed for long shelf life without refrigeration, and may be marketed with much of the water removed to lower transportation costs.

The emphasis will be on whole-meal packages that can be easily prepared in the home. There also may be a general emphasis on reducing water content because of energy costs for transportation. The housewife will add water; the meal can then be placed in the microwave for short time preparation.

Emphasis will continue on diet-type meals that are highly nutritious. What is lacking in the natural food will be added. The housewife will buy meats in the exact cuts that she desires: chicken will be sold by pieces; beef and pork will be cut to serving sizes.

There may be more foods sold in the form of flakes, chips, powders, and other forms that are storable but tasty when prepared. Fresh fruits and vegetables will become nonexistent except as specialty foods.

Julia Child. In the future, convenience foods will continue, of course. I have no idea what form they will take because I am concerned with fresh raw produce which, I think, will continue to improve. There is so much interest now in good food and good cooking among a growing number of people in this country, that public demand will increasingly force an upgrading in quality all along the line.

We have already made great strides in growing techniques, marketing, and other aspects of getting the raw materials from the field to the kitchen. I see no reason why this encouraging trend will not continue.

Furthermore, once the public gets used to good food, it is not going to accept inferior substitutes. I hope I am right in predicting a bright gastronomical future.

Dr. Hans Fisher. Food-eating habits are primarily determined by odor and taste perception, and such habits are difficult to change or break. Therefore, in my estimation of the future, we will be eating a modification of the same types of foods we are eating now. The modifications will develop in two directions: one will be in the direction that lends itself to quick and easy preparation in fast-food outlets; the other will be in the direction of less processing and a return to the more natural state in which the fruits, vegetables and cereals are normally harvested.

The food industry will respond to increased nutrition-consciousness on the part of the public by adjusting to the demand for leaving in the nutrients that are a natural part of the food. This involves reducing the processing conditions that remove nutrients—and then necessitate adding them back in the form of supplements at a later stage. At the same time, our rushed society will increasingly eat foods from fast-food chains, and will, most likely, acquire specific taste requirements for these foods, regardless of their nutritional quality. In time, these fast foods will also be modified to maximize their nutritional content.

Dr. Jean Mayer. It would be pleasant to be able to say that we will be eating more fresh, farm-grown foods in the future. However, it is likely that the American diet will contain as many, if not more, processed foods. It is also likely that more attention will be paid to their nutritional value and to their effects on health maintenance.

Entirely new foods, developed to meet the needs of a growing world population—new types of plants, new breeds of animals, algae and single-cell protein foods—will find their way into every market. Aquaculture (fish farming) will provide us with more, and probably some new, sources of animal protein. As knowledge of nutrition advances, foods can be more closely tailored to meet optimal nutritional requirements.

Nathan Pritikin. In the future we will eat less meat and more plant foods. These are healthier, cheaper to produce, and use less land to provide the necessary calories and nutrients.

We will also be eating many foods unfamiliar to us now. Photosynthetic algae, microorganisms grown on petroleum, lettuce growing hydroponically in small cellophane bags in the supermarket, freeze-dried fruits and vegetables, and new varieties of grains bred to meet certain specifications for size, color, shape and nutritional content—these are just a few of the possible foods we will be eating in the future. Even Jules Verne could not begin to describe the exact nature of our culinary future, but I can tell you with certainty that it will be exciting.

Dr. Carol I. Waslien. For the majority of the world, the kinds of foods eaten will remain unchanged—although relative quantities of meat and wheat will probably continue to increase. In developed countries I would anticipate that an increasing number of "fabricated foods" would appear in the diet, i.e., meat or cheese substitutes based on whey (yeast protein isolates used as emulsifiers), to add texture or to substitute for animal protein.

CANCER

*F*OR AMERICANS LIVING at the turn of the century, cancer presented relatively little threat. In 1900, tuberculosis ranked as the number one killer, with such illnesses as pneumonia and influenza, heart disease, and infectious childhood diseases following close behind. Cancer was only eighth on the deadly list.

Today cancer is the second leading cause of death in the United States; only heart disease kills more people each year. While improved medicine and hygiene have controlled such diseases as tuberculosis, cancer has not yielded so easily. In 1976, for instance, Americans died of cancer at the rate of almost 1,000 a day. According to estimates by the National Cancer Institute, one in four Americans will develop cancer. However, many cancers have encouraging survival rates, especially if they are detected and treated in the early stages.

Cancer may seem more threatening than ever, but it is by no means a new disease. An Egyptian papyrus dating from 1500 B.C. describes cancer symptoms, and ancient Greek doctors working under Hippocrates reported finding cancers, such as stomach and breast tumors, that are common today. Galen, a renowned Greek physician, classified different types of tumors as early as A.D. 164 and advocated treating cancers through diet, ointments, purges and surgery.

In 1775, Percivall Pott, a British physician, was the first to hypothesize that exposure to a particular substance could cause cancer. Pott noticed that chimney sweeps developed scrotal cancer in unusually high numbers. He theorized that the soot and ashes, in which the chimney sweeps worked, tended to lodge in the wrinkled skin around the testicles, thus making the boys particularly susceptible to scrotal cancer.

Since Pott's early observations, researchers have isolated a wide array of carcinogens ranging from asbestos to X rays. Scientists now know that some substances can cause cancers, but they still do not know precisely *how* cancers are caused. One fact is known, however: cancer is not a single disease but a group of more than a hundred diseases all characterized by abnormal cell growth. The new cell growths or "neoplasms" take the form of tumors in most cancers, tumors that can be either benign or malignant. Malignant cancer tumors generally grow more quickly than the normal cells from which they are derived. The growing malignancies usually do not remain within the organs or tissues in which they originate; instead, they tend to spread from their original sites to other parts of the body.

Cancers can occur in almost any part of the body. Some parts are much more susceptible than others, though, and some cancers have much higher survival rates than others. Moreover, the incidence and fatality of individual cancers vary markedly among different groups of people. In general, cancers are diseases of aging, striking the middle-aged and elderly far more often than children and young adults. No one is immune, however, and some cancers prey primarily on the young. About half of all those who develop acute lymphocytic leukemia, for example, are under seven years old.

Overall, nonwhites have higher cancer mortality rates than whites in the United States, and those who live in industrial areas have higher rates than rural populations. A fair-skinned white living in the rural South, however, will have a much higher chance of developing skin cancer than a black living in a city. This occurs partly because melanin, a pigment produced in greater quantity by cells in skins of darker peoples, seems to provide protection from ultraviolet rays.

Some cancer incidence rates vary radically according to sex. For instance, while breast cancer occurs in both sexes, it develops in males at only about 1 percent of the frequency that it develops in females; in females, breast cancer is the leading cause of cancer fatalities. In contrast, lung cancer claims far more fatalities among men than among women.

Perhaps one of the most frightening aspects of cancer is that there is no hard-and-fast rule to predict who will develop the disease. Some factors, such as smoking or working in a high-risk occupation, are known to predispose people toward developing certain cancers. Yet sometimes factors that predispose people toward developing one cancer may reduce their risk of developing another type. Cancer of the uterus, for example, tends to be higher in women who have had children. Breast cancer, on the other hand, tends to develop more frequently among women who have had few or no pregnancies.

Despite the tremendous complexity of cancers, some progress has been made in recent years in reducing cancer mortalities. Between 1968 and 1978, cancer mortality tended to increase somewhat for those over fifty-five, but it decreased substantially for younger groups: cancer deaths fell more than 30 percent for those under fifteen years of age, and about 20 percent for those between fifteen and forty-five years of age.

Early detection of cancer can literally mean the difference between life and death. Physicians advise that all people be aware of the American Cancer Society's early warning signals and consult their doctors if any of the symptoms develop:

- Change in bowel or bladder habits
- A sore that does not heal
- Unusual bleeding or discharge
- Thickening or lump in breast or elsewhere
- Indigestion or difficulty in swallowing
- Obvious change in wart or mole
- Nagging cough or hoarseness

CONTRIBUTORS

Edward J. Beattie, Jr., M.D., General Director and Chief Medical Officer, Memorial Hospital for Cancer and Allied Diseases, New York, New York

Paul P. Carbone, M.D., Professor and Chairman, Department of Human Oncology, University of Wisconsin; Director, Wisconsin Clinical Cancer Center, Madison, Wisconsin

Lawrence Garfinkel, Vice-President for Epidemiology and Statistics, American Cancer Society, New York, New York

Arthur I. Holleb, M.D., Senior Vice-President for Medical Affairs, American Cancer Society; former Associate Chief Medical Officer and Attending Surgeon, Department of Surgery, Sloan-Kettering Cancer Center, New York, New York

Edmund Klein, M.D., Roswell Park Memorial Institute, Department of Health, State of New York, Buffalo, New York

Alfred G. Knudson, Jr., M.D., Ph.D., President, The Fox Chase Cancer Center, Philadelphia, Pennsylvania

Charles G. Moertel, M.D., Director, Mayo Comprehensive Cancer Center; Professor and Chairman, Department of Oncology, Mayo Clinic and Mayo Medical School, Rochester, Minnesota

Guy R. Newell, M.D., Professor of Epidemiology and Director, Cancer Prevention, University of Texas System Cancer Center, Houston, Texas

Richard A. Passwater, Ph.D., Director of Research, Solgar Nutritional Research Center, Berlin, Maryland

Linus Pauling, winner of Nobel Prizes in chemistry (1954) and peace (1962); advocate of chemotherapy in treatment of certain mental illnesses

Arif Stephan Rechtschaffen, M.D., President, Omega Institute for Holistic Studies; Medical Director, Springs Health Center, Lebanon Springs, New York

Richard A. Rifkind, M.D., Member, Sloan-Kettering Institute; Director, Sloan-Kettering Division, Graduate School of Medical Science, Memorial Sloan-Kettering Cancer Center, New York, New York

Dr. Franklin C. Salisbury, J.D., Executive Director and Founder, National Foundation for Cancer Research, Bethesda, Maryland

James K. Selkirk, Ph.D., Cancer and Toxicology Section, Biology Division, Oak Ridge National Laboratory, Oak Ridge, Tennessee

C. Norman Shealy, M.D., Ph.D., Founder and Director, Pain and Health Rehabilitation Center™, LaCrosse, Wisconsin; founding and immediate past President, American Holistic Medical Association

Dr. Albert Szent-Györgyi, Marine Biology Laboratories, Woods Hole, Massachusetts

Jack E. White, M.D., F.A.C.S., Director, Howard University Cancer Center, Washington, D.C.

HAS ANYONE IN THE WORLD DISCOVERED ANYTHING THAT COULD BE THE BEGINNING OF A CURE FOR CANCER? IS ANYONE EVEN CLOSE?

Arthur I. Holleb, M.D. People with cancer are being cured every day. Through early detection and prompt treatment many patients are considered cured—that is, they are alive and *free of recurrent disease* at least five years after treatment. However, since most scientists agree that cancer is not one disease, but rather a hundred or more different diseases—and since there is no identifiable common denominator among the many forms of the disease—we cannot expect, with present knowledge, to find a single cure for cancer.

The American Cancer Society estimates that in the year 1981 there were about two million people in this country who could be considered cured of cancer. The prospects for even higher cure rates are good. New technological advances give physicians the opportunity to recognize cancer earlier than ever before, at a stage that promises cure rates never before achievable. For example: breast cancer is currently the number one cancer among American women, in terms of both incidence and mortality. If breast cancer is localized to the breast, 85 percent of the patients are alive at the end of five years. When mammography, a low dose X ray of the breast, detects a cancer so early that it is too small to be felt by the most experienced physician (a "minimal" or in situ cancer), the cure rate approaches 100 percent. Progress in the treatment of cancer—new forms of chemotherapy, more sophisticated techniques of radiation therapy, and advances in surgical management, used individually or in combination—have raised the cure rates for a number of different cancers.

For a variety of reasons some cancers are more difficult to cure than others. Yet, over the past forty years I have witnessed one cancer after another begin to succumb to laboratory and clinical research. The successes include what were once uniformly fatal cancers: acute lymphocytic leukemia in children, Wilms' tumor of the kidney, choriocarcinoma, Hodgkin's disease, certain cancers of the testicle, osteogenic sarcoma and others. The more common cancers like breast, colon and uterus are also beginning to yield. Unfortunately, lung cancer, the most prevalent cancer among American men, is hardly yielding at all. And if current trends persist, it will also kill more women than any other cancer, by the late 1980s. However, it is a highly *preventable* cancer. Its primary cause is well known: cigarette smoking. If people did not start smoking, and if smokers quit early, most lung cancers could be prevented.

Edmund Klein, M.D. A number of ways to cure cancer have been discovered and new methods of treatment are being developed continuously. At present one out of every three patients stricken with cancer will be cured—approximately 250,000 people a year in the United States alone. That is 50,000 more people than were cured even a few years ago, when only one out of four cancer patients was saved. Furthermore, with presently available knowledge and facilities, it is estimated that up to 50 percent of cancer patients could be cured, if they were diagnosed early enough and treated adequately.

From these figures it is obvious that available methods for treating cancer are curative in some cases and not in others. It should be kept in mind that there are many different types of cancer, just as there are different types of infectious diseases. Therefore, a treatment method that may be highly effective for one kind of cancer may be only partially effective, or not effective at all, for other types. The treatment methods that are most effective include surgery, radiation therapy (X ray or nuclear radiation) and chemotherapy. More recently, immunotherapy has been explored.

Newer treatment methods and improvements of previously developed therapies are under study in the clinic and the research laboratory. These studies include treatment approaches based on the continuous input from basic science research in biochemistry, molecular biology, virology, immunology, genetics, and almost every scientific discipline from fundamental physics and chemistry to advanced electronics. The newest areas of research include materials that are found in healthy individuals and that defend the body against foreign invaders, such as viruses. These materials are known as interferons and lymphokines and can now be produced in large quantities in test-tube systems, usually employing human cells grown outside the body in tissue culture.

The most striking progress in the recent past has been made in chemotherapy, which has led to discovering new treatment methods and cures. Chemotherapy employs drugs that are more destructive to cancer cells than to normal tissues and that may be used in addition to surgery or radiation treatment. Chemotherapy is largely responsible for long-term survival and cures in a number of types of widespread cancers, particularly in children and young adults. For example: twelve types of cancer which had been considered hopeless and were rapidly fatal can now be treated effectively. As a result of chemotherapy (sometimes combined with surgery or X ray), better than five year survival has been attained in a large percentage of the following cancers: breast cancer (75 percent); acute leukemia in children (50 percent); Hodgkin's disease (75 percent to 90 percent); cancer of the testes (80 percent); bone cancer (50 percent); and a number of less common types of cancer, such as choriocarcinoma, a cancer arising from the uterus in pregnancy.

A great deal of progress has been made in helping patients with cancer, even when a cure is not yet available. Continuously improved methods of chemotherapy treatment have resulted in temporary disappearance of widespread cancers, have kept the cancer from spreading, or slowed its growth—thus making patients more comfortable, reducing pain and increasing survival. Many patients who were bedridden and in distress are now able to resume a normal life. Other recent advances, such as special types of blood transfusions that control hemorrhage (uncontrollable bleeding) and otherwise fatal infections, have made it possible to tide patients over critical phases until new treatments become effective, thus literally providing a new lease on life for the patient.

It takes time, usually at least three to five years, to find out how effective a new treatment method is, or if it is effective at all. Therefore, the full curative potential of many forms of treatment that, at present, are known to be temporarily beneficial can only be fully assessed by careful studies over a number of years.

Some types of cancer can be kept under control even though they are not cured. An example is leukemia; with continued treatment the patient can lead a normal life indefinitely, without any signs of the disease. In a way this is similar to diabetes; dietary, drug or insulin treatment can keep the patient free of symptoms or the serious consequences of the disease.

The advances in cancer treatment and the promising new leads have come about through the increasing rate of research. Cancer research is expensive. Currently we are spending about $1,000,000,000 per year of public funds in the United States alone. However, this amount seems miniscule when you realize that Americans spend $3,500,000 per year for chewing gum. The cost of research is dwarfed even more by the cost of treating cancer patients—more than $22,000,000,000 per year—and this does not measure the incalculable cost in human suffering and loss of life.

The great progress, recently, in medicine in general and the cancer field in particular, especially in the past few decades, has far exceeded the combined progress made during the preceding thousands of years. Nevertheless, much more work remains to be done. The United States has led the world in this effort both through government and private support of cancer research. It is this research that provides the leads for prevention and early diagnosis as well as effective treatment and cures of cancer.

Alfred G. Knudson, Jr., M.D., Ph.D. Almost 50 percent of the cancers that occur in the United States are cured. Most of the failures concern cancers that are too far advanced at the time of diagnosis or whose biology renders them aggressive even early on. What is needed are new ideas for both prevention and treatment.

The greatest hope lies in learning more about the fundamental steps by which a normal cell becomes a cancer cell. Recent advances in biology have been so dramatic that there is now real hope that such an understanding may be achieved in the near future. Discoveries on the origin of cancer by mutation and by viral transformation make it likely that these old rivals in the theory of cancer are two features of the same problem. It now appears reasonable to suppose that tumor viruses cause cancer by the activation of certain genes in the host or by introducing viral genes that are very similar and perhaps originally derived from host genes. Chemical carcinogens and some kinds of radiation may induce cancer by altering these same genes. With the new recombinant DNA technology it is probable that the nature of such changes will be characterized in the next few years. This knowledge would provide, for the first time, a foundation for rational programs of prevention and treatment.

Arif Stephan Rechtschaffen, M.D. There are many notable advances taking place in the field of cancer. However, it is important to understand that "cure" in cancer is not like a "magic bullet" or antibiotic for pneumonia. The answer to cancer will not be a single drug or technique, but an integrated synthesis enabling the body to overcome the cancer.

The most promising work is focusing on two areas: first, on uncovering the lapse in the body's defense mechanisms that allows the initial growth; and second, on uncovering the mechanisms for strengthening the body's capacity to respond. The following treatments, which deal mostly with immune system mechanisms, are all of great significance.

1. Immunotherapy—utilizing blocking agents and testing techniques developed by Dr. Lawrence Burton in the Bahamas.
2. Autogenous vaccine—based on the theory of the role of progenitor cryptocides, according to Drs. Eleanor Jackson and Virginia Livingston-Wheeler.
3. Thymus fractions—mostly done in Europe, to enhance the immune system.

4. Lysozyme enzymes—Dr. Otto Lobstein, in Chicago, has researched the protective effects of body enzymes.
5. Specific antibodies—Dr. Rottino, in New York, has noted those antibodies associated with cancer which may be used diagnostically and therapeutically.

Immunotherapy really holds the key to successful treatment. Both vitamin C and interferon play significant roles here as well.

Richard A. Rifkind, M.D. Cancer research has identified specific gene sequences, and their protein products, that are active in malignant transformed cells (the "src" and "leuk" genes). This fact, coupled with the power of recombinant DNA technology, strongly suggest that we may be close to understanding the unique features of cancer cells. This is the beginning of being "close to a cure." This research involves the work of many independent labs and investigators.

Dr. Franklin C. Salisbury, J.D. Dr. Albert Szent-Györgyi and his colleagues at the National Foundation for Cancer Research have applied the principles of the quantum sciences to biology and have discovered that human cells follow many principles of solid state physics. He has concluded that a cancer cell is a healthy cell which differs from other normal cells in these important ways: the sophisticated mechanisms used by the cell to operate have been upset and the ability of the cell to carry on functions other than random growth have been destroyed. By applying electronic technologies, now available for the first time, this hypothesis is being studied in over twenty-four different laboratories at prestigious universities and science-oriented corporations. While not all the scientists in the National Foundation for Cancer Research accept the Szent-Györgyi hypothesis, not one has come up with proof that it is not factual. Hundreds of scientific papers that support Szent-Györgyi's hypothesis have been published in recognized journals.

Three compounds based on principles developed by the research program of the National Foundation for Cancer Research were synthesized in 1981 and are undergoing extensive tests in vitro and in animal models. A limited amount of patient-testing is being carried on in other countries. It is the opinion of the executive director of the National Foundation for Cancer Research that this work can be described as bringing us close not only to the understanding of cancer but to doing something about it.

James K. Selkirk, Ph.D. Cancer is a very ancient disease. The fossil record shows dinosaur bones with essentially the same types of tumors seen today. Therefore, we face an enemy that has been in existence for tens of millions of years. Only in the last few decades has science been able to make a concerted attempt to understand this disease and rid the

world of it. The fact that cancer remains one of the world's major killers
is evidence of our limited success in combating this ravaging disease.

Since no living organism, such as a bacteria or virus, has been associated with human cancer, and since cancer itself appears to be a whole
family of tissue-specific diseases that appear to be biologically distinct
from one another, we must begin to view the problem of cancer as a
malfunction of basic biochemical controls inherent within the cell, including its nucleus where the genetic material resides. Unregulated
growth appears to be the only common characteristic that can be ascribed
to all cancers. For reasons that remain obscure, cancer cells fail to heed
normal control signals of the organism to restrain growth when normal
tissue boundaries are reached. The cells continue to grow; and then
interrupt normal functions of the organ or tissue. However, in spite of
abundant research performed during the last fifty years, it is readily
apparent that we do not yet know what really causes cancer. Previous
research, covering a broad range of living species, has indicated that
carcinogenesis mechanisms dealing with viruses, chemicals, hormones
and defective genetics may be causative factors. However, this body of
evidence often applies only to one or to a few species. It is not yet
possible to directly extrapolate the findings to man. Therefore, we are
faced with searching for a cure for a disease without having established
its origin.

The search for a cure appears to be divided into two broad categories.
The first approach is empirical: biochemical research and medicine try
various chemical, physical and biological agents that might have some
therapeutic effect in destroying the cancer cells. This second approach is
the origin for many of the drugs used today with some degree of
success. These chemicals attempt to exploit the metabolic differences in
cancer cells, due to their unusual growth characteristics, and render
them more susceptible to toxic substances. However, no family of drugs
has been discovered that has a uniform curative capability. From this
standpoint, it is difficult to ascertain whether we are close to a cure for
cancer. Test substances are being selected from large screening programs for cancer-static effect. Yet we have little knowledge of the
underlying cause of the disease. A cure discovered by this approach
would be quite fortuitous.

The second approach is directed toward finding the inherent cause of
cancer by understanding the molecular biology of cell division, differentiation and growth and determining where the critical controls are and
what can cause them to malfunction. This approach is being pursued by
almost every scientific discipline. Increasingly, it adds to our base of
knowledge concerning the biological events surrounding the transformation of a normal cell to a cancer cell and its progression to a tumor.
While these studies do not usually search for a cure directly, they
continually discover new facets of this insidious process. This work has
not yet produced sufficient information to lead to a cure. However,

knowledge has grown in such rapid proportions over the last ten years that we are hopeful major advances in understanding and combating cancer will be made in the not too distant future.

Understanding the molecular biology of the cancer process will help direct development of better drug therapies, and every year basic research comes closer to finding out where, how and why the malignant process begins. If the rate of overall research into cancer continues to increase, we can foresee a meeting of the empirical and molecular biological approaches to cancer research which will culminate in understanding and conquering this disease.

Dr. Albert Szent-Gyöorgyi. Yes, discoveries have been made that could be the beginning of a cure for cancer. This information is not yet published. However, I know it through confidential sources.

WHAT PART DOES DIET PLAY IN REDUCING OR INCREASING ONE'S CHANCES OF GETTING CANCER?

Edward J. Beattie, Jr., M.D. What we eat, and do not eat, has a profound effect on the body's immune system (which fights disease), the aging process, general health, and whether we will contract cancer—yet surprisingly little is known about what constitutes a proper diet and the subject is incredibly complex.

Dr. Ernst Wynder, the distinguished epidemiologist, believes that nutrition in its broadest sense relates to, but does not cause, about 60 percent of the cancers in women and about 40 percent of the cancers in men. The most important cancers to which diet is related are: malignant lesions of the breast, uterus, liver, esophagus, stomach, colon and rectum.

Nutrition exerts mostly an *indirect* effect on cancer, either by setting the stage for cancer-causing substances, by promoting their activity, or by protecting us from them. Many of the agents considered carcinogens (cancer-causing) are actually precarcinogens and may be detoxified by the liver into harmless substances or activated into genuine carcinogens.

Nutrition relates to cancer in three ways:

1. Nutritional deficiencies that lead to biochemical malfunctions which start the neoplastic process leading to cancer.
2. Nutritional excesses that induce metabolic abnormalities which initiate, or promote, cancer.
3. Nutrients, additives and contaminants which promote or speed up carcinogenesis or which, in relatively few cases, are actual carcinogens such as the aflatoxin molds, nitrosamines, and polycyclic hydrocarbons.

Commenting on the reluctance of many physicians to accept the role of diet in causing and preventing cancer, Dr. Wynder wrote in a professional paper: "It should come as no surprise that a factor (nutrition) which can influence hormone production and retention, constituents and bulk of stool, the makeup of cell membranes and other cellular components, as well as affecting immunological factors can be related to carcinogenesis (the causing of cancer)."

Paul P. Carbone, M.D. At the present time, except for drastic lifelong changes in eating habits, i.e., vegetarianism, abstinence from smoking, tobacco (chewing) and alcohol, changes in diet will not influence the incidence of cancer.

While experimental and clinical data suggest that exogenous factors may be important, there is little support from clinical trials that decreasing fat as protein, or ingesting vitamin C or vitamin A, will alter cancer incidence. Current clinical trials are underway but as yet, there are no supporting data.

Lawrence Garfinkel. Some researchers believe that a certain percentage of cancers may be attributed to diet, dietery habits, methods of cooking and additives. Other researchers claim that the evidence is not strong enough to draw these conclusions.

The American Cancer Society has been concerned about the role diet may have in relationship to cancer, and has been closely monitoring reports in the scientific literature on the subject. It has sponsored several meetings on nutrition and cancer, the last in 1978.

There is much research still being conducted on various aspects of diet and diet additives, and the American Cancer Society is supporting some of this research.

Charles G. Moertel, M.D. At the present time, there is very little hard information regarding the role of dietary constituents in either causing or preventing cancer. Consequently there are no specific and well-founded dietary recommendations that can or should be made.

There is strong circumstantial evidence that dietary patterns probably play a role in the development of certain cancers. For example, native Japanese have a high incidence of stomach cancer but a very low incidence of colorectal cancer. The reverse is true for native born Americans. On the other hand, Japanese born in this country also have a high incidence of colorectal cancer and a low incidence of stomach cancer. This evidence suggests that dietary factors play a role in the causation of both cancers. Attempts to identify specific elements of the diet that are at fault, however, have thus far proved futile. Even in very primitive societies where extraordinarily high rates of cancer of the esophagus or liver are observed, presumably related to diet, years of study by skilled epidemiologists have not proved fruitful in identifying causal agents.

These problems of identification are greatly compounded in our highly complex Western society with our vast array of foods and food additives, plus numerous other industrial and environmental exposures. Finally, we cannot rely upon experimental animal studies, since they are often conflicting and cannot be directly translated to man.

Two of the most popular theories have involved the role of dietary fat and fiber in the induction of cancer of the large bowel. Unfortunately, here again, the evidence is very soft. High fat and low fiber contents are characteristic of the Western diet and we do have a high incidence of bowel cancer. There are, however, other more primitive societies that have still higher dietary fat content and still lower dietary fiber, but paradoxically have very low incidences of bowel cancer. Some epidemiologic studies in this country have associated a high dietary fat intake and high blood cholesterol levels with an increased incidence of colorectal cancer. However, other studies by equally competent epidemiologists have shown that people with a high blood cholesterol, and presumably a high dietary fat intake, have a significantly reduced incidence of colorectal cancer.

In spite of the dogmatic pronouncements of some scientists, it would seem premature to make any dietary recommendations for the prevention of cancer. Our knowledge is too rudimentary and the costs of such radical changes in our food economy would be too great. Also, we must still admit the possibility that a dietary change that would suppress one type of cancer could be conducive to the formation of others.

Guy R. Newell, M.D. Although the role of nutritional factors in the prevention of cancer has not been defined, both epidemiologic and experimental evidence suggests that they may be quite important. Increasing numbers of several classes of chemicals reportedly inhibit or delay the formation of tumors in animals exposed to cancer-causing agents. These preventive chemicals include the retinoids, butylated hydroxytoluene or hydroxyanisole, disulfiram, ethoxyquin, protease inhibitors, some prostaglandins, cyclic nucleotides, selenium compounds, and others. Several of these are contained in commonly eaten foods. This overall concept has generally been called "chemoprevention" or "intervention of carcinogenesis."

From a more practical point of view, some interesting observations have been made concerning the possible anticancer effects of certain fruits and vegetables. Cabbage, broccoli, cauliflower and other members of the Brassicaceae family, as well as spinach, dill and celery, are potent inducers of the microsomail mixed-function oxidase system. Increased carcinogenic detoxifying enzymes can result from ingestion of these foods. A decreased risk of colon cancer has been noted in individuals who frequently ingest cabbage, brussel sprouts and broccoli. Flavones, found in citrus fruits, can also increase the activity of these metabolic reactions.

The proposed importance of dietary fiber in protecting against diseases of the bowel, including cancer, has received a great deal of publicity. Fiber may be defined as consisting of plant wall and nonnutritive residues; this encompasses all substances resistant to animal digestive enzymes.

Finally, food additives, such as butylated hydroxyanisole (BHA) and butylated hydroxytoluene (BHT) are used as food preservatives. These compounds are antioxidants and can inhibit the tumorigenic response to a number of chemical carcinogens in animals.

Richard A. Passwater, Ph.D. Most likely your diet plays a significant role in whether or not you get cancer. But we cannot answer that question with certainty, or quantify exactly how large a part diet plays in cancer, until we fully understand cancer. However, we do see certain patterns in cancer incidence that appear to be linked to diet.

The strongest links to cancer may relate to what is missing from our diet, rather than what is included in our diet. There is a strong suggestion that certain nutritional deficiencies increase our chances of getting cancer. This may be because these nutritional deficiencies impair our immune system and other protection mechanisms.

The news media have concentrated more attention on how excesses of various dietary components have been linked to higher cancer incidence. Both the deficiency and excess links argue well for a moderate and diverse diet. A well-nourished individual can handle moderate amounts of any food without increasing his (or her) cancer susceptibility. In contrast, a poorly nourished person eating excessive fats, alcohol, artificial sweeteners, artificial flavors and colors, etc. might tip the scales toward cancer. The concept of moderation in diet (as well as life-style) is supported by the evidence that religious groups such as the Seventh Day Adventists and Mormons have lower cancer rates.

The diet–cancer link itself is supported by the fact that cancer incidence changes when population groups change from a traditional diet to a new diet. This has been observed when Japanese immigrants to the United States switch to our diet. A similar change in cancer incidence can be seen within countries that have switched from their traditional diet to a westernized diet. This is not to say that one national diet is necessarily better than another, only that the types of cancers linked to the diet are different. For example; Japanese diets are associated with higher stomach cancer rates, but lower breast cancer rates.

Stronger evidence of the diet–cancer link is available in terms of nutritional deficiencies because a greater amount of experimental evidence exists from animal studies, in addition to the population studies. Deficiencies of vitamins A, C, E, as well as most of the B-complex vitamins, and the minerals selenium and magnesium, have been shown to increase the susceptibility of animals to cancer. The deficiency does not cause cancer, it only lowers our resistance to cancer.

I am sure we will learn more about the relationship between diet and cancer during the coming decade.

Linus Pauling. Several epidemiological studies have shown that a high intake of vitamin C and vitamin A, or of vegetables and fruits rich in these subtances, decreases the incidence of cancer significantly.

My estimate is that an intake of 1,000 milligrams of vitamin C per day and 10,000 international units of vitamin A per day reduces the incidence of cancer, at each age, to less than one-half of its usual value.

Dr. Franklin C. Salisbury, J.D. There is no question but that diet plays an important part in keeping cells healthy and, hence; a proper diet can reduce one's chances of getting cancer. However, no one knows theoretically or experimentally just what a proper diet is. For instance, Dr. Albert Szent-Györgyi, who won the Nobel prize for his discovery of vitamin C, teaches that a diet deficient in vitamin C increases one's chances of getting cancer. Other experts disagree. Unquestionably, more work needs to be done in this field.

C. Norman Shealy, M.D., Ph.D. There are a number of highly suggestive statistics in relation to diet and cancer. The most striking is the association between fat intake and the incidence of cancer of the colon and cancer of the breast. The higher the fat intake the greater the chances of having these two types of cancer. Beyond this, at the present time, the proof is not utterly convincing.

However, really good nutrition consists of eating a wide variety of real food. Food that contains white sugar, white flour and artificially hydrogenated fat is not "real food," because it has been highly chemically processed and altered. If one reads labels carefully and avoids sugar (sucrose, beet or cane sugar, glucose or corn sweeteners), white flour and artificially or partially hydrogenated fats, one has probably gone as far as one can, in today's society, in eating a good diet. Certainly, the evidence for high doses of vitamin C in preventing cancer is not conclusive. Nevertheless, the work of Linus Pauling and Ewan Cameron is beginning to be highly suggestive that large doses of vitamin C may be preventive or assist in the recovery process.

Jack E. White, M.D., F.A.C.S. Evidence from epidemiological studies indicates that diet plays a significant role in the causation of cancer. Specifically, diets with low fiber and high fat content appear to increase the chances for development of cancer of the large bowel. High fat diets seem to increase the probabilities of breast cancer. Oriental diets, or diets containing large amounts of smoked fish, appear to increase the chances for development of gastric cancer. Therefore, the chances of getting these types of cancers should be reduced by making the indicated changes in diet.

HEART DISEASE

SUDDEN DEATH—that is what heart disease means to many people. It may be symbolized by the jogger who collapses halfway through his laps or by the elderly shopper who suffers a fatal heart attack while strolling through the supermarket. Heart disease can strike quickly and often unexpectedly. Even the phrase *heart attack* creates the image of a sudden, fatal assault on the body.

To some extent this ominous image is justified. As William Harvey, the seventeenth-century physician who discovered the principle of circulation, described it, the heart is the "first principle of life." If the heart fails, if the vital flow of blood and oxygen to the body is disrupted, life is endangered. As late as the 1950s, a doctor who discovered that a heart attack victim's breathing and heart had stopped would declare the patient clinically dead.

Faced with the same situation today, a doctor will begin working furiously to bring the patient back to life. Thanks to the discovery of such life-support techniques as cardiopulmonary resuscitation (CPR), trained personnel can temporarily maintain life through artificial respiration and manual heart stimulation. More advanced life-support systems, as those found in hospitals and ambulances, can prolong life for much longer periods.

The immediate availability of emergency care can often make the difference between sudden death and slow healing. Each year, about 600,000 Americans die from heart attacks. More than half these deaths occur suddenly—before the victims reach a hospital. In fact, most heart attack fatalities occur within an hour after the attack.

Time is vital in treating heart attack victims because the brain will begin to die within minutes if the heart does not provide oxygenated blood. A person's chances of survival increase considerably if he or she recognizes the signals of a heart attack and obtains aid immediately. Heart attacks are often signaled by pain or pressure in the center of the chest lasting two minutes or more and possibly radiating toward the jaw, shoulder or arm. Nausea, sweating, weakness or shortness of breath frequently accompany the pain.

Who is likely to suffer a heart attack? Almost anyone, especially if he or she lives long enough. Heart disease is the most common cause of death in the United States, as well as in many other industrialized countries. Each year in the United States heart disease kills about 1.5 times as many people as cancer and about 12 times as many as motor vehicle accidents. These statistics for heart disease include such conditions as rheumatic heart disease and congenital heart defects, but coronary heart disease is the most common form.

As people age, their chances of developing heart disease increase dramatically. In 1977, for example, Americans between thirty-five and thirty-nine years of age died from heart disease at the rate of about 70 per 100,000; for those sixty to sixty-four years of age the death rate from heart disease soared to 678 per 100,000, and rates continued to climb steeply for those over sixty-five. In general, men had higher mortality rates from heart disease than women, and blacks had higher rates than whites.

Yet there is some encouraging news. Overall, the rate of death due to heart disease has decreased in recent years. Between 1950 and 1970, the age-adjusted death rate fell by about 1 percent a year, and rates have continued to decline significantly in the 1970s. Some researchers suggest that the reason for this decline is that more people are taking the threat of heart disease seriously. Free blood-pressure clinics, special low-cholesterol diets, antismoking campaigns, exercise programs, and CPR training courses—these are just some of the counterattacks being launched against heart attacks.

CONTRIBUTORS

Dr. Lawrence S. Cohen, Professor of Medicine and Cardiology, Yale University School of Medicine, New Haven, Connecticut

Michael E. DeBakey, M.D., Baylor College of Medicine, Houston, Texas

Roman W. DeSanctis, M.D., Professor of Medicine, Harvard Medical School and Massachusetts General Hospital, Boston, Massachusetts; Physician and Director, Coronary Care Unit, Massachusetts General Hospital

Joseph T. Doyle, M.D., Professor of Medicine and Head of the Division of Cardiology, Albany Medical Center, Albany, New York

Donald Brian Effler, M.D., Chief of Thoracic-Cardiovascular Surgery, Cleveland Clinic Foundation, 1950–1975; Senior Cardiovascular Surgeon, St. Joseph's Hospital Health Center, Syracuse, New York

David G. Greene, M.D., Professor of Medicine and Associate Professor of Physiology, State University of New York, Buffalo, New York

J. Willis Hurst, M.D., Candler Professor of Medicine (cardiology), Chairman of the Department of Medicine, and Chief of Medicine, Emory University Hospital and Grady Memorial Hospital, Atlanta, Georgia

Dwight C. McGoon, M.D., Professor of Surgery, Mayo Medical School, Rochester, Minnesota

Nathan Pritikin, nutritional scientist and author

Raymond D. Pruitt, M.D., Professor of Medicine and Dean Emeritus, Mayo Medical School, Rochester, Minnesota; Consultant in Cardiovascular Diseases, Mayo Clinic, Rochester, Minnesota

Richard O. Russell, Jr., M.D., Clinical Professor of Medicine, Department of Medicine, Division of Cardiology, University of Alabama, Birmingham, Alabama

David C. Sabiston, Jr., M.D., James Duke Professor of Surgery and Chairman of the Department, Duke University Medical Center, Durham, North Carolina

HAS ANYONE FOUND A CURE FOR HEART ATTACKS? IS ANYONE EVEN CLOSE?

Dr. Lawrence S. Cohen. To date there is no cure for heart attacks. Certain risk factors, however, have been identified that predispose individuals to the development of heart attacks. These factors are: hypertension, cigarette smoking, high blood cholesterol, diabetes mellitus, sedentary lifestyle, obesity and a pressured lifestyle. All of these risk factors, with the possible exception of diabetes mellitus, are susceptible to change if the individual is aware of them and comes under medical care. Obviously, the earlier in life these risk factors are modified, the more likely that the change will have an impact on potentially preventing heart attacks.

Quite recently, a technique called intracoronary administration of streptokinase has been developed. With this technique, some patients who are in the midst of a heart attack may be candidates for prompt emergency therapy to dissolve the causative clot within the coronary artery. Dissolution of the clot may prevent the heart attack from evolving. This therapy will be available for only a fraction of patients having a heart attack and for the present, prevention is still the goal.

Michael E. DeBakey, M.D. Heart attacks are caused by occlusion or blockage of blood flow through the coronary arteries, which supply arterial blood to the heart. The disease that causes this blockage in the arteries is arteriosclerosis or atherosclerosis, often referred to as hardening of the arteries.

Atherosclerosis is believed to begin with damage to the innermost layer of cells lining the artery, termed the intima. Just how this occurs, and the precise cause, are not known. Once the lesion develops, the following conditions occur: focal accumulation of cholesterol; an increase in the quantity of smooth muscle cells, collagen and elastic tissue; thickening and a plaquelike formation. In time, this lesion progresses and produces narrowing of the lumen of the artery and, ultimately, complete occlusion; this process causes blockage of blood flow.

While there is no cure yet known for heart attacks, much progress has been made in treating heart attack victims, both by medical and surgical means.

Roman W. DeSanctis, M.D. The most honest answer to both of these questions—is there a cure for heart attacks or is anyone close to finding one—is no.

The medical term for what is properly called a heart attack is "myocardial infarction." Myocardial infarction results when the blood supply to an area of heart muscle is suddenly shut off by the formation of a blood clot (thrombus) in the arteries supplying that heart muscle. Acutely deprived of its oxygen, the affected heart muscle dies and is replaced with scar tissue. Almost always, the clot forms at a point of narrowing in the artery caused by arteriosclerosis.

Unfortunately, there is no sure way of preventing either the underlying arteriosclerosis or the formation of the clot; nor are we particularly close to a solution for this problem, which ranks not only as the number one cause of death in the United States, but which also afflicts so many people in their most productive years. On the other hand, there is room for cautious optimism.

Since 1973, there has been a slight but steady decline in the number of annual deaths from coronary arteriosclerosis. Although there are many reasons for this, we would like to think that a major factor has been the increasing emphasis on preventive medicine; because the ultimate cure of any disease resides first and foremost in its prevention. Furthermore, preventive medicine is relatively inexpensive. Therefore, the medical profession has stressed the adoption of habits and practices that may diminish the likelihood of the development of arteriosclerosis. These include: keeping body weight in a desirable range, not smoking, detecting high blood pressure early and treating it vigorously, exercising regularly, and consuming a diet that is low in animal fat and cholesterol. Favorable modification of these so-called risk factors is particularly important in people with a strong family history of premature coronary artery disease. We are also trying to develop simple methods for screening large population groups to pick out individuals who might have significant unrecognized coronary artery disease, with the hope of preventing fatal heart attacks by appropriate medical or surgical intervention. We are also developing methods for reducing the size of a heart attack, if it does occur.

Although we can look forward to preventing both arteriosclerosis and blood clot formation by using specific drug therapy, such treatment is not presently on the horizon.

Donald B. Effler, M.D. The answer to both questions is no—no one has found a cure for heart attacks nor is anyone even close.

Heart attacks are caused by arteriosclerosis (hardening of the arteries) in main coronary arteries. This is a degenerative disease and it has no single cause and no cure to date.

The best results for prevention of heart attacks today comes from early diagnosis and preventive treatment. Early diagnosis includes coronary arteriography to demonstrate the threatening occlusion in a major coronary artery. For the majority of patients, successful therapy combines medications with coronary bypass graft surgery.

The combined medical-surgical treatment described above does not cure coronary artery disease but it can be extremely helpful in preventing heart attacks.

Dwight C. McGoon, M.D. A precise answer cannot be given because the question is internally inconsistent and also because "heart attack" is such a vague term. Everyone would recognize the unreality of a question such as: "Is there any cure for a bullet passing through the brain?" This is something that has happened, an event. It cannot be "cured." It can only be prevented, or its effect made less significant. A heart attack is also an event that has occurred and it cannot be "cured" as such.

What is the meaning of "heart attack"? Any period of improper function of the heart could be referred to as heart attack, i.e., during very rapid or very slow beating, or during the experience of severe heart pain (angina) or weak heart action. The most common use of the term refers to an episode in which a section of the muscle of the heart dies (myocardial infarction), usually because the coronary artery bringing blood flow to that section of heart muscle has become severely narrowed or plugged up. So, when we think of a heart attack, we immediately think of obstruction of a coronary artery (arteriosclerosis). When we think of a cure for heart attack, we know that the dead muscle cannot be brought back to life. Therefore, we think of seeking ways to prevent the heart attack by preventing this blockage of the coronary artery (coronary arteriosclerosis). Since many factors seem to accelerate the process of arteriosclerosis, such as smoking, high blood pressure, sedentary living and obesity, it seems logical that the incidence of heart attacks should be reduced if people would stop smoking, if high blood pressure were discovered early and corrected by treatment, and if people would exercise and eat sparingly. It is difficult to prove that these measures prevent heart attacks, but it is a fact that in very recent years, since these measures have been emphasized and widely practiced, the incidence of deaths from heart attacks has declined. Possibly these measures have caused a decline in the occurrence of heart attacks, and possibly other measures can be detected that could be used to reduce further this incidence. However, arteriosclerosis seems to be a universal part of aging, and even if the process is being slowed down by proper habits of living, it seems unlikely that it will be eliminated entirely, at least in the foreseeable future.

Another consideration relating to this question is the possibility that the effects of a heart attack, i.e., the effects of a blocked coronary artery, can be minimized so that not so much of the heart muscle will die, and so that the person himself or herself will not die. Much has been accomplished along these lines, and research continues. However, nothing approaching a "cure" has resulted from this approach. Since heart muscle dies quickly after its blood supply has been shut off, the short time available (twenty to forty minutes) to implement treatment after the heart attack has started will probably prevent the universal "cure" of heart attacks by such measures.

Operations that allow blood to be detoured around an obstructed coronary artery can be done with great safety. Evidence is accumulating that such operations do reduce the likelihood of later heart attacks. However, for many people a heart attack may occur "out of the blue"— as the first evidence that blockage of the coronary arteries is developing. Much work is being done to develop a simple and accurate test to detect the presence of coronary artery disease before a heart attack occurs. But it does not seem very practical to consider that a heart operation will be indicated for such a large proportion of the population in hopes that some future heart attack could be prevented.

To sum up: it can be said that a "cure" for heart attacks is not available, but that much progress with this problem is being made.

Nathan Pritikin. Once a heart attack has occurred, it cannot be "cured" or its effects undone, although a person who has had a heart attack can do much, through diet and exercise, to decrease the chances of future attacks. More importantly, however, most heart attacks can be prevented by a proper diet and exercise regimen.

There is increasing evidence that the buildup of arterial plaques that cause heart attacks can be reversed by following a diet that is so low in fat and cholesterol that the plaques are absorbed. There is no other method that has even come close to curing heart vessel disease.

Raymond D. Pruitt, M.D. The term "heart attack," as used by physicians and non-physicians alike, commonly describes an event that results from obstruction to the blood supply of the heart. That obstruction was produced by thickening of the walls of the coronary arteries and had

developed over a period of many years. The heart attack itself may or
may not be attended by formation of a clot in the narrowed channel of
one or more of these coronary arteries. The patient so affected may
develop one or both of two clinical events.

In the first event, a part of the heart muscle may be injured to the
point that it is totally destroyed and, if the patient survives the attack,
will be replaced by scar tissue. This is known medically as acute myocardial infarction. What may happen to the patient so affected? If a
sufficiently large part of the heart muscle is destroyed by the infarction,
the patient may die within a period ranging from minutes to days,
because of the heart's inability to perform adequately its pumping
function. A patient affected with such a large infarct may survive
the immediate period, but be left with a scar of such magnitude that the
heart is never able to regain sufficient pumping function to permit
the patient to resume a normal level of physical activity. A patient who
experiences a smaller infarct, and who is spared a catastrophic irregu-
larity of the heartbeat during the acute phase, may recover and be
entirely free of symptoms for years or decades thereafter.

In the second event, the lack of blood supply to the heart may induce
changes in the rhythm of the heart so severe that its pumping function
is rendered useless and the patient "drops dead." This patient will very
likely remain dead unless cardiopulmonary resuscitation (CPR) is initiated
within a matter of a very few minutes. If such treatment is accomplished
promptly, this patient also may be free of heart symptoms for a longer
or shorter time.

Whatever may have been the nature of the patient's heart attack, are
we justified in referring to long-term survival as "cure"? Strictly speaking, the answer in the majority of instances must be no. As indicated
already, the underlying cause of most heart attacks is obstruction of the
coronary arteries that supply the blood to the heart. Even when the
heart attack is attended by clot formation in a coronary artery, preexisting disease is commonly present at the site where the clot forms or
is lodged. A diseased coronary artery cannot be restored to a completely
normal state by any medical measures currently available. Such restoration, one may argue, would be an essential component of a "cure." In
this sense, then, the cure for heart attacks has not been found, and will
not exist until prevention of the coronary sclerosis, which is responsible
for the obstructive changes in the vessels, becomes a reality. Such
prevention may be a long time coming.

What about the second half of the question: "Is anyone even close?"

If, as implied in the preceding comments, the cure resides in prevention of coronary artery disease, then the much-publicized identification
of risk factors for coronary disease, and improved understanding of and
control of these factors, merit comment. Noteworthy is the observation
that among these several risk factors, control of hypertension is nearly
within our grasp. Such control depends not so much on what the

individual does for him/herself, but upon the administration of more effective medications for the treatment of hypertension. These medications did not exist three decades ago. Improved understanding of lipid metabolism may at some future time eventuate in production of medicines that will afford a similarly effective approach to control of high blood fats. As for elimination of cigarette smoking and achieving physical fitness, the patient must continue to assume the principal responsibility. Altering a genetic predisposition to coronary disease is an item on the future agenda of medical science.

It would be unrealistic, however, to suggest that the advances discussed above constitute a near-miss on a cure.

If one approaches the question of cure from the standpoint of partial cure, rather than from the standpoint of prevention of the underlying coronary sclerosis, a more convincing case can be made. The most striking example is that of the individual who has coronary disease, is totally free of symptoms, experiences a fatal disturbance in the rhythm of the heart but is fortunate enough to have immediate cardiopulmonary resuscitation. Thereafter, a carefully designed and monitored program of cardiac medications may prevent recurrence of the rhythm "catastrophy," and the patient who was without heart symptoms before his attack may continue, unabated, a life of normal activities and responsibilities. The control of heart standstill by the ever-improving technology of cardiac pacing offers a similar approximation of cure for the patient who suffers from defective performance of the heart pacemaker that nature gave him.

A successfully executed cardiopulmonary resuscitation followed by effective control of the rhythm of the heart is, then, along with ever-better cardiac pacing, an approximation of cure of a heart attack. Such treatment is available now in the coronary care units of our hospitals. If the impact of these developments on reducing mortality from heart attacks has not been impressively great, the reason is not that rhythmic death is uncommon. Roughly 50 percent of patients dying with heart attacks fail to survive long enough to reach the hospital. Emergency squads are working heroically to bring this effective treatment to the patient who experiences an attack outside of the hospital. Ever-increasing efforts are also under way to bring it to the patient within the extremely short period when lifesaving measures can be performed. Herein resides the major current and future challenge.

Surgical treatment as an approximation to cure merits two illustrations. First is the patient having cardiac pain of recent onset, characterized by "unstable angina," i.e., pain occurring both at rest and with exertion. Visualization of the coronary arteries in such a patient may disclose critically placed obstructions in the coronary circulation that can be bypassed. By such an approach, a heart attack in the form of an acute myocardial infarction may be averted. A small percentage of coronary bypass operations are performed on patients with the specific problem just delineated. The majority of such operations, however, are undertaken in an effort to relieve severe or intractable pain of angina pectoris, often with gratifying results for the patient. Whether bypass surgery under these latter circumstances prolongs life and prevents future heart attacks is disputed.

A second illustration of surgical treatment, albeit a strained one, is the surgical excision of a bulging scar in the wall of the left ventricle, when this scar has seriously reduced the capacity of the heart as a pump. Although the patient undergoing such treatment will still have significant heart disease, the degree of improvement effected by removal of the bulging scar, called a ventricular aneurysm, may indeed be dramatic.

Today, we have no cure for heart attacks—no magic bullet, no vaccine, no insulin, no penicillin. Nonetheless, significant progress has been and is being made in understanding and coping with the complex and diverse medical problems subsumed by the phrase "heart attack." Let us get on with the job.

Dr. Richard O. Russell, Jr., M.D. To date I believe that most authorities would agree that no one has found a cure for heart attacks. Fear of this dread illness pervades the population of the civilized world, both east and west. Many individuals believe that this concern has been one of the factors that has led to the marked increase in participation in exercise, particularly jogging. While no one can hold forth the promise of preventing a heart attack by an increase in physical activity and avoidance of a totally sedentary lifestyle, this is certainly considered to be an important factor in our maintaining good general health. Other factors include: stopping or cutting down on smoking, particularly cigarettes; maintenance of both correct weight and the ingestion of a nutritionally well-balanced diet; control of blood pressure elevation; control of stress and strain in one's lifestyle, so far as is possible; and treatment of diabetes mellitus if this is present. Other factors that cannot be changed or that are less easily controlled (family prevalence of heart disease or the vicarious inhalation of cigarette smoke) have been shown to play a role in both heart disease and heart attack.

Much research is going on, worldwide, in an effort to understand arteriosclerosis and it is reasonable to be optimistic that a better understanding of this process may help us to know how to prevent heart attacks.

Perhaps closer at hand, is information that may contribute to the reduction in size and extent of damage once a heart attack has occurred. Intensified research programs are presently being conducted. These hold forth the reasonable hope that, if a patient can be treated in the early minutes to hours following the onset of a heart attack, its potentially serious consequences may be sharply reduced. However, once the heart attack has occurred and damaged the heart, this area of damage or scar formation cannot be cured. Fortunately, however, the heart and other body mechanisms make compensation for the damaged area to the extent that many individuals can lead a normal life once they have recovered from the heart attack. It is generally held that alteration of an individual's lifestyle to incorporate some of the hygienic measures mentioned in the first paragraph will improve the individual's opportunity for a longer, happier and more productive life in the years following a heart attack.

David C. Sabiston, Jr., M.D. In answer to the question as to whether or not a cure for heart attacks has been found, the answer must be no. However, it should be emphasized that the term "heart attacks" has a number of definitions—and that heart attacks can have many different causes.

The most important feature of the issue, is the fact that, today, there are many ways to reduce the likelihood of an individual developing a heart attack. In other words, quite specific measures can be undertaken to reduce the incidence and likelihood of heart attacks.

One very important aspect is the cessation of cigarette smoking. (Cigarette smoking has clearly been demonstrated to be associated with an increased incidence of heart attacks.) Moreoever, patients who have heart attacks can reduce the rate of subsequent attacks, and therefore the risk of death, by prompt cessation of cigarette smoking.

The control of high blood pressure is also important in reducing the risk of heart attacks and the same is true of the control of obesity. Most authorities in the field believe that a reduction of the total amount of fat in the daily diet aids in prophylaxis against heart attacks, especially a reduction in those fats containing large amounts of saturated fatty acids. Finally, in patients with significant obstructive coronary-artery arterial disease, it has been proven that coronary artery bypass surgical procedures correct the anginal pain often associated with this condition. They also extend the length of life in selected groups of patients. In the future, advances in transplantation of the heart may offer significant relief to a number of individuals with heart attacks. Recent progress in perfection of an artificial heart further heightens the likelihood that this approach may be lifesaving in a significant number of patients with severely damaged hearts.

IS IT TRUE THAT EVERYONE'S HEART GROWS WEAKER EACH YEAR NO MATTER HOW MUCH HE OR SHE EXERCISES?

Roman W. DeSanctis, M.D. The precise answer to this question is not known, but there does appear to be a modest decline in cardiac performance with advancing age. The evidence for this comes from studies in which the response of the heart to exercise has been assessed in healthy populations. These studies show that the hearts of elderly people do not contract as vigorously during exercise as do those of the young. However, this reduction in cardiac function does not appear to be of any real consequence, although it may be one of many factors contributing to the general decline in the ability to perform maximum physical exercise that is associated with aging. If heart failure does develop in elderly people, it is invariably due to some other associated disease of the heart, and not to the effects of the aging process *per se* upon the heart. Indeed, considering the fact that the heart beats somewhere between two and one-half and three billion times in an average lifetime, it is remarkable that the heart muscle holds up as well as it does through the years!

Whether exercise prevents the age-related deterioration in cardiac function is as yet unknown. Serial studies of cardiac performance over a period of years in athletes, as contrasted with nonathletes, have not been made. Our best guess is that even people who exercise regularly will undergo a slight decline in the function of the heart with advancing years; but their overall level of cardiac performance will likely remain better than that of physically inactive persons of equivalent age.

Joseph T. Doyle, M.D. The healthy heart continues to pump blood efficiently even in advanced old age. A normal feature of advancing age is, however, a slight, but progressive, reduction in maximum oxygen uptake from the lungs, in maximum heart rate and in the maximum amount of blood the heart can eject with each beat. The tempo as well as the extent of these changes can be partially offset by maintaining a high degree of physical fitness.

David G. Greene, M.D. While it is true that advancing years may be associated with diminished exercise capability as a result of diminishing capacity of the heart, lungs, muscles and other organs, many persons are able to maintain fitness into middle age and some even as senior citizens. If one has deteriorated in youth because of inactivity, one can regain a measure of heart function through an appropriate exercise program. One of the striking things about physical fitness and cardiovascular function is how rapidly it changes over a period of weeks in response to exercise or inactivity. Astronauts, after a period of inactivity and weightlessness, need exercise to restore their usual fitness after return to earth.

So far, we have been discussing the normal circulation and its response to training and inactivity. Similar comments are also true of the heart after various injuries and diseases. After a heart attack, a properly graded exercise program may help some patients regain a large measure of physical fitness.

J. Willis Hurst, M.D. It seems wise for healthy individuals to remain physically and mentally active throughout their lives. Medical advice should be obtained to guide them since apparently healthy persons may be unaware of the presence of heart disease.

There is no scientific evidence that exercise alone will increase the length of one's life. It is likely that all of the following will prolong an individual's life: appropriate exercise; abstaining from the use of tobacco; eating properly; and maintaining a normal body weight. There is certainly no evidence that super exercise, such as running five miles a day, is better for one's health than walking briskly for one to two miles daily. The complications of exercise are: bone and muscle injury; angina pectoris due to coronary disease; and unexpected sudden death. Marathon runners get a host of serious problems and many of them are related to the development of increased body temperature during the run.

The strength of the skeletal muscles can be improved with exercise and a trained person can do more than an untrained person, without increasing the heart rate excessively. One cannot stave off skeletal muscle deterioration indefinitely regardless of how faithfully one trains. The muscles will finally become weaker.

Furthermore, it should be understood that when one exercises, the skeletal muscles need more blood than when one is at rest. The normal heart can increase its output of blood to meet the requirements of exercise. The heart's output is determined by: the strength of heart muscle contraction (squeeze); the load of blood returning to the heart; and the resistance of the flow of the blood from the heart. The cardiac output of blood decreases with age. The exact amount of the decrease varies from subject to subject but approximates about 1 percent per year after mid-life. The pressure in the left ventricle of an elderly individual increases abnormally with exercise presumably due to increased "stiffness" of the heart muscle.

The decrease in the cardiac output of blood in older subjects is not necessarily harmful. This is so because the body no longer needs to maintain a youthful cardiac output, since there is a decrease in total body muscle mass and a decrease in metabolic rate in older subjects. Therefore the old heart does not need to be able to increase its output of blood as a young heart does.

In effect, the old heart acts like an untrained heart. The heart does less in old persons because it does not need to do more. While the subject has not been studied extensively, there is evidence that the heart of a healthy old person who undergoes proper physical training, can be brought to do more than it did before the training began. Despite this the aging process will continue.

Ultimately, the answer to the question—is it true that everyone's heart grows weaker each year no matter how much they exercise—is yes (at least after middle age). However, the good news is that this probably does not matter very much since the heart does not have to be any stronger than the skeletal muscles and other organs demand. The body is wise. A beautiful balance is achieved between the ability of the normal heart and the needs of the body.

BIRTH CONTROL

*B*ECAUSE IT LIES at the sensitive nexus of so many social currents, birth control remains one of the central social dilemmas of our society. Some who are traditional in their approach see birth control as a religious issue: sex without the possibility of conception is sinful; the decision of whether the sperm will fertilize the egg lies in the hands of God; and it is immoral to interfere with a natural process.

Others have a socioscientific interest in promoting birth control. They reason that because the resources of the earth are finite, it is wise to plan ahead to ensure that population growth does not outstrip the planet's ability to provide for its inhabitants. They argue that population control—through birth control—is particularly essential to countries with lower standards of living, whose resources should be harnessed to improve the quality of life for all rather than desperately trying to feed an ever-increasing number of hungry people.

And a third perspective on birth control, which is particularly noticeable in our country, can be called the feminist perspective. This argues that a woman must have the right to biological control of her own body. If a woman cannot decide when and with whom she would like to have a child, then all of her other rights—social, economic and political—are meaningless. Some feminists also argue that the very terms in which the argument is usually phrased—whether a *woman* has the right to birth control—indicates the basic sexism of our society. They maintain that the decision to have a child should be borne equally by man and woman—and that the responsibility for birth control should lie equally with both sexes.

Regardless of one's own perspective, the question of birth control is of interest to the entire population of our country. The fact remains that, in spite of recent advances in contraception, we have not yet developed an ideal method of controlled contraception. While our highly sophisticated country may spend millions of dollars a year on the exploration of space or on research to combat cancer, only $5 million a year is spent on research to find a better means of contraception.

According to the experts who discuss the subject in the following section, partly because of the scientific complexities and partly because of the tangled web of social, religious and political opinions that often inhibit the most direct efforts toward mass marketing of contraceptives, it will be at least five—and more likely ten—years before a contraceptive device with minimal side effects will be available in this country.

CONTRIBUTORS

Carl Djerassi, Professor of Chemistry, Stanford University; recipient of the National Medal of Science (1973) for the synthesis of the first oral contraceptive; author, *The Politics of Contraception*

Oscar Harkavy, Ph.D., Program Officer in Charge, Population Office, The Ford Foundation, New York, New York

George Zeidenstein, President, The Population Council, New York, New York

WHAT RESEARCH IS BEING DONE TO DEVELOP A SAFER BIRTH CONTROL PILL FOR WOMEN? WHEN WILL A SIMILAR PILL FOR MEN BE ON THE MARKET?

Carl Djerassi. The safety of drugs in general and of birth control methods in particular, cannot be considered in absolute terms. For instance, will a birth control pill of 90 percent contraceptive effectiveness that is totally devoid of any side effects be "safer" than steroid oral contraceptive pills which are nearly 100 percent effective but do have some side effects? Is an unwanted pregnancy not a component of "safety"? Therefore, before answering a question about a safer birth control pill, one needs to reply with another question: Safer than what?

A considerable amount of work was carried out during the middle and late 1970s to reduce the dosage of the active ingredients in the standard oral contraceptive pills. There is little doubt that the side effects associated with the smaller dosages currently used are considerably lower (both qualitatively and quantitatively) than those associated with original higher dosage oral contraceptives. Furthermore, extensive studies have shown that steroid oral contraceptives have beneficial side effects such as reduction in pelvic inflammatory disease, toxic shock syndrome, rheumatoid arthritis, certain uterine and ovarian cancers, to name just a few.

However, the question may really mean to ask: when will a completely different type of oral contraceptive for women become available? In this case, my own guess is that this will not happen before the 1990s, at the very earliest. The detailed reasons for this dim prognosis are associated not just with scientific questions but with an entire array of political ones. As a result, the development of a fundamentally new chemical birth control agent, that can be used by millions of women, takes a minimum of fifteen years from laboratory discovery to final clinical application and government approval.

In light of the above statement, it should not be surprising that a male contraceptive pill would take at least as long. In fact, it will take longer. There are several reasons for this. First: the man continuously produces new sperm whose lifetime exceeds seventy days. Second: less is known about the male reproductive system. Finally: less money and fewer efforts are being spent worldwide in the field of male contraception. As a result, a chemical birth control pill that can be used by millions of men, will not be developed before the turn of the century.

Oscar Harkavy, Ph.D. Contraceptive pills, now used by an estimated 150 million women around the world, consist of a combination of two steroid hormones: estrogen and progestin. When pills were first marketed in the early 1960s, they contained 150 micrograms of estrogen and 10 milligrams of progestin. Research by the pharmaceutical industry has produced a 99 percent effective pill, containing sharply reduced doses of these steroids: typically 20 to 50 micrograms of estrogen and 1 milligram of progestin. This has resulted in a much safer product because the most important health risks from use of the pill—heart attacks, stroke and blood clots in the lung—are substantially reduced as the amount of the steroids contained in the pills is reduced. While an estimated 3.7 of every 100,000 pill users in the United States suffer pill-related deaths each year, this total would be cut in half if pill users did not smoke and if women with such predisposing conditions to cardio-vascular disease as high blood pressure, high cholesterol and diabetes avoided the pill.[1]

Nonprofit organizations with government and philanthropic support are currently developing and testing novel methods of long-lasting contraceptive steroid administration, obviating the need for daily pill taking. These include: subdermal implants (plastic capsules inserted under the skin) that will provide 99 percent effective contraception for a period of five to seven years; steroid-releasing intrauterine devices,

1. Howard W. Ory, Alan Rosenfield, and Lynn C. Landman, "The Pill at 20: An Assessment," *Family Planning Perspectives*, November–December 1980, 278-282.

with a five year life span, that are 98 to 99 percent effective; and contraceptive vaginal rings to be inserted like diaphragms, with an estimated contraceptive action of six months and 98 to 99 percent effectiveness. Because these methods use a very low dose of steroid hormone it is expected that they will be at least as safe as modern low dose contraceptive pills. These new products may be available within two to three years.

Researchers are in the early stages of experimentation with new classes of compounds that they have reason to believe will be safer than methods using steroids. One such class of compounds is chemical analogs of so-called releasing factors; hormones produced by the brain, identified by the initials, LHRH, that stand for luteinizing hormone-releasing hormone. These compounds prevent ovulation in women and also stop sperm production in men. Fundamental research is also going forward on a number of other leads to improved female contraception, including an antipregnancy vaccine. New technologies in biology, such as monoclonal antibodies and gene-splicing, may considerably speed up progress in developing new methods of contraception. It will be a number of years, however, before scientists will ascertain whether this fundamental research will result in improved safer methods of contraception.

The results of research on a potential contraceptive pill for males has been generally disappointing so far. Compounds that suppress sperm production typically also decrease the production of testosterone, which, in turn, lowers libido. Furthermore, in cases where small amounts of sperm are produced, it is not known if they are normal. As indicated above, research is also going forward on LHRH analogs as a possible male contraceptive. It is too early to predict whether an acceptable product will result. Some scientists are enthusiastic about the potential of gossypol, a derivative of cottonseed oil. In China, gossypol pills have been administered to some 4,000 men, some of whom have been taking the pills for as long as six years. Repeated side effects have been relatively minor. A number of laboratories throughout the world are now testing gossypol on animals before beginning trials on humans. If gossypol continues to show promise as it is tested, a male pill may be on the market in ten to fifteen years.[2]

George Zeidenstein. The currently marketed birth control pills for women are very safe for women under age thirty. In fact, for them, the risks of taking the pill are much less than those associated with pregnancy. After age thirty, women who smoke should not take the pill, and even those who do not smoke should not take it after thirty-five. After that age, other methods of contraception are safer than the pill.

2.   Linda Atkinson, Bruce Schearer, Oscar Harkavy, and Richard Lincoln, "Prospects for Improved Contraception," *International Family Planning Perspectives*, June 1980, pp. 43–59.

The drugs in the current pill stop a woman's ovary from releasing an egg, thereby preventing pregnancy. But they also produce many other changes in body chemistry, and in a very few women these can give rise to such side effects as: heart attacks, strokes, other circulatory system diseases, gall bladder diseases, liver hepatomas and increases in blood pressure. The incidence of these side effects is rare and there is hope that they can be reduced still further by modifying the drugs used in the pill.

New versions of the pill are being developed and tested that will cause fewer changes in body metabolism. Some new approaches being tested use a small amount of contraceptive drug, others release the drug at a more constant rate, thus preventing high levels from accumulating in the blood stream, while still others employ new types of drugs. Currently, research is being conducted to determine whether a pill that contains a natural, rather than a synthetic, estrogen is safer.

New birth control pills incorporating these improvements are likely to cause fewer changes in body chemistry. But whether they will, in fact, give rise to fewer side effects is uncertain. Since these side effects are so rare, proving that they are lessened with the new pills will require studies involving tens of thousands of women over many years. Thus, the enhanced safety of the new pills will need to be assumed until the results of long-term studies confirm this expectation.

Some of this research is being conducted by pharmaceutical companies in the United States and Europe, and some is being conducted by public contraceptive development programs funded by governments and foundations. The largest research effort in this area, at present, is being carried out by a special center that is part of the National Institute of Health of the United States government. In comparison with other areas of health, however, only a small amount of money is being devoted to this objective—less than $5 million annually by all groups. Despite the modest expenditures, prospects for the development of one or more new versions of a safer pill within the next five years are very good.

Other studies are being performed to determine whether hormones can be delivered into the body in a safer way. Recent observations suggest that there are very few effects on health when a progestin (one of the components of the pill) is administered subcutaneously in an implant; this device has proved to be a very effective method of birth control. Hormone-containing rubber rings, similar to the outer rim of the diaphragm, can also be used to deliver contraceptives into the vagina. This route of administration may prove to be safer than by mouth. Thus, different hormone combinations and other routes of delivery may result in effective contraception that is safer than the current pill.

Unfortunately, prospects for a birth control pill for men are less encouraging. Extensive testing of contraceptive drugs in men, over the past ten years, has failed to identify a safe and effective agent. At least three new approaches are now being pursued by public and private contraceptive development groups, but it is unlikely that any of these could yield a marketable new product for men in less than ten years. It is obvious that scientists need to learn more about male reproductive physiology and processes. Such basic research is considered necessary for improving the prospects of developing male contraceptive methods. So far progress has been made on basic issues of gametogenesis, sperm ultrastructure, zona pellucida composition, male hormone action and testicular function—all necessary knowledge in the quest for a safe, effective and convenient systemic male contraceptive.

HOSPITALS

N O ONE IS MORE INTERESTED in hospitals than prospective hospital patients. They know their health—and possibly their lives—may depend on whether they choose a good hospital.

But how good are any of the nation's more than 7,000 hospitals? The answer very much depends upon what health care consumers want from a hospital. The average taxpayer looking for economical health care will not have much good to say about any American hospital—or the health care system in general. Health care expenditures have taken up increasingly large proportions of the country's gross national product in recent years: from 6.2 percent in 1965 to more than 9 percent in 1980. Hospital costs consume the lion's share of these health care expenditures. In 1978, Americans spent $167.9 billion on hospital care and less than half that amount, $76 billion, on the next greatest medical expense, physicians' services.

Throughout the last decade, the cost of health care frequently outpaced the general rise in the consumer price index. While inflation pushed up the prices of just about everything, the cost of hospital care led the rest. According to estimates by the Social Security Administration, the amount spent on hospital care per person in the United States more than tripled between 1970 and 1980.

What does all this money buy? The good news about American hospitals does not lie in the ledger sheets but in the new treatments developed and in the impressive medical advances made. At its best, hospital care in the United States ranks among the finest in the world.

Hospital administrators and staff trace a good part of the rising costs of hospital care to the up-to-date technology used in American hospitals. New equipment, new employees to use the equipment, advanced training, more intensive care for the seriously ill—all add up to higher costs.

As a group, taxpayers tend to be outraged at these costs. Individually, however, most people want the best that money can buy when they themselves need hospital care. And patients do not pay all their own bills. A 1977 survey estimated that 90 percent of the population was covered by some type of insurance plan. "Third parties," such as insurance companies, private industry, government agencies and philanthropic organizations, pay for roughly two-thirds of all personal health expenditures. As critics point out, both health care providers and health care consumers tend to spend more freely when they know the bills will be paid by a third party. Cost-conscious patients commonly request costly hospitalization for procedures that could be done in a physician's office because their insurance plans reimburse them only for hospital expenses.

Virtually everyone is hospitalized at some time in his life, whether for emergency or for elective treatment. Yet many people do not realize the wide range of health services available and therefore do not use the hospitals as effectively as possible. A prime example is the patient who goes to an emergency room in the middle of the night with a non-emergency condition; such conditions can be treated much more easily—and inexpensively—at an outpatient clinic during the day.

When it is absolutely necessary to go to a hospital, there are several different types to choose from. Private, nonprofit, community hospitals provide most of the nation's short-term hospital care. These hospitals are usually small (with fewer than 200 beds) and are designed to serve patients from the surrounding community.

Patients who require unusual or highly sophisticated treatment may be referred to a large public hospital or to a teaching hospital that is affiliated with a medical school. Public hospitals, which include city, state and federal hospitals, along with special institutions such as Veterans' Administration hospitals, sometimes suffer from a poor image. Government hospitals may seem less attractive than private community hospitals, but they are generally larger and offer more services.

Hospitals affiliated with medical schools exist to teach and conduct research as well as to serve the community. Patients at these institutions may benefit from the most advanced techniques available, but they also may miss the personalized attention that they might receive in their community hospital.

Thus a good hospital for a tonsillectomy might not be quite so good for brain surgery—and vice versa. One universal recommendation is that people investigate all the available hospitals in their area *while they are well* in order to be able to choose the hospital that best suits their needs should they become ill.

CONTRIBUTORS

James W. Bartlett, M.D., Medical Director, Strong Memorial Hospital, University of Rochester, Rochester, New York

Harold A. Cohen, Executive Director, State of Maryland Health Services Cost Review Commission, Baltimore, Maryland

Scott Fleming, Senior Vice-President, Kaiser-Permanente Medical Care Program, Oakland, California

James R. Flynn, Senior Vice-President, Riverside Methodist Hospital, Columbia, Ohio

Victor R. Fuchs, Professor of Economics, Stanford University, Stanford, California

Robert M. Heyssel, M.D., Executive Vice-President and Director, The Johns Hopkins Hospital, Baltimore, Maryland

Robert M. Magnuson, President and Chief Executive Officer, Memorial Hospital of DuPage County, Elmhurst, Illinois

John A. Maloney, Associate Administrator, Walter Reed Army Medical Center, Washington, D.C.

J. Alexander McMahon, President, American Hospital Association, Chicago, Illinois

Rodger E. Mendenhall, M.S., Dayton Mental Health and Development Center, Dayton, Ohio

Charles M. O'Brien, Jr., Hospital Administrator, Georgetown University Hospital, Washington, D.C.

John Pekkanen, author, *The Best Doctors in the U.S.*

Melvin H. Rudov, Ph.D., President, Affiliated Risk Control Administrators of Pennsylvania, Inc., Pittsburgh, Pennsylvania

David D. Thompson, M.D., Director, The New York Hospital, New York, New York

WHY ARE HOSPITAL COSTS SO HIGH?

James W. Bartlett, M.D. This complicated question of high hospital costs involves several answers:

1. Hospitals, responding to community needs, have greatly broadened the range of services provided. Thus, the hospital of today provides much more than the hospital of yesterday and costs are higher, accordingly.
2. All costs have been rising rapidly.
3. The pricing system by which hospital costs are usually measured does not reflect true costs. In many cases prices have been pushed up above actual costs by accounting and reimbursement practices that require the "paying" patients to make up for the charitable

care provided those who are unable to pay; and for hospital under-reimbursement built into many regulated insurance rates.

4.   What were formerly hidden or unpaid costs, such as depreciation, are not reflected in the actual costs.

5.   Stand-by costs—the cost of being there, waiting to be needed, and able to meet most if not all emergencies—are also added into hospital bills.

Is it possible, in view of all of the above, that hospital costs are not as high as generally believed and represent a real value received by the society they serve?

Harold A. Cohen. This question of costs generally reflects the feeling that our society is not getting its money's worth for the share of our resources being devoted to hospital care—a feeling with which I agree. Why then do we continue to collectively expend what we individually question?

The answer, I believe, is fairly straightforward: no one is forced to act as if he will have less money to spend on other things when he causes money to be spent on health care. Economists refer to these other things as "opportunity costs." In the hospital sector we have devised a market that almost totally protects decision-makers from the opportunity costs of their decisions.

Patients, physicians, hospitals and even, by design, most government programs, are encouraged to overlook these true costs.

One factor contributes immensely to Americans consuming as much hospital care as we do; the lifestyles we lead. These include our behavior relative to smoking, drinking, driving, eating, exercise, stress, etc. All these private decisions have huge implications for the likelihood that we will be consumers of costly hospital care. Because of the largely socialized nature of the payment (as opposed to the provision) of hospital care, individuals do not pay the costs of their lifestyles.

Furthermore, when we face the decision to consume hospital care, most of us are fully insured. We do not decide whether to spend $5,000 on an operation or to spend that $5,000 on other things. We do not shop to buy the operation for less money. We do not even face the true cost of the insurance we buy because the tax laws mask most of those costs. Thus, as employees, we may give up close to $2,000 in before-tax wages for $1,000 worth of nontaxed health insurance.

The physicians who make most of the decisions that influence hospital costs are not employees of the hospital and are paid separately from the hospital. Their incentives are to increase hospital costs as long as that increases their own income or makes it easier for them to earn that income. In fact, physicians earn much more money per hour when their patients are hospitalized. Imagine how inefficient most businesses would be if their managers earned more money by helping to raise general company costs.

Hospitals, caught between the insufficiently constrained desires of patients and the largely unrestrained desires of physicians, are then paid by most major payers according to their actual costs, or according to charges set by the hospital's board. Due to insurance, there is no competition to restrain charges and programs apply extremely weak limits to the costs which will be paid. Thus, hospitals' profits do not decline if their costs rise—the basic restraint to inefficiency in our economy.

Finally, government has responded to these problems not by altering the underlying causes—starting with the tax laws—but by creating agencies, such as local health planning bodies, that decide whether a certain hospital project is "needed." The local residents benefit from the project, if it is approved. But people from all over the country pay the project's costs—through the socialized payment system. Hence, the opportunity costs, or the things we as a society forego because of the amount of resources spent on hospital care, are still not considered.

Scott Fleming. Many factors contribute to the pronounced increase in the cost of hospitalization that has occurred over the last fifteen to twenty years.

1. General inflation. Increases in the cost of foods, medicines, energy and other supplies that hospitals buy, is one significant factor that affects hospitals just as it affects individuals and organizations throughout our economy. The "market basket" of goods and services purchased by hospitals contains elements that have increased in cost faster than general inflation.

2. Personal compensation for hospital workers. The biggest single cost incurred by hospitals has escalated for three primary reasons: general escalation of wage and salary costs throughout the economy; a significant "catchup" that has moved hospital workers from a substandard compensation level to parity (and some would say more than parity) with comparable employment in other sectors of the economy; escalation in the skill levels, specialization and number of workers required to support the rapidly expanding health care technology discussed below.

3. Escalation in health-care technology. The sophistication, complexity and cost of diagnostic and therapeutic techniques that constitute contemporary medical care in modern United States hospitals have increased dramatically, and continue to increase explosively. These scientific and technological advances, which vastly increase the effectiveness of medical care, often require costly equipment, expensive construction and highly trained, well-compensated personnel. For example, the average rate of

use of laboratory procedures has been increasing 10 to 15 percent per year.

4. Demographic changes. Health care needs and consequent costs are markedly higher for older people, especially in their postretirement years, than for the younger, working population. Basic demographic changes, including lower death rates and increased life expectancy, have greatly increased the proportion of our nation's population in older age groups; this demographic trend will continue well into the next century.

In addition to these fundamental forces (which include demographic and technological components that are virtually certain to continue strong upward pressure on hospital costs regardless of general inflation) other factors deserve mention.

5. Inappropriate utilization of services. The only major cost factor that involves a significant degree of economic waste is unnecessary or excessive use of expensive hospitalization. Despite extensive efforts to control this, by government and by well-motivated physicians and hospital administrators, unnecessary or inappropriate use of hospitals remains an important problem. Aspects of inappropriate use include: elective surgery for conditions for which alternate therapy is available, hospitalization for diagnosis or treatment that could be handled at much lower cost in the physician's office, necessary hospital stays unduly prolonged, etc.

This conclusion is supported by the fact that, after adjusting for demographic and health status differences, well-established successful group practice prepayment plans (one form of "health maintenance organization") consistently serve their enrollees with only about 75 percent as much inpatient hospitalization as persons covered by other forms of private health insurance. Responsible studies, indicating that quality of care provided through such organizations is at least as good (if not better) than that provided through the traditional fee-for-service system, show that these savings on hospital utilization are real economic savings and do not reflect skimping on necessary or appropriate hospital care.

Unless our society is prepared to limit scientific and technological progress in the health care field—or limit access, particularly by older persons, to advances in medical science and technology—there is no realistic prospect that hospital cost escalation will drop to or below the general rate of inflation in the foreseeable future.

Over the long term, "health promotion" and widespread adoption of healthier lifestyles could have a moderating effect on the proportion of our national resources required for hospitalization. Another important factor would be a major increase in the percentage of the population enrolled in health maintenance organizations or other alternatives to the traditional fee-for-service health care system. This could create competition in the marketplace for personal health care services. In turn, competition might reduce waste and inefficiency within the system and bring hospital utilization rates down to levels more comparable to those achieved by the most efficient organizations. However, while these factors could significantly moderate the total cost of hospital services used in our society, they would not reduce the average daily cost-per-patient.

Ironically, more appropriate use of hospital services, which reduces the total cost of care for a given population, tends to increase average hospital costs per patient day. The reason is simply this: patients who don't really need to be in the hospital are less costly to care for; and the latter days of an unduly long hospital stay are also less costly. Thus, a hospital that manages to eliminate unnecessary hospitalization, and that does not keep patients in the hospital any longer than medically necessary, will be providing more intensive and more costly care to those patients who are in the hospital. Indeed, a significant nationwide trend of fewer admissions and declining lengths of stay (after adjusting for aging of the population), has also contributed to increasing hospital cost when measured on the basis of costs per patient day.

6. Cost shifting. When Medicare and Medicaid originally took effect in 1966, they provided a source of payment for many persons who had previously received charity care or who had been unable to pay full charges for hospital services. Thus, these programs eased the financial situation of hospitals. However, in recent years, stringent efforts by government to limit cost increases in the Medicare and Medicaid programs often produce underpayment for services provided to Medicare and Medicaid beneficiaries. In order to meet their financial requirements, hospitals must recover this underpayment by increasing charges to persons who pay their own bills or who have private insurance or other private sector health care coverage.

7. Method of payment for health services. A very large portion of the payment for hospital services in the United States is on a cost reimbursement basis. This not only covers costs incurred by hospitals, whether such costs are really necessary or not, but actually rewards hospitals with increased revenue as a result of cost increases. Thus, the system provides little incentive for cost control.

Under the dominant fee-for-service system, physicians are rewarded for rendering more services; they also earn more net income per hour for hospital services than for services rendered in their offices. These circumstances tend to increase hospital use.

In addition, United States residents are relying more on physicians for health care than they did in the past.

8. Health insurance. Since World War II, stimulated by government tax and labor policies, employer-sponsored group health insurance has become very widespread. This protects a large portion of our population from the direct impact of health care costs—another factor that has undoubtedly contributed to the increasing cost of health care services.

James R. Flynn. All of the following factors relate to high hospital costs.

1. Health care services are labor intensive. Therefore, escalating wages and benefits are direct and leading factors in escalating health care costs.
2. The health industry is a major user of sophisticated technology equaling or even outpacing the space program. The need to keep up with current technology has legal implications for health care institutions, in terms of staying up with "the current state of the art"; and has moral implications for the family seeking care, when they demand "only the best" for a member of the family. Today, society fully expects to benefit from the full range of medical and health care technology, not only to relieve pain but to extend life.
3. Reimbursement formulas are inequitable; formulas spawned by Medicare and Medicaid do not pay their full share of the costs; thereby forcing hospitals into high cost financing for capital improvements.
4. The health care industry is one of the most regulated industries on the American scene. Although it is often referred to as a voluntary hospital system, it is, in fact, anything but voluntary. The oppressive regulations (federal and state), governing the manner in which services are provided, as well as how reimbursement is made, lead to a morass of bureaucracy that is frightfully expensive.
5. We are entering an era of competition in health care that can only escalate costs. People are confused about how the forces of supply and demand will work in the health care field. Ultimately, this competition will lead to a duplication of facilities and services in the name of free choice, and will perpetuate the escalating cost to the public.
6. Society's propensity to sue and demand compensation for non-negligent acts has caused a layer of medical practice to be performed that is clearly defensive. This increases the number of tests performed, the days of patient care in the hospital and the number of follow-up visits that patients receive—all increasing costs unnecessarily.

7. Clearly the unions' increased attempts to organize health care workers have had an impact on health care costs.

8. The health care industry, by virtue of its major cost components (labor, supplies, equipment and debt service) has been directly influenced by the country's general economic inflationary pattern over the past six years. While the health care industry may be recession proof, it is not inflation proof.

Victor R. Fuchs. A good way to begin to understand the problem of high hospital costs is to reverse the question and ask: "Why aren't hospital costs higher than they are?" As soon as the question is put in this form we see that the people whose decisions determine hospital costs have no incentive to keep them down. The patient who has hospital insurance (currently 92 percent of all hospital bills are paid by third parties) wants the best possible care regardless of cost. The physician wants his or her patient to get the best possible care. The administrator of the hospital wants to run a high quality institution, which means an endless pursuit of new, better and more expensive technology.

The nurses and other personnel who work in the hospital naturally want better wages. The manufacturers of drugs, instruments and other technology want to develop new products; and want to sell as many as possible to the hospital.

In short, hospital costs are as high as they are primarily because nearly all the incentives push the system in that direction.

The only groups that have an immediate stake in holding down costs are the third-party payers—i.e., the government and the private insurance companies. These third parties, however, are inhibited in their efforts to control costs because they have explicitly or implicitly promised their beneficiaries that they will get all the care they "need," and it is the physician and other health professionals who determine "need." It is only when those who ultimately pay the bills (the taxpayers in the case of government, and employers and employees in the case of most private insurance) begin to resist ever-escalating health costs that some restraint is introduced.

Robert M. Heyssel, M.D. The question of hospital costs could have been phrased better, as: "Why have hospital costs gone up at a rate that is almost two times greater than the general rate of inflation over the last decade and a half?"

Hospitals, like any other institution, are caught by the same inflationary aspects as the general economy: energy, food prices, materials prices, etc. The reason, however, that hospitals have outstripped the rest of the economy in the growth in their prices depends upon two other factors. The first is the growth of wages in the hospital industry. This reflects the fact that two decades ago many hospital workers were paid less than the minimum wage and so there was a considerable catchup phenomenon. It also reflects the fact that, in an increasingly complex medical environment, hospitals have been forced to hire more highly specialized people in order to provide services.

That leads to the second, and probably the major, reason for hospital cost rises—the burgeoning of technology in hospitals over the years. Here is a most graphic example: obviously, it costs much less money to allow patients to die of leukemia in three months, without really doing anything effective, than it does to prolong the same patients' lives for two years or perhaps even to cure the patients with very expensive treatments such as bone marrow transplants, chemotherapy, radiation therapy and others. In addition to that, the growth of such technologically oriented procedures as open heart surgery, total hip replacement, total knee replacement, renal transplantation, etc., has forced costs up. Technology is not only a matter of the large procedures I have mentioned. It also involves growth in the amount of laboratory testing, to more accurately diagnose and treat disease and monitor the cause of treatment. All these factors, then, have conspired to make hospital rates increase markedly and run ahead of the general economy.

Robert M. Magnuson. Hospital costs are not unreasonable considering the services rendered. Comparing today's hospital costs with costs of previous periods is extremely misleading since what is provided today has changed dramatically. The result of the changes is a higher quality of life for more people.

Costs can be considered in two ways. The first is in overall expenditures, and much of the increase here reflects the fact that more and more services are provided to more people. Access to health care in this country is virtually universal. The public considers health care as a fundamental right.

The second way of looking at costs is on a per occurrence basis. The increases here reflect a significantly improved service and a service that is subject to the forces of inflation as well. Technology allows physicians to detect, treat and increasingly, to cure maladies that were only recently untreatable or that previously required more painful or more dangerous methods. But the rapid technological advances also mean additional equipment costs, more skilled personnel and more training. American hospitals average 3.4 employees per occupied bed, and a large portion of them are highly trained technical and professional persons.

Other factors add to the increase in hospital costs. Hospitals must be built and maintained with the highest degree of safety and include state-of-the-art equipment. Hospitals are subject to the forces of the open market (including inflation). They must also pay competitive wages, and the going price for goods and services including energy, food and supplies. Laws and regulations control almost every aspect of hospital operations. The costs of complying with these requirements are built into hospital rates.

John A. Maloney. To adequately answer the question of hospital costs, one needs to look at the history of hospitals. For several centuries hospitals were operated by religious groups or orders, by charitable foundations and by government entities. Until the middle of this century, there were very few proprietary hospitals. The largest increase in proprietary hospitals has been during the last fifteen years.

Until recent years, the largest cost in operating a hospital was labor cost. Several years ago it was about two-thirds of the total operating cost. However, for centuries, people who worked in hospitals did it for religious or service reasons, not for the monetary rewards. Until the early 1960s, hospital salaries and wages were low, in comparison to industrial and commercial enterprises. Nonprofit and governmental hospitals had not been required to operate under the Fair Labor Standards Act which also required that the federal minimum wage be paid employees. This was one of the causes for the increase in hospital costs. Many of the lower salaried employees (food service, housekeeping, clerical workers) were being paid 20 to 30 percent less than the minimum wage. This meant that not only did their wages have to be increased, but that the supervisory and the paraprofessional personnel salaries also had to be increased.

Another factor increased hospital costs: most of the nonprofit hospitals operated their own nurses training schools (most were three-year diploma schools). Much of the first year student's training was didactic in nature. However, the last two were spent in "hands on" nursing care, especially the senior year. Because of the pressures of nursing associations and accrediting bodies many of the schools have ceased to operate. Those that continue have very little "on the job" training; 95 percent of the student training is spent in didactics. These students have had to be replaced by other nursing personnel who are paid at the prevailing wage.

Because of the low wages and, sometimes, the poor working conditions, hospital employees were "ripe" for union organization. When a hospital in a particular area was organized, the wages and benefits in that institution increased. Since the hospital labor market, especially nurses and paraprofessionals, is highly competitive, this resulted in the nonunion hospitals having to increase wages and benefits also.

It is true that, during the last few years, the labor costs in hospitals have been decreased (to just slightly above 50 percent). Many positions have been replaced or decreased through automation. However, the cost of this automation, itself, has kept costs higher.

Another factor: hospital and medical equipment is continuously changing and being improved. A hospital may buy a piece of equipment and use it for a year or two and suddenly a better piece of equipment will be developed. A case in point is the new CAT scan which suddenly made older models obsolete. The newer scans are in the $1 million price range while older models were available at half the cost—but could only give half the results.

As long as the inflationary spiral continues it is inevitable that hospital costs will continue to rise, but, hopefully, not as fast as they have in the past.

J. Alexander McMahon. The factors involved in hospital costs are many and complex. Just as individual consumers have found their budgets pressed by inflation, hospitals also have been hit by rising prices in basic goods and services such as food, supplies, utilities, laundry and maintenance costs. Hospitals have been particularly hard hit by skyrocketing oil prices, which affect not only direct energy expense, but the cost of the many petroleum-based products used extensively in hospitals.

The largest single expense in the delivery of health care is labor. As in other industries, inflationary trends in wages have had a major impact on hospital costs. A nationwide shortage of hospital nurses has created additional labor expense for hospitals, since many have been forced to hire nurses from temporary employment agencies to meet staffing needs, spend advertising dollars to recruit nurses, and offer higher salaries and increased benefits to attract and retain them.

Labor costs have also risen as a result of the need for more highly skilled personnel required to perform complex procedures and work with sophisticated hospital technology. These advancements, in themselves, have contributed to higher costs, along with increased capability for saving lives and improving medical care. Sophisticated diagnostic tests and procedures continue to evolve. These can dramatically improve the quality of health care but, also, can often involve additional costs.

Other factors contributing to high hospital costs are public expectations and payment mechanisms. Naturally, patients expect that no expense will be spared in their treatment or that of someone they love. The traditional focus on providing optimum health care has not encouraged consumers or physicians to make decisions regarding what is possible on the basis of what is affordable. Moreover, most of the population is covered by either private insurers or government health programs, and so they are shielded from the cost realities of that care because they do not pay for hospital care directly, as they do for other commodities. Consequently, some people use health services less judiciously than they might if they were paying full cost. Use of emergency rooms for noncrisis care is an example.

An additional societal factor in hospital costs is the increasing number of elderly people in the population. Older citizens go to hospitals more often, stay longer, and require more intensive services while hospitalized.

Government's role in health care has also meant higher costs. The Medicaid and Medicare programs have created many financial difficulties for hospitals, including inadequate payment for services to beneficiaries. Excessive government regulation and procedural requirements have made it necessary for many hospitals to employ full-time staff simply to process government paper.

Many of the contributing factors to increasing hospital costs are difficult or impossible to control. Others can be, and are, modified by the conscious efforts of hospitals, physicians and consumers to make the most judicious use possible of all resources—without compromising quality of care.

Rodger E. Mendenhall, B.A., M.S. Why high hospital costs? This is a complex question. A list of major contributing factors would have to include the following:

1. Inflation. Hospitals face the same inflation we all experience for food, utilities, gasoline, vehicles, interest, facility costs, etc. Special equipment and supply costs will cause hospital costs to rise at a rate about 3 percent higher than the consumer price index.
2. Labor costs. Increased specialization, higher educational requirements, expansion of sophisticated services, new technology, and product improvement all lead to higher labor costs. Couple this labor intensity with twenty-four-hour service and you have an industry where about 60 percent of the cost is labor. In other businesses such costs are closer to 25 percent. A salary increase in a hospital will, therefore, increase costs about 2½ times faster than in other enterprises.
3. Governmental regulatory intervention—this, and its accompanying paperwork, increases daily hospital charges by approximately 6 percent.
4. Rising demand is requiring new and expensive expansion. Among major unavoidable causes are higher birth rates; more intensive care required by older population groups; inpatient care that treats a more seriously ill population—because improved ambulatory services, emergency services, and clinical services have reduced admissions to the more complex medical cases.

There are avoidable causes of expensive expansion. There is unnecesary duplication of services caused by pride, perceived need for completeness, staff convenience or "profit," in hospitals within close proximity. There are constant increases in benefits—and therefore in demand—caused by negotiated labor contracts. Hospitals offer unnecessary services to potential "customers" because "customers" *want* the services—not because they *need* them.

Charles M. O'Brien, Jr. Many of the reasons for hospital cost increases are well known. These include the overall rate of inflation with concomitant increases in pay rates, fuel, food, medicines and supplies, coupled with the rapid development of sophisticated medical technology.

Other reasons are less obvious, but have a direct bearing on the additional cost of hospitalization. For example, the hospital industry is the most regulated in the country and the cost of complying with various federal, state and local regulations is passed on to the consumer.

Increased unionization of hospital employees has resulted in higher wages and expanded fringe benefits. Loss of revenue caused by strikes is also a factor.

Physician specialization and changing practice patterns also affect hospital costs. Higher malpractice premiums are the natural result of more lawsuits being brought by patients and higher damages being awarded to claimants. The cost of these premiums must be borne by the hospital.

It should be noted that higher expectations on the part of consumers have forced hospitals to provide more amenities such as color television, private phones, attractively decorated facilities and other niceties that may be desirable but that do add to the consumer's total cost of hospitalization.

Melvin H. Rudov, Ph.D. There is no singular answer to this question since a number of disparate factors contribute to hospital costs. Thus, in answering this question, we have to go down the list of some of these factors and point out what they are and how it is that they contribute, not only to high hospital costs, but to continuing escalations in these costs.

A. Regulation. Over 90 percent of all hospital costs are usually paid through a reimbursement agency rather than directly by the patient. Approximately 40 percent of these are paid for by Medicare and Medicaid. The federal government rarely gives up any money without stipulating the rules under which that money is given. Hence, a very complex set of regulations is imposed upon hospitals participating in these government programs. Adhering to these programs requires increases in costs that the hospital would not otherwise incur. An example would be the Professional Standards Review Organization (PSRO) program, which has resulted in hospitals hiring coordinators (usually nurses) who review the kinds of care given in hospitals. The government requires that all hospitals participate in these functions. Therefore, a hospital that is not practicing overutilization still must go through the same activities as a hospital that has been. In addition, after participating in the program and reducing their overutilization, the hospitals must continue to do the same level of monitoring, and thus the costs for utilization monitoring continue.

In addition to the federal government, state health departments usually impose strict sets of requirements on the plant and equipment as well as on the operations of all health care facilities. A similar set of regulations is imposed by the Joint Commission on Accreditation of Hospitals (JCAH). Although some would regard these as self-imposed regulations since the JCAH was formed by the American Hospital Association, an argument could be made that once formed, the hospitals of this country lost control of this accrediting agency. This agency imposes an additional set of regulations, many of them having to do with plant and equipment. The regulations of the state health departments and the JCAH continue to grow year after year. Many of these requirements are extremely worthwhile, but sometimes their effects are economically deleterious. It is not uncommon for a new hospital to be constructed only to find that it is no longer in compliance with the codes imposed by these regulatory agencies. The redesign and reconstruction efforts can sometimes add millions to the original costs.

The fact that these regulatory functions have a great deal of overlap is not being addressed in most parts of the nation. It has only recently been addressed in some areas, where there has been agreement with the JCAH and state health departments to conduct their inspections at the same time. We would probably be better off if they just conducted a joint inspection rather than separate ones with overlap, but again these activities increase hospital costs. The costs stem from complying with recommendations made by these agencies. They also stem from the hours spent by hospital personnel first in the preparation for the site visit, then the conduct of the site visit, and finally in the review of the findings of the survey.

B. *Personnel Costs.* Usually, approximately 50 percent of the hospital's budget is personnel-related costs. Until now, approximately half of the employees of the hospitals have been nurses, and nurses have been underpaid. Recently substantial increases in nurses' salaries have escalated hospital costs. One of the factors that is going to cause huge increases in hospital costs in the near future is the extreme shortage of nurses in this country. The only means for countering this shortage is to offer yet higher salaries.

But nurses have not been the only underpaid hospital personnel. Most other hospital employees (including laundry workers, dietary workers and custodial personnel) have traditionally been underpaid. The number of hospitals in which these personnel have become unionized is increasing yearly, and labor strikes for higher wages and benefits have become commonplace. Thus, we can expect personnel costs to be a significant factor in increases in hospital costs in the coming years.

C. *Manpower Categories.* It has been reported that there are probably at least seventy-five job categories in hospitals that did not exist ten years ago. These categories of employees come about basically from two sources. One is the increase in technology requiring specifically trained personnel to perform certain tasks. The second source is the desire to unburden some existing personnel of some of their lower-level tasks; so new categories of paraprofessional and technician personnel are being invented, frequently to help in the reassignment of such tasks.

An example of this burgeoning of categories of staff is that dealing with respiration therapy. Prior to the respiration therapy devices, there were no respiration therapists. When the devices started coming onto the market, nurses were taught to administer respiration therapy. As nurses became more and more involved in many other tasks, someone decided that it made sense to teach a technician how to operate the equipment, and the field of respiration therapy was born.

One of the advantages that accrues when you have personnel who are capable of many tasks is that you can shift those personnel around as tasks need to be done. The more categories of employees with focused abilities you have, the more this kind of flexibility abates; and your efficiency abates as well. Therefore, if you need someone to work with the IV team, you cannot use (or at least should not use) a respiration therapist for this task. The result is increased amounts of employee downtime, and decreased amounts of flexibility in assigning your staff to the various hospital tasks. An additional problem comes from the laws of institutionalism. If you are going to have a respiration therapist, you need two more for the other shifts, plus another for weekends, holidays, vacations and sick leave. Then you need a supervisor and the supervisor needs a secretary, and they all need office space and continuing education.

D. *Hospital Associations.* I would now like to address two very unpopular topics. The first of these topics is hospital organizations. Hospitals form councils and associations to which they pay dues and sometimes these dues are extremely hefty. The concept is a good one, in that there are some things that hospitals can do in groups much better and less expensively than they can do as individual hospitals. However, when these groups are formed, they frequently take on an identity and set of needs for themselves, and frequently the original purpose of the council or association is lost. The association continues to grow so that the president of the association can get a higher salary, but the growth is not always related to the hospitals' needs for programs offered by the council or association.

Sometimes the council or association starts programs because of relationships that they get themselves into, and these are clearly not the best programs for the hospitals. One of the ways that I interface with hospitals is through their insurance programs. Many hospital associations have put together insurance programs that are no longer the best programs that the hospitals could have. But the people offering these programs get their grips on the hospital association's personnel, and a bond is formed between them that is stronger than the bond between the hospital association and the hospitals themselves. Hospitals are very lax in auditing and monitoring the functions of their councils and associations.

E. *Administrative Competence.* If the above statement is going to cause some furor, then the next one is going to cause more. I have worked with some extremely competent hospital administrators who are also extremely dedicated to their jobs. But the truth of the matter is that the bulk of the people administering hospitals are incompetent, and some of the increases that we see in hospital costs are directly due to the fact that these people are not administering their hospitals well. Many hospital administrators around the country have never received any didactic training in their field, yet the management of a hospital can be an extremely complex occupation. Even for those who have been didactically trained, it is questionable that the training has been sufficient or properly oriented to achieve its purpose.

Sometimes the lack of competence is politically motivated. A large number of hospital administrators are fired yearly because they have run afoul of a single member of the medical staff or a member of the board. Since this is the case, there are a fair number of hospital administrators who play it safe and try not to be too innovative or exert too much control.

F. *Incentives.* Until recently, there have not been many incentives to try to control hospital costs, and even now the incentives are too weak. A lot of this stems from the method of reimbursement that intermediaries utilize to handle hospital costs. To put it simply: what hospitals have been doing is to run themselves without a tremendous regard for costs, and at the end of the year tell the reimbursement agencies how much their costs have been. Since most hospitals do not buck up against reimbursement maximums, there has never been much of an incentive for most hospitals to keep their costs low.

When President Carter indicated that he was going to do something to control costs in hospitals, the hospitals, through the American Hospital Association, came up with a "Voluntary Effort" in which the hospitals were supposed to meet their own standards without regulation. These standards were higher than President Carter's, and from the records that I have seen, the hospitals have never been able to meet their own standards.

Within the last few years, there have been a number of experiments with reimbursement, to try to curtail hospital costs. One of these appears to be somewhat successful. In essence, the hospital agrees (before a given year) what its costs will be for that year. It then must run the hospital within those reimbursement guidelines or find the monies through some other means. There are some difficulties in trying to run a hospital under such constraints, but they are too vast to be treated in this discussion.

G. *Planning.* Actually, although there are common references to the American health-care delivery system, we do not have anything that should be dignified by the word "system." Hospitals essentially came into being because someone decided that we needed one—going from door to door collecting money in order to put up a building. At least in urban areas, this was accomplished without reference to "clinical needs" of the community. Hospitals were started because we did not have enough "Catholic beds," no hospitals would accept "Jewish doctors," a given order of nuns had no place to call their own, or people residing in one community decided that they did not want to go across town for hospital care or visitations. In the past, when a hospital decided that it was going to expand, it could do so without any reference to the needs of the community. When a hospital wished to buy expensive equipment, it could do so without any reference to whether or not the hospital down the street was buying the same set of equipment. In the 1960s, the government started the Comprehensive Health Planning Agency Program, which was supposed to try to get hospitals to work together in planning their plant and equipment acquisitions. That mechanism failed and was replaced in the 1970s by the Health Systems Agency Program, which was supposed to do the same thing, but which was given more teeth with which to do it. That program is also judged by many to have been a failure, and the Reagan administration wants to cancel the program.

Even under this program, we have had hospitals built that did not need to be built, additions to hospitals being built that did not need to be built, and equipment proposed that could have been shared. As this program is being canceled, we are still in a state of being overbedded and overequipped. Moreover, we do not have plans for a future organizational means of trying to control the lack of integration between extremely expensive facilities and equipment.

This lack of planning has created an unhealthy air of competition between hospitals. To make sure that they get a large share of obstetrical cases, one hospital I know has a candlelight dinner arranged for new patients who have their babies in that hospital. A very nice touch—but is it necessary? In California, where competition is extremely high, hospitals fight over physicians (remember, physicians are the hospital's salesmen). It is not uncommon for physicians who accept staff privilege, or who meet admission goals, to be rewarded with automobiles, trips to Hawaii, and other perks.

There is no way that anyone can consider the above items complete, or the terse analysis accompanying them to be a thorough analysis of each of these items. They are just some of many that contribute to high hospital costs. In other words, if some fix were placed on each of these items, a great deal of the problem would disappear.

WHAT SHOULD A PERSON LOOK FOR IN SELECTING A HOSPITAL?

James W. Bartlett, M.D. A hospital is a special place organized principally around caring for patients. Care is provided by a large number of well-trained persons including nurses, physicians, social workers, technicians and many other health care professionals. The patient's physician coordinates the care, including the decision to hospitalize. He also coordinates the care, treatment and diagnostic activities that are carried on during the hospitalization, and the time when discharge is ready. Therefore, the major factor in selecting a hospital is to become the patient of a good doctor or group of doctors.

Often doctors and hospitals are so closely associated that a physician or group practices only at a particular hospital. Again, the quality of the physician is the first consideration. After that, it is important that the full range of facilities required for good care are available at the hospital that that physician uses; that the technical and consultative persons and equipment that may be needed are ready; that the hospital is fully accredited by the JCAH; and that the hospital is well-staffed.

Hospitalization involves not only the patient but the patient's family. Therefore, it is also important to consider, whenever possible, the facilities the hospital offers to assist the family in coping with the illness and in mobilizing the resources that will be needed for the patient's recuperation.

In summary, first choose a good doctor and then discuss the choice of hospital with that physician. Or, if you choose a hospital first, be sure you establish a doctor–patient relationship as promptly as possible with a well-qualified member of that hospital's medical staff.

Harold A. Cohen. Since I, like most Americans, am protected against the cost of health care via insurance, the concerns I have would relate to quality. Quality should be measured largely by patient outcomes rather than by process or credentials. There is evidence that quality is related to how often a procedure is performed. One would also want to know how prepared the hospital is to handle any complication that arises from the procedure. While I am protected against the dollar cost of the hospitalization, I am not insured against the cost of the time and inconvenience of being hospitalized.

As a result of the above considerations—and depending upon how unusual an illness I had—I would want to know how often the procedure I might require is performed at the hospitals I was investigating; what the overall diagnosis and procedure-specific infection rates are; what the diagnosis and procedure-specific death rate is; what the readmission rate is; what the average length of stay is; and information regarding the medical staff's areas of expertise relative to potential complication.

While I am not a big fan of the JCAH, I would want to know why any hospital I went to was not accredited. The specific questions regarding nursing and physician coverage and availability of specialty services would depend upon the specific illness I had.

In short, we are doing ourselves a disservice if we simply pick a physician and go wherever that physician has privileges.

Scott Fleming. The question reflects an erroneous perception of how our nation's health care system generally functions. *Patients select doctors; doctors select hospitals.* Indeed, even emergency admissions must be ordered or approved by a doctor on the hospital staff.

If a patient wishes to utilize a specific hospital, the patient should identify a suitable physician who is a member of the medical staff of that hospital. Because many physicians in traditional practice have admitting privileges at more than one hospital, the patient should also be sure that the physician understands the patient's specific hospital preference.

Most good-quality hospitals strive to maintain accredited status with the JCAH. Such accreditation indicates that the institution meets reasonable, minimum standards. If possible, confirm that any hospital that you plan to use has full (two year) accreditation.

Affiliation, as a teaching hospital, with a well-regarded medical school is generally good evidence that the institution maintains high standards with respect to technical aspects of quality medical care. On the other hand, teaching hospitals tend to be significantly more expensive than general community hospitals; and some teaching hospitals, although excellent in terms of technical quality, may lack amenities that are important to some patients. Also, the technical "quality" available in major teaching hospitals may exceed the realistic needs of most patients for most episodes of hospitalization. An appendectomy, gall bladder or hernia operation, or most other common causes for hospital admissions, can be handled in a thoroughly satisfactory fashion in most accredited hospitals; the supersophistication available in a large teaching institution is simply not relevant to the ordinary needs of most patients.

Factors such as geographic convenience and reasonably easy access for visiting family members are also important. Other personal preference factors include sponsorship, e.g., religious or nonsectarian affiliation, and proprietary or nonprofit status. Historically, there has, with some justification, been a skeptical attitude toward proprietary or investor-owned hospitals, as compared with nonprofit hospitals. However, good quality medical care is available in many proprietary hospitals, and there are, undoubtedly, poor-quality nonprofit hospitals.

The professional competence of your physician and your physician's judgment in selecting referral specialists and consultants will generally have more bearing on the quality of care you receive than will the characteristics of the hospital itself. As a generalization, well-qualified physicians tend to be associated with good-quality institutions.

Most patients will be well-advised to devote their effort to selecting a good physician who is qualified in the medical specialty appropriate to their probable health care needs. They should discuss hospital preferences with their physician. The physician will know more than the patient can reasonably expect to learn about the hospitals in the community and their suitability to the probable needs of the patient.

James R. Flynn. In selecting a hospital, the lay person should look for the following:

1. A physician or specialist who practices at the hospital of choice or preference.
2. The hospital's reputation and image for caring and for servicing the public.
3. The hospital's ability to meet standards set by the Joint Committee on Accreditation, Medicare, etc., followed by its ability to exceed minimum standards. Inherent in a hospital's reputation is its projected image of cleanliness, modern well-kept physical facilities, the reputation of the medical staff in general.
4. Reasonable charges for services. The public must become price sensitive in terms of selecting health care, even if covered by third-party payers. The ultimate price paid for the total health care package will influence premiums paid and will ultimately affect the patient, even if he/she enjoys a company-sponsored health care policy. Sooner or later, the effects of high health care costs come back to haunt the consumer. Sometimes this occurs indirectly through the price of goods paid for, such as automobiles, etc., where the health cost component is rising at a tremendous rate. High costs also affect the consumer because the insurance premium paid by the individual directly reflects the escalating health care cost.

Robert M. Heyssel, M.D. In truth, most patients do not select a hospital; they select a physician who has privileges at one or more area hospitals. As a generalization, it is fair to say that a well-trained competent physician will not practice in a hospital that is inadequately equipped and that has inadequate nursing and other personnel to take care of the problems of the patients whom the physician deals with. Therefore, selection of the physician is probably the more important issue.

In this regard, it is generally true that physicians who have a certificate from one of the specialty boards are better trained and more capable of taking care of an illness than noncertified physicians. One should be wary of the physician who claims to be board qualified as opposed to being board certified. Qualification simply means the physician went through some training but either failed to pass the examinations, never took them or did not train in an accredited program. One can find out about certification, or the specialization of a physician, from the county or other medical society in the political jurisdiction in which the physician lives.

With regard to the hospital itself, accreditation of the hospital by the JCAH (granted every two years) is the surest way to be certain that individual hospitals are properly administered, meet life-safety codes, have proper sanitary procedures, have appropriate nursing care for the patients they are caring for, and follow at least minimal standards in all these and other areas of administration and medical practice. Joint Commission accreditation also means that the hospital must have in place a quality assurance program which assures that there is peer review and staff review of the practice of each individual physician there. While not foolproof, this should mean that no physicians are performing procedures they are not qualified to do nor are they taking care of patients they are not qualified to care for.

Finally, Joint Commission accreditation and physician qualifications aside, some hospitals, for certain and particularly special services, clearly have a better track record than others. For instance, in the field of open heart surgery, it has been clearly shown that hospitals that do 250 or more procedures a year have a lower mortality rate and better overall results than programs in hospitals that are smaller, let us say, 50 to 100 procedures a year. This simply implies that the more a hospital does of a particular complicated procedure or therapeutic approach, the better at doing it both physicians and hospital staff become. In general, those hospitals that are larger, that are affiliated with teaching programs in medical schools and that have graduate medical education programs (residents) will be better places to look to for such things as kidney transplantation, open heart surgery, certain complicated neurosurgical procedures, etc.

Robert M. Magnuson. First, we must recognize that hospitals are similar to other service industries in that the person may not truly have a choice. Frequently, geographic limitations dictate that a choice is not feasible. More commonly, though, the person's choice of physician determines which hospitals are available to him. Physicians have privileges only at specific hospitals and it is the physicians who actually admit the patient.

Asking your personal physician about his preference can be helpful, since he can relay his experience with previous patients. Additionally, your trust in your physician should extend to his preference for a hospital since it is important that he feels comfortable with the facilities, equipment, services and personnel that will be required for your particular illness.

Hospitals are highly regulated and monitored, so they are generally considered safe places. An additional indication of a hospital's merits is accreditation by the JCAH. Achieving accreditation from this voluntary organization means that the hospital has gone beyond the minimal fire, safety and health codes and is striving to continually improve the quality of patient care provided.

Selecting a hospital before you need one is, again, similar to selecting any service organization since so much of what they provide is intangible. Inquiring among friends who have used a hospital, or asking your physician, will probably yield the most useful information.

John A. Maloney. The selection of a hospital is not, in most cases, left up to the consumer to decide. For example, if you intend to purchase a car you may be able to shop around for the best buy between Ford, GMC, AMC and even foreign manufacturers such as Toyota or Volkswagen. However, the selection of the hospital is usually determined by the selection of your physician. Most physicians are on the active staff of one hospital and in some urban areas on the active staff of several. Since most physicians have their offices located near their hospital of preference you will be admitted to their hospital since it is more convenient for your physician.

If you disagree with your physician's choice your only alternative is to choose a different physician. To avoid this problem, it might well be advantageous to select your hospital first and then select your physician from the members of that hospital's medical staff.

In selecting a hospital there are several things one should keep in mind. First, is the hospital accredited by the JCAH, an accrediting agency made up of members from the American College of Physicians, American College of Surgeons, American Medical Association and the American Hospital Association? Approval by this agency assures you that the physical plant meets all national, state and local fire and safety codes and that the medical, nursing and paraprofessional staffs are practicing medicine and surgery in a scientific and ethical manner. Does the hospital have twenty-four-hour physician coverage in its emergency room? Does it have intensive and coronary care units? If you are planning specialized surgery, coronary bypass, organ transplant (kidney) etc., what is their success rate in comparison to the national average? Many community hospitals have these facilities available and it is not necessary to travel to one of the large national medical centers to receive highly specialized surgical and medical treatment any longer.

I am reminded of the time, several years ago when, as administrator of a community hospital in one of the southeastern states, a patient needed some highly specialized eye surgery. The patient was a wealthy dowager and money was no object. Her doctor suggested she see an ophthalmologist in a town 60 miles away who was well qualified to perform the necessary surgery. The patient declined the doctor's advice and opted for a medical center in the northeast some 600 miles away. On arrival at the medical center she was advised that they were flying in a specialist to perform her operation. Lo and behold, the specialist turned out to be the ophthalmologist that her doctor had wanted her to see in the first place. Not only did she have the expense of travel to the medical center, but also the expense of flying in the specialist plus the higher cost of staying at the medical center which, at the time, was probably twenty to thirty dollars per day higher than the community hospital located only 60 miles away from her home.

I cite this example to prove to you that it is possible to have a Mayo Clinic or a Johns Hopkins in your own backyard and not know it—unless you have made the investigation I have suggested.

J. Alexander McMahon. The choice of a hospital may be a decision that can be pondered well in advance, or it may need to be made in a split second. If you are unconscious or unable to think clearly because of illness or injury, someone else, even a stranger, may make this decision for you. Different hospitals serve different functions and it is important to familiarize yourself with the various types of hospitals in your area.

Most hospitals have annual reports, brochures or other publications that describe the facilities, staff and services. The public information or community relations office of a large hospital, or the administrator's office of a hospital that does not have such a department, can provide additional information or sometimes even a tour of the facility.

Check to see if the hospital is accredited. The JCAH evaluates hospitals to see if they adhere to guidelines regarding facilities, staff, services and administration. Accreditation or lack of it does not tell you everything you need to know to judge the quality of a hospital, and some qualified hospitals do not choose to be accredited, but it does say that certain standards have been met.

Ask whether the medical staff consists mostly of primary care physicians or if specialists are available on a round-the-clock basis. Inquire about the quantity and training levels of other staff, such as nurses and specialists in anesthesia, radiology and laboratory procedures. Check into affiliations or agreements with larger hospitals that would enable you to be transferred smoothly to a facility with more extensive services should the need arise.

Investigate the special capabilities of hospitals in your area, such as coronary care or burn treatment, so that in the event of a crisis, you can save valuable time by knowing exactly where to go. Most hospitals have some type of emergency services, but such services can vary from first-aid care to a full-scale trauma center. Some are minimally staffed at night, so that the time of an emergency may determine where you should seek care.

For nonemergency hospitalization, physicians often play a major role in the selection of a hospital. Thus, in selecting a physician, you should consider the hospitals at which he or she has staff privileges. As a health care consumer you do have the right to question a physician's choice if you are not completely comfortable with it, and to inquire on your own about the facilities and capabilities of a particular hospital.

The majority of common medical and surgical procedures can be handled by most local community hospitals, large or small, and your physician may suggest a particular one. If you have a more serious problem that requires highly specialized care, your physician may choose, or you may decide to seek, beyond the closest hospital to one with a broader range of services and expertise. Although size is by no means an indicator of quality, large hospitals often have more physician specialists, more diagnostic equipment and sophisticated facilities for handling critical care.

The most important consideration in the choice of a hospital is to select the facility that can provide the most appropriate level of care for your specific need. Investigate the alternatives in advance so that in the event you need hospital care, you, or someone who knows your preference, can make an informed choice.

Rodger E. Mendenhall, B.A., M.S. This question presumes that a choice in hospitals is available. Under such circumstances, three considerations are of the highest priority and are outlined below:

1. Determine reputation of hospital and professional staff for services needed, particularly if unusual specialization is required.
   Suggestions:
   A. Discuss with your own physician
   B. Check with local medical society
2. After the above step, select the hospital available that will offer you the most comfortable environment for your personal lifestyle.
   Possible considerations:
   A. Experiences of previous patients
   B. Consultation with a visiting pastor for impressions
   C. Religious preference
   D. Geographic location/convenience
   E. Visiting hour convenience

   Additional considerations include asking for a hospital brochure and recognizing that you may prefer a hospital without a teaching component.
3. After the above two steps, if a choice is still available, consider costs; there will be a difference:
   Suggestions:
   A. Don't select a more complex hospital than your medical needs require.
   B. Compare room rates as an indicator. There will be a correlation between room rates and total costs.
   C. See if outpatient or walk-in services are available and would meet your needs.
   D. See if a self-help ward is available and would meet your requirements.

E. Be sure your insurance is acceptable to the hospital of your choice.

F. If you need financial assistance, discuss it with your doctor and the hospitals involved—there will be great differences in the hospitals' responses.

Charles M. O'Brien, Jr. Essentially the matter of selecting a hospital depends on the person's medical condition and on his or her individual preferences. Many patients prefer a medical facility close to home and family. Some desire the more relaxed atmosphere of a small community hospital rather than the faster pace of a large urban hospital.

In general, my advice would be to choose a hospital that is accredited by the JCAH, an organization of medical professionals which periodically surveys hospitals to ensure compliance with high standards of medical care. Additionally, the hospital should be licensed by the local city or county health department.

A university teaching affiliation is an indication that a hospital has access to the latest technology and expertise in specialized areas. Such hospitals are also more likely to have the most highly trained medical, nursing and ancillary personnel.

Lastly, the reputation that a hospital has with physicians and former patients in the community can provide valuable information regarding the quality of its services.

John Pekkanen. The most important thing to look for, when selecting a hospital, is a hospital with a university affiliation, a teaching hospital. There is little doubt in my mind that university hospitals offer the best medical care in this country, despite the fact that they are often less commodious than many private hospitals.

Teaching hospitals are superior because they demand the best of their staff. The environment within them continually scrutinizes and criticizes medical opinions and procedures, and physicians who practice there must be able to meet this continuing scrutiny.

Moreover, no university-affiliated hospital will allow physicians who are not board certified or board eligible to practice there. Although board certification is a minimum requirement for a physician, it is an important one; and any physician who is practicing medicine without it should be avoided unless there are extraordinary circumstances. At many private hospitals, board certification is not a requirement for physicians to practice.

I also think the best hospitals are large, in excess of 400 beds. The larger size usually means a wider array of medical technologies, and more importantly, a greater depth and breadth of medical expertise.

Accreditation by the JCAH is a minimum requirement and can easily be checked by asking the hospital. If the hospital does not have it, avoid that hospital.

Finally, I would choose a hospital with American-educated interns and residents. This is not snobbery, but simply a realization of the fact that United States-trained physicians do much better on standardized medical examinations than do foreign-trained physicians. The only exceptions to this are physicians taught and trained in Canada and England, both of which offer superb medical training.

David D. Thompson, M.D. Here are the important points that relate to selecting a hospital:

1. Be sure your doctor is on the staff of a first-rate hospital.
2. Select a hospital connected to a leading medical school.
3. Be aware of back-up facilities and specialists at the hospital.
4. Select one that is accredited by the JCAH.
5. Recognize that residency programs are important for round-the-clock care.
6. Depending on your ailment, select a hospital that specializes in the treatment of that ailment.

MENTAL HEALTH

*T*HE FOLLOWING SECTION on mental health offers a fascinating selection of material about how the brain functions and about the interrelation of the brain and the body.

Paul MacLean, of the National Institute of Mental Health, asserts that human beings actually have a triune—or three-part—brain. We have maintained three different brain structures that correspond to three different levels of evolutionary development. The reptile structure is responsible for running our physical routines and activities; our early mammal brain governs the areas of family, play, and emotional feelings; and our late mammal brain governs the higher, symbolic activities such as speaking, reading, writing and counting.

A similar interplay between psychology and physical functioning is thought to exist in the area of sexual dysfunction. F. Paul Pearsall, of the psychology department of Sinai Hospital of Detroit, says that although many sexual dysfunctions appear to have physical causes, in fact, medical problems underlie very few cases of sexual dysfunction. Dr. Pearsall—and many other experts in the field—maintain that psychological issues, such as conflicts of expectations and communications problems between partners, account for the vast majority of sexual dysfunctions..

Paul J. Rosch states some iconoclastic findings of his own in the area of stress. He writes that modern man's response to stress dates back to primitive times. When primitive man was faced by stress, the body reacted by stimulating the nervous system and pumping adrenalin into the bloodstream. These responses sharpened primitive man's physical senses and allowed him to respond better to the cause of his stress, which was usually some kind of physical threat. But in modern man (whose stress is more likely to be psychologically oriented) these physiological responses to stress do not help to solve the problem in the least. In fact, this psychophysiological reaction to stress may actually *damage* the body, in part because stress (and its response) can easily occur three or four times in a single day (for an urban inhabitant) rather than once in a great while (as it did for primitive man).

Nutritional consultant Randolph Bufano describes another form of interplay between mind and body. He says that placebos (or pills that contain no drugs, but that patients think *do* contain drugs) cause 35 percent of patients to improve in health. He offers this as testimony to the fact that the inner belief is vital to the healing process. In addition, an individual's belief in the placebo causes the brain to secrete the chemical agents necessary to help combat the illness. Michael L. Culbert, an authority on cancer, says that mental stress is involved in a wide variety of cancer cases and that researchers have found a statistically cancer-prone personality type.

The ultimate interplay between mind and body control is in the field of biofeedback. This relatively new practice is based on the discovery that people can control biological processes that were previously thought (in Western society) to be involuntary. These processes include blood pressure, heart rate, muscle tension and body surface temperature. Biofeedback is being explored enthusiastically and has been shown to have real, positive effects in the control of such diseases as migraines.

The experts in the following pages offer a diversity of opinion in the areas of psychology and sexual problems.

INTELLIGENCE

ALTHOUGH PSYCHOLOGISTS and other researchers have been trying to quantify human intelligence for more than a century, many questions remain about the nature of intelligence and about how it can be measured. Is intelligence the capacity to master specific intellectual skills, such as reading and understanding abstract concepts? Or is it a more general ability, such as knowing how to adapt to one's social environment, whether it be at a job, in a classroom, or on a ghetto street? Much controversy has surrounded the concept, and some researchers now define intelligence simply as that which intelligence tests are designed to measure.

Despite the lack of agreement about what intelligence actually is or what intelligence tests really measure, standardized intelligence tests are used to estimate intellectual capabilities and to help predict later success. The first such use was in 1905, when French psychologist Alfred Binet and psychiatrist Théodore Simon devised tests to discover which schoolchildren were intelligent enough to be taught in the general classrooms and which should be relegated to special learning programs.

The Binet-Simon tests analyzed the mental age of each child and compared it to the child's chronological age. Later, intelligence test scores were expressed as *intelligence quotients*, or IQs: mental age divided by chronological age and then multiplied by 100. Thus if a ten-year-old had the mental age of a 12-year-old, his IQ would be 1.2 × 100, or 120, an above-average IQ. An average child's IQ would be about 100, while a mentally deficient or retarded child would probably score about 70 or below.

In the United States, Lewis Terman of Stanford University changed and expanded the Binet-Simon scale to create the Revised Stanford-Binet Tests, which, along with tests devised by the psychologist David Wechsler, are among the most popular intelligence tests in use today. These intelligence tests are designed to be administered to one person at a time, but in 1914 Terman also devised the Army Alpha Tests, which were given to nearly two million recruits during World War I. The army recruit tests were the forerunners of other group tests, such as the College Entrance Examinations, that can be quickly administered to large groups of people.

Studies have shown that these intelligence tests have some predictive validity, especially in such areas as determining academic success. Critics charge, however, that the tests are geared toward members of the mainstream culture and discriminate against persons who have grown up in minority socioeconomic groups or in poor learning environments. As the following answers illustrate, controversy still exists as to how much of a person's intelligence is predetermined by heredity and how much is the product of his or her social environment and training.

CONTRIBUTORS

F. G. Brown, Professor of Psychology, Iowa State University, Ames, Iowa

John E. Corbally, President, John D. and Catherine T. MacArthur Foundation, Northbrook, Illinois

Marian C. Diamond, Department of Physiology–Anatomy, University of California, Berkeley, California

Carmen J. Finley, Ph.D., Principal Research Scientist, American Institutes for Research, Palo Alto, California

Charles J. Furst, Ph.D., Psychologist University of California, Los Angeles, California

William T. Greenough, Professor of Psychology and Anatomical Sciences, University of Illinois at Urbana–Champaign

Arthur R. Jensen, Professor of Educational Psychology, University of California, Berkeley, California

Jerre Levy, Ph.D., Associate Professor, Committee on Biopsychology, Department of Behavioral Sciences, University of Chicago, Chicago, Illinois

Paul D. MacLean, M.D., Chief, Laboratory of Brain Evolution and Behavior, National Institute of Mental Health, Bethesda, Maryland

Prof. Emeritus J. McVicker Hunt, University of Illinois at Urbana–Champaign

Dr. Perry Miller, Professor of Education and Psychology, Boston State College, Boston, Massachusetts

Richard M. Restak, M.D., neurologist, Washington, D.C.; author of *The Brain—The Last Frontier*

E. Paul Torrance, Alumni Foundation Distinguished Professor, University of Georgia, Athens, Georgia

Elliot S. Valenstein, Professor of Psychology and Neuroscience, University of Michigan, Ann Arbor, Michigan

HOW MUCH OF OUR BRAIN DO WE USE?

Charles J. Furst, Ph.D. As one who has studied the human brain for some years, I have always been puzzled by statements to the effect that we only use 50 percent (or 25 percent or 10 percent) of our brain capacity. I suppose these statements—totally unsupported by any real evidence in the scientific literature—reflect wonder at the realization that the brain has considerable flexibility in recovering from injury. These statements suggest the imaginative extrapolation that if we could only tap the presumably unused parts of the brain we would be very smart indeed.

The facts from which these speculations are drawn are simply that people can recover from massive brain wounds, even though the neural tissue does not regenerate. This is especially true if the brain damage occurs early in childhood, when apparently the developing brain is plastic enough to reassign functions from one area to another (doubling-up language and visuo-spatial functions in the right hemisphere, for example, if the left is damaged). It has been found through the recently developed technique of brain scans that some adults with a childhood condition known as hydrocephalus are apparently normal even though they have only a fraction of the normal amount of brain tissue. The ability for the brain to reorganize diminishes or vanishes at puberty, but even in adults, significant areas of the cerebral cortex can be damaged with surprisingly little effect, in some cases.

It would not only be sheer guesswork at this point but would also, perhaps, be somewhat meaningless scientifically, to estimate the percentage of the human brain that is actually used—after all, the liver and other organs have spare capacity, but it would be difficult to say how much of this is unused in its normal operation. Nevertheless, an evening's collaborative research in conjunction with a colleague—Prof. Edward Sadalla of Arizona State University—has produced the following results:

Activity	Percent of Brain Engaged
Sleeping	
Deep sleep	2%
Dreaming	50%

Activity	Percent of Brain Engaged
Driving a car	
Freeway	4%
Traffic	20%
Golf	3%
Eating a Big Mac	1%
Watching television	
Commercial television	30%
Educational television	5%
Sex	
Males	5%
Females	25%
Gin Rummy	40%
Listing tax deductions	90%

Jerre Levy, Ph.D. We very often hear the claim that people only use a small portion of their brains, and that with proper training, individuals could be taught to use their entire brains. There is no doubt that training and education can have powerful effects in teaching us to see situations clearly, in helping us to discriminate relevant from irrelevant considerations, in aiding us to remember and recall important aspects of our experiences that we can bring to bear in making current decisions, and in improving the clarity and depth of our thinking.

However, the statement that "people only use a small portion of their brains" implies that we typically rely on some restricted anatomical portion of the brain mass, with the remainder of the brain being in an idle and inactive state. This implication is false. Any perception, motivation or idea we have involves the integrated activities of the whole brain, including both the deep underlying regions that play a special role in emotion and the outer covering of the brain, the cortex, that is highly elaborated in human beings and plays a special role in thinking.

So to answer the question, "How much of our brain do we use?" the answer must be: We always use the entire brain. The real issue is how efficiently we use that marvelous biological computer in our heads. If we are tired, inattentive or distracted, efficiency is low, and we think and perform more poorly than we do when we are rested, attentive and undistracted. Our maximum capacities go unrealized, also, if we have failed to get the proper stimulation and education in infancy and childhood, and if we fail to keep our thinking capacities challenged and active in adulthood.

Some educators, being aware of scientific research showing differences in function for the two sides of the brain—with the left brain hemisphere specialized for language and the right brain hemisphere specialized for face recognition and visualization—have worried that schools are biased toward teaching only the left side of the brain. There is little justification for such fears. A good teacher necessarily stimulates the whole brain and engages specialized abilities of both the left and right hemispheres. A child who is appropriately taught to appreciate literature, learns to understand the language and its beauty, but also learns to feel the emotions of fictional characters, to visualize their expressions and bodily movements, to "see" the environments in which they find themselves, and to experience the moods the author paints with words. The teen-ager who solves algebraic problems, if taught well, imagines the geometric forms described by the equations.

As adults, if we wish to fulfill our abilities and humanity, we must read and think, seek challenges for our intellect, and have the will and commitment to continue our education for the rest of our lives. Just as muscles become weak without exercise, so will our brains become poor and inefficient if fed only on a diet of lighthearted entertainment. In spite of the simple momentary pleasures such entertainment may bring, deep satisfaction and meaning in living comes from fulfilling our human potential; from continuing, throughout our whole lives, to grow in emotional depth, in empathy with others, in knowledge of ourselves, of others, and of our universe. If we do so, we not only use our whole brain, as all animals do, but we live up to the gift of our human evolution and follow the commands of our religious heritage.

Paul D. MacLean, M.D. How much of our brain do we use? Although this question is impossible to answer, think of it this way: Based on present knowledge, human beings had their large brains for thousands of years before there was a language of words. And it is only about two thousand years since people first saw the empty spaces between their fingers that led to the concept of zero and a workable language of numbers. With such modern developments as television, computers, and the like, who is to say what other languages, what metalanguages, what transcendent speech, may still be in the making?

Are our nerve cells of the brain working to their full capacity, just as managers could wish workers in industry and government to do? Modern methods are not good enough to say. When recording the activity of individual nerve cells under experimental conditions, one encounters families of cells that all seem to be doing the same thing, e.g., responding faithfully to a flash of light. The majority of nerve cells, however, appear to be idling. Even so, such idling activity may be necessary for wakefulness and alertness or may contribute to some particular function not apparent to the investigator.

In 1929, when Berger extended the recording of brain waves to human beings, he introduced a noninvasive method that has since been extensively used for detecting what parts of the brain are working, not working, or working abnormally. But as for revealing how much of our brains we actually use, the viewing of brain waves is somewhat comparable to standing outside a banquet room and attempting to detect what is being said at the different tables. Recently, positron emission tomography has provided another noninvasive technique that greatly supplements the information obtained by electroencephalography.

The question might be better stated as: "How much of our *brains* do we use?" In its evolution, the human brain has evolved and expanded to its great size while retaining the basic features of three formations that reflect an ancestral relationship to reptiles, early mammals and recent mammals. Radically different in structure and chemistry, and in an evolutionary sense countless generations apart, the three formations constitute a hierarchy of three brains in one—a triune brain. There is clinical evidence that the two older formations do not have the capacity for verbal communication, suggesting a major reason for ignorance of ourselves.

Recent findings are beginning to suggest that the reptilianlike brain is essential for regulating an animal's master routine and subroutines, as well as the four main kinds of expression used in nonverbal communication. The part of the brain identified with early mammals (limbic system) has been crucial for the evolution of the family, play, and emotional feelings and expression regarding all aspects of life. The evolutionary newest brain reaches its greatest proportions in human beings, in whom it is essential for speech and the capacity for reading, writing and arithmetic. Hopefully, it will eventually devise some means of improving communication with the two older brains and make it possible to get the best use out of the triune combination.

E. Paul Torrance. Ordinarily, we use only an infinitesimally small part of our brain. When challenged or highly motivated, we use a larger portion of our brain. However, if we have not practiced and developed the mental skills that are challenged, we may not be able to respond adequately to these challenges.

Of our total mental activity, by far the greater part goes on out of consciousness. We fail to use and develop those mental activities that occur out of consciousness. This unconscious activity includes such things as autonomic functioning, dreaming, daydreaming, reflexes, psychodynamic defense mechanisms, habitual behavior, memory search, pattern recognition, conceptualization, hunches and intuition, creative imagination and the like.

Generally, education has failed to recognize the existence of these unconscious activities and has failed to provide practice in their use.

Elliot S. Valenstein. It is often said that most people generally use only 20, 30 or 40 percent of their brains. The fact is that such figures are completely made up and have no basis in scientific fact.

Contrary to popular opinion, it is not possible at present to make any measurements that could justify a quantified statement about the percentage of the brain that is being used. It is not true, as many persons believe, that the nerve cells (neurons) that make up the brain are inactive except when used. Actually, the great majority of the billions of cells in the brain are firing spontaneously at all times even when a person is asleep or in a coma.

Much of the brain is concerned with controlling internal organs that regulate digestion, respiration, temperature control and other "housekeeping" functions and these must go on even when we are asleep. Other parts of the brain control our muscles and movements and therefore the brain of an athlete might consume as much or even more energy than Einstein's brain did when he was developing the theory of relativity.

In the past, a number of scientists have investigated the activity of the whole brain by determining the amount of energy utilized. This was accomplished by measuring the amount of oxygen consumed by the brain. It was found that there was no difference in oxygen consumed by the brain of a person actively engaged in solving a mathematical problem or that of a person asleep. There was also no difference in brain oxygen consumption between normals and schizophrenics. The brains of very young children consume more oxygen per gram of tissue than that of young adults not because they are more actively engaged in thought, but in part because more energy is required for supporting a growing brain. There is no decrease in oxygen consumption in the elderly providing they are healthy, but the brains of the senile usually consume less oxygen because there is often a decrease in the brain's blood supply.

Although measurements of activity of the total brain have not proven very useful, more recent investigations have looked at the relative activity of different regions of the brain. This approach has been helped dramatically by the development of brain scanning techniques for visualizing the relative activity of different parts of the brain. Thus, when a person is reading, the parts of the brain that process visual information and language are most active. To date, however, it has not proven possible to use such information to distinguish between a person actively thinking about the implications of the written material and one who does not even comprehend the text.

There are several techniques that make it possible to distinguish the activity of the brain of a person who is mentally alert from one who is relaxed or asleep. In general, the nerve cells of a person in a drowsy state tend to fire in synchrony and therefore produce a synchronous electrographic pattern with a characteristic rhythm. Also, recent reports based on brain scanning techniques have indicated that the most frontal part of the brain is very active when a person is thinking and this same region is relatively inactive when mentally relaxed. It is possible that future advances will provide some degree of quantification that would reflect differences in amount of time people are engaged in active thought. At present, however, information about relative activity of different brain regions can only make crude distinctions between mentally alert and drowsy states, and can tell us nothing about the quality of the thought processes.

For the present, any statement about the percentage of brain used by most people should be viewed as nothing more than a way to exhort us to try harder and to realize more of our potential. We would all agree that there are few people who could not increase their mental capacities, but this conviction is not based on any measurements of brain activity.

CAN A PERSON ACTUALLY INCREASE HIS OR HER INTELLIGENCE?

Professor Emeritus J. McVicker Hunt. The answer to this question depends upon how one defines "intelligence." If one means by "intelligence," as some do, the genetic or hereditary variations in efficiency of functioning, the answer is no. On the other hand, no measures for such genetic variations exist. No tests of innate intelligence exist. Such variations are always inferred.

If, however, one defines "intelligence" as whatever it is that tests of intelligence measure, or the measurable aspects of functioning or ability, the answer is yes. Unfortunately, by the time a person could become deliberately concerned with increasing his or her intelligence, the degree of plasticity remaining would be very limited. Even so, by increasing one's language skill, the range of problems with which one is familiar and conversant and the fund of one's knowledge, scores earned on tests of intelligence and general intellectual competence would increase to some limited degree.

On the other hand, there is great plasticity in both intellectual and motivational development at birth. From the evidence available, one can safely infer that the variations in average measures for people of the various social classes are almost entirely a function of the development-fostering quality of the rearing conditions in the homes of the people. I am also confident that the predominant share of the differences between the test performances of people of the various races have this same source. At an orphanage in Tehran, training caregivers how to foster the intellectual and motivational development of comparable groups of foundlings served to increase an estimate of their IQ, at about two years of age, by forty-seven points. Estimates were derived from a cohort of sensorimotor skills derived from Piaget. The foundlings reared by the trained caregivers attained the top steps on five of the seven Piaget-inspired scales at mean ages younger than home-reared children from predominantly professional families. The foundlings were estimated to have an average IQ of approximately 130 at this age. They were also socially attractive and well motivated.

Arthur R. Jensen. There is no good evidence that a person can increase his general intelligence to a significant degree, although it is possible, to some extent, to enhance one's scores on particular mental tests by means of coaching and practice on similar tests. However, through study and well-directed effort, it is possible to learn to use one's innate intelligence more effectively in pursuing one's goals—just as an athlete can improve his performance by acquiring and perfecting certain skills, without necessarily increasing his overall muscular strength or other physical capacities per se.

Individuals should be less concerned about their own intelligence, which they can do little about anyway, and think more in terms of the products of mental effort, namely, actual achievements, which can be positively affected by one's education, interests, ideals, effort and persistence.

Richard M. Restak, M.D. Of course people can increase their intelligence. Intelligence is a measure of adaptability. The more adaptable individual is able to improve his or her performance and success. Although there is a biological basis for intelligence, and some outer limitations exist regarding the degree to which intellectual performance can be enhanced, a person can improve IQ and intellectual ability by coaching, reading and other formal instruction. Recent evaluations of students who have taken the Scholastic Aptitude Test show that scores can be improved by twenty to forty points depending on the student's motivation and time investment in preparation for the test.

Two further points need emphasis. First, there is no necessary correlation between IQ and occupational or professional success. Despite claims to the contrary, scholastic standing—one measure of IQ—does not correlate with later occupational success. Personality, motivation, socioeconomic standing, "contacts,"—all contribute significantly to later performance.

E. Paul Torrance. As intelligence has been and is being measured, there is much evidence that a person can actually increase his or her intelligence. In fact, the evidence shows that almost any intellectual function can be improved through practice. In addition, systematic and deliberate problem-solving procedures enable people to behave more intelligently and more creatively—and even increase the chances of producing original, inventive ideas. This has been documented in several experimental studies, most of which have been conducted since 1960.

HOW EFFECTIVE ARE STANDARDIZED TESTS IN DETERMINING A PERSON'S INTELLIGENCE OR SUCCESS IN LIFE?

F. G. Brown. Standardized tests, particularly individually administered intelligence tests, are the best available method for determining an individual's intelligence. They are the best method because they are carefully constructed to measure characteristics that clearly are signs of intelligence, are administered to all persons under the same conditions, are scored objectively (i.e., use agreed upon answers and scoring procedures), and meet various statistical criteria of quality. How effective they are in determining a person's intelligence cannot be precisely determined as there is no one definition of intelligence and, even if there were, there would be no way to measure a person's "true" intelligence. However, the better tests are good measures of skills most people would consider to be signs of intelligence, and are quite accurate predictors of the types of performance that require use of intellectual abilities, such as success in school.

Whether standardized ability tests can predict success in life is also a debatable question. One obvious problem is: What is meant by "success in life." If by success we mean occupational and vocational achievement, the scores on ability tests are related to success. But their effect is indirect. That is, standardized ability and achievement tests predict how well people will do in school. In turn, how well people do in school is a major determiner of what occupations and jobs will be open to them. For example, to become a physician one has to first complete medical school—and to be admitted to medical school one must have completed an undergraduate program, with relatively high grades. To the extent that test scores predict educational success, and to the extent that educational success allows access to certain careers, to that extent test scores predict life success.

Another way to view the relationship between test scores and success is to consider the scores obtained by people who enter various occupations. There are data which show that the average and minimal level of mental ability of workers differs widely between occupations. These differences parallel the educational requirements of the occupations; that is, the average mental ability of persons in occupations requiring extensive education or training is higher than that of people in occupations requiring less education or training. Again, this reflects the fact that entrance into certain occupations is dependent on meeting certain educational requirements. Whether people can meet these requirements depends on their ability.

However, within any occupation there are people having various levels of mental ability above the minimum for that occupation. Furthermore, differences in ability above the minimum seem to be unrelated to success in the occupation. It should also be noted that there are numerous occupations where the types of mental abilities measured by standardized tests play only a small part in determining success. Professional athletics, performing arts and mechanical trades are some examples.

Carmen J. Finley, Ph.D. A distinction must be made between using standardized tests for classifying groups of people and using them for guidance of an individual. Tests can be very effective in ranking a heterogenous group of individuals with respect to intelligence, and they are better than any other competitive single indicator. However, standardized tests, like any other technique used to assess individuals, must be used with care and knowledge of the tests' strengths and weaknesses. In recent years much criticism has been leveled against standardized tests. Many of the problems the critics attribute to these tests (i.e., lack of precision, the inability to measure the whole person, bias against economically or socially "different" groups) may have some basis in fact. But what these critics do not take into account is that the problem arises only when people try to use tests for purposes beyond that for which they are intended.

Another fact that is often neglected is that tests should rarely, if ever, be used alone when we are trying to determine such things as a person's intelligence or his/her chances for success in later life. Standardized tests represent only one of many techniques that should contribute to the evaluation of an individual. Observations, judgments of others, anecdotal records, individual conferences, self-evaluation, evaluation by peers, attitudes and past performance are only a few of the other measures that should be taken into account. While any one measure or indicator cannot be expected to be perfectly reliable, a number of different indicators, followed over a period of time, can be of value in estimating a person's intelligence and later success in life.

Some critics of standardized tests have recommended a moratorium on all testing. Such an extreme action would be like "throwing out the baby with the bathwater." Human judgment must enter into the use of any evaluation tool, whether it be a standardized test or some other. Some standardized tests are better than others. People who use standardized tests must know how to judge the adequacy of any given test for any given purpose. Problems that have been noted in the use and abuse of standardized tests will not be solved by abolishing them. The answer lies in improving the quality of tests and educating test users and the public in the proper selection and use of tests.

There is also variation in test-wiseness and ease with which individuals take tests; and many temporary conditions of the individual can adversely affect test results (fatigue, illness, text-anxiety, etc.). Test users must also be able to judge the extent to which these factors may be affecting an individual's score.

The effectiveness of standardized tests in determining a person's intelligence or later success in life lies not in the test itself, but rather in the skill and judgment of the user. However, for most people, standardized tests are really quite effective.

William T. Greenough. While I am less well-qualified than many others to comment upon the predictive value of *human* intelligence tests, I can say that the performance of *animals* on various problem-solving or learning tests may be greatly affected by the physical and social characteristics of the rearing environment.

Among the best demonstrations of this are observations that feral animals reared in natural surroundings are typically superior to laboratory-reared counterparts on discrimination and other learning tests. Similarly, animals reared in "enriched" laboratory environments—for rats, these involve large, toy-equipped cages and several playmates—generally learn mazes, visual discriminations and other complex tasks more rapidly than do animals housed in standard laboratory cages. We can only surmise that these artificial laboratory tests tap behavioral abilities that would facilitate survival in the wild.

In humans, there is ample evidence that the quality of childhood experience affects both intelligence test performance and success in later life. However, to the extent that the individual's experience can alter subsequent test performance, a test at a specific point in time cannot be viewed as a stable predictor of later intellectual performance.

Professor Emeritus J. McVicker Hunt. If "intelligence" is to have any operational meaning, standardized tests define that meaning. On the other hand, scores on intelligence tests are only roughly correlated with measures of success in life. The Stanford-Binet tests were designed to predict performance in school, and they do predict; not perfectly, by any means, but the correlations are in the range of +.60 to +.75. Such prediction, however, is not very important. It would be much better to have tests that would define the specifics of the skills and knowledge that each child has, to enable teachers to anticipate the kinds of educational experiences from which the child can profit most.

Considerable evidence indicates that tests of intelligence, particularly in the early years, chiefly measure skill with such symbolic processes as language and numbers. These are the skills in which the children of parents with little education and low incomes show the largest deficiencies. Unfortunately, it is not widely recognized that the foundations for the development of skill with language and numbers start very early—in the development of vocal imitation as a source of phonology and in opportunities to hear the sounds of words timed with perception of the things they represent.

Dr. Perry Miller. This is really a two-part question and a most fascinating one. First, I feel that, in general, standardized tests are most effective in determining a person's intelligence as long as we have a test or instrument that has a high degree of validity and reliability; that is, as long as the test really demonstrates that it measures what it claims to measure and does so with a high degree of consistency. For example, suppose I constructed a test of intelligence, but the only tasks involved were those of hitting a baseball. More than likely, I would not have a very valid or reliable test of intelligence. I would not want the American League or National League to get angry with me but, nevertheless, this kind of test of intelligence would not be of any value simply because there is probably little relationship between how you hit a baseball and your degree or level of intelligence. Again, the test has to show that it can measure what it claims to measure. Validity and reliability of a test are the two main ingredients that go into the recipe of test-making. They are ingredients that can be established and determined by a combination of test construction techniques and various mathematical procedures involving that branch of mathematics that we call statistics.

Now, measuring a person's intelligence is something we can do most effectively today—but determining a person's success in life is a whole other issue and not so easy to do. If a person has a high level of intelligence—a high IQ—we tend to say that this person is going to make out OK and will be successful in his or her endeavors. But, trying to determine success is a very hazardous activity. There is a whole host of factors at work, called "nonintellective factors," that influence success. For example; enthusiasm, desire, drive and perseverance. These are great influencing factors and have very little to do with a person's existing level of intelligence. Also, a person's level of mental health or emotional well-being is important. I have seen a lot of crazy people walking around with Ph.D.'s or other advanced degrees. Because of their poor level of mental health they tend not to enjoy any significant amount of success.

In general, I think that we can speculate about people's success but we really cannot make certified determinations through the use of intelligence tests or otherwise, because success is influenced by so many factors other than intelligence. And these just don't lend themselves to existing measurement techniques.

Richard M. Restak, M.D. Standardized tests are of limited effectiveness in determining either intelligence or success. The most important determinants involve an individual's ambitions. This is partly a result of the experiences he has had, particularly in regard to the role models he has encountered. The absence of appropriate role models accounts for the deleterious effects created by socioeconomic deprivation. Not that the person cannot learn to excel, but rather, he is not exposed to the kind of confirming experiences that stimulate success.

In my neuropsychiatric practice, I daily encounter people who have high IQ's and enhanced aptitudes—but have not the emotional maturity to apply themselves to the hard work required to make a success of anything. This is another area where standardized tests fail to pick out the person who will eventually reach enhanced levels of achievement.

Finally, "happiness" is not correlated with IQ. Often, the "smartest" individuals are crippled by neurotic inhibitions, conceit, lack of tact or social awkwardness. Their expectations are unrealistic and this leads to poor self-esteem and, as a result, poor adaption and little success in life.

DOES INTELLIGENCE DECLINE
AFTER THE AGE OF FIFTY?

F. G. Brown. General intelligence, as measured by scores on intelligence tests, does decline after the age of fifty. In fact, the evidence suggests that intelligence test scores begin to decline much earlier. For example, Wechsler's (1981) data indicate that intelligence test scores reach a peak at ages twenty-five to thirty-four and decline with increasing age thereafter. However, the average scores of persons aged forty-five to fifty-four are at the same level as persons aged eighteen to nineteen.

While this decline with age is well established, several factors must be taken into account when determining what these data mean. First: these data are based on cross-sectional samples. That is, all persons were tested during the same year. As a consequence, persons in the various age groups differed widely in the amount of education they had had, with older persons having had less education than the younger age groups. Thus, differences in intelligence test scores may reflect differences in the amount of education.

Another consideration is what specific ability is being tested. Scores on intelligence tests reflect performance on various types of tasks. Performance on some of these tasks, especially those requiring rapid response and those involving perceptual skills, decline relatively rapidly with increasing age. Scores on other tasks which rely more on general reasoning and verbal abilities (such as vocabulary, comparing concepts, fund of information) do not decline, and may even increase after age fifty.

Yet another consideration is how much use a person makes of a particular ability or skill. Studies have shown that whether a particular ability increases or decreases with age depends on whether a person continues to use that ability. For example, performance on vocabulary tests (a good measure of general intelligence) remains stable or increases with age if a person continues to use that ability, either on the job or in his leisure time activities. However, if a person does not continue to use an ability, it will probably decline with age.

Finally, one must be concerned with what is meant by intelligence. The data we have been talking about refer to intelligence as the psychologist describes and measures it. But the average person probably uses a broader definition of intelligence than the psychologist, a definition that includes "common sense" knowledge and the ability to deal with the problems of everyday living, not just performance on certain intellectual tasks. While I know of no good data, one might expect these abilities to increase with age unless illness or disability interferes with the ability to reason and function normally.

John E. Corbally. In responding to any question about intelligence declining after the age of fifty, I can only answer: I hope not!

Marian C. Diamond. In answering this question, one must ask what is meant by intelligence. If we use the dictionary's definition, then we refer to the power of understanding. Many psychological tests have been given to individuals past fifty and the results indicate that active people do not show a decrease in intelligence compared with those who are less active.

Laboratory investigations with animals have demonstrated that the outer layers of the brain, the cerebral cortex, can grow at any age in response to enriched conditions. Since the structure of the brain has been shown to increase at any age, we believe its potential to learn exists throughout the lifetime of the animal. There is no reason to believe that the human brain acts any differently. We all know people over ninety who are still very mentally alert and active. Of course, if the general health of the individual has degenerated, then the matter is quite different. It is the total health of the individual that is important in maintaining an active body and brain.

William T. Greenough. Some evidence indicates a decline in certain aspects of human mental performance in later life, although the ages at which such declines become apparent vary widely across individuals. Many abilities do not decline in nonpathological aging, and at least some measures, such as vocabulary, may increase virtually throughout life. It may be that the degree to which abilities decline, in cases where physical condition is comparable, depends upon the degree to which they are practiced. Many of our most productive scientists are beyond the age of fifty, and their talents certainly depend to a significant degree upon the breadth and depth of their scientific experience. Indeed, increasing evidence indicates that the mind, like the body, requires exercise to maintain its fitness.

Studies of the brain in animals have revealed possible substrates of this process. When young adult and middle-aged rats are provided the opportunity for "mental exercise," either by placing them in complex surroundings for a time or training them on mazes or other tasks, certain regions of their brains actually increase in size and the nerve cells in these regions develop new processes of the type which connect with other nerve cells. In fact, the adult brain is now widely viewed as quite dynamic, its very structure responding to the demands of the organism's surroundings. There is also evidence that nerve cells of the human brain grow new processes after middle age. Thus a proper response, in cases of good health, is that mental ability in middle age may decline to the extent that it is allowed to do so.

Arthur R. Jensen. The mental abilities that psychologists identify as "intelligence" and can measure with reasonable accuracy by means of appropriate tests show little, if any, decline (on the average) until well past age fifty. Certain types of abilities and skills, which are termed "crystalized" intelligence, show no decline in normally healthy persons, and may even increase up into the seventies. Crystalized intelligence consists of one's fund of knowledge, general and specialized, as well as highly practiced skills that one has cumulated over a lifetime.

On the other hand, there is "fluid" intelligence, which involves the ability to learn things that are entirely new to one's experience; to solve novel or unfamiliar problems; and to memorize things. Fluid intelligence does seem to show a gradual decline in middle age, and a more rapid decline in old age. One's brain cells gradually die off and the brain actually shrinks in size and weight with advancing age. The rate of mental decline is mainly affected by the person's health, especially the condition of the vascular system and the blood and oxygen supply to the brain. In addition to maintaining good health while growing older, there are indications that maintaining interests and pursuits that demand mental activity may, to some extent, stave off intellectual decline.

Dr. Perry Miller. I do not think that intelligence declines after the age of fifty. What many behavioral scientists think, and I happen to be one of them, is that, with the onset of so-called middle age and old age, "impaired efficiency" begins to occur. In other words, the intellect per se does not decline or deteriorate but the person in general begins to slow-up because of the beginning of physical problems (arthritis, cardiac problems, etc.). There are some psychologists who think that intelligence reaches the peak of its development between the ages of about thirty to fifty; and then it remains on a plateau for the remainder of one's life unless senility begins to occur. Of course with senility there is, unfortunately, a deterioration of one's intellectual abilities.

It should be remembered that intelligence is not an absolute quantity; it is a variable quantity; it is always subject to change; and in the case of physically healthy people, both children and adults, it is always subject to improvement and expansion.

I am almost fifty-three years old and I am much more competent intellectually today than I was as a freshman in college at age seventeen. As long as there is no disease present, human intellect can be like good wine: the older it gets the better it is.

MENTAL ILLNESS AND ATTITUDES

What is "MENTAL ILLNESS" or "mental health," and what is the difference between them? Is there interplay between physical and mental illnesses? How are mental illnesses best treated?

These are some of the basic problems that experts tackle in the following section. Although people often like to think of those with mental illnesses as somehow distinctly different from the mentally healthy—just as those with measles are obviously different from the physically healthy—the experts' answers show that mental illness may indeed be just a state of mind. Many people undergo brief periods of mental illness and then appear to be completely recovered; others suffer from mental disorders most or all of their lives.

Unlike measles victims, who have spots, fever and other conveniently explicit symptoms, the mentally ill can appear to be just like the rest of the population. In fact, the mentally ill make up a sizable proportion of the American population. No exact figures are available, but a 1975 study estimated that at least 15 percent of all Americans suffer from some type of mental disorder. These disorders include such diverse problems as psychoses, neuroses, drug or alcohol dependence, mental retardation and severe personality disorders.

Although many people may suffer mental disorders at some time in their lives, society has traditionally had trouble deciding who the mentally ill are, what is wrong with them, and how they should be treated. At various points in history, a person who habitually acted in a bizarre manner might have been thought to be possessed by devils, stricken by

God, damaged by early childhood experiences, afflicted by a biochemical disorder or just plain eccentric.

Until about thirty years ago, the unfortunate few judged to be severely mentally ill were usually packed off to large, government-run mental hospitals or asylums. Since mental illnesses were generally considered to be permanent disorders, once a person was diagnosed as severely ill and sent to an asylum, he or she could expect to spend months, years or even an entire lifetime in the institution.

Some people spend most of their lives in mental institutions, but in the last few decades the number of institutionalized patients has dropped dramatically. In 1940, for example, there were 479 mental hospital patients per 100,000 people in the United States. The rate fell to less than 400 by 1955 and continued to fall throughout the 1950s, reaching 194 per 100,000 by 1970.

"Wonder drugs" developed in the 1950s opened the way for this exodus. Tranquilizers, antipsychotic drugs and other medications revolutionized the care of the mentally ill. Doctors found, for example, that antipsychotic drugs could relieve many of the symptoms of schizophrenia, a type of psychosis characterized by disturbed moods and disordered interpretations of reality, such as hallucinations and delusions. Today, patients diagnosed as schizophrenic still make up the largest group in mental hospitals, but with the help of antipsychotic medications and community health programs, many schizophrenics can function in the community. Since long periods in institutions can lessen patients' ability to cope with the outside world, mental-health-care providers now try to keep hospital stays at a minimum.

But what becomes of the mental patients who do not require the constraints of mental hospitals but who do need help in meeting everyday needs? Ideally, these patients receive ongoing help in the community. In 1963, Congress passed the Mental Retardation Facilities and Community Mental Health Construction Act to underwrite a system of community mental-health care throughout the country. Thus, while large mental hospitals were shutting down their wards due to increasing costs and decreasing numbers of permanently institutionalized patients, hundreds of community health care centers were opening. As fewer patients remained in institutions, more received help in psychiatric outpatient clinics, general hospitals, nursing homes, halfway houses and other community services.

Critics, however, claim that patients' releases from mental hospitals are often motivated more by financial concerns than by consideration for the patients' or the community's welfare. Emptied mental institutions, they argue, result in more still-symptomatic patients wandering the streets and more "bag ladies" huddling in the subways.

Chronically ill mental patients present different problems than those who suffer only brief periods of mental illness or those whose mental disorders are not disabling. The basic dilemmas of mental-health care, however, affect people with a wide range of disorders, as well as the community as a whole. Wonder drugs have radically changed mental-health care, but the debate about what mental illness is, what causes it, and how it should be treated still continues, as the answers on the following pages illustrate.

CONTRIBUTORS

Prof. George W. Albee, Psychology, University of Vermont, Burlington, Vermont

Kenneth Anchor, Ph.D., A.B.P.P., Associate Professor of Psychology and Director, Vanderbilt University–Veteran's Administration Medical Center Internship in Professional Psychology, Nashville, Tennesee; founding editor, *The American Journal of Clinical Biofeedback*

David E. Anderson, Ph.D., Department of Psychology, Allegheny College, Meadville, Pennsylvania

M. H. Anderson, M.D., Evansville, Illinois

Richard W. Anderson, M.D., Psychiatrist, Scripps Clinic and Research Foundation, La Jolla, California

John V. Basmajian, M.D., Professor of Medicine, McMaster University; Director of Rehabilitation Medicine, Chedoke–McMaster Hospital, Hamilton, Ontario; former President (1979), Biofeedback Society of America; editor, *Biofeedback*

Edward J. Beattie, Jr., M.D., General Director and Chief Medical Officer, Memorial Hospital for Cancer and Allied Diseases, New York, New York; author of *Toward the Conquest of Cancer*

Randolph Bufano, nutritional consultant

Thomas G. Burish, Ph.D., Associate Professor of Psychology and Director of Clinical Training, Vanderbilt University, Nashville, Tennessee

Arthur Canter, Professor of Psychiatry, University of Iowa College of Medicine, Iowa City, Iowa

John G. Carlson, Ph.D., Professor of Psychology, University of Hawaii, Honolulu, Hawaii

Michael L. Culbert, Chairman of the Board, Committee for Freedom of Choice in Cancer Therapy, Inc.

Albert Ellis, Ph.D., Executive Director, Institute for Rational Emotive Therapy, New York, New York

Sol L. Garfield, Ph.D., Professor of Psychology, Washington University, St. Louis, Missouri

Robert R. Holt, Professor of Psychology, New York University, New York, New York

David W. Jacobs, M.D., Director, Biofeedback Institute of San Diego, San Diego Medical Center, San Diego, California

Arnold A. Lazarus, Ph.D., Professor, Graduate School of Applied and Professional Psychology, Rutgers, the State University, New Brunswick, New Jersey; Director, Multimodal Therapy Institute, Kingston, New Jersey

Harry Levinson, President, The Levinson Institute; Lecturer, Harvard Medical School, Cambridge, Massachusetts

Joel F. Lubar, Ph.D., Professor of Psychology, University of Tennessee, Knoxville, Tennessee

Judd Marmor, M.D., Los Angeles, California; past President, American Psychiatric Association

Rollo May, Ph.D., psychoanalyst and author

Thomas B. Mulholland, Ph.D., Veterans Administration Hospital, Bedford, Massachusetts

Eli Robins, M.D., Wallace Renard Professor of Psychiatry, Washington University School of Medicine, St. Louis, Missouri

Paul J. Rosch, M.D., President, American Institute of Stress, Yonkers, New York; Adjunct Clinical Professor, Division of Behavioral Medicine, New York Medical College, New York, New York; President-Elect, New York State Society of Internal Medicine

C. Norman Shealy, M.D., Ph.D., Founder and Director, Pain and Health Rehabilitation Center™, LaCrosse, Wisconsin; founding and immediate past President, American Holistic Medical Association

B. F. Skinner, leading exponent of the school of psychology known as Behaviorism; author of *Beyond Freedom and Dignity*, *About Behaviorism*, and other books

Solomon S. Steiner, Ph.D., Professor of Psychology, The City College of The City University of New York, New York, New York

John A. Talbott, M.D., Professor of Psychiatry, Cornell University College of Medicine, Ithaca, New York

Edward Taub, Ph.D., Chief Behavioral Biology Center, Institute for Behavioral Research, Silver Spring, Maryland

Jack E. White, M.D., F.A.C.S., Director, Howard University Cancer Center, Washington, D.C.

WHAT IS GOOD MENTAL HEALTH AND HOW DOES ONE ATTAIN IT?

Robert R. Holt. Good mental health means the ability to function adequately in all important human respects, up to the limits of one's capacities. It is a complex outcome of the reasonably good operation of many of the human being's vital subsystems. It is necessarily defined by use of some rather vague terms like "adequately" and "reasonably good," because the concept of health is fundamentally a value, not an objective attribute (like weight) that can be precisely measured.

One attains good mental health, basically, by virtue of several fortunate happenstances: first, having a more or less normal, complete and smoothly operating body; second, being endowed with a minimum of intelligence, capacity for normal emotional response and other psychological abilities; third, being born into a family of reasonably normal, loving and competent parents who do not traumatically abuse you. Finally, it is also helpful to be born at a time and in a place where certain basic conditions and supplies are present: peace and social stability; enough economic security so that essential food, shelter and clothing are available and so that at least one parent is not overworked or emotionally drained by anxiety; and a neighborhood with at least one friend and free from such dangers as kidnappers, drug pushers or other criminals who prey directly on children. No one of these ingredients is indispensable, yet all are important.

It does not seem to be especially critical to be loved and tended to by a "good enough" mother or mother-substitute for the early months (and perhaps years) of life—nor does it seem critical that one be exposed to an interestingly varied environment at some point in childhood. Of course, children who have been kept in dark closets for many years do not attain full mental health on being rescued; however, they have usually suffered severe emotional deprivation and often brutal abuse as well.

Perhaps the answer can be summarized, without too much distortion, in these few words: the main psychological prerequisite for mental health is to experience love, not hate, as a child.

Arnold A. Lazarus, Ph.D. To put it succinctly, good mental health consists of acceptance without complacency. The healthy (or adaptive) person realizes that he or she is fallible. There are no strivings for perfection, no self-downing, no falsely catastrophic cognitions. Yet, the person is aware of shortcomings and limitations, and endeavors to remedy them, if possible. A mentally healthy person is generally tolerant and nonjudgmental, but he or she is certainly assertive (not aggressive) and will stand up for what he/she believes to be his or her reasonable rights. Such people have high frustration tolerance thresholds. They are not hypersensitive to criticism, rejection or disapproval. They tend to react, whereas neurotics typically over-react.

The mentally healthy person takes emotional risks. They are inclined to be forthright, authentic, empathic and compassionate. They have acquired a broad range of coping behaviors; they can control most of their negative emotions; they enjoy many sensual and sensory delights (food, art, music, sex, nature); they have a positive self-image and enjoy optimistic fantasies; they attempt to reason logically and rationally and are open to feedback; they form close love-bonds and meaningful friendships; they take care of their physical health (they exercise, eat sensibly, and avoid tobacco and other harmful drugs).

How does one attain the foregoing? Some people are fortunate enough to inherit extremely easygoing, stable temperaments. The rest of us have to work very hard at increasing our levels of frustration tolerance, at decreasing our over-critical faculties, and at acquiring a variety of personal and interpersonal skills. Contrary to popular opinion, these ends are most unlikely to be achieved solely through the development of "insight." Most people require coaching, training, teaching and modeling to enable them to cope with life's demands.

Harry Levinson. Mental health is not a state that one attains, but essentially a process in which one is always engaged. Several years ago, a group of colleagues and I evolved a definition of mental health by interviewing the senior staff of The Menninger Foundation. We found that mentally healthy people, as described by those experts, were characterized by a wide variety of sources of gratification; flexibility under stress; the ability to recognize and accept their own assets and limitations; the ability to treat other people as individuals. Also, they were active and productive, they did what they did because they wanted to, and enjoyed doing it rather than being driven.

Certainly, people can invest themselves in a wide variety of things and, by doing so, have psychological anchors when there are stresses. If there are significant losses in one area, then they have gratification and support in another. Under those conditions, they are much better able to think well of themselves—and, therefore, will think well of others.

People who are able to do these things are likely to invest themselves in gratifying and productive work. If people cannot evolve a variety of gratifications and good relationships with other people, if they cannot, as Freud put it, work effectively and love effectively, then usually, it will take professional help to relieve the barriers to that kind of achievement.

John A. Talbott, M.D. Good mental health has been a subject of some controversy in the field of psychiatry. As with the definition of health, the mere absence of disease does not seem sufficient. What is necessary to be healthy in a more positive way, however, is more elusive. Does it or must it include the potential for continuing personal growth; ability to form close and intimate relationships; capability to respond to new, unexpected or potentially stressful situations adaptively; capacity to work, love and play; ability to be flexible and spontaneous and shift gears from hard-driving, concentrated, focused behavior to a laid-back, tolerant, relaxed mode as the situation demands?

I would answer that good mental health, while hard to define, is a concept we all implicitly agree on. Its parts include all of the factors mentioned above, but the whole is more important than the parts. Good mental health involves: the person's sense of being alright with him or herself; the fact that one's children, parents, and friends sense that the person is alright; and an individual's ability to behave personally and interpersonally as a responsive and responsible individual.

Now having said that, how do you attain good mental health? A good question. For some, early childhood experiences in the family seem to engender it; for others, adolescent or adult experiences seem pivotal; while for others, more formal attempts at correction and development through psychotherapy or psychoanalysis seem critical. But certainly, for those who wish to change, the knowledge of what's wrong and of how they would like to behave and feel, is half the battle. If actually getting to the desired end seems overly difficult, or seems to be taking too long a time—that may indicate the time is ripe to seek a professional guide for the process.

WHAT EFFECT DO MENTAL ATTITUDE AND OTHER PSYCHOLOGICAL FACTORS HAVE ON SUCH AILMENTS AS CANCER, EARLY AGING, HEART DISEASE, ETCETERA?

Edward J. Beattie, Jr., M.D. If there is anyone who doubts that the mind has a profound effect on the body's physiological mechanisms, let him think back to the last time he was in danger—perhaps an automobile accident narrowly avoided. Adrenalin and epinephrine pour into your bloodstream, your heart rate increases, blood pressure shoots up, reflexes quicken, and your mouth tastes like copper. The brain has shouted "Danger!" and the body responds. In fact, it is well known that a person's mental outlook can affect health and play a role in the outcome of illness. Undue stress, depression and a negative outlook can upset hormonal balance, overstimulate the autonomic nervous system and alter the output of corticosteroids that weaken the individual's immune system— our primary defense against disease. Emotions alter the endocrine gland system's output of substances vital to health and well-being.

I am not familiar with any scientific studies that show that mental attitude affects the aging process, although this may well be true. My guess is that a well-adjusted person with a sound philosophy of life, a happy family life and work he enjoys, is very apt to be healthier and live into a rewarding old age than a less well-adjusted individual.

There is now good evidence that things such as blood pressure, once thought not to be consciously controllable, may in fact be controlled to some degree by the mind. Far Eastern religious men have shown astonishing ability to control body processes formerly believed impossible to control.

There is also no question but that psychological factors trigger biochemical responses in the body. For instance: when a witch doctor places a hex on an intended victim, that person often dies when he learns of the curse, because of his belief that the hex causes death. The same is often true when the voodoo doctor sticks pins in a doll representing the victim. In a more scientific approach, well-documented research shows that a placebo (a pill or injection with no pharmacological effect) can cause the brain to release secretions that deaden pain. The individual does not know the pill itself has no effect but *believes* it will kill pain; the *belief* causes the brain to order the release of endorphins and encephalins which, in fact, provide physiological relief. This is why terribly injured accident victims usually feel no pain until much later.

A patient's belief in the competence and healing power of the physician also affects the outcome of an illness. This is why "bedside manner" is so vital to the healing process. A warm, sympathetic, compassionate, caring physician has a far better chance of healing his patient than a brusque, unfeeling, unpleasant doctor, who communicates as little as possible.

The brain, quite literally, can telegraph orders to the body's tiny but efficient chemical factories to fill prescriptions for chemicals—drugs—to fight disease and ease pain. In partnership with medical therapy, a positive mental outlook is an important weapon in defeating disease. There are, of course, diseases that are not reversible despite diligent medical care and a good mental attitude; but even here, faith and a positive outlook make the best of life.

In the years ahead we will, I am sure, increase our knowledge of the brain's effects on the body and how to marshal this important weapon against disease.

Randolph Bufano. Mental attitude has a very great effect on physical well-being; and pessimism or optimism often determine whether a given stress will eventuate increased illness or recaptured health. This has led some, notably Christian Scientists, to claim that illness is wrong thinking and health right thinking. It has led others to place their lives at the whim of faith-healers. Without going this far, even the most orthodox physicians allow that numerous diseases respond to a positive mental attitude; and they have observed such response in ailments ranging from headache to cancer. It seems that the brain is a pharmacy of agents, mediated by the endorphins and the central nervous system; and that the brain is capable of motivating these agents.

The well-known placebo effect is evidence of the importance of mental attitude to medicine: 35 percent of patients given a placebo improve in health, suggesting that inner belief is vital to the healing process. There is also a *negative* placebo effect. Again, hypnosis is used in orthodox hospitals and clinics to sooth pain and even to control bleeding. Furthermore, biofeedback experiments have demonstrated beyond dispute, what yogis have known for thousands of years—that with practice, we can attune our physiological processes to conscious mental cues, thereby extending the domain of bodily functions under voluntary control.

On the other hand, mental attitude is readily improved by physical measures such as taking vitamins or going for a walk; and the functioning of the mind is dependent on the chemical state of the brain. I conclude that the relation of the body and mind, while far from completely understood, is certainly intimate, and that it is clear either can react upon the other for good or ill.

Michael L. Culbert. Mental stress is implied in a wide variety of cancer cases and in certain areas of cardiovascular calamities. It is known that grief and despair can impair immune functioning and that negative attitudes may interrupt hormonal balance, leading to metabolic dysfunction.

Cancer outbreaks have frequently been traced to times of extreme mental and emotional trauma. The evolution of a "cancer psychological profile" for much of cancer indicates that sustained patterns of mental behavior and attitudes play important roles in the induction of malignancy. It is doubtful that mental conditions *alone* "cause" cancer, but they undoubtedly help set the stage for it.

Albert Ellis, Ph.D. No one really knows, as yet, what the relationship is between psychological factors and illness; although there are many theorists and practitioners who dogmatically claim that the effects of mental attitudes on all physical illness are crucial or enormous. This view probably contains some truth but also, alas, much falsehood.

It has been reasonably well established that certain illnesses (e.g., high blood pressure) are sometimes, and particularly in individual predisposed cases, somewhat affected by people's psychological outlook and their emotional reactions. But other factors—especially heredity, nutrition, exercise, etc.—are also very important in causing cancer, early aging, heart disease and other physical ailments; and the interaction of these factors with the psychological and philosophic attitudes of afflicted people is probably more important than either of these elements alone.

Robert R. Holt. A good deal of psychological and medical research indicates that several psychological attitudes are strongly related to longevity, and to mortality from such major illnesses as cancer and heart disease.

The one best predictor of how long men live is the degree to which they enjoy their work. Cancer patients who live the shortest time after the disease's onset tend to have preexisting feelings of hopelessness and helplessness. Conversely, strong attitudes or feelings of personal competence, of self-respect and of autonomy (feeling that you are master of your own fate) are often found in people who are relatively free from disease or who recover from bouts of cancer, heart attacks, stroke, etc.

It pays to develop deep interests and strong attachments to people, and to cultivate a determination to enjoy and cling to life!

Judd Marmor, M.D. The question of psychological factors and their effect on illness is global in scope, and therefore difficult to answer.

There *is* growing evidence that mental attitudes and psychological stress have an effect on the body's immune system. This may indirectly affect resistance to cancer and the rate at which it may spread. I know of no reliable evidence, however, that mental stress in and of itself can *cause* cancer. Similarly, clinical experience over the years clearly indicates that mental and emotional stress does play a contributory role in a wide variety of physical disorders such as heart disease, hypertension, hyperthyroidism, etc.

The important thing to remember, however, is that the causation of disease is always multifactorial and involves the individual's genetic predisposition, life patterns, eating habits and environmental factors as well as psychological stresses.

Eli Robins, M.D. My answer to the question of psychological factors and their effects on illness and early aging, must be: There are few effects; and even these few have not been demonstrated unequivocally.

Paul J. Rosch, M.D. Relationships between emotional states and cancer have been recognized since the time of Galen, who noted that women with an excess of black bile or melancholy (Greek, *melaschole*) tended to have more cancer than individuals in whom other humors predominated. Investigations in the past two decades verify the observations that certain emotional states or personality types clearly predispose to a variety of malignancies. These predisposing tendencies may be summarized as: (1) loss of an important emotional relationship; (2) feelings of helplessness and hopelessness; (3) loss of *raison d'etre*; and (4) the inability to express emotions. Recent studies suggest that psychological tests designed to demonstrate the above tendencies can predict with a surprising degree of accuracy, the likelihood of malignancy—for relatively asymptomatic individuals merely undergoing diagnostic test for different types of cancer (pap smear, breast biopsy, abnormal chest X-ray).

Equally important is the observation that the emotional status of the patient appears to play a considerable role in influencing the clinical course of malignant tumors; and just as negative or distressful factors can accelerate tumor growth, so is it likely that positive emotions (faith, humor, love, creativity) exert opposite effects. In those well-documented cases, where cancer has disappeared spontaneously without the assistance of any outside agency, the strong positive faith of an individual can usually be demonstrated. From a theoretical point of view, it would be almost inconceivable that stress or emotional factors would not play an important role in malignancy. Emotional stress profoundly influences the competency of the immune system, levels of interferon and, indeed, almost every other element known to have an important role in the development and outcome of the malignant process.

The relationship between stress and aging is equally intriguing. Chronologic age is quite a bit different than biologic age; and the latter phenomenon is characterized by a variety of degenerative phenomena known to be associated with acute and chronic stress. Premature aging can be produced by stressing laboratory animals; and results in microscopic evidence of pigment changes, and "wear and tear" pathology so characteristic of the stress response. It may well be that we all inherit a finite amount of "adaptational energy" that can be used up prematurely, resulting in a spectrum of stress-related disorders or premature degeneration of a generalized nature. It also seems likely that the devitalizing effects of daily distress can be offset or retarded by stress-reducing measures (meditation, behavioral modification, regular exercise, etc.) or by the good stress that comes with good emotional health (as evidenced by those individuals with powerful positive emotions such as creativity and pride of accomplishment). Good examples: symphony conductors, musicians, artists and entertainers—who may be unbelievably youthful despite their years, simply because they are creative and are involved in activities that they enjoy and that give pleasure to others.

From an evolutionary point of view, a species could survive only if it could reproduce itself. In the case of humans, a characteristic feature of the reproductive act involves doing something enjoyable that gives pleasure to others. In man's highly developed cerebral cortex, it would seem reasonable and logical that the achievement of this emotional state would similarly be rewarded with good health and therefore longevity (in the absence of other negative emotions). To sum up: We consistently see that individuals in a variety of occupations, who achieve intense joy and satisfaction from efforts that give pleasure to others, have a youthful vitality that bears no relationship to their actual age. Conversely, many individuals lack such revitalizing stimuli and succumb to accelerated arteriosclerosis because of an inability to adapt to the stress imposed by modern civilization.

The relationship between stress and heart disease is much more certain and demonstrable. Primitive man responded to severe stress, such as fear, in an appropriate fashion. This involved the stimulation of the sympathetic nervous system and the release of adrenalin, which admirably prepared him to deal with an adversary in terms of "fright or flight." The physiological responses that ensued under such situations included an elevation of blood pressure; dilation of the pupils; increased flow of blood to the brain, arms, legs, and a shunting away of blood from the intestines; the pouring of fats and sugars into the blood stream; increased coagulability of the blood, etc. All of these responses were purposeful and allowed primitive man to see better, think better, fight better, run away faster, get more energy—and minimized the risk of blood loss due to hemorrhage. The problem is that the nature of stress for man today is more apt to be a psychological, rather than a physical threat—e.g., being stuck in a traffic jam on the way to an important appointment, having a fight with the boss or your mate— and such responses are now no longer appropriate but actually harmfull. The stresses occur not once every fortnight, as in the case of our ancestors, but often several times a day; invoking the identical stereotyped archaic response with the subsequent development of hypertension, heart attacks, strokes, peptic ulcer, diabetes, etc.

With respect to heart disease, specifically, it now seems quite clear that the most important risk factor is the stressful Type A behavior pattern. Such individuals are characterized by a great sense of time urgency, a need to cram more and more into less and less; by latent hostility; by an inability to relax; and they produce an excessive secretion of adrenalin and other stress hormones. It is likely that such individuals become addicted to their own adrenalin "highs" and unconsciously seek ways to perpetuate this feeling which leaves them in a state of constant arousal.

It now seems likely that elevated cholesterol, increased smoking, and many other so-called risk factors thought to be related to heart attacks, are significant only in that they occur as manifestations of Type A behavior. Attempts to reduce the incidence of heart disease by reducing cholesterol with diet or drugs, or by reducing smoking, have failed to produce any significant results. On the other hand, successful modification of Type A behavior has proven to be a very effective strategy. Even the beneficial effects of jogging on cholesterol, high-density lipoproteins and heart attacks are probably due more to the behavioral modification that occurs as a result of such activity than to the exercise itself. The successful prevention and treatment of heart disease may lie more in stress-reducing techniques such as meditation than in medication.

C. Norman Shealy, M.D. The single most important factor in determining health is mental attitude and belief system. The attitude, when positive, helps one to choose health life habits. In order of their importance, these are: (1) not smoking; (2) moderation in alcohol intake (maximum of two ounces of spirits or equivalent per day); (3) maintaining weight within 10 percent of ideal; (4) minimizing fat, salt, sugar and white flour in the diet; (5) obtaining adequate physical exercise.

All the positive thinking in the world, about factors other than those innumerated, is not likely to substitute for these basic, good health habits. However, when one does have these habits and a healthy will to live, both optimal health and longevity are the result.

Fear, anger, guilt and depression (psychological or emotional stresses), weaken the immune system and cause tremendous distress in the natural homeostatic defense mechanisms. All diseases are ultimately the result of total life stress—physical, chemical and emotional or psychological. Positive attitudes and belief systems help one to avoid the negative psychological and emotional stresses—and help one choose to avoid those that are physical and chemical.

B. F. Skinner. If by "psychological factors" you mean feelings and states of mind, the answer to the question is—no effect whatsoever.

So-called "psychosomatic symptoms" are due to the environmental factors which are said to be responsible for feelings and states of mind—factors such as inconsistent reinforcement, lack of reinforcement or unusual emotional or motivational variables.

Jack E. White, M.D., F.A.C.S. Stress, especially mental stress, may play an indirect role in the causation of cancer by causing one to drink more alcohol, to smoke more, etc. Stress of all types, including physiological stress, undoubtedly plays a significant role in the production and maintenance of heart disease. Similarly, it is probably a major factor in aging.

In all of these disorders, a positive attitude contributes to recovery from, or living with, these diseases.

WHAT IS THE MOST SUCCESSFUL CURE FOR MENTAL ILLNESS?

Professor George W. Albee. The question of what is the most successful cure for mental illness is impossible to answer intelligently. Try to answer the question: "What is the most successful cure for physical illness?"

Most forms of mental disorders should not be called "illnesses" because there is no identifiable defect or organic condition associated with them. They are learned behaviors.

For functional disorders, I would say cognitively oriented behavior therapy works best.

M. H. Anderson, M.D. The most successful cure for mental illness is a compassionate, empathizing, well-trained psychiatrist.

Richard W. Anderson, M.D. The most successful treatments for mental illness to date have been psychoactive drugs. Antipsychotics, developed in the early 1950s, have moved the treatment of all but the most refractory schizophrenic patients from the chronic mental hospital to community hospitals, other care facilities and outpatient centers. A few years later, the clinical development of new treatments for depression, namely monoamine oxidase inhibitors and tricyclic (and recently tetracyclic) antidepressants made office treatment possible for many depressive patients; now only the decompensated or suicidal must be hospitalized. Most recently lithium therapy, available in the United States for the past ten years, and elsewhere for more than thirty years, has proven to be our most effective agent in the control of manic attacks.

A close relationship with the physician is important for patients receiving any of these medications; since compliance is more likely, and side effects can be managed with dose adjustments or drug changes. Psychotherapy per se is not the treatment of choice for the management of mental illness.

Sol L. Garfield, Ph.D. The term "mental illness" is a vague and overly general designation, lacking precise meaning. There are many types of organic and psychological disorders which may be included in this catch-all classification. These range from progressive deteriorating organic brain disorders to relatively mild anxieties, fears and feelings of depression. Some have no cures, and some improve with or without treatment.

"Cure" is also a poorly defined term, particularly when dealing with mental or psychological disturbance. The analogy with physical illness is an easily made but frequently inappropriate one, since many of the loosely labeled mental illnesses do not clearly resemble physical illnesses.

One needs to ask about specific disorders in order to be given information on the possibilities of treatment and positive outcome.

Arnold A. Lazarus, Ph.D. Some authorities do not believe in the existence of mental illness. They point out that several physical lesions and biochemical imbalances can result in unusual or bizarre behaviors, but the basis is organic or physical.

Nevertheless, to answer this very broad question of "cures": the most successful approach to so-called mental illness is one that uses medication (if and when necessary) in conjunction with a broad-based reeductive psychobehavioral treatment regimen. Thus, if a patient requires medication but is treated solely by psychotherapy, success is unlikely to ensue. On the other hand, organic psychiatrists who use appropriate drug treatments but ignore the network of psychological excesses and deficiencies that most people exhibit, only address part of the overall problem.

It is my considered opinion (based on outcome and follow-up studies) that the most successful therapy is one that examines and treats any biological factors and then addresses six specific psychological modalities: (1) excesses and deficits in the patient's overt behaviors (e.g., faculty habits, compulsive actions, withdrawal tendencies, etc.); (2) negative emotions (especially anxiety, depression, guilt and hostility); (3) unpleasant sensations (such as tension, tremors, dizziness, muscle spasms, etc.); (4) problems in imagery (e.g., a poor self-image, a lack of positive imagery, mental pictures of failure, gloom and doom); (5) faulty cognitions (e.g., irrational ideas, distorted values, attitudes and beliefs); (6) interpersonal problems (e.g., inability to form close attachments, family difficulties, issues relating to excessive needs for power and control, etc.).

This broad-spectrum or multimodal orientation assumes that people are troubled by a multitude of specific problems that need to be dealt with by a similar multitude of specific treatments. The orientation is *educational*. The more the patient learns during therapy—the more adequate coping responses he or she acquires—the less likely relapse will follow.

DOES PSYCHOTHERAPY WORK—TO WHAT DEGREE AND FOR WHAT PROBLEMS?

M. H. Anderson, M.D. For most neurotics, psychotherapy works very well and, as with surgeons and surgery, the success is somewhat related to the therapists' competency. For psychotics, it frequently is more effective when used with chemotherapy and other somatic aids.

Richard W. Anderson, M.D. Psychotherapy does work, and works best for problems of adjustment. Those problems associated with marriage, child-rearing, work adjustment and socialization are all helped by a wide variety of individual and group therapies.

Although developed by Freud and others for the treatment of neurosis, psychotherapy is of limited value. Character change comes slowly, often only after long and arduous "working through" of transference— the attribution to the physician of traits first experienced in the past with significant persons. Thus, therapy that holds the hope of personality change is expensive, time consuming, and is usually available only to the well-insured or affluent. Little wonder then, that the newer therapies for the neuroses have ignored the past and aimed at behavior change in the present; these are the behavior therapies. Antianxiety drugs, another form of therapy, are of limited value in short-term use, and their extended administration carries with it the risk of habituation and dependence.

However, the therapeutic aspects of the doctor-patient relationship should not be overlooked in any field of medicine, for its supportive benefits are in themselves strong medicine. If I am suffering, what better help can I have than a strong, interested, knowledgeable and kind person on my side?

Albert Ellis, Ph.D. Yes, psychotherapy works mildly or moderately well for most clients who experience it and it works beautifully and profoundly for a few clients. Who are these few? Mainly, those who: find for themselves a very sane, sensible, down-to-earth therapist; acknowledge, with the therapist's help, that they themselves have, to a great extent, created and still are creating their own emotional problems— and do not "cop out" by blaming their parents, their society, or anyone else; work intensively again with their therapist's guidance, to accept the discomfort that therapy normally entails—the extended, and often intense, discomfort of forcing themselves—yes, *forcing themselves*—to practice—yes, *practice*—thinking, feeling and behaving in more functional ways; and continue to work hard, usually for the rest of their lives, to maintain the gains they achieved during therapy—and to do so mostly on their own, with relatively little help from their therapist.

Psychotherapy works for many different kinds of emotional problems and behavioral dysfunctions—particularly for neurotic symptoms like anxiety, depression, hostility, self-hatred and self-pity.

Sol L. Garfield, Ph.D. Psychotherapy is referred to, by many people, as if it were a unitary process and there was only one type of psychotherapy. Actually, there are probably over 200 different types or kinds of psychotherapy. Furthermore, they are dispensed by a variety of psychotherapists with varying kinds of backgrounds and varying kinds of training. Different kinds of psychotherapy also vary in terms of the frequency of sessions and the length of therapy. Some are brief, and some take years. Thus, one must be cautious in making generalized statements about psychotherapy.

Keeping what has been said in mind and recognizing that generalizations are difficult, a few statements can be offered based on the current research in the field. Psychotherapy, conducted by a competent therapist, appears to produce some positive results in perhaps 65 percent of the cases treated. For most individuals treated, the positive effects range from modest to moderate. A few, perhaps, around fifteen percent, may show really marked improvement. A much smaller number, depending upon the type of problem and the therapist, may even get worse. Problems of moderate anxiety and depression appear to respond most readily to certain types of psychotherapy. Specific fears or phobias may respond fairly well to behavioral therapies. For the most part, severe disorders such as schizophrenia do not respond well to psychotherapy.

Harry Levinson. Psychotherapy is a blanket term for a wide variety of verbal discussions between a person seeking psychological help and a therapist or person who provides that help. There are, therefore, varying degrees of helplessness depending on the skill and competence of the therapist, and the ability of the person seeking help to make use of the help being offered.

Taken on the whole, the research on psychotherapy indicates that it is indeed helpful for a wide variety of psychological problems, ranging from severe mental disorder to the milder problems of everyday living. Some people lose their symptoms. Others are able to adapt more effectively to their environments. And still others are able to work more creatively and productively than they did before. As with other forms of treatment, some persons find great success and help with one therapist after having failed with others. Some have profited not at all. People who cannot become aware of their own feelings are not likely to profit from psychotherapy.

Judd Marmor, M.D. There has been an accumulating body of evidence in recent years demonstrating that psychotherapy does work for a wide variety of mental and emotional disorders. The degree to which it works cannot be arbitrarily stated because it varies with the type of psycho-therapy used, the skills of the therapist, the personality of the patient and the severity of the disorder.

In general, psychotherapy is most effective in neurotic disorders but even in psychotic disorders, where psychotrophic medications are indi-cated, the adjunctive use of psychotherapy has been shown to be both necessary and helpful.

Rollo May, Ph.D. Yes, psychotherapy works. However, the answer also depends on what one means by "work." Does it make some people happier? Yes. Does it help them integrate their capacities? Yes. Does it support them in times of need? Yes.

What it does not do is to perform cures or give people genius that they did not have before.

WHAT IS BIOFEEDBACK?
HOW IS IT USED AND BY WHOM?

Kenneth Anchor, Ph.D. Biofeedback is a term referring to a series of discoveries, many within the past decade, which demonstrate that hu-mans have remarkable capacity to establish control over various physio-logical functions—some of which were previously thought to be beyond voluntary self-regulation. Biofeedback involves the measurement of certain ongoing physiological processes (such as blood pressure, heart rate, muscle tension, galvanic skin response or surface body tempera-ture) and mirroring this information back, instantaneously and continu-ously, to the person whose bodily functions are being monitored. This feedback most often occurs through a device such as a meter, display of colored lights or a musical tone transmitted by a loudspeaker. With such visual and/or auditory feedback, it has been found that for many bodily functions, people can learn to control them at will. For example; it has been found that—by measuring a person's heart beat, and transmitting this information back to that individual—given enough time, and with the proper series of training sessions and professional consultation, one can learn to control the heart rate.

Another form of biofeedback measures level of muscular activity, detected with metal discs pasted to the surface of the skin. These signals are then amplified and converted to an audible tone that alters with changes in the muscular tension level. Treatment begins with a series of sessions that focus on listening to this tone. Through these sessions—in combined with home practice, professional consultation and activities designed to work this skill into a person's everyday life—most people can learn to relax muscles to depths seldom found in Western populations. With such muscular self-regulation training, tension headaches have been eliminated for some individuals; and in some instances, nerve damaged muscles have been rehabilitated.

Temperature feedback refers to the use of a small sensor, attached to the skin, which detects and reports temperature changes caused by variations of blood flow beneath the skin surface. Through this method, people are able to learn to alter blood flow to various parts of the body. This type of biofeedback has been used to control migraine headaches, and to correct certain circulatory system disorders that produce complaints such as cold hands or feet.

It is important to recognize that the biofeedback instruments serve as learning devices reflecting information not otherwise possible back to the individual. Biofeedback is a technique for teaching voluntary control. This method is most likely to succeed if the individual is sufficiently motivated to take an active role in, and to accept responsibility for, the treatment. The individual is best advised to "think small," that is, to expect small gradual changes in the frequency, intensity, and duration of whatever stress-related disorder is addressed.

Qualified professional practitioners from a variety of health disciplines, most notably clinical psychologists, have taken an active role in conducting research with biofeedback methods. Many, but by no means all, biofeedback techniques have been found to be a useful addition to the armamentarium of therapeutic strategies offered by practitioners in clinics, hospitals, schools, industrial settings, pain treatment facilities and other settings. Some manufacturers are producing small home training units for use by clients.

David E. Anderson, Ph.D. Biofeedback is simply the feeding back of biological information to the person whose biology it is. Feedback is a shorthand term for something being returned or "fed back" to the thing from which it came. The expression developed in the field of engineering to define control systems that operate via feedback mechanisms; that is, those systems that operate by their ability to detect changes in the environment and then make internal adjustments so that their functions remain optimal. The most common example is the home thermostat and its ability to maintain a certain temperature by burning a heating unit on or off when conditions demand it. The terms "feedback" and "feedback control systems" were borrowed by physiologists and psychologists when they began theorizing about how the functions of the body were performed.

Biological feedback systems have been known for some time as they operate within the body. There are hundreds of individual feedback systems in the human body. Information about the external environment is sensed by any of the five senses and relayed to the brain where it is integrated with other relevant information; and when the sensed information is significant enough, commands are generated for appropriate body changes. Responses of scratching an itch, hitting a baseball with a bat, pupil accommodation for near and far vision—are all examples of feedback control systems. The body responds to external and internal changes by using its self-regulating control systems. All that biofeedback does is to make available to the conscious mind information about internal systems that is usually not available to us. Most of us, for example, are not consciously aware of the temperature of our fingertips. There are systems that regulate this temperature, but the regulation is usually done without our conscious awareness. Biofeedback, usually using electronic devices outside the body, makes such information available. And when such information about some aspect of the physiological functioning of the body is made available, it is possible to attain increased voluntary control over that function. One can learn to control bodily processes that were previously under nonvoluntary, unconscious control.

The wide public interest aroused in the development of biofeedback in the past ten years derived, in part at least, from the apparent exotic possibilities it created. The early experiments, on the enhancement of alpha activity in the brain, attracted the attention of those for whom the attainment of higher states of consciousness was the main aim in life. Not unnaturally, this interpretation of the "meaning" of biofeedback produced an adverse reaction among the more hardheaded research scientists and therapists. They had become interested in the possibility that biofeedback offered for investigating the control of internal physiological processes not readily accessible to observation, and of applying these techniques to the amelioration of certain physiological disorders. The situation has now changed to the point where a considerable scientific literature has accumulated which enables a sober appraisal of the process to conclude that biofeedback does have legitimate scientific and therapeutic uses.

Biofeedback is currently in wide use in the treatment of what are often called "disorders of autonomic function." These include cardiac abnormalities, hypertension, migraine, gastrointestinal disorders and Raynaud's disease (decreased blood circulation in the fingers). To date, biofeedback has involved learning to control heart rate, blood pressure, skin temperature, brain waves and muscle tension. However, a variety of other physiological functions, including gastrointestinal processes and salivation, are also likely candidates.

Research is currently underway exploring the use of biofeedback in reducing anxiety and in the treatment of asthma, hyperactivity, hypertension and insomnia. And recently, some practitioners have begun to use biofeedback in the rehabilitation of physical functions after accidents or strokes.

Biofeedback is the application of electronic technology for observation of variations in aspects of an individual's physiological functions. Subtle changes in heart rate, blood pressure, skin temperature, muscle tension and brain electrical activity can be detected to assist in training individuals to decrease stress responses and increase relaxation. Many authorities believe that such techniques may be useful for the prevention, or amelioration, of stress-related diseases, and in rehabilitation from stroke and other neurological disorders.

Physicians, psychologists and others are actively engaged in research to determine the extent to which biofeedback procedures can be utilized—either alone or in combination with other behavioral interventions, such as meditation and progressive relaxation—to increase self-control of bodily functions and reverse psychophysiological disorders.

John V. Basmajian, M.D. Biofeedback is a new technique that involves attaching electronic and other devices to a person (without harming him/her) under the supervision of trained medical and behavioral therapists and scientists. The instruments instantly reveal the physiologic state of various deranged internal bodily processes, to both the patient and the therapist.

Using the information displayed by suitable visual and audible monitors, the person uses willpower to bring the body's responses toward standard normal levels—under the coaching of a trained professional, in a series of brief training sessions. In many cases, this results in marked improvement of various types of illness. Many diseases and conditions for which it was first advocated are now known to respond only weakly. Others are being actively investigated and may be added to the above list when proof exists.

Biofeedback is based on scientific principles established since World War II by specialists in medical electronic research. While at first it appears "miraculous" when it succeeds, biofeedback is a rational application of scientific knowledge revealed by modern electronics research.

Thomas G. Burish, Ph.D. Biofeedback refers to the process whereby an organism is given *feedback* about one or more *biological* processes. The goal of most biofeedback applications is to enable the organism to learn to reliably and voluntarily control physiological activities. For example: a person with hypertension (high blood pressure) might learn to decrease his or her blood pressure by watching a meter giving feedback on moment-by-moment changes in blood pressure level, and then learning to control meter readings.

There are many different types of biofeedback, each of which has a somewhat different purpose. Generally, each type of biofeedback is aimed at helping a person learn to control one of two different types of physiological responses, both of which are related to promoting the physical or emotional health of the individual: (1) responses not usually under voluntary control by the person; and (2) responses that are usually under voluntary control but for which control has been lost due to injury or disease.

Biofeedback is provided by a number of different health care professionals, including psychologists, physicians, rehabilitation therapists and psychiatrists.

Arthur Canter. Biofeedback is a special case of the "information feedback principle"—which states that an action cannot be controlled unless information about the action is available to the controller. Biofeedback refers to the use of instrumentation to permit the person to "watch" or "hear" fluctuations in such functions as blood pressure, heart beats or muscle cell activity.

The typical biofeedback apparatus is a miniaturized complex electronic machine that transforms the variations in body activity picked up by sensors attached to the person into electrical signals—filters them, amplifies them, selects the wanted from the unwanted signals, quantifies the strength or size of the wanted signals—and translates them into a form recognizable by the subject, such as a sound of varying pitch or different colored lights. The person's own body activity provides the source for the signal; and the changes in the body activity produced by that person alter the signal. If the person can change the signal by something he or she voluntarily does, or withholds from doing, it will be reflected by changes in the signal. In this manner, the person may learn to gain voluntary control of specific biological activities not previously controlled.

For example, the pain of tension headaches is directly related to the induction and degree of tension in muscles of the head and/or neck. By attaching instruments to the person—which measure electrical activity of the target muscles (EMG) and immediately provide a signal to the subject about the level of electrical activity, as it increases or decreases—the person can learn which "relaxing" actions or thoughts result in lowered EMG level and which do not. By trial and error, after a number of training sessions, the person will learn those relaxation responses which effectively reduce the pain generated by the muscle tension.

Biofeedback treatment is best carried out under the direction and supervision of a licensed health professional (e.g., psychologist, physician, physical therapist, etc.) who has been trained in the use of biofeedback in addition to his or her own area of expertise.

John G. Carlson, Ph.D. In the most general sense, biofeedback means receiving information, feedback, from a part of one's own body; that is, from a *bio*logical process. The feedback is ordinarily not otherwise available. In this sense, even standing in front of a mirror as you watch yourself raise a corner of one eyebrow is a kind of biofeedback; visual cues are provided in the mirror, due to muscle movements that might otherwise give you only a few internal sensations. In its most recent scientific usage, the term biofeedback also connotes the use of sophisticated electronic instruments that: (1) monitor a biological response (such as, muscle twitches, brain waves, heart rate or skin temperature); (2) amplify the biological signal; (3) transform the signal into sounds, lights, movements of a meter or other cues that provide immediate information. In turn, the person may use the feedback to help guide changes in the biological response in a desired direction—just as watching your eyebrow in a mirror may help you to learn some control over its movements.

Some biofeedback researchers believe that a kind of voluntary control may be attained by these means over internal responses that normally are out of a person's range of awareness and direct self-control. Other researchers contend that the biofeedback is only an indirect aid to bodily self-control and that a person's beliefs, expectations, thoughts and images are important in the bodily changes obtained during biofeedback training.

Despite the theoretical issues, biofeedback has been used increasingly in therapeutic settings to aid in the treatment of both specific and more general disorders. For example, Dr. John Basmajian has developed biofeedback methods for alleviating dysfunctions of the nerves and muscles due to strokes, in paralyses, and other such disorders. And Dr. M. B. Sterman has used brain wave biofeedback for treating epileptic seizures.

Some clinical researchers maintain that biofeedback may play an important role in alleviating a general pattern of disorders that are stress related. For instance, while developing biofeedback techniques to relieve the specific muscle strain of tension headache, Drs. Johann Stoyva and Thomas Budzynski theorized that some forms of biofeedback may assist a person in achieving a generalized state of bodily relaxation. In turn, the relaxation may help an individual to control stress-induced disorders such as chronic anxiety, essential hypertension, insomnia and muscle-tension related pain. In these uses, biofeedback is often combined with a variety of other relaxation techniques and even psychotherapy.

It now appears that the most common and successful uses of biofeedback are in conjunction with a variety of self-control techniques in the treatment of both specific and more general stress-related disorders.

David W. Jacobs, M.D. Biofeedback is a collective name for a series of techniques that are used to self-regulate body processes that normally we do not control. The technique involves placing in a feedback loop a person by means of an electronic device attached to the body. This feedback loop (machine to person—person to machine) is useful in learning to regulate a body process not normally available to control.

This technique was originally developed in the late 1960s and has since been the subject of intense investigation by a series of investigators. Within the last decade it has come into widespread clinical use. The single best source of information about biofeedback can be obtained from the Biofeedback Society of America in Colorado. The Society, which represents both researchers and clinicians, has issued a series of task force reports that examine in detail the many applications to which biofeedback has been put.

To date, the most interesting applications of biofeedback have been in the field of medicine. Many diseases that are stress-related lend themselves to biofeedback treatment. Generally speaking, the clinical applications for medical treatment have been carried on in the offices of psychologists and physicians, although the treatment procedures themselves may be done by biofeedback technicians. Treatment normally consists of a series of weekly sessions of biofeedback training at the office, supplemented by home training for generalized relaxation, stress management and self-regulation for physical control. The treatment procedures vary from office to office but, generally, are short-term (three to six months) and are problem-oriented.

In addition to the medical uses of biofeedback, there has been a great deal of interest exhibited in the application of biofeedback for preventive purposes. A number of investigators are currently examining the potential benefits of biofeedback-induced "stress innoculation" for school children of varying ages. Conclusions regarding the effectiveness of these techniques will have to wait for long-term follow-up studies. The initial data are quite encouraging.

A second interesting application has been in the field of sports medicine. Some investigators are now attempting to determine whether biofeedback induced self-regulation is useful in the training of athletes to enhance their performance and prevent injury.

The field of physiological self-regulation has many other potential applications in psychology, medicine and other fields. It is really in its infancy.

Joel F. Lubar, Ph.D. The advent of biofeedback has been one of the most exciting health care developments to occur in this part of the twentieth century. This is a new applied field, a part of a new discipline called behavioral medicine developed from the basic areas of brain research, psychology and medicine. It deals with the monitoring of our internal states, our state of health, and the management of many physical disorders through cognitive and behavioral methods—in contrast to a primary reliance on medication. With the advent of integrated circuitry, microprocessors and modern computer technology, electronic devices— or biofeedback instruments—have been developed for this purpose and perfected to a very high degree of sophistication.

Ten years ago there was considerable publicity devoted to biofeedback, with popular articles appearing almost monthly in many major national magazines and newspapers. At that time, extravagant claims were made that by using biofeedback we could control our health and live a long life, simply through our own management of disease processes. Although this is an idealized goal, in reality it takes considerable practice to develop and maintain these important skills.

Currently, there is solid research progress throughout the world toward consolidating some of the many new areas that have been opened up by biofeedback. More than 5000 papers on applications of biofeedback have been published since 1968. The list of applications of this technique is enormous. For example; one area of biofeedback application is directed towards neuromuscular rehabilitation. Here, feedback is provided to patients for muscles which may appear to be paralyzed, but, in fact, have some residual function. Muscle or electromyographic (EMG) feedback of this kind has been helpful in the rehabilitation of patients with spinal cord injuries, and for the rehabilitation of patients who have suffered stroke or mechanical injury and are trying to regain the use of a hand or leg. Other forms of EMG feedback are being used to train people with speech disorders (including stuttering), and for individuals suffering from cerebral palsy. Many patients who could not be helped in the past are now able to walk better, and regain more normal function, following injury or disease to motor nerves and muscles.

Another area of biofeedback application includes the control of tension and migraine headaches. The techniques for controlling migraine headaches were developed ten years ago at the Menninger Foundation by Drs. Green, Sargeant and Walters. These techniques are deceptively simple and involve training patients to increase the temperature of the hands and feet in order to divert blood flow from specific engorged cerebral vessels involved in migraine headaches. Clinicians who have worked with migraine headaches report that many patients having this problem suffer from cold hands and cold feet. Patients with tension headaches train on instruments designed to register excessive muscle activity. Many tension headaches occur not only as a result of pain in the head from tensed muscles, but also from pain beginning in the shoulder muscles, upper or lower back, and neck. To determine exactly which muscles are involved in a person's tension headache requires much skill and ingenuity. But with proper exercise, relaxation and biofeedback techniques, considerable relief has been brought to many sufferers.

The control of blood pressure and cardiac arrhythmias is now becoming a commonplace biofeedback application. Impressive results have been obtained by Dr. Bernard Engel, at the National Institute of Health, as well as many other researchers here and in Europe. One contributing factor in hypertension is psychological stress in everyday life. Training procedures can be used to help patients deal with such stress. These include relaxation exercises, autogenic training, and various visual imagery. All of these, combined with biofeedback, lead to some very potent and enduring alterations in disease and stress patterns. Sometimes patients wish to change their life style as well. The best biofeedback programs for hypertension are those that take a total view of the individual. This approach helps them to change life styles through psychotherapy or counseling, integrated with biofeedback; and to help them find ways of dealing with work, or family situations, or events that might be stressful.

Other areas of biofeedback research, which have recently become appropriate for clinical application, include the treatment of epileptic seizures through training individuals to control certain aspects of the electrical activity of their brain (the EEG). This work has been carried out by this writer at the University of Tennessee and by Dr. M. B. Sterman at the Sepulveda V.A. Hospital in Los Angeles, as well as by more than twenty-five other laboratories in the United States, Canada and Europe. EEG training, similar to that used for epileptics, has also been used for the management of hyperkinesis and hyperactivity in children. EEG feedback training is now being employed as a method for increasing attention span in children with specific learning disabilities, and for helping excessively anxious individuals achieve states of deep relaxation.

One of the most important aspects of biofeedback training is that different bodily systems are linked together. That is: EEG, skeletal-motor responses and also responses mediated by a system known as the autonomic nervous system, work in patterns. The autonomic nervous system controls secretion of glands, diameter of blood vessels, sweating, heart rate, blood pressure, digestion and more than 1100 varieties of regulatory functions in our bodies.

Although for many decades it had been believed that the autonomic nervous system could not be conditioned, or trained, current research indicates that this is no longer true; with proper methodology and instrumentation, different components of the autonomic nervous system can be brought under behavioral control. After all, individuals with ulcers, lower back pain, essential hypertension, migraine headache and certain lower gastrointestinal tract disorders have already learned to condition their autonomic nervous systems exquisitely, as part of their reaction to stress. Biofeedback provides a way to "de-condition" over-reactive stress responses, and substitutes a more normal regulatory response of our bodily systems in stressful situations.

Since many internal body systems are physiologically linked together, the best results are obtained when several of these systems are trained, either successively or simultaneously. For example: to achieve a state of extremely deep relaxation requires the use of hand warming techniques (thermal biofeedback); decreasing muscle tension in head, trunk and limb muscles (through EMG feedback); and reducing the frequency of the EEG brain wave activity to a level more consistent with relaxed states and thoughts. Such training also includes patterns of breathing. Biofeedback clinics across the country are using multiple modalities of feedback to achieve potent and long-term results.

The use of biofeedback belongs to no one field. It is being used by dentists to decrease bruxism or grinding of teeth and to help reduce pain due to malocclusion and abnormalities in the function of the temporol mandibular joint (TMJ), all very common problems for dental patients. It is used by physical therapists for a variety of muscle rehabilitative tasks and by cardiologists who are interested in the control of blood pressure and cardiac arrythmias. It is employed by clinical psychophysiologists, social workers, psychologists, and psychiatrists who are working with stress management, deep relaxation, and the control of migraine and tension headaches; by speech therapists who are dealing with stuttering and other speech difficulties; and by clinical psychophysiologists for the management of hyperactivity in children. Biofeedback has been employed by many specialists for increasing alertness and attention in children with learning disabilities. Insurance companies have become well-acquainted with biofeedback and its results, and are now generally including biofeedback as one of the areas for which coverage is being provided. Governmental agencies and state agencies that deal with patient services have also learned about biofeedback and support both research and patient care using this new modality.

Thomas B. Mulholland, Ph.D. Biofeedback is a safe, noninvasive procedure which combines physiological measurements, electronic technology and behavioral training methods. Physiological processes can be measured with miniaturized electronic circuits so that a person can see or hear the changes that occur in his or her physiology. By means of behavioral training methods, a person can use the feedback information to practice self-control of his or her physiology.

Biofeedback is used in research and in the treatment of diseases or disorders of physiological functions. It is almost always an adjunctive therapy; that is , a part of a total treatment program.

Biofeedback is used by psychologists, physicians, dentists and by ancillary service professionals, i.e., nurses, physical therapists and dental technicians.

Solomon S. Steiner, Ph.D. Biofeedback is a term that includes a wide variety of techniques. These techniques detect and amplify information derived from specific physiological processes which is then transformed into a modality readily discerned by the subject (sometimes patient). The subject is then taught how to use this information to influence the physiological process in the desired fashion. (If someone can be taught to play tennis, why can he not be taught to regulate his blood pressure?)

Frequently, the physiological process is presumed to be influenced by the nervous system, and the specific physiological response generally eludes clear or accurate perception. This is not always the case; in a very real sense, when one gets on a bathroom scale to measure one's weight, one is using a biofeedback technique. Large changes in weight are directly perceivable by the subject. Small day-to-day fluctuations of weight are generally not accurately perceived by most subjects. However, the bathroom scale does detect them, amplifies these changes, and transduces them to a visual display readily perceived and understood by the subject (number of pounds and ounces or kilograms). It should be further noted that, in this example, one need not assume the weight gain or loss is under direct control of the nervous system. The indirect control (altering feeding behavior) suffices in a well-motivated subject, to produce the desirable outcome of weight loss.

Edward Taub, Ph.D. The purpose of biofeedback methods is to enable people to establish voluntary control over important bodily, or physiological, processes of which they are normally unaware; and which were previously thought to be involuntary. Examples of biofeedback: a setup where a light becomes brighter when hand temperature increases or dims when hand temperature decreases; or, a tone that becomes louder when blood pressure goes up or becomes softer when blood pressure goes down. In effect, an internal physiological process is controlling an information display. A person is not usually aware of the level of his blood pressure or whether it is elevated. However, through biofeedback, he can become aware of this aspect of his physiological functioning. The main principle is to make the operation of bodily processes, which a person cannot usually sense, easily detectable. A person can, thereby, frequently establish voluntary control over these processes.

Biofeedback is frequently employed clinically with disorders that are stress-related; the type of condition which in the past has been termed psychosomatic. Biofeedback is a particularly effective means of training people to develop the ability to relax. Biofeedback is also used for the treatment of conditions that may not be stress-related: physical rehabilitation following stroke and other types of central nervous system injury; torticollis or wryneck; various types of tics including blepharospasm (tic of the eyelid); some cardiac arrhythmias; and fecal incontinence due to incorrect timing of the anal sphincters.

Biofeedback techniques have been used clinically for approximately ten years. There is research evidence available that biofeedback is an effective treatment, in many cases, for the conditions listed above. For other common applications of biofeedback, controlled research evidence of efficacy is not yet fully available; sometimes because the particular application is so recent, and sometimes because the target condition is particularly difficult to assess. The latter include anxiety states, phobias, chronic pain states, insomnia, epilepsy, temporal mandibular joint syndrome (grinding or clenching of teeth) and arthritis. Some practitioners feel that learning relaxation through biofeedback can improve the quality of daily life. That is, it can enhance "wellness," in individuals not suffering from any disease.

Biofeedback is appropriately administered by professionals who are already licensed or certified to treat patients with pathological conditions. The professionals that are currently most commonly involved in the clinical use of biofeedback techniques are: psychologists, physicians, physical therapists and occupational therapists.

SEXUAL PROBLEMS

*T*HE ADVENT OF the Pill in 1960 marked the beginning of a period of radical change in American attitudes toward sex. Suddenly, sex was not so much for procreation as it was for recreation.

But it was not all fun and games. As sex came out of the marriage bed, out of the closet, and generally out into the open, a host of problems came out along with it. At first, there were few practical approaches to dealing with sexual difficulties.

At the turn of the century, Sigmund Freud had provided theories about the origins of sexual feelings and sexual failures, and in the 1940s and 1950s, Alfred Kinsey had issued reports on the nation's sexual norms. Those who felt themselves to be sexually abnormal or inadequate, however, had trouble finding help. Even most medical schools did not offer training in treating sexual problems.

It was not until 1970, when Masters and Johnson released their ground-breaking study, *Human Sexual Inadequacy*, that sexual therapy was widely recognized. By 1980, there were thousands of sex therapists working in the United States.

The recognition of sexual therapy and the increased interest in effective oral contraceptives are just two aspects of the current movement toward more joy of sex. For better or worse, the country's attitudes about sex have altered dramatically during the last twenty years. Sexually explicit literature has moved out of brown wrappers and into neighborhood book stores and corner newsstands. Sex education has begun to play a part in school curricula and has created controversy in many communities. Perhaps most significant of all, young people are having sex more often at earlier ages. According to studies by the National Institute of Child Health and Human Development, the number of fifteen-year-old girls who had experienced intercourse increased from 14 percent to 18 percent betwen 1971 and 1976; the number of sexually experienced seventeen-year-old girls jumped from 27 percent to 41 percent during the same period.

Because the basic problems of sex are timeless, it is easy to forget how recent are developments such as oral contraceptives and sex therapy and how quickly things have changed and may continue to change. On the next pages, experts survey the problems and progress in sex therapy and suggest what advances may be made in years to come.

CONTRIBUTORS

Larry E. Beutler, Ph.D., A.B.P.P., Professor of Psychiatry and Psychology, Chief of Clinical Psychology, and Director of Clinical Research, Department of Psychiatry, University of Arizona College of Medicine, Tuscon, Arizona

Janet Shibley Hyde, Ph.D., Dennison University, Granville, Ohio

Dr. David R. Mace, Professor Emeritus of Sociology, Bowman Gray School of Medicine, Winston-Salem, North Carolina

James W. Maddock, Ph.D., licensed consulting psychologist, Meta Resources, P.A., St. Paul, Minnesota; Adjunct Associate Professor, Department of Family Social Science and School of Public Health, University of Minnesota, Minneapolis, Minnesota

John F. O'Connor, M.D., New York, New York

F. Paul Pearsall, Ph.D., Chief, Problems of Daily Living Clinic, Department of Psychiatry, Sinai Hospital, Detroit, Michigan

Dr. Patricia Schiller, Executive Director, American Association of Sex Educators, Counselors and Therapists, Washington, D.C.

Dr. Peter A. Wish, Director, New England Institute of Family Relations, Inc., Framingham, Massachusetts

WHAT ARE THE MOST COMMON SEXUAL PROBLEMS AMONG MEN AND WOMEN? WHAT KINDS OF THERAPY ARE AVAILABLE, AND WHAT ARE THE SUCCESS RATES?

Larry E. Beutler, Ph.D. Men and women are subject to a variety of sexual difficulties and dysfunctions that represent a complex interplay between psychological stress and physical conditions. Among men, the most common problems are: the inability to initiate and/or sustain sufficient erection to complete intercourse; inability to ejaculate; and very rapid ejaculation which prevents the completion of the sexual act to the couple's mutual gratification. Among women, the most common sexual dysfunctions are: the failure to achieve orgasm; absence of sexual pleasure; and pain accompanying sexual intercourse.

Nearly one out of every two men, by the age of forty-five, has experienced a period in which he has had difficulty initiating or maintaining an erection. By age seventy-five, one in three has had prolonged periods of such difficulty. This age effect suggests that some of the biological processes of aging have a significantly deleterious, but not universal, effect upon sexual ability.

The incidence and prevalence of ejaculatory difficulties are more difficult to estimate than are those of impotence, since their definition necessitates understanding certain characteristics of the partner's sexual response. Premature ejaculation refers to the condition in which ejaculation consistently and regularly occurs either prior to penetration or within one or two thrusts after penetration. Many individuals who believe that they are suffering from premature ejaculation are, in fact, experiencing difficulties related to sexual expectations and/or sexual foreplay. They may either have excessive expectations of their own sexual stamina, or sexual foreplay may not be sufficient to arouse their partner so that both can achieve satisfactory climax prior to ejaculation. Only rarely is either premature ejaculation or delayed ejaculation a consequence of some physiological deficiency, imbalance or disease.

In contrast, there are many medical diseases and physiological deficiencies that may result in erectile failure. These include circulatory difficulties in which blood flow to the penis is insufficient; neurological difficulties in which either sensory experience is impaired or the nerves stimulating blood flow and retention in the penis are damaged; traumatic injury affecting the nerves around the groin or damaging the tissues within the penis; hormone imbalances caused by systemic disease or iatrogenic effects associated with the use of certain drugs.

Approximately one-third of sexually active women fail to achieve orgasm regularly. Nonetheless, for most women this does not cause the degree of sexual dissatisfaction and anxiety that a similar experience does among men. Traditionally, women have not placed as great an emphasis on orgasm as have men, although this pattern may be changing as women have become more educated about their sexual capacities. While a woman's inability to achieve orgasm does not impair the act of intercourse, it is often a source of frustration and dissatisfaction. Such orgasmic failure among women is typically the result of anxiety or distress, either around the sexual act itself or around some aspect of the relationship with their sexual partner.

Vaginal pain upon intercourse (dyspareunia) may occur either because of lesions within the vaginal cavity or constriction of the muscles in anticipation of pain. In some cases, a woman's vagina is simply not sufficiently flexible or large to accommodate her sexual partner's penis and this can produce pain during intercourse. If such pain occurs with shallow penetration the cause is more often organic than psychological, while the opposite is true of pain occurring only during deep thrust.

In vaginismus, on the other hand, the woman is typically found to be physiologically normal, but whenever penetration is attempted the vaginal entroitus snaps shut in anticipation of pain and, therefore, prevents intercourse. While vaginismus is characteristically psychological, it sometimes begins as a secondary reaction to a pain produced by physical problems such as scarring or infection. Vaginismus is to be differentiated from simple phobic avoidance of intercourse. The latter typically reflects a pronounced and often generalized negative feeling and attitude toward the sexual partner, unassociated with physical pain.

Disturbances in sexual desire or inability to achieve sexual fulfillment and pleasure, while usually attributed to women, are also found among men. There is no known organic basis for this difficulty and incidence rates are very difficult to obtain. Predominantly, the difficulty is caused by some struggle within the sexual union, reflecting hostilities, resentments or fears between the sexual partners. When the lack of sexual enjoyment transcends relationships with specific sexual partners, it may indicate a more deeply rooted psychological conflict over sex.

Most sexual dysfunctions are the result of emotional stress, difficulties in interpersonal relationships or internal conflicts. However, the frequent presence of physiological disease, associated with the development of male impotence, pain during intercourse, and more rarely orgasmic failure among women, point to the necessity of a thorough medical evaluation before any treatment decisions are implemented.

Among individuals who experience sexual dysfunction as a result of medical conditions, a variety of treatments are available. Organic impotence has been treated through special surgical procedures that either channel increased blood volume to the penis, or that implant a prosthetic device within the penis which lends it enough additional turgidity to allow penetration. Some cases of organic impotence are the result of hormone imbalances and have been treated successfully through hormone injections. Similarly, introital dyspareunia, a vaginal pain frequently associated with lesions within the uterine canal, can be appropriately treated surgically. The technical success of such medical treatments is over 90 percent among appropriately diagnosed cases. However, in those cases where there are also contributions from psychological and/or marital stress and conflict, sexual dissatisfaction may remain.

Many sexual dysfunctions occur because of "performance anxiety": this refers to an exaggerated fear of failure, either because of having failed previously, or because of excessive concern with one's partner's satisfaction. Such sexual dysfunctions are usually successfully treated with a variety of behavioral restraining procedures developed or refined by Masters and Johnson. Men with psychogenic sexual impotence, for example, who have been able to maintain stable interpersonal relationships without unduly exaggerated depression or other psychological disturbance, can be treated successfully 70 to 80 percent of the time. Similar rates of success have been noted for men with premature ejaculations, and women with vaginismus. In each case, the treatment consists of systematic exercises that allow one to experience sexual pleasure in the absence of excessive performance demands, and to decondition the anxiety associated with sexual performance. In most instances, both members of the sexual union are engaged in the treatment process—since sex involves an interrelationship rather than simply the responses of one individual.

In those instances where sexual dysfunction accompanies some broader-ranging psychological disturbance such as depression and anxiety, treatment rates are somewhat lower. In these cases, treatment is oriented not to the sexual dysfunction, per se, but to the broader-ranging psychological disturbance. In many cases, for example, the sexual disturbance reflects conflict in the interpersonal relationship of the sexual partners. Marital therapy and, sometimes, individual psychotherapy or behavior therapy is indicated. In many cases, these treatments are supplemented by the use of medications designed to reduce anxiety or depression. In most instances, when the psychological conflict and distress is alleviated, sexual functioning returns.

Janet Shibley Hyde, Ph.D. In 1970, with the publication of Masters and Johnson's *Human Sexual Inadequacy*, we were given access to a comprehensive body of data on sexual problems. (I am interpreting "sexual problems" to mean problems of behavior, technically termed as sexual dysfunctions, and not other sexual problems such as unplanned pregnancy or sexually transmitted diseases.) In the 790 cases of people seeking therapy from Masters and Johnson, the most common problems in men were erectile dysfunction (impotence, or the inability to have or maintain an erection), and premature ejaculation. The most common problem in women was orgasmic dysfunction, the inability to have an orgasm. However, in the last couple of years, many sex therapists report that the above problems are becoming less usual among those seeking therapy, and that problems of sexual desire—a disinterest in sex, or a lack of arousal—have become the most frequent problem.

There are two major categories of therapy for sex dysfunctions: (1) psychoanalytic or psychodynamic therapy and (2) behavior therapy. Psychoanalytic therapy is based on the assumption that sex dysfunctions are symptoms of underlying unconscious conflict. Therapy consists of uncovering these conflicts and resolving them; the assumption is that the sex problem will go away when the conflict is resolved. Typically, therapy is lengthy.

Behavior therapy, on the other hand, is based on learning therapy. The assumption is that sex problems are a result of learning, and therefore can be unlearned. This therapy is, typically, of shorter duration. Masters and Johnson's therapy can be classified as behavior therapy. They initially reported a success rate of about 80 percent, although the rates varied depending on the problem. For example, premature ejaculation is relatively easy to cure and has a very high success rate while primary erectile dysfunction (a man who has never had an erection) is relatively difficult and has a low success rate. Masters and Johnson's rate of success, however, has been questioned recently. Helen Singer Kaplan, using combined behavior therapy and psychodynamic therapy, achieves a success rate around 60 percent, and that is probably the more realistic figure.

Dr. David R. Mace. All sexual relationships that cause difficulty have one common problem—the inability of the partners to communicate to each other their feelings, both positive and negative. Only when feelings are freely and openly communicated can real needs be identified and met. Failure to do this inevitably creates anxiety; and anxiety, apart from relatively rare physiological defects, is the basic cause of all so-called sexual problems.

Of course, open communication of feelings may lead to the recognition that the persons concerned cannot in fact meet each other's sexual needs; but it is much better to know this at the outset than to suffer the pain of discovering it through later failure.

Sometimes partners cannot, by themselves, achieve the kind of openness that honest communication requires. In this case, either a sexual or marital therapist, suitably qualified, can be very helpful—provided the therapy is relationally oriented, which means involving both partners, separately and together.

James W. Maddock, Ph.D. Probably the most common of all sex-related problems of men and women is the struggle to maintain a close, intimate, long-term relationship between two people of different sexes, i.e., marriage.

While never easy, the task, today, is substantially complicated by significant changes in social expectations and behavior patterns of both sexes, particularly women. The stress created by these changes, in turn, leads to unhappiness, conflict and disillusionment in many marriages; and may ultimately contribute to the decision to divorce. Help for troubled marriages is available in the form of marital therapy, or marriage counseling. Therapeutic approaches to marital problems vary and include: traditional psychoanalytic analysis of one or both partners; training procedures for behavior modification; and strategic maneuvering of the couple's patterns of communication. Success rates for marital therapy are difficult to specify, due to limited outcome research and lack of uniform criteria for judging success. Surveys of outcome research tend to suggest that approximately two-thirds of the couples seeking help show noticeable improvement in their relationship.

Diminished sexual desire often occurs in connection with general intimacy problems between men and women. This is a second—and increasingly common—problem. One or both partners may show little or no interest in sexual contact, even though the capacity to function sexually remains unimpaired. Sometimes, desire problems have a gradual onset that reflects a kind of sexual boredom—a problem often remedied by counseling that assists the partners in creatively varying their sexual routines. At other times, this difficulty may occur suddenly or dramatically—to the surprise of the partners, who may still intellectually want to be sexually active. Treatment of sexual desire problems always includes a thorough medical checkup—to eliminate the 10 to 15 percent of cases involving a physical factor, such as imbalance of sex hormones, or a situational factor, such as side effects from a prescription drug. However, the majority of cases requires a combination of marital therapy and a structured program of sexual behavior modification. Recognized as a distinct sexual disorder only in recent years, the sexual desire syndrome has not been systematically treated long enough to be evaluated thoroughly. Available reports suggest that the majority of couples receiving therapy shows improvement. However, a significant number of these still complain that they are not *fully* satisfied due to a continuing discrepancy between the partners' relative levels of sexual interest.

A third category of common sexual problems clusters around anxieties about sexual performance. Some of these anxieties result in a specific sexual dysfunction, such as difficulty in becoming aroused or in reaching orgasm. Others produce generalized anxiety, which may in turn lead to various nonsexual symptoms: nervous irritability or sleeplessness, depression, irrational fears or physical complaints. As a result of varying degrees of anxiety, men may suffer from an inability to produce or maintain an erection. Or, they may have problems with the timing of orgasm and ejaculation, i.e., reaching climax too quickly or, at the other extreme, ejaculating only after long and laborious periods of stimulation. Sexual performance problems of women most commonly take the form of difficulty in becoming aroused, i.e., experiencing pelvic congestion and vaginal lubrication, or in failure to reach orgasm. A smaller amount of women suffer from pain during sexual activity or from an involuntary cramping of the pelvic muscles that can prevent sexual intercourse from occurring.

While approaches to sex therapy vary considerably, most have the following factors in common: attempting to help partners feel permission to think, talk and act in a positive manner about sex; providing up-to-date information on sexual physiology and behavior; emphasizing the responsibility of each partner for his or her own sexual satisfaction; improving communication between the partners about sexual feelings, fantasies and desires; modifying sexual behavior through the use of carefully planned "homework assignments," which the partners practice privately between therapy sessions. In spite of the relative brevity of this kind of sex therapy—typical programs extend through six to twenty sessions—most treatment is successful. Reported results range from over 90 percent effectiveness in overcoming lack of orgasm in women, and premature ejaculation in men, to 75 to 85 percent success in dealing with difficulties of sexual arousal in women and erectile problems in men. And almost all couples receiving sex therapy show some improvement in their overall sexual relationship.

John F. O'Connor, M.D. The following chart outlines the sexual difficulties, stemming from psychological factors, that men and women experience. It also evaluates the effectiveness of available treatments and therapies.

INCIDENCE OF OCURRENCE	MEN	WOMEN
Most Common	Premature Ejaculation Secondary Impotence	Primary Anorgasmia Sexual Apathy
Common	Primary Impotence Retarded Ejaculation	Secondary Anorgasmia Dyspareunia Vaginismus
Rare	Male Dyspareunia Penile Anaesthesia	Vaginal Anaesthesia

TREATMENT	
Type	*Effectiveness*
Masters and Johnson Treatment	80%
Behavioral Therapy	60% +
Hypnosis (Adjunct Therapy)*	?
Woman's Group Therapy	90% +
Man's Group Therapy	80% +
Psychoanalysis/Psychotherapy	60% +

*Hypnosis ranges from no success to above 60%. However, the data is sketchy and not well presented.

F. Paul Pearsall, Ph.D. Over the last decade, researchers and therapists have come to realize that the most commonly experienced problems with sexuality rest with differences in levels of sexual interest and desire. Masters and Johnson, pioneers in the short-term therapy approach to sexual difficulties, estimate that more than 50 percent of couples in the United States have some type of sexual difficulty or incompatibility. More than 5,000 sex clinics in the country typically identify and label those problems with terms implying some type of genital difficulty. Further history taking, however, often reveals that different levels of interest in sexuality and related communication problems underlie most genital manifestations of sexual distress.

Of course, problems such as difficulties with erections, involuntary vaginal muscle contractions before coitus, difficulties with ejaculatory control and inability or difficulty in experiencing orgasmic release are also problems encountered in clinics dealing with sexual distress. In an important, though low percentage of cases, medical or metabolic problems account for genital difficulties. Substance abuse, poor cardiovascular health or generally being out of condition can all affect sexual life. Any person seeking help in a clinic claiming to specialize in sexual difficulties, should make sure that that clinic rules out medical problems; and also describes an interest and competence in dealing with communication problems and individual differences in sexual interest.

Success rates in clinics dealing with sexual distress are typically reported as very high. Some clinics estimate that more than 80 percent of persons who come to them for help, experience improvement in their sexual lives. There is little data, however, to support either the long-term stability of such changes, or the veracity of this high percentage. Researchers are now examining new forms of sex therapy, including group therapy for couples—and, in some clinics, use of surrogates and educational programs utilizing explicit films. Other areas of current interest include working with the physically impaired, and other sexual minority groups, to enhance sexual health for all persons.

When sexuality is seen as a totality of a person's maleness or femaleness —and as related to the person's entire health picture, including communication systems, stress present or absent in daily living, and the effect of transitional life crises on personal development—then sexual health or the ability to relate intimately and responsibly with a partner of choice comes closer to an everyday reality.

Dr. Patricia Schiller. The most common sexual problems among men are: premature ejaculation; secondary impotence; ejaculatory incompetence. The most common sexual problems among women are: being nonorgastic; vaginismus; pain during intercourse.

No one style of treatment is equally effective for everyone. The best therapy is the kind that works for a particular client. However, most therapists follow the basic method pioneered by sex researchers Dr. William H. Masters and Virginia Johnson. In "sensate focus exercises" a couple caress each other's bodies in privacy, learning to give and receive sensual feelings. But they are freed from the pressure to perform, because genital touching and intercourse are forbidden at this stage. In office sessions, couples are taught how to tell each other what pleases them sexually. And they learn ways to deal with specific problems.

Some experts believe therapy should be done only by a male/female team, but many therapists work alone. Some require clients to take two weeks away from job and home, and to go through an intensive training program. Others see patients several times a week for a month or two and have them go on occasional weekend "honeymoons" to practice what they have learned. Still others think it sufficient to see a patient once or twice a week for several months. In general, the results seem to be much the same no matter which approach is taken. Fees may range from $35 to $60 an hour for treatment by a single therapist; $100 or more an hour for two therapists.

Patients and clients need to be informed concerning the process of sex therapy. It is advisable for those seeking therapy to consider several important factors. Does the therapist: require patients to have a medical exam to rule out physical problems that may be causing sexual difficulties; take a thorough sexual history; give "homework assignments" in sexual communication and touching; guarantee complete privacy and confidentiality; adhere to an ethical code that prohibits sexual intimacy with a patient; refrain from imposing his or her personal sexual values on a patient? Selection of a therapist should depend upon a positive evaluation of these factors.

Dr. Peter A. Wish. Masters and Johnson estimate that 50 percent of all couples at some time have a sexual problem severe enough to benefit from professional help. For men these difficulties (dysfunctions) include premature ejaculation, inability to ejaculate, impotence and inhibited sexual desire. For women, common dysfunctions include lack of or difficulty in achieving orgasm, painful intercourse and lack of arousal.

Sexual dysfunctions can result from physical problems like diabetes (impotence); diseases of the nervous system (multiple sclerosis, tumors, etc.); or, drugs, alcohol or medications. Most problems, however, are psychological and involve emotions like guilt, depression and anxiety. Other causes include a lack of information, misinformation, traumas such as rape and incest, and fears of loss, abandonment, rejection and "fear of failure."

Treatment of sexual dysfunctions (sex therapy) is usually short-term. Sessions include verbal psychotherapy and at-home exercises designed to increase communication, decrease anxiety and enhance sexual pleasure. These exercises are then discussed with the therapist at the next session. In reputable treatment centers, at no time does any sexual activity take place at the therapist's office—or in the presence of the therapist.

Sex therapies are highly successful. In some conditions, treatment success is higher than 90 percent. When entering therapy, however, one should not hesitate to ask what training and qualifications the therapist has. One indication of competence is certification by the American Association of Sex Educators, Counselors and Therapists in Washington, D.C.

INDUSTRY AND TECHNOLOGY

DURING THE 1950s and 1960s, the United States was envied throughout the world as the paradigm of technological progress. American cars, American machinery, and (in the 1960s) American computers were exported all around the world. Foreign experts poured into our country to study the American system.

The 1970s began with a slow erosion of the American share of the market in certain areas of electronic goods—Japanese television sets, then cameras, and finally stereo equipment entered the American marketplace and pushed often inferior American goods out. The automobile had always held a privileged position in the American economy and imagination, but by the end of the decade the Japanese had beaten us even in this market: in the year 1980, for the first time, the Japanese produced more automobiles than did the United States.

The Economist, a strongly pro-American journal that is highly respected in the international banking community, warned that if current trends continue, Japan will supplant the United States as the world's largest economy by the end of the decade. And in a recent essay in *The New York Times*, Professor Robert Reich of Harvard University declared that the Japanese are about to surpass us in the emerging technologies of computers, lasers and industrial robots.

The experts who speak out in the following pages offer a more balanced perspective on the new developments and applications of technology, and on the role of the United States in the new technological world to come.

The United States is leading the world into the second phase of postindustrial society. According to this viewpoint, industrial society was characterized by the century or so in which the leading nations focused on manufacturing goods. The first phase of postindustrial society was characterized by the switch in emphasis from manufacturing to the service professions, such as law, accounting and real-estate development. In the second phase of postindustrial society, information itself becomes the central commodity in a nation's economy. More than 50 percent of our work force is now occupied in different aspects of information handling—from computer-related activities to the telecommunications industry to professionals in the various media.

The United States leads the world in high-technology applications that are ushering in the information era. Within the next couple of years computerized work stations will become commonplace. Corporate managers, working at keyboards and video terminals, will be able instantly to recall whatever information they need from company computers, as well as to hold audiovisual conversations with several colleagues in different parts of the country simultaneously.

Another area in which the United States currently holds a technological lead is in the use of space. Commercial satellites have dramatically reduced the cost of developing private corporate phone systems and have permitted the broadcasting of hundreds of television stations directly into a person's home. The development of the space shuttle marks the opening of a new frontier in the exploitation of the commercial potential of space with the ability to perform scientific operations inexpensively in space, and to set up manned and unmanned space stations.

A third area in which the United States leads the world is biotechnology. Breakthroughs in the areas of cloning and transplanting genetic material will be applied to the production of drugs and may well result in the development of new organisms to perform such activities as disposing of chemical wastes. Agricultural scientists also expect to create new food strains that will produce dramatically higher yields and help to feed the world's growing population.

In the following pages, our panel of experts gives us its views on the importance of technology and the role that the United States will play in the new technological world to come.

INDUSTRY

IN THE LAST THREE YEARS, automakers have cut production and laid-off workers. According to industry analysts, the American auto industry employs about one out of five American workers. Some of these people work directly in producing, selling and servicing cars; many more work indirectly in businesses ranging from advertising to steel. All depend upon auto production to keep their own earnings in high gear. So when the auto industry slows down, the unemployment rate in Detroit is felt throughout the country.

The nation's dependence upon the automobile is more than economic. When sleek, powerful cars were Americans' best-loved toys, the auto industry seemed to stand for all that was right in American industrial know-how. Henry Ford became famous for introducing the first assembly line into the nation's factories and for promising the average citizen an affordable car. Until the 1970s, the Big Three—General Motors, Ford and Chrysler—not only maintained a solid standing among the top American corporations, but also enjoyed a reputation for well-paid workers and well-made products.

This reputation began to come apart in the 1970s, however, as American cars began accumulating poor repair and recall records, and Detroit's large, low-mileage machines no longer met the nation's new energy needs. More and more consumers turned to imported automobiles, and particularly to Japanese models. While the market shares of Ford and Chrysler declined, the number of Japanese cars sold in the United States increased from 0.8 million in 1975 to 1.9 million in 1980. It suddenly seemed that Detroit's assembly lines, and by association similar assembly lines throughout the country, could no longer make the grade.

Today consumers often ask nostalgically, "Why can't America make things the way it used to?" Yet America's industries, like most of its institutions, have changed tremendously since the first factory—a textile business staffed by nine children who tended seventy-two spindles—opened in the United States in 1790.

During the 1800s, the United States was still primarily an agricultural nation, but the invention of the steam engine, the introduction of the business corporation, and the massive waves of immigration helped to foster industries' rapid expansion. Ambitious businessmen were quick to take advantage of such vast supplies of natural resources as land, water, coal and iron. Unfortunately, they took advantage of their workers, as well, more than one-third of whom were children. In the 1830s, for example, owners of the Lowell Mills in Massachusetts commonly worked their women and girl laborers thirteen hours a day, six days a week, and paid them less than twenty-five cents a day. And the Lowell Mills owners were considered progressive employers.

As might be expected, many industries brought their owners huge profits, and the employers, in turn, were able to offer more jobs to new immigrants and out-of-work farmers. Between 1880 and 1980, capital investments in machines more than doubled. Advanced machinery and the introduction of the assembly line made factories even more profitable. By the 1920s, Calvin Coolidge could confidently say, "The business of America is business."

Yet the nation that so abruptly switched from farming to manufacturing began to shift again after World War II. This time the shift was away from manufacturing and mining and toward the so-called service industries: trade, transportation, real estate, utilities, government and other businesses that *do* things rather than *make* things. In 1919, people in these service professions accounted for little more than half of those employed in fields other than agriculture. By 1975, employees in service industries accounted for an estimated 70 percent of all nonagricultural employees.

Not only did blue-collar workers in manufacturing lose much of their manpower to the service industries; they also lost much of their prestige. Today, thousands of jobs in skilled labor remain unfilled while workers in other fields are unemployed.

Many industrial analysts say that it is time for the United States to reemphasize the basic craftsmanship and industrial know-how for which it was once famous, time to improve worker morale, and time to make "Made in USA" a symbol of quality again.

Currently, Japanese and West German manufacturers offer stiff competition to American manufacturers in fields ranging from cars to calculators. While foreign companies once sent their personnel to the

United States to study American expertise, American corporations are now trying to learn from their international competitors.

What are the strengths and weaknesses of American industries? Why have American car manufacturers in particular fallen behind while their competitors have gained sales both in the United States and in other countries? International experts offer their analyses in the following pages.

CONTRIBUTORS

Tetsuo Arakawa, President, Nissan, U.S.A.

Dr. Jack Baranson, President, Developing World Industry and Technology (DEWIT); author of *The Japanese Challenge to U.S. Industry*

James D. Calderwood, Joseph A. DeBell Professor of Business Economics and International Trade, School of Business Administration, University of Southern California, Los Angeles, California

Kenneth W. Clarkson, Director, Law and Economics Center; Professor of Economics, University of Miami, Coral Gables, Florida

Dr. Clifford M. Hardin, Director, Center for the Study of American Business, Washington University, St. Louis, Missouri

Marion Hayes Hull, Director, Telecommunications Programs, Booker T. Washington Foundation, Washington, D.C.

F. James McDonald, President and Chief Operating Officer, General Motors Corporation, Detroit, Michigan

Richard T. Pascale, co-author of *The Art of Japanese Management*

Donald E. Petersen, President, Ford Motor Company

Ian M. Ross, President, Bell Laboratories, Murray Hill, New Jersey

WHAT ARE THE GREATEST STRENGTHS OF AMERICAN INDUSTRY? IN WHAT AREAS DO WE NEED THE MOST IMPROVEMENT?

Dr. Jack Baranson. Our ultimate strength lies in our ability to organize and manage industrial systems, but we now face intensified competition from both industrialized economies (Japan and Europe) and the more advanced of newly industrializing countries (like Brazil, Mexico, Korea). We need to improve our economy's ability to adjust more rapidly and more effectively to economic and technical changes in the world economy.

There are two major deficiencies in this regard. One is the faltering will of United States industrial management to invest in innovation at the level and rate now necessary to meet international competition. The other deficiency lies in our financial structures—in their support of innovation and in the willingness of banks and stockholders to take the kinds of risks associated with dynamic innovation.

James D. Calderwood. One cannot generalize about "American industry." That is the first important point to be made. Instead, it is necessary to identify different types of industries and corporations and evaluate each. Basically, they can be described under the following categories:

1. Highly innovative, efficient, technologically sophisticated industries such as the computer, aerospace, pharmaceutical and oilfield equipment industries
2. "Old" industries, such as the steel and automobile industries, which do not seem to move with the times, have stodgy management, and are experiencing problems as they seek to adjust to foreign competition
3. Corporations with anonymous professional management, like A.T.&T. and Sears, Roebuck
4. Corporations that are the shadow of a dominant leader such as Occidental Petroleum under Armand Hammer and I.T.&T. when it was under Harold Geneen

The *strengths* of certain American industries include:

1. Skilled, professional management
2. Innovative leadership
3. Emphasis on research and development
4. A skilled labor supply
5. A huge domestic market (making possible the economies of scale)
6. A growing sense of social responsibility on the part of many leaders

Improvement is needed in industries and corporations that:

1. Overlook export opportunities
2. Place too much emphasis on maximization of short-term profit at the expense of long-range objectives
3. Fail to communicate with employees (to develop team effort that increases productivity)
4. Ignore the basic rule of marketing: to give consumers what they want and not what management thinks they ought to have (e.g., the record of the automobile industry)
5. Emphasize "free enterprise" and the importance of keeping government at arm's length, but rush to government for protection and help when their business gets into trouble (e.g., Lockheed, Chrysler, steel industry)

Kenneth W. Clarkson. American industry has one great resource—its talent. First, United States industrial firms have developed the most advanced technology in the world. For decades, United States firms have systematically exported more technologically oriented products than any other country.

Second, American industry has developed the greatest concentration of problem solvers, managers and supporting personnel in the world. The collective knowledge and ability of these individuals represent a form of "human capital" that is far more important than the traditional physical capital shown in a firm's balance sheet. It is the flow of ideas from this human capital that develops new products, helps decision makers solve business problems, and results in economic growth.

Unfortunately, it is the same human capital that creates problems for industry, for its workers, and for consumers of its products. Given any system of costs and rewards, industry decision makers will attempt to maximize their welfare—the difference between rewards and costs, broadly interpreted. In a free enterprise system, the industry decisions that maximize this difference in general also generate the highest output for members of society. The introduction of restrictions, however, such as quotas restricting imports, licenses restricting the entry of new firms, and regulations governing new products modifies the structure of costs and rewards. Then, highly talented managers may take actions that result in gains to their own firms at the expense of other firms—specifically, those companies that could provide competition. These actions also penalize consumers, who must forego the opportunity to acquire some goods and services and who must pay a higher price for those that remain in the market.

Elimination of these rules and regulations would direct industry talent to more productive activities—activities that would result in improved performance and increased welfare of consumers.

Dr. Clifford M. Hardin. The greatest strengths of American industry are: experience; pools of well-trained and educated workers; managerial competence; and scientific backup.

The improvement that is most needed is: modernization of existing plants to take maximum advantage of new technologies and efficiencies.

Marion Hayes Hull. The greatest strength of American industry is the fact that it is recognized around the world as a leader in industrialization.

American industry probably needs the most improvement in devising strategies for controlling technology. One of the greatest problems we have in America today, inflation, is due in part to the lack of coordination between technology developers, policy makers and economists.

F. James McDonald. In the final analysis, the greatest strength of American industry is the workers in its offices and factories. That is the foundation upon which we must build our success in the marketplace.

Technology is not the principal problem. The greatest challenge before the American auto industry is to apply this technology to achieve greater production efficiencies than our foreign competition.

We Americans have, I believe, learned some hard lessons in the past few years. And that is a major reason why I am so optimistic in looking at the future. Today, our country is moving in new and more promising directions, reversing a trend of more than three decades. While Japan and West Germany, and much of the rest of the world, were rebuilding after World War II, the United States seemed to be doing the reverse. Government spending reached the point where it represented about one-third of our Gross National Product—nearly twice as much as it did in the earliest years after World War II.

We are pleased to see movement in the direction of easing of the heavy burden of regulatory costs that have buried American industry. General Motors alone—just one company—spends about $2 billion a year in complying with these regulations.

We believe that government programs should focus on reducing inflation, restoring this country's economic vitality, providing incentives for business expansion, and reducing government regulations substantially. Such programs would provide new stimulus for the nation's economy and the automobile business.

Richard T. Pascale. An executive in the automotive industry recently told me, "We are still well ahead of the Japanese technologically, but where they are far superior to us is in getting people to work together. And that gives them the competitive edge."

In American organizations we do not pay enough attention to the relationships between people. One symptom of this problem is our penchant for announcements and decisions. It is almost essential for a manager to appear tough and decisive—the macho syndrome. But not *all* situations benefit from this tendency. For example, when an organization is merging its sales and marketing departments, there is often a lot of ego and politics involved. Instead of announcing the merger in advance, it is far wiser to get the key people working together informally, to let them experience a few successes as a team. Then, after the new relationship has started to evolve, "announce" the change. "Decide" on the new organization after it is already an internal reality.

Unfortunately, managers who are willing to bring about change in this way are not as prevalent in American corporations as they should be. In this country, we tend to promote the wrong people. We put a high value on toughness, decisiveness, financial wizardry—skills that, unfortunately, have little to do with moving an organization. And we overlook the less aggressive types who tend to share recognition and work skillfully through people.

There are a number of great American companies that have sustained themselves over time and are in fact beating the Japanese today (e.g., IBM, Boeing, Caterpillar). These companies are surprisingly "Japanese" in their approach—not because they ever tried to be, or even thought about it, but because there are only so many things that can be done to make an organization work. Therefore, most of the great corporations around the world tend to resemble each other. They do not think in terms of short-term financial performance, but rather in terms of long-term strategic superiority. They do not promote financial wizards, but choose as their senior managers individuals who have proven they can get the job done in the trenches. They promote from within. They cultivate good mentors. These, then, are the qualities that make for success in industry, American or foreign.

Ian M. Ross. The greatest strength of American industry has traditionally been the technology that underlies its products. Better products, based on superior technology, enjoyed a distinct competitive edge in domestic markets and created a positive balance of international trade.

Historically, "Yankee ingenuity"—the genius of the backyard tinkerer or basement inventor—made us worldwide leaders in many industries. As science and engineering advanced, however, research and development grew too complex and costly for individuals to pursue. As a result, people, equipment and funds were pooled in university, industrial and government laboratories. Innovation continued to flourish in these institutional environments, and America built substantial leads in many fields—agriculture, aircraft, automobiles, chemicals, computers, machine tools, pharmaceuticals, steel, telecommunications, textiles and others. The rapid growth and vitality of such industries gave us a standard of living unmatched anywhere else on earth.

I believe that American science and technology are still second to none. The transistor, the computer and the laser—three advances that have revolutionized industry—are American inventions. The key scientific and engineering advances in microelectronics and software—the foundation of the emerging information age—continue to flow from American laboratories. We are ahead of foreign competitors in these technologies, and should remain so. Our leadership, here, may hold the key to controlling costs, increasing productivity and reducing energy consumption in many industries. Such progress, in turn, is essential to revitalization of the economy and a more favorable balance of trade. Further, American preeminence in the information-age technologies is critical to collecting and communicating worldwide financial, political and military information, and, thus, is vital to our well-being and security. In the future, international competition for position, prestige and ideological acceptance will also depend on how effectively a particular nation employs modern communications and information technologies.

In these respects, American industry is quite strong, and our future prospects are bright indeed. But there are weaknesses elsewhere, and warning lights that we must not ignore. For example, the quality of research and development abroad now rivals that of the United States in many disciplines. Fully one-third of the patents now issued in this country are awarded to foreign inventors. Since the 1960s, American investment in research and development—as a percentage of the Gross National Product—has declined, while the opposite pattern has prevailed in Japan and some Western European nations. Clearly, if such trends continue, American leadership in key scientific and engineering fields will be jeopardized, creating a "knowledge gap" that could have severe repercussions in the decades ahead.

To maintain American superiority in high-technology industries, we must preserve and strengthen the research and development infrastructure that underpins them. Ample federal support for research in our universities is essential. Similarly, tax credits and other incentives may be needed to spur research and development and plant modernization among industries whose market leadership has been threatened or lost. In other cases, more streamlined regulatory procedures could accelerate the introduction of more competitive products by American manufacturers.

Such issues, so widely debated today, suggest that government still has lessons to learn in orchestrating public and private interests. Industry must avoid the all-too-frequent temptation to opt for short-term gain instead of taking long-term risks—where payoff has historically been far greater. A unique but intangible strength of American industry has been precisely this kind of daring and initiative—a willingness to take the long-range view, to believe in the future, and to roll up our sleeves and work hard to make it happen. I do not believe we have lost this spirit. But I think the time has come for industry and government to work together to rekindle it.

WHY HASN'T THE UNITED STATES, WITH ALL ITS EXPERTISE IN BUILDING AUTOMOBILES, BEEN ABLE TO COMPETE WITH GERMAN AND JAPANESE MANUFACTURED CARS?

Tetsuo Arakawa. The important point at issue here is not the American automobile industry's inabilty to compete with the Germans and

Japanese, but rather, the fact that, until recently, they have not chosen to do so.

Traditionally, the domestic car manufacturers in the United States have concentrated their efforts toward building large cars, which accounted for the majority of new car sales. The small-car segment of the market—which represented only a small percentage of sales—was left essentially to the imports.

When the market shifted—first, with the Arab oil embargo in the early 1970s, and then more abruptly some years later, following the revolution in Iran—the American automakers found themselves with most of their resources committed to large cars while consumers were demanding small cars.

The domestic industry has already begun producing new generations of small cars which compete very effectively with the imports. This trend will undoubtedly continue as the American manufacturers develop new technologies and construct new production plants.

Dr. Jack Baranson. There has been a progressive erosion of the United States competitive position vis-à-vis Japan and Germany in terms of product designs, production efficiencies and international marketing capabilities. These emerging differences are attributable in part to relative deficiencies in United States industrial management and partly to the relative disadvantages of certain environmental factors.

Japan poses by far the more formidable challenge. Its relative strength is based upon the following factors: (1) the impressive capabilities of Japanese industry, which have developed over the past fifteen years, to design and engineer high quality and cost-competitive automotive products; (2) the ability to maintain a broad spectrum of products—in a variety of configurations for different segments of world markets—and still remain cost effective, even in the face of intensive competition; (3) an aggressiveness in marketing on a global basis, and a responsiveness to special tastes and demands of segments of the world market; (4) the quality and productivity of its labor force, reinforced by a highly effective management and industrial organization—including component supplier industries that are responsive to continuing changes in automotive design and to the need for progressive upgrading of industrial facilities; (5) the continuing rationalization and modernization of plants and equipment, including investments in automation, and persistent concern with cost effectiveness and meticulous quality control (in contrast, the United States automotive industry has only begun, belatedly, to redesign vehicles to meet emerging demands for fuel-efficient vehicles and to robotize and automate facilities to reduce production costs); (6) an economic and financial environment conducive to risk-taking and ready to supply the capital resources needed to maintain and advance technological capabilities; and (7) government-industry relations that are highly supportive of Japanese enterprise and its competitive position in world trade (in contrast to the adversary position that often characterizes United States government-industry relations).

Richard T. Pascale. My expertise is in understanding the Japanese competitive advantage, so I will address the question from that perspective. First, I do not believe their success is due to the exotic elements to which the media has given so much attention—elements such as calisthenics, company songs or quality circles.

The Japanese have a competitive advantage because they are beating us at our own game. Much of their success derives from a superior product/market strategy, superior quality and superior production control systems.

They are doing exactly the things Americans have always prided themselves on—only doing them better. They foresaw the increasing demand for small cars before American companies were willing to face this. In the golden days of Alfred Sloane, General Motors (GM) would have responded to the developing market by creating a new division that specialized in small cars. But the 1970s were not the 1930s and GM was entrenched in its large dealership network that regarded small cars as low-margin orphans in the product line. GM's four divisions (Chevrolet, Pontiac, Cadillac and Oldsmobile) would have been demoralized by the addition of a fifth. These divisions had every reason to want small cars to fail—they were outside the usual areas of expertise, they were not what dealers wanted, and their profit margins were low. As a result, the four divisions consistently exerted halfhearted efforts in behalf of the small cars.

A second facet of Japanese management is equally significant. Japanese firms do a much better job than most American firms in drawing on the human potential at all levels within an organization. In the United States, we tend to look for a few big brains at the top to call all the shots. In contrast, the Japanese use the "little brain" approach, believing that a lot of little brains are better than a few big ones. So they create an environment that gets everyone thinking, each day, about how to do their jobs better, and believing the system will listen if they have an improvement to offer.

Donald E. Petersen. Expertise is not the issue. For example, much attention has been given to new front-wheel drive cars and the use of electronics. The facts are that in the 1980 model year, American small cars and Japanese imports had essentially the same percentage of front-wheel drive vehicles; and, in electronics, American cars lead technologically in the development and application of on-board electronic engine controls.

The present problem in the United States—of substantially reduced sales of United States-made cars, and the perception of superior Japanese expertise—can be traced to the massive increases in oil and gasoline prices following the 1979 Iranian revolution. The sales surge in Japanese imports (German imports total less than 3 percent of the market) at the expense of the United States manufacturers, is primarily the result of the dramatic shift in consumer demand—to small, fuel-efficient cars and away from larger cars and V-8 engines that were in heavy demand through early 1979. The increase in fuel prices and the shift in consumer preference were made more radical by past United States government policies to maintain artificially low gasoline prices. Thus, while the United States companies are in the middle of an $80 billion product-conversion program, they are vulnerable to strong competition from Japanese imports, designed for home market conditions that include very high gasoline prices.

Examples of the new American products, resulting from this $80 billion effort, are Ford's new Escort and Lynx, Chrysler's new K-cars, and General Motors' X-cars. All of these cars have been very well received by today's highly discriminating consumers.

In Europe, where gasoline prices have been high for many years, the United States companies have offered lines of small, fuel-efficient cars that meet consumer requirements—and have been doing so for quite some time. In Germany, General Motors and Ford sell 28 percent of the cars; German companies sell 46 percent; other European companies, 16 percent; and Japanese imports sell 10 percent. In Japan, the total protection offered to local manufacturers in the past, and present restrictive practices, help hold all car imports to minimal levels (less than 1.5 percent of the market in 1980 for all European and United States manufacturers).

TECHNOLOGY

AMERICANS HAVE ALWAYS had a love-hate relationship with science and technology. In the late 1950s—spurred on by *Sputnik I*—our country poured millions of dollars into science education in the schools. Science and technology were part of modern life, we were told, and these twins of the modern age would solve all of man's problems.

In the 1960s, the pendulum swung back. The "flower children" of our college campuses were only one manifestation of a general notion that somehow science was evil. Scientists came to be associated primarily with the manufacture of napalm and the atom bomb.

Now that we are on the threshold of the information age, the pendulum seems to have swung back again toward technology and science. Computer technology is beginning to influence every aspect of our lives. School children now play video games rather than make-believe. Advanced chips the size of a fingernail can process, in a microsecond, information that would have taken first-generation computers minutes to process. Home computers have captured the popular imagination as well as the imagination of Wall Street: witness the extraordinary 400 percent rise in price of Apple Computer stock on its first day on the market.

Biotechnology has also captured the public imagination—from stern sermons warning against man's interfering with natural processes to happy farmers who will soon be sowing new strains of wheat and corn "bred" by microscopic manipulations of the genetic material in familiar strains of these agricultural staples.

In the following pages experts offer their images of what the future will bring. Tetsuo Arakawa, of Nissan USA (the makers of Datsun automobiles), predicts that the miles of wiring and switches in our current cars will soon be replaced by a central computer. Computer- and laser-operated guidance systems will prevent the cars of the future from having accidents.

Harvey Brooks, of Harvard University, discusses the most advanced of high-technology areas in laymen's terms in order that we may all catch a glimpse of the techniques of our nation's most advanced laboratories. He maintains that the most advanced technology is used in scientific experimentation itself, particularly in the areas of high-energy particle physics and radio astronomy, and in molecular genetic research.

In this section, our experts give us a preview of the exciting future that American technology will help make possible.

CONTRIBUTORS

Tetsuo Arakawa, President, Nissan, U.S.A.

Prof. Harvey Brooks, Benjamin Pierce Professor of Technology and Public Policy, Harvard University, Cambridge, Massachusetts

Rondo Cameron, Kenan University Professor, Emory University, Atlanta, Georgia

E. E. David, Jr., Exxon Research and Engineering Co., Florham Park, New Jersey

William H. Dutton, Annenberg School of Communications, Los Angeles, California

John C. Lilly, M.D., Director, Human–Dolphin Foundation, Malibu, California

Leon C. Martel, futurist; author (with Herman Kahn and William Brown) of *The Next 200 Years*

Donald E. Petersen, President, Ford Motor Company

Ian M. Ross, President, Bell Laboratories, Murray Hill, New Jersey

Theodor D. Sterling, University Research Professor, Computing Science and Faculty of Interdisciplinary Studies, Simon Fraser University, Burnaby, British-Columbia, Canada

Alvin M. Weinberg, Director, Institute for Energy Analysis of the Oak Ridge Associated Universities, Oak Ridge, Tennessee

WHAT IS THE MOST ADVANCED TECHNOLOGY ON EARTH TODAY AND FOR WHAT IS IT USED?

Professor Harvey Brooks. The answer to this question depends upon how one defines the term "advanced technology." One definition might be complex or sophisticated. Another definition might be most related

to, and dependent upon, recent advances at the frontiers of fundamental science. In either sense, the most advanced technologies are
those used in scientific research itself—technologies that have not yet
reached the stage of being applied for economic or social purposes, and
for which practical applications may not even be foreseeable.

In this respect, the most "advanced technology on earth today" would
be the collection of techniques used in research in high-energy particle
physics. These include the design and construction of high-energy
particle accelerators, especially those for the highest attainable particle
energies. They also include the whole range of extremely sophisticated
particle-detection and event-selection measurement techniques used in
connection with such accelerators.

Probably the next order of advancement would be represented by
the Very Large Array radio-astronomy observatory in Arizona, dedicated a few years ago. Next in order would come the techniques used
for research in molecular genetics, especially the recombinant DNA
technology—and some of the recent efforts to partially automate this
for the purpose of accelerating laboratory experimentation by orders of
magnitude.

If one looks only at technologies that have reached at least a preliminary stage of commercial application, then one would come up with a
somewhat different list. I would probably single out the field of optical
communications technology—which makes use of high quality optical
fibers and optical signal processing and offers extremely high rates of
information transfer. So far this technology has received only limited
commercial application, usually within fairly localized areas.

If this technology is considered too limited in application (at present)
to qualify, then I would choose the field of microchip information
storage and processing. This is being used to construct more compact,
sophisticated and "transparent" computers, but will also be integrated
into numerous industrial processes and consumer durables such as
automobiles and washing machines.

The area of biotechnology, which includes the exploitation of recombinant DNA techniques and "engineered" microorganisms, may ultimately prove to be the most revolutionary of all the advanced technologies now being discussed. However, it is largely in the laboratory
stage, and its development and applicability in the future have to be
classed as very speculative. Potentially, the new techniques can be used
to: reduce the cost of many rare drugs and biochemical substances;
make these drugs and substances more readily available; manufacture
modifications of existing biochemicals with new properties for therapeutic purposes, including possible new approaches to cancer therapy.
Additionally, there are many possibilites for increasing agricultural
productivity while decreasing use of chemical inputs such as fertilizers
and pesticides. And finally, there is the possibility of revolutionizing
many industrial chemical manufacturing processes—through the substi-

tution of artificial biological processes (that occur under mild conditions) for chemical processes (that require high temperatures and pressures). But I must emphasize that all this is very speculative and it is difficult to foresee how fast it will come about or what the economics will look like.

Rondo Cameron. The most advanced technology on earth today is an integrated system of elements including rocket propulsion, aerodynamics, electronic communication, high-powered computers, specially designed metals and materials—and other elements, as well. It is used for the exploration of space.

E. E. David, Jr. Electronics: this is the most advanced technology available today.

Electronics is concerned, primarily, with passing information in various forms (visual, sound, text) between people and from archives to people. This technology also has uses important in the fields of education, training, and amusement—and in the marketing of goods and services.

Finally, electronics is critical for the defense of the free world, and for collecting intelligence relating to the institutions of possible adversaries.

William H. Dutton. Buckminster Fuller once suggested that the human body is our most advanced technology. However, our understanding of biological processes seems much less adequate than our understanding of computer technology. Therefore, computer technology is our most advanced in that we have a relatively good understanding of its operations —the equipment, people and procedures.

Not only are computer systems the most advanced technology on earth today, they are also likely to underlie other sophisticated systems. Most technological breakthroughs of the recent past—including the Space Shuttle Transport, nuclear power plants and weapons systems— are quire dependent on computer technology.

Computers are also a reasonable candidate for "most advanced technology" in the sense that they are—by definition, as well as by use— general purpose machines. Their utilization extends to nearly every field of endeavor, from art to communication to manufacturing.

Theodor D. Sterling. The most advanced technology on earth today is the technology to answer questions.

Underlying the power, the strength, the growth, the very survival of human society, and with it of humans, is the ability of mankind to ask questions about the world in which we live and to answer those questions in a way that enables us to manipulate our world to satisfy our needs—both real and imagined. As the product of human inquiry is an ever advancing technology, it is not surprising that the technology is utilized to serve the process of scientific inquiry as well. Instruments and techniques to provide answers to questions vary from elaborate experimental operations to elaborate calculating machines to do the elaborate calculations necessary to obtain sure knowledge about the world around us from whatever information has been gathered. The most advanced calculating machine is the modern computer, invented in order to help answer such questions as "What trajectory will a particular star take?" The art of human inquiry includes the art of querying man's opinions and predicting, from a sample of responses, in which directions man's actions will be exercised.

We should keep in mind that the technology to answer questions refers not only to physical instruments. To be sure, some exquisite instruments have been built to serve man's curiosity and man's needs to obtain information. Perhaps the best examples of such instruments are the explorer spacecrafts that fly out to the furthest planets and return beautiful photographs of the various shapes and features of the icy silence and majesty of these distant places. But perhaps even more intricate is the method of use that underlies this magnificent hardware. The word "software" is the name coined to describe the underlying organization of computer programs and operations—the unseen procedures—through which the buzzing and booming confusion of information gathered by instruments is integrated into useful knowledge. And this software, as well, is a powerful technology. Examples range from our wonderful number system to the things we do with it—such as the calculus, or the geometry of space, or the inferences by which large conclusions are drawn from small samples of observations.

The hardware and software of the question-answering technology are interwoven, often so tightly that it is not possible to tell where one ends and the other starts. To return again to our explorer spacecraft. The computer programs that reduce the spacecraft's view to a series of signals—and the programs that reconstitute these signals into visible vistas, such as of the rings of Saturn—are a highly sophisticated technology in their own right, no less sophisticated than the microcomputers on which they are implemented.

Alvin M. Weinberg. By any standard, the most advanced technology today is that associated with computers. There are now ideas for computers that will be able to process 100 billion operations per second! This is about 100 to 1,000 times faster than the fastest existing computers.

What the long-term implication of such an extraordinary advance will be I can hardly perceive. Should this technology become the basis for a new, extremely efficient, *defensive* weapon system—capable, say, of knocking out incoming missiles with a 99 percent probability—the entire strategic confrontation would be changed. And possibly the terrible threat of nuclear warfare would be reduced.

But this is all still very much in the realm of speculation, and we cannot count on such a development.

WHAT DO YOU THINK WILL BE SOME OF THE ELECTRONIC MIRACLES OF THE FUTURE?

Tetsuo Arakawa. In the automotive field, which provides most of my insight into the future of electronics, computers and micro-processors will probably have the greatest impact.

The miles of wiring and numerous electric switches found in the cars of today will be replaced by a central computer. This computer will be linked by a single wire to a series of processors which will control virtually every function of the automobile, from the operation of the taillights to the flow of fuel to the engine.

In the area of safety, individual radar and microwave systems will sense potential obstacles and provide collision avoidance. That same safety system will also be combined with television cameras and the central computer to allow a vehicle to drive itself automatically.

Although most of these systems already exist, the "miracle" will occur when they become practical enough—as regards both sophistication and cost—to be utilized in individual vehicles.

Rondo Cameron. Mankind can look forward to all of the following "miracles:"

1. Generation of electrical power by means of solar energy from artificial satellites
2. Inhabited artificial satellites
3. Interplanetary travel by humans

E. E. David, Jr. One "miracle" of the future will focus on curing diseases and improving health conditions by genetic intervention. This will involve the use of recombinant DNA techniques to improve manufacturing (make it more economical, with fewer harmful or noneconomical by-products), and to remove harmful elements from the food, water and atmospheric systems. Major improvements in agricultural productivity are also in prospect, via DNA techniques; and ocean farming will become feasible.

Electronic control systems will result in much more selective use of resources—mineral, energy and human. The increase in productivity that will result from using all of these elements more effectively will provide major increases in standards of living and, hopefully, decrease conflict between nations and classes.

John C. Lilly, M.D. I think that some of the electronic miracles of the future will include:

1. Computerlike machines that will be more intelligent than any one human person. These machines will process "spoken" questions (from any human voice; in any of the major languages of earth) and will answer, instantly, in the same or any other language (instantaneous translation).

2. Small portable electronic machines that can translate the human voice into sounds appropriate for communicating with dolphins, baleen whales and elephants. These machines will also pick up and translate the sounds of their replies, resulting in the evolution of true high level abstract interspecies communication.

3. Entirely new electronic discoveries on the physical nature of the signals subserving mental telepathy—Extra-Sensory Perception (ESP)—with development of amplifiers, transmitters and receivers for this new energy—analogous to radio but not identical with electromagnetic radiation. Instead, it will represent a new physics and a new influence on masses of people.

Leon C. Martel, Ph.D. Energy and food are necessities that, at present, require new supplies every day. But the "miracles" of the future will change all this.

Future historians will look back with barely concealed amusement at our concern about "energy crises" in the 1970s and 1980s. By the middle of the twenty-first century—perhaps sooner—we will have eternal sources of energy coming on line. These will consist of some combination of solar, geothermal and man-made fusion. We do not now know which will come first, which will be most important. This will depend on research and development and capital costs for installation of major projects. But, once these sources come on line, the energy problem will be solved for all time. Energy will become, like food, a *renewable* resource.

Food *is* a renewable resource. New crops follow old crops. The United States, with 2 percent of its labor force on the farm, grows enough food for itself and for export to many countries in the world. As American agricultural technology spreads to other countries, their farms will increase yield, as many are already doing; *and*, as future technology becomes available, it will dwarf what is being accomplished today.

The most dramatic future development will be the increased use of special environments (greenhouses, nutrient film solutions, etc.) for growing food. These herald a virtual future revolution in agriculture: the eventual end of traditional farming on open fields. Future generations may well wonder why it took us so long to realize that there were more valuable uses for our land than ploughing it and farming it.

Donald E. Petersen. High-powered computing at a low cost, voice synthesis, voice recognition and cable television will give us the technologies, the human interface and the network to have a virtually paperless society. New products to support this scenario could include:

- Home and office video communications terminals
- Home and office electronic data storage units
- Bank and point-of-sale terminals for money transactions
- Teaching machines for schools and home
- Development of vehicle guidance systems (route guidance, drive-by-wire, etc.)
- Major advances in vehicle safety systems (possibly prompted by development of the guidance systems) such as collision avoidance and radar braking

Limited oil reserves and the social barriers to increased use of coal and nuclear power will create higher energy costs and the need for home energy converters. New products to support this scenario could include:

- Wind-powered energy converters for home use
- Solar-powered energy converters for home use
- Biomass energy converters for home use
- Small hydroelectric generators

High energy costs will lead to more energy-efficient, compact homes, factories and offices and more energy-efficient production processes. New products for use here might include:

- Production equipment that does not require high ceilings and large floor space
- Compact appliances for home use
- Waste heat (from production process) energy converters and distribution systems
- Compact office equipment modules
- Home, factory and office energy management modules
- Energy-efficient appliances and equipment

High energy costs will lead to the need to transport goods and personnel more efficiently. New products to support this could include:

- Mass transportation communication/scheduling systems to optimize routing and scheduling of buses and to pool vehicles on a demand basis
- Systems for demand-controlled scheduling of planes and trains
- System for scheduling truck-borne goods to avoid deadheading rigs

- System of traffic control to avoid energy-consuming traffic jams
- Use of solar power for supplemental vehicle/accessory loads

The need for increased national productivity will lead to a need for a flexible work force and more automation. New products required for this include:

- New automatable processes
- Automatic machines to execute the new processes
- Products designed for the new processes
- Teaching machines to broaden the skills of the work force
- Modular assembly of cars and trucks

Ian M. Ross. Through promising work in many fields, the miracles so frequently predicted by futurists may indeed come true. Physics and chemistry, for example, may help meet future energy needs through photovoltaics or nuclear fusion. These sciences could also enable materials experts to "molecularly engineer" synthetic materials as substitutes for scarce and expensive material resources: e.g., cobalt, gold, copper and platinum. Biotechnology could someday give us vaccines against cancer and hepatitis, and revolutionize agriculture through development of synthetic fertilizers and genetic engineering of healthier, more productive livestock. Finally, the new technology referred to as robotics should enable us to build machines capable of handling hazardous industrial tasks and relieving us of routine household chores.

But in my view, a technological miracle of far broader dimensions is already upon us—the dawning of the Information Age. Already, half our work force, more than agriculture and manufacturing combined, is engaged in handling information—generating, analyzing, storing or distributing it. This information revolution is transforming society through basic changes in our jobs and lifestyles. Indeed, the paperless office of the future and computerized home communications centers are information-age miracles not to be hoped for, but expected.

I am confident these expectations will be realized, because advances in solid-state electronics—the foundation of the information age—are accelerating at a pace unparalleled in any other field. Every year since 1960, we have doubled the number of components on the silicon chips used in communications and information-processing systems. Today, we can cram 150,000 transistors on a sliver of silicon, and pack the power of yesterday's room-sized computers on chips that cost just a few dollars and occupy less space than a postage stamp. Tomorrow, we will see chips that can store one million bits of information, and computers that may operate one hundred times faster than those we have now. Equally exciting advances are being made in lightwave communications systems, which transmit information as pulses of light through hair-thin glass fibers. Future lightwave systems may transmit hundreds of millions of bits of information per second—the information equivalent of the Encyclopedia Britannica.

Such capabilities, integrated into a nationwide, software-controlled communications network, will bring the full promise of the Information Age to every American household and business. In their homes, people will have fingertip access to banking, shopping, education, entertainment, and other kinds of information. Businesses will have sophisticated teleconferencing facilities; and streamlined systems that handle a growing volume of voice, data, video and facsimile information far more efficiently than ever before.

To assure that the benefits of information-age technology are widely available, we must make machines easier for people to use. We are doing so in a variety of ways: increasingly intelligent terminals, simpler computer languages, improved computer graphics and display techniques. Ultimately, research in speech synthesis and voice recognition may lead to machines capable of responding to inquiries and commands in ordinary English. With such simplified access to data bases, people—at home and at work—will find machines easy and even fun to use.

As we move further into the age of information, these technological miracles—and others as yet unforeseen—will improve the quality of life, increase productivity, and contribute to the well-being of society as a whole.

SPACE

SOCIAL SCIENTISTS AND policy planners frequently debate the merits of our national space program. Some say that it is a crime to spend billions of dollars on space exploration when our country's problems here on earth are unsolved. Our inner cities are crying for funds for major capital improvements, and almost one-fifth of our population is denied an adequate diet and health care because of lack of money.

Others maintain that curiosity about space is a basic human response dating back to ancient times. They also say that space exploration brings out a latent patriotism that the country sorely needs expressed. Above all, proponents point to discoveries and inventions that begin with space-program research and end up improving the quality of our daily lives.

Regardless of one's point of view, the space program seems to be here to stay and is now entering a new phase: that of exploitation rather than just exploration. At least partly because of budgetary pressures and the need to show that space exploration is in some sense *practical*, NASA has reoriented itself toward proving the success of the space shuttle program. NASA officials now estimate that the shuttle—the first reusable space vehicle—will be able to take off for orbit approximately once a month.

Having a shuttle taking off for space on a regular schedule opens up whole new areas of commercial use: from performing special scientific experiments under conditions of superlow gravity to setting up manned space stations in inner space that could be used as jumping-off points for exploration of outer space. The use of the shuttle also suggests the possibilities of lowering the cost of putting new satellites into orbit, the ultrasensitive combing of the earth's surface for new mineral deposits and information about weather patterns, and the commission of laser antisatellite weaponry.

Experts in the following pages tell what to expect in the coming decades from space exploration and exploitation.

CONTRIBUTORS

Isaac Asimov, biochemist; writer of science and science fiction works, New York, New York

Dr. Mark R. Chartrand, Executive Director, National Space Institute, Washington, D.C.

Stephen M. Cobaugh, International President, United States Space Education Association, Elizabethtown, Pennnsylvania

Dr. W. David Cummings, Executive Director, Universities Space Research Association, Columbia, Maryland

Dr. Jerry Grey, Administrator, Public Policy, American Institute of Aeronautics and Astronautics, New York, New York

Daniel M. Lentz, F.B.I.S., Director, Dividends from Space, Milwaukee, Wisconsin

Dr. John F. McCarthy, Jr., Director, NASA Lewis Research Center, Cleveland, Ohio

Dr. Brian O'Leary, writer, lecturer, and former astronaut, Princeton, New Jersey

Sen. Harrison "Jack" Schmitt (R-NM), Apollo 17 lunar module pilot and geologist

WHAT IS THE FUTURE OF THE UNITED STATES SPACE PROGRAM? WHAT ARE THE SPACE PROGRAM'S GOALS FOR THE NEXT TWENTY YEARS?

Dr. Mark R. Chartrand. As of August 1981, there are no announced goals for the United States space program other than the general goals of using space for the benefit of earth, primarily through use of the space shuttle. The science advisor to the president is now making a study of space policy, and a report is expected soon.

Possible goals for the space program include: a permanent, manned space station for research; increasing transfer of space-borne communications and remote-sensing projects to private industry; occasional planetary exploration; and investigation of the use of the space environment (microgravity, vacuum, free solar energy) for manufacture of specialized materials and products.

The increased sophistication and power of commercial communications satellites will enable direct-to-home broadcast of television from space, better and safer navigation for private and commercial aircraft and shipping, and eventually better person-to-person communication.

In about a decade it may be possible to plan mining ventures on the surface of the moon, or on the asteroids—perhaps transporting entire small asteroids to earth orbit for refining. While space colonies may become feasible within the next few decades, no pressing need to build them has yet been advanced.

On the military side, the continued development of laser antisatellite weapons and other "satellite killers" offers the potential of altering the current strategic policy of "mutually-assured destruction" to one of mutually-assured protection—since most space-borne weapons are effective only against other objects in space, not against ground targets. The military and intelligence services will make increasing use of remote-sensing satellites and communications and navigation satellites.

In general, however, the thrust of the space program over the decade will be one of increasing use of the space environment as a milieu for human activity.

Stephen M. Cobaugh. The space shuttle will provide routine access to space for the United States during the next twenty years. This access will provide capabilities never before available in the exploration of outer space. Among its abilities are: deployment and retrieval of satellites; earth resources observation; new military and scientific uses. NASA envisions a fleet of five space shuttles that will comprise the Space Transportation System (STS). The shuttle should eliminate the need for expendable rocket boosters and will reduce the cost of space exploration.

The shuttle will be the forefront for other space activities before the end of the century. There are several different scenarios being studied at NASA for post-shuttle activities. All of the options being considered will depend on congressional funding and future evaluation of the agency's long-term objectives and goals.

One possible objective is the construction of a Low Earth Orbital Base Camp. The base would begin with a rudimentary platform of solar arrays. Science and applications platforms, like the European Space Agency's spacelab (that will be flown on space shuttle missions as a payload), could be added. The construction elements, as well as access and return of scientists, would be provided by the space shuttle. The shuttle could transport a manned module for permanent occupation by 1990. This timetable would require congressional approval within the next couple of federal budgets. This early space station will resemble a "tinker toy," with additional elements being added as needed.

By the end of the century, the United States should have an operational base camp. This could be the first of many additional space stations. Also, by this time, there should be a permanent station with "company modules"—owned by various aerospace companies—that will provide manufacturing and industrial facilities.

This so-called base camp could serve as a launching location for space probes and planetary spacecraft of a large scale. They could be built in space from components carried into orbit by the space shuttle. In effect, the camp would become the Kennedy Space Center of the future. It would eliminate the need for large propulsion rockets to escape the earth's gravity.

The Low Earth Orbital Base Camp would not be a destination in itself. It would simply serve as a testing location for putting still larger stations into higher earth orbit.

The Office of Space Flight at NASA Headquarters has produced a set of long-term goals: (1) upgrading the space shuttle and spacelab into routing operation, which includes modifications to the thermal protection system and certain hardware; (2) the development of a man-tended, but multi-function facility in low earth orbit; (3) a manned operation in low earth orbit and a platform in geosynchronous orbit; (4) the development of a manned permanent facility at geostationary orbit by the end of the century.

NASA does not envision a manned return to the moon in this century. Although the United States has the technological capability for a manned mission to Mars, it is unlikely (for budgetary reasons) that such a project would be undertaken. Instead, the agency will concentrate on terrestrial application of what it has learned from past Apollo flights, Skylab and the current STS program.

The agency is planning several unmanned probes to study the other planets. It is likely that by the 1990s, a robot spacecraft will explore the surface of Mars. The space telescope, an orbital telescope, will provide remarkable views of distant stars in the mid-1980s—views that were never before possible.

The conquest of space has paralleled American exploration of the West—where settlement always followed military and pioneer groups. Space exploration should lead to human settlement. These colonies, spurred by current and future objectives of the space program, will extend human expansion beyond the perimeters of earth in a permanent way.

Dr. W. David Cummings. United States space policies and long-range plans are still in the process of being formulated. What follows is simply my best guess about our future in space.

The success of the space shuttle means that the focus of space activities for the next two decades will be on near-earth space, i.e., the space above the earth's atmosphere that can be easily accessed by the space shuttle. The political need to reap benefits from the investment in the space shuttle dictates that direction for the space program over the next twenty years. The rate of progress in this direction will depend on such things as how rapidly the economy improves and the strength of competitive involvement in space by foreign countries.

We will continue to explore the viability of near-earth space for scientific, commercial and military purposes. The space shuttle is a transportation system and is not optimized as a research laboratory. There will be a need for an unmanned research platform in earth orbit—to which, and from which, the space shuttle will carry scientific payloads. There is also likely to be a manned operations center in orbit. One way or the other, the space shuttle will soon have something to shuttle to and from in space.

The focus will eventually shift from finding applications of near-earth space that benefit those who reside on the earth's surface, to finding applications that benefit activities in near-earth space itself. In anticipation of this, our space exploration program will be driven by the need to inventory space resources that can be used in near-earth space. In the next two decades, we will want to further investigate the potential resources of the moon, for example, as well as explore earth-approaching asteroids and comets.

Dr. Jerry Grey. There is no question that satellite communications are here to stay. Investment in satellites and ground stations is expected to be in the $20 to $40 billion range by 1990, and will still be accelerating.

No other segment of the United States space program has yet become self-supporting, and hence they all depend to some degree on federal funds. Weather forecasting and military reconnaissance/navigation via satellite, as well as pure scientific research, are generally accepted as functions of the federal government, and will therefore continue to be supported. Space industry awaits the results of experiments to be conducted in the 1980s, but appears to be promising; considerable private-sector (and overseas) interest is already in evidence. Earth-resources sensing from orbit has been demonstrated to be possible, both technically and operationally, but may not prove to be *commercially* viable.

Overall, the future of a United States space program seems to be assured. The diversity and level of that program will depend in good part on the degree to which it is supported by the federal government—except for the already booming satellite communications industry.

There are as many "space program goals" as there are advocacy groups on space. They number in the hundreds. The possibilities include: permanent occupancy of space by people (in an orbiting space station); an established, consistent program for scientific exploration of the sun, the planets, the stars, and the earth's atmosphere; commitment to a specific program of earth observations; and establishment of an operational capability for multipurpose use of the geostationary orbit.

Daniel M. Lentz, F.B.I.S. In the next twenty years, the United States space program will rely heavily upon the space shuttle. Within the first five years, the program will develop from initial testing of the system to earth surveys, satellite repair and bases for unmanned exploration of the planets. By the end of the twenty-year period, the shuttle will be used in construction of small manned space stations, and as a supply source for the completed stations.

Space stations will serve as laboratories that will produce many new materials, report on potential natural disasters, determine man's ability to live in space and set the groundwork for the period after 2001— manned exploration of Mars, of the other planets and finally of the universe!

Dr. John F. McCarthy, Jr. The United States space program is evolving from one of exploration to one of exploitation. The initial efforts were aimed at overcoming the technological difficulties associated with the development of aerospace vehicles, both manned and unmanned, that could reliably perform space missions. The important technical problems have been solved. The challenge now facing the United States space program is one of economics. The initial thrust in this direction has been the space shuttle program, which was launched to allow for economical space transportation by the use of reusable space modules.

Within the next thirty years, the space shuttle will allow exploitation of space by providing transportation for huge volumes of space cargo. The shuttle bay measures fifteen feet in diameter by sixty-five feet in length—with an eventual payload capability of 65,000 lbs. to near-earth orbit. This capability will be extremely useful to both the military and civilian communities. For example, NASA has launched a program called Large Space Structures (LSS) for the purpose of assembling huge structures in space, such as antennas, solar arrays, platforms for a variety of sensors, etc. These large space structures could be transported to geosynchronous orbit to perform a variety of missions: space communications, early warning for the military, air traffic control, etc.

In addition, the space shuttle will allow for inspection and retrieval of satellites—for repair in orbit or return to earth. Manufacturing in space, to take advantage of zero gravity and the hard vacuum, will also be possible. Scientists will be able to perform experiments and make observations of outer space without the attenuation of the atmosphere.

These are only a few of the opportunities that will be possible because of the shuttle. In fact, the next twenty years should be very exciting for the United States space program.

Senator Harrison "Jack" Schmitt. These two questions—about the future of the space program and its goals—are really one and the same. The Reagan Administration is now presented with the opportunity to articulate a purpose for United States activities in space, a purpose that establishes once and for all a permanent commitment to compete continuously and successfully in the development of space. Such a statement of purpose does not need to have dollars attached to it, in the short term. However, this statement must carry with it the realization that our public and private investments in space will, of necessity, increase with time. Without such investments, the opportunities for public and commercial satellite services, for commercial space-made materials, for research and education in space, and for keeping the peace and defending freedom will be lost to others whose historical perspective is superior to our own.

Among the short-term essential national capabilities that must be maintained, are: full development of the space shuttle; improved aeronautical and remote-sensing technologies; fulfillment of international obligations; and continuance of basic space science.

In the longer term, the permanence of a United States commitment to space could be reflected in the fiscal year 1984 budget—with a start on a multipurpose American station in space for use by 1990. Clearly this is the ultimate near-earth nondefense utility of the space shuttle and we should plan to get on with it. Also, in the longer term, the peace-keeping and defense uses of space will become more obvious to the unduly conservative Pentagon. Defense application of the space shuttle includes: increased reconnaissance and intelligence capabilities; increased research and development of space defense weapons such as lasers; and, possibly, small manned battle observation satellites that can improve command functions in the event of conventional hostilities.

There is a new test of our heart and soul and will. It is the new ocean of space.

WHAT IS THE LIKELIHOOD THAT LIFE FORMS SIMILAR TO THOSE ON EARTH HAVE DEVELOPED ON OTHER PLANETS?

Isaac Asimov. There are so many stars in the universe that vast numbers must resemble the sun. If planetary systems are common, and many astronomers think they are, there must be vast numbers of earthlike planets circling sunlike stars. Many scientists think that life will inevitably form under earthlike conditions; and if that is the case, there may be uncounted billions of planets in the universe that bear life forms. (Some scientists, however, suspect that life may be comparatively rare.) If the optimists are correct, it may be that there are hundreds of thousands of intelligent life forms on various planets in our own galaxy.

How similar would these extraterrestrial life forms be to those on earth? Given earthlike conditions, it seems reasonable to suppose that life forms would be based on proteins and nucleic acids undergoing chemical changes in a water background as on earth. There may be other basic chemical foundations for life, but scientists have no evidence that others may exist.

Even granted basic chemistries similar to life on earth, however, there are astronomically great numbers of different genes and gene combinations possible. Even on earth, slight changes in nucleic acid molecular detail give rise to life forms as different as oak trees and giraffes, penguins and lobsters, mushrooms and squid. The potentialities of difference are so great that it is extremely unlikely we will ever encounter an extraterrestrial life form that will have the slightest similarity to a human being, for instance.

Dr. Jerry Grey. There is a finite probability that extraterrestrial life forms, similar to those on earth, do exist. The specific magnitude of that probability is debatable—and is often debated in forums and publications on the Search for Extraterrestrial Intelligence (SETI). It ranges from absolute certainty to high improbability, depending on (a) the number of potentially habitable planets in the universe, and (b) the likelihood that intelligent life will develop on any such planets.

We are only in the very early stages of the search. For example: an intelligent extraterrestrial life form would need to be within forty light-years of the earth in order to know, from the radio waves Guglielmo Marconi began transmitting eighty years ago, that intelligent life exists here. And forty light-years is only a minute dust-speck in the universe. As Philip Morrison, one of SETI's founders, said, "This is a program for the centuries."

Daniel M. Lentz, F.B.I.S. I feel that the likelihood of life forms like those on earth is 100 percent. Looking at the billions of stars that we can see and realizing that, for each of these, there are hundreds that we cannot see—the numbers are so great that they make it unlikely that humanlike life has not evolved, perhaps to a greater extent than life on earth.

Dr. John F. McCarthy, Jr. The planet with the highest probability of supporting life as we know it on earth is Mars, because the temperature extremes and the possible existence of water could support organic matter. Therefore, NASA (in its Viking program) supported research to determine the presence of life on Mars. Unfortunately, all data received were negative, and it is highly unlikely that life as we know it on earth exists on Mars.

In addition to the Viking experiments, NASA has supported a low-level program called Search for Extraterrestrial Intelligence (SETI). In this program, receivers were constructed to receive signals from outer space across a wide range of frequencies. Again, the results to date have been negative, and there is some pressure to cancel the program completely.

In view of the dearth of evidence based on Viking and SETI findings, it is unlikely that life forms similar to those on earth have developed on other planets. However, the remote possibility does exist, and we should continue to probe—in every way we know—for the evidence of existence of life on other planets.

Dr. Brian O'Leary. This is a highly controversial and speculative topic. The question of life forms on other planets can be subdivided into other, related questions. Did life originate on earth or was it emplaced (seeded) either deliberately or accidentally from somewhere else? The latter possibility ensures a yes answer to the question; and I believe there is a very good chance that this is true.

The question of the spontaneous generation of life on earth—from complex organic molecules—is a challenging one. So far, laboratory experiments have been unable to mimic this crucial step in evolution. But, if life was indeed created on earth, there is a very good possibility that this could also have happened independently on other planets— probably not in our solar system (conditions are too hostile on the other planets in the solar system), but on some of billions of hypothetical earthlike planets circling the billion trillion or so single stars in the known universe. Theories of planetary evolution favor the possibility of the formation of planetary systems circling stars, and there is some observational evidence for this.

If there is life out there, and it has a common origin, we would expect the basic chemistry to be similar (DNA, RNA, etc.); but the morphology (appearance) will be as different and diverse as life forms on earth. Without a common origin, the chemistry *and* appearance will be different. In any case, it will be a surprise!

Finally, if a technologically advanced civilization—or civilizations— exists, it will probably be far ahead of us. We are just beginning to emerge as galactic citizens.

Senator Harrison "Jack" Schmitt. The probability that life forms similar to those on earth have developed on the planets of our solar system is very, very low—because of their extremely hostile non-earthlike environments, which appear to have existed since the solar system was born 4.6 billion years ago. There is a slightly higher probability that a few *simple life forms* may have developed on Mars and/or Venus in the first one billion years of their evolution as planets, when their environments were similar to that in which life was beginning on earth. However, there is as yet no evidence that such life forms could have survived the subsequent hostile environmental changes to which Mars and Venus have been subjected.

On the other hand, the probability of life forms similar to those on earth developing on earthlike planets that revolve around other sunlike stars in the universe is very, very high. Statistically, earthlike conditions must have existed hundreds of thousands of times during the 14 billion years or more that the universe has existed.

THINK TANKS

*I*N A COMPLEX, POSTINDUSTRIAL society like ours—in which information handling rather than production of objects has become the primary focus of our economy—there is a tremendous demand for guided research to help in the decision-making process. Government involvement in so many areas of our lives, as well as the increasing complexity of international politics, has generated a tremendous increase in the demand for focused studies of the different options available to various government agencies. Traditional scholars in our universities, with their emphasis on teaching and academic research, were ill equipped to handle this demand. As a result, think tanks have come into existence— bodies of researchers drawn from various fields—whose function is to address the policy issues of the day and to lay out the options.

In the pages that follow, a number of experts discuss the work and operations of a variety of think tanks in this country.

CONTRIBUTORS

William J. Baroody, Jr., President, American Enterprise Institute for Public Research, Washington, D.C.

Edwin J. Feulner, Jr., President, The Heritage Foundation, Washington, D.C.

Michael J. Pelczar, Jr., President, The Council of Graduate Schools in the United States, Washington, D.C.

Gail L. Potter, President, Hudson Institute, Inc., Croton-on-Hudson, New York

WHAT IS A "THINK TANK" AND
WHAT DO PEOPLE DO THERE?

William J. Baroody, Jr. Policy makers themselves rarely originate the concepts underlying the laws by which people are governed. They choose among practical options derived from the ideas, speculation and theories of intellectual men and women. At public policy research institutions, thoughtful men and women explore issues in depth and formulate these practical options.

A think tank is like a college or university. Its scholars and fellows conduct research and perform an educational function much like professors. In the case of a think tank, however, the student body consists of government officials, business leaders and the general public.

There are many kinds of think tanks. Some, such as the Rand Corporation, are contracted to do research on specific issues for their clients (including government). Others, such as Georgetown University's Center for Strategic and International Studies, focus on a single area of interest, such as foreign policy. Still others, like the American Enterprise Institute, the Brookings Institution or the Hoover Institute at Stanford, conduct ongoing research in many areas of public policy. The American Enterprise Institute researches areas that include economic policy, health policy, foreign policy, defense policy, tax policy, legal policy, legislative analyses, government regulation, social institutions and political and social processes.

The general goals of think tank research are: (1) to identify where and why the system is not working; (2) to propose alternative solutions for correcting those problems; and (3) to identify issues that should be addressed by public policy. A good think tank is guided by one theme: that the competition of ideas is fundamental to a free society. It does not dictate opinions to its scholars and fellows. Rather, "academic freedom" is the principle that is adhered to, diligently.

Edwin J. Feulner, Jr. The term, think tank, has taken on a specific meaning in the modern American political context. A think tank is an institution that employs academics, government officials, journalists and other public policymakers. It provides an opportunity for these individuals to translate academic or theoretical ideas into practical public policy options. Think tanks work as idea generating centers, and not as lobbyists or direct pressure groups. While there are some think tanks in other countries, they tend to be American institutions.

Some of the major think tanks in the United States consider broad public policy issues, such as foreign policy and national security questions (The Center for Strategic and International Studies at Georgetown University, to name one). A second category of think tanks works in specific areas, such as criminal justice issues (e.g., Center for Criminal Justice Policy and Management, University of San Diego). The third, and perhaps most influential group, covers all issues—foreign, economic and social policy (e.g., The Hoover Institution at Stanford University).

Professional personnel at a think tank may be professors from colleges and universities. Some may be in residence at the think tank, others may be used as consultants or project directors for specific programs.

Another key component of personnel is the former government official, who uses the think tank as a base to analyze and review the governmental programs that he previously administered. These individuals can also monitor their successors in government and review their performance. In this role, the think tank functions as an "alternative government," "government in exile" or "shadow government"— e.g., The Brookings Institution for Democrats; American Enterprise Institute for Republicans (AIE).

Think tanks may even house journalists who have taken a leave of absence from their jobs—perhaps to write a book, free from the day-to-day pressures of deadlines.

Most think tanks are independent corporate bodies with their own boards of trustees. However, some have university connections; others are governmental units (e.g., The Congressional Office of Technology Assessment). Most think tanks are tax-exempt under IRS regulations. Their sources of funding may be individual contributions, corporate or union contributions, donations from foundations, or grants or contracts from governments. Some of these funds may be designated for specific projects, others may be for the think tank's general operations. Presumably, when the funds are designated for a specific research project, the results of the project are not predetermined. That is, the role of the think tank is to look at the question, analyze it, and present alternative conclusions.

The written products of think tanks may be books (hundreds a year), monographs, scholarly journals (e.g., Woodrow Wilson Center's *Wilson Quarterly*; Heritage's *Policy Review*), magazines (AEI's *Public Opinion*), or policy papers. Think tank personnel are considered experts in their own subject areas and they frequently participate in television, radio, magazine and newspaper discussion of their fields. Think tank personnel also often testify as experts before congressional committees, and in panels and meetings at colleges and universities.

The think tanks that are involved with policy issues tend to take on an ideological cast. That is, if their product tends to be liberal—or conservative—the organization tends to be considered liberal (e.g., Brookings Institution) or conservative (e.g., The Heritage Foundation).

Think tanks are a fairly new ingredient in the public policy process. They provide an opportunity for individuals to promote their own viewpoint, to support it with intellectual arguments, and to try to influence the government and the national news media to act in accord with their views. As policy issues have become more complex, the role of think tanks has become more important; they are now a substantial force in our governmental process.

Michael J. Pelczar, Jr. The term, think tank, as currently used in the United States, refers to an organization made up of a staff representing a variety of disciplines—who are engaged in long-range speculation about the future.

The issues which the staff addresses are generally of a global nature, e.g., world food supply, world population, energy supply and demand. Periodically, extensive reports are issued by these organizations. The reports describe various scenarios that may emerge in the future and thus provide topics for discussion and debate by various groups in society. In addition to final reports, think tanks sponsor seminars and other types of discussion groups for the purpose of assessing new ideas.

Gail L. Potter. A think tank is a policy-oriented research center that attempts to supply government and business policy makers, planners and administrators with the best possible analysis of subjects of concern to them. Think-tank research does not aim to conform to academic canons of quality. It is conducted under time pressures, and uses many kinds of information as a basis for formulating conclusions. Almost necessarily, a think tank conducts future studies, since it is under future conditions that policies will be implemented.

The function of a think tank, to borrow Walter Lippmann's phrase, is "outsiders advising insiders." Think-tank researchers must be generalists to a greater extent than most other brainworkers, and this quality is augmented by use of multi-disciplinary research teams. The think tank provides a client with a different perspective; a broader and longer-range context; a greater capacity for drawing useful analogies; and, often, a greater independence of judgment than can be obtained in-house.

With broader experience and fewer scholarly inhibitions than academics, a think tank has usually been more of an idea factory than a university. For these and other reasons, such as full-time year-round research staffs and access to top-notch consultants, think tanks justify their high costs relative to academic research operations. However, as policy-analysis and futures-studies programs have proliferated in universities, think tanks seem generally to have become somewhat more academic and less daring, at least in relation to government clients, in recent years.

Think-tank research works best in relation to responsible, serious clients in organizations where decision making is relatively concentrated —and in challenging fashionable theories and conventional wisdom sometimes promulgated by the educated public.

ENVIRONMENT

*P*ERHAPS NOTHING AROUSES greater frustration and confusion than the linked subjects of energy and environmental protection. Several years ago we were treated daily to headlines proclaiming that the United States was at the mercy of the Arab nations and that our country could never attain energy independence. The next cycle of headlines trumpeted news of the world oil glut and announced that the energy problem had disappeared because Americans, for the moment, were beginning to conserve energy. The one type of report that never seems to appear is that of the planning of a responsible national energy policy, and of the steps necessary to carry it out.

The experts in the following section tackle the challenging problems of energy, the environment, and the use of the world's resources. Polls show that most Americans favor protecting the environment; these same polls show that most Americans would like this country to become free from the control of OPEC. While these may appear to be separate issues, they are in fact interrelated.

Coal, for example, brings together the issues of energy development and environmental protection. The United States currently has enough coal reserves to supply our country's energy needs (at current levels of consumption) for the next three hundred years. Patriots (and the major energy companies, who have bought up most of our country's coal reserves) tout coal as the perfect solution to the problem of dependence on foreign oil. However, the financial and environmental costs of introducing and utilizing coal may be higher than many of us are willing to pay.

The experts in the following section address the problems of our vanishing farmland, the diminishing supplies of fresh water, and the steps necessary for the development of alternative energy supplies.

ENERGY ALTERNATIVES

*T*ODAY, ENERGY IS ON EVERYONE'S MIND. Discussions about housing now concern BTU's (British Thermal Unit = the amount of heat required to raise the temperature of one pound of water one degree Fahrenheit.) and proper insulation; talks about cars stress mileage statistics; complaints about prices center on the soaring costs of fuels. Recently, when American relations with Mideast oil-producing nations grew especially tense, Americans even asked, "Will we go to war for oil?"

Few people want to fight World War III over oil fields, but almost everyone agrees that the United States needs steady, dependable supplies of energy to fuel the economy. The Department of Energy predicts that in upcoming years the nation will demand even more energy—up to more than 111,000 trillion BTUs by the year 2000.

How will the nation satisfy its energy appetite? In the past, petroleum products supplied roughly half of America's energy needs. For decades, petroleum was cheap and plentiful—the United States paid only $1.30 per barrel for imported crude oil in the early 1970s. There were petroleum heated homes, powered industries, and fueled station wagons for long Sunday drives. Few people stopped to think that, while petroleum was the country's single largest source of energy, the United States possessed less than 5 percent of the world's petroleum supplies. Thus the nation depended to a large extent upon its foreign oil suppliers. When the supplies were cut off in the 1973–74 Arab oil embargo, energy luxuries like the traditional Sunday drive came to a screeching halt. More supply shortages coupled with hard-hitting price increases—

the cost of a barrel of crude oil soared an incredible 3,200 percent in the 1970s to a high of $40 to $45 per barrel—convinced many Americans that energy, like charity, should begin at home. The following table, based on figures from the Department of Energy, illustrates how rapidly our energy consumption has grown just in the last decades:

UNITED STATES CONSUMPTION OF ENERGY IN TRILLIONS OF BTU'S

Year	Coal	Natural Gas	Petroleum	Electricity	Total
1950	12,891	5,970	13,320	1,440	33,621
1955	11,519	9,000	17,260	1,410	39,189
1960	10,116	12,390	19,920	1,656	44,082
1965	11,889	15,770	23,250	2,104	53,013
1970	12,660	21,800	29,520	2,900	66,880
1975	12,821	19,950	32,730	5,190	70,691
1979 (est.)	15,080	19,860	37,020	5,990	77,950

Limited petroleum resources have forced the nation to reevaluate its energy alternatives. Some of these alternatives are as old as the first camp fire; burning wood has regained popularity in the United States, especially in areas such as Vermont that have extensive forests and cold winters. Technological advances offer newer alternatives, but some of these, such as nuclear power, have so far generated more controversy than energy.

A 1980 report by the Department of Energy took stock of the nation's energy natural resources. It predicted that, at current rates of production and use, the United States has eight more years worth of petroleum, ten more years worth of natural gas, forty-five more years worth of uranium, and 299 more years worth of coal.

Does this mean coal will become the energy source of the future? According to another study, this one compiled over a period of four years by the National Academy of Sciences, coal will be just one of the fuels needed to meet the next three decades' energy needs. The $4 million study, released in 1980, stressed that synthetic fuels (derived from oil and shale) and nuclear power will be needed along with coal; together, these fuel sources could supply most of the nation's energy. The study acknowledged the contributions of sources such as petroleum and solar and geothermal power, but it stated that only coal and nuclear energy provide "reasonably assured ability to support significant electrical generating capacity over the next three decades."

Yet as confident as this conclusion sounds, some of the 350 contributors to the study disagreed with the findings, and the question of what fuel sources to use in the future is still being energetically debated. Most experts agree that any successful domestic energy policy will depend in part on Americans' willingness to curb their energy use and to find alternatives to petroleum. The following questions and answers explore the choices and look at how Americans are warming up to alternative energy sources.

CONTRIBUTORS

Ralph E. Bailey, Chairman, Conoco, Inc., Stamford, Connecticut

Larry Bogart, National Coordinator, Citizens' Energy Council, Allendale, New York

John F. Bookout, President, Shell Oil Company, Houston, Texas

Kenneth R. Bordner, Director, Conservation and Renewable Energy Inquiry and Referral Service, Silver Spring, Maryland

H. Laurance Fuller, President, Amoco Oil, Chicago, Illinois

Michel T. Halbouty, consulting geologist and petroleum engineer, Houston, Texas

Dr. Craig Bond Hatfield, Professor of Geology, The University of Toledo, Toledo, Ohio

Martin Peterson, Board of Directors, Alternative Energy Resources Organization; registered professional engineer, Billings, Montana

John C. Sawhill, former U.S. Deputy Secretary of Energy; Chairman, U.S. Synthetic Fuels Corporation, Washington, D.C.

Edwin F. Shelley, Director, Center for Energy Policy and Research, New York Institute of Technology, Old Westbury, New York

Earl C. Tanner, Director, Plasma Physics Laboratory, Princeton University, Princeton, New Jersey

WHEN WILL ALTERNATE SOURCES OF ENERGY BE MADE AVAILABLE TO THE GENERAL PUBLIC, AND WHICH KINDS?

Ralph E. Bailey. If alternative energy sources are taken to mean anything other than oil, natural gas or electricity (generated by coal, nuclear power or hydropower), then numerous alternative energy sources are publicly available today. Individuals can attach solar collectors on their roofs, purchase wood-burning stoves, and use gasohol (which is 10 percent alcohol derived from corn) to fuel their automobiles.

The reason more alternative energy sources are not utilized, or existing alternatives are not utilized more, is a matter of economics. Some alternatives—such as fusion, solar electricity generation (photovoltaics) and coal synthetics from bituminous coals—are not technically proven. But in many other instances, such as solar water and space heating, shale oil and coal synthetics from subbituminous coals, the alternatives are not more widely available because of unfavorable economics. Alternative energy sources begin to become available when there is enough confidence in their potential viability to stimulate investment. They become widely available only after commercial viability is established.

The four major categories of alternatives can be classified as (1) synthetics from shale oil, coal or tar sands, (2) synthetics from biomass, (3) photovoltaics and (4) fusion. The first two (both synthetics) yield liquids and gases, and the processes are well defined. The latter two would yield electricity, and the technology is not proven.

Among the two types of synthetics, those derived from shale oil, coal or tar sands appear to be cheaper to produce (assuming equal tax treatment) and closer to economic viability. Numerous companies have invested in bench scale tests and pilot programs. But the required front end capital investment for a commercial scale facility is estimated to be in the billions of dollars. Few organizations can afford to risk such sums without having a reasonable certainty that the capital investment can be recovered fairly quickly. However, until commercial size facilities are actually built, the economics cannot be definitively ascertained.

My personal assessment is that if the federal government allows adequately accelerated depreciation, the first commercial scale units could be in operation by the mid to late 1980s.

Larry Bogart. If the multi-national oil companies, which dominate energy policy, do not restrict competition, photovoltaic cells—designed for roof tops, and capable of generating enough electricity for all a home's needs, by conversion of sunlight—should be as cheap as conventional power from a central-station generating plant by the end of the 1980s. Low-cost loans or grants, like programs of the Tennesee Valley Authority, could make solar hot water systems generally available within a few years. Lacking federal incentive programs, alternate energy will be limited to the "do-it-yourself" people.

John F. Bookout. Energy from sources alternative to oil and natural gas has been available to America's general public for many years. Coal and wood are good examples of alternative energy sources. Another is hydroelectric energy, which has been around since the mid-nineteenth century. Commercial generation of electricity by nuclear power in the United States began in 1960.

It is the exotic sources of potential energy and their wider use that excite public attention: solar, wind, biomass, geothermal and others. Technology for their development is just emerging. Generating efficiency has a long way to go. Therefore, the cost of power from these sources still hampers their use. Economics ultimately will dictate whether every home will have its own heating-cooling-electrical plant or if commercial generators will tap these sources to produce and sell electricity.

Shell Oil Company's energy forecasts do not expect major contributions from these sources before the year 2000. The principal alternative sources of energy that will augment conventional supplies of oil and gas should be nuclear power, coal and shale oil into the twenty-first century.

Nuclear generation of electricity is becoming important to the United States. By the year 2000, nuclear plants should generate 20 percent of the nation's electricity. This will provide between 8 and 9 percent of total domestic energy needs.

America's capacity to produce coal is growing about 5 percent annually —and by 2000 should be 2 billion tons per year. Much of this coal will be burned to produce electricity. Some will be turned into liquids to supplement crude oil supplies, and some into gas to supplement natural gas supplies.

Shale oil should begin to emerge as an energy source by about 1986. By 2000 it should contribute about 10 percent of the total domestic liquid supplies.

Martin Peterson. A variety of alternate energy sources are already available, but most require infusion of considerable capital—an impossible task at elevated interest rates. For most of the alternate energy technologies to become economically feasible, and therefore available to the general public, three things must occur.

One, conventional fuel prices in America need to rise and be on par with Europe and Japan. This, of course, makes the alternate energy technologies less expensive, if only by comparison.

Two, the state of the art must advance—beyond the equipment built by the backyard experimenter and laboratory technician—to commercially available equipment mass-produced by industry. Like refrigerators, the equipment must become more reliable and less complicated. For instance, few lay people understand the principles of refrigeration, but we all own a refrigerating unit. The same will be true of solar collectors and windmills.

Three, the interest rates must drop significantly. Since nearly all alternate energy systems require a high initial capital investment, the American economic system requires that all or most of the cost be financed over the life of the system, on borrowed money. At excessively high interest rates, this initial investment will not generate enough savings to financially benefit the purchaser. Therefore, there is no economic incentive to install such systems.

I see the first two criteria occurring naturally in the next five years. The third criteria, however, is the stickler because it depends on the country's basic economic health. If interest rates do drop to more reasonable levels within five years, we could see an alternate energy boom on par with the introduction of automobiles into America's lifestyle in the 1910s and 1920s—after Henry Ford began mass-producing his machines. We would all have an alternate energy system on our homes and businesses because we could not afford to be without one.

John C. Sawhill. The most promising sources of alternative fuels for Americans are the liquids and gases we can create from our vast domestic resources of coal and oil shale. These fuels should become available in the 1990s.

Earl C. Tanner. New sources of energy will become available to the general public, in significant quantity, on a schedule that depends as much on political and economic considerations as it does on technological advance.

For example, if foreign oil is suddenly cut off, we shall see a very rapid development of synthetic fuels from coal, shale and biomass. The manufacturing processes will not be optimized, economically or environmentally, but the fuel will flow in five years—and will become quite abundant in ten to fifteen years. If, on the other hand, imported oil continues in good supply, synthetic hydrocarbon liquids will play a relatively minor role in the 1990s. Thereafter, environmental considerations will determine the extent of the development of these fuels.

The breeder reactor could conceivably be deployed by about the year 2000, if research is vigorously and consistently supported for the next twenty years. It could then play a dominant role in electrical generation and synthetic fuel (hydrogen) production some twenty to thirty years later. However, it is quite possible that government or public opposition may preclude the use of the breeder altogether.

The new solar technologies (those other than hydropower) are extremely diverse, ranging from flat-plate collectors, biomass, photovoltaics, wind, thermal electric, ocean thermal gradients, salinity gradients, waves and currents on up to giant space satellites. I expect some of these technologies to be common enough during the 1990s to supply a small percentage of national energy needs. Technological breakthroughs could increase this fraction to 10 percent or more by the first decade of the twenty-first century.

Geothermal energy is not really new, since it already supplies large blocks of power in San Francisco and elsewhere. Its use will increase slowly in the 1980s and 1990s, and will supply only a small percent of national needs.

Fusion can probably be deployed early in the twenty-first century, but only if the Fusion Energy Engineering Act of 1980 is fully and vigorously implemented at the funding levels specified in the legislation. Twenty to thirty years after initial deployment, fusion could dominate U.S. energy production, both electrical and nonelectrical.

HOW MANY AMERICANS NOW MAKE USE OF SOLAR ENERGY AND OTHER ALTERNATE ENERGY SOURCES?

Larry Bogart. About 5 percent of the public uses solar energy, if one includes households that, primarily, use wood for space heating. (Since trees require sunlight to grow, wood is considered an indirect solar energy source.) With higher prices for oil and natural gas, we will see more new homes incorporating passive solar systems.

Kenneth R. Bordner. It is difficult to provide a completely accurate number of the people using renewable energy—since no actual count has ever been made of alternate energy systems. Estimates vary widely, depending upon the source of the estimate and the scope of the survey. (For example: Are solar swimming pool heaters counted? Or fireplaces? Or homes with large south-facing windows?)

According to recent Department of Energy estimates, there are 350,000 homes in America with some form of solar space heating or hot water system. Using the Census Bureau average of 2.75 people per American household, 350,000 solar systems translate into 962,500 people living in a building with a solar system.

An estimated 10,000 small windmills are now in operation across the country, generating electricity for the 27,500 people who live in those homes (Census Bureau average). If windmills used for other purposes, such as waterpumping, are included, the number of wind systems nationwide climbs to 150,000, according to the American Wind Energy Association.

In the last few years, the use of wood has also risen rapidly. The Wood Heating Alliance estimates that six million homes, housing 16.5 million people (Census Bureau), are heated, at least in part, by wood stoves. And 18 million homes have at least one working fireplace.

These figures do not include people using solar cells to produce electricity directly from sunlight (photovoltaics), nor ocean energy (energy from tides, waves and temperature gradients in the ocean), nor gasohol, nor small-scale low-head hydroelectric systems. (Large-scale hydroelectric plants have been used for decades to produce electricity across the country.)

Although these figures may be only estimates, the trend is clear. As the prices of conventional fuels escalate, Americans are converting to renewable sources of energy.

Michel T. Halbouty. There is no accurate way to estimate the number of Americans who use solar and alternate energy sources today. Anyone who burns wood for heating or cooking, inserts gasohol in his car, consumes electricity produced from coal, nuclear or hydroelectric power, has a windmill, or has passive or active solar features built into his home uses alternate sources of energy.

Electric power provides 38 percent of the nation's total energy supply, and of that amount, 12 percent is generated from nuclear energy and 14 percent comes from hydroelectric generating stations. Biomass provides 2 percent of our country's energy needs, and solar power contributes less than 1 percent of the total energy supply.

Certainly, as more and more people become aware of energy conservation—and of actual money saved by using alternate energy sources—the numbers of people using these sources will increase. But to state any specific number of Americans today using alternates to oil and gas energy is unreliable. How would anyone know, without extensively investigating every segment of this country? Even the people themselves probably do not realize how much they do use alternate sources of energy. Think about it.

Edwin F. Shelley. Solar energy and most alternate energy sources ultimately come from the sun. They are renewable, since the sun rises every day. Fossil fuels such as coal, oil, gas and uranium are nonrenewable and, once used, are gone forever.

Renewable energy from the sun can be used in two general ways. The first is *direct* interception of the sun's rays to heat water for domestic or industrial use; to heat living spaces in buildings; to cool buildings by a heat-driven refrigeration system; to generate electricity using photovoltaic cells that convert sunlight directly to electricity (these power most space satellites); or, to generate electricity by heating water until it becomes steam, which then drives an ordinary turbine-generator.

Taking advantage of this direct use of solar rays, three-quarters of a million Americans live in homes designed especially to be heated in large part by the sun (so-called passive solar homes) or in homes using solar collectors to heat the domestic hot water or the living spaces of the home. (Domestic hot water heating systems alone numbered 125,000 in the United States by early 1981). Several hundred thousand people use some 60,000 solar collector systems to heat their swimming pools.

Although no significant number of buildings are cooled, as yet, by solar energy, and not much electricity is generated directly by solar power, considerable experimental work is under way. Photovoltaic cells now power only a few thousand remote installations, such as telephone relay stations, but economically competitive photovoltaic systems for home and industrial use are expected to be available before the end of this decade.

The second way of using solar energy is much more widespread. This involves the *indirect* use of the sun's rays in three ways: by growing trees and other crops that are then burned to produce heat or electricity; by using the wind, produced by uneven heating of the land by the sun, to turn windmills and thus pump water or generate electricity; and by using the falling water of dammed-up rivers to generate hydroelectric power. The water in the rivers is constantly replenished by rain, which is simply water evaporated from the oceans by the sun, held temporarily in clouds, and eventually deposited on the land.

Taking advantage of these indirect ways of using solar energy, approximately 15 million Americans make use of solar energy by deriving all or part of their heat from some 5 million wood-burning stoves. Another half-million people derive a significant amount of their energy from approximately 150,000 windmills in use today. More than 50,000

Americans now fuel their automobiles with gasohol, 10 percent of which is alcohol distilled from solar-grown crops. A very small but growing number of people make use of methane gas or electricity derived from garbage and other biomass sources. Finally, more than 25 million Americans depend on electricity from hydroelectric power plants, the most common way of utilizing renewable solar energy today.

Altogether, then, 40 million Americans now make use of solar energy and other alternate energy sources in one form or another.

WHY DOESN'T THE UNITED STATES MAKE FAR GREATER USE OF ITS COAL SUPPLIES IN ORDER TO REDUCE OUR DEPENDENCE ON MIDEAST OIL?

H. Laurance Fuller. Over the next twenty years, the United States is expected to increase its use of coal—at the same time that the use of crude oil is declining and the use of natural gas is remaining about constant. Coal's contribution to total energy supply is forecast to increase from the 1980 figure of 15.6 quadrillion BTU's to 30 quadrillion BTU's in the year 2000. This represents an increase in coal's share of the energy market from 21 percent to about 32 percent.

The transition to an economy that utilizes more coal will take time—because more facilities must be built to utilize coal, including electrical utility plants and industrial boiler plants. These facilities are expensive: large coal-fired utility plants cost over a billion dollars. Another problem is that environmental regulations severely restrict the use of coal in new facilities. For example, these regulations require that flue gas desulfurization be employed on new electrical power plants even if low sulfur coal is burned. Unfortunately, coal cannot be used directly as a transportation fuel in modern vehicles.

In the future, we expect that coal will still be used, primarily, as a fuel to produce electrical power and steam, just as it is today. Small amounts of coal will probably be converted to synthetic fuels, but the high cost of manufacturing synthetic fuels from coal will be the limiting factor.

Dr. Craig Bond Hatfield. If we could mine the amount of coal for liquefaction that is necessary to replace the 2.5 billion barrels of oil we imported in 1980—and given the optimistic but feasible condition that one ton of coal will yield three barrels of liquid product—we would liquify, each year, an amount of coal as great as the total amount mined for all purposes in 1980. This would necessitate *doubling* the 1980 U.S. coal production rate, in order to maintain present coal consumption for electric power generation and other current uses. But this is not easy to accomplish.

Rapid expansion of coal mining faces formidable roadblocks. A new mine capable of producing just two million tons per year can require seven years of development time. Significant expansion of existing mines is also time-consuming.

Each year in the United States, coal mining accidents kill more than 100 miners and injure thousands more. Many hydrocarbons abundant in coal are especially carcinogenic—and have resulted in high rates of skin cancer among employees of coal liquefaction plants. In light of these hazards, and considering the roadblocks raised to prevent construction of nuclear power plants, which have yet to cause a single death, the probability of unimpeded development of synfuels from coal seems slim.

If we ignore the dangers, and commit ourselves without reservation to coal liquefaction, there are other problems. During the 1950s, eight years were spent in building and perfecting a South African coal liquefaction plant known as Sasol, which yields 10,000 barrels per day of liquid hydrocarbons. In 1973, South Africa began Sasol Two, which was not ready to begin operation until late 1980. This awesome industrial complex covers more than a square mile and converts coal into 55,000 barrels per day of liquid product. That output, however, is only about 1/300th of what United States daily oil consumption was in 1980.

Major oil companies and the Department of Energy, among others, are planning similar facilities for coal liquefaction in the United States, and tests are being conducted at pilot plants. If such demonstration models prove successful, it is possible that, by 1990, we could have three or four coal liquefaction complexes even more colossal than South Africa's Sasol Two. If, by 1990, we build four of them, each twice the size of Sasol Two, the construction cost would exceed the entire $20,000,000,000 earmarked by our government (in 1980) for launching domestic synthetic fuels industries—and these four behemoths could provide us with the equivalent of only about 3 percent of our daily 1980 oil consumption.

For this to occur by 1990, we would also have to avoid the very possible delays in plant construction and expanded mining operations imposed by environmental and conservation concerns. The time required just to complete a conventional coal-fired power plant has now grown to nearly ten years. Difficulty in acquiring—from various levels of government—the permits necessary to locate a new power plant has even resulted in some cancellations of such plans by industry.

Other problems include inadequate rail facilities for greatly expanded coal transportation and the risks attached to the kind of giant long-term investments that would be required by industry—risks made even greater because we do not really know how changing economics will affect the profitability of such ventures.

In short, this is not a job that is likely to be accomplished quickly.

Finally, there is the most significant question of all: whether it is in our best interests to consume our remaining fuel resources at an increasing rate. The United States Geological Survey has estimated that the

United States has about 1.7 trillion tons of coal within 3,000 feet of the surface. Unfortunately, only about 12 percent of this coal (approximately 200 billion tons) is recoverable with existing technology and pricing structures. Most of our total coal resources are unobtainable because they are too deeply buried to be economically mined; because they occur in very thin beds that can be mined only with extreme difficulty and cost; or, because they underlie man-made or natural features that prohibit exploitation.

At the 1980 production rate of about 800 million tons per year, the available 200 billion tons of United States coal would last more than two centuries. If, on the other hand, we could increase the United States coal production rate to more than two billion tons per year by 1985—which was the coal consumption goal called for by President Ford in 1976— then our available coal reserves would last us less than one century (assuming production rate would not climb beyond the two billion tons per year, but would remain constant at that level).

However, if the United States could manage to resume and maintain the roughly 7 percent annual increase in domestic coal production rate that we achieved from 1860 until 1910, then our 200 billion tons of coal would be exhausted in less than fifty years. The United States coal production rate stopped increasing, and was roughly constant, from 1910 until the 1970s because our increasing fuel consumption was supplied by oil and natural gas. Now, in the case of petroleum, we are learning the consequences of exponentially increasing consumption of a finite resource. Domestic coal resources would be essentially exhausted, and thus would not be a fuel option available to us today, if our 7 percent annual growth in coal production had not terminated from 1910 until recently.

There is a sensible alternative that the United States and much of the rest of the world seems to have discovered recently. We can, through conservation, terminate and even reverse our 120 year history of increasing per capita energy consumption. If, in addition, we can stop population growth, the coming conservation imposed by finite fuel resources may even be experienced without famine.

Edwin F. Shelley. There are four reasons for the current failure to make greater use of coal supplies in the United States.

The first is the serious pollution problem created by the burning of coal. When coal is burned it generates large quantities of carbon dioxide. The accumulation of carbon dioxide in the upper atmosphere reduces the amount of heat that normally escapes from the earth into space, and this accumulation threatens to radically alter the earth's climate. Burning coal also liberates oxides of sulphur and nitrogen, which pollute the air we breathe, and which dissolve in atmospheric water and produce acid rain. Acid rain destroys fish, harms vegetation and can endanger the health of people far from the coal-burning source.

The second problem is the high cost, and limited effectiveness, of presently available smokestack scrubbers and other equipment designed to reduce the amount of pollutants released—and the high cost of equipment and labor needed to convert power plants from oil or gas to coal.

The third obstacle to more extensive use of coal is the difficulty now being experienced by utilities in raising capital funds for conversion of plants to coals. Investor uncertainty about the financial impact of nuclear plant outages and accidents (where the utility owns a nuclear plant in addition to its oil, gas or coal-burning plants), coupled with present high interest rates, tends to discourage investment in electric utilities.

Finally, the increasing cost of coal—because of increasing wage and safety demands and because of the natural tendency for different forms of energy to reach the same price per unit of heating value—has added to the uncertainty about the economic benefits of switching to coal.

Nevertheless, coal seems destined to become more and more important to the United States as technology reduces its disadvantages, and as the economic and political burden of dependence on Mideast oil becomes more and more unacceptable. It is even anticipated in some quarters that coal will eventually be used as the base for a new type of synthetic fuel that would be economically competitive with conventional fossil fuels.

NUCLEAR POWER

AMERICAN INDUSTRY HAS invested huge amounts of money in nuclear power plants. The country now has sixty-nine operable plants, and eighty-three more are in various stages of planning. Scientists are hard at work perfecting the technology of nuclear fusion (the joining of atomic particles), which should result in a safer and more efficient means of producing energy. It seems safe to say that as long as our national policy is committed to making America energy independent, federal funds will continue to support the nuclear industry.

The following essays by experts in the field give a balanced account of the state of our domestic nuclear power industry and the hazards that are inherent in nuclear power. Michael Stevenson, a nuclear physicist affiliated with the Los Alamos National Laboratory, asserts that the rate of exposure to radiation for an individual living within one mile of a reactor is significantly less than that absorbed from natural sources. In fact, the background radiation emitted by the stones in Grand Central Station in New York City is actually higher than allowed by government regulations.

At the other end of the spectrum, Larry Bogart, national coordinator of the Citizens Energy Council, maintains that no responsible figures are available on the exposure levels of nuclear radiation in its entire cycle (including mining and milling), and that there is no such thing as a level of exposure that is "too small" to make a difference to an individual's health.

This section on nuclear power gives everyone a chance to absorb the facts about the nuclear industry and to come to his or her own *informed* opinion about the future of nuclear power in our country.

CONTRIBUTORS

Larry Bogart, National Coordinator, Citizens Energy Council, Allendale, New York

Joseph M. Hendrie, Chairman, Nuclear Regulatory Commission, Washington, D.C.

H. G. MacPherson, consultant on nuclear energy; formerly Deputy Director, Oak Ridge National Laboratories and Director, Institute for Energy Analysis, Oak Ridge, Tennessee

Dr. Michael G. Stevenson, Los Alamos National Laboratory, Los Alamos, New Mexico

HOW MANY NUCLEAR PLANTS ARE THERE IN THE UNITED STATES? WHERE ARE THEY?

Larry Bogart. In May 1981, there were sixty-nine operable nuclear plants licensed by the Nuclear Regulatory Commission. They produced 10.4 percent of United States electric power. Eighty-three plants are under construction, or proposed, but no new plants have been ordered since 1978. Nuclear plants are concentrated along the Atlantic seaboard and the Middle West.

Joseph M. Hendrie. As of April 17, 1981, sixty-nine nuclear power plants were licensed for full-power operation in twenty-six states. One was licensed for fuel loading and low-power testing, and one for fuel loading and zero-power testing. Eighty-three others have been granted a construction permit.

H. G. MacPherson. There are seventy operable nuclear power plants in the United States as of mid-1981, and at least fifty more are in various stages of construction. Most of them are located in the eastern part of the country. The following eight states each have four or more reactors, and together they account for one-half of the total: Illinois, New York, Alabama, Michigan, Pennsylvania, South Carolina, Wisconsin and Virginia. Each individual reactor is required to be located in a low population zone, generally extending several miles from the reactor.

Dr. Michael G. Stevenson. As of June 1981, there were seventy nuclear power plants producing electricity for public use in the United States. These plants produced 136 billion kilowatt hours of electricity during the first six months of 1981.

There are an additional eighty commercial nuclear power plants under construction in the United States. The combined power rating of these plants, plus those now operating, is 140,000 kilowatts. The plants are located in thirty-six states in nearly all areas of the country, but most are in the eastern part (about 75 percent are east of the Mississippi).

HOW MUCH RADIATION IS ESCAPING INTO THE AIR?
IS THERE A SAFE LEVEL OF RADIATION?

Larry Bogart. All nuclear plants emit radioactive gas and liquids into the environment at concentrations permitted by regulatory authorities. The average nuclear plant has ten "incidents" a year where these maximum permissible concentrations are exceeded. No one knows how much radioactive material is dispersed into the environment at the plants—and throughout the nuclear fuel cycle beginning with uranium mining and milling.

Because there is no safe level of radioactive exposure, it appears the nuclear power industry may be killing 400 people per plant per year but the effects are long delayed.

Joseph M. Hendrie. In 1978 (the last year for which figures have been compiled), licensed nuclear power plants released about 3 million curies of radioactive noble gases (such as krypton) and about 19 curies of radioactive iodine and particulates. The dose of radiation that the average person in the United States receives, as a result of these releases, is much less than 1 millirem per year. This compares with an average annual dose to each individual in the United States of 100 millirems from natural background sources, such as cosmic radiation, radiation from brick and other building materials, and radiation from within the human body.

Scientists do not agree on whether there is a safe level of radiation or what that level might be. However, at low-level incremental exposures slightly above natural background, such as those resulting from nuclear power plant operations, there have been no observable human effects.

H. G. MacPherson. Reactors typically liberate thousands of curies of radioactive noble gases each year, but these are quickly dispersed so that the radiation dose to people is very small. Regulations require that if a person should stay outdoors at the plant boundary all year he should receive less than five millirems of radiation. All operating plants meet this requirement, by a large margin.

There is no firm evidence of any deleterious effect of radiation for exposures of less than 25,000 millirems. However, some responsible scientists believe, on purely theoretical grounds, that there is no safe level of radiation. The effect, if any, is so small that it would require tests involving millions of people to detect a significant effect of 5,000 millirems.

Dr. Michael G. Stevenson. We live in a sea of radiation, nearly all of which comes from completely natural sources. Of this natural "background" radiation at sea level, about one-half comes from the earth, that is, from the rocks and soil, and about one-half comes from outside the earth in the form of high-energy cosmic radiation. The dose to humans exposed to radiation is usually expressed in units called rems. A rem is a unit of measurement based on the effect of radiation on human tissue. Since doses received by people are usually small, they are often expressed in units of 1/1000 rem, or millirems (mrem).

The annual dose an individual receives from cosmic radiation depends strongly on altitude. At sea level, the dose an average person receives from cosmic rays is about forty-five mrem. At the mile-high altitude of Denver, Colorado, the average dose received in a year is about ninety-five mrem, more than double the sea level dose.

The background radiation from terrestrial sources depends not so much on geographical location, but more on where one lives and works. For example, granite is one of the most radioactive rocks, and the background radiation level in some granite or marble buildings, such as Grand Central Station in Manhattan, is actually higher than allowed by government regulations. As another example, the level of background radiation in a brick house is about 30 percent higher than in a wood-frame house.

In addition to these natural sources of radiation, most people are periodically exposed to radiation from dental and medical X rays. Typically, a person receives a dose of about 10 mrem from a chest X ray. The total dose that most Americans receive from all sources is about 150 mrem per year.

The amount of radiation escaping from a nuclear power plant is much smaller than this. Doses to an individual living next to a nuclear plant are not allowed to be greater than five mrem in one year from radiation released from the plant. In practice, the doses received will be much smaller. For example, the additional dose to an individual living and working about one mile from a nuclear plant will be about 1/2 mrem per year. Overall, the total *lifetime* dose to the average American, from nuclear plants, should be less than 1 percent of his or her *annual* dose from natural background radiation; that is, about three days' worth.

Although such low levels of radiation are very easy to detect with instruments, their effect on humans is very difficult to determine. It takes a dose of about 50,000 mrem to an individual before there are any medically observable effects, and about 500,000 before death is likely. There seems to be no statistically significant variation in death rates that can be attributed to high levels of natural background radiation. For example, total death rates in Colorado are much lower than for East Coast states, despite the much higher level of natural background radiation.

A commonly used assumption is that the health effects due to radiation are linear with dose. That is, a dose of 1/1000 mrem received by all of 1000 people is assumed to cause the same health effects as a dose of 1 mrem received by a single person. Some experts argue that the effects are worse at low levels than this linear assumption implies; others argue that there is a threshold of dose below which there are no health effects whatsoever. Assuming that the linear assumption is correct, only about 1 out of every 2000 cancer deaths is due to radiation from all sources, including background. With 200 nuclear plants operating in the United States, then only one of every 200,000 cancer deaths each year could be attributed to radiation from nuclear plants. This number is so small that it could never be detected.

WHAT HAS BEEN THE AVERAGE AGE OF DEATH BEFORE AND AFTER NUCLEAR PLANTS? ARE AMERICANS LIVING SHORTER LIVES BECAUSE OF NUCLEAR PLANTS?

Joseph M. Hendrie. The average age of death of Americans has, of course, risen substantially through the years. I am not aware of any studies comparing the average age of death before nuclear plants were introduced with the average age afterwards.

H. G. MacPherson. The life span of Americans has been increasing continuously. For example, in 1955, before there were any nuclear power plants, the average life span was 69.6 years, and in 1977 was 73.2 years. The average life span of people in nuclear communities such as Oak Ridge, Tennessee, is longer than the national average, although this is not related to nuclear activities.

Dr. Michael G. Stevenson. Fortunately, the life span of Americans continues to increase. In 1950, before the implementation of commercial nuclear power, the average life expectancy was 68.2. In 1978, it was 73.3. Of course, this cannot be attributed to nuclear power in a direct sense. However, nuclear plants are thought to provide less total risk to the public than, for example, large coal-fired systems for generating electricity.

[This response is based on my own technical expertise and in no way represents the position of the Laboratory, the University of California, or the U.S. Department of Energy.]

WHAT ARE THE CHANCES THAT THERE WILL BE A NUCLEAR ACCIDENT EVEN MORE SERIOUS THAN THREE-MILE ISLAND? WHAT WOULD HAPPEN IN THE EVENT OF SUCH A MAJOR ACCIDENT?

Larry Bogart. Apart from the constant contamination that will rise when it becomes necessary to dismantle the nuclear plants themselves, there is constant danger from severe nuclear accidents. A Class 9 accident, which would result in the escape of millions of curies of fresh fission products downwind, could be the greatest man-made catastrophe in history—because nuclear plants were unwisely sited close to dense populations. Escaping fission products, which are 1 million to 1 billion times more lethal than industrial poisons like cyanide, could cause health effects, at distances up to 100 miles away.

Members of the presidential Kemeny Commission which investigated Three-Mile Island believe there will be an accident more severe than Three-Mile Island soon because of basic design defects, inability of utilities to operate plants safely and failure of the Nuclear Regulatory Commission to enforce regulations.

Joseph M. Hendrie. It is difficult to provide a quantitative estimate of the risk of such an accident. However, the Nuclear Regulatory Commission's rule of thumb for achieving the "adequate protection" and "no unreasonable risk" standards for nuclear power plants (set out in the Atomic Energy Act) is that the risk to individuals should be small compared to other risks in life, and that nuclear plants should present no more societal risk than other methods available for providing bulk electricity.

Many changes have been made since the Three-Mile Island accident to prevent one like it, or a worse accident—with larger releases of radioactivity. The Nuclear Regulatory Commission has required utilities that own nuclear plants to improve operator training, operating procedures, plant staffing, safety instrumentation, radiation monitoring, control room layouts, emergency planning and numerous other features of nuclear plants.

H. G. MacPherson. Three-Mile Island was a serious accident in two ways. It was a financial disaster for the utility operating it because it lost the production of one plant indefinitely, and of another for two years, besides incurring many hundreds of millions of dollars cost of cleaning up. It also caused a severe psychological trauma to many of the local residents. However, no one was physically damaged by the accident.

Future accidents will be no more severe financially, since General Public Utilities suffered about as much as possible. The psychological effect of the next accident may be less as a result of greater familiarity with radiation. However, there can be accidents that are more serious in hurting people. There is perhaps one chance in a thousand that there will be a nuclear accident in the next twenty years that kills as many as ten people.

Although accidents of this severity are commonplace in other human activities, it is difficult to predict the public reaction to another serious reactor accident, if one should occur.

Dr. Michael G. Stevenson. The Three-Mile Island, Unit 2, accident, although serious in terms of damage to the reactor core, did not cause any significant physical health effects.

For an accident to have large public health consequences, at least some melting of the core would be required. This evidently did not occur at Three-Mile Island. A presidential commission, led by Professor Kemeny of Dartmouth College, investigated the Three-Mile Island accident and concluded that even if core melting had occurred, the probability is low that a large amount of radioactivity would escape. The Reactor Safety Study, conducted in 1974 by Professor Norman Rasmussen of the Massachusetts Institute of Technology, concluded that an accident involving core melting might occur once in 200 years with 100 reactors operating. Even then, only one out of 100 of these core melt accidents would cause more than one fatality.

CONSERVATION AND FUTURE RESOURCES

Wial THERE BE ENOUGH FOOD, energy and natural resources for the future? Some people just wonder about these questions; others actively study the probabilities and try to influence the outcome.

The experts in this section fall into the latter group. Some refer in their answers to a major government study: *The Global 2000 Report to the President*. This report, prepared during the Carter administration, projects what the world will be like in the year 2000, assuming that technology continues to develop at its present rate, that the rules of supply and demand continue to regulate prices, and that international trade continues to be relatively undisrupted. Given this status quo, the report offers the following bleak forecast:

- water supplies decreased 35 percent
- deserts expanded 20 percent
- number of animal and plant species down 15 to 20 percent
- human population swelled to 50 percent more than its 1975 level

The authors of this report do not pretend to predict that the world will continue to change at the same rate and in the same direction as it has in the past. Instead, they project what life on earth will be like in 2000 given the trends of the late 1900s. By looking ahead, researchers hope to change the present and thus make the future more livable.

Yet forecasts of the future vary enormously, and tremendous controversy exists about what steps—if any—should be taken to preserve the world's resources. Take the case of the snail darter, a fish about three inches long. This small species of perch swam into public attention during one of the nation's biggest environmental battles. The snail darter live in the Little Tennessee River, where the multi-million-dollar Tellico Dam was under construction. Environmentalists argued that the dam would destroy the snail darter's habitat and that there were equally economical alternatives to the dam. The dam's proponents countered that human benefits from the Tennessee Valley Authority's project greatly outweighed any harm that might be done to the snail darter. The Supreme Court, basing its decision upon the 1973 Endangered Species Act, decided in favor of the fish, and the dam could not be completed even though more than $100 million worth of work had already been done.

For some Americans, the snail darter's case came to symbolize environmentalists' cause gone to extremes, fighting to protect plants and animals without considering the costs to humans. Others saw the snail darter's victory as a long-awaited public realization of the damage that man has done to his world and as a first step toward reversing that damage. Like the hunters who mowed down seemingly endless herds of buffalo, modern Americans, environmentalists argue, are generally too shortsighted to know how their actions will change the shape of the future.

Lately, news reports have covered cases of environmental damage done many years ago but only recently recognized. In 1942, for example, the Hooker Chemicals & Plastics Corporation began disposing of containers of chemical wastes in the unused Love Canal in upstate New York. At the time, this disposal method was legal and seemed relatively safe. More than thirty years later, however, residents of the Love Canal area noticed bubbling pools of chemicals in their backyards and noxious fumes in their basements. The waste containers had corroded, and the leaking chemicals were a hazard to the community. Women in the Love Canal area suffered abnormally high rates of miscarriage; their children had high incidences of birth defects.

The plight of Love Canal's neighbors attracted nationwide attention. It is by no means unusual, however, for Americans to live next door to chemical waste dumps. In recent years, the Environmental Protection Agency has found more than 30,000 industrial waste dumps in the United States. Many of these dumps contain toxic chemicals that were disposed of without the proper safeguards to protect them from leaking into the environment.

In the face of the Love Canal experience and many other environmental hazards, some scientists urgently argue for technological containment and for greater safeguards to protect natural resources. Other researchers, however, point to the world's need for more food and energy resources. They contend that technology must be improved and expanded to provide even basic necessities for future generations.

What steps will be taken to protect and enhance which of our resources? The answer may depend on how nations view the problems of the future and thus how they set their priorities. Will providing energy be the single greatest challenge? Or protecting natural resources? Or supplying food for the hungry? The following experts offer their forecasts.

CONTRIBUTORS

Dr. Gilbert H. Ahlgren, retired agronomist and university chancellor, Danbury, Wisconsin

Ralph E. Bailey, Chairman, Conoco, Inc., Stamford, Connecticut

Douglas J. Bennet, Jr., former Administrator, U.S. Agency for International Development, Washington, D.C.

John F. Bookout, President, Shell Oil Company, Houston, Texas

Prof. Daniel W. Bromley, Department of Agricultural Economics, University of Wisconsin, Madison, Wisconsin

Emery N. Castle, President, Resources for the Future, Washington, D.C.

H. Laurance Fuller, President, Amoco Oil, Chicago, Illinois

Michel T. Halbouty, consulting geologist and petroleum engineer, Houston, Texas

Dr. Clifford M. Hardin, Center for the Study of American Business, Washington University, St. Louis, Missouri

Richard A. Kunin, M.D., President, Orthomolecular Medical Society; author of *Mega-Nutrition*

Sylvia Lane, Professor, Department of Agricultural Economics, University of California, Davis, California

Michael McCloskey, Executive Director, Sierra Club, San Francisco, California

John W. Megown, agricultural consultant; Chairman, Iowa Agriculture Promotion Board, Cedar Rapids, Iowa

E. Joe Middlebrooks, Dean, College of Engineering, Utah State University, Logan, Utah

Rufus E. Miles, Jr., Senior Fellow, Woodrow Wilson School of Public and International Affairs, Princeton University, Princeton, New Jersey; author of *Awakening from the American Dream*

Russell W. Peterson, President, National Audubon Society, New York, New York

Triloki N. Saraf, Representative of the Food and Agriculture Organization of the United Nations

John C. Sawhill, former U.S. Deputy Secretary of Energy; Chairman, U.S. Synthetic Fuels Corporation, Washington, D.C.

Arthur Simon, Executive Director, Bread for the World, New York, New York

Dr. Carol I. Waslien, Executive Officer, League for International Food Education, Washington, D.C.

Richard G. Woods, consultant and former U.S. Senate staff member; editor of *Future Dimensions of World Food and Population*

George Zeidenstein, President, The Population Council, New York, New York

WHAT IS THE WORLD RUNNING OUT OF IN OUR ENVIRONMENT AND AT WHAT RATE?

Douglas J. Bennet, Jr. We do not know how responsible and successful our societies will be in conserving and recycling nonrenewable resources, and in creating renewable resources. There are no reliable projections for damage to the ozone layer; consumption of oil compared with new finds; the damage done by chemicals to water supply; the ultimate effects of our present rampant global deforestation, topsoil loss and so forth. What we can project is that pressure on all of these resources will increase dramatically in the years ahead—as population increases and as demand accelerates with higher incomes around the world.

Long before we actually run out of any resources, the price is likely to go so high that severe adjustments will be required in our lifestyles. The question is whether or not we have the wisdom to start making those adjustments now so that they can be gentler ones.

Professor Daniel W. Bromley. I am rather concerned about the availability of water of sufficient quality to permit traditional uses over the long run.

In the poorer countries of the world, human wastes currently cause serious water quality problems for the vast majority of individuals—not only in rural areas but in urban centers as well. We have yet to respond to this problem in a fashion that will bring much relief.

In the industrialized countries, toxic chemicals pose a more serious threat. We are only now discovering a number of chemical residues that are capable of rendering totally unfit the majority of freshwater sources. A resource which we have taken for granted for so long may someday be unusable.

The worst of both situations may occur if chemical companies continue to relocate to the poorer countries—to avoid the more strict environmental laws in the industrialized world. In this case, the world's poor become doubly cursed.

Emery N. Castle. Natural resource specialists often classify resources as renewable and nonrenewable and this is a useful distinction for many purposes. However, it may also be a misleading distinction—unless it is recognized that all life as we know it is dependent upon the sun, which is gradually being consumed. Thus, in an ultimate sense and in the very long run, all resources are nonrenewable and are "running out."

Of the principal nonrenewable resources we probably are consuming the liquid fossil fuels more rapidly than the other nonrenewables. But it must be remembered that no one knows just how much of any resource is available at a particular time. Resources change not only with use but also with discovery—and discovery is a function of the amount of time, effort and treasure that is devoted to the search for a resource. Furthermore, the value of a resource will affect the rate of use.

We may be in greater danger of damaging some of the common property environmental resources—the atmosphere, the oceans and the soil—than we are of running out of the more conventional resources, nearly all of which have substitutes that can perform the same service, often better and more cheaply than the original.

Sylvia Lane. The world is running out of the endangered species of wildlife—the California Condor, for instance. It is also running out of various species of fish that cannot be replaced. The rate of attrition varies with each species—and for some, like the snail-darter, it is already too late. The world is also running out of: scarce mineral resources and fossil fuel resources (the United States is a major user of petroleum); arable soil; clean water; forests and some plant species, but again at varying rates.

As anything grows scarcer (if it is marketable) its price increases; less of it tends to be purchased and used; and less costly products, when available, are substituted. Thus, it is impossible to say at what rate we are running out of anything without knowing what substitutes are, and will, become available—and the rate of substitution that will prevail in each instance.

Discoveries of new technologies and the improvement of technologies have made richer life-styles possible for many people in the world since Malthus gave his dire predictions. Despite population growth, we may be able to maintain a habitable environment far into the future.

Michael McCloskey. The world is running out of species of plants and animals in the wild from which most modern foodstuffs are derived. According to *The Global 2000 Report to the President*, "four-fifths of the world's food supplies are derived from less than two dozen plant and animal species." These remaining wild gene stocks are rapidly disappearing as their habitat is being cleared for development.

Such wild stocks are critical for breeding new strains of pest-resistant plants and animals. Wilderness areas must be reserved to protect this base for the world's food supply. 15 to 20 percent of all species on earth could be extinguished in the next twenty years by the accelerating pace of development.

John W. Megown. The number one thing our own country is running out of is farmland—due to erosion and to land development.

The loss of agricultural land is a much worse problem than the energy problem. Norman Berg, Chief of the Department of Agriculture Soil Conservation Service, says, "Ten years from now, Americans could be as concerned over the loss of the nation's prime and important farmlands as they are today over shortages of oil and gasoline."

The rich, precious topsoil of our countryside is being washed into rivers and streams and blown into roadside ditches. In Iowa, one inch of topsoil is lost every twelve years, and it takes 250 to 1,000 years to rebuild one inch of topsoil. In addition, it has been estimated that we lose three million acres a year to land conversion.

It is essential that we not let the best resource in the world, our farmland, slip through our fingers. No-till and limited tillage practices must be adopted, and intelligent land-use policies must be developed to save our farmland.

E. Joe Middlebrooks. The problems associated with misuse, contamination and waste of our water supply are among the most serious problems confronting the United States, potentially more dangerous than the energy crisis. As with energy, experts have been cautioning the public for many years that there is an impending crisis. At our present rate of growth, by the turn of the century almost every section of the country will experience water shortages unless we make drastic changes in our current practices.

Intermittent droughts in various parts of the country; limited snowfall in the Rocky Mountains that leaves many of the western states vulnerable to water shortages; excess pumping of underground water in the arid western states and high plains are but a few examples of the difficulties currently facing the nation. Water mains in the older cities leak profusely, and it will cost billions of dollars to correct this waste. The groundwater supplies of many communities are being contaminated with chemicals and toxic wastes rendering them unfit for human use. This practice must be averted to avoid further diminishing our limited water supply. Conservation techniques must be implemented if we are to avoid a calamity.

The use and distribution of water has become a legal issue because of the extensive controversies arising from various distribution and use plans. For example, the proposed peripheral canal in California—transporting water from northern California to Los Angeles—has caused a great deal of controversy. Farmers have resisted the installation of coal slurry pipelines that would consume large volumes of water. Some farmers have already been forced out of business in Colorado because of the lack of water for irrigating crops. Farmers in the high plains of Nebraska, South Dakota and Texas will be forced out of business because of the depletion of the underground water tables by irrigated agriculture. The water table is dropping rapidly and the continued use of these underground water supplies will cost more and will probably also increase the cost of food. In fact, the costs of pumping the water from greater depth will probably drive the farmers out of business before the water supply is exhausted.

There are many acres of arable land that would not require irrigation, and it is likely that some plan involving the phasing out of irrigated agriculture and the use of water for other purposes will result. This is particularly true in the arid areas of the West where energy development will continue to grow. Currently, agriculture uses approximately 90 percent of the water used in the West. However, the energy development companies can afford to outbid farmers for the water and consequently, farmers will be forced out of business. It is possible that the use of new technology—such as drip irrigation—can save enough water to allow the West to continue to develop without a serious redeployment of agriculture or depreciation of agricultural activity in the western United States.

As it becomes necessary to repair existing water systems and the competition for water increases, the price of water will increase. Higher water bills will encourage all users to be more conservation conscious. Hopefully, these conservation efforts and reuse schemes will result in our averting a disaster. But, without provisions for conservation and reuse, the United States and the world will be facing a water crisis by the turn of the century.

Russell W. Peterson. The world is running out of time, that most precious of all resources. We are running out of the time we need to change dangerous present trends in population growth, resource depletion and environmental degradation. These closely related, interacting forces require an immediate worldwide response if the human species is not to exceed the capacity of the earth to support us.

According to the 1980 *Global 2000 Report to the President*, prepared with help from a dozen federal agencies, present trends must be changed without delay. If not, the outlook for food and other necessities of life in the year 2000 will be worse for many than it is today: 100 million human beings will be added each year to the world's population, and 90 percent of this growth will be in the poorest countries; the need for fuel wood (on which 25 percent of humanity depends) will exceed available supplies by 25 percent before the turn of the century; agricultural soils will deteriorate worldwide due to erosion, loss of organic matter, spread of deserts, salinization and other causes; and hundreds of thousands of species of plants and animals, perhaps 20 percent of all species that now exist, will be irretrievably lost as the world's rain forests are cut down.

These are projections, not predictions, based on the assumption that national policies will remain essentially unchanged. Policies are in fact beginning to change; in some countries, forests are being replanted after cutting, family planning is becoming better understood and practiced, and soil loss is being halted. But the rate of change must be faster, because the time left to make the necessary changes is short. We have less than a generation, maybe even less than a decade, to get ourselves and our world on a life-supporting path.

Triloki N. Saraf. Clean air, clean water and fertile farm soil are running out at an alarming rate.

Clean air and water are diminishing not only because of automobile and industrial pollution and chemical wastes, but also because of accelerated urbanization. Inadequate progress and efforts in the treatment of polluted air and water are worsening the situation. Soil degradation is taking place because of marginal lands being brought under cultivation. Underground water resources are diminishing because of over-exploitation.

[The views offered are personal views and do not necessarily represent the views of the Food and Agriculture Organization of the United Nations.]

IS THERE ENOUGH FOOD TO SUPPORT THE WORLD'S PRESENT POPULATION? WHAT WILL THE SITUATION BE IN THE YEAR 2000?

Dr. Gilbert H. Ahlgren. Food and population are directly linked. Of all the essentials for life, food is the first requirement and the most basic. Accordingly, food supply and population growth and stability go hand in hand.

In 1960 the world population was about three billon, and by the year 2000 it is expected to double to six billion. Such rapid growth will place a severe stress on food supplies. The industrialized nations of Western Europe, North America, Australia, New Zealand and Japan have available or can obtain sufficient food to supply 3000 calories or more daily to each individual. In Latin America, Africa, western Asia, Communist Asia and the non-Communist Far East, food is in short supply. This is the area that gives rise to the statement that "two-thirds of the people of the world go to bed hungry every night."

Bringing the food budget into balance to meet the needs is perhaps the greatest challenge the world has ever faced. Best estimates indicate that food supplies must be more than doubled, perhaps tripled, by the beginning of the next century if the growing needs are to be met at no more than minimal levels.

There is now about one acre of land available for crop production for each person. By the year 2000 this will drop to one-half acre. In addition, there are the food resources obtained from the ocean, lakes and streams, but these contribute less than 1 percent of our total supply.

The world appears to have adequate resources in the way of land, water, climate and knowledge to feed the six billion inhabitants expected in the year 2000. However, improved crop production techniques must be applied much more widely, food preservation and distribution upgraded, and resource shifts made realities.

Some actions that a hungry world can take to accomplish this gigantic task still exist, but major efforts must be made, and world cooperation is a requirement.

New land may be brought into cultivation. Thoughtful estimates indicate this ranges from one to two billion acres, but most is in the tropical areas where soil improvement and management is much more difficult and costly than in the temperate zones. Also, our oceans and other water resources can be managed or farmed to double, perhaps, the output from this source.

More intensive use of the present cropland is the best hope for a steady increase in production, however. Much will depend on more widespread use of scientific agricultural advances. These include new varieties of crops, fertilizer use, irrigation, pest and weed control, mechanization and double cropping. Doubling production from this source is possible if the incentives are favorable.

There probably will be a steady shift from livestock agriculture toward crops for direct human consumption. Crops for direct consumption provide from five to ten times more calories than when converted to food by way of livestock. However, it must be recalled that already—on a world basis—over 90 percent of all food is consumed directly as plants or their products.

Increased attention can also be given to reducing food waste as it is harvested, processed, stored and distributed. Some statistics place total food losses in these areas at from 10 to 20 percent.

There are many unknowns in any predictions of food production. For example, will global water resources be adequate? As water table levels decline in some major cropping areas, will means be found for replenishment? A major drought could occur. What priority will the food producer receive for energy if supplies are disrupted and scarce? Will there be enough fertilizer in the right place at the right time? Can severe outbreaks of disease and pests be controlled so that huge crop losses will not occur? Is there an adequate political and social resolve among the nations of the world to meet the food supply challenge? These questions can only be left to speculation.

The world will not be free of hunger at any time in the foreseeable future. Even in the industrialized nations diets may be less varied and palatable as fewer livestock products are available. In the long run, there appears little reason for optimism for a world capable of adequately feeding its human population—unless that population can stabilize soon.

Douglas J. Bennet, Jr. Today, the world produces about 3,000 calories per day for every man, woman and child on the planet—enough for a reasonably adequate diet. The problem is that these calories are maldistributed. Some of us enjoy rich, calorie inefficient diets, with a good deal of meat and protein, while others go hungry.

By the year 2000, current estimates suggest that there will be both more food and more people, so that per capita availabilities will be scarcely greater than they are today. The maldistribution problem will probably be even greater because rising per capita incomes in some parts of the world, including our own, will mean greater and greater demand for the kind of diet most Americans now take for granted. In sub-Saharan Africa, and in other very large parts of the world, scarcity and famine will continue *if* there is not a substantial acceleration of production above present trends.

My own view is that such an acceleration is entirely possible—provided we capture the benefits of modern agricultural technology, make an adequate investment to put that technology to work, and ensure that the developing countries provide adequate incentives to their farmers.

Emery N. Castle. Is there enough food for everyone in the world to eat what—and as much as—they would like? No. Is there enough food to permit the world's present population to exist? Yes.

Based on the experience of the past two decades, I am cautiously optimistic about the year 2000. Per capita consumption of calories increased during the 1970s in spite of severe energy problems and mismanagement of agriculture and food policy by many countries. Agricultural research has increased and the rate of population growth has slowed dramatically in many populous countries. Even so, the outcome in the year 2000 is by no means clear and will be influenced greatly by the level of world poverty generally.

If incomes can be increased so that food can be purchased, it appears there are enough natural resources available to permit substantial increases in output. Useful production also can be increased through improvements in food distribution and storage.

Dr. Clifford M. Hardin. The present population of the world is being fed in some manner. There is, however, serious malnutrition—especially in those countries with exploding populations.

Part of the problem is uneven distribution. Even so, it is probable that not enough food is being produced to meet the real nutritional needs of all people. The United States and other advanced countries simply cannot begin to produce enough food to meet the nutritional needs of the world—even if some magic way can be found to finance it. If starvation and malnutrition are to be stemmed, the developing countries simply have to learn to produce more from their own soil.

It is my conviction that sufficient food-producing resources and technology exist today to provide for the feeding of whatever number of people may live in the year 2000, in a manner better than mankind has ever been fed. That is not a prediction, but rather, a statement of potential that can be realized if the majority of developing countries advance as far as a few already have. Taiwan and Korea are cases in point.

The situation in the year 2000 will depend on whether the political leadership in developing countries is sufficiently strong and enlightened to bring about the necessary improvements.

Richard A. Kunin, M.D. Food supply is adequate for the present but will be inadequate—at the present rate of population growth—unless new areas of cultivation and new varieties of edible plants are discovered. Fortunately, these are definitely being developed at the present time.

Sylvia Lane. There is enough food to support the world's present population. The problem lies in the fact that the very poor cannot afford to buy enough food or do not have any other means of access to it. "According to the World Bank, approximately 800 million people in the non-Socialist developing world live in such absolute poverty that they cannot provide themselves with even a minimally adequate diet."*

In physical terms, there may still be enough food to provide a minimally adequate diet for all the world's inhabitants in the year 2000, despite present rates of population growth. But, unless there are unprecedented and unanticipated increases in food production on the part of the developing countries themselves, the number of those who are undernourished will increase markedly—under a pessimistic set of assumptions, the number may double.

John W. Megown. It is not a matter of having enough food to support the world's present and future population. The real problem is: what type of food will be available; and will it be available where needed.

The world is not short of carbohydrates, but it is short of protein-rich foods.

It is very expensive to ship whole grains, like wheat and corn, to the countries that need food. Furthermore, the content of starch in whole grains is very high and the protein is low.

Corn is generally not considered to be a particularly good food for humans, but it does have the potential of being an excellent high-protein foodstuff, if modified and concentrated. One bushel of corn, when processed to make alcohol, produces—in addition to the alcohol—eighteen to twenty pounds of food-stuff that has a protein content of 27 to 32 percent. The original corn contained only 8 to 10 percent protein. The concentrated product can be shipped at much less cost than whole grains.

*Quoted from the *Preliminary Report of the Presidential Commission on World Hunger*, Washington, D.C., December 1979.

By processing feed grains in this way, the United States might be able to better supply the food needs of the world. And the alcohol (used as a fuel) might help to solve the energy crisis, now and into the next century.

Triloki N. Saraf. Theoretically, there is enough food produced to support the world's present population. However, millions are starving or malnourished because they are too poor to buy food. There is over-consumption in some rich countries and malnourishment in poor countries. Poor countries consume cereals directly as food—in rich countries cereals are converted into meat. This indirect consumption requires greater quantities of cereals being used to feed one human being.

The problem of malnutrition could be solved if only about 2 percent of the world food output could be redirected to the malnourished. This, however, is unrealistic. The only solution to the world food problem is for developing countries to become self-reliant in food production—and create conditions under which all sections of their populations have sufficient incomes to meet their nutritional needs.

There will, and should, be enough food in the year 2000 with the world population exceeding 6 billion. But, that will require a rapid increase in food production in developing countries. This, in turn, requires that certain measures be taken, both by developing and developed countries, including: an adequate increase in agricultural investments and inputs; research and development; external assistance and transfer of agricultural technologies; and improvement in food storage facilities, agricultural trade arrangements, and income distribution among and within countries.

[The views offered are personal views and do not necessarily represent the views of the Food and Agriculture Organization of the United Nations.]

Arthur Simon. There is enough food *produced* to provide every person in the world with at least minimally adequate nutrition, and that situation can be expected to obtain in the year 2000, as well. However, providing such nutrition to everyone would require a massive shift in the diets of the affluent (less meat, more cereals) and a system of distribution that defies all reasonable expectation. Consequently, increased food production of food in developing countries is a critical aspect of improving the distribution of food. But increased production by itself will not greatly reduce hunger, because those with money can buy the food they need, while those with too little money cannot.

The relationship between income and hunger helps us to understand the graph below: this shows per capita food production rising slightly since 1960 in developing countries as a whole, despite a drop in per capita food production between 1979 and 1981. The graph appears to indicate that the problem of hunger is easing, and in some countries

FOOD AND POPULATION BALANCE
IN THE DEVELOPING COUNTRIES
Indexes, 1961–1965 Average = 100

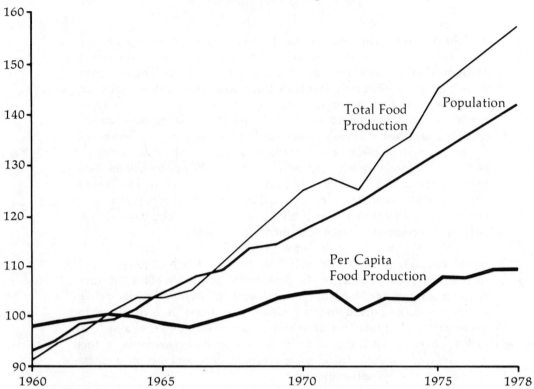

SOURCE: AID data for non-communist countries only
U.S. International Development Cooperation

that is the case. The graph fails, however, in two respects. First, averages conceal disparities and do not reflect the fact that many countries, notably most of those in Africa, are steadily dropping in per capita food production. Second, as some people in the developing countries become affluent or even less poor, they buy more food. Increases in food production do not necessarily provide more food for those who are malnourished. Sometimes more food produced means more export sales—or more food for a minority of persons with rising standards of living—but less food for the rest of the population. In developing countries as a whole the demand for food (that is, effective market demand, reflecting purchasing power) is rising faster than food production.

This explains why developing countries are increasing food imports at an alarming rate; from scarcely a trickle before the middle of this century to an estimated 96 million metric tons for crop year 1980–81, according to the United Nations Food and Agriculture Organization. If the trend were to continue, they would import 185 million metric tons by the year 2000. The trend will not continue that long, however, because low-income developing countries cannot afford to pay for such imports. A "crash point" would come first. Consequently, it makes sense—both on moral and economic grounds—for the United States to do much more than it has been doing to encourage more self-reliant, equitable growth in the developing countries.

Dr. Carol I. Waslien. In light of current trends in food production and population growth, it can be anticipated that regional shortages of food will continue into the twenty-first century, most strikingly in Africa south of the Sahara. I do not envisage worldwide shortage and I would anticipate that the overall food supply of most countries would have improved.

Inadequate purchasing power is the major constraint to adequate food intake, while inadequate intake of vitamins and minerals may more often be related to lack of information on the nutrient content of foods.

Richard G. Woods. In general, sufficient food is available for the world's people, but the production and distribution of food is highly uneven. While the North American granary produces food in such quantities that marketing of surpluses is frequently a problem, many underdeveloped nations, with little to sell internationally in exchange for food, pursue a domestic "cheap food" policy prompted by the political pressures of urban masses. The result is that domestic agriculture in poor countries is undermined by lack of incentives; so farmers continue relatively unproductive agronomic methods.

Even where developing countries produce enough food for their people, it is common to find inadequate distribution of food because of such handicaps as poor markets, insufficient roads and transportation, and inadequate food storage facilities. Simple transfer of food from rich to poor countries, while sometimes necessary to prevent disaster, does nothing to alter the vulnerability of the food-deficit countries.

The know-how and the resources exist to feed the people of the world now, and in the year 2000. Whether or not mankind succeeds with this task depends most of all on appropriate political behavior.

Success will require substantial cooperation and coordination on the part of organizations, governments, and factions within countries. Will the thirty to forty food-deficit countries have the political courage to foster domestic agriculture and related infrastructure in order to become more self-reliant? Will the more affluent countries be willing to part with sufficient resources to provide much-needed development aid? Will development assistance be administered in such a way as to be effective? Will trade barriers be removed so as to facilitate international exchange? Will critical agricultural research be undertaken soon enough to pay dividends when they are most needed? Will private enterprise be permitted, by governments in the developing world, to make its contributions to the solution of food problems? Will political leaders refrain from using food as a weapon against their adversaries when disruption of the food supply could cause real nutritional hardship or even starvation? Will prime farmland be protected from depletion and loss to nonfarming uses? Will the many public and private foreign assistance organizations coordinate and stabilize their programs to maximize their effectiveness?

The manner in which questions such as these are answered in the years ahead will determine the extent of human well-being insofar as food is concerned.

George Zeidenstein. The world is not one political, economic or social unit. Therefore, the adequacy of food supply must be assessed at national, household and individual levels—as well as at the global level.

The global food supply appears to be adequate to feed the world's current population, but food production is grossly deficient in developing countries. The situation at the global level is unlikely to worsen, but improvements in food-deficient developing countries will require greater acceleration in their food production than they have ever achieved in the past.

During 1963–75, global food production increased at about 2.6 percent per year while the world's population increased at about 1.9 percent per year. In fact, *per capita* food production has been increasing—and global food production has been higher than the annual rate of the world's population growth.

At the national level, the annual rate of increase in food production—even in developing countries—has kept pace with the annual rate of population growth. But, due to slight improvements in per capita food consumption, developing countries imported about 45 million tons of food grains per year during 1977–79 (in comparison with about 15 million tons per year during 1960–63). Annual food imports averaged about 1 million tons for India and 6 million tons for thirty-seven other low-income developing countries. Food imports were equivalent to about 4 percent of their annual consumption.

Food import is not limited to developing countries. During 1977–79, average annual food imports were estimated to be about 26 million tons for countries in Western Europe, 12 million tons for Eastern Europe, 18 million tons for the Soviet Union, and 9 million tons for China. Most countries, except North America, Oceania, Thailand and Argentina, imported food during this period.

Food trade has increased considerably over the years, reaching about 181 million tons or 14 percent of global production in 1979. This has created major pressure on grain handling and distribution facilities—which are more important constraints than food procurement itself.

There are major differences in food consumption between rich and poor households within a country—and sometimes between individuals within the same household. The potential food consumption at the individual level depends upon the availability of food at the right place, right time and right price. But actual food consumption depends, in addition, upon people's dietary preferences and their social customs. In many countries, deficiencies in food consumption, within the same household, are greater among women and children than among men.

Because the minimum requirement of food varies among individuals, it is difficult to estimate accurately the number of people below the critical level of food intake; however, this number is estimated to have been about 415 million people in developing countries during 1974–76. In many developed countries—for example, in the United States—it is estimated that more calories of energy are used in food production and distribution than the food itself yields at the table. Per capita food consumption in developed countries is estimated at about 700 kilograms per year during 1977–79, which is about three times higher than the corresponding average for developing countries (211 kilograms per person per year).

There are many uncertainties in projecting the adequacy of food supply for the year 2000. The total food requirement at the global level in 2000 will simply be the product of the projected world population and the anticipated per capita food consumption. The anticipated deficit (or surplus) will be the difference between the anticipated food production and the total food requirement. Thus, the adequacy of food supply by the year 2000 will depend upon: the increase in total population, increase in per capita food consumption, and the anticipated increase in food production.

There are indications that the annual rate of population growth has started declining and will continue to decline. The speed of this decline will determine the eventual size of the global population and, consequently, the total food requirement in the long run. But, the speed of decline in the population growth rate will have very little effect on the size of the world's population in the year 2000. Due to built-in momentum of growth, the world's population in the year 2000 is likely to be somewhere between 5.9 billion and 6.4 billion, depending on whether replacement-level fertility is reached by the year 2000 or by 2040. A difference of about 500 million people, at the current level of per capita food consumption of about 333 kilograms per year (weighted average), will require about 166 million tons of additional food grains. The actual impact will be less—because most of this population growth will be concentrated in developing countries with lower per capita food consumption.

Global population in the year 2000 is more likely to be around 6.2 billion, that is, an increase of about 50 percent during the next two decades. (This assumes that replacement-level fertility will be reached by 2020–2025). Therefore, global food production must also increase by about 50 percent during the next two decades to maintain the current level of per capita food consumption.

Total food production during 1963–75 increased at an average rate of 2.6 percent per year. A continuation of this rate of increase in annual food production during the next two decades would increase global food production by about 67 percent and, thus, would be more than sufficient to maintain current levels of per capita consumption. The situation in the year 2000 is unlikely to worsen, even with a slight decline in the annual rate of increase in total food production. With some acceleration, especially in developing countries, the per capita food supply by the year 2000 is likely to improve.

However, in developing countries, the gap between production and overall consumption is likely to be greater than the current deficit. Per capita food consumption in these countries is likely to increase during the next two decades. The extent of this increase will depend upon the rate of their economic growth and upon more equitable distribution of its benefits within countries.

The economic conditions of people, their level of food consumption, and their demographic behavior are all interrelated. For example: improvement in people's economic conditions within a country is likely to increase per capita demand for food. At the same time it is also likely to modify their demographic behavior. Therefore, the net effect of an increase in per capita food consumption on the total food requirement in developing countries will not be of the same order of magnitude as would be expected under the assumption that increase in income and population growth are factors that operate independently. However, according to one estimate, the deficit of cereals for ninety developing countries for the year 2000 is projected to be about 88 million tons, which is about 10 percent of their anticipated domestic consumption.

The technical know-how is more than adequate to increase food production to meet global requirements for the year 2000. The better-off or the middle-income developing countries could meet their food deficit by purchasing food supplied in the open market at international prices. The low-income developing countries would not be able to use this option due to lack of financial resources in foreign exchange. This option will be further restricted due to increased demand for food in food-deficient developed countries in Western Europe, Eastern Europe, the USSR and other centrally planned economies. Food aid from developed countries to the low-income countries might provide some short-term relief, but it cannot provide a long-term solution because of the financial costs of transporting and distributing food supplies. (These costs are sometimes higher than the cost of the commodities themselves.) Thus, the adequacy of food supply in the low-income developing countries in the year 2000 will depend upon the extent to which the rate of annual food production in these countries is accelerated.

The thirty-eight developing countries classified as "low-income," contain about 30 percent of the world's population. According to one study, food production in these countries by the year 1990 is projected to be about 374 million tons, while consumption is projected at between 386 million and 448 million tons—depending upon the level of increase in income-related per capita consumption. Therefore, this study projected a food deficit of 12 to 74 million tons by the year 1990, provided food production during 1975–90 in these countries continued to increase at the same rate as it did during 1960–75.

Therefore, an acceleration in food production will be required to meet the demand for food generated by economic development. The rate of economic development in these countries, however, will also have some implications for the rate of population growth during the next two decades.

There *is* a potential for increasing food production in these countries— by increasing the output per unit of land. (For example, the area under irrigation in India is estimated to be about 135 million acres, compared with 40 million acres in the United States.) However, there are many constraints to such an increase, some of which can be removed by simple transfer of financial and technical resources from rich to poor countries. But an acceleration of food production will require a strong political will and important changes in social organization, especially in customs governing inheritance, tenancy and ownership of land.

WILL WE HAVE ENOUGH ENERGY SOURCES FOR COOKING, HEATING AND OTHER DOMESTIC USES TWENTY YEARS FROM NOW?

Ralph E. Bailey. By definition, there will be enough energy in twenty years. Prices will be bid up to the point where supply matches demand. The issues are (1) the cost of energy, and (2) the sources of energy.

The real cost of energy (after adjusting for inflation) will rise over the next twenty years. Currently, we are heavily dependent on oil and natural gas—and increasing prices will be necessary merely to maintain present domestic production over time from these depleting resources, irrespective of pricing actions taken by foreign oil producers.

Increasing real prices for oil and natural gas have several implications. (1) Nonenergy substitutes become more practical. The major nonenergy substitute is capital. Examples of capital substituting for energy include extra insulation to reduce heating requirements, and radial tires (instead of cheaper bias ply) to improve automobile fuel-use efficiency. (2) Coal becomes relatively more attractive over a wider range of applications. Coal has an economic advantage in large facilities run at high operating rates (such as base load capacity for electricity generation) where lower fuel costs can offset higher capital investments. As oil and natural gas prices rise, coal becomes more advantageous in smaller (industrial) facilities. (3) Electricity (generated by fuels other than oil and gas) becomes more competitive versus direct oil or gas use. (4) Unconventional energy sources begin to become economically viable. (5) Assuming oil imports also increase in price, import dependence should decline as alternatives become more competitive.

As a result of increasing real prices for oil over time, twenty years from now (1) society will be less energy intensive; (2) oil and gas consumption will decrease as a percentage of total energy use, but will still be significant; (3) coal consumption will grow strongly as electricity comprises a greater share of total energy, coal use in industry expands, and some coal synthetics are likely to become commercially viable; (4) the need for energy sources such as nuclear power to fuel electricity generation will increase (though the prospects for nuclear power remain clouded); (5) some unconventional energy sources, most likely including shale oil and some coal synthetics, should become commercially viable; and (6) oil imports are likely to decline.

Douglas J. Bennet, Jr. Twenty years from now, most Americans will have enough energy resources for domestic use—provided they can pay the bill. Even today, however, in large parts of the world fuel wood, the standard domestic energy source, is becoming scarcer and scarcer. We anticipate a 50 percent reduction in the globe's tropical forests by the year 2000, largely because of fuel wood cutting.

In developing countries, the enormous cost of finding fuel—and environmental damage from deforestation—will retard economic development. This, in turn, will seriously damage our own capacity to export.

John F. Bookout. Yes—twenty years from now, we *will* have energy resources sufficient for domestic use.

Energy demand is expected to grow at a lower rate than in the past, and energy supplies should increase between now and the year 2000, according to Shell Oil Company forecasts.

In the American domestic market, new home construction standards, appliance improvements and some consumer constraints should continue the trend, begun in 1972, toward lower growth rates in energy demand.

The growing popularity of diesel automobiles and more efficient gasoline-powered cars, plus other conservation efforts, should reduce energy demand for personal transportation.

Energy supply over the next twenty years should meet demand, but much will come from new sources. Of total domestic oil and liquid supplies in the year 2000, 37 percent should come through new technology: enhanced recovery, shale oil and coal liquids. Crude imports should decline mainly due to the use of coal liquids and shale oil.

Natural gas availability and use should decline about 20 percent over the next twenty years. Synthetic gas (from coal) and natural gas (from underground formations, which create production difficulties) should contribute about 30 percent of total domestic supply.

Emery N. Castle. Yes, there will be plenty of energy for domestic purposes twenty years from now. The only question is whether there will be sufficient energy—and at a low enough cost—to permit the kind of industrial growth here, in other industrial countries, and in the third world, that has characterized the United States during the past two or three decades.

I am quite optimistic that there will be enough energy, at a sufficiently favorable price, to permit quite substantial economic growth. That optimism is based on two considerations. First, recent experience has demonstrated that realistic energy prices will bring about responses both in the use of energy as well as in its supply. Second, the pattern of growth and change will reflect the availability and cost of energy—and both (energy availability and cost) will also affect the kinds of innovations that are forthcoming as well as our patterns of consumption.

Therefore, I believe we will have enough energy for cooking and heating, but the way we cook and heat may change as a result of a relatively more scarce resource.

H. Laurance Fuller. Yes, we believe that domestic energy supplies, coupled with some level of imports of oil and natural gas, will be sufficient to satisfy United States requirements for energy over the next twenty years and beyond.

We estimate that United States demand for energy will increase at about 1 percent per year during the next twenty years. We believe that demand for oil will decline at an average rate of about 1 percent per year during this period, and that demand for natural gas will remain about constant. We forecast domestic production of oil—including modest amounts of synthetic oil derived from oil shale, tar sands, coal and additional crude oil recovered by advanced techniques—will remain essentially constant over the next twenty years. We expect that the quantities of oil imported from other countries will be somewhat lower in the year 2000 than they are today. There may be a slight decline in domestic natural gas production, but increased quantities of natural gas should be available from Canada and Mexico.

In the future, more of our total energy will be supplied by coal, nuclear power and renewable energy forms such as hydropower and solar power. Coal supplied about 21 percent of United States energy in 1980, but is forecast to supply almost 32 percent in 2000. Nuclear power is expected to increase its share from 3 percent to about 8 percent, and hydropower, geothermal and solar from 4 percent to about 7 percent.

Michel T. Halbouty. The United States has a composite energy base (mix) which will produce enough energy for our domestic residential, industrial and military complex needs well beyond twenty years from now.

We have scarcely begun to develop and produce all of our vast natural resources. The United States is one of the richest energy nations in the world. Our energy potential for future production of oil and gas is tremendous. Our coal reserves alone could provide us with consumable energy for another 400 years. Our capacity for nuclear power is huge. Approximately 12 percent of the United States electric energy is provided by the seventy-two current operating reactors. Without this energy source we would need an additional 2 million barrels of oil per day.

Using present day nuclear reactors, we can generate electric power for another fifty to sixty years. However, by applying the breeder reactor, this time frame can be expanded to several centuries. And synthetics and renewable energy sources hold great promise for our energy future.

John W. Megown. We will not have sufficient energy for cooking, heating and other domestic uses, such as transportation, twenty years from now, if the United States continues to depend largely on the use of petroleum and natural gas.

It is absolutely essential that alternative energy sources be developed as quickly as possible.

At the present time, government has not given, and is not giving, adequate support to the development of synthetic fuels and agricultural energy sources to help solve the developing energy crisis.

For instance, the production of ethanol and methanol from grain, food wastes, lumber waste, forage crops, sewerage, etc., could help to greatly reduce this nation's dependence on petroleum and natural gas. However, it is a matter of commitment as to whether, or not, we will find the ways to have enough energy during the next twenty years and beyond.

Unfortunately, a dangerous sense of complacency prevails in this country, and this could slow down the process of solving this problem.

Rufus E. Miles, Jr. A simple answer to the question is: "Yes, we will have enough energy, but it will cost much more than it does today." Higher costs will mean that consumers will have to take far greater care to avoid wasting energy than they have been accustomed to taking in the past.

During the rest of the twentieth century, conservation of energy by domestic, commercial, industrial and governmental (including military) users is, by all odds, the most effective strategy for both individuals and the nation in achieving an adequate level of comfort and mobility at acceptable cost. Simultaneously, conservation can reduce the nation's vulnerability to the economic chaos that could occur from the abrupt cut-off of oil imports. Conservation is not now receiving the emphasis it deserves.

It is not useful to try to frighten people into thinking that we will run out of any one energy source, suddenly, some time in the next two decades. This can only lead to an overemphasis on crash programs to provide such substitute sources as fission and fusion energy and synthetic fuels. It is also unwise to overemphasize the very rapid exploration and exploitation of all remaining domestic oil reserves. Both oil and natural gas should be used with an increasing realization of how precious they are—and with a sense of responsibility for preserving as much as possible of what remains for our children and grandchildren. Thus, it is important to use great care and imagination in saving all the energy we can.

Higher prices alone will move us in this direction, but not nearly as fast as this combination of motives would: high prices, deep concern for the welfare of our children and grandchildren, and the realization that energy conservation may contribute mightily to the avoidance of World War III—a war that could be ignited by excessive Western dependence on Middle East oil.

Triloki N. Saraf. There will be enough energy supplies for domestic use in the year 2000. Coal alone will be enough if adequate investment in coal conversion technology takes place.

However, in order to assure sustained energy supplies beyond the year 2000, certain measures have to be taken now and in the near future: conservation measures; exploration of new supplies of fossil fuel sources; research and development of renewable energy sources (solar, geothermal, tidal wave, wind power, biomass, etc.); and investments in synthetic fuels as well as in hydro and nuclear power projects.

The greatest environmental danger is large-scale denudation of forests in developing countries, to produce wood for cooking and other domestic uses.

[The views offered are personal views and do not necessarily represent the views of the Food and Agriculture Organization of the United Nations.]

John C. Sawhill. The problem is not an energy shortage; it is an oil shortage. Twenty years from now we will be well on our way to substituting a variety of other fuels for oil.

Therefore, the answer to the question of whether or not we will have energy sources available for domestic use twenty years from now is—yes.

POLITICS, GOVERNMENT AND FOREIGN AFFAIRS

*T*HE UNITED STATES GOVERNMENT has grown in size and complexity in the last 50 years, and many Americans want to know who really runs our country. Does the average citizen still have impact on what happens in Washington? Most of our contributors imply that we can have impact on our government; we just have to be more organized than we used to be in reaching our legislators and our president. Several cite the growing importance of special interest groups, whose lobbyists vie for access to congressmen and senators and work very hard to get the laws they want and quash the ones not in their interest. Another expert feels that our government is still working pretty much as the Constitution ordained with each of the three branches—administrative, legislative and judicial—functioning in the traditional system of checks and balances, with all three very responsive to the electorate. Curtis B. Gans points out that on one level, the people, through their votes and public opinion polls, remain sovereign, but that on other levels, official organs of government, interest groups, business, labor and the media have direct control or influence on what happens in the United States. Leon Jaworski, however, singles out the Supreme Court as wielding the greatest power in shaping the nature of our democracy.

Several contributors go on to explain how the Supreme Court chooses the cases it hears. Others present new ways of selecting our presidents which might prove more efficient and less costly and possibly produce candidates the electorate could vote for instead of against. Yet, most experts agree that changing either the term or the method we use to elect a president is extremely unlikely in the near future since getting agreement on any single method would be difficult.

Watergate, Koreagate, Abscam—names that suggest pervading corruption—have disillusioned many Americans. Stuart E. Eizenstat says that, on the whole, elected officials are dedicated, not corrupt, while Hugh S. Sidey asks: Could corporate officials pass the conflict of interest scrutiny that Cabinet officers must undergo? Other contributors to this section are not as confident about the integrity of our politicians, urging new, enforceable laws that are truly enforced. Exposure and public trial for corrupt officials are the only deterrents, says Leon Jaworski.

Americans are also concerned with our country's performance on the international level. Contributors outline some of the most serious problems in this area, including the arms race, renewed nationalism on the part of the United States and other countries which often puts national interests before world peace, learning to deal with other countries as a great but no longer dominant power, and an exaggerated reliance on military force to achieve national objectives. Tad Szulc says we have a lack of credibility in the eyes of other countries, while Prof. Donald Brandon cites a lack of a diplomatic tradition which should combine short and long term objectives, principle and power, idealism and realism.

Most of our experts support the United Nations and plead for greater support from and use by the United States and other major powers. Although several say the effectiveness of the UN may have deteriorated in the past decade, they point out we would have been worse off without it.

The major thrust of both American diplomacy and the UN is, of course, to avert war. How serious is the threat of a major war and who will be the combatants? A war between China and Russia is not seen as probable by most of our contributors, although tensions exist. They add that Russia's satellites could well be a hindrance in a war, not a benefit. Harrison E. Salisbury, however, disagrees and offers a different view on this question. Almost all, including Salisbury, see selling arms to China as detrimental to the cause of peace and to the United States.

Our experts also discuss the vulnerability of our nuclear plants to saboteurs and terrorists. And, in tune with the recent worldwide protests and concern about nuclear war, they give their views on the results of such a war. Not surprisingly, most see unspeakable horror, both in the number of casualties and the condition of the world afterward. Yet, a few of our experts do see recovery after a nuclear holocaust as possible.

Espionage in real life can be stranger than fiction. Our contributors will tell you how many spies we have in this country, what they are out to do, and what you can do if you think you are being spied upon by anybody—the FBI, the CIA or foreign agents.

AMERICAN POLITICS

*B*EGINNING A FULL TEN MONTHS before the November 1980 elections, Jimmy Carter, Ronald Reagan, John Anderson and a host of other presidential hopefuls lavished attention upon the American electorate. From Carter's initial vow to beat Ted Kennedy in the primaries ("I'll whip his ass") to Reagan's persuasive presentation in the final debates ("Are you better off than you were four years ago?"), the candidates argued, appealed, threatened and exhorted to win votes. In the end, however, only about half of all Americans eligible to vote bothered to cast their ballots.

Have Americans become apathetic about politics in general—and presidential elections in particular? Historically, the ballot has been a prized right of citizenship and the symbol of democratic politics at work. Blacks endured threats and violence in order to cast their votes at segregated polling sites; women went to jail to earn the right to vote. Today political pressure has expanded the electorate to include all citizens over eighteen years of age, regardless of race, sex or income. Yet the proportion of eligible voters who actually cast their ballots has failed to show corresponding growth. In 1880, for example, an estimated 79.4 percent of all eligible voters cast their ballots in the election that brought James Garfield to office. In 1980, on the other hand, only about 53.2 percent of the eligible electorate participated in the presidential election.

Wooing voters to the polls is an increasing problem in a system that depends upon voter interest and participation. Candidates have begun to measure their strength not only by how many supporters they have but also by how likely their supporters are to translate backing into ballots. By these calculations, a candidate with widespread support among senior citizens may be better off than a candidate with equally widespread support among young voters. A census survey of voters in the 1976 election showed that over 60 percent of those sixty-five years of age and older reported voting, but only about 38 percent of those eighteen to twenty years of age cast ballots.

Winning the popular vote, however, is only half of the presidential hopeful's battle. Democrat Samuel Tilden discovered that in 1876 when he won the majority of votes in the presidential election but his opponent, Rutherford Hayes, moved into the White House. Incumbent President Grover Cleveland realized it when he had to give up his office to Benjamin Harrison even though Harrison had won fewer popular votes. In the most recent election, Jimmy Carter acknowledged it when he conceded defeat to Ronald Reagan even before many of the polls in the Western states had closed. No matter how many votes Carter could have won in the West, he knew he would still lose in the electoral college.

The electoral college remains as the last hurdle in the race for the highest office. Even after all the party primaries—and candidates fought a record number of thirty-four state primaries in the 1980 election— and all of the anxiety at the polls, it is still the electoral college that finally determines who will be president. Voters at the polls do not actually cast their ballots for the president and vice-president but for the party representatives from their state who will vote in the electoral college. Since each state is allowed as many representatives in the electoral college as it has in Congress, some populous states have far more influence in the electoral college than others. When too many of these large states are lost, the whole election is lost.

In all but three elections, the electoral college has decided on the same candidates as the popular voters. According to the Constitution, however, the members of the electoral college can vote for people other than the candidates they are pledged to. Therefore, whatever the returns of the November election, the new president is not officially elected until the president of the Senate counts the electoral college votes on 6 January. If there is a tie in the electoral college, the House of Representatives decides the election.

Despite all the safeguards built into the American political system, no one has yet found a way to eliminate corruption from public office. The scandals that ousted former President Richard Nixon and former Vice-President Spiro Agnew have brought government officials under a more watchful public eye. Yet, as Nixon's supporters argued, scandals have touched the government many times in the past and will probably continue to do so in the future. If the recent Abscam convictions are any evidence, corruption is still a serious problem.

Some people claim that they have become so disenchanted by American politics that they have lost interest even in voting. Others stress the importance of voting and of working within the system to improve it. In this section, experts discuss the problems of contemporary American politics: how the government works, whether it works effectively and ways it might work better.

CONTRIBUTORS

John E. Aldrich, Associate Professor of Political Science, University of Minnesota, Minneapolis, Minnesota; author, *Before the Convention Stategies and Choices in Presidential Nomination Campaigns*

James David Barber, James. B. Duke Professor of Political Science and Policy Studies, Duke University, Durham, North Carolina

William Buchanan, Professor of Politics, Washington and Lee University, Lexington, Virginia

Bruce A. Campbell, Director, Survey Research Center, University of Georgia, Athens, Georgia

C. Joe Carter, Ph.D., Professor of Government, Adams State College, Alamosa, Colorado

Reo M. Christenson, Professor of Political Science, Miami University, Oxford, Ohio

Alan Clem, Professor of Political Science, University of South Dakota, Vermillion, South Dakota

David Cohen, President, Common Cause, Washington, D.C.

Stuart E. Eizenstat, formerly Chief Domestic Policy Adviser with the Carter Administration; now practicing law in Washington, D.C.

Curtis B. Gans, Director, Committee for the Study of the American Electorate, Washington, D.C.

Leon Jaworski, lawyer; formerly Director, Watergate Special Prosecution Force, and Special Counsel, House Committee on Standards of Official Conduct

Malcolm E. Jewell, Professor of Political Science, University of Kentucky, Lexington, Kentucky

Hugh S. Sidey, correspondent and author, Washington, D.C.

Susan Welch, Happold Professor of Political Science, University of Nebraska, Lincoln, Nebraska

WHO ACTUALLY GOVERNS THE UNITED STATES?

C. Joe Carter, Ph.D. The United States of America is actually governed by a large number of special interest groups. These include farmers, ranchers, teachers, laborers, skilled workers, professionals, environmentalists, organized religions and businesses. The special organizations provide information, financial backing and campaign workers to help office seekers become officeholders. They do not have to ask for favors or support as they have cultivated friends in government who sympathize with their goals and keep their welfare in mind.

Every person in this country is represented by several groups and these groups know who their friends are when legislation is pending or a policy change is being considered.

David Cohen. We Americans are living in a special interest state. The special interests are economic, occupational and regional, as well as state and local governments. Together, they now dominate government policy-making on domestic issues. They form political action committees (PACs) to funnel campaign contributions to elected office-holders which give them special access and enable them to influence actions in Congress. The escalating amounts of money devoted to influencing the system and the intensity of the competing and conflicting demands of these interest groups—both private and public—have led to government by interest veto. The power they gain fuels inflation, squeezes subsidies out of tight budgets, and continues a tax system based on narrow favors rather than on equity. As a result, our representative government is rapidly becoming a government of the PACs, by the PACs and for the PACs.

Stuart E. Eizenstat. Our system of government, with its divided powers at the national level—with the executive, legislative and judicial branches sharing governmental authority—and its federal system of authority dispersed between national, state and local governments, precludes a simple answer to this question. Governing authority in America is shared to a greater degree than in any other democracy, among the president, Congress, the courts, governors, mayors and county officials.

While the citizens of the United States are at one level the governed, it has been my experience in the federal government that those who govern are, in fact, very responsive to the will of the electorate. This is particularly true of Congress, where public opinions are frequently translated into action in a very direct way. In this way, the public has a meaningful impact on the process of governing.

From the time of the New Deal until Watergate the power of the presidency in the process of governing grew at the expense of the power of Congress. Watergate shifted the pendulum of governing power back to the Congress—as it eliminated the president's authority to impose wage and price controls, phased out his authority to invoke credit controls, limited his ability to ship arms abroad and imposed legislative vetoes on his executive branch.

But the president sets the nation's governing agenda. He is the only one who can set clear priorities for the United States. When a president is able to effectively articulate a sense of direction he, more than any other person or institution, can move the country in the direction he desires.

Curtis B. Gans. On one level, the public as a whole and the voting electorate remain sovereign. For in relation to the war in Vietnam, the Nixon presidency and Watergate, the public set the limits to the use and abuse of power and the overall direction of public policy—through their votes and their answers to public opinion polling.

On another level, the official organs of government still govern, proposing and enacting the laws and then implementing and interpreting them.

On still another level, major interest groups, large corporations, banks, unions, certain powerful issue interests—petroleum producers and environmentalists to name two—have some control over the course of American government because they set the terms of debate and the transcendent economic interests involved in that debate.

But if there is a significant change in American democracy in recent times, it is the degree to which the media (especially television) define the national agenda and have increasing say in running the nation.

Leon Jaworski. In the final analysis the people govern the United States. But their power of governance is resorted to all too sparingly.

In *Federalist* Number 51, attributed to James Madison, it is said: "In framing a government which is to be administered by men over men, the great difficulty lies in this. You must first enable the government to control the governed, and in the next place oblige it to control itself."

The people on some occasions have exercised the prerogative of governing. I was a witness to what the collective participation of individuals can produce in representative government. During the Watergate investigation Nixon did not have in mind the appointment of a special prosecutor. He was determined to let his own Department of Justice appointees wind up the investigation which, of course, would have then been under his domination. But the American people would have none of that. The avalanche of protests that came to members of Congress and directly to the White House was so overwhelming that Nixon was forced to change his course. His chief of staff, Alexander Haig, told me that the public's reaction to Nixon's plan was so overwhelmingly adverse and its widespread disapproval so unanticipated that Nixon had to abandon his plan. In Haig's words, "The reaction was almost revolutionary." This accounted for my appointment as special prosecutor—an appointment that never would have come about but for the unwillingness of the American people to accept the wrong of stifling an investigation they believed to be in the interest of good government.

President Franklin Roosevelt, stung by the decisions of the United States Supreme Court declaring some of his New Deal programs to be unconstitutional, espoused an enlargement of the Court's membership so as to have the power to make additional appointments of justices favorable to his political, social and economic views. In this way Roosevelt hoped to have enough friendly votes on the Court to keep his programs from being ruled unconstitutional. An aroused American public protested. So strong was the collective disapproval of the public that President Roosevelt abandoned his efforts.

Of the institutions of government, the United States Supreme Court exercises the strongest power. The Court can nullify acts of Congress as well as acts of the president on the ground of unconstitutionality and has done so on a number of occasions. Most recently the Court told President Nixon that his claim of executive privilege would not be allowed and compelled him to surrender tape recordings he had been maintaining under his control.

IS THERE A BETTER WAY TO SELECT PRESIDENTS OF THE UNITED STATES THAN THE PLAN WHICH WE NOW FOLLOW?

John H. Aldrich. Few object to the way we choose between Democratic and Republican presidential candidates except over details (with the notable exception of the great barriers erected against independent or third-party candidates). The way we choose these two party nominees, however, is controversial. Our current method is unique and very complicated. Surely there are many possible plans for selecting presidential nominees. Many of them are simpler, and some of them must be better than today's method. Much of the controversy centers on the long, complicated series of presidential primaries with all their hoopla, media attention, and so on. Primaries originated in opposition to a strong leader-dominated party convention system. Many argue today that the pendulum has swung too far, so that political parties have too little control over the selection of their own nominees. Even more agree that today's system could and should be improved, if not scrapped outright.

Each of us, if we took the time to think about it, could come up with a new and better plan. Unfortunately, what I think is better, you might believe to be worse. The problem is that we have many goals and many values that we desire to see achieved in the way we select presidents, and these goals and values conflict with each other. Moreover, each virtue is, to some people or in some circumstances, a defect. Total agreement, therefore, is unlikely.

Let us imagine a debate between a defender of our current plan and an opponent who favors, say, a stronger role for political parties and their leaders. Our plan today, says the defender, is permeable; that is, a much wider variety of candidates can hope realistically to win, at least in comparison to a leader-dominated party plan. Yes, says the opponent, but all that means is that inexperienced candidates can win, or those ill equipped to be president, or those holding extreme or unusual beliefs. But, continues the defender, today's system is open to public participation, and experience has shown that the public, not party bosses, chooses nominees today. No other country lets the public choose nominees. Yes, says the opponent, but that means that the most politically informed and knowledgeable cannot take advantage of that knowledge in selecting presidential candidates. Today, there is too much emphasis on a candidate's ability to come across well on television and the other media and too little emphasis on the many other skills a good president must have. Further, the presidential primary season is far too long and demanding of candidates and voters alike. Well, yes, the defender agrees, but if the public is to choose, the campaign must be long enough for voters to learn about the candidates and their beliefs, and television and the other media are crucial for providing voters with that necessary information. The opponent responds by saying, that is all well and good but the campaigns have been all but over after the first primary in New Hampshire and one or two other early primaries, well before most of the public has had a chance to learn about candidates, and long before most could vote in their state's primary. The defender responds that it is precisely the small and early primaries that make it possible for the relatively unknown candidate to launch his (or someday her) campaign and have a chance at winning—that's what makes today's plan open and permeable.

And now we are back at the beginning of the argument, ready to go around again. There is no stopping this debate, because both sides have good, solid arguments. We cannot design the perfect plan.

We can improve our current plan, however. It is important that the public plays a great role in selecting nominees, that it has sufficient information about the candidates to make wise choices, and that a relatively large number of candidates have a reasonable hope of winning. It is also important that political parties retain some say over their standard bearer, that those who know the candidates and the demands of the presidency play a role in selecting nominees, that those true to the principles of a political party have the best chance of winning its nomination (without foreclosing the infusion of new ideas and leaders), and that citizens express their preferences in timely fashion.

One way that all of this can be achieved involves a four-part change of today's plan. First, as for timeliness, it should be required that all phases of the selection process begin no sooner than three (or two, or even four, but surely not our current six or seven) months before the nominating convention. Further, party meetings that conduct straw ballots or other ways of measuring candidate popularity should be banned until the three-month period begins (in November 1979, Florida Democrats and Republicans took straw votes, with the national media watching closely). Second, retain the current system in which each state can hold its primary whenever it chooses, as long as it keeps within the three month rule. This will help keep the system open to the relatively unknown candidate (as a national primary or even a series of regional primaries would not) and will not produce the biases regional primaries might induce. And, most importantly, it would keep the public playing a major role and retain some measure of state-level influence. Third, to temper the public's role and strengthen that of the party, require that one-quarter of all delegates who attend conventions and select the nominees be automatically awarded to major elective officials (all members of Congress and governors, for example, as well as others). These elective officials would not be bound to vote for any particular candidate by the results of their state's primaries. This would provide a large bloc of publicly responsible, free acting individuals who would be unlikely to go against strong sentiment for one candidate in the public (who retain, after all, three-quarters of the delegate votes) but who would temper the expressed, if chaotic, public will with more—and more up-to-date—information. Finally, to help get information out to the public as soon as possible, it should be required that all serious candidates (such as those who file with the Federal Election Commission) supply the government with a campaign platform, biography and statement of purposes and goals. The government, then, should make this information quickly available to all, and the information should be published in major newspapers shortly before their state's primary.

This plan seems workable and compatible with a large number of desirable goals. It is not perfect. Indeed, it rather smacks of compromise, but so too does our Constitution and our entire 206 year political history. But when values conflict, the only two choices are compromise or extinction of one value or the other. Besides, this is my plan; you undoubtedly have a better one.

James David Barber. Yes, there is a better way to select presidents of the United States than the plan which we now follow.

William Buchanan. A better way would be one that enables the voters to express satisfaction or discontent with the incumbents' administrations and policies, indicate generalized preferences for alternatives, and insure that those elected will be effective in accomplishing whatever they propose to do. This would require a better mechanism for achieving a consensus on major policy directions among executive and congressional leaders. Until recent decades the winning political party provided this mechanism.

The importance of television both in campaigning and in communicating political ideas, the passage of finance laws that favor political action committees over parties, the weakening of loyalty to Democratic and Republican symbolism, the growth of presidential primaries, the transformation of national conventions into media spectacles and the fragmentation of congressional leadership all have atrophied the ability of the party to link the two branches of government.

Improving the situation requires no major constitutional revisions but rather the alteration of particular federal and state campaign and election finance laws and party regulations, so that they would reward those politicians, executive and legislative, who work with one another for common national objectives and discourage those who are loyal only to a single area, interest or idea. An incoming president could then hope for a year or two of cooperative deliberation. The Johnson Great Society programs proved defective and I am confident that those of the Reagan "honeymoon" will turn out to be no less so.

It would be convenient if the institutions that provide this coordinative mechanism should continue to bear the names, Republican and Democrat—but that is not too important.

Bruce A. Campbell. To ask whether a better way exists to select presidents implies that the present method is in some way unsatisfactory. Clearly, our method works perfectly from one point of view, since it has in fact produced a president every four years for nearly two centuries now. Therefore, the implication of the question must be that the wrong sort of person has been elected, that somehow our current system allows poor candidates to be elected while the better people are doomed to failure.

Perhaps there are impartial, nonpartisan ways to decide whether a given president is a good one or a poor one, but that seems doubtful. And in any event, it is not at all clear that good and poor presidential material can be reliably identified before a president takes office. Who can say, at this point in Reagan's administration, whether history will record him as one of the successes or one of the failures?

It seems to me, therefore, that the only way to distinguish good from poor ways of selecting presidents must involve the question of who controls the process. Methods of selection vary in the extent of popular participation, from totally democratic to totally elitist. Therefore, what one considers to be a good or poor system emanates from whether one's political philosophy is democratic or elitist.

This criterion can be applied to the two major controversies of the selection process: nomination and campaign financing. In the case of the nominating process, the basic debate is between the advocates of the primary system and those who support a convention system. The basic argument for the former is that it is more democratic—it puts the nominating process directly into the hands of the people. The latter system is defended by those who prefer to rely on the expertise of the party regulars, who presumably have a more thorough knowledge of the candidates and can make a wiser choice.

The controversy over campaign finance legislation has similar dimensions. Do we limit contributions and spending so that candidates must appeal to a broad spectrum of the electorate in order to support their campaigns and so that elections cannot be bought by massive infusions of money, or do we take a laissez-faire attitude and let those with great wealth give their support as they choose?

In both of these instances, the "better" system can easily be identified. The democrat would prefer a primary system and thorough campaign finance limitations, while the elitist would choose the convention system and no hindrances on campaign financing. Moreover, both could make arguments based on constitutional principles to defend their positions.

Thus, both from the point of view of selecting better presidents and from the constitutional point of view, no system can be declared necessarily to be better than any other. The choice depends on whether one wishes to maximize democratic or elitist values. I therefore suspect that much of the current controversy on this issue revolves more around the question of the amount of trust accorded, by the democrats to the few and by the elitists to the many, rather than anything else.

C. Joe Carter, Ph.D. There are several popular plans for changing the method of electing the president of the United States. One with great promise is the selection of electoral college members by majority vote in the 435 United States representative districts. This would combine a good feature of the old electoral college method and add some new twists. The district plan would help neutralize the impact of single-party states. It would add responsibility to the political leaders of the different districts to get out the vote for the most important office in the country. The individual voter would feel closer to the action when his/her vote counted more on the district level.

Reo M. Christenson. Yes, there is a better way to select the president of the United States.

We should confine presidential primaries to a two-month period (April and May, probably) and permit party professionals (in Congress, in gubernatorial chairs, from state and national party committees) to comprise and select 25 to 35 percent of the total convention delegates. Party professionals are better judges of political talent than are the casually interested, relatively uninformed voters. This is an essential step in the urgent need to reinvigorate the political parties.

Direct election of the president, with a runoff if no candidate wins 40 percent of the total vote, is probably preferable to election by an electoral college, for reasons too numerous to list here.

Alan Clem. The contingent election process in event of electoral college deadlock should be changed. The decision should be made by simple majority vote in a joint session of Congress between the top two electoral vote getters.

Electoral vote system is preferable to popular vote system for a number of reasons, in my opinion. However, I would suggest this compromise: declare winner if any ticket receives a clear (50 percent

+1) popular vote majority; if no ticket receives a majority, use the electoral college system as at present but make electoral votes automatic, not dependent on individual electors.

David Cohen. Today the political parties hold the shakiest position as influencers of policy. Elected officials, the media and citizens do not take them seriously. For decades they have grown weaker. Political parties neither deliver promises they make in the general election nor do they serve as recruiters and testers of political leadership. The parties must take seriously their task of building coalitions. The first step is to knit the congressional party to the presidential party. There are three steps that should be taken and they can be initiated by the political party.

1. Elected and party leaders need to play a direct role in the nominating process. Party rules need to be changed to ensure that elected officials and party leaders are guaranteed participants at the nominating conventions.
2. After the presidential election, each party should convene a meeting of the same grouping of elected and party officials who participated in the national convention to thrash out a short list of legislative priorities for the next two years.
3. An additional way to build coherence in the congressional parties and to sharpen public understanding of party programs would be to have televised debates in the Congress on the parties' agenda items.

To carry out wide-ranging changes that blend the values of advocacy with the ability to compromise, parties must take responsibility for their campaign promises and those of their officeholders.

Curtis B. Gans. Basically, were I to choose between the present method of choosing our presidential nominees and the methods used either in the past in the United States or those used by other countries, I would stick with the present system as affording a maximum degree of participation, flexibility and safety.

On the other hand, there are ways in which it could be improved, although not in the ways currently part of the conventional political wisdom. It would not, in fact, serve either the health of the political party or the welfare of American governance either to group the primaries in any way or to shorten the political season. The former would make it impossible for anyone other than the already rich or powerful to enter and the latter would make it impossible for any outsider who entered to be revealed for his feet of clay.

There are, however, a number of positive reforms that might be undertaken to rekindle some health and strength in the political party and reduce the centripetal force of narrow single-issue interests. The first would be to abandon the two-party reforms undertaken by President Carter to protect his presidency. This means abolishing the new rule that makes it impossible for a candidate to enter primaries if he has not filed sixty days before the primary and abolishing the other Carter rule that forces the convention which is held at one point in time to follow exactly the votes of the primaries held at another point in time.

Second, it would be both wise and useful to return the convention to its proper role as a potentially deliberative body, and to make it difficult for a convention to be captured by any one faction, by reinstating a two-thirds rule, by decoupling some of the delegates from the results of the primaries or by insuring some seats for elected party officials at the convention.

Third, it would be useful to attack what is the central affliction of the political party—the degree to which modern media technology has made parties obsolete. For now all a candidate needs is his pollster, money and a media technician to gain access to great power. He arrives on the political scene neither a product of nor beholden to a political party or to a set of issues and programs he is compelled to enact. His mandate is personal and not collective, and the present legislative chaos is the result. By forcing all televised political commercials to be live as in some European countries, one might reduce though not totally eliminate the destructive force of money and media on American politics.

Beyond that, if the media had a short course in more objective coverage of elections and more concern about the stakes involved in the elections, the polity also would be better off.

All of which is to suggest that to reform the present system, which has its virtues in high levels of participation, an involved electorate and the potential for orderly debate and change, and its vices in media domination and weak parties, it would be well to address the root causes—the media and the convention—rather than the symptoms—the primaries.

Malcolm E. Jewell. The presidential selection process consists of two steps: nomination and election. Both of these need to be improved.

At present the nominees are chosen in conventions, following a long hectic season of state primaries and conventions. While these do permit the popularity of candidates to be tested at the polls, the voice of the people is distorted in a number of ways: by the great expense of campaigns, the heavy influence of the media, the exaggerated importance attached to early primaries, the advantage enjoyed by candidates who have time and resources for very extensive campaigning.

One solution to the nomination problem would be a national presidential primary. If no one had a majority, there could be a runoff, or a final decision made by a national convention from among the leaders in the primary. This should guarantee that the nominee more nearly reflected popular preferences. Many observers, however, prefer that party professionals and officeholders be given a bigger role in the convention and that the importance of primaries be reduced, in the belief that the strongest candidate be chosen; that is, the candidate with the broadest appeal within and outside the party.

In the general election, the direct voice of the voters is presently distorted by the mechanism of the electoral college. The outcome is determined by electoral votes, cast as a bloc in each state, and if no one wins a majority of electoral votes, the House of Representatives will make the decision.

This system is outdated and, although it has generally worked well, there is always the possibility that the winner will not be the person who has the largest number of popular votes. While it is possible to tinker with this system, the simplest and best election method would be a direct popular election of the president. Every vote would be equal, and the winner would be the person with the most votes. We would end the risk of a president being chosen who was not really the popular choice and whose effectiveness as president would inevitably be undermined by that fact. Abolition of the electoral college has public support, but it would require a constitutional amendment, which Congress has failed to adopt in the past.

Hugh S. Sidey. I think we should have regional primaries and there should be a time limit on them. Thus, we would have fewer and faster primaries. That would cut down cost and hopefully heighten interest. Beyond that, I would like to see a system which leaves some of the selection process open for convention decision. Surely there must be some formula that could combine the new democratic ideas with the old notion of the bosses; some system that would give us an accurate reflection of party sentiment across the nation but also would leave some authority for those party functionaries who may have a better notion of which men or women would be the best candidates and presidents.

WHY ARE SO MANY GOVERNMENT OFFICIALS CORRUPT? WHAT CAN BE DONE ABOUT THIS PROBLEM?

James David Barber. The major reason so many government officials are corrupt is the public opinion poll which corrupts their thinking. The spurious concreteness of such polls, pretending as they do that people know what they do not know, distorts the politicians' perceptions, encouraging them to follow when they should lead. The fact that some 70 percent will express an opinion on anything—largely to be helpful, one suspects—miseducates those whose opinions must be taken responsibly, not casually and anonymously.

Nothing can be done short of a (quite unlikely) conversion experience on the part of the pollers: a determination to discard the type of pretense represented in the wording of the very question above, and to display in all its lurid reality what they know to be the truth; that the public is largely uninformed with respect to the most elementary political realities, uncommitted to the most essential democratic values and uninterested in discovering even the rudiments of choices beyond their (largely misperceived) self-interest. Then it conceivably might be possible to begin to design a civic education for self-government based on an honest assessment of the public mind.

Alan Clem. Why are so many government officials corrupt? They think they can get away with it! Most people will sin if the reward is high enough and likelihood of capture and/or censure is low enough.

Some people are more prone to corruption than others. Daniel Elagar (*American Federalism*) presents an interesting regional perspective on this with his three culture thesis—moralistic, individualistic and traditionalistic. And John Fenton (*Midwest Politics*), among others, has applied it to specific states, comparing, for instance, Wisconsin's issue-oriented politics to Indiana's job-oriented politics.

Writing reasonable, enforceable laws and then enforcing them is one way to curb corruption by government officials.

Stuart E. Eizenstat. I do not believe many government officials are corrupt. The nation's elected representatives as a whole are very dedicated, hard-working and honest, and maintain their jobs at a substantial financial and family sacrifice.

For the very few corrupt officials, I believe that the current law, including the special prosecutor's law, are adequate.

Leon Jaworski. The greatest deterrent to official corruption is exposure, trial and conviction. In recent years there have been increased efforts to expose white-collar crime and as a consequence there should be a decrease in corruption in public office. The Abscam activity should have a salutary impact on the amount of corruption on the national level especially. It is public vigilance that will determine how much corruption there will be—vigilance participated in by the news media in particular.

Proportionately speaking, there are not many government officials who are corrupt. Granted that even a few are too many, a vast majority of our government officials are honest.

The failure on the part of Congress in years past to act swiftly and effectively in disciplining its own members has had some unfavorable effect on the misbehavior of some members of Congress. More recently, the House of Representatives Ethics Committee has been doing a much better job along this line and undoubtedly its new approach will have a helpful effect.

Hugh S. Sidey. I am not at all sure that there is a greater percentage of government officials who are corrupt than of people in the private sector. Public persons are subject to greater scrutiny. Therefore, I judge that more of them get caught. Their work for the most part must be out in the open or at least there is some part of the record that can be checked by journalists, other interested politicians and special interest groups. Beyond that, I also believe we hold many of our public servants to a code of behavior not always required in the private sector.

What would a check of the income tax returns of all the heads of our major banks reveal? We want such disclosure of our senators and we are critical of some of the things we find. Cabinet officers must pass conflict of interest scrutiny. Could corporate heads? College students by the thousands simply walked away from the loan obligations they incurred from the federal government. The number of welfare cheaters and "double dippers" (recipients of both government or military pensions *and* social security) and food stamp frauds is monumental. Is that worse than what we find in government? I doubt it.

Yet, I am certain there are times (Watergate) and places (Chicago, perhaps?) where government corruption is serious. I don't know that there is any special cure other than diligence. If the public is indifferent to public concerns, underpays its servants and makes them second-class citizens, there is no doubt that corruption will follow.

Surely, the nature of public service invites some who look for illegal ways to profit. Government is a formless endeavor, not easily pigeon-holed or organized. It is a people business. Thus, I suspect some people feel they can hide in this misty atmosphere while they do their thing. Again, the answer is constant concern, constant awareness.

But to be honest with you, my main concern these days is that our search for perfection, at least on the federal level, is driving out talented people. Anyone who is creative and dynamic in today's world has had some dealings with the government, probably has made some money which is sheltered or protected and even may have attacked certain government restrictions and regulations. Such behavior in this climate is enough to eliminate these people from public appointment.

Susan Welch. One must question the assumption that "so many" are corrupt. Probably the incidence of corruption and dishonesty among government officials is no greater than among business leaders, academics or other professionals. Corruption among public officials is probably less today than in decades past when public expectations about, and awareness of, the ethical standards of their elected leaders were not so high. One reason why corruption by public officials seems so frequent is the publicity given such behavior and the efforts made (rightly) by the press and others to expose it. This publicity and watchfulness are much greater than similar efforts and publicity directed toward business leaders engaging in corrupt or illegal activities, toward middle-class Americans who chisel on their income tax, or toward workers who steal from their employers, for example. Probably only the efforts directed toward exposing welfare cheats rival those directed toward exposing official corruption.

Still, dishonest behavior on the part of government officials is serious, and any such behavior is too much. Why does it occur? For one thing, opportunities for private gain at taxpayer expense are more available for many public officials than for blue-collar workers or other kinds of employees. Some individuals are not mature or honest enough to handle the power, glamour and deference that goes with at least some public offices and soon use these conditions for personal gain. Remember, however, that in many instances it takes two to create a situation of corruption—someone has to offer the bribe or favor as well as to receive it. There are always private citizens, corporations or other entities willing to corrupt public officials in return for gains for themselves. Private citizens are partly responsible for corruption in other ways too. Voters who opt for a candidate with a handsome face, smooth speaking style, or glib television ad without looking at the quality of the person must share some of the blame. Some voters are willing to ignore even proven charges of corruption because their representative has, in their view, done good things for the district or state.

The public also has not been consistent in putting pressure on its public officials to improve standards of public conduct through legislation and otherwise. Outright bribery is of course illegal everywhere and probably reasonably rare despite "Koreagate." But there is often little regulation of conflict of interest situations where by a public act an official can increase his or her own financial holdings. While Congress has passed strong conflict of interest laws for our federal judiciary and executive branch, it has not seen fit to demand the same high standards for itself, nor have lawmakers in many states and localities. Likewise laws regulating collection and use of campaign funds are quite lax in many states and locales.

On the whole, however, laws by themselves will not work without a watchful citizenry ready to demand and enforce through its voting behavior high standards of conduct from its public officials. Certainly this is possible. Some states, such as Minnesota or Oregon, seem to have a history of clean government while in other states such as Maryland, New Jersey, or Illinois, corruption is endemic. The reasons for these differences have been the subject of interesting speculations and studies in the past and will undoubtedly continue to be so in the future.

INTERNATIONAL RELATIONS

*I*F THERE HAS BEEN a central theme to American foreign policy since the Spanish-American War it has been one of contradiction. Since the turn of the century, the United States has alternated between policies that have reflected, on the one hand, our deep desire for isolation and neutrality and, on the other, our often unsought responsibility as a world power.

While Theodore Roosevelt managed to create the state of Panama, and consequently the canal, in a moment of expansionist fervor, his concerns were largely domestic. It was Woodrow Wilson who became embroiled in and eventually defeated by America's first entry into a major world conflict. After Germany's defeat in World War I, Wilson hoped to end all wars with a "peace without victory" backed up by the League of Nations. But the country retreated from involvement and, in 1920, elected Warren G. Harding who decided against American membership in the League and signed a separate peace agreement with Germany. America returned to normal.

From Harding through the Depression and the election of Franklin Roosevelt, America maintained an awkward neutrality as tensions rose again in Europe and in Asia. America was finally forced into war by the Japanese attack on Pearl Harbor on 7 December 1941. But even when Congress declared war the next day, there was still one dissenting vote, a faint echo of isolationism.

The end of World War II, the devastation of Western Europe and the Soviet occupation of Eastern Europe created a sudden vacuum that the United States had no choice but to fill. From 1945 until 1960, American foreign policy was dominated by the threat of Soviet expansionism and the need to contain it.

The major U.S.-Soviet confrontation took place in 1962, when John Kennedy successfully forced the Soviets to withdraw offensive missiles from Cuba. After Kennedy's assassination in 1963, Lyndon Johnson increased his predecessor's commitment to Vietnam, and by 1968 there were over 500,000 American troops fighting in that country. Vietnam replaced the Soviets as the dominant theme of American foreign policy well into the 1970s, leaving in its wake a period of neo-isolationism—called by some the Vietnam syndrome—that lasted the entire decade.

The end of America's neo-isolationism came with the seizing of fifty-three Americans by the new Islamic republic in Iran in November 1979. Their release a little over a year later, and the election of Ronald Reagan, seemed to mark, at least for the time being, the final end of the Vietnam syndrome.

In the following pages, experts answer questions about current international problems and the future course of American foreign policy.

CONTRIBUTORS

Chadwick F. Alger, Mershon Professor of Political Science and Public Policy, The Ohio State University, Columbus, Ohio

Lincoln P. Bloomfield, Professor of Political Science, Massachusetts Institute of Technology, Cambridge, Massachusetts; former member (1979–80) of the National Security Council in charge of global issues

Prof. Donald Brandon, University of San Francisco, San Francisco, California; author of *American Foreign Policy: Beyond Utopianism and Realism*

Dr. Ben Cashman, Chairman, Department of Political Science, Seattle University, Seattle, Washington

H. Paul Castleberry, Professor of Political Science, Washington State University, Pullman, Washington

Ellen C. Collier, Specialist, U.S. foreign policy, Foreign Affairs and National Defense Division, Congressional Research Service, Library of Congress

Norman Cousins, former Editor of the *Saturday Review*; Adjunct Professor, School of Medicine, University of California, Los Angeles, California

Roger Enloe, President, U.N. We Believe, New York, New York

Dan H. Fenn, Jr., Director, John F. Kennedy Library, Boston, Massachusetts; Lecturer, Harvard Business School, Cambridge, Massachusetts

Howard Frazier, Executive Director, Promoting Enduring Peace, Woodmont, Connecticut

Walter F. Hahn, Editor-in-Chief, *Strategic Review*, Cambridge, Massachusetts

Walter Hoffman, National Chairman, Campaign for U.N. Reform; Chairman, Executive Committee, World Federalists Association; former Chairman, Arms Control and Disarmament Committee, American Bar Association

Henry Cabot Lodge, former U.S. Senator, vice-presidential candidate and U.S. Ambassador to Vietnam

Dr. Pat McGowan, Professor of Political Science, Arizona State University, Tempe, Arizona

Dr. Ronald I. Meltzer, Department of Political Science, State University of New York at Buffalo, Buffalo, New York

Lynn H. Miller, Associate Professor of Political Science, Temple University, Philadelphia, Pennsylvania

J. Carter Murphy, Professor of Economics, Southern Methodist University, Dallas, Texas

Tad Szulc, columnist, author and foreign affairs commentator, Washington, D.C.

Paul C. Warnke, former Director, U.S. Arms Control and Disarmament Agency; former Chief Delegate to the SALT talks; former Assistant Secretary of Defense for International Security Affairs; now practicing law in Washington, D.C.

Urban Whitaker, Professor of International Relations, San Francisco State University, San Francisco, California

Francis O. Wilcox, Director–General, Atlantic Council of the United States, Washington, D.C.; Dean Emeritus, Johns Hopkins School of Advanced International Studies; formerly Assistant U.S. Secretary of State in the Eisenhower Administration

Robert K. Woetzel, Ph.D., J.S.D., Senior Professor of International Law and Politics, Boston College-Jesuit University, Chestnut Hill, Massachusetts; President, Foundation for the Establishment of an International Criminal Court and International Criminal Law Commission, United Nations Affiliate

WHAT IS THE MOST SERIOUS PROBLEM THE UNITED STATES FACES IN ITS DEALINGS WITH OTHER COUNTRIES? WHAT CAN WE DO ABOUT IT?

Professor Donald Brandon. In his classic *Democracy in America*, Alexis de Tocqueville expressed doubts that the United States would be able to conduct a wise foreign policy. He argued that democracies by definition would lack the qualities of patience, foresight, etc., necessary for success in world affairs. In his words, ". . . a democracy can only with great difficulty regulate the details of an important undertaking, persevere in a fixed design, and work out its execution in spite of serious obstacles."

Politicians in a democracy cater to uninformed, impatient popular moods and passions which prevent establishment and implementation of coherent foreign policies which look beyond short-run aims and interests.

A century and a half later, America is still plagued by the absence of a tradition in world affairs which combines short- and long-run perspectives, principle and power, idealism and realism. The United States still alternates between utopianism and Realpolitik. At this time Jimmy Carter's largely idealistic approach is being followed by an excessively nationalistic, power-oriented foreign policy of Ronald Reagan's administration. If Carter was somewhat naive about the human rights aspect of American foreign policy, Reagan is pursuing a course which goes to the other extreme in putting power above principle.

America has inspired peoples around the globe with its principles and its progress, but it has all too often failed to bring its practice into adequate harmony with its ideals.

To overcome this deficiency in America's approach to world affairs will require the efforts of leaders in education, politics and, above all, the media. If they do not show the way in the creation of a more mature tradition in foreign policy no other groups will. Pressure groups and public opinion need to be enlightened regarding the failure both of excessive idealism and of narrow nationalism in United States diplomatic history. While wisdom is required for specific issues such as arms control, trade and aid policies and the like, the major problem of the United States in its dealings with other countries is the absence of a sound, balanced diplomatic tradition.

H. Paul Castleberry. The most serious problem the United States faces in dealing with other countries is to effect an abatement of the arms race, including the proliferation and spread of nuclear weapons. The arms race is diverting resources worldwide that are sorely needed for economic development and the building of a viable social order. And increasing levels of arms are producing the capability for unparalleled destruction of life and property, and for the first time in history, are creating a serious threat to civilization itself.

A realistic appraisal of the state of the union and the goals and policies of other nations makes abatement of the arms race improbable. The current mood of the American public and the Congress, and the goals and policies of the Reagan administration, are supportive of increasing levels of military capability and more threatening weapons systems in this country and among its allies. The behavior of the Soviet Union and its allies, whether aggressive or merely responsive to U.S. actions, is beyond our control. Additionally, there are scores of conflicts for which third-world leaders are convinced they must have arms, and the number of tension areas increases each year.

What can the United States do? First, we must reassess our goals in keeping with the fact, attested to by all recent administrations, that we live in an interdependent world for which unilateral solutions and even solutions undertaken by the United States and the other major industrial powers are inadequate, if not impossible. We must recognize that there is no alternative to détente with the Soviet Union. There must be a revival of SALT II, together with an attempt to make disarmament and arms control mutually advantageous to all concerned. Most of all, we must become sensitive to the conditions that cause men to seek arms, and to support with renewed vigor the quest for improved means of effecting peaceful change and the pacific settlement of international disputes. In general, we must undertake to strengthen and support the United Nations system and those regional organizations that are designed to serve similar ends. The latter have often been used for purposes that serve only selective security ends or in the case of the Organization of American States (OAS), for example, to provide fig leaves for Great Power intervention. It is in the long-range interest of the United States to use the OAS as auxiliary to achieving the goals set forth in the United Nations Charter, per commitments made under Chapter VIII of that document, rather than as an instrument for legitimizing unilateral decisions unilaterally arrived at, as illustrated in the Bay of Pigs action, the Cuban missile crisis, the intervention in the Dominican Republic and various other cases.

In sum, what the United States can do to abate the arms race necessitates a return to the principles of the United Nations Charter in the context of a more highly restricted interpretation of Article 51 (a measure taken so as not to impair a nation's right to attack, and right to self-defense). In addition, we must attempt to make disarmament and arms control attractive to potential adversaries as well as to allies and to members of the third world. Finally, the United States must somehow muster the will and the courage, whatever the costs risked in domestic politics by the administration in power, to curb the behavior of client states and weak allies that increasingly demonstrate the capacity to jeopardize this nation's vital interests, of which the avoidance of World War III is the most fundamental.

Ellen C. Collier. The most serious problem the United States faces in its dealings with other countries is the possible use of nuclear weapons. Because any use of nuclear weapons could lead to immediate devastation, nuclear warfare presents a more dangerous potential than other serious problems such as environmental pollution, overpopulation and economic imbalances.

There are four approaches that might reduce the likelihood of the use of nuclear weapons. (1) The United States needs to build its conventional defenses so that it does not have to depend on nuclear weapons. (2) It needs to maintain enough strategic forces to serve as a deterrent yet seek arms control agreement to place quantitative and qualitative limits on the growth of nuclear weaponry. (3) The international community needs to continue to develop procedures such as the safeguards program of the International Atomic Energy Agency aimed at preventing nuclear materials in commercial and research reactors from being stolen by terrorists or diverted by governments into weapons. (4) The international community needs to make efforts to develop international law that makes the first use of nuclear weapons illegal.

[These views are personal and do not represent the views of the Congressional Research Service or the Library of Congress.]

Norman Cousins. The most serious problem faced by the United States in dealing with other countries is that both the United States and other countries are attempting to resolve their difficulties in the nationalistic context. The main problems in the world today all have a global dimension but no effective global instruments exist for dealing with them. We are living in a primitive condition of world society and are rushing headlong into a man-made holocaust of unimaginable proportions. The machinery we now employ to meet foreign policy problems is guided by a mammoth fallacy; namely, that national force is the best and also the only means of achieving national security.

Dan H. Fenn, Jr. The most serious foreign policy problem facing the United States is adjusting to the changing realities, such as the fractionating of so-called Communist countries, the North-South division, the shifting bases of what constitutes actual as opposed to apparent power and influence, and the economic situation at home which increasingly depends on and impacts on other national economies.

Dr. Pat McGowan. The foundations of current American foreign policy, such as the NATO alliance, were established during the period 1945–50 when the United States exercised unprecedented economic, diplomatic and military power. Our foreign policy as established by the Truman administration had three fundamental objectives: to contain the supposed expansionist drives of the Soviet Union and other Communist countries; to link firmly the advanced capitalist countries of Western Europe and Japan to the political and economic leadership of the United States, and to speed their recovery from World War II; to open up the colonial empires and other less developed countries to United States trade, investment and diplomatic influence. The intellectual justification for these policies, which led to strong domestic consensus in support of them, was based upon anticommunism, defense of the free world and traditional American anticolonialism.

Up to 1965, these policies generally met with success at home and abroad. However, with the onset of the Vietnam War the domestic consensus disintegrated. Abroad each policy encountered increasing obstacles. The third world, now independent, began to see United

States activities as imperialism, not friendly assistance. Europe and Japan, fully recovered economically, became strong competitors of the United States in the world market and no longer willing to accept unquestioningly United States political and military leadership. Finally, the Communist "bloc" broke up and the Soviet Union, if not China, achieved superpower status, able to exercise its power and influence worldwide and to threaten the United States with thermonuclear destruction in the same fashion that the United States had threatened the Soviets since at least 1950.

In brief, since 1965 the world has become increasingly complex, yet the ideas and institutions of United States foreign policy are little changed from the era of American hegemony (1945–1965). This is the most serious problem facing the United States in its relations with other countries. For example, as in the 1950s, we still worry more about communism in the third world than development. We still tend to ignore the legitimate national aspirations for autonomy among our European and Japanese allies. And we still deal with the Soviet Union in a confrontationist/containment mode and are not able to develop different relations with different Communist states depending upon our mutual common and divergent interests.

How to deal with other countries as a great but no longer dominant power is the most serious foreign policy problem facing the United States in the 1980s. I suspect we will only find our way through trial and error and thus, we must keep the goal firmly before us and encourage public debate over the options that confront us.

Dr. Ronald I. Meltzer. The most serious challenge the United States faces in its foreign relations is the need to develop the necessary principles and arrangements to gain effective collective management of global problems. The world has become increasingly complex and interdependent, and more of the goals and requirements of individual societies—including the United States—have become intertwined with and reliant upon developments occurring elsewhere. Thus, despite continuing vast differences found among the world's many nations, contemporary societies across the globe possess an underlying shared fate. This fundamental condition is apparent in its most basic and perilous context: surviving in a thermonuclear age. It can also be seen in virtually every realm of public policy and government activity, from maintaining peace and security throughout the world to protecting individual dignities, from preserving the global environment and resources to achieving economic and social well-being. Some observers have labeled these ever-accumulating and complex demands associated with the world's human, political and natural environment as the "global problematique." In effect, what is involved is a set of interrelated global problems, military, economic, humanitarian and ecological, that cannot be ignored, nor managed alone by individual states. Instead, these wide-ranging difficulties and evolving urgencies require collective action and responsibility within the international community.

Despite the critical need to address and resolve such global issues as nuclear proliferation, resource depletion and scarcity, and economic underdevelopment, it is very difficult to muster the necessary political will and leadership to construct effective collective management of these problems.

Several factors account for this dilemma, including increased domestic sensitivities and instabilities that inhibit more far-reaching global policies as well as persistent differences among various groups of nation-states. As a great power with tremendous stakes in the unfolding international order, the United States should give highest priority to establishing the basis and direction for the collective management of global problems. Short-term national approaches can no longer suffice. New multilateral policies and arrangements must be formulated and collective management must be established and proceed in a manner that is responsive to all the different groups of countries and to global order considerations. Far from being utopian, this challenge goes to the core of every nation's basic interests and security. There are growing signs of international recognition and activity concerning this challenge, even among the most adversary of states. But the process needs to be accelerated and broadened significantly. The United States must play a positive leadership role in committing itself to achievement of effective and equitable collective management of global problems and in mobilizing international action toward this end. In the long run, there is really no alternative.

Lynn H. Miller. In immediate, concrete terms, the most serious problem facing the United States and the world lies in the exaggerated reliance on military force to achieve national objectives. Specifically, the vast increase in armaments called for by the Reagan administration is likely to accelerate both the arms race between the superpowers and efforts by many secondary powers to obtain nuclear weapons of their own, making the world increasingly dangerous in the near future. Nuclear arms are, above all others, futile as instruments for achieving national values because their use can only annihilate those conditions of civilization they are purported to protect; therefore, it is imperative that the major nuclear powers negotiate a radical reduction in their stockpiles as soon as possible. Only then will they be in a position to move jointly to discourage other nations from pouring their treasures into weapons of mass destruction.

At a more abstract level, the United States must come to a far greater understanding than in the past that it cannot speak or act for all humankind; that as the home of only about 6 percent of the world's population, it is egocentric in the extreme to suppose that the goals of those on the rest of the planet are not in many cases worthy reflections of real human needs, even though they are not always our own. As the wealthiest, most powerful nation on earth, the United States needs to listen to, and where possible, address the needs of the poor and unpowerful, not only because they are generally legitimate in their own right, but because it is only in so doing that we—and they—can develop the habit of living together in the global community beyond which no nation, no group of people, can ever again expect to live for long in splendid isolation.

J. Carter Murphy. If a single, central problem in United States foreign relations is to be named, the problem certainly must be the concept of national sovereignty itself. Unfortunately, the doctrine that nations are sovereign—which is to say, loosely, that each nation has an unlimited right to defend its self-interest as it alone defines that interest—is deeply embedded in people's minds everywhere. In such an environment, sustained peace among 140 or so nations is impossible. The situation has become, of course, especially perilous in view of the proliferation of nuclear means of mass destruction.

World government, with a single police force and judicial system, can perhaps someday provide an answer to the problem. At present, however, the only world government possible would be one of tyranny. A world government that can tolerate a high degree of individual liberty and that can proceed in a way that is responsive to an electorate awaits the cultivation of a new social milieu. In that milieu people who now view each other as aliens must view each other as members of a common community; in particular, people must see their several interests overlapping those of other people who are distant in place and custom in a social fabric that is near global in scope. Such a milieu is probably materializing under the forces of expanding trade, tourism and communication. The evolution, however, is, and will remain, slow.

In the meanwhile, there are a few safeguards that can be employed. Among them are the following:

1. Assign no social function to government that is not essential to government. In particular, let free dealings in open markets between individuals and nonsovereign associations of individuals govern economic affairs to the maximum extent possible.
2. Solidify harmonies of interest among nations in treaties and other agreements wherever possible, and build international institutions which serve common national interests.
3. Use power and the threat of power sparingly in international relations. Governments should never use more economic or political pressure than is necessary to obtain precisely defined and essential objectives.
4. Work at building the bridges of cross-cultural understanding in such forms as private charities, educational and other cultural exchanges, and free and open trade and investment.

Tad Szulc. The United States will continue to be damaged by its credibility problem. Thus far the credibility problem has stemmed—probably since the early 1960s—from our own confusion concerning American goals, needs and capabilities. Between the 1960s and the 1980s, the sheer power of the United States helped to make up to a degree for the credibility gap. Because the overall power equation is changing this lack of credibility will be accentuated in the 1980s and the 1990s. Leadership, or degrees of it, are only possible if (a) the U.S. knows where it is going; and (b) if the world understands this direction.

I am talking about the entire range of political, economic and military problems in an increasingly competitive world. My own sense is that, as a society, the United States is not thinking ahead, and muddles through from improvisation to improvisation. This includes the condition of American industry in relation to other industrialized states. Clearly, an upgrading in United States political, economic, labor and academic leadership would help. In sum, we can deal satisfactorily with other countries only if we solve our domestic problems in what really amounts to common-sense solutions and approaches.

Urban Whitaker. The most serious problem is internal: our slow pace in developing our understanding of the inevitability of the various aspects of developing world government. Our most serious external problem is the blindness (born of poverty and accumulated mistreatment) of the long-time numerical majority that now emerges as an active political majority in the new world order.

Francis O. Wilcox. The most serious problem facing the United States in its relations with other countries lies in the ever-present possibility of a nuclear war. Compared to a nuclear holocaust all our other problems are relatively unimportant. I believe we have a reasonably good chance of avoiding one since both the United States and the Soviet Union are anxious to be spared the terrible consequences of such a conflict.

Closely related to the threat of nuclear war is the threat of Soviet expansionism, particularly in the developing countries, which they hope to bring about by intimidation and diplomatic pressures backed up by overwhelming military power. The task ahead of us, therefore—if we are to meet this dual problem—is to move ahead with a vigorous program of improving our nuclear capacity and strengthening our conventional forces so we can negotiate with the Soviet Union from a position of strength. In these efforts we must have the strong support of our friends and allies.

Robert K. Woetzel, Ph.D., J.S.D. The basic problem the United States faces today is a lack of value orientation that conforms to the consensus of mankind. This country persists in following nineteenth-century pat-

terns of balance of power without recognizing, as the United Nations
majorities indicate, that interdependence is compatible with independence, poses no threat to the identity of peoples, and leads to greater
freedom of choice. Furthermore, to receive good will, as the United
States did for the Marshall Plan, requires sharing of resources and
technology; U.S. nationalistic use of food as a weapon has only been
reciprocated by the use of oil by the Arabs to pressure us.

We must recognize that the common interest of mankind requires a
value orientation that stresses multilateral solutions to common needs.
Exercises of strength, "showing the flag" and handwringing will not
solve problems of imbalance nor impress anybody but will only lead to
retaliation and contempt. Consequently, the United States should prefer
multilateral aid to bilateral programs, adjust its economic programs
such as those regarding inflation and unemployment to the needs of
others as well as our own, and abstain from intervention and competition in arms. Instead of an empire, America should stand proudly and
firmly as a civilization, with culture rather than material strength as a
priority in our values, while we also attempt to raise the intellectual
levels of our political leadership, which have sunk to abysmal lows in the
eyes of the world, to the heights of genius which our people have shown
themselves capable of in the arts, sciences and humanities. The business-
man's ethic by which this government operates today that "what's
good for General Motors is good for the United States" is both untrue
and an obstacle to worldwide recognition of the qualities of our nation.
Even normally conservative institutions like the Roman Catholic church
have recognized the need for progressive changes; how then can a
government still insist on the perpetuation of outdated values, methods
and conceptions based on social Darwinism and "survival of the fittest"?

BY THE YEAR 2000, WHAT WILL THE ROLE
OF THE UNITED STATES BE AS A WORLD POWER?
WILL WE BE STRONGER OR WEAKER THAN WE NOW ARE?

Ellen C. Collier. If the United States acts wisely between the 1980s and
the year 2000, the nation should remain a leader in the cause of freedom
and be stronger both economically and militarily. Wealth of resources
and technological skills give the United States a head start which will be
difficult to overtake unless the United States rests on its laurels and
ceases to work hard, innovate, and solve its problems. The challenges the
United States will face as a leader will continue to grow more difficult,
however, because other countries—adversaries, allies and the noncom-
mitted alike—will also become stronger. Leadership will no longer be
automatic but will require setting an example in the solution of American
domestic problems; continued engagement in international efforts to

solve transnational problems; and winning support by the strength of ideas and the merits of solutions.

[These views are personal and do not represent the views of the Congressional Research Service or the Library of Congress.]

Dan H. Fenn, Jr. By the year 2000 the role of the United States as a world power will be stronger because I have faith in our skill in conforming to a changing world and adjusting our leadership style—despite the current aberration—to one which will attract and appeal to followers.

Walter F. Hahn. National power, however it is measured, clearly is a relative phenomenon on the international stage, which is dependent on the strength of other actors on that stage. Moreover, such power has to be defined in terms of its effective application; i.e., the ability to influence the international environment in a way conducive to the given nation's interests.

My guess is that the United States may emerge by the year 2000 even more powerful than it is today in both absolute and relative terms, but paradoxically weaker in its ability to influence the international environment. If the United States can weather the next, critical decade of competition with the Soviet Union—which looms as the climactic phase in an almost desperate Soviet expansionism—we may well witness a subsequent decline in relative Soviet power, prodded by multiplying and intensifying problems internal to the Soviet domain. And no other nation, including China, can hope in the next twenty years to close in any meaningful way the technological gap separating it from the United States.

At the same time, however, two trends are likely to hit their peak in the 1990s: the emergence and growth of regional actors and the proliferation of military technology, including nuclear weaponry. These trends will produce an environment in which the effective use of American power will be progressively contained. In fact, what may emerge is a "systemic revolution" of global scope featuring a fundamental revision of the international system as we know it today.

Henry Cabot Lodge. I hope that the United States will, by the year 2000, be able to operate as a world power in case of need, even though it may never be necessary. Modern wars are often conducted in underdeveloped countries; and to be strong requires a political precinct-type organization which can reach the undercover terrorists rather than the conventional soldier to whom we have become accustomed. The army would be a shield behind which the war would be carried out. If we learn how to set up such a guerrilla infrastructure and run it, we would be stronger than we are now.

Tad Szulc. In general terms, I think, the United States role in year 2000 as a world power will be diminished as a result of a continued evolution in global conditions. I am referring less to a military loss of strength vis-à-vis the Soviet Union (by 2000, I think, an essential equilibrium will have been created) than to economic and political changes.

Firstly, America will find itself in an ongoing economic competition for ever-expanding third-world markets with Japan and Western Europe; America may even compete badly unless there is serious reindustrialization in this country and a modernization in production methods and marketing approach. All of this defines economic strength and influence. Secondly, the United States (as the rest of the industrialized, non-communist world) probably will remain at the mercy of oil producers unless it opts for a more or less permanent recession to keep down consumption, which is not a very rational solution. This creates other economic and political dependencies. Thirdly, there will be the emergence of new economic regional power centers—Mexico, Brazil, India and South Korea/Taiwan/Singapore complex—in the third world, substantially changing economic and political relationships as we know them now. In this sense, I anticipate a realignment of power in the world, which need not threaten American interests if American policies are adequate and responsive to a new state of affairs. This new state of affairs will simply mean that approximately 5 billion people in the world in year 2000 will have acquired living standards, capabilities and strengths which, by definition, will diminish the relative power of a nation of, say, 250 million (the United States) no matter how improved its economic-social base will have become.

I see greater problems for the Soviet Union: the Soviet system's inability to perform credibly in economic (nonmilitary) affairs will have worsened even more by year 2000; Moscow's economic-ideological-political hold on Eastern Europe will continue to slip (even if violent countermeasures are applied by the Russians in the meantime). In economic terms, the Soviet Union will be unable to compete worldwide with America, Japan, Western Europe and even the new economic centers in the third world.

Paul C. Warnke. Unless we exercise execrably bad judgment, the United States by the year 2000 will still be the strongest world power. Contrary to some alarmists' assertions, we have not become militarily inferior to the Soviet Union and have the resources and the political will to see that this does not occur.

Moreover, it is only in the area of military strength that the Soviet Union is remotely a match for the United States. The basic strength of our economy, our industrial skills, our political freedom and the appeal that our democratic institutions have for people throughout the world give us a degree of influence which the Soviets can only envy.

One real danger to the strength of our position is that we may seriously damage our economic strength by enormous expenditures on weapons systems that contribute little or nothing to our security. Another misjudgment by which we might diminish our role as a world power is by treating the phenomenon of turmoil and change in the developing countries as if it were a part of the Soviet military threat. If we repeatedly align ourselves with an unpopular and untenable status quo, we may substantially forfeit our credibility and our goodwill.

Urban Whitaker. There will be little change that soon in the degree of power, but significant change in the nature of the power and the way in which it is used. We will be stronger if we accept and understand the shift from military to economic power—on the timeworn physical scale—and the more important shift from more meaningful physical power toward more meaningful psychological power.

Francis O. Wilcox. Only a seer could answer this question satisfactorily. This much is clear. The United States will be stronger than it is now—stronger economically and militarily. But we must remember that power is relative and that many other nations will be moving into positions of greater power and influence in the world in the next twenty years. Japan has already taken its place among the great powers. Countries like Brazil, Mexico, China, Nigeria and India are on the way. In this evolving situation the United States will cease to be the dominant power that we have been since World War II. But if we work closely with our friends and allies, if we really help the developing countries in their quest for security and stability, and if we improve our image as a country that supports the ideals of freedom and independence, then we can continue our role as leader of the free nations.

Robert K. Woetzel, Ph.D., J.S.D. By the year 2000 a transformed United States with a planned economy and cultural values rather than capitalist incentives, closer to the evolution of other states, will play a major role of leadership especially due to its advanced technology and reservoir of experts. The present-day confrontations between the military-industrial complex here and foreign hegemonism will have given way to closer cooperation because of economic interdependence and population growth. Managerial reigning elites in different states will be forced to yield to values based on human rights and responsibilities rather than on wealth and power. One life will count as much as another in terms of human dignity and while the Marxist ideal of "withering away of the state" and "to give according to need and take according to ability" may not have been perfectly realized, priorities of wealth and individualistic aggrandizement of power as well as transnational corporate terrorism, racism, colonialism and militarism will be overcome by more comprehensive theories of the common good based on self-determination, monitoring through international organizations, such as commissions of inquiry, and mechanisms of implementation like international tribunals. The prime focus will be the welfare of the individual in the group rather than xenophobic nationalism and its attendant evils. The only remaining threat will be civil conflict, or rebellions by alienated elements which should not pose too great a problem for an organized humanity. In this sense the United States will be a stronger force for peace than its current confrontationist policies allow.

WHAT IS THE UNITED NATIONS DOING TO FURTHER WORLD PEACE? HOW CAN THE UNITED NATIONS BE MADE INTO A MORE EFFECTIVE ORGANIZATION?

Chadwick F. Alger. The United Nations is contributing to world peace in three fundamental ways. First, when international conflicts result in violence, the UN provides a forum through which concerned parties can try to stop or limit the violence. On numerous occasions the UN has successfully limited violence through the use of peacekeeping forces in the Congo (now Zaire), the Middle East and Cyprus and through a variety of kinds of mediation and negotiation. There also have been more numerous occasions when the UN has not succeeded in stopping violence or when involved parties have prevented the UN from becoming involved. Second, it offers numerous arenas for nonviolent conflict, as a substitute for conflict with guns. In this way it serves the same function as national, state and local representative bodies in the United States. An example would be the years of conflict in the UN associated with the successful efforts of colonial territories to acquire independence. It is very important that virtually all countries have acquired UN membership as they have become independent. Third, the UN offers opportunity for cooperative activities that can help to solve underlying problems that cause violence. A few examples are economic and social development programs in the third world; procedures and regulations for global telecommunication, mail, maritime traffic and air traffic; and the drafting of human rights declarations and conventions that express a global moral consensus about the quality of human life on the planet toward which all should aspire. These documents have dealt with civil and political rights, economic and social rights, racism, colonialism, women, etc. An achievement of overwhelming significance has been a draft law of the sea treaty that provides standards for maritime traffic and exploitation of the mineral and food resources of the sea and offers innovative procedures for settling disputes. If this treaty is ratified by a significant number of countries, it will help to avoid future wars over the resources of the sea.

The UN becomes more effective as its members (national governments) use it as a means for joining with other members in efforts to solve common problems. The UN can most effectively cope with these problems before violence erupts. A fundamental problem the UN faces is that national governments tend to avoid joint problem solving through UN auspices until it is too late to avoid violence. While most governments reflect this avoidance, the big powers, including the United States, are the most reluctant to use the UN. Because of their great economic and military power, they tend to think they can solve problems by themselves, or with a few friendly countries. But in an age of global interdependence this tends to be an illusion. For example, presently the United States is undermining UN effectiveness by its unwillingness to take part in global negotiations in the UN that would respond to the belief of third-world countries that the global economic system is rigged against their interests. From their point of view, the global economic system was organized by the industrialized nations to serve their own interests while third-world countries were still colonies. They believe the third world will remain poor until the global economic system is made more equitable. Were the United States to take part in these negotiations it would increase the likelihood that global economic disputes would be solved peacefully and it would also strengthen the UN.

UN effectiveness would also be enhanced if the people of the world were more cognizant of UN activities and potential that relate to their everyday needs and interests. This would lead to public pressure for more active participation in the UN by member governments and less tendency of these governments to jealously protect their prerogatives from UN intrusion. The UN is gradually being strengthened by increasing participation of nongovernmental organizations in UN conferences. But most people do not know enough about concrete UN activities to be able to insist that their government use the UN to seek cooperative solutions to global problems—inflation, unemployment, energy, atmospheric pollution, etc. For example, Americans learn almost nothing about the UN from the media, they seldom know about UN organizations and activities relevant to problems they confront in everyday life, and they rarely ask their legislative representatives or governmental leaders to pursue a specific policy in the UN. Without active concern by citizens it is unlikely that the United States will begin to energetically use the UN in order to work with other countries in solving global problems. Thus, the lack of attention to the UN and lack of knowledge about the UN by Americans is an important deterrent to UN effectiveness. This is also true of people throughout the world.

Lincoln P. Bloomfield. The UN should be thought of as two quite different institutions. One is a set of meeting rooms in which the original 51 member states, now 155, have faithfully mirrored the external world, warts and all, which they inhabit. The other UN is a set of sometimes indispensable programs and activities in practical fields of common concern which together make up a kind of primitive world order.

The first UN, because of the great power veto in the Security Council, has had little direct effect on the conflict-ridden reality of Cold War, armed clashes and vast military arsenals. But it has had a role in maintaining international peace and security in several crucial situations. Since the mid-1950s under a new form of international intervention called "peacekeeping" noncombat military units under a UN flag have helped implement cease-fire agreements for the Middle East and Cyprus, preserved the integrity of the Congo (now Zaire), and will police the birth of Namibia (formerly Southwest Africa) when final agreement is reached on its future.

The second, "functional" UN is far more active. It has played an important role in devising cooperative solutions to global problems of environment, energy, nuclear spread, technology transfer, trade, monetary policy and other items on the "interdependence agenda." But progress here is limited by North-South differences, particularly demands by the 115 or so developing countries for a far greater share of the wealth, technology and markets of the 24 advanced industrialized democracies (and to a lesser extent the Soviet Union and Eastern Europe). This new international economic order is resisted by the United States and other rich countries, while the leap of several oil-rich countries into the ranks of the wealthy has somewhat confused the lineup.

Meanwhile, the UN "family" of fourteen Specialized Agencies has achieved great progress in less publicized sectors, for example the eradication of smallpox by the World Health Organization, the global navigational safety standards of the Intergovernmental Maritime Consultative Organization, reforestation by the UN Food and Agricultural Organization, and the routine but indispensable cooperation on international mails through the Universal Postal Union and on telecommunications through the International Telecommunications Union.

Progress in the two "UNs" depends both on East-West mutual toleration, and on practical bargains between rich and poor (whose interaction also of course affects superpower relations). It is said that if the UN system did not exist it would have to be invented without delay. What is most needed is a keener sense of unity for the solution of common problems—including the avoidance of global catastrophe—in a world of enormous diversity and variety.

Dr. Ben Cashman. The UN has deteriorated as an effective organization for furthering world peace. This reflects the lack of use of the appropriate organs by the major powers to resolve differences and the changed membership where the majority is more concerned with global economic inequalities. The United States and the Soviet Union must bear major responsibility for the demise of the UN because these two nations, beginning in the early 1960s, ceased to use this organization as one of the important instruments for the conduct of foreign policy. The UN continues to be an effective body in the areas of social, cultural, health and some economic areas, and the alleviation of problems in these areas is clearly linked to an eventual world at peace.

The UN can only be made an effective organization if its members utilize its facilities and agencies. In short, it is as good or as bad as its members make it. It is not a governmental body with the accompanying sanction power possessed by nations with legislative, executive and judicial functions. To be effective, the UN must use the various powers it now possesses in the charter to solve current conflicts and it must do this by consensus since unanimity is impossible.

H. Paul Castleberry. From the social scientist's point of view, what the UN is doing to further world peace is a matter of conjecture. There is no way to know how much more violence there would have been during the past thirty-five years if the UN had not existed.

Although the hypothesis is unprovable, students of international relations almost universally assume that all the major programs of the UN make a contribution to "furthering world peace," from its debates and draft conventions on human rights and arms control to its countless resolutions, field missions, and peacekeeping forces regarding the pacific settlement, abatement, or containment of international conflicts. No less important is its work in the quest for a new international economic order, population control, and economic development. The work of its Specialized Agencies (now approximately fifteen in number) makes an enormous contribution to contemporary international order, while underscoring the interdependence of states and providing constructive experiments in the essential task of further integrating the state system.

The UN cannot be made into a more effective organization apart from the will of its members, particularly the most powerful members, including the major industrial powers, key members of OPEC and at least some of the developing states. Thus far, the members of the UN, including the power elite, are unwilling to support more than a weak confederation of sovereign states. Ivory tower projects pointing to the necessity for world federation, or even less ambitious fundamental reforms, are thus essentially irrelevant. Even so, there is much that can be done, within the framework of the Charter's goals and principles, to make the UN a more effective organization.

1. Its more powerful members have the means, given the will, to assure enforcement of a host of UN resolutions that deal with specific international conflicts. For example, America is in a position to make major contributions to compliance by such states as Israel and South Africa. The great powers could also make more

extensive use of the UN in resolving conflicts in which they are directly involved. The "spill over" effects might be impressive, providing means, for example, for avoiding such disasters as the United States involvement in Vietnam.

2. The power elite could also make the UN a more effective organization in the field of economic development. Thus, the United States could vastly augment the achievements of United Nations Development Program and the UN financial institutions by channeling more of its economic aid through those organizations, thus reversing its preference for a bilateral approach to this problem. In terms of the proportion of its GNP diverted to such "official development assistance," the United States ranks about fifteenth among the major contributors. Meanwhile, the 1 percent contribution goal repeatedly set by the General Assembly has not been approximated.

3. In the quest for world peace, the UN would be a more effective organization if more members accepted compulsory jurisdiction of the International Court, as did the U.S. Senate in 1946 with the Connally Reservation. At present, fewer than half of them do. Although America is among that number, every president since Harry Truman has failed in his effort to drop the damaging Connally Reservation.

4. The organization would be more effective if its members, by example and by pressing other states to do so, adhered to the host of UN resolutions and treaties on such subjects as human rights, disarmament and arms control.

This list of ways and means for making the UN a more effective organization is far from complete. The literature is replete with reports of blue ribbon panels of experts that have underscored these and additional means for making the UN more effective, without significantly modifying the nature of the contemporary state system. What has been lacking during the past thirty-five years is commitment, especially by the relatively few states, including America, that have the power to make significant contributions to these ends. In earlier years, the United States was potentially the leadership center for major strengthening of the UN system, but with the voting power of the third world and its anticolonialism and, particularly, concern for the Palestinians, the UN has lost its most vigorous supporters within this country.

Prospects for making the UN a more effective organization are thus remote. In consequence, the UN will continue to be a center of conflict, only infrequently the source of conflict resolution, and paradoxically, the most impressive organization man has yet devised to seek to develop a consensus on fundamental values without which the human prospect is more dim than at any time in history.

Roger Enloe. Since its inception, the UN has pursued various approaches in the quest for world peace.

On a day-to-day basis, the UN, as the only worldwide political forum, serves an essential role as a meeting place where complaints can be aired and tensions vented. An incalculable number of potential crises have surely been averted through its auspices.

The General Assembly, though not empowered to create or enforce mandates, has at times used its power as a mirror of world opinion by condemning hostile acts. Most recently, a large majority condemnation of the invasion of Afghanistan has had a tremendous impact on the Soviet Union.

The secretary-general has used his good offices to seek solutions to problems through personal mediation of conflicts or through the use of representatives.

Finally, the Security Council can attempt peaceful solutions to crises through enforceable measures or by installing peacekeeping troops to guarantee cease-fires. Such troops are presently engaged in Kashmir, Cyprus and the Middle East. However, since a permanent member of the council (China, France, Great Britain, the United States, and the Soviet Union) can veto a council decision, concrete action by the UN is stymied in the absence of superpower acquiescence or approval.

It is often said that the UN is only as effective as its members wish it to be. Though this may seem weak-kneed to some critics, it is based upon world reality. No nation is ready to relinquish sovereign rights to a world organization. Likewise, the permanent members' veto power, which blocks many possible UN responses to problems, reflects the existing world balance of power. If the superpowers had no veto rights, they could simply ignore the council's decisions they deemed harmful and soon the validity of the UN would be destroyed.

This said, there are measures which could favorably affect the performance of the organization: if nations would treat the UN with greater respect; if there was more action and less rhetoric; and if it were treated as an instrument for the common good rather than merely as a stage for nationalistic exploits.

If there were no UN, then we would have to create one. And if the UN was perfect, then so too would be the world, and it could finally and justly close its doors.

Howard Frazier. Maintaining peace throughout the world is the primary goal of the UN. Since its founding in 1945 it has helped settle disputes in over seventy troubled places around the world through the efforts of the Security Council, the General Assembly, and the behind-the-scenes negotiations of the secretary-general.

Methods for preventing or terminating conflicts take many forms. In some disputes the UN acts through peacekeeping forces, observer or fact-finding missions dispatched by the Security Council or General

Assembly, plebiscite supervision, good offices missions, conciliation panels, mediators and special representatives. In other instances, it provides the forum for debate and negotiation and a channel for quiet diplomacy.

Peacekeeping operations are authorized by the Security Council (or in exceptional cases by the General Assembly) with the consent of the parties, in order to enable the United Nations to assist in bringing about the cessation of hostilities, preventing their recurrence and normalizing conditions. There are two types of such operations: United Nations military observer missions and United Nations peacekeeping forces.

Military observer missions—as in the Middle East and in Kashmir— are composed of unarmed officers made available to the United Nations, on the secretary-general's request, by member states. An observer mission's function is to observe and report to the secretary-general (who, in turn, informs the Security Council) on the maintenance of the cease-fire, to investigate violations and to do what it can to improve the situation.

Peacekeeping forces are composed of contingents of armed troops made available by member states selected by the secretary-general. They are arranged in consultation with the Security Council and the parties, and with due regard for the principle of equitable geographical representation.

These forces typically assist in preventing the recurrence of fighting, restoring and maintaining law and order and promoting a return to normal conditions. To this end, peacekeeping forces are authorized, when necessary, to use negotiation, persuasion, observation and fact-finding. They run patrols or interpose physically between the opposing parties. They may use force only as a last resort for self-defense. They must at all times maintain complete impartiality and avoid any action that might affect the claims or positions of the parties. United Nations peacekeeping forces have played a significant role in the Middle East and Cyprus.

The Commission to Study the Organization of Peace has made various recommendations for making the United Nations a more effective organization. Please see their twentieth report, entitled *The United Nations: The Next Twenty-five Years*, for a complete study on this problem.

Walter Hoffman. The UN has attempted to promote world peace by acting as a forum for airing and negotiating grievances. On occasion, it has provided small, ad hoc peacekeeping forces to maintain peace in a troubled area of the world, but only when the country where the troops have to be stationed has consented. By holding conferences it has also focused the world's attention on and made recommendations to resolve such major global problems as environmental pollution, the world food crisis and overpopulation.

Unfortunately, the UN has failed to achieve its primary purpose of "saving succeeding generations from the scourge of war," as attested to by numerous wars in Southeast Asia and the Middle East. The UN has no permanent peace force, no mediation and conciliation service, and no means of verifying compliance with disarmament agreements. It is bogged down by the veto in the Security Council and by an inequitable one-nation, one-vote system of voting in the General Assembly. Its International Court of Justice is seldom used and lacks the means to enforce its decisions, as was vividly illustrated in the case of the American hostages in Iran. In short, the UN is too weak to do the job assigned to it.

There is much that can be done to change this situation and make the UN into a more effective organization. The following is a partial list of what can and should be done:

1. Create a regional UN mediation and conciliation service with a trained staff ready to mediate disputes as soon as they arise.
2. Establish a permanent UN peace force trained to put out brush-fire wars.
3. Create an international arms control verification agency with on-site inspection authority to verify national compliance with arms control agreements.
4. Grant authority to the UN itself to bring cases before the International Court of Justice (ICJ) and modify the veto power in the Security Council so that it cannot be used to block enforcement of the decisions of the ICJ.
5. Adopt weighted voting in the General Assembly so that appropriate weight will be given to population and contributions to the UN.
6. Create a special international criminal court to try persons accused of aerial hijacking and other forms of international terrorism.
7. Appoint a UN high commissioner for human rights.
8. Create an international ocean authority to regulate the high seas.
9. Reorganize all UN development work under a single UN development authority.
10. Strengthen the UN Environment Program.
11. Develop supplemental, autonomous sources of revenue for the UN system.

Unfortunately, people are accustomed to a weak, ineffective organization and therefore believe they must rely on national strength and large military expenditures for security. In truth, history reveals that such reliance has never provided real security, but rather has led to widespread war. In our nuclear age, such a war would mean cataclysmic disaster.

As former UN Secretary-General U Thant said in 1972, "The ultimate crisis before the United Nations is the crisis of authority, and nations, unfortunately, are reluctant to give to the United Nations the authority it needs to resolve global problems."

Dr. Ronald I. Meltzer. The UN has become an increasingly important—and often beleaguered—fixture of contemporary world politics. At the same time the world has become more complex and heterogeneous, the UN has been assigned increased responsibilities and faced growing demands among its member states. Thus, the UN has been called upon to assume greater tasks in an environment that has become less hospitable to multilateral governance. Nonetheless, the UN continues to further world peace, a preeminent goal of the UN Charter, in a number of important ways. First, it provides common global arenas for discussing international problems and conflicts. In this capacity, the UN can mobilize needed attention and provide for an exchange of views concerning these matters. The Security Council can offer the bases and occasions for the peaceful settlement of disputes which cannot be found elsewhere in the international community. Second, the UN can issue recommendations, reports and policies aimed at resolving international conflicts and impending crises. In this role, the UN can legitimize norms, confirm international agreements, and set standards in support of world peace. Third, the UN can offer the vehicle and foundation for providing direct services to maintain global peace and security. These activities can range from peacekeeping troops to fact-finding missions, from third-party mediation to the supervision of truces and cease-fires.

These broad areas of UN involvement in peace and security affairs have been put into practice in almost every case and situation of international conflict since 1945. Past experience has shown that the UN has been most effective when both the immediate parties to the dispute and the great powers are willing to seek peaceful resolutions to their problems. It has also been most useful in cases where the UN presence can be kept limited, impartial and uninvolved in subnational or internal disputes.

Clearly, world peace is a multidimensional problem that transcends simple military considerations. Only the UN, with its wide-ranging activities and jurisdictions in political, security, economic and humanitarian affairs, can encompass the full requirements and terms of international peace. The UN can improve its operations and upgrade its capacities to resolve disputes in a number of ways. For example, it can strengthen its peacekeeping machinery and use of the Security Council. It also can provide greater access to mediation and broaden its role and initiative in conflict management. But in the end, it is how the member states approach and use the UN that will determine its capabilities in dealing with world peace. This underlying condition is both an opportunity and a limit for the functioning of the UN in international peace and security affairs.

Lynn H. Miller. In a direct sense, very little, if furthering world peace means simply stopping inter-state conflicts. But indirectly, the UN serves as an important forum for addressing the issues of poverty, resources use and distribution, the variety of threats to the globe's environment, and even, occasionally, tyranny, repression and other injustices—all of which lie at the root of violence and war.

Yet the UN is an extremely weak institution for wielding political authority in the name of the world community. It is weak because it was designed to perpetuate the state system (defined as one of self-help by all its national actors who maintain the right, most disastrously for human life, to use force as they see fit) rather than to modify that sytem by creating a central, global police power. Such a hypothetical authority presumably could maintain the peace with much the same kind of success as national or local police forces do. There are dangers inherent in such an arrangement to the liberties of various groups, although they probably are no greater than in any governmental monopoly over the use of force. The alternative, self-help system of the nation-states wherein the UN largely does the bidding of its members (on those occasions when the members can agree upon what it ought to do) cannot be tolerated much longer in a world in which the power to destroy the world remains dispersed in an ever-greater number of hands.

Whatever global institution may be created in the ashes of a major nuclear war will, it seems likely, provide much stronger controls over the indiscriminate use of force than does the UN. Whether we have the wisdom to create such supranational controls before that catastrophe, and thus help prevent it, remains an open question, although we certainly have the experience at less than the global level to do so. The union of the thirteen confederated states of North America in 1789 provides one example; the recent progress of traditional European rivals in forming themselves into a community where war among themselves is now almost unthinkable is another. What is needed first is the recognition that each nation's fate is inextricably tied to that of all humankind.

Urban Whitaker. The United Nations is not, and never has been, an "it" or a "they." It is a "we." The relevant question therefore is: what are we, in concert with the changing panorama of other peoples, doing to further world peace. We can become a more effective United Nations— and we will—only as we come to recognize the facts of the "one world" that inevitably emerges.

Francis O. Wilcox. We live in an interdependent world. Since many of the problems we face are global in nature—food, population, refugees, outer space, drugs, pollution of the environment, disaster relief, terrorism, energy, trade, the oceans, health, the maintenance of peace, arms control, etc.—they must be dealt with by a global organization like the UN. It has often been said that if the UN did not exist it would have to be invented.

In the maintenance of peace and security the UN record has been a spotty one. As most people expected, it has been unable to handle great-power conflicts. It has, however, been quite useful in a good many local conflicts with its peace observation and peacekeeping activities. The Congo crisis, Cyprus and the Middle East War, are well-known examples. It has also helped solve a good many disputes over the years, but many more have gone unresolved.

The UN was based on the assumption that the great powers would be willing to work together to maintain world peace. That is still a valid assumption. The most effective way of making the UN function more effectively would be to improve relations between the United States and the Soviet Union. The UN can do almost anything the great powers want it to do.

Meantime the UN could be made more effective by: (1) strengthening the machinery for the peaceful settlement of disputes; (2) streamlining the work of the General Assembly; (3) avoiding the formal voting process wherever possible; (4) strengthening the regional organizations like the Organization of the American States and the Organization for African Unity; (5) electing a strong and effective secretary-general; and (6) using smaller groups of states—coalitions of the willing—to get agreement on problems of special interest to those states.

LAW AND THE SUPREME COURT

ONE WAY ORDINARY CITIZENS can find answers to legal questions is to hire a lawyer. There are more lawyers in the United States today than ever before, so obtaining legal counsel should not be very difficult. Hiring a good lawyer, however, can be costly. Good lawyers can command as much as $200 an hour in some cities, and the superstars of the legal profession charge even higher fees.

A less expensive alternative is to look at the legal system itself, how the courts work, and what civil rights citizens have. Anyone planning to go to court will probably need an attorney to guide him through the judicial maze, but a basic knowledge of the law and of legal questions is fundamental for all Americans. The following section addresses two basic aspects of American law: property rights and the role of the Supreme Court in the judicial system.

The famous jurist Oliver Wendell Holmes, Jr. described law as "what the courts will do in fact." This definition may not satisfy those who want to know exactly what their legal rights may be in a given situation, but it illustrates both the changing nature of law and the power of the courts in deciding legal questions. A question that reaches a judge or jury will be determined by the court, and the court's decision, unless overturned, will be law.

The immense power of the courts originated in 1789 when the authors of the Constitution awarded the Supreme Court a sweeping jurisdiction: "The judicial Power of the United States, shall be vested in one supreme court, and in such inferior courts as the Congress may from time to time ordain and establish. . . . The judicial Power shall extend to all Cases in Law and Equity, arising under this Constitution, the Laws of the United States, and treaties made, or which shall be made, under their Authority."

The leaders of the Revolution intended to create a judicial branch equal in power to that of the executive branch and of the legislative branch so that the tripod of checks and balances would remain steady. Yet at first it was unclear exactly how far the court's jurisdiction over "all cases in Law and Equity" extended and whether the court actually wielded any power at all.

This question was decided in 1803 by the case of *Marbury* v. *Madison*. Then Supreme Court Chief Justice John Marshall established the principle that the court was indeed supreme because it had the final power to interpret the Constitution. "It is emphatically the province and duty of the judicial department to say what the law is," Marshall argued. "Those who apply the rule to particular cases must of necessity expound and interpret that rule."

The most famous recent test of the "province and duty of the judicial department" occurred in the tug-of-war between the federal courts and President Nixon regarding the notorious Watergate tapes. The courts ordered the president to turn over the tapes; President Nixon claimed that executive privilege protected the tapes from the long arm of the law. After lengthy legal wrangling, the Supreme Court decided in *United States* v. *Nixon* (1974) that even the chief executive must obey the law, and the legal system, along with public outrage, defeated the president.

While the judicial system bases its powers upon the steadfast Constitution, the laws and the courts themselves may vary with differing interpretations of the Constitution. In fact, nothing more aptly illustrates the nation's changing laws than the actions of its highest court. In 1896, for example, the Supreme Court ruled in *Plessy* v. *Ferguson* that according to the "separate but equal" doctrine, racial segregation did not necessarily deny blacks equal protection. In 1954, however, the Court decided in *Brown* v. *Board of Education of Topeka* that separate was unequal for black students and that school segregation was unconstitutional. Similarly, the Supreme Court decided in 1873 that women could be barred from the bar because their proper place was in the home. By 1981, however, women made up about 10 percent of all lawyers, and President Reagan appointed Sandra O'Connor as the first woman to join the ranks of the "nine old men" at the head of the nation's courts.

The courts can and do effect immense changes in society, but their power has limits because they cannot initiate change in the way that the legislative or executive branches can. If an issue is not challenged in court, the court cannot rule on it. And, of course, not all court challenges reach the Supreme Court. How does the court decide which cases to hear? What rights do citizens have in such a vital area as property ownership? The following section offers experts' judgments on these issues.

CONTRIBUTORS

Prof. Anthony D'Amato, Northwestern University Law School, Chicago, Illinois

Larry L. Berg, Ph.D., Director, Institute of Politics and Government, University of Southern California, Los Angeles, California

James L. Blawie, Professor of Law, University of Santa Clara School of Law, Santa Clara, California

Richard C. Cortner, Professor of Political Science, University of Arizona, Tucson, Arizona

Eugene Gressman, Kenan Professor of Law, University of North Carolina, Chapel Hill, North Carolina; co-author of *Supreme Court Practice* (Bureau of National Affairs, fifth edition, 1978)

Dr. Ferinez Phelps, Department of Political Science, Columbus College, Columbus, Georgia

Rev. Richard J. Regan, S.J., Associate Professor, Fordham University, Bronx, New York

S. Sidney Ulmer, Alumni Professor, University of Kentucky, Lexington, Kentucky

HOW DOES THE SUPREME COURT OF THE UNITED STATES DECIDE WHICH CASES TO HEAR?

Professor Anthony D'Amato. The easy answer to this question today is that the Supreme Court simply takes whatever cases it finds in its own unfettered discretion to be interesting.

The system was not quite set up to work that way. There used to be an appeals procedure and a certiorari procedure, the former being mandatory and the latter discretionary. But over the years and through a series of procedural maneuvers, some highly questionable to legal scholars, the Supreme Court has emasculated the appeals procedure so that it is only a very pale shadow of its former self. Very few cases are appealed now—so few that law students hardly bother learning what the rules for appeals are. Only a limited number of cases even in theory can be appealed, and the Supreme Court's appellate docket is highly restrictive.

So we are left with the certiorari docket. Thousands of cases go up to the Supreme Court with a "Petition for Certiorari," which is a small lawyer's brief asking the Court to hear the cases. The judges look through these petitions (or their law clerks screen them first), and if four judges vote to hear a case, then "certiorari is granted" and the case is set for hearing before the entire Court.

Sometimes judges have voted *against* certiorari not because they didn't find the case interesting or important, but because they believed that the result in the lower court, which they liked, would probably be reversed by the Supreme Court if the Court got to hear the case!

Of course, the justices will not agree that they only take cases interesting to them. They use terms such as socially important, or cases that resolve disagreements in federal courts, or other such phrases. But in fact there are no legal limits on the Court's discretion to hear cases, and since the Supreme Court is the highest legal authority in the nation, we are left with the bald proposition that the Court can take any case it wants to take.

Since every case has already been appealed (before the Court is asked to review it), no one's rights are denied because the Court decides not to hear a case. However, some legal scholars wish the whole matter of certiorari could be more principled.

Larry L. Berg, Ph.D. To decide which case to hear, four or more members of the Supreme Court must agree that the case should be brought before the Court for review.

James L. Blawie. There are two answers to this question: one mechanical and formal, and the other realistic and informal.

Cases to be considered by the Supreme Court are chosen by the Rule of Four. If four members of the Court, assembled or unassembled, indicate that a particular case should be heard in full, or disposed of by memorandum decision, the case is set for the Court's attention. If fewer than four justices select the case for hearing, review is denied. It is not unusual for a case to fail in this process, and yet for a very similar case with nearly indistinguishable facts to be selected a year or two later. The change may be due to new court membership, a shift in thinking of one or more members, change in economic or social conditions, new indication that a problem which appeared of little importance has become of critical moment, and so on.

Realistically, the Court can hear only about one to two hundred cases in one session as it is presently constituted. A bare minimum of even the very important cases is thus able to be selected for hearing. The cases which attract the attention of the justices are likely to concern questions which appeal to them in a subjective manner as containing critically important elements. But justices, just as other persons, differ considerably in those matters which they regard as of critical importance.

A few cases may require resolution on other grounds also. It may be that two or more federal court circuits have made diametrically opposed decisions on important legal issues, with resulting heavy impact on police, business, civil rights or the like. The justices may believe that the conflict must be resolved. Some cases may have a high political content, leading the judges to reject some as too hot to handle at the moment, while others are accepted for hearing because Congress has obviously bargained for a resolution of a question at the Supreme Court level, for example. There is also an element of "the buck stops here" thinking which goes into the selection of cases. If Congress, the executive, and the states have acted wrongly or failed to act over a great period of time; and if further, critical legal and constitutional issues are involved, which if unresolved will create unrest and dislocation, the Supreme Court is much more likely to accept a case for hearing. This notion is usually expressed in the axiom that the Court is the balance wheel of the federal union.

Remarkably, history indicates that justices who go to the Supreme Court bench under political obligation, or with certain understandings with others outside the Court, rarely act, once seated, in a manner dictated other than by their own subjective convictions and legal training and experience.

Eugene Gressman. The Supreme Court generally hears only those cases that at least four of the nine justices think are important enough to be heard fully on the merits. This is known as the Rule of Four.

There is no statute or court rule that formally establishes the Rule of Four. It is an informal and long-standing practice. It first became a matter of public knowledge during congressional hearings in 1924, but it probably came into existence shortly after 1891, when the Court was first given discretionary jurisdiction.

The Rule of Four reflects the highly discretionary nature of the Supreme Court's jurisdiction. There is no absolute right to a full Supreme Court review of the merits of a case. Indeed, it would be physically impossible for the nine justices to decide the merits of all the nearly 5000 cases that are filed each year in the Court. Experience has shown that they have the time and energies to hear fully only some 150 to 175 of that vast number each year. Thus there must be a sifting-out process, a method for selecting those relatively few cases the Court can afford to hear. That is the point where the Rule of Four comes into operation.

The selection process is highly subjective in nature. Each justice's vote to grant or deny full review is based on a subjective view of the importance of a given case, importance either to the national interests or to the proper administration of justice. Often the nine justices are in total agreement about the importance or the lack of importance of a case. But there are significant numbers of cases where they disagree. In such situations, the Court has developed the common sense rule that if a substantial minority of the justices think the case important enough to review fully, the other justices will accede to the minority's viewpoint as to importance. That is how the Rule of Four operates in practice.

There is no other practical way to control the Court's overburdened docket than by use of collective wisdom as to the national importance of the issues presented in any given case. The role of the Supreme Court in our form of government is to resolve the important constitutional and legal issues that beset our way of life. Its function is not to resolve issues that are of parochial concern to the litigants only. To fulfill its proper function, the Court must make subjective assessments as to the cases that give it the best opportunity to fulfill its constitutional purpose. The Rule of Four is but one aspect of that process.

The Reverend Richard J. Regan, S.J. Article III, section 2, of the U.S. Constitution defines the jurisdiction of the Supreme Court. The Supreme Court has jurisdiction to try cases *de novo* (original jurisdiction) when a state is a party or when a case involves a foreign ambassador, consul or other public minister. Only a few cases, typically cases between two or more states, come before the Court under its original jurisdiction. The Court has jurisdiction to review lower court decisions (appellate jurisdiction) in cases involving federal questions but not originating in the Supreme Court.

Article III empowers Congress to regulate the Court's appellate jurisdiction, and Congress has done so since 1789. Congress authorizes appeals as a matter of right to the Supreme Court from decisions of federal courts of appeals invalidating either acts of Congress or state statutes and from decisions of highest state courts invalidating acts of Congress or sustaining state statutes against federal claims. From other decisions of federal courts of appeals and highest state courts involving federal questions, Congress authorizes petitions to the Court for discretionary review (certiorari). Rule 19 of the Court indicates the considerations favorable to granting certiorari. The first such consideration is one where a lower court decision involves a conflict between federal courts of appeals, a conflict between a federal court of appeals and a state court, or a conflict between state courts on a federal question. Other favorable considerations are those where lower court decisions depart significantly from the accepted and usual course of judicial proceedings or conflict squarely with applicable Supreme Court decisions.

A final consideration is whether or not a lower court decision involves an important question of federal law. Petitioner and respondent submit briefs arguing for and against review, and the justices meet in private session to decide whether or not to grant review. The outcome of this vote is determined by the so-called Rule of Four, i.e., a petition for certiorari will be granted if and only if at least four justices favor review. In practice, less than 10 percent of the petitions for certiorari are granted. For the statutory bases of Supreme Court jurisdiction, see Title 28 United States Code, Sections 1251, 1254 and 1257.

S. Sidney Ulmer. Appeals and certiorari cases constitute about 98 percent of the Supreme Court's docket each term. Unlike cases originating in the Court, cases falling in these two categories have been decided first by a lower state or federal court. Congress has mandated that the Supreme Court hear certain cases (appeals) and has given the Court complete discretion to hear others (certiorari). In any given term, better than 90 percent of the Court's docket will be made up of requests for certiorari—for discretionary review. Whether to hear an appeal or grant a request for certiorari is decided via the so-called Rule of Four. If as many as four of nine justices so wish, the case is heard. Otherwise, review is denied.

In a typical term, the Supreme Court will hear about 150 cases of the 4–5,000 docketed. Normally, the Court provides neither votes nor explanations for its action in certiorari cases, which reflects its complete discretion to hear or not to hear such cases. Rejection of an appeal, however, requires an explanation since such decisions, technically, are not discretionary. Sometimes, the Court simply finds that the appeal fails to meet the conditions of the jurisdictional statute. More often, the explanation is that the appeal does not raise a "substantial federal question," a Court imposed condition that must be met in appeals cases. Because of the necessity of determining whether such conditions have been satisfied, a measure of discretion is inherent in deciding whether to review appeals cases.

Under certain conditions, the expenses of filing a case for Supreme Court review will be borne by the Court itself. At present, about one-half of the cases docketed each term fall in this category. Whether a case is paid or unpaid (*in forma pauperis*) is correlated with the granting and denying of review. If the case is paid, the probability is about 5 in 100 that a hearing will be granted. If the case is not paid, the chance of review is only 1 in 100. Other factors that influence the decision to hear a case include compliance with procedural requirements, the importance of the question or questions raised by the decision below, whether the federal government is the party petitioning for review, and the personal interests or attitudes of the judges in exercising their discretion.

CAN PEOPLE BE FORCED TO SELL THEIR LAND TO THE FEDERAL OR STATE GOVERNMENT? WHAT RIGHTS DO CITIZENS HAVE IN SUCH SITUATIONS?

Professor Anthony D'Amato. Citizens certainly can be forced to sell their land to the government! Any property a citizen owns is subject to certain overriding rights that the government retains.

In some countries, governments simply take any private land that they desire. In the United States, however, there are certain restrictions.

As the question indicates, in the United States the government must *buy* the land. Not only that, but the government must buy the land at fair market value. The constitutional requirement, expressed in the Fifth Amendment, is that the government must pay "just compensation." Normally "just compensation" is fair market value, but sometimes a market value cannot be readily assigned to certain parcels of land. In those cases, the government will indicate a price, and if the landowner feels that the price is inadequate, he or she may bring suit against the government charging that the indicated price is not "just compensation" for the land. The court's decision, of course, is final.

Another big restriction on the government, whether it be the federal or the state government, is that the land must be taken "for public use." Those words, too, are contained in the Fifth Amendment to the Constitution. Many states have similar clauses in their state constitutions. Some state constitutions have even more restrictions, defining in more detail what is meant by "public use" or "public purpose." A citizen should not neglect to look at his or her own state constitution as well as looking at the Fifth Amendment to the federal Constitution.

If a private person who has connections with your state legislature manages to convince the legislature to pass a bill taking your land and assigning it to his—even at a fair price—that bill would be unconstitutional. There has to be a public purpose before your land can be condemned by the government. However, the Supreme Court has held that a private developer working with a city to rebuild part of the city through rezoning and other redevelopment and rebuilding, is sufficiently "public" in purpose that private land can be condemned under such a scheme. Thus, the government itself does not necessarily have to take over the land. The land may be condemned for redevelopment and rezoning (under government approval), or for utility companies (which after all serve a public purpose), or for other "public" means.

A landowner whose land is appropriated by the government may sue the government either on the question of the fairness of the price, or on the question of whether the taking was truly for a public purpose.

Larry L. Berg, Ph.D. There is no doubt that in most situations people can be forced to sell property to the government through the process of eminent domain. People do have the right to due process in the proceedings and fair compensation for property, and it must be taken only for a public purpose.

James L. Blawie. Of course people can be forced to sell their land to the federal or state government. People may also be forced to sell their land or other property interests to a variety of public utilities, railroad companies, airports and other semipublic and private companies determined by the legislature and courts to affect in some way the public interest. The due process clause of the Fifth Amendment applies to federal proceedings of this type, and that of the Fourteenth Amendment of the Constitution applies similarly where states and their subagencies are concerned.

In brief, citizens have the right to have the value of their land determined by fair and objective procedures, ultimately by a judge and jury if that proves necessary. By payment of the figure thus determined, the public agency may take title to the property for all purposes, and may also purchase any subinterest in the same property which may belong to another person. Litigation is seldom necessary, because the negotiated price is likely to be at or above the appraised value of all interests in the subject property.

Most relevant statutes provide for some means of reimbursing the owner, at least in part, for the loss of value to adjacent land, for attorneys' and other professional fees, and for certain related expenses.

Richard C. Cortner. Individuals can be forced to sell their land or property to both the federal and state governments, since both levels of government possess the power to take private property for public purposes—a power called the power of eminent domain. In exercising the power of eminent domain, however, both the state and federal governments are constitutionally required to provide just compensation for private property taken for public purposes. The Fifth Amendment of the Bill of Rights thus provides in part that private property shall not "be taken for public use, without just compensation." While this provision originally applied only to the federal government, the Supreme Court held in *Chicago, Burlington & Quincy Railroad Co.* v. *Chicago* in 1897 that state and local units of government were also required to provide just compensation for private property taken for public purposes by the due process clause of the Fourteenth Amendment of the Constitution. In addition to these just compensation requirements of the federal Constitution, most state constitutions contain similar provisions.

If an individual has his property condemned by either the federal or state government, the individual ordinarily will be offered compensation by the government involved. If that offer is not satisfactory to the individual, the issue of what constitutes just compensation for the property will ultimately be determined in a court of law.

Dr. Ferinez Phelps. Yes, people can be forced to sell their land to the federal or state government. The citizen has the right to a jury trial to determine the value of the land, which is subject to condemnation proceedings because those governments have the power of eminent domain; and the power sometimes is extended to public utilities.

The Reverend Richard J. Regan, S.J. State and federal governments can exercise the right of eminent domain over private property. But the Fifth Amendment of the United States Constitution limits the federal government to taking private property "for public use" with "just compensation," and the Fourteenth Amendment has been interpreted to apply this clause to condemnations by state governments.

The Supreme Court has construed public use broadly enough to include condemnations to assist private commercial and residential developers. Just compensation is the current fair market value of the condemned property. Whether or not government regulation beyond formal appropriation or protracted occupation constitutes "taking" of

private property is complicated. The magnitude of economic loss resulting to the property owner from government regulation is apparently
the key consideration. The Court has interpreted government regulation
which destroys the primary use to which private property has been
committed and from which it cannot be economically diverted as an
unconstitutional "taking" but has not so interpreted zoning or environmental regulations affecting future use.

Legislative statutes and administrative rules prescribe the procedures
by which private property may be condemned and compensated.

THE SECRET SERVICE

*T*HE SECRET SERVICE is the type of government agency about which little is normally heard. Secret Service agents quietly go about their business of protecting the president and his immediate family, as well as former presidents and their spouses, and visiting heads of state.

Ever since the 1960 election—in which President Kennedy defeated Nixon reputedly because he projected a better image during their televised debates—we have been in the era of the "electronic presidency." Candidates running for office—and presidents interested in maintaining their power once they have been elected—have felt the need to create exciting visual images in order to ensure that they are covered frequently by network news. Grabbing the eye of the television-watching public means frequent public appearances in which candidates get out and mingle with the crowds.

The burden of difficulties arising from all of this interest in grabbing media attention falls on one body more strongly than any other: the Secret Service. Their advice to a president—stay secluded as much as possible in order to lessen the danger of kidnap or assassination—runs counter to the suggestions of presidential media counselors, whose advice is to appear in public as often as possible.

In the following section, James A. Boyle, special agent and spokesman for the United States Secret Service, gives a more detailed outline of the general activities of this governmental body.

CONTRIBUTOR

James A. Boyle, Special Agent and Spokesman, U.S. Secret Service, Washington, D.C.

HOW MANY PEOPLE ARE BEING PROTECTED BY THE UNITED STATES SECRET SERVICE TODAY? WHO ARE THEY? WHY ARE THEY BEING PROTECTED? HOW MUCH DOES IT COST THE TAXPAYER?

James A. Boyle. The Secret Service is presently providing protection on a permanent, full-time basis to 20 persons. In addition to these permanent protectees, we annually provide protection to an average of 115 heads of state and heads of government during their stay in the United States.

In 1901, following the assassination of President McKinley (the third president to be assassinated in thirty-seven years), Congress assigned the Secret Service the responsibility to provide protection to the president.

Since that time our protective responsibilities have increased, each time by act of Congress, to include the following individuals:

(a) the president of the United States and his immediate family; (b) the vice-president and his immediate family; (c) the president-elect and his immediate family; (d) former presidents and their wives; (e) the widow of a former president until her death or remarriage; (f) children of a former president until they reach sixteen years of age; (g) major presidential and vice presidential candidates and nominees and their spouses; (h) visiting heads of a foreign state or foreign government; and (i) at the direction of the president, other distinguished foreign visitors to the United States and official representatives of the United States performing special missions abroad.

The general Secret Service budget request for fiscal year 1981 totaled $175,000,000, and was applied to the investigative, protective, administrative, research and support functions.

For reasons of security we do not identify the amount expended for any particular protective effort. This information, while provided to Congress for approval in executive session, is protected by law from public release.

ESPIONAGE

*I*N 1941, WHEN Franklin Roosevelt asked William "Wild Bill" Donovan to organize the Office of Strategic Services (OSS), the forerunner of our current intelligence-gathering community, he told him, "You will have to begin with nothing. We have no intelligence service."

A slight exaggeration, perhaps, but close to the truth. Without the sanction of war, espionage had been looked on as something distasteful and ultimately un-American. Secretary of State Henry Stimson summed up the prevailing attitude in 1929 when he closed the Black Chamber, our only cryptographic bureau. "Gentlemen do not read each other's mail," he said.

Americans spied a great deal in wartime. George Washington spent over $17,000 on spies during the Revolution. In the Civil War, both the North and the South used spies, including several women.

But it took World War II and the rise of the Soviet Union to turn American espionage into a growth industry. The Central Intelligence Agency (CIA) was created by the National Security Act of 1947 and was designated as the coordinator of all intelligence-gathering agencies. Its charter was vague enough to give it a wide operational latitude. "The CIA will," it read in part, "perform such other functions and duties related to intelligence affecting the national security."

There were few external controls over agency conduct by either the executive or legislative branch, and even its budget and number of personnel were excluded from public disclosure. Current estimates are that the CIA employs about 80,000 people with a budget of $1.5–$2 billion a year. The *total* budget for all intelligence-gathering agencies may run as high as $8–$10 billion a year.

Given the controversy surrounding the agency and America's histori-cal aversion to spying, it is difficult if not impossible to judge what the role of a secret agency ought to be in an open, democratic society. The normal checks and balances of government do not apply—in some cases, *cannot* apply—and have more often than not proven ineffective.

It may be that the only real constraint on CIA activity is the character of the director and that of the president he serves. Some observers, including some presidents, have argued that the agency ought to be unrestrained in its protection of national security.

American espionage is a fact of international life, to be used or abused by each new administration. Our intelligence community provides in-formation and analysis of world events and keeps the secrets secret. Undoubtedly, on some future occasion, it will also provide us with another tool of our national policy, one that lies in that gray area between a diplomatic protest and sending in the marines. That is the kind of area where it operates best.

In the following section, intelligence experts answer some of the most frequently asked questions about espionage.

CONTRIBUTORS

Walter F. Hahn, Editor-in-Chief, *Strategic Review*, Cambridge, Massachu-setts

Lyman B. Kirkpatrick, Jr., former Executive Director/Controller of the Central Intelligence Agency; Professor of Political Science and Uni-versity Professor, Brown University, Providence, Rhode Island

Peggy Shaker, National Coordinator, Campaign for Political Rights, Washington, D.C.

Charles E. Wilson, Public Affairs Official, Central Intelligence Agency, Washington, D.C.

HOW MANY SPIES OF FOREIGN NATIONS ARE THOUGHT TO BE IN THE UNITED STATES? WHAT DO THEY DO?

Walter F. Hahn. Not having access to FBI files, I have no idea of the number of spies of foreign nations active in the United States. What do they do? They spy, of course.

Lyman B. Kirkpatrick, Jr. The number of spies of foreign nations in the United States is a matter for conjecture. The FBI on occasion publishes the number of Soviet agents suspected of operating domesti-cally but rarely publicizes the activities of the other socialist nations or of the other nations of the world.

The most positive information available is that the Soviets maintain a fairly constant cadre of about 500 to 700 intelligence and security personnel under official cover in the United States. These individuals are assigned either to the Soviet embassy or consulates, to the United Nations mission, or are working in the United Nations secretariat. It is likely that nearly all of them are known to the FBI and the CIA. How many other Soviet agents are under deep cover, having entered the United States with false passports and established themselves in some innocuous activity, is most difficult to assess. However, from cases such as that of Colonel Rudolph Abel, it is known that these deep cover networks may be extensive. During World War II there were eight such networks mainly in and around the federal government.

It is assumed that other major nations have at least intelligence observers in their embassies and that the satellite nations have sizable intelligence staffs, as do some of the Middle Eastern powers and Asiatic nations.

The primary mission of all of the intelligence personnel in the United States is to discover American intentions with regard to their nations and to report on the latest weapons being developed.

WHAT CAN A PERSON DO WHO SUSPECTS HE OR SHE IS BEING SPIED UPON BY THE FBI, THE CIA OR BY FOREIGN AGENTS?

Lyman B. Kirkpatrick, Jr. The first step is to advise the local office of the FBI of the individual's suspicion. If the individual indeed is the object of an internal security investigation, obviously, the FBI will neither confirm nor deny that it may be involved. However, this is very rare and today involves only those suspected of being foreign agents or criminals. It is most unlikely that any American in the United States will be spied upon by the CIA as that agency is forbidden by law from any internal security function. There were some violations of this law in the 1970s, but these have been stopped by presidential order.

If the individual is being spied upon by foreign agents, then both the FBI and the CIA would be interested. Inasmuch as it would be in the United States, the FBI would have primary jurisdiction and would investigate the case, bringing in the CIA if evidence led the investigation to individuals outside the United States. Usually foreign agents in the United States are interested in individual Americans only to gain access to specified classified information, in which case the American should report his suspicions to his employer, who in turn can discuss the matter with proper federal authorities. Foreign agents may, on occasion, attempt to recruit American citizens to act as agents for them. This, obviously, is a matter of major interest to the FBI and should be reported to that organization only.

Peggy Shaker. In order to give advice on what a person should do if he/she suspects that he/she is being spied on by the CIA, FBI or foreign agents, it is very important to find out if the person thinks the surveillance is connected to lawful political activity or if it might be the result of criminal activity on the individual's part. Foreign agents have no jurisdiction over criminal activity in the United States and technically are not permitted to investigate the conduct of Americans or resident aliens in the United States. (Our intelligence services have, however, been known to overlook the activities of foreign agents in America and some people feel that United States intelligence services even condone and cooperate with such activities.)

If the person who believes himself or herself to be under surveillance is not engaged in unlawful activity, the course of action is clear.

First, document as well as you can the activities which have led you to believe you are under surveillance. Obtain written and notarized affidavits from witnesses to suspicious events, such as disruption of mail service, phone service or suspicious actions by individuals. If you are the subject of a suspicious burglary, be sure to report the incident to the police and request that a copy of the police report include your suspicions. While the documentation of such incidents may not serve to stop surveillance, it does build a record which will enable investigators to help you when enough evidence has been accumulated; it will also help you to convince others that there is actually something happening to you.

Second, check with others who work with you or are associated with you, especially in political activity. Find out if there have been any suspicious incidents which could be related to surveillance affecting them or others they know. Compare notes in order to discover a trend.

Third, if you suspect your phone may be tapped, request that the phone company do a "sweep" to discover illegal devices. Put the request in writing and send it to an official of the company. Such sweeps seldom discover taps, but they may uncover private taps or bugs. If there is a government bug or tap on your phone, the chances are that you will not find any evidence of the device or the tap because of the sophisticated nature of the technology involved. Government officials who wish to tap a phone usually do so with the consent of the telephone company or with the assistance of one of the company's employees.

Fourth, if you are experiencing a lot of trouble with your mail, complain in writing to an official of the post office. Keep all correspondence along with transcripts of any conversations you have with the official.

Fifth, file a request under the Freedom of Information (FOI) and Privacy Acts with the FBI, the CIA and any other agency which you think may be involved. The FOI and Privacy Acts have provisions under which the government may withhold information if it endangers an ongoing investigation or will lead to the revelation of sources and methods. However, you may find out if you have been a subject of investigation in the past. Some FOI Act requests do not get answered as speedily as Congress intended; be persistent and file appeals on rulings which you feel are not accurate or fair.

Consider contacting an attorney to find out if you have cause to file a suit against the agency in question. If you are not able to hire an attorney, approach your local legal aid society, a law school nearby, or any one of a number of civil liberties organizations including the American Civil Liberties Union, the National Emergency Civil Liberties Committee, the National Lawyers Guild or the Center for Constitutional Rights.

Remember, if you are engaged in lawful political activity, any surveillance of you by a governmental agency is likely to be illegal. Contact others in your community who may have concerns about stopping such activity and pool resources. Approach members of the city council, the state legislature and Congress with your concerns. (If your evidence shows enough to document your suspicions, ask your representatives for assistance in stopping the specific surveillance.) For information on who can help and what you can do, contact: Campaign for Political Rights in Washington, D.C.

If you are engaged in criminal activity and believe yourself to be under surveillance by a law enforcement officer, contact your attorney.

Surveillance by foreign agents is harder to deal with and very dangerous. One of the best ways to deal with this kind of surveillance is to interest members of the press in your case. Often, if the presence of agents is revealed, they will discontinue their harassment.

Depending on the seriousness of the situation, you may want to consider approaching a sympathetic law enforcement official with your problem. Again, approach your representative if you want some kind of assurance that the governmental officials you are asking for assistance will in fact deal with you fairly. (You do not want to become a pawn in an international espionage game.)

Above all, remember that the United States government is increasingly using the rationale of national security to justify increased surveillance of American citizens at home and abroad. Those who travel abroad may be especially subject to some form of such surveillance. The most important advice we can give is this: do not let surveillance of your lawful activity deter you from traveling, exercising freedom of speech and association or writing. If such a threat does deter you, then those freedoms have been undermined and undervalued with very little effort on the part of the government.

Charles E. Wilson. If one suspects that he or she is being spied upon by foreign agents, one should report as soon as possible to the FBI, which is the principal investigative arm of the U.S. Department of

Justice. For immediate assistance or aid in contacting the FBI, one should notify one's local law enforcement authorities.

If one suspects that he or she is being illegally spied upon by either the FBI or CIA, one has recourse within both the administrative and legislative branches of the federal government. The first is the president's Intelligence Oversight Board which is responsible for reporting to the president any intelligence activities that raise serious questions of propriety or legality, and for forwarding to the U.S. attorney general reports on activities that raise questions of legality.

A second avenue for action is to notify one's congressman or senator, who in turn will have access to the intelligence oversight committees that exist in Congress. They are the House Permanent Select Committee on Intelligence and the Senate Select Committee on Intelligence. These organs are also equipped to act appropriately in cases of illegality or impropriety.

Finally, one could report one's suspicions to the inspector general of the CIA, who is charged to monitor the legality and propriety of activities carried out by his agency, or to the director of the FBI or to the attorney general of the United States.

THREAT OF WAR

WHEN THE TWENTIETH CENTURY began, the United States was basking in the glory of its spectacularly successful ten-week war with Spain. Less gloriously, American forces were still fighting in the Pacific, suppressing a revolt of Philippine nationalists. In 1908, Theodore Roosevelt told Congress, "If we desire to secure peace, one of the most powerful instruments of our rising prosperity, it must be known that we are at all times ready for war."

Although generations of Americans have been involved in combat, the United States has had a comparatively fortunate position in recent decades: all of our battles have been fought over other people's land. With the exception of Pearl Harbor, the American countryside has remained relatively untouched while American troops went to the aid of other imperiled countries. As a result of this long immunity from fighting, many Americans do not take the threat of war very seriously. Some defense planners, however, warn this may be a mistake.

To add might to the military, President Reagan proposes the largest peacetime buildup of American forces ever. Planning to spend an estimated $1.5 trillion between fiscal 1981 and 1986, he schedules hefty boosts for everything from highly advanced nuclear weaponry to everyday spare parts. For example, the navy has been reduced from the more than 800 active ships it had in 1964 to less than 500. Some ships are kept in port because there are not enough sailors to staff them. Reagan plans to bring the fleet up to 600 ships by 1990 and to begin programs, such as increasing pay and improving benefits, to encourage people to join and stay in the military.

What threat, real or imagined, causes America to prepare so heavily for war in time of peace? As the questions in this section illustrate, American concerns center on the Soviets or on Soviet-inspired aggressors. The other major world power, China, has become a strange political roommate, if not exactly a bedfellow. For example, former secretary of state Alexander Haig offered the People's Republic of China the opportunity to buy arms from the United States.

What will happen if more nations become involved in nuclear arming? Can the United States still preserve peace by being, as Teddy Roosevelt proposed, "at all times ready for war"? In this section, experts examine the possibility of nuclear terrorism and the threat of future wars.

CONTRIBUTORS

H. Alexander, Ph.D., author and consultant, now working on a biography of A.N. Kosygin

Larry Bogart, National Coordinator, Citizens Energy Council, Allendale, New Jersey

William P. Bundy, Editor, *Foreign Affairs*, New York, New York

John R. Christiansen, Professor of Sociology and Social Work, Brigham Young University, Provo, Utah; contract researcher for various U.S. civil defense agencies

Walter C. Clemens, Jr., Professor of Political Science, Boston University, Boston, Massachusetts

Dr. J. I. Coffey, Distinguished Service Professor of Public and International Affairs, University of Pittsburgh, Pittsburgh, Pennsylvania

David D. Finley, Professor of Political Science, Colorado College, Colorado Springs, Colorado

Howard Frazier, Executive Director, Promoting Enduring Peace, Woodmont, Connecticut

Dr. Roger Hamburg, Professor of Political Science, Indiana University at South Bend, South Bend, Indiana

Jerry F. Hough, Professor of Political and Policy Sciences, Duke University, Durham, North Carolina; member, associate staff, Brookings Institution

Klaus Knorr, Professor Emeritus, Woodrow Wilson School of Public and International Affairs, Princeton University, Princeton, New Jersey

Henry Cabot Lodge, former U.S. Senator, vice-presidential candidate and U.S. Ambassador to Vietnam

H. G. MacPherson, consultant on nuclear energy; formerly Deputy Director of Oak Ridge National Laboratories and Director of the Institute for Energy Analysis, Oak Ridge, Tennessee

Richard P. Pollock, Center for Science in the Public Interest, Washington, D.C.; formerly Director, Ralph Nader's Critical Mass Energy Project

Harrison E. Salisbury, specialist on Soviet affairs and historian, New York, New York

Barbara G. Salmore, Professor of Political Science, Drew University, Madison, New Jersey

Dr. Michael G. Stevenson, Deputy Division Leader, Energy Division, Los Alamos National Laboratory, Los Alamos, New Mexico

Dr. Charles W. Thomas, international affairs consultant, New York, New York

W. Scott Thompson, Associate Professor of International Politics, The Fletcher School of Law and Diplomacy, Tufts University, Medford, Massachusetts

Paul C. Warnke, former Director, U.S. Arms Control and Disarmament Agency; former Chief Delegate to the SALT talks; former Assistant Secretary of Defense for International Security Affairs; now practicing law in Washington, D.C.

MANY MILITARY EXPERTS THINK THE NEXT BIG WAR WILL BE BETWEEN RUSSIA AND CHINA. HOW LIKELY IS THIS? WHAT ARE THE CONSEQUENCES LIKELY TO BE FOR THOSE COUNTRIES AND FOR THE REST OF THE WORLD?

H. Alexander, Ph.D. There is a 10 percent chance that Russia and China will go to war with each other before the end of this century, and only a 5 percent chance it will be a nuclear war. In either a nuclear or nonnuclear war Russia would occupy large areas of northern China. However, Russia does not have enough troops to occupy and hold all of China. So a war between the two Communist states could last for decades. A war of attrition would be hard on both countries. Both could decline in power vis-à-vis the West and the third world as the war dragged on.

If the United States furnished extensive arms to China, that would produce jobs and profits for aerospace companies. However, the Chinese do not have enough cash or credit for large purchases.

A nuclear war between the two countries could contaminate large parts of the northern hemisphere with radioactive fallout. Alaska and parts of the western United States could suffer millions of deaths.

William P. Bundy. There is no question that the relations between China and Russia remain in a state of considerable tension, over a host of territorial issues all along their common border (including the Sinkiang area and the disputed islands on the Ussuri River). Basically, the Russians see China as a threat to some border areas such as Mongolia, and even in the longer term to the whole Soviet position in eastern Siberia—much of which was taken over by Russia under treaties essentially imposed by force. And the massive Russian military buildup along the Chinese border, together with the nuclear threats uttered, for example, in 1969, have given the Chinese serious concern over Russian intentions. There is a deep national antagonism between the two nations, and this antagonism includes an ideological element arising from the different forms of communism adopted by each.

Yet in spite of these important underlying factors, a direct frontal war between the two would be an enormous undertaking for either party, and I would judge that the chances of this have receded somewhat in the last decade, to the point where it appears unlikely at least for the near or medium term future.

More serious, however, is the possibility of the two being drawn into conflict as a result of developments elsewhere, notably in Southeast Asia. If the Chinese had pushed their "punitive" action against Vietnam further in February 1979, they probably would have approached or even reached a "flash point" where the Soviet leaders would have felt impelled to show their support of Vietnam by some degree of military action along the main northern border of China. Once initiated, such an action would have been hard to confine or terminate, and could have resulted conceivably in major fighting, although probably not a serious Russian invasion designed to occupy large areas of China or overthrow its regime. I think a recurrence of this type of situation is at least not unlikely in the next few years, although I do not rate it as probable.

Walter C. Clemens, Jr. Border skirmishes are quire possible, but a big war is not likely. Both sides realize that they could not win such a war, even if it were restricted to conventional arms. The Chinese nuclear force is much smaller than Russia's, but probably quite adequate for deterrence.

David D. Finley. China is no military match for the Soviet Union now, nor is she likely to become one for a long time. While Russians have undoubtedly thought about preemptive war against China to foreclose a future threat, the prospective costs for the Soviet Union clearly exceed the benefits. The present directions of Chinese policy do not pose any vital threat to Russia, and thus a big war between the two is unlikely.

Many conflicting interests divide Russia and China however, and they will probably remain political adversaries. That is in the best interest of the United States. We gain the chance to cultivate normal relations with both and then exercise stabilizing political leverage against either by virtue of our relationship with the third corner of the triangle.

Other consequences of this scenario include further diffusion of international power in contrast to the bipolar Cold War and continued disintegration of Communist ideology as a unifying political force in the world.

Should China and Russia go to general war despite the mutual disadvantages of such a course, there would be great danger that it would become a nuclear war and that it would expand unpredictably to involve Europe and the United States and Japan.

Jerry F. Hough. Such a war seems quite unlikely. China is militarily very weak, and even Mao Zedong backed down when the Soviet Union began to threaten in 1969. The present leadership is less assertive. The Soviet Union has plenty on its hands without adding China to its troubles.

In fact, my expectation is that there will be a return to more normal relations between the Soviet Union and China, especially after Brezhnev goes. I don't think that they will become close allies, let alone that China will become a Soviet satellite. Rather I see the kind of peaceful coexistence that has existed between the United States and the Soviet Union— or maybe even the relationship between Europe and the Soviet Union. The fundamental conflicts of interests that would produce war, let alone the present level of hostility, don't exist.

If there were a war between the Soviet Union and the United States, it would overwhelmingly be in the Chinese interest to opt out in order to avoid nuclear attack. I think that movement towards a Soviet-American war would be preceded by a Soviet-Chinese nonaggression pact, just as World War II was preceded by a Soviet-Nazi Pact.

Henry Cabot Lodge. A possible development (much discussed today) is the effort of smaller Communist states to detach themselves from Moscow. This effort could be of far-reaching importance. If China became a highly developed industrial and world power, with all the equipment of a modern state, it would, of course, have fundamental consequences for the world. At the present moment it does not seem likely.

General Marshall left behind him a number of lessons, one of which was that the Marshall plan promoted the security of the United States *by strengthening our friends*. We did not seek to profit at the expense of a war-torn Europe, but rather to relieve its woes. We will do well never to forget the wisdom of the approach. True national security is achieved not just by military power—necessary though that regrettably is—but by taking actions which subtract from the number of our potential enemies and add to the number and strength of our friends, be they military or civil.

Harrison E. Salisbury. This is the most likely of the big wars. It has been on the front burner at least once (1969) and constantly moves back and forth in Soviet strategic planning. There exists a substantial body of

Soviet military opinion which holds that Russia must fight China sooner or later so better do it soon when China is weak rather than later when she is nuclearly armed and able to devastate the Soviet Union while the Soviet Union devastates her.

In my belief if such a war starts it will quickly escalate to pull the rest of Asia and very soon the United States and Europe into it.

Dr. Charles W. Thomas. A war of aggression started by one party as a result of a deliberate policy choice is extremely unlikely. What political goal could be worth such costs? A war begun accidentally as a result of border tensions and the buildup of forces near the border is perhaps the most likely way for limited action to begin but unlikely (though certainly not impossible) to escalate to higher levels of violence. A surgical nuclear strike by the Soviets on Chinese nuclear facilities is improbable because Russia had its best opportunity to do this ten to fifteen years ago and is not likely to pursue such a policy now due to the uncertainties of achieving 100 percent success.

The probability of a large military conflict between the Soviet Union and the People's Republic of China is low. However, improbable things happen in international affairs. Given high levels of tension, Soviet paranoia concerning China, newly acquired military sophistication in China, and perhaps a "sparking" factor such as political unrest in Siberia or northern China and the improbable may become the possible.

A large-scale conventional conflict would have enormous but non-violent consequences outside the combat zone. The only likely combat spillover would involve the United States and Japanese reconnaissance activities near the combat zone and, of course, some danger to merchant ships and warships in the Pacific near the Chinese or Soviet coastlines. The main consequences would be diplomatic and economic: the value of the dollar dropping and gold and oil rising, for example; or the diplomatic efforts of the belligerents to gain United States support or at least friendly neutrality. For the belligerents the social and economic costs would be staggering—all the more noticeable since neither side would be likely to emerge as a clear victor.

In the event of nuclear war, the consequences are nearly incalculable. Japan and the Koreas would receive near-lethal doses of radiation. America and Europe also would receive significant levels of radiation; but this would be highly dependent on prevailing winds and rainfall just after the attack. Levels of radiation would also vary greatly according to the percentage of strikes that were air-burst or ground-burst.

The Soviet industrial and military structure east of the Urals would be decimated. Thousands would eventually die not just from direct military action but from hunger and disease as a result of the destruction of the transport infrastructure and medical support facilities. The destruction of Siberian oil, gas and mining facilities would mean longer-term social distress for all of the Soviet Union. Some targets west of the Urals would be attacked. How many would be hit would depend on extremely complex equations of Chinese long-range accuracy and the efficacy of Soviet missile defense around Moscow.

China, of course, would be devastated. The Soviets' overwhelming superiority in nuclear weapons would permit them to send Chinese industry and agriculture back to the middle ages. Very little would be left that might be called a coherent Chinese society.

IN THE EVENT OF WAR BETWEEN RUSSIA AND THE UNITED STATES, WHAT WILL COUNTRIES LIKE POLAND, RUMANIA, CZECHOSLOVAKIA AND OTHERS DO—FIGHT FOR RUSSIA OR FIGHT AGAINST RUSSIA?

H. Alexander, Ph.D. Depending on the circumstances, length and intensity, different countries will go in different directions. Few could have predicted in 1913 that England and Italy would end up on the same side in World War I. In some scenarios Poland and Rumania might fight against the Soviet Union. I do not think that Polish and Rumanian troops are considered by Russian general staff to be reliable for fighting outside their own borders. However, if a victory were quickly won by the Red Army agaiut the NATO armies, these troops would be more reliable because everybody likes to be on the winning side.

I don't know about Czechoslovakia.

Walter C. Clemens, Jr. If there is a war between Russia and the United States, Eastern Europe will be overshadowed by the massive exchanges between the superpowers.

But there are few war scenarios in which one can plausibly argue that the East European forces (with the possible exceptions of Bulgaria and East Germany) could be counted on to fight as reliable partners of the Soviet armed forces.

In the countries mentioned, the armed forces might well work against the Soviet Union in most scenarios one can imagine.

David D. Finley. None of the East European socialist states would be eager to fight for the Soviet Union in a conflict against the United States. The specific circumstances of such a war, however, would determine what, if any, choice they would have. In the event of a land war in Europe, each of the countries named would likely resist an invasion of its territory, especially by Germans, despite general distaste for the Soviet hegemony. And the East European military establishments, integrated in the Warsaw Pact under Soviet command, would have little choice but to fight for the Soviet Union at least at the outset of hostilities, despite any public opinion to the contrary. In offensive operations against NATO, most East European forces would be unreliable and would likely be used in flank defense and support roles while the Soviet forces in Germany would carry primary offensive responsibility. Any East European military action against Russia probably would be of a partisan, guerrilla nature. Its extent might be related to the tide of the conflict. In a land war which saw Soviet retreat, one might expect considerable such activity. There is stronger anti-Soviet sentiment in some Warsaw Pact countries than others. It is strongest in Rumania and Poland, weakest in Bulgaria.

In sum, the East European members of the Warsaw Pact are unreliable Soviet allies; they don't want to fight for anybody but they have little latitude for choice.

Dr. Roger Hamburg. I think that if the war occurs because of a Soviet attack in Western Europe, Poland, Rumania and Czechoslovakia would be of doubtful military and political usefulness. They would certainly not be used as regular national armies. I can see few contingencies in particular in which the Rumanians would fight. The East Germans and particularly Bulgarians are another question, particularly the latter who are historically very pro-Russian. They might be more useful, particularly if officered at the highest levels by Soviet officers or officers of their own nationality thoroughly integrated into the Warsaw Pact command structure. Most East European countries involved would not fight *against* Russia but they would at best be reluctant combatants who couldn't be considered a reliable part of the Soviet order of battle, particularly if the Warsaw Pact did not achieve a rapid victory. If the war could reliably be pictured as against West Germany, Warsaw Pact states, especially Poland and Czechoslovakia, might react with more enthusiasm.

Outside of Europe things are more speculative. The Soviets, as far as I know, have not had any great success in drawing East Europeans into bloc obligations (except the East Germans in Yemen). Whether a "racial appeal" to them in the event of a serious simultaneous flare-up on the Sino-Soviet border in the wake of a Soviet-American conflict would be successful is possible.

Jerry F. Hough. It depends on the nature of the war. If there is nuclear war, it will be in every country's interests to try to opt out, and Eastern Europe is no exception. Of course, our theater nuclear strategy involves attacks on Soviet staging and supply points, and that may well involve nuclear attacks on Poland and Czechoslovakia. That would, no doubt, affect the attitudes of their people.

If the Soviet leadership thought that a war would remain nonnuclear and that it could launch a conventional attack on Europe, it might get East European involvement with some kind of promise, but surely no one believes that a successful Soviet attack on Western Europe would stay nonnuclear. If any conventional war began to involve serious fighting, Soviet generals could not assume that the East Europeans (especially the Poles and Rumanians) would fight for Russia. They would not be likely to fight against Russia either, simply dissolve.

The Soviet nightmare—and the explanation they give for such a large army—is that NATO troops would intervene to support a rebellion in Eastern Europe and that China would take advantage of the situation in the east. The Soviets have an army which they hope could handle that in a nonnuclear fashion. Obviously if that scenario involved a rebellion in Poland, the Polish army would be on the other side or at the very least, dissolved. If it involved a rebellion in East Germany, some of the East European armies might well fight to prevent the reunification of Germany under NATO.

If we talk about the more likely type of scenarios such as the Soviet and American armies facing each other on a third-world border (say, the Syrian-Israeli border), then there might well be small East European units in the Soviet-led forces (as there were small Allied units on the American side in Korea), but I would not expect that Soviet generals would trust them to do serious fighting.

Harrison E. Salisbury. The Warsaw Pact countries will fight, albeit grudgingly and unenthusiastically, on the Soviet side—if they get a chance. In my opinion any war between the United States and the Soviet Union will either be nuclear from the start or escalate to that stage in the briefest time. The Warsaw countries will have no time to play a significant role one way or another; they are undoubtedly targeted as are Canada and other American allies to go up in the same nuclear smoke we do.

Dr. Charles W. Thomas. The course chosen by the East Europeans in the event of a North Atlantic Treaty Organization-Warsaw Treaty Organization (NATO-WTO) central conflict is contingent on a variety of factors, of which five stand out as decisive. It will be assumed here that the various armed services will indeed follow the orders of their national political leaders. This is, however, only an assumption. Many scenarios are conceivable in which the political leaders may choose one course, and the armed services another.

First, the individual national political environments at the time of war. Political, social or economic unrest in any given nation at the time of conflict initiation would make it an unreliable ally. Poland in 1981, for example, would present the Soviets with a very large uncertainty factor.

Second, the length of the crisis period preceding the outbreak of hostilities. In a "cold start" surprise war with very little time to think the East Europeans would find themselves caught up in standard operating procedures that would make their immediate involvement automatic. A lengthy period of prewar tension might offer the East Europeans time to reflect on and initiate alternatives to direct involvement.

Third, whether the WTO is the aggressor or the object of NATO aggression. The East Europeans will certainly defend their homelands, but might not participate so willingly in aggression.

Fourth, if the Soviets attack NATO and are quickly and decisively successful, the East Europeans will likely remain loyal to the WTO. However, no immediate successes and the possibility of a war of attrition might well encourage the East Europeans to withhold or withdraw their support.

Fifth, for NATO to threaten devastation (either nuclear or conventional) of Eastern Europe but withhold it might encourage an anti-Soviet policy. For NATO to unleash immediate destruction on Eastern Europe would probably cement the WTO alliance.

The question should certainly contain a third alternative for the East Europeans: some form of neutrality is also a policy option. The choice *not* to help the Soviet Union does not lead automatically to becoming hostile to the Soviets. A far more likely choice would be either friendly or belligerent neutrality; both of which would do immeasurable damage to the Soviet cause.

ISN'T SUPPLYING ARMS TO CHINA AND HELPING TO BUILD CHINA'S MILITARY STRENGTH A GOOD WAY TO HALT RUSSIAN AGGRESSION?

William P. Bundy. I have no doubt that the policy pursued toward the People's Republic of China since 1972 has been a wise one. That policy has moved from reconciliation to formal diplomatic relations and the development of a host of ties in economic and cultural matters. And at the present time the United States is apparently prepared to supply military supporting equipment as well as dual-purpose technology that has predominantly civilian application but might be used to some degree for military purposes (for example, technology for satellite photography).

However, I am dubious that it would be wise—at least under present circumstances—to go any further in the direction of supplying arms to China and helping to build China's military strength. The principal concern of the Chinese is and should be to deter any Russian aggression against China itself, and with that objective we can be fully sympathetic. The Chinese military establishment has deteriorated seriously in the last fifteen years, and its needs form an important part of the program of the present regime associated with Deng Xiaoping, although the best information is that military rebuilding is being subordinated to pressing economic needs and that Chinese military leaders are far from satisfied with the allocation.

But China has many sources to which it can turn for arms supplies on a purchasing basis, and there seems to be no pressing need for the

United States to offer special or sophisticated weapons where its situation is unique.

And, above all, there is a serious question whether a United States arms relationship with China would contribute to its deterrent military power in any degree that would offset the alarm such a relationship might arouse in Moscow. As I can testify at first hand, the Soviet Union is neurotic about the threat from China, and especially so about the possibility of anything resembling a military alliance that involved China with the United States and possibly also with Japan and Western Europe.

In present circumstances at least, I believe that American arms supplies to China would have a strong chance of arousing a vehement and excessive Soviet reaction long before those supplies would in fact do anything significant to improve China's military posture. And there is a good chance that such supplies would engage, or appear to engage, the United States in support for Chinese actions, notably in Southeast Asia, that might in themselves be disturbing and toward which we would wish to preserve a hands-off policy.

In short, I believe that any United States supply of arms to China is best held in abeyance for the present. China has all it can do to defend itself, and does not seem to be in serious danger of direct Russian aggression. Nor can it be militarily effective on other fronts, unless possibly at the expense of its essential economic program—which indeed we are supporting and should support. The possibility of United States arms supplies should be kept in reserve, as a measure to be taken if and when Soviet expansionism becomes more acute and threatening.

Walter C. Clemens, Jr. No, China's massive presence is sufficient to inhibit Moscow whether or not the Chinese have a large supply of modern arms.

Given China's past record of turbulent domestic politics and China's history as an imperial power, I consider it unwise to build up China's military capacity. We should limit ourselves to cultural, scientific and human exchange programs and to the same kinds of commercial exchanges carried on by the West Europeans and Japanese.

David D. Finley. Helping build Chinese military strength does promise to increase incrementally Soviet preoccupation with their Chinese threat. But China is militarily weak as compared to Russia, and the United States is not likely to give her enough help to change that balance appreciably. Since Russian expansion will probably be political rather than military and directed south rather than east or west, it is hard to envision a major correlation between American military aid to China and Soviet restraint. On the other hand, extensive American military aid to China would reduce the prospect for effective political and economic development of the complex Soviet-American relationship. A full-blown Sino-American military alliance would probably be a net destabilizing force in international relations, and it would assume greater identity of interests between the United States and China than presently exists. Thus the cultivation of greater Sino-American cooperation offers political leverage for both the United States and China, but it can be more useful for America if it is primarily nonmilitary.

Jerry F. Hough. The basic problem with our supplying arms to China—unless we want to give them weapons systems that can deliver atomic weapons or absolutely massive quantities of conventional weapons—is that nothing we can do will affect the military balance between the Soviet Union and China. Hence our military aid to China does not really accomplish anything militarily, but it offends the Soviet Union and perhaps increases the likelihood that it will attack. This is why former Secretary of State Cyrus Vance is right in calling it little more than "bear-baiting."

One can go further. The present level of Soviet-Chinese hostility is not really in our interests. It results in the Soviet Union having built up a huge army on the Chinese border (rather than in having shifted troops from elsewhere). In the case of a rise in the danger of a Soviet-American war, the Soviet Union is highly likely to issue an ultimatum to China, get a nonaggression pact, and then have this army available to transfer to other fronts. The Soviet Union is now facing a demographic crisis (the number of eighteen-year-olds by 1985 will be 25 percent less in number than in 1980), and if hostility to China lessened, the Soviet Union would almost surely reduce the size of its army rather than shift it to Europe (barring a Northern Ireland situation in Poland). That would be in the American interest.

In cases such as Afghanistan or Cambodia, the Soviet-Chinese conflict has not halted Russian aggression. Rather it has given the Soviet Union an additional reason to take an aggressive action.

The time has come for the United States to think seriously about military realities and the nature of war in the nuclear age. By retaining outmoded geopolitical concepts and applying them in a knee-jerk manner, we significantly lessen our security.

Harrison E. Salisbury. Russian aggression against whom? China? Perhaps. It also can serve as a trigger for Soviet attack against China. If the United States is going to arm China, better attack China before she is armed—so goes the thinking of many Soviet military strategists.

Dr. Charles W. Thomas. Is supplying arms to China (People's Republic of China) a good way to halt Soviet aggression *against whom*? Supplying arms to the People's Republic of China will not stop Soviet force projection in third world conflict zones such as the Middle East or Africa. In China itself it might possibly help. However, it is extremely unlikely that the Soviets would ever be willing to pay the unthinkable costs of

invading the People's Republic of China regardless of the level of sophistication of its armed services. If the Soviets seriously wished to attack the
People's Republic of China it would be with nuclear weapons. Arming
China might prevent the Soviets from launching limited punitive attacks
along the border. It is unlikely to prevent Soviet aggression in northern
Asia (Japan or Korea) unless the arming policy is accompanied by security
treaties—an unlikely event at present.

Russia certainly has no desire to fight a two-front war, against both
China and NATO. However, the Soviet Union really does not face this
prospect unless the arming policy is accompanied by NATO/United
States-People's Republic of China security agreements. The Soviets
could still attack NATO confident that Chinese self-interest would keep
them waiting to see who wins. Only if NATO begins to win would the
Soviets face the prospect of a two-front war. This would be an extremely
dangerous moment. If anything were to encourage the Soviets to escalate to nuclear weapons it would be the prospect of a Chinese invasion.

Arming the People's Republic of China will certainly have no effect on
Cuban proxies ranging throughout Africa. However, arming China
might act as a considerable deterrent to any Soviet notion of employing
the Vietnamese as proxies in Southeast Asia.

These answers, of course, beg a number of important considerations:
Can the West arm China significantly at a reasonable price? Will China
remain anti-Soviet? Will the desire to arm China increase pressure on
Russia to attack now before the balance swings even further against
her?

Paul C. Warnke. For us to supply substantial military assistance to
the People's Republic of China would hurt American security interests.
China is under no present threat of Soviet attack and the risks involved
in trying to control China militarily should continue to deter any such
action. Rather than serving to restrain Soviet military aggression, a
decision by the United States to become a major arms supplier to China
could precipitate Soviet efforts to consolidate its territorial holdings in
the Far East, to increase its political pressures on Japan, and to suppress
forcibly any efforts by the countries of Eastern Europe to exercise
greater political and economic autonomy.

The existence of the "China card" serves our interests because each of
the Communist giants would like to avoid being odd man out in the
United States-Soviet Union-China triangular relationship. To play that
card by providing American arms to China would be to deprive it of any
value in motivating the Soviet leadership to pursue a more constructive
policy in Asia and elsewhere.

In addition, events in Iran and other former recipients of our military
assistance have demonstrated the risk that American weapons may fall
into the hands of successor governments less well disposed toward us.

HOW SAFE ARE OUR NUCLEAR INSTALLATIONS FROM TERRORIST ATTACK?

Larry Bogart. The greatest fear connected with nuclear power plants is the inability to protect these plants from sabotage, either from within or externally. It is admitted that terrorists could trigger a major accident at a nuclear plant. If this involved tons of highly radioactive spent fuel being stored at the plant, it could be a disabling blow to the entire nation and compel evacuation of an area larger than New England.

Klaus Knorr. Great care has been taken to safeguard these installations from terrorist attack. But nobody will claim that all of them are absolutely safe at any one time.

H. G. MacPherson. Reactor plants are less vulnerable to terrorist attack than many other types of plants because of the great strength built into the containment building and the thick steel walls of the reactor vessel and piping. An attack that might release damaging amounts of radiation would require the cooperation of engineers who know in detail how to deactivate the many redundant protective systems. The Nuclear Regulatory Commission requires each plant to meet rigid standards of physical security, and they are planning to test the effectiveness of these measures. Nevertheless, no facility can be totally immune from a well-planned, large-scale terrorist attack.

Richard P. Pollock. The physical protection of nuclear facilities has been one of the more worrisome aspects of our nuclear energy and nuclear production sector. In 1977 the United States General Accounting Office (GAO), the watchdog agency of Congress, examined the physical security of fifteen nuclear installations that handle weapons-grade nuclear material. None of the fifteen plants was capable of warding off a "dedicated group" of saboteurs, the minimum credible threat then designated by the United States government for terrorist activity.

A minimum credible threat to nuclear facilities is considered to be three individuals, one who is an insider and two outsiders. None of the nuclear installations reviewed by GAO could withstand this minimal threat. A maximum credible threat is of fifteen dedicated individuals, of whom three would be insiders.

Since the GAO's findings, little movement has been achieved toward adding protection to our very vulnerable nuclear plants. In 1978 the Nuclear Regulatory Commission's Office of Nuclear Material Safety and Safeguards expressed this concern in a whole series of memoranda.

Related to actual terrorist attack is the theft of nuclear materials. Only 11 pounds of highly enriched uranium or 4.4 pounds of plutonium are needed to manufacture a crude nuclear bomb. In 1977 the Congress'

Office of Technology Assessment estimated that a small group of people could construct such a weapon for several thousand dollars if they could obtain the nuclear materials.

In 1977 the first report of missing uranium was released by the Energy Research and Development Administration (ERDA), now part of the Department of Energy. ERDA officials testified before the House Subcommittee on Energy and Power that about seventeen tons of weapons-grade uranium and plutonium could not be accounted for. "This is the kind of subject that sends chills up my spine," said Representative John Dingell during the hearing. According to Representative Morris K. Udall, chairman of the House Interior and Insular Affairs Committee, "We may never know whether there was a diversion (theft) but it's darn hard to prove that there wasn't."

Barbara G. Salmore. American nuclear installations are not as safe from terrorist attacks as most people probably imagine or wish them to be. Military installations, containing nuclear weapons for use in the national defense, are very secure. However, this is not the case at those facilities serving peaceful purposes, such as the electrical power plants fueled by nuclear energy, which dot the country. Plants such as these are manned by private security guards with limited training, who are generally not equipped to hold out against a well-armed, determined group of attackers.

However, there are at least two reasons to believe that incidents of nuclear terrorism are quite unlikely to occur. First, there is the simple fact that no terrorist group has yet opted to use weapons of mass destruction. An authoritative Ford Foundation study discovered only two relatively minor incidents at nuclear facilities involving political terrorists (in Argentina in 1973 and France in 1975). Other weapons of mass destruction—chemical and biological agents—have never been used by terrorist groups. If terrorists have not seized the opportunity to go nuclear, or use other similarly terrible weapons to date, what reason is there to expect them to suddenly find this an attractive option today or tomorrow?

Second, even if terrorists in the United States did adopt a nuclear strategy, there are numbers of technical obstacles they would face. The low-enriched uranium used in most commercial light-water reactors cannot be made to explode, and the spent fuel is so dangerous and cumbersome to handle that it is unlikely to be stolen.

The easiest route for terrorists would be to occupy a peaceful use nuclear power plant. The mere threat to begin a core meltdown, or to release contaminants into the air, would probably cause widespread panic and concern, as seen in the Three Mile Island incident in 1979. However, as noted, political terrorists have never opted for strategies producing untargeted, widespread and wanton destruction. It is much easier and cheaper to use conventional terrorist methods such as explosives, hijacking, and targeted kidnapping, assassination or hostage-taking.

It would seem the public should be more concerned about innocent malfunction, such as that portrayed in movies like *The China Syndrome*, or in real life, as at Three Mile Island, which, unlike nuclear terrorism, occurs with uncomfortable frequency.

Dr. Michael G. Stevenson. Both commercial and governmental nuclear installations are heavily protected against terrorist attack. Commercial facilities are required by the United States Nuclear Regulatory Commission to have several layers of security, including armed guards and searches of people entering protected areas. Defense-related nuclear installations are also heavily guarded and have many protective systems, the details of which are generally classified.

In addition to heavy security, a nuclear power plant has a tremendous inherent ability to both deter and contain any damage from a terrorist attack. The sealed and locked containment building consists of a steel liner inside several feet of reinforced concrete designed to withstand the direct impact of such objects as a crashing commercial jet aircraft. Inside this, the reactor core is contained in a steel pressure vessel eight to ten inches thick.

A nuclear power plant should be one of the installations least vulnerable to terrorist attack.

[This response is based on my own technical expertise and in no way represents the position of the Laboratory, the University of California, or the U.S. Department of Energy.]

W. Scott Thompson. American nuclear installations at home are adequately protected from any terrorism action that can be envisaged today. Installations abroad, however, are nowhere near as safe, less for reasons of the physical protection present than because of the political situation. The physical protection at some sites in Europe is not as good as in America, but the key danger comes from the access to politically sensitive decision-making levels by Communist party officials and/or terrorist groups. As seen in mid-1981, domestic politics in general can also be a factor, as in Japan, where the question of American nuclear weapons caused a national furor and threatened the disposition of nuclear materials even in ships in Japanese ports. Any such furor degrades the overall security of the installations. Only if the domestic situation within the United States deteriorates so that terrorist groups could infiltrate the government and/or key military commands, and gain preliminary access to weapons compounds by political means, do our nuclear installations become unsafe.

IF WE GET INTO AN ALL-OUT NUCLEAR WAR, HOW MANY PEOPLE WOULD BE LIKELY TO PERISH IN THE UNITED STATES AND AROUND THE WORLD? HOW MANY WOULD SURVIVE? WHAT WOULD THE WORLD BE LIKE FOR THE SURVIVORS OF A NUCLEAR WAR?

John R. Christiansen. It must be remembered that for years the policy of the United States has been deliberately *not* to protect the civilian population from nuclear attack. This part of the Mutually Assured Destruction (MAD) Policy was initiated under the hope that the Soviet Union would do the same. Russia has chosen *not* to keep its population vulnerable to attack. Presently, America would lose about 60 percent of its population in an all-out attack. Russia, Sweden, Switzerland, Norway, the People's Republic of China and many other developed nations—all of whom have developed effective civil defense systems—would lose no more than 6 percent of their populations, given adequate warning which is most likely. Most of the rest of the world's population would be relatively safe.

Depending upon the targets, the survivors would be relatively non-affected (most of the world) or relatively destitute—as would the United States under present circumstances. The United States, with a continued policy of no civil defense adequate for dealing with an attack, would become a third-world nation. With an adequate civil defense system, comparable to that of the Soviet Union, it would become a viable, equally productive nation within three years following a nuclear attack.

Dr. J. I. Coffey. I see no reason to change former Secretary of Defense McNamara's estimate that, in such a war, 100 million Americans, 100 million Soviets and 100 million Europeans would perish. So also might 100 million people elsewhere, depending, for example, on whether nuclear weapons were used in the Middle East, against United States bases in Japan and the Philippines or against Soviet positions in, say, Vietnam, or whether the Soviet Union struck at targets in the People's Republic of China.

I see no reason to envisage a nuclear holocaust; hence, for most of the remaining 4 billion survivors, the geographical environment would be much the same, barring increased radiation from fallout. The survivors in the United States, the Soviet Union and Europe might not, however, survive long, as I do not believe societies there can withstand the tremendous shock of large-scale nuclear war. More significantly, the political environment would change dramatically, with the disappearance of the two superpowers (and many of the advanced industrial nations) as "viable twentieth-century societies," to once more quote Mr. McNamara. Thus, I see a world in turmoil for at least a generation, with more dying in that subsequent period from the indirect consequences of an all-out nuclear war than were killed in the actual exchange of warheads.

Howard Frazier. The United States has 31,000 strategic and tactical warheads, equivalent to 600,000 atom bombs like the one that was dropped on Hiroshima. According to a study made by the Congressional Office of Technology Assessment dated May 1979, up to 165 million Americans could die under conditions that would be "the economic equivalent of the Middle Ages."

Estimates regarding the number of people that would be killed around the world vary from half the world's population to every person in the world. Professor Philip Handler, president of the National Academy of Sciences, has stated: "A qualitatively new phenomenon would result. The depletion of the stratospheric ozone . . . global in scope . . . would persist for years, resulting in such intense ultraviolet irradiation of the earth's surface as to cause crop failure by direct damage to plants and by major alterations of climate and . . . markedly increase the incidence of skin cancer in those exposed." Professor John Somerville in an article in *The Churchman* (August, 1979) stated: "It is already objectively clear that the nuclear weapons which now exist in the arsenals of the opposing 'superpowers' are capable, if used, of annihilating all forms of life and all vestiges of civilization in a new kind of holocaust for which a new term had to be invented: omnicide. This is abundantly confirmed in the overkill statistics of weapons technology."

"The living would envy the dead" has been said of survivors of a nuclear holocaust. John Hersey in his book *Hiroshima* described some of the survivors of the Hiroshima bombing as follows:

> . . . There were about 20 men . . . all in exactly the same nightmarish state: Their faces were wholly burned, their eye sockets were hollow, the fluid from their melted eyes had run down their cheeks . . . their mouths were mere swollen puss-covered wounds, which they could not bear to stretch enough to admit the spout of a teapot . . .

Civilization as we know it would no longer exist. There would not be doctors and nurses to care for sick people. Water and air would be contaminated. Food would be scarce. There is some thought that the only people who could survive would be those in third-world countries, people who have lived close to the earth all of their lives. Someone asked Albert Einstein how the Third World War would be fought. He said he didn't know but if nuclear weapons were used then the Fourth World War would be fought with bows and arrows.

Ultimately, as Albert Einstein said, "The unleashed power of the atom has changed everything except our ways of thinking. Thus we are drifting toward a catastrophe beyond comparison. We shall require a substantially new manner of thinking if mankind is to survive."

Klaus Knorr. Nobody really knows the exact figures. The extent of human destruction depends on the nature and scope of nuclear attacks, as well as other factors. But if such a war is not designed to minimize human casualties, upward of one hundred million people are likely to die, at once or over a period of time.

The entire world would be seriously damaged by nuclear devastation in the United States, Soviet Union and probably Europe, not only by nuclear fallout but also by the damage done to the world's economic capacity, and also from the resulting political and military chaos in various parts of the world. Yet gradually the world would recover.

AMERICAN
LIFE

EVER SINCE ALEXIS DE TOCQUEVILLE came to America in the 1830s to study the "American character," our country has been a fertile field for study by writers and social commentators. One feature that has always stood out in our national character has been our steady impetus for change.

Social change in this country has been particularly turbulent in the last two decades. In the 1950s and early 1960s, Americans exuded a fresh self-confidence and an attitude that there was no challenge too great for us to overcome. By the late 1960s and the 1970s, however, the country was gripped by a new mood of pessimism and doubt. The popular television shows of these two different periods are good indicators of the changes that our country has undergone.

"Lassie" and "Life with Father" were two of the most popular and typical television shows of the 1950s and early 1960s. In both the action was basically the same week after week: the half-hour began with the setting up of a problem; twenty minutes later we reached the climax; and then, in a burst of dramatic activity, the problem was resolved in the final minutes of the show. Regardless of our involvement in the action of the show, we all knew that there was no situation that was too tough for June Lockhart's loving smile or the worldly-wise look of father.

The self-contained action of the show and the underlying attitude that no matter what happened, there was no problem too grave to be handled by a wise father or a loving mother, were indicative of the dominant national attitude of self-confidence and a feeling of control of the world around us.

"All in the Family" of the 1970s, however, exhibited an entirely new feeling about the complexity of life. The family portrayed was not a typical television white Anglo-Saxon Protestant family, but a working-class family living in Queens, New York. There was a constant tension between the generations, and the problems the show dealt with were imported from the outside world and were larger than the show. There was some kind of resolution within the half-hour, but the viewer was left with lingering questions and doubts about the issues raised.

In short, "All in the Family" projected an image of an America that was less than ideal. We were left with the sense that life's daily problems are not resolvable within a pat, half-hour formula, and that life is not always easy, but at best must be lived with a sense of humor.

The essays in the following section attempt to make sense of the many different changes our country is going through. In a lucid essay on the future of the family, Robert Francoeur writes that our country is undergoing a shift from a male-dominated society to an egalitarian society in which men and women assume equal power. Because of the increasing psychological and economic independence of women, a pronounced de-emphasis on marriage and childbirth is taking place. The traditional family will be replaced more and more by a new pluralism of intimacy networks such as the "extended family of friends" structure that is now so common among twenty- and thirty-year-olds living in our cities. Dr. Francoeur suggests that 10 to 15 percent of the population will struggle to hold on to traditional values in the face of these changes; 20 percent will explore these new patterns; and two-thirds of the population will be utterly confused by these changes.

The section on minorities and women is filled with fresh ideas about these important subjects. Edward Chang asserts that minorities are certainly better off than they were in the past—they are no longer denied the right to purchase a house, enter college, or move freely around the country. Edna Bonacich takes a more radical stance—she maintains that most minorities are members of the country's working class; therefore, their situation will never improve under the current capitalist system. And Wilmoth Carter takes a middle stance—more blacks have entered the middle class, but the plight of the black underclass has grown more dismal; she maintains that one's sense of whether there has been improvement for minorities depends upon which class of minorities is most visible.

The essays in the following section offer a stimulating and refreshing selection of opinions on a range of subjects that are of crucial importance to our country in the coming decade.

ATTITUDES
AND
EXPECTATIONS

THE WAY WE WERE, the way we are, the way we will be—those are the subjects of the following section on American life. But before reading the experts' answers, ask yourself some questions:

- Are you over twenty-one?
- Are you a woman?
- Do you live in a metropolitan area?
- Are you white?
- Do you belong to a Protestant church?
- Are you married?
- Do you have two children?
- Do you work outside the home?
- Do you own a television and watch it fairly often?
- Do you exercise occasionally, but not very often?

If you answer yes to most or all of the above questions, move over—you belong to a big group. The average American is not necessarily a suburban or city-dwelling white, Protestant mother of two who holds a job and watches television more often than she goes jogging. In fact, there probably is no such thing as the "average American," even though we commonly pry into the habits, income, ideas and other aspects of the average American's life. After all, along with the millions of metropolitan, middle-class mothers, such as the one described above, there are also millions of divorced fathers, married farmers, unemployed youths, homemakers with large families, elderly widows and widowers, Roman

Catholics, Jews, young singles, blacks, Asians, children of all races and religions, and many other groups.

The very diversity of Americans makes it necessary to generalize when talking about the American way of life. While it is not possible to account for every individual, it is possible to evaluate changes, see patterns and note trends.

Thus we can guess that the average American is an adult. The United States Department of Commerce says that the majority of us are no longer kids—and we are not getting any younger either. In 1970, 40 percent of the population was under age twenty-one; the government estimates that by 1990 only 32 percent of Americans will be on the wrinkle-free side of twenty-one. As the baby boom grows up, the proportion of young adults—those aged twenty-one to thirty-nine—is expected to go up. In 1970, these young adults made up only 24 percent of the population compared to a projected 30 percent by 1990.

If strength is measured in numbers, women are the stronger sex in America—more than half the population is female. More than 80 percent of the population is white, and an estimated two-thirds are Protestant. It is not too risky, therefore, to depict the average American as a white, Protestant woman who, like most Americans, lives in a metropolitan area.

From there on, however, characterizing her life becomes more difficult. More than 90 percent of the people in our society marry at some time in their lives, so we can guess that she has entered wedlock—although with the current divorce rates there is no guarantee she will stay there. The average couple today has 1.8 children, although for ease of discussion the average family is usually rounded out to four.

The Bureau of Labor Statistics estimates that in 1979 it cost the average American family of four about $20,517 a year to live in an urban area and that food made up about a quarter of all their expenses. How do the Averages pay their bills? Chances are both husband and wife work. In 1980 more than half of all married women with children under the age of eighteen held jobs. If they are like most couples, she does not earn as much as he does, but between them they manage to keep up, well, an average middle-class income.

Between working and caring for the two children, Ms. Average is busy. She knows that exercise is important to her health and, on the whole, her family exercises more than similar families did ten years ago. But virtually all families own televisions, and only some families exercise regularly, so the Averages have to be careful to watch their weight.

The only thing that separates the Averages from other Americans is that, in real life, no one is average, and the American way of life is actually made up of more than 200 million individual lives. In the following section, experts discuss basic questions about where and how most Americans live. Equally important, however, experts discuss the crises that individuals face in their daily lives, as well as the personal joys. In the final analysis, America wants to know how the average

American can achieve more-than-average happiness. The experts offer their answers.

CONTRIBUTORS

Helen Bottel, syndicated columnist, and Suzanne Bottel Peppers, Sacramento, California

Dr. Doris K. Campbell, formerly Professor of Psychology, East Tennessee University, and Silliman University, The Philippines

Kenneth E. Clark, Professor of Psychology, University of Rochester, Rochester, New York

Stephen Fleck, M.D., Professor of Psychiatry and Public Health, Yale University School of Medicine, New Haven, Connecticut

Norval D. Glenn, Professor of Sociology, University of Texas, Austin, Texas

Walter W. Haines, Professor of Economics, New York University, New York, New York

Prof. Leonard J. Hausman, Florence Heller Graduate School for Advanced Studies in Social Welfare, Brandeis University, Waltham, Massachusetts; Director of the university's Master's Program in Human Management

Dr. Ralph W. Hood, Jr., Department of Psychology, University of Tennessee, Chattanooga, Tennessee

Walter Klopfer, Ph.D., Professor of Psychology, Portland State University; clinical psychologist, Portland, Oregon

Prof. George C. Myers, Director, Center for Demographic Studies, Duke University, Durham, North Carolina

Maxine Schnall, Founder and Executive Director of Wives' Self-Help Foundation, Inc., Philadelphia, Pennsylvania; author of *Limits: A Search for New Values*

Rudy Ray Seward, Ph.D., Associate Professor of Sociology, North Texas State University, Denton, Texas

Gail Sheehy, author of *Passages* and *Pathfinders*

John A. Talbott, M.D., Professor of Psychiatry, Cornell University College of Medicine, Ithaca, New York

Charles N. Weaver, Professor of Management, St. Mary's University, San Antonio, Texas

WHAT CONTRIBUTES MOST TO A HAPPY LIFE— A SATISFYING JOB, INTELLECTUAL CURIOSITY, SEX, RELIGION, SOCIAL RELATIONSHIPS, A SPOUSE, CHILDREN, GOOD HEALTH, A GOOD INCOME?

Suzanne Bottel Peppers. I would like to add a tenth item to the list of components in the question: a keen sense of humor. The ability to laugh at oneself and with others, to amuse and be amused, is high on my list.

Humor enhances. Without it, intellectual curiosity grows pompous; family, social and sex relationships dull. Certainly health and good cheer go together, one drawing from the other. And I could never appreciate a job or a religion which pushed eternal seriousness.

Looking at the other nine components, I believe intellectual curiosity contributes most to a happy life because, as with laughter, it betters chances for success with the other eight.

Intellectually curious people seldom bore, if, that is, they listen as well as talk. Generally open and accepting, they form deep relationships; spouse, family and friends appreciate them and usually don't drift away. But should rejection or loss come, an inquiring mind is too busy for prolonged loneliness. Interesting, well-paying jobs most often go to the brainy. And sometimes curiosity takes the sameness out of sex. As for religion and health: exploration becomes enlightenment.

Even if intellectual curiosity had no effect on other areas of a happy life, I'd still make it my first choice. Husband, children and friends are extremely important to me. I like my work. But if my mind went inactive, I'd dislike myself, and then no one could love me. Goodbye, happy life!

Dr. Doris K. Campbell. My belief is that one does not find happiness in an active pursuit of those things that are perceived to be necessary for a happy life, whether they are money, recognition, fame, achievement in one's field of work, good health or a satisfying sexual relationship. In other words, I believe that one does not directly pursue (and attain) happiness for its own sake.

A truly happy life is elusive and not always attainable. It is possible one does not always realize when one is leading a happy life. At times one may be surprised by joy, or one may attain self-actualization and a peak experience as described by humanist psychologist Abraham Maslow. In experiences such as these one may have a glimpse of what actually contributes to happiness.

I do believe, however, that one would not attain these experiences of happiness without some basic essentials. They are a sense of harmony or congruence within one's self, ego integrity or self-consistency. Believing in one's self-worth and the value of what one is doing is closely related to, if not a part of, this inner harmony. A sense of belonging to the brotherhood of man and an interest in the welfare of one's fellow men are also relevant in this context. The capstone which completes the picture is an appreciation and enjoyment of life, a sincere religious faith or religious transcendence.

In this context it seems to me that the things people usually pursue to find happiness fall into proper perspective. I am referring to productivity and achievement in one's work, an adequate income, good health, a supportive home and family and understanding friends. Some or all of these can contribute to a happy life, but no one of these is absolutely essential.

A happy life is not to be bought or sought. It comes as a sort of by-product. Perhaps what I am trying to say can best be summarized in the words of Jesus: Seek first the Kingdom of God (the kingdom within you), and all these things will be added unto you.

Kenneth E. Clark. The characteristics that are most important for happiness vary over a lifespan. Rather than detailing them through all of the ages, I would like to comment most directly on what makes a person review his or her own life as one that was a happy one. In the studies made of Terman's men and women of genius, those persons in their later years reported that their family relations were critical to their having had happy lives. They also indicated that the degree of achievement they had reached was important, particularly in terms of utilizing their unusual talents. That group was healthier than average and indicated gratification for that. Most of the evidence that comes from other sources supports these points, namely that one needs a sense of fulfillment in terms of having made a contribution to others in some way in order to be happy and contented.

Most studies of this sort deal with persons whose intellectual attainments are significant. Many persons end up very happy because one feature of their life is very good. Thus, having happy children, or being fully dedicated to a religious belief, or having a happy marital relationship, or having close friends turns out to be important. All of these are important for all persons but some individuals can sustain themselves with less intellectual involvement, a less satisfying job, with less of an income, and with poorer health because of the personal associations they have with other persons in terms of their own set values with regard to religion.

If one seeks a simple answer, I would say that the most important characteristic for a person to achieve in order to have a happy life is the thing that the person is convinced is the most important aspect of his or her life. Thus for each individual, the answer is different. For me, variety has been one of the greatest sources of satisfaction in my life. I would hope that every person would have as many and varied experiences as I have had, and can find equal joy in those activities and in the memories of them.

Stephen Fleck, M.D. What may be considered a happy life in one culture might be a most difficult, if not unhappy one, in another society. A great many variables enter into the self-assessment of one's life, and even within a particular society very different life-styles and circumstances can be compatible with a sense of a happy life provided that the particular culture or society allows for such variations.

In our pluralistic society, for instance, a celibate priest may consider his life a happy one, as may a nun, but a profligate scoundrel who stays within the outer edges of lawfulness also may consider himself or herself happy.

In our country, success in relationships, intimate relationships in particular, and work or career are usually the two yardsticks by which most people consider their happiness or, at least, success in life. Good health and absence of economic hardship would also be basic ingredients, but in and of themselves they seem to have little to do with one's sense of having a happy life, although their absence is felt painfully and unhappily.

Educated people are also happier, or at least, more satisfied with their lives than the less educated, according to survey statistics. Because exploration and curiosity through all our senses seem to be quite basic in human nature, it could be argued that the greater peoples' capacities and freedom to pursue and widen their horizons through exploring and analyzing themselves and their environments, the better the chances for happiness.

Norval D. Glenn. Of the characteristics mentioned in the question, a spouse seems to be, by a large margin, the most important contributor to a happy life for most adults in American society. Of course, having a spouse contributes to a happy life only if the marriage is satisfactory; a poor marriage is not better than no marriage at all. The happiest adults in this country are, as a whole, the married persons with good marriages, next are the unmarried persons (never-married, divorced and widowed), and last are the married persons with poor marriages.

Of the remaining possible contributors to happiness named in the question, a satisfying job, religious devoutness, social relationships, sex within a close relationship (but, for most persons, not casual sex), a good income and good health are all apparently fairly strong contributors to happiness, although all rank far below having a good marriage. To my knowledge, there is no good evidence on what effect intellectual curiosity has on happiness, although I would guess that it has a distinctly positive effect. It is not possible to rank these characteristics with precision according to their relative importance, but good health and social relationships are among the most important, and a good income is perhaps the least important. Having a moderate rather than a very low income does make an important difference, but above the moderate level, increments of income seem to have little effect on happiness.

There is an abundance of recent evidence on the effects of children on their parents' happiness in American society, and on the average, those effects seem to be slightly negative. I emphasize on the average because some parents derive a great deal of happiness from their children, although that effect has apparently not been the usual one in this country in recent years. While the children are at home, their negative effects on their parents' happiness seem to be on the quality of the parental marriage and on the closeness of social relationships of the parents with persons outside of the family. After the children leave home, their effects on their parents' happiness seem to be neutral for most segments of the population but seem to be distinctly negative for parents who are black males or highly educated white males. The reasons for this are a mystery.

Dr. Ralph W. Hood, Jr. The options listed are less relevant to producing a happy life than what integrates all these options—the ability to believe that one is meaningfully participating in life. One's ability to find a meaningful life can be through religion, interpersonal relationships, intellectual curiosity or whatever, but any of these alone will not suffice. What most people think makes for a happy life, good income, etc., in fact just makes for conditions under which one can feel meaningfully involved in life. This is why sometimes the paradoxical effect of low income, poor health, etc., is to make one happy—when such adverse conditions force one to confront or discover meaning in life.

Maxine Schnall. The sources of happiness in life fall into four categories of equal rank as indicated in the following chart.

Relational	Achievement	Survival	Spiritual
Social relationships	Satisfying job	Good health	Religion
Spouse	Hobbies or	Good income	Intellectual
Children	Individualistic		curiosity
Sex	pursuits		

Although these four categories are of equal rank, an individual deprived of a source of happiness in any one category may attach undue importance to that particular one or may try to compensate for the loss by focusing excessive energy and thought on a different set of needs. For example, a person who loses a spouse through death or divorce may become a workaholic obsessed with career success. But the relational need for intimate love is one that only another human relationship, not work, can fulfill.

When any of these categories becomes so predominant in a person's life that it precludes another, the result is a neurotic imbalance that inhibits happiness. The driven overachiever who forfeits relational or spiritual needs for success ends up feeling lonely and alienated. By the same token, happiness cannot be attained through the satisfaction of relational needs alone, as the women's movement has shown, but must also derive from individualistic pursuits that confirm one's identity.

Rudy Ray Seward, Ph.D. Clearly, good health helps in doing the things necessary for accomplishment and so sets a kind of base line for happiness. But the importance of health increases with age because it becomes the focus of attention more often. The existence of poor or declining physical health is a primary determinant of suicide, and that is surely a dramatic expression of an unhappy life.

Assuming people have good health, what other factors promote the feeling of safety, security and comfort? Happiness often becomes dependent upon meeting the need for intimacy based upon enduring commitments. For most people marriage offers a means to fulfill this need, so it is considered central to the good life. The conjugal bond can be a source of comfort and support, as well as the focal point of everyday life. This may explain why married people on the average have better health and live longer; less often do they die in automobile accidents, commit suicide or get murdered. This is not the result of selection factors, such as the possibility that healthier people are more likely to marry. Support in marriage includes help in meeting emotional, sensory and survival needs. Together these integrate an individual into a close association which regulates the person's life, forcing one to take a spouse into account in what are often the person's most significant activities. In survey research, a strong association is found between marital happiness and overall happiness, especially for women. The marriage relationship often serves as an important prophylaxis. For a variety of social variables relating to psychopathology, martial status has consistently surfaced as the crucial factor. Married people are less often found among psychiatric patients; divorced and separated persons are consistently overrepresented among those requiring such care. The widowed and never-married fall in an intermediate category. This striking pattern is stable across different age groups; it is reasonably stable for both males and females and for blacks and whites.

Of course, marriages often fail and spouses do not lack ingenuity in finding ways to irritate and abuse one another. For that matter, lack of success in other areas of life can offset the potential advantages of marriage. Poverty offsets the usual advantages of marriage. Marriage for couples with incomes below the poverty level doesn't protect against feelings of loneliness, unhappiness or general life dissatisfaction. Having young children reduces the level of marital satisfaction for parents from the levels reported by newlyweds and their marriage does not totally recover until the children leave home.

But the attraction to marriage remains strong throughout the population. Almost all divorced people will eventually remarry, and many people outside of marriage attempt to create marriagelike bonds. This is seen in living together patterns among couples of all ages, and the urge of people in all kinds of settings (at work, in homes for the aged, in churches, etc.) to establish relationships which are similar to kinship relations—treating each other as if they were members of the family, by granting privileges and establishing obligations.

Gail Sheehy. Like the dance of brilliant reflections on a clear pond, well-being is a shimmer that accumulates from many important life choices made over the years by a mind that is not often muddied by pretense or ignorance and a heart open enough to sense people in their depths and to intuit the meaning of most situations.

Well-being is more than happiness. In its narrow sense, as Freud defined it, happiness generally conveys relief from pent-up frustration or deprivation of pleasure. Although the need may have reached great intensity, its satisfaction is most often instantaneous. By definition, then, happiness is only fleeting. Well-being, though, registers deep in our unconscious. It is an accumulated attitude, a sustained background tone of equanimity behind the more intense contrasts of daily events, behind even periods of unhappiness.

In 1977 I set out to locate adults who felt exceptionally good about themselves, to compare their experiences and especially to explore the qualities of mind and heart they cultivate in themselves and call upon at important crossroads. For this study, I developed a questionnaire with a complex instrument to measure well-being.

Broadly speaking, my survey found older is more contented than younger, married is happier than unmarried, and professionals are more satisfied with their lives than the working class. Income, however, is less closely correlated with overall well-being than age, the capacity to love and be loved, and the enjoyment found in one's work.

Merely scoring high on the well-being scale did not insure that one would *sustain* well-being. After intensive interviewing, I developed three subjective criteria that finally enabled me to identify the pathfinders—those models for lives truly worth living: (1) Did the person have the courage to change? (2) Did the person have a concern for his or her intimates, not leaving broken bodies in the wake of a search for well-being? (3) Did the person have a commitment to a purpose beyond his or her pleasure and advancement?

The most important thing about all of the qualities of personality that fortify pathfinders in resolving life crises is this: None is innate. We can strengthen each of these qualities by our own effects. Insofar as we are prepared to accept our humanness and struggle with it, we are all incipient pathfinders.

John A. Talbott, M.D. Probably fortunately for us as a species, the answer to what contributes most to a happy life is different for every person. People spend entire, satisfying lifetimes working as forest rangers; involved in the Girl Scouts, soccer leagues or disco dancing; trying to untangle puzzling genetic problems; or being good and devoted spouses. Society certainly shapes some preferences through status or stigma as well as monetary incentives or disincentives. For instance, for men in this society, a satisfying job probably remains most contributory to their perception of a happy life, while for women their former reliance on the role of spouse and mother is no longer sufficient.

And there are changes over time. For instance, while a good income and good health may have been enough a century ago, more people now would probably insist on including other factors that contribute to more

personal self-fulfillment; i.e., intellectual fulfillment, family contentment, close friends, etc. In addition, our American hunger to be all
things probably leads most of us to reply that while one factor is most
important, a balance between all of the possibilities is optimal.

Charles N. Weaver. There is increasing evidence that job satisfaction
may not be uniquely important to the overall happiness of either males
or females in most occupations. Employees whose happiness is significantly related to job satisfaction are also likely to experience satisfaction
in other parts of life. Thus, happiness seems to be a generalized phenomenon, according to which employees are either generally satisfied
or dissatisfied across a broad totality of life, with relatively few employees experiencing a significant satisfaction-happiness relationship in
only one or a few aspects of life. If this interpretation is accurate, the
happiness of most employees would rarely come entirely from a satisfying job, with little or no support from other domains of life.

IS IT POSSIBLE TO PREDICT WHICH PEOPLE
WILL GET DIVORCED? HAVE AUTO ACCIDENTS?
BE SUCCESSFUL IN BUSINESS? BECOME CRIMINALS?
WHY OR WHY NOT?

Stephen Fleck, M.D. The many variables involved make it difficult, if
not impossible, to make predictions about an individual person's future,
or future behavior. For instance, two youngsters start different grass
fires, neither of them intending any particular harm. One of them is
unlucky because the wind carries the fire to a shed causing damage
above a certain dollar value. He is labeled a delinquent, maybe even
punished by the court, and goes to a so-called reform school where he
learns about asocial behavior. This may be the beginning of a criminal
career for him. The other boy's fire did not cause any particular damage
and after he gets a parental scolding, the incident does not jeopardize his
future. Comparable differences in familial or societal responses to undesirable behaviors are common and these are examples of unpredictable
variables.

Yet habitual past behavior can indicate a person's future conduct to
some extent, particularly with regard to accidents and criminality. It is
possible, furthermore, to identify some other risk factors related to such
behaviors which could be used by individuals and those responsible for
them to guard against undesirable contingencies, possibly with the
assistance of some counseling or psychotherapy.

People who have experienced parental divorce are more likely to have
unsuccessful marriages than are individuals whose parents were stably,
if not satisfactorily, married. In our country marriages undertaken by
teenagers and in general by immature people, show a significantly

greater risk of ending in divorce than marriages undertaken by people twenty-two years or older. Similarly, marriages based on legitimizing an unexpected—not necessarily unwanted—pregnancy are terminated more often by divorce than are other marriages, even though the intent to get married may have antedated the conception.

A particular form of criminality, violence against other persons, while not predictable on an individual basis, is strongly correlated with having experienced violence in one's family of origin. This includes violence in the form of corporal punishment, no matter how well intended in the minds of a parent or parents.

I have no knowledge of how to predict success in business or whether or not it is predictable.

Dr. Ralph W. Hood, Jr. As a social scientist it is obvious to me that we can predict gross categories of events such as divorce rates, auto accidents, etc. However, with respect to the individual, such is not the case. Ultimately, I firmly believe persons are free and hence, their specific actions always are unpredictable in principle. The fact that a certain percentage of persons of type X can be expected to be criminals is predictable, but whether or not person X will become a criminal is ultimately unpredictable. Yet the common fallacy of using statistical data to predict individual behavior is rampant. Statistical data predict for groups of persons, never a particular person. Personal lives are always lived as exceptions or as unique events beyond the laws of probability that hold for groups of persons.

Walter G. Klopfer, Ph.D. It is possible to predict all these things. People who are young (especially teenagers), who have known each other only briefly, who have recently broken up with someone else, who are immature and emotionally unstable are candidates for divorce. People who drink excessively, drive at high speeds, drive when emotionally upset, are under the influence of drugs are likely to have auto accidents. People who have a financial cushion, other sources of income, training in economics, accounting and management and an assertive, confident manner, are most successful in business. People who are poor, retarded, unskilled and have been abused physically and/or psychologically by their parents often become criminals.

WHERE IN THE UNITED STATES DO WE FIND THE RICHEST PEOPLE? THE POOREST PEOPLE?

Walter W. Haines. The states with highest per capita personal income in 1980 were Alaska ($12,406), District of Columbia ($11,883), Connecticut ($11,445), California ($10,856), New Jersey ($10,755) and Wyoming ($10,692). Nevada and Delaware were among the top five in

1960, and New York and Hawaii made it in 1970; the list changes from year to year. At the low end of the scale are Utah ($7,485), Alabama ($7,484), South Dakota ($7,452), Arkansas ($7,180) and Mississippi ($6,508). Kentucky was among the lowest five in 1960, and South Carolina in 1970. Mississippi has been by far the poorest state for at least four decades. While the richer states are widely scattered geographically, almost all of the states in the Southeast are among the poorest in the nation; no one of them except Florida and Virginia ranked higher than thirty-sixth in 1980.

The richest counties are not necessarily in the richest states. The first ten in per capita personal income in 1979 were:

Cimarron, Oklahoma	$20,100
Witchita, Kansas	18,599
Loving, Texas	17,882
Haskell, Kansas	16,605
Arlington, Virginia	16,027
Falls Church, Virginia	15,480
Glasscock, Texas	15,075
Greeley, Kansas	15,060
Texas, Oklahoma	14,965
Juneau, Alaska	14,605

And while Mississippi had twenty counties with per capita personal incomes below $5,000 in 1979, it did not come close to having the poorest. That distinction went to Alaska, the richest state. Texas, with two of the richest counties, also had two of the poorest. The lowest counties in 1979 were:

Hayes, Nebraska	$3,668
Maverick, Texas	3,663
San Juan, Utah	3,661
Starr, Texas	3,640
Loup, Nebraska	3,626
McCreary, Kentucky	3,592
Owsley, Kentucky	3,411
Shannon, South Dakota	3,280
Wiboux, Montana	3,265
Wade Hampton, Alaska	2,737

In terms of the richest individuals, the Internal Revenue Service reports that in 1978 a total of 2,041 income tax returns reported an adjusted gross income of $1,000,000 or more. These millionaires lived in every state of the union except for Idaho and South Dakota. Mississippi had 3, but Alaska had only 1. At the other extreme California had 352, New York 316, Texas 233, Florida 125 and Illinois 113.

Much of these large incomes is derived from dividends, interest, partnership and other business income, and the sale of capital assets, but 273 persons received $1,000,000 or more in salary and wages. *The New York Times* named twelve business executives who were paid over $1,000,000 by their companies in 1978. Topping the list was David J. Mahoney, chairman of Norton Simon, Inc., who earned $2,037,055. Mr. Mahoney lives in New York City. Of the other eleven, three are officers of the Ford Motor Company, living in Grosse Point, Bloomfield Hills and Dearborn, all in Michigan; two are executives of Boeing in Seattle, Washington; two live in Dallas, Texas, and the rest in Chicago, Illinois, Farmington, Connecticut, Villanova and Buck Hills Falls, both in Pennsylvania.

One might also be interested in knowing where in the economic structure the rich and the poor are. The very rich tend to be property owners whose unearned income comes in the form of rent, interest and profits. In terms of earned income, the Bureau of the Census reports that the highest-paid workers in the United States in 1978 were self-employed physicians, dentists and related practitioners (with a mean annual income of $43,684), followed by salaried doctors ($38,944), and male salaried managers and administrators in manufacturing enterprises ($28,412). Women earn much less, female managers receiving only $13,432 per year. Other female workers do better; college and university teachers top the list at $17,013, with female computer specialists earning $15,415 (compared to $20,204 for males).

At the bottom of the list of occupations for men are farm laborers and supervisors ($8,359) and food service workers ($8,803). Among women, farm labor is also the lowest ($3,097), with private household workers not far ahead ($3,457).

All of these occupational figures are for full-time workers. Much lower income is earned by part-time workers and migrant workers. Blacks, Hispanics, native Americans and illegal aliens earn relatively little, with the unemployed at the bottom of the ladder.

Professor Leonard J. Hausman. Geographically, a disproportionate number of the richest people's principal residences are in New York City, Houston-Dallas and southern California. The richest people concentrate in investment banking, mining (oil, natural gas, etc.) and real estate development. There are very rich in other industries too, such as soft drinks. And some very rich people are in illegal industries, drugs and gambling. They are usually entrepreneurs and managers of very big private corporations.

The poorest people are concentrated in the rural south, although this is changing. And one cannot ignore the very large concentration of the poor in inner cities. The very poorest people still are in agriculture and in various illegal places of work, e.g., urban "sweatshops." Illegal aliens must be included in this category.

Professor George C. Myers. If by richest, you mean the persons with the most capital assets, then such people would be found in several areas of southern California, parts of Florida and the New York/Connecticut metropolitan and suburban areas. I have the suspicion that many of the elderly persons within such areas would have the most assets. But, we mustn't overlook the tremendous land assets of farmers in the Midwest, Texas and Oklahoma; nor holders of oil rights.

The poorest people are certainly located in central portions of cities and those located in marginal farming areas. I've often thought that the poorest persons I have ever met are located in portions of upstate New York.

MARRIAGE
AND FAMILY

*I*F CURRENT TRENDS continue, half of all young Americans' marriages are expected to end in divorce. The other half are predicted to last throughout the couples' lifetimes. The statistics speak for themselves. The Bureau of the Census records that the divorce and annulment rate per year in 1940 was about 2 per 1,000 people; the rate reached 3.5 per 1,000 by 1970. During the next nine years, divorces rose another 50 percent to reach an unprecedented rate of 5.3 per 1,000 by 1979.

As the divorce rate has more than doubled in twenty years, people have begun to question whether the nuclear family is as stable an element in society as it had once been thought to be. Divorced couples and their immediate families are the ones most involved in the painful process of marital breakups, but other people, such as grandparents, in-laws, relatives and friends, are also affected when a family splits apart. Children are often the hardest hit. In 1979 alone, divorce and accompanying custody arrangements changed the lives of more than a million children in the United States. Currently, only about three-quarters of all American children live in two-parent homes.

As sociologists point out the two-parent family in which the father works and the mother stays home taking care of the children is no longer "typical." Not only are more couples getting divorced and more children living in one-parent homes, but more wives are working. An estimated 47 percent of all married women held jobs in 1977 as compared to 40 percent in 1970. Also, couples tend to be having fewer children, and many couples are opting not to have children at all.

While marriage and family life are changing, Americans have by no means abandoned these institutions. In 1979 the marriage rate reached its highest point in five years, and marriages that year outnumbered divorces by more than a million. As the following table illustrates, the percentages of married people have declined somewhat in recent years, but married couples still make up by far the largest group in the adult population.

MARITAL STATUS OF ADULTS 18 YEARS OLD AND OVER

	1965	1970	1975	1978
Single	14.9%	16.2%	17.5%	19.3%
Widowed	9.0	8.9	8.3	8.0
Divorced	2.9	3.2	4.6	5.7
Married	73.2	71.7	69.6	67.0

SOURCE: U.S. Bureau of the Census

Furthermore, while the divorce rate is climbing, so is the rate of second and even third marriages. In 1976, for example, the government estimated that one in every three marriages for people married between 1970 and 1979 would end in divorce; in addition, 35 to 45 percent of those who divorced would remarry but later divorce again.

As divorce becomes more and more predictable, society's attention is turning back to the married, especially to those who manage to stay married through better and worse, richer and poorer, and even until death. Divorce has never been easier, cheaper or more socially acceptable. Why then do so many marriages endure? Are the couples who enjoy long, happy marriages skillful, persistent, lucky, or all three?

The following experts' answers discuss all facets of marriage and family life. They examine the marriages that break up along with those that endure; they look at current problems of coping with marriages and children as well as the future of the family as an institution. Statistics show how the family has changed in the past few decades; the experts offer insights into how it may—or may not—change in years to come.

CONTRIBUTORS

Dr. Joyce Brothers, psychologist, author, news commentator

Bettye M. Caldwell, Ph.D., Donaghey Distinguished Professor of Education, Center for Child Development and Education, University of Arkansas, Little Rock, Arkansas

Victor G. Cicirelli, Professor of Developmental and Aging Psychology, Purdue University, West Lafayette, Indiana

Prof. Manuel Diaz, Graduate School of Social Services, Fordham University, New York, New York

Robert T. Francoeur, Ph.D., A.C.S., Professor of Human Sexuality and Embryology, Fairleigh-Dickinson University, Madison, New Jersey; author of *Becoming a Sexual Person*

Jane T. Howard, author, New York, New York

Edward M. Levine, Professor of Sociology, Loyola University, Chicago, Illinois

Dr. David R. Mace, Professor Emeritus of Sociology, Bowman Gray School of Medicine, Winston-Salem, North Carolina

Prof. Brendan A. Maher, Harvard University, Cambridge, Massachusetts

John F. McDermott, Jr., M.D., Professor and Chairman, Department of Psychiatry, University of Hawaii School of Medicine, Honolulu, Hawaii

Letty Cottin Pogrebin, writer, lecturer and Founding Editor of *Ms.* magazine; author of *Growing Up Free: Raising Your Children in the 80s*

Dr. Robert M. Rice, Director of Policy Analysis and Development, Family Service Association of America, New York, New York

Rudy Ray Seward, Ph.D., Associate Professor of Sociology, North Texas State University, Denton, Texas

Gail Sheehy, author of *Passages* and *Pathfinders*

Dr. Peter A. Wish, Director, New England Institute of Family Relations, Inc., Framingham, Massachusetts

ACCORDING TO EXPERTS AND COUPLES MARRIED A LONG TIME, WHAT ARE THE BEST INGREDIENTS FOR A LONG AND HAPPY MARRIAGE?

Victor G. Cicirelli. There is probably no single general formula for a long and simultaneously happy marriage; it varies with the match of the personalities and the situation that couples find themselves in. However, some general factors that increase the probability of a long and happy marriage are intimacy, understanding and deep commitment to each other. Willingness to compromise when there are differences, and goals that are meaningful to both partners are also important. There must be a balance between sharing of feelings, mutual interests, and common goals and a respect for the marital partner's individual privacy and personal interests and goals. Some couples spend a lifetime doing everything together, while others have their own lives and careers and come together for a limited amount of time and sharing of experiences. But in both cases, if the marriage is to succeed, there must be a sense of intimacy, of closeness, feelings of understanding, and willingness to help the other.

Letty Cottin Pogrebin. The greater the degree of sharing between wife and husband (in decision-making, economic contribution to the household, discipline of the children, etc.) the more likely the marriage is to be satisfying to both partners, and the less likely there will be domestic violence and abuse.

In my own marriage of more than seventeen years, the ingredients seem to be egalitarian decision-making, mutual respect, active communication and conversation, and complete lack of boredom. Both of us have deep commitments to our children and family unit, but we also each have very involving work lives. We are each other's best friends.

Dr. Robert M. Rice. Several research studies suggest the most dangerous periods for marriages are those of considerable change. All marriages have change points in their lives—the advent of children, moving to a new town, or responsibility for aging parents, for example. Changes can be up (a job promotion) or down (a job layoff).

Long and happy marriages have capacities in their relationships which help them over the rough periods of change. Often, couples turn to elements in their marriage that continue to be stable. For example, many couples maintain an ongoing romance. There are unchanging aspects to relationships that are deeply understood and utilized in marriage. Often, couples have a common religious belief or a common ethnic heritage. Many couples are surrounded by kin who can be counted upon to provide support in bad times. Sometimes a home location can be an important support because of neighborhood or community ties.

Probably most important of all these unchanging elements is an understood commitment between a couple that, no matter the stress, the marriage will continue. The marriage vows stress this, and long-lasting marriages reflect it.

Rudy Ray Seward, Ph.D. Many of the components which increase the chances for a stable and successful marriage exist prior to the wedding. Selecting a mate who has the same racial background, socioeconomic status, religious affiliations, intelligence level and age as oneself is strongly associated with marital success. In general, the greater the similarity between the spouses on these foundations for agreement factors and a host of others, the higher will be the quality of the marriage. In addition, certain resources which the couple brings to marriage, such as educational attainment, social standing, physical and emotional health, and approval from family and friends, improve the prospects. Finally, the longer and better a prenuptial couple is acquainted with one another affords an advantage.

Having all the right characteristics is no guarantee of harmonious wedlock, unfortunately. It just helps. But our emphasis on romantic love as the primary basis for marriage often obscures this advantage, so young people short-circuit the selection process and choose mates on the basis of very imperfect information about them. An extreme example is the person who is drawn to love and marriage as a way to escape or solve a personal problem. Wedlock ought to be an end in itself; even if love is blind, marriage definitely is not.

The strong attraction which brings a couple together will hopefully develop into an attachment based upon the mutual satisfaction of many needs. After the halo from courtship excitement wears off the basis for a strong relationship will then still endure. A reciprocal fulfillment of needs in marriage should contribute to both intellectual and emotional growth for each spouse, creating a one-of-a-kind relationship between them. One survey of successfully married, middle-class couples—ones who had never even considered divorce—revealed several distinct kinds of unions. For some couples conflict was a continual part of their relationships; for others marriage involved minimal interaction and served mainly the separate convenience of each; for a few the union was total with all important aspects of life shared in a vital way. No one model for success could be found. Even the ingredients for a long and happy marriage varied.

After the wedding, social and economic factors continue to play a crucial role. The importance of being like one another after marriage works to an advantage in interpersonal characteristics. The more consensus on values, congruence on role perceptions, and similarity of personality traits, the better off the couple is. A key to discovering similarities—links in the chain of mutual compatibility—is communication, the bloodline for most human relationships, and certainly crucial for the nourishment of a marriage. Will your spouse be fascinating—or at least a pleasure—to talk to from now until old age? Most specifically, successful communication can increase the empathy between a couple, which in turn contributes to even more similarities, and promotes the ability to manage practical problems. The one thing constant in marriage is change. The goodness of fit between a couple can easily decline over time because of the changes which affect one or both spouses. Couples who enjoy a firm mutality, adequate support resources and communication efficiency will be the best equipped to have a long and happy marriage.

Gail Sheehy. People of high well-being overwhelmingly had relationships in which love was mutual, a key ingredient for a happy marriage.

Beneath the treacherous currents of self-love runs a wellspring of clear intensity—the feelings of pure gladness or sadness in watching someone else live. This, to me, is the meaning of mutual love.

A sense of confidence about who we are is essential to developing this most fragile and imprecise form of creativity—the capacity for loving mutually. As our identity becomes more secure, the capacity for loving seems to expand. People often believe quite the opposite: that if a mate is not dependent, he or she might leave. Yet it may be the strong sense of their individual identities that allows a man and woman to accept the emotional risks of intimacy. If one person's feelings change, the other will not be left in total collapse.

Mutuality of loving does not mean that two people always will want the same things at the same time. Any two healthy people will change from stage to stage and find themselves sometimes out of synch. As their primary needs are met, they will want things from life and from each other that go beyond their early romantic ideals. As one of the pathfinders I found said, "It takes a while to learn not only to let a person be where they are, but to enjoy their differentness."

Dr. Peter A. Wish. According to a recent in-depth study of over 650 couples, happily married from fifteen to twenty-five years, vital marriages have several key ingredients.

1. Make your marriage the number one priority in your life. Make your spouse the most important person to you while you protect, preserve and strengthen the marriage bond.
2. Enjoy sex together. Enhance your love life by communicating to your partner what pleases you, and keep yourself physically appealing.
3. Don't take each other for granted. Praise each other's efforts by compliments about looks and good deeds. Be nice to each other.
4. Accept your spouse for what he or she is and is not. Don't try to remold your partner; it doesn't work.
5. Have a positive self-image. Don't be hopelessly dependent on each other. Maintain your independence and individuality.
6. Keep lines of communication open. Vent your feelings including anger and frustration. And share your happiness.
7. Be sensitive to your partner's needs and desires.

WHAT IS THE MAIN CAUSE OF FAMILIES BREAKING UP?

Professor Manuel Diaz. Economic pressures that undermine the well-being of the family. In competitive societies such as the United States the family has little or no chance to function as an economic unit. The emphasis shifts to the individual. Decisions are based on personal, not familial needs.

Jane T. Howard. We live longer and move oftener and have many more choices than previous generations faced. Parenthood was never optional, for large numbers of people, until this century.

Dr. Robert M. Rice. The usual expected answers to this question are "sex" and "money." Actually, American family life is so diverse that this way of answering the question proves fruitless. To further complicate matters, there are certain known crises at various stages of family life which relate to the ages of family members and which therefore vary from time to time. For example, there is stress in raising young children which is different from what parents experience when their children are in their teens. It is different, again, for a couple to have to face that their children are leaving them to form homes of their own.

Another way of answering the question is to think about how our society may encourage the breakup of so many families. Probably the fundamental answer is an assumption in modern America that people have a right to many choices in their family lives which can be made in order to find satisfaction. There are both problems and opportunities for this social assumption of the happiness ethic. Although our society allows us the flexibility to tailor our lives effectively, this very flexibility may result in families breaking up. With an emphasis on happiness, Americans sometimes have difficulty weathering the bad times in families. No families operate without some strain. Ironically, the very optimism about family life which assumes there is always a better way of living, or of solving all problems, also leads to the breakup of many families.

WHAT CAN PARENTS DO TO IMPROVE THEIR CHILDREN'S CHANCES OF HAVING A SUCCESSFUL LIFE?

Robert T. Francoeur, Ph.D., A.C.S. In the first two-thirds of this century, adults and children alike could find comfort and support in a near monolithic structure of social standards that clearly defined our male/female relationships, sexual mores, marital pattern, sex roles and values. That support no longer exists in our growing pluralistic, patchwork society. The next few decades will accelerate our daily confrontation with choices and options, some of them completely new and without precedent in our past experience.

With this kind of future facing our children, it seems obvious to me that we can help our children survive and succeed in the years ahead by educating them from their earliest years in the skills of making decisions. Parents need to provide direction and guidance, but at the same time they have to provide an environment rich in the opportunities of growing up as an autonomous and socially responsible adult. Teaching young people how to deal with options means teaching them how to isolate central issues or questions, how to analyze the options they can pick from, how to weigh the costs and benefits of each option, how to arrive at a decision and then how to live with the consequences of the decision they have made. Training in the skills of decision making can begin very early in life on such a simple, innocuous level as deciding what skirt goes with what blouse and shoes, what to wear to school, or which of two television shows to watch.

It is much easier to be strict and authoritarian in child-rearing than it is to encourage a child to consider the options and make his or her own decision. Guidance and support is important for a young child, and parents can supply that even as they daily challenge their child in small ways to become a mature, self-actuating, socially responsible person. In the years ahead, a child raised in a very strict, authoritarian and rigidly structured family will find him or herself continually confronted with choices and options they are unprepared to deal with either intellectually or emotionally. They may even "drown psychologically" in "decisional overload," finding themselves pulled along in currents of change they cannot understand, control or participate in. If, on the other hand, they have slowly developed their decision-making skills in simple childhood problems, they will still make mistakes, but they will feel much more in control of their lives and future, much more prepared for the unexpected and more able to cope and succeed.

Our ancestors had to cope with the industrial revolution. Our children will have to cope with an information revolution: the computer, the word processor, the electronic age. Parents who really want to help their children prepare for a full, rich life in the years ahead will help them develop the communication skills they will need to be successful. Computer literacy will be an important aspect of these communication skills.

Finally, and in no way less important than the need for decision-making and communication skills, children need to be taught in non-verbal ways from their earliest years, a comfortableness and appreciation of their wholeness as human persons. Touch is the most basic form of communication. Cuddling, stroking, nurturing warm touch is essential for our balanced, full development. Human and animal research clearly shows that infants deprived of this nurturance grow into antisocial, maladapted and violence-oriented adults. Infants and adolescents who grow up with a lot of nurturance become warm, peaceful, loving adults, whether they be rats, monkeys or humans. A positive pleasurable embracing attitude towards our human body, towards our sexuality, our emotions and feelings is something adults can encourage or deny in so many nonverbal ways to a growing child. The antisensual and antisexual bias of the Victorian Age is behind us. So is a sexual ethic based on reproduction and marital status. As parents, we may still feel its influence, but we need to prepare our children with positive values and a sense of personal and social responsibility that will help them live fully as human sexual persons in a world filled with choices and options.

Edward M. Levine. Modern parents are confronted with a painful dilemma concerning their responsibilities toward their children. On the one hand, they enjoy the comforts and status afforded by two incomes as well as the independent satisfactions gained because of the augmented income. Some parents, of course, must work to make ends meet, and most single parents have no alternative to working. On the other hand, when both parents work, children are neglected; and it is inaccurate to assume that day care centers or parental surrogates can properly meet children's emotional needs so as to assure their healthy emotional development or adequately meet their socialization needs.

Children must have their parents' involvement with them on a continuing basis—when they need and want it, not at their parents' convenience. Otherwise, they will fail to adopt fundamental values that facilitate their learning how to become self-disciplined, to be properly mindful of other persons' needs, rights and prerogatives, and to guide their lives in terms of future goals. Furthermore, without having instilled such basic standards, children grow up to be impulse-dominated, an underlying cause of the psychopathology termed "character disorder" or "character defect." These psychological difficulties frequently lead to self-impairing and antisocial behavior, including drug use, educational underperformance, the inability to get along well with others (particularly with members of the opposite sex), and to depression and anxiety. These are the all too predictable outcomes of absentee-parenting and of parental neglect as well as parents' failure to act as parents, their unwillingness to firmly, consistently, and effectively set meaningful standards for their children and help them over time adopt and use these standards in ways that enable them to define and pursue their self-interest in self-productive ways.

More than ever before, there is a compelling need for parents to assure their children of a sound family life, to establish meaningful rules and regulations for them, and to be appropriately attentive to them from infancy into and through adolescence. The more that parents are remiss in assuming such responsibilities, the more emotional and behavioral problems will befall their children.

Dr. David R. Mace. The ideal setting for the healthy development of a child is to be raised in a home where the parents are united in a deep, strong, loving and open relationship to each other. In other words, the key to effective parenthood lies in the quality of the parental marriage.

What children need most is the emotional security which comes from knowing that they are loved and cared for by a father and a mother who manifestly love each other, and who demonstrate their united love for the child in an open, honest relationship—not a relationship which is free from conflicts, but one in which conflicts are recognized as "grow points," to be used for the progressive improvement of the relationship concerned.

The child of such a home will have the two essential requirements for success in life: a strong and secure self-esteem, and an effective coping system for the management of interpersonal relationships.

Professor Brendan A. Maher. Parents can improve their children's chances of having a successful life by first realizing that nobody else can do the job of parents but themselves. Not the school, not the experts on child development, not the guidance counselors and not the magazine writers—none of these can provide the example and the guidance that comes from a child's own parents. Everything that diminishes the parents' relationship with the children diminishes the child's chances of living the kind of life that is truly successful.

The important impact of parents comes from both example and from the training of children in the habits of self-discipline and respect for others that will be necessary to them in adult life. Children are greatly influenced by the model of behavior that their parents provide. A father who regards moneymaking and business success, or career success, as the only reason for living will be imitated by his children. If, in the pursuit of these ends he neglects his family and takes pleasure in the outmaneuvering of rivals by any means possible, then his children also will learn that lesson. A mother who is more concerned with achieving social success in the neighborhood than with her children will teach her children to think the same way. In brief, whatever the values and behavior we hope to see in our children, that we must do ourselves.

But example alone is not sufficient. The mastery of competence in whatever direction a child's talents may lie requires practice, study and patience. No new method of teaching and no faith in the power of spontaneous love of learning can be trusted to produce the competencies upon which self-esteem and the possibility of contribution rest. Learning is hard and sometimes boring. Parents can help this by taking a close interest in their child's work, by praising accomplishments—especially the accomplishment of recovering from failure and persisting nevertheless. Failures need sympathy and support, not punishment or abuse.

Children differ in their talents and their temperament. What is easy for one is less so for another and each one must ultimately find the tasks that suit his or her personality. Children may not wish to follow their parents' footsteps in choosing a career. Failure to accept this is often a source of conflict and misery; it must be accepted gracefully if the child is to find his or her own success.

In brief, love, example, firm kindness and tolerance of differences may provide the setting in which a child may develop toward a successful adulthood. Above all, it must be remembered that children grow up and leave home. The leaving will be the better if the parent has a life that has not become completely dependent upon the child's continued presence.

Finally, little worth having comes easily. Parents must work at being parents: the child must work to acquire the characteristics that will be needed later in life. Indulgence is not kindness, and is a poor preparation for the demands of adult life.

John F. McDermott, Jr., M.D. Parents must give their children a steady feeling of being wanted and loved if they are to grow up to deal with the world realistically and develop satisfying friendships and intimacies with other people. But beyond this basic core of becoming a person there is another layer of the personality which can be developed.

Parents can help children develop their own personal sense of confidence in themselves, confidence that they can do something well and that they will find their niche in society. It can be boiled down to a sense of mastery which is achieved over a long period of time and with some struggle, but with lots of support. Parents should begin to search early for their youngsters' own special talents and inclinations and encourage their development by making sure there is plenty of opportunity to increase and master them. As your children grow they will begin to realize themselves which of these talents they are most motivated to use in life, and which ones have a market waiting for them.

Too many well-meaning parents see only their own dreams in their children and mistake it for the child's. A chip off the old block is just that and nothing more. Find your child's dream and help develop it. Don't mistake theirs for yours, even if it is for their own good.

Rudy Ray Seward, Ph.D. Today parents are in the unenviable position of virtually having complete responsibility for their children but only partial authority over them. Because of the attention focused upon parenthood by both social science research as well as professional practitioners, the expectations for role performance are often very high— parents find themselves being compared with the professionals and not their fellow amateurs. In some instances we only can conclude that parents are expected to succeed where the experts have failed. Concomitantly, competition for the child's attention and time has become fierce, with heavy school and peer group demands plus the intrusion of television.

With rising expectations—children are to be reared not only differently than their parents but better—and with declining plus more thinly spread resources, parental contributions to their offspring's success might appear to be dwindling. Yet the parent-child relationship because of its intensity, intimacy and continuity, especially during the early years, has a decisive (although clearly not exclusive) influence upon the child's life. Parents who understand and accept their children for what they are can help them perform up to their potential academically throughout their schooling. Such parents provide care without over-protection or usurping the child's autonomy, and are more likely to share family recreation, ideas and confidence than the parents of low achievers. The former group encourage achievement without sacrificing approval, trust or affection toward their children. This warm, under-standing and moderately nonrestrictive relationship helps academically, and contributes to leadership and creative thinking in children too. Having certain materials (e.g., encyclopedias, magazines, books, collec-tions) in the home and participating in certain activities (e.g., hobbies, private lessons, membership in formally organized groups) increase the chances of success. Even the occupations children choose are influenced; most of them select jobs which are person-oriented. The alternatives in parent-child associations are related to aggressiveness, antisocial be-havior, and more involvement in disciplinary actions among children.

Unfortunately, no precise formula exists. These findings suggest only a general pattern, not specific behavior. Neither permissiveness nor restrictiveness has been found to result in maladjusted children unless either orientation becomes intense. Extreme parental restrictiveness, authoritarianism and punitiveness, without acceptance and warmth, lead toward a less positive self-concept for the child and weaker emo-tional and social development. Efforts to push independence in children too soon can also strongly reduce success in some areas. Children who are encouraged or allowed to exercise too much power in the home will tend to remain insensitive to the needs of others. Consistency becomes a key factor. The specific standards, as long as they are applied in moderation, are less critical than the fact that they remain constant from day to day. As children mature they must be given responsibilities commensurate with abilities. Their proper handling of these plus other accomplishments needs to be recognized. Finally they should receive unconditional acceptance and love quite independent of these achieve-ments.

WILL THE FAMILY BE A STRONGER OR WEAKER LIVING UNIT IN THE YEAR 2000? WILL THERE BE MORE SINGLE PARENTS? MORE DIVORCES?

Dr. Joyce Brothers. I believe the family will grow stronger. But families won't be the same in the future as they are today. Already they are changing. There are fewer children in each family unit than there were even a decade ago. And there are fewer mothers making mothering a full-time career. Indeed, the fear of overpopulation has caused many young couples to renounce parenthood entirely.

Many of these same young adults have been experimenting with alternatives to the nuclear family which separates responsibility for the larger community from responsibility for family members.

The most popular alternative to the family has been the commune, in which adults and children live together as one extended family. Is the commune the form our most intimate relationships will take in the future?

Probably not. The commune is as special in its appeal as the celibate monastic community and not everyone is adapted to communal living. Moreover, the commune has serious limitations for the children brought up within it. Though they are spared many of the emotional conflicts they experience in the nuclear family, they become very dependent on their peers and on the communal way of life.

The extended family for the future will probably be what Margaret Mead called the "cluster" community. In the cluster community the family would keep its identity but would live closely with other families of many different kinds. The cluster group might share a large house, a group of cottages or homes around a courtyard. In such sharing, independence would not be sacrificed to interdependence as it is in the commune. But neither would family units be isolated and alone, as they are in a society of nuclear families.

An ideal setting for the emergence of cluster groups is the academic community. There, young people and old come together for varying lengths of time and might learn a new life style along with their academic subjects. But the families might also cluster around a factory, a company, a series of tennis courts, a pool, a church, or any other common interest. Although there will be many single and divorced adults, the adults who do marry and remarry will form a stronger union because they will be marrying not because they have no alternative or because of community pressure but because they want stability in a rapidly changing world.

Bettye M. Caldwell, Ph.D. By the year 2000 we will probably have broken the habit of using the word family in the singular when we are referring to demographic conditions. We already have "families" rather than "the family." I think that families will continue to be very strong living units, but I agree with the many futurists who say that there will be many mutations and changes in styles of living between now and the year 2000. What has been called the traditional family, which some people challenge was never quite as widespread as we tend to assume, will undoubtedly occur with diminished frequency. However, it is my conviction that people will continue to look for satisfactions in traditional family units and that every young couple who begins a new family unit will enter into that arrangement with the expectation that it will indeed last and fulfill many of the aspects of the myth that has been with us for many years.

Unquestionably there will be more single parents and more divorces. The rate is changing so fast now, and always in an upward direction. It is always conceivable that something could happen to reverse this trend, but I would think it very unlikely.

Victor G. Cicirelli. The current trend toward single parenthood and divorce in all likelihood will continue to increase in the foreseeable future in the United States. There will also be an increase in remarriage (and series of remarriages) and couples living together without marriage (occurring with the middle-aged and elderly as well as the young). Although severely divergent forms (e.g., communes, group living, polygamy, and gay marriage) exist in relatively small numbers, they too will increase to some extent.

Without attempting to judge these alternative family forms, they may have the practical consequence of disrupting the degree of closeness and the helping relationships between family members. The divergent family forms do not seem to produce the needed degree of commitment, since individuals can easily obtain divorces or move in and out of a relationship that requires no legal binding or other formal obligation. If the trend toward small families continues, there may be fewer siblings as well.

In short, increasing diversity of family forms may lead to decreasing closeness and commitment of family members to each other, making the family a weaker unit in the year 2000. Greater self-reliance may be the only alternative to dependence on family members.

Professor Manuel Diaz. The family will be weaker because the emerging Information Society (the second post-Industrial Era), will place more emphasis on the individual as a programmable social unit than on the family as an economic unit.

On the other hand, this should imply a greater need for mutual support systems, since the individual will be ever more isolated and alienated than is true now.

Robert T. Francoeur, Ph.D., A.C.S. By the year 2000, our whole understanding of family will be greatly changed from what we have known in the recent past. There are many factors for this radical shift, including, among others, an increasing life expectancy, the increasing and irreversible economic and psychological independence of women, an improved contraceptive technology, the greater affluence and leisure-orientation of the majority of Americans, and a growing emphasis on population control.

One of the more obvious changes will be a dramatic increase in the number of women who remain childless. By 2000, over a third of white women and about a quarter of minority women will remain childless, whether or not they marry. Those couples who do have children will likely average a little over one child per couple. The harsh economic demands of child-rearing, coupled with the factors mentioned above, will trigger this shift away from parenthood and child-rearing in an increasingly adult-oriented society. Single parents, unmarried mothers and men who adopt, hire surrogate mothers or retain custody after a divorce, will be much more common than in the early 1980s.

With an expanding life expectancy and the economic independence of women, the pressure to marry will drop significantly. Considering the psychological problems and emotional adjustments men are now experiencing in accepting the shift from a patriarchal to an egalitarian pattern of male/female relationship, the majority of Americans who do marry will likely end up in divorce and remarriage. Men, in particular, will be looking for traditional values in the women they marry even though intellectually they disavow these values and attitudes. When they do not find them in marriage, the frustration will trigger a divorce and renewed quest for "an old-fashioned girl."

At the same time that 10 to 15 percent of the population struggles to hold on to the traditional values, 20 percent of Americans will be openly living new lifestyles and finding new patterns of intimate relationships. Many of these will not work out in the long term, but people will learn from their mistakes. The majority of Americans, at least two-thirds of the population, will be very confused and perplexed by all the changes in relationship and lifestyle patterns. Open, flexible and nonexclusive relations will be difficult for most people to accept, even though all the environmental factors will make such male/female lifestyles much more functional than in the past.

By the first decade of the twenty-first century, many people will have adapted to the new pluralism of intimate networks, including gay, single parent, childless and multilateral "intentional families" which will then provide the emotional, social, familial, psychological and economic support once provided by the blood kinship family. People will meet their real needs for intimacy in a variety of relationships which will vary with different life stages, some being sexually intimate, others emotionally intimate. For many, a long-term commitment and marriage will be a central core in their new intentional family or intimate network, with a variety of satellite or supporting relationships. As society becomes comfortable with this pluralism, new support mechanisms will emerge giving a new strength to the new family styles.

Jane T. Howard. In the year 2000, the family will be weaker unless we learn to define the word family a lot more generously. I suspect that divorces and single-parent households will proliferate, and so we will need to build and cherish ties based on choice, honoring them as much as we honor ties of blood.

Letty Cottin Pogrebin. The family will be a redefined living unit, encompassing people—both adults and children, or just adults—who choose to live together, love one another and be responsible for one another's well-being. Families will be functional, not ideological. They will be constellations for companionship as well as economic linkages. Families will not need dependency and power as unifying concepts, as has been the case with traditional male-dominated nuclear households. Old-style family life has ceased to deliver nourishment and satisfaction to all its members; it only serves to support the male. Therefore, in the interest of equity, economic necessity and psychological health, the egalitarian, nonpatriarchal family is the living unit of the future.

The number of single parents, divorces, etc., is not symptomatic of moral decline, as some would have it. Rather, this phenomenon is a measure of the failure of patriarchal marriage as an institution, and the need to address human needs from a reality base, not from some nostalgic idyll of "Life With Father."

In sum, the family, in diverse permutations—married couples, men together, women together, single parents with children, groups of single parents, extended age-groupings related to one another or not—will survive into the twenty-first century because economic and political reality will make such arrangements the only solutions that are utilitarian and rewarding to all who enter them.

MINORITIES AND WOMEN

T HE MAJORITY OF US are blends of many minorities: Italians, Chinese, white Anglo-Saxon Protestants, Irish, Portuguese, Hungarians—whatever the ethnic background or mixture, some Americans are bound to claim it.

But only about one in six Americans is a member of a minority group in the usual sense: a group set apart, often by race, and often discriminated against. These minorities include blacks, Hispanic Americans, Asians, Pacific Islanders and American Indians. Racial minorities represent a small but growing proportion of the total population. In the last decade, minorities increased from 12.5 percent to 16.8 percent of the total population.

Within the minority population, blacks make up by far the largest majority. According to 1978 figures from the Bureau of the Census, blacks comprise about 90 percent of the population of "blacks and other races." Blacks also tend to be more disadvantaged than the "other races" included in the minority grouping, but all of the minority groups share a history of discrimination in the United States.

Women actually make up the majority of American citizens: about 52 out of every 100 Americans are women. In recent years, however, many white women have identified with the struggles of minority groups because both women and minorities often seek equality with white males.

One major battlefront for both has been the field of employment and economic opportunity. Despite all the campaigns for black economic opportunity, blacks, as the answers in the following section point out, are still far from achieving an equal share in American prosperity. Since 1947 black families' median incomes have averaged only about 60 percent of white families' median incomes, and even less in recent years. Similarly, women workers, on the average, bring home far less than men, earning only about sixty cents for every dollar men earn.

The Civil Rights Act of 1964 guarantees equal pay for equal work, but so far women and minorities have not been able to achieve equal employment. Traditionally, white men have monopolized most of the high-paying jobs while women and blacks filled the jobs at the low end of the wage scale. Things are changing, but many jobs are still predominantly female or black. In hospitals, for example, black women in white jackets are usually mistaken for nurses—even if their name plates identify them as doctors. It is not surprising. In 1977, figures from the Bureau of Labor Statistics showed that only 11.2 percent of all physicians were women; 9.2 percent were black. In contrast, 92.8 percent of all nurses were women; 11.5 percent were black. Similar imbalances could be seen in other fields. For instance, only 4.4 percent of all bank officials were black; 27.3 were female. Among the low-paid tellers, however, 90 percent of the workers were female; 7.6 percent were black.

Minority groups cite a long history of racial bias as one of the factors limiting their earning potential. Women's groups cite sex discrimination along with the practical problems of trying to work, raise children and manage a home.

Throughout the 1970s more American women, both black and white, encountered these problems because more women held jobs than ever before. The year 1980 marked the first time in American history that more women worked outside the home than worked within as homemakers. Approximately 52 percent of all women belonged to the labor force; about 45 percent held jobs full time. Even more revolutionary, an estimated 45 percent of all married women with children under age six held full- or part-time jobs outside the home.

In many families, wives and mothers no longer view jobs as options; they are necessities if their families are going to maintain their economic status. A wife's income may make the difference between living at the poverty level or enjoying a few luxuries. Among black families, the only group to achieve income parity with their white counterparts in the 1970s were young couples in the North and West in which both husband and wife worked.

The following section examines the effects of working women on American economics and family life and looks at the gains—and losses— of minority groups throughout the United States. One indication of women's newfound political strength is that Americans want to know what advantages or disadvantages women—who as recently as 1924 could not vote—would face as presidents of the United States. Are women and racial minorities finally achieving recognition and opportunities equal to other American citizens? Experts offer some insights.

CONTRIBUTORS

Dr. Sharon N. Barnartt, Assistant Professor, Department of Sociology and Social Work, Gallaudet College, Washington, D.C.

Edna Bonacich, Professor of Sociology, University of California, Riverside, California

Melvin S. Brooks, Associate Professor of Sociology, Southern Illinois University, Carbondale, Illinois

C. Emory Burton, Chairman, Sociology Department, University of Alabama, Huntsville, Alabama

Leonard A. Carlson, Department of Economics, Emory University, Atlanta, Georgia

Wilmoth A. Carter, Ph.D., Vice-President of Academic Affairs and Research, Shaw University, Raleigh, North Carolina

Dr. Ben Cashman, Chairman, Department of Political Science, Seattle University, Seattle, Washington

Dr. Edward C. Chang, Chairman, Department of Psychology and Special Education, Albany State College, Albany, Georgia

A. Lee Coleman, Professor of Sociology, University of Kentucky, Lexington, Kentucky

Frances R. Cousens, Ph.D., Emeritus Professor of Sociology, University of Michigan, Dearborn, Michigan

Arlene K. Daniels, Professor, Department of Sociology, Northwestern University, Evanston, Illinois

Muriel Fox, Founder, past Chairwoman, National Organization for Women (NOW); past President, the Women's Forum and the NOW Legal Defense and Education Fund; Executive Vice-President, Carl Byoir and Associates, Inc.

Victor M. Goode, Executive Director, National Conference of Black Lawyers, New York, New York

Marion Hayes Hull, Director, Telecommunications Programs, Booker T. Washington Foundation, Washington, D.C.

Maurice Jackson, Ph.D., Professor of Sociology, University of California, Riverside, California

Dr. Robert C. Johnson, Chairman, Board of Directors, Institute of Black Studies, Inc., St. Louis, Missouri

Vernon E. Jordan, Jr., President, National Urban League, New York, New York

C. Eric Lincoln, Professor of Religion and Culture, Duke University, Durham, North Carolina

Marabel Morgan, author of *The Total Woman*

Florence Z. Perman, Director, Federal Women's Program, U.S. Department of Health and Human Services, Washington, D.C.

Lillian B. Rubin, Ph.D., sociologist and psychologist, El Cerrito, California

Phyllis Schlafly, author, television and radio commentator; President of Eagle Forum, Alton, Illinois

ARE MINORITY GROUPS IN THE UNITED STATES BETTER OR WORSE OFF THAN THEY WERE IN THE PAST? WILL THEY BE BETTER OR WORSE OFF IN THE FUTURE?

Edna Bonacich. Better off is a complex concept, especially if one compares the present to an undefined past. For example, the black situation may be better now than it was in 1860 or 1930 but worse than it was ten years ago. It may be worse economically, but better in terms of self-respect, communal solidarity and political awareness. Lumping all minority groups together presents additional problems since the situation of new immigrants, for instance, is different in important ways from the situation of older minority communities. My answer, therefore, will not be comprehensive but limited to a couple of particular cases.

If we consider the economic situation of blacks over the last few decades, the picture appears to be mixed. On the one hand, some blacks have apparently been able to enter the middle class, with rising numbers and proportions of white-collar workers. On the other hand, the existence of a large unemployed or underemployed population living in severe poverty and hopelessness continues unabated. Statistics suggest that the black median income may have risen slightly as a proportion of the white median income, but the absolute dollar discrepancy has increased. Thus, while a minority of blacks may be better off economically, the black community as a whole is revealing greater internal class differentiation, with many people no better off, and perhaps worse off, than their families of several decades ago.

In the noneconomic realm, some strides have been made in reducing the worst forms of overt racism. Open, intentional segregation is against the law and people are more conscious of the political costs of making public racial slurs. But many of these changes are more symbolic than real, and when real change is in the offing, as in serious efforts to desegregate the nation's schools, racism easily resurfaces. The recent rise of the Ku Klux Klan and Nazi Party, and the emergence in academic circles of a return to biological explanations of human social behavior, bode ill for the small gains made in this area.

Groups like Asian Americans and Latinos are in a different situation from blacks (or Native American Indians) because their numbers have been greatly augmented by new immigrants. Since new immigrants suffer important handicaps, of language, adjustment to a new society, lack of citizenship rights, and, in some cases, severe political disability (as when they are here illegally), the arrival of immigrants in large numbers tends to push community averages downwards. On the other hand, some members of these communities may themselves be able to take advantage of the plight of new immigrants to increase their own wealth. These communities, like the black community, may become increasingly polarized along class lines.

I believe that the condition of minority groups in this country will never improve in a significant way for the vast majority of their members so long as we retain a capitalist economic system. Problems of poverty and unemployment appear to be endemic to this kind of economy, and invariably are maldistributed along ethnic or racial lines. Some reforms are possible under capitalism, but we have witnessed their limits under recent liberal Democratic regimes. Conservative policies unmask the "natural" tendency of capitalist economies, which is to emphasize profitability over such human values as equality. Profit-making depends on the exploitation of workers. Such policies as reduction in the minimum wage, the diminution of welfare programs, or reduction in health and safety standards, all aid profits but hurt workers, especially those workers caught at the bottom of the system who are disproportionately minority members.

The capitalist system is supported by an ideology which states that increasing profits will benefit everyone, since profits will be reinvested in the creation of job opportunities. A healthy business climate, it is stated, is good for business and workers alike. There is no inherent conflict between capital and labor. I see this set of beliefs as a myth which helps to sustain the system and limits the ability of those who are hurt by it to question it. In fact the pursuit of profits is directly and inherently at odds with the interests of workers. Wealth tends to pile up in the hands of those who command profits, namely the owners of productive property, while poverty continues without alleviation. This is not a product of the failure of reform efforts, but is an inherent feature of a system that depends upon the accumulation of profits.

In conclusion, since most minority group members are working class, rather than owners and employers of capital, and tend to occupy the most disadvantaged position within the working class, class conflict between capital and labor is felt especially harshly by them. So long as our economic system sets profitability as its highest criterion of success, I can see no end to the disadvantaged position of most minority group members.

Melvin S. Brooks. The largest minority groups in the United States, which are also the poorest, are worse off now than in the 1960s and early 1970s. The major factors determining how well off they are are level of unemployment, degree of inflation and political climate. Prior to about 1942, however, they were worse off than now.

Whether they will be better or worse off in the future will depend largely on the above three factors. In the next two or three years, I anticipate little net change in unemployment and inflation, but I believe that the direction of governmental policy changes, especially economic, will worsen the plight of the poor and others who rank in the lower half economically. This, of course, includes most blacks, Latin Americans and Indians, and also the handicapped and aged.

However, in the more distant future, I expect the political climate to become more favorable to the less well off, which should improve the situation of our major minorities unless unemployment and inflation remain high.

I believe the situation of Jews, Japanese Americans and Chinese Americans has changed little the last ten years and will continue to change little compared to that of most Americans. Their situation might improve slightly because of their better than average educational and work records.

C. Emory Burton. There is no question that minority groups in the United States are better off in the early 1980s than they were about twenty years ago. Civil rights legislation, particularly in 1964 and 1965, has rather effectively served to remove legal barriers restricting full participation in American life on the part of minorities. Even in most parts of the South, blacks and other minorities are fairly well integrated into most areas of employment, housing, education, etc.

But important qualifications need to be made to this seemingly optimistic picture. Because of the nation's long history of discrimination against minorities, serious inequities remain. The median black family earns slightly more than half what is earned by the median white family. The black jobless rate is almost twice the white jobless rate. Almost half of all black youngsters less than eighteen years old live in poverty. The number of minorities in public office, while substantially higher than a decade ago, is far less than their numbers would warrant.

Whether minorities will be better or worse off in the future is difficult to answer. It might be argued that since there has been improvement in the last twenty years or so, a continuation of these trends would lead to an improvement in the status of minority citizens. But a discernible white backlash has developed, as seen in opposition to the social programs that benefit minorities, and even in a resurgence of the Ku Klux Klan.

It is possible, therefore, that minority groups could actually be worse off in the future. A more optimistic guess would be that the setbacks will only be temporary, and that several forces will work to gradually improve their lot. Among these forces are well-organized and aggressive black organizations; growing political power on the part of blacks (and other minorities); a renewed concern for the condition of our cities, where most minorities live; and an enlightened self-interest that makes the majority aware that our nation is so interdependent that improvement of the lot of our disadvantaged citizens is likely to improve the lot of all of us.

Leonard A. Carlson. The simple answer to the question of whether minority groups are better off in material terms is absolutely yes. Income per capita in the United States has risen decade by decade and minority groups, like other residents of the United States, have shared in that prosperity. The harder question is how minority groups have fared relative to the majority. In general, most but not all minority groups have lower average incomes than the population at large. The reasons for the relative poverty of minority groups is a hotly debated subject. Most minority groups began with relatively less property, fewer skills and a lower level of education than the population at large. These disadvantages would have a left a legacy of poverty which would in the best of circumstances have required more than one generation to remove. In addition, minority groups have often faced discrimination in hiring, education and in public policy that further hindered their progress. Despite these handicaps, many minority groups have made substantial economic progress relative to the entire population. On balance, minorities are better off today relative to the population at large than they were in the past. Not all groups, however, have fared equally well and not all trends are positive. In particular, let us consider the fate of blacks, European immigrants, Hispanic Americans, Asians and Indians.

At the time of emancipation, most black American families had virtually no property or formal education. They were handicapped economically by living in a poor region (the rural South) and by legal discrimination. Blacks have made steady progress toward economic equality. By 1900, the average income of a black family in the United States was perhaps 35 percent of the national average and by 1950, the average black family had an income equal to roughly 50 percent of the average white family. Since 1970, it has been approximately 60 percent of the white average.

New immigrants from Europe often experienced difficulties and a period of struggle. Not surprisingly, those immigrants who did not speak English and/or had the fewest skills often were relegated to unskilled jobs and faced the greatest discrimination. The second and third generations have fared far better. The average incomes of these groups have typically converged to that of native white Americans. Indeed, some immigrant groups have achieved higher incomes per capita than the population at large, while others have closed the gap but still lag the population at large. The relative successes of these groups are in part tied to the types of opportunities available to them when they arrived in the United States, which varied markedly between groups and historical epochs.

Hispanic Americans have had diverse economic experiences. On the one hand, many immigrants from Mexico or other Spanish-speaking nations entered low-skilled jobs and faced elements of discrimination. For these people, economic progress has sometimes been slow. On the other hand, some Hispanic Americans have had experiences similar to European immigrants. Spanish-speaking immigrants who are relatively skilled have been able to insulate themselves from discrimination and make substantial economic progress.

Asian Americans, especially Chinese and Japanese immigrants, since World War II have managed to achieve levels of income per capita, education and professional achievement which actually exceed those of the population at large despite legal limitations on the ownership of property imposed in many western states in the first decades of the twentieth century and, for the Japanese, internment and loss of property during World War II.

Native Americans (Indians) remain a disproportionately rural people and, by and large, they are among the poorest of Americans. In many cases economic opportunities are relatively limited near Indian reservations and Indians have been reluctant to leave the reservations and abandon ties of kinship and culture to seek opportunities in cities. Agricultural development has often been hindered by inept or inconsistent federal policies. In 1970, the per capita income of Indians was about the same as that of black Americans.

The prospects for the future of minorities in the United States depend in large measure upon the course of development in the economy as a whole. Demographic factors, such as the age of the population and family size, are also related to economic status. Poverty tends to beget poverty; nonetheless, well-educated and well-trained members of minority groups, despite recurring discrimination and other handicaps, will probably continue to progress to higher-level jobs and achieve economic success. The unanswered question, in my opinion, is what will happen to the unskilled and disadvantaged. Jobs for people with few skills may become scarcer as the economic technology develops, and people with few skills and little work experience will, I suspect, continue to be in a difficult situation. The ability of individuals now in poverty to climb out of that trap will depend in part on whether the economy is able to generate jobs that allow for upward mobility and to provide educational opportunities which are meaningful and attractive to members of minority groups whose legacy of frustration, discrimination and failure make work and education seem like fruitless alternatives. It will depend as well on the willingness of members of minority groups to utilize available economic opportunities and to press for their own interests.

Wilmoth A. Carter, Ph.D. Using changes in education, occupation and income as indices of the well-being of minorities, one must conclude that minorities are better off today. This contention is substantiated by viewing these item indices as they apply to blacks, the largest minority in the United States and the one most likely to rank at the bottom of any ladder of minorities.

Even though differentials and gaps still exist between blacks and whites, these are narrowing as accessibility of blacks increases relative to existent educational, economic and occupational opportunities. This is manifest in changes observed through census data and can be summarized as follows: The proportion of blacks and whites enrolled in school is about the same; the percentage of young adult blacks completing high school has risen more sharply than for whites; there has been a sharp rise in the proportion of blacks who are enrolled in college. Such reduction in the educational differentials gives evidence of one type of improvement.

Trends in occupational changes indicate increases for blacks in white collar, professional, clerical and skilled jobs. The increase in black professionals, while still somewhat minimal, has been accompanied by a corresponding decrease in the traditional service occupations of blacks, especially in the South. Moreover, there has been an increase in black-owned businesses, such as banks and insurance companies, although the number of such remains small.

The widest gap between blacks and whites has probably been in the area of income. Fluctuations in the median incomes of blacks and whites were many in the 1960s and 1970s, but the overall income differential between them widened after 1969. The distribution of income in the black community has failed to keep pace with the trend in economic well-being therein, thus leaving a broad base of low-income persons at the bottom while blacks at the middle level have incomes more nearly equal to their white counterparts. The perception that all blacks are worse off than before is a myth possibly stemming from the distance between classes in the black community and giving the appearance of their standing at the same economic level as before.

The rate at which the status of blacks has changed may be a "jogging" one and the differential between those at the top and bottom just as great as before but only if two classes are viewed. With more persons becoming middle class, and middle-class blacks gaining in mobility and landing at the same level as their white counterparts, one must conclude that blacks as a minority group are better off and will become increasingly upwardly mobile in the future.

Dr. Ben Cashman. More real progress has been made since 1954 in improving the legal and political positions of minorities in the United States than in the entire previous history of this country. This is not to say, however, that full equality has been achieved, but if the record of the past three decades is maintained and expanded upon, the future will be better for minorities. There continue to be severe economic inequalities for minorities, particularly blacks and those who are transient agricultural workers. The future should improve the economic situation for all minorities as new skills are developed and more job opportunities are opened. The economic factors are the critical issues and genuine equality will not exist until jobs of all kinds are open to prospective employees, regardless of race, color or creed, because they have the skills necessary for a position and are not given it or denied it because of membership in a minority group.

Dr. Edward C. Chang. Generally speaking, minority groups are better off today politically, economically and socially than they were in the past.

Gone are the days when a minority person because of race could be denied the right to purchase a house, to enter a college or to move freely. Today, we see both black and white parents attending the same PTA meeting, participating in the same community projects, and gathering together as friends or neighbors. In the past, minority groups were largely excluded from the political process; today, we witness more and more minority persons being elected or appointed to governmental office at all levels. In many instances, minority groups in recent years not only have made a significant difference in a close political election, but have also influenced many governmental policies and decisions.

Although it is true that, as compared to whites, minority groups are still far behind in both median income and educational level, it is also true that many minority individuals are wealthier than most white Americans. We cannot deny that racial discrimination still exists in many aspects of American life, nor can we wash away prejudice from the human mind in a short period of time. On the other hand, we cannot dispute the fact that talented and qualified minority individuals are being sought and recruited to fill positions in both public and private organizations. Thus, it seems reasonable to say that minorities, as a group, still have a long way to go toward achieving full equality; as an individual, however, a hard-working and competent minority person no longer has to see his talent wasted and his effort going down the drain simply because of his skin color.

For some minority groups, the most important gain perhaps is the resurgence of a sense of self-esteem, self-identity and the development of self-worth. Recent empirical studies have in fact shown that black people's attitudes toward themselves have become more favorable. For instance, studies essentially replicating the classic Clark and Clark (1939) paradigm* have found that black children now prefer black dolls to white dolls; a reversal of earlier findings that black children would prefer to play with white dolls when given a choice. My own research on the racial attitudes of black college students also corroborates other researchers' findings that the attitudes of these students toward themselves have become more positive and favorable. Instead of accepting

*Clark, K., and Clark, M. The Development of Consciousness of Self and the Emergence of Racial Identification in Negro Preschool Children. *Journal of Social Psychology* 10 (1939): 591–599.

negative stereotypes about their race as those college students in the 1950s, they now reject such stereotypes.

Will minority groups be better off in the future? The answer appears to be a qualified yes. It is unlikely, barring a national disaster such as severe economic depression, that the clock will be turned back to a time during which minority groups were an acceptable target of prejudice and discrimination. But many things can happen. The best safeguard for a better future in America is for every American, whether he is a member of the minority or majority, to be treated equally according to his or her ability and potentials. Minority groups have come a long way in the course of their struggle for liberty and equality. To achieve a better future, they must continue to strive for equal rights and equal opportunities through hard work, discipline and a sense of dignity and moral values; they must do their part to work for better interracial relations and increase their own level of attractiveness to white Americans, without compromising their own identity and cultural heritage.

A. Lee Coleman. My answer is a rather unqualified yes, minority groups are better off today than they were in the past, to the question *as phrased*—that is, all minority groups lumped together and evaluated on the basis of all the possible criteria combined and comparing their collective situation at present with that of the earliest period in which they were a significant minority group in the United States.

Having said that, I must immediately recognize that it is a value judgment based on implicit criteria. Others could—and no doubt do—reach different conclusions based on a different ranking of criteria.

If one gives exclusive or predominant weight to subjective criteria (quality of life, happiness, life satisfaction, the feeling or perception on the part of minority group members of having made progress collectively, etc.) it is perhaps more difficult to reach the conclusion that I have stated. One can always find or emphasize gaps between the situations of minority members and the dominants, or new reference groups or individuals with which to compare one's individual or collective situation unfavorably. My implicit criteria include both objective and subjective measures. But even using mostly subjective criteria I believe most experts would come out on the side of some change for the better, and most minority group members would choose their group's present status over that of periods in the past. Clearly, though, there have been short-range ups and downs; it has not been all linear progress.

Another perspective on the question would be provided by evaluating the situation of the several United States minority groups separately. Obviously there has been great variation between groups both in long-range progress and in their situations at given times. Some have gone from substantial discrimination to very little at present, while the situation of others has not changed a great deal. If it can be concluded that native Americans (Indians) are better off than in the past it would probably have to be based on just the last decade or so of the 100 years they have had minority group status.

Whether minority groups will be better or worse off in the future is largely a matter of faith or one's general outlook, it seems to me. Economic and political trends and events (at the world, national and local levels) that cannot be predicted are likely to be more determining than are our social science principles based on our contemporary society.

My answer is a cautious yes. But this is not to suggest that minority-dominant status, differences and perceptions based on race and/or ethnicity are likely to disappear completely in the foreseeable future. And obviously the situations of particular groups will vary substantially, with those already the most integrated, the most established and most equal, and the least "visible" biologically, socially and culturally being the most likely to hold or better their present status—or to disappear almost entirely into the dominant group.

Frances R. Cousens, Ph.D. If the term minority refers to all Americans who are not members of the white Anglo-Saxon Protestant (WASP) dominant group and if the past refers to any period prior to 1950, it can be said that minorities are better off now. With some prejudiced individuals present, it is important that systematic discrimination is no longer as characteristic of our society as was the case prior to 1950.

Since World War II, minorities have made progress in education, access to better jobs and higher incomes. The reason is legislation and court rulings prohibiting discrimination. However, not all minorities have benefitted equally from such legislation and litigation. Of the two racial minorities, Orientals have fared much better than blacks in achieving middle-class status. Although the income of black families rose more rapidly for a time, it has never remotely equalled that of whites. Despite a greater number of two-income families, blacks have achieved no more than about 60 percent of whites' income.

Orientals, like Jews, have experienced prejudice and discrimination, most virulent early in the century. Also, like Jews, their strong family and group pride, and their emphasis on education and achievement were well suited to America's work ethic and they prospered. Hispanics, our newest and fastest growing minority, have made even less progress than blacks because of language and other cultural differences.

After decades of neglect, blacks began to demand and, ultimately, achieve greater equality in the 1960s only to see it eroded in the economic stress of the 1970s. The last hired and first fired, their taste of success made subsequent frustration even more painful.

The future of minorities will reflect economic conditions. However, one measure of progress is likely to remain: we will probably not return to considering mistreatment of minorities as either normal or impervious to change. Antidiscrimination agencies, often "paper tigers," and affirmative action programs are being weakened but will not disappear, albeit their existence has more symbolic than actual value.

Women, like minorities, have been granted greater opportunities and are, generally, making more progress in the labor market. Once hired as tokens, they are proving their capabilities in many former all-male occupations. It is ironic, however, that such gains by white women are often at the expense of black men. It is a choice which no society should be forced to make.

Victor M. Goode. Minority groups in America, particularly Afro-Americans, are worse off today than twenty-five years ago. A variety of factors have contributed to this condition. However, at the head of that varied list is the ever present specter of institutional racism and its resultant class implications.

Despite the reality of racism in the American social structure since the inception of this country, blacks have somehow managed to resist it, fight it and retain a strong sense of cultural identity, community, moral purpose and capacity for self-help.

During the last twenty-five years many forces have worked to weaken this resilient social infrastructure and to exacerbate the traditional oppression we have faced with respect to jobs, housing, education, health care and the criminal justice system. The process of monopoly formation and the centralization of capital and political power in this country have radically changed the character of the black institutional process.

Inner-city mayors find themselves presiding over bankrupt municipalities. Blacks in the labor force find themselves competing in what is now an international pool of unskilled and semiskilled labor, but most importantly black culture is being rapidly destroyed by its headlong absorption into the mass culture commodity phenomenon that is sweeping the country.

It is the qualitative change in this critical trilogy of politics, economics and culture that is the key to understanding blacks' worsening quantitative position in American society. I won't repeat the litany of statistics that verify this point. Suffice it to say that in most statistical social indices that measure quality of life, blacks in the last twenty years have slipped deeper onto the bottom rungs of the American social order. Prejudice, where it has given way, has simply transformed itself into an institutional form of racism that grinds away in an almost reflexive fashion utilizing the most sophisticated and powerful instruments in the social order.

Our future in the proverbial belly of the whale is not immediately hopeful, but neither is it completely lost. One quantitative change of great significance is the current enrollment of nearly one million Afro-Americans in various institutions of higher education. This cadre of talent has some very heavy responsibilities to bear. In large measure our prospects for the future depend upon their ability and their commitment to the common purpose of our evolution as a people.

They must provide us with a clearer understanding of the way in which this political economic structure works. With this clarity they must offer us political programs that are tactically flexible yet united to the strategic purpose of our liberation from oppression. Lastly, their efforts must flow from a vision of a new social order and a new economic order that recognizes and reflects the interdependence of people and nations here and abroad. If this reservoir of energy and skill can be tapped, our future will be ours.

Marion Hayes Hull. This question is impossible to answer without defining the minority group to which you are referring and in which era in the past you are referring. If you mean black Americans, it is obvious they are better off than blacks were during slavery. However, in some ways—political and economic—some experts would argue that blacks were better off during the Reconstruction Period in the United States than they are today.

In terms of the future, one would have to be a prophet to predict whether minorities (whatever that means) will be better off in the future.

Maurice Jackson, Ph.D. Changes in the situation of minorities (American Indians, Asian Americans, blacks and Hispanics) in this country are more superficial than deep-rooted. There have been relative improvements in education (more minorities in higher education), employment (more professionals), politics (more elected officials), athletics (more professional players), voting (more registered voters), availability and quality of knowledge about minorities (more ethnic study programs), and identity (removal of some degree of stigma from race labels). However, these changes have not been systematic and thoroughgoing. They tend to be either small in scale, isolated, offset by other changes, short-term or in the process of being reversed. It must be remembered that many changes have been made with less than full societal support, and some, such as those sought by affirmative action and busing, have met vigorous, organized opposition. They have not brought minorities to parity with the majority insofar as competitive relations are concerned.

Some members of minority groups—the few in highly visible positions—have benefited far more than the vast majorities within the various minorities. There is a cabinet member here, a judge there, a mayor here, and a professional there. Given the history of minorities in this country, the presence of even a few minority persons in certain situations and positions is very striking.

These few successful minority persons tend not to occupy controlling command positions in society. They are not making policy in the government, mass media, business or the military. To take one example from the governmental sector, there are more minority elected political officials, but proportionately the number is still low. In addition, the number and proportion of appointed officials from minority groups remain low. To the extent that appointed officials are middle-class and white and to the extent they make important policy decisions, they are likely to reflect middle-class Anglo concerns and not those of the whole society. This results in minority problems, concerns, interests and needs being either ignored or assigned less importance.

Taking another example from the nongovernmental sector, there are very few minorities who own and control mass media facilities and organizations or who produce, direct and edit the news. This is a serious limitation since the mass media influence public opinion and social policy. Minorities are not able to present self or group images that they think reflect their lives in a realistic way.

The net effect of these changes, then, has been to widen the gap between the elite and mass of minorities, but not to make it possible for either to live without racial constraints. On their part, most minorities continue to be plagued by low-level jobs, greater unemployment, ill health, underutilization of service, welfare and low home ownership. They have major concerns for public safety ranging from high rates of crime and violence to police shootings and killings, not to mention indiscriminate acts of racial violence. Threats of violence appear to be stronger than in the recent past from groups such as the Ku Klux Klan and Nazi-type organizations with enormous material resources.

The problems are widespread. There is not just one "South Bronx"—there are many. They are populated in this land by the great mass of minorities whose situations and life circumstances have remained unchanged. A recent task force has concluded that conditions in Watts are the same as they were before the 1965 riot. To underscore what is happening, one only needs to be reminded that not only the federal government, but many of America's great cities are reducing services and programs.

Minorities do have special problems and needs. They have not and do not typically participate as fully free individuals in this society. They have not enjoyed such benefits as homesteading, home equity, depletion allowances and farm subsidies. This means that minorities need these special advantages available to (and taken for granted by) the majority throughout the history of this country, along with tax credits, depreciation possibilities and the like. The evidence suggests a need for more support rather than less from both governmental and nongovernmental sectors. Furthermore, short-term cost-effectiveness and other business considerations cannot be the sole criteria for evaluating programs and services for minorities. Special programs and services are indicators of good will and resolve, as well as the bases for improvement, especially economic.

The severity of the minority situation is maintained, at least, by common explanations that serve to justify the existence of minority problems. It is claimed that members of the majority either benefit from the oppressed situation of minorities, or that members of the majority are protecting their economic interests. It may be true that there are short-term benefits, but racial oppression is not beneficial for the society at large nor for any group in the long run. Another justification for minority problems is that, bluntly, minorities are less intelligent, according to questionable genetic and intelligence-testing theories. To entertain such thoughts is degrading in the first place, and their invalidity has been amply documented by many studies, past and present. Denial of the special histories and present circumstances of minorities exacerbates the situation further. In this regard, it appears that America is not taking a hard look at its minorities. Taken together, these quasi explanations obscure the issues and absolve the society of any responsibility for dealing with minority problems.

The existence of minority problems is especially crucial in the United States, where individual freedom is so highly valued. In a free open democratic society no one should be constrained by personal conditions beyond one's control, i.e., race or color. Racial domination, for whatever reasons and at any time, is antithetical to such a society. Minority activities are still highly circumscribed and constrained by irrational forces. The nature of limitations for them is twofold: (1) relatively limited and partial inclusion for the minority elite and (2) relative exclusion of the mass of minorities. The limitations are real. They mean that America will not be a truly open and free democratic society until the minority problem is faced and solved so that their participation in society is not constrained by race or color. Until then, it is not yet time for cheers.

Dr. Robert C. Johnson. Since the term minority groups encompasses such a large number and diverse group of peoples (Afro-Americans, Spanish-speaking Americans, American Indians, Americans of Asian extraction, Jewish Americans and others) I will address myself to that group of which I am more qualified to speak, i.e., Afro-Americans.

The history of black Americans in the United States has been characterized by periods of progress followed by setbacks of a political, social and economic nature. Periods following the American Revolution, the Civil War and World War II are illustrative of this phenomenon. However, since space does not permit a definitive historical analysis of the progress and setbacks of black Americans, it is instructive to limit our discussion to the period of recent history, that is, within the past two decades. Since the concept of progress is relative, it is necessary to establish benchmarks; that is, one must ask, "Progress compared to what or to whom?" There are at least three ways to assess the development of black Americans in recent times. One is to compare the current status of black Americans to their past position in society. The second manner of assessing progress is to examine the status of black Americans relative to that of the majority population in terms of their share of national wealth and resources. And thirdly, we can ascertain where black Americans are relative to their needs and circumstances in the larger society. Various elements of these three approaches will be used in this analysis.

In absolute terms black Americans are faring better at this point in their history than during other times. More blacks have moved into higher occupational professions. They enjoy a longer lifespan on the average. The infant mortality rate is lower than it has been in the past, and blacks have achieved higher levels of educational attainment.

While in absolute statistical terms the situation of black Americans appears to have improved, when we examine their position relative to the majority population we find that a gap continues to exist and in some cases has widened. Black unemployment is still twice as high as that of white unemployment; blacks are three times as likely to be in poverty as are whites; black babies still die at twice the rate of white babies; the black lifespan is several years shorter than that of the white; black median family income is only 57 percent that of white family median income. In 1978 if blacks had received a proportion of the national income commensurate with their size of the population they would have been 60.2 billion dollars richer in that year alone (159.3 billion versus 99.1 billion). Blacks, while making up 12 to 15 percent of the national population, only received 1.3 percent of the 107 billion dollars that were earned in 1976 from property, interest and dividend income. Blacks are less likely to own their own homes and are more likely to live in substandard housing. Blacks are underrepresented in every level of professional and managerial category in spite of their recent educational achievements. In sum, it can be said that relative to the majority population blacks continue to lag behind in many critical areas and on most statistical indices. Not only does the gap remain constant but in many cases it is even widening.

From the third perspective, we see that the gains ushered in by the social activism of the civil rights movement are insufficient to meet the critical needs and adverse conditions facing the black community. Whereas manifestations of overt discrimination are no longer visible, institutional racism remains vibrant and continues to undermine the quality of life for black Americans in the United States. The failings of social and economic subsystems and institutions make the efforts by black Americans to improve their lot extremely difficult. Social and economic pressures systematically undermine black family life, contribute to the institutional and systematic decimation of black males, render black children homeless and parentless, and subject members of the black community to increased levels of crime and violence. Hence the gains that blacks have achieved over the past two decades have started to put a dent in the morass of problems facing the black community, but they have not eradicated these problems. The magnitude and complexity of the concerns facing black Americans require far greater resources and efforts than have been allocated to date, and which are currently being proposed to address these concerns.

What does the future bode for black Americans? New technologies bringing about the automation of industries and the society, new economic constraints, the scarcities of many natural resources, and a changing world political order are changes in the larger society that pose serious challenges to the prosperity of all Americans but especially to those already sitting marginally on the economic and social perimeters.

Unless certain actions occur the prospects for improving the lot of black Americans will remain dim. Black political action and social-economic organization are needed to prevent further erosion of the tenuous gains made over the past two decades. More internal efforts will need to be undertaken to increase the economic self-sufficiency, productivity and well-being of black Americans. The emergence of political powers among African and other third-world nations also makes it important that black Americans establish international linkages to enable them to overcome the dim prospects. If changes are not made in the larger society and in the black community as well, the changing economic and technological conditions noted above will lock a significant proportion of black Americans into permanent poverty creating for certain a so-called black underclass.

Vernon E. Jordan, Jr. While some minority groups who have had a history of being victimized by discrimination have largely entered the American mainstream, blacks by and large have not.

While a relatively small number of blacks have overcome the hurdles to win decent jobs and homes, racial prejudice is still a major impediment in their lives. Despite the removal of overt segregation, black citizens are still at a gross disadvantage.

In jobs, blacks are still twice as likely as whites to be in low-pay, low-skill jobs and less than half as likely as whites to be in the jobs that count in America. Black unemployment rates are two and a half times those for white workers.

In income, the black middle class comes to barely a tenth of all black families, and even they are earning middle-class incomes because two or more family members are working. Median black family income is only 57 percent that for whites—lower than it was in 1966!

In education, the majority of blacks in college are in two-year schools while most whites are in four-year colleges that put them on career ladders denied to blacks. In some cities more black kids drop out of high school than graduate.

In housing, far more blacks than whites live in deficient housing. Blacks pay more for less housing than whites. A 1979 Housing and Urban Development study documented the fact that the typical house-hunter or apartment-seeker can expect to run into discrimination.

I have faith that this will change in the future but it will take a determined effort on the part of all who profess American ideals of equality to achieve change. My confidence is based on the fact that Americans will realize that separate and unequal economic and social conditions are as repellent as the separate and unequal segregated facilities of the past.

C. Eric Lincoln. To generalize about minority groups is a hazardous undertaking. Not only do different minority groups have different histories which affect their relative well-being and the rate of change for better or worse, but segments of the same minorities register different levels of gain or loss. For example, Jews as a minority group have fared substantially better than blacks, but some blacks are much better off than others with whom they previously shared a common status.

Perhaps the best way to answer the question is to say that if the group can be said to benefit by the improved circumstances of an identifiable segment of its membership, then most minority groups in the United States are somewhat better off than they have been. On the other hand, if we are dealing with statistical group "averages," then some are worse off relative to the national average. The black minority is a case in point.

Whether things will be better or worse in the future depends upon a complex of factors which include the national well-being, the opportunities for group self-improvement, group incentive, the quality and intensity of intergroup competition and the quality of alternatives to group self-exertion.

Florence Z. Perman. The middle class of minority groups are better off. Laws prohibiting discrimination in housing, employment, voting, education and credit have made a dramatic difference for a significant number. These laws have changed our society and improved the lives of many minorities. Their status and the future will depend on the economic state of the country.

The high percentage of unemployed minority youth, especially among blacks, and the poverty of the many families headed by a woman suggest that many are not better off, but the middle class has increased and their situation has improved.

IN THE LAST TWENTY YEARS, THE NUMBER OF WORKING WOMEN IN THE UNITED STATES HAS INCREASED DRAMATICALLY. HOW HAS THIS INCREASE AFFECTED THE ECONOMY? FAMILY LIFE?

Dr. Sharon N. Barnartt. The principal effect of the increase in the number of working women is that it has permitted our economy to expand substantially. This has happened because women have filled many of the new jobs created by this expansion. This did not happen just because there were not enough men—of any age or ethnic group—to fill these new jobs. Rather, women brought with them certain characteristics to these new jobs which could not be found among unemployed men. These characteristics include higher levels of education than can be found among unemployed men and the willingness to work—usually for low pay—in jobs which are considered in this society to be female jobs. Since about half of all new jobs created in the last two decades have been in traditionally female areas, women's willingness (and men's apparent unwillingness, except in a few areas) to accept these low-paying jobs has been extremely important for our economic growth. Corporations cannot expand without clerical or secretarial help, hospitals must have nurses and technicians, and schools must have teachers, to cite just a few examples of areas which have grown rapidly in recent years. At present there is no question that our economy would collapse if all working women left their jobs, and if women had not been pulled into the labor force to fill many of the new jobs, the rate of economic growth after World War II would definitely have been much slower.

It is important to realize that two types of changes in our economy have not occurred with the increase in numbers of women workers. For one thing, women's salaries have not become equal to men's; in fact, the gap between the average male and average female salary has increased slightly in the past two decades. Also, women have not, for the most part, infiltrated the ranks of male jobs. Rather, the traditional separation of the sexes into "male" and "female" jobs has continued, with only a small percentage of either sex working in an opposite-sex job.

It is difficult to assess the effect working women have had on families without also asking how changes in family life have affected the desire or ability of married women to work. It is clear that family patterns have been changing drastically since before the beginning of this century. Divorce rates have been increasing, and both the numbers of children women have and the number of years between their births have been decreasing. Combined with the added female life expectancy of over thirty years since 1900, these changes have both freed women from the most intense of their family responsibilities and changed the complexion of families in our society.

If we ask if working women by themselves have caused any of these changes, the answer is no. However, it is likely that the increasing number of working women will not stop these changes. Women who are working may be more able to terminate a bad marriage than are nonworking women who depend upon their husbands for economic support—although the large number of female heads of households who are below the poverty line suggests that this is not as true as we like to believe. Working women also tend to have fewer children than nonworking women, although this is a trait they share with educated women, whether or not they are working. It is more likely that women's working has taken advantage of, and perhaps reinforced, changes in families which had already begun occurring, than that women's working has caused any of these changes.

Muriel Fox. The harmful effects of both inflation and recession have been softened considerably by the increase of women in our work force. I believe, most especially, that we could have plunged into a serious recession or even a depression if it were not for the cushion provided by two-income families. To cite just one example, three out of five home mortgages granted today are based upon the incomes of both husband and wife—whereas the income of wives was not even figured in the computation for mortgages just a decade ago!

As for family life in the United States, it's still in a state of transition and readjustment caused by many factors (inflation, growing influence of the media and young peer groups, rising divorce rates, declining birth and death rates and the decay of community support systems) in addition to the adjustments resulting from women entering the work force.

Many problems facing American families today result from the failure of government and industry and other institutions to recognize how drastically American families have changed. These institutions still continue to address an outmoded stereotype of "The American Family." This stereotype—picturing a family comprising breadwinner father, homemaker mother and two or more dependent children—actually describes only 7 percent of American families today. The other 93 percent are poorly served by existing support systems.

I am hopeful that American industry, especially, is beginning to address these new needs through innovations such as cafeteria benefits, flextime, parental leave for new fathers, career status for part-time workers, and growing support for a variety of child care options.

I am also hopeful that families are on the way to becoming stronger, freer, more loving, more supportive of the needs and aspirations of their individual members. This new strength and supportiveness is partly a result of increased confidence gained by women with the help of the women's movement.

Marabel Morgan. Show me a woman who works 9 to 5 and I'll show you a tired woman at 5:30. A woman has only so much energy and stamina, and often she is exhausted by the time she comes home from work, with nothing left over for the family.

In many cases I realize that working mothers are unwilling conscripts, forced into the work force by death or divorce, or because their incomes are necessary to supplement the family income. I have talked with so many women who have said, "I'd love to stay home and raise the kids full time, but I can't afford it." Unfortunately, the very young and impressionable children are the losers.

Child educators draw the parallel between unsupervised homes and wayward youngsters. I believe that the increase of teen-age sex, drug use and violent crime in our nation is one of the results of parents not spending quality and quantity time with their children, teaching them values and standards, yes, and also just being with them—showing them love and acceptance.

A child thinks that if you love someone, you will want to spend time with that someone. Psychiatrists point out the vital need of a mother's presence with her child during the first five formative years. One study indicated that the most creative time of a person's life is between ages four and seven. Imagine that!

Young children need guidance and lots of it. We all know that. Teenagers need even more. My two girls are now eleven and sixteen, and I can see that the older they get, the more guidance they need.

It takes time to communicate with a child, especially as he or she grows through those turbulent teen years. Children don't always voice their deepest feelings in the first sentence. They wait to see if Mom or Dad has time to hear them out.

It also takes time to show love. Sitting on a ball field bleacher, planning a pizza party or baking a cake together takes a parent's time, but it's in activities together that children feel their parents' love.

Granted, for most working women, their job is not an option, but a necessity. Those mothers have no alternative if there is to be bread on the table. I believe children can rally behind such mothers and actually grow in character, seeing the sacrifice their mother is making on their behalf. The mother's part, however, must be to train those children in the hours after work even when she is exhausted.

Of course, a woman with the option of staying home to raise her very young children is in a different category. Too many housewives with that choice are busy in careers or community affairs, improving the streets while their kids are out running them. Later on they may regret the time they chose to spend away from their children.

Many mothers forced into the work force would give their right arm to be home, yearning to have the time to be a good parent. How ironic it is then, that women who feel their time at home is boring or a trap, stampede out of the house "in search of." Is it a case of the grass is always greener syndrome?

In my opinion, the women who have the option of staying home while their children are very young but don't, do an injustice to their family in general, and to their children in particular. With the institutional family in this country in peril, I believe a wholehearted commitment to the children could bring about a great turnaround.

Florence Z. Perman. The number of jobs in the 1970s increased dramatically and many of them were filled by women. Availability of women made this growth possible. Since many of these women were married their added income increased the purchasing power of the family; at the minimum kept the family's status from falling because of the high inflation. Increased income created demand for more services, better goods.

Family life changed in families where women worked. There was greater stress on women who continued to do most of the household chores. The relationship of the husband and wife probably became more equal in terms of family decisions and how to spend the family income. Unhappy marriages probably ended in divorce or separation more quickly than if the wife had not worked—economic independence provided options. Women's financial contribution has lessened the pressure on the husband as the sole income provider. Preschool children have less time with a parent, which puts greater pressure on both parents when they come home from work or on weekends.

Lillian B. Rubin, Ph.D. Let me leave the question of the impact of working women on the economy to the economists and focus instead on the second half of your question: How has the large increase of women in the work force affected family life?

First, a caveat about causal relationships. Experts disagree about which way the causal arrow goes, some arguing that the family in both its structure and function is a direct response to the structure of the economy and its needs; others treating the family as if it were an autonomous institution whose internal arrangements are a result of some rather mysterious natural force. In fact, like all social institutions, the family (and its individual members) lives in a reciprocal relationship to the institutions around it—each influencing the other in ways that often are outside conscious human intention. Thus, for example, medical advances that have dramatically increased longevity, and the development of modern birth control methods which make it possible to regulate with some certainty the number and spacing of children, are responsible for demographic changes that have profound effects on what happens inside the family which, in turn, affects the family's relationship to the economy. Similarly, certain political developments—for example, the rise of an articulate feminist movement which itself is related both to these demographic shifts and to the expanding economy of the 1950s and 1960s— enter into a complex reciprocal relationship with both family and economy.

The point I am making is that there are many factors affecting family life today, and the increasing number of women in the work force is both a product of those factors and, at the same time, is itself a force for change in both the family and the economy.

One major change made possible by women's increasing economic independence has been the postponement of marriage among large segments of American women, as indicated by the steadily rising age at first marriage over the last two decades—from a low of 20.1 years in 1956 to 22.1 years in 1979. This is not to suggest that, on the average, women's earning capacity has yet come anywhere near to men's. Indeed, quite the contrary. In 1979, the median income of full-time women workers in their prime working years (25-64) was only about 58 percent of the income of comparably aged men. Still, one consequence of the feminist agitation of the last two decades has been to bring increasing numbers of women into occupations that once were the almost exclusive province of men—occupations that afford the kind of income that makes marriage a choice not a necessity.

Obviously, as women become more independent financially, important shifts take place in the internal psychological and power dynamics of the family. Sometimes those shifts culminate in divorce as women feel freer from economic bondage to terminate an unsatisfactory marriage. More often, however, the marriage partners find ways to accommodate the shifting balance of power. Indeed, both women and men often experience relief and exhilaration at the prospect of laying down their stereotypically feminine and masculine encumbrances. For men, for example, the prospect of not having to be the sole breadwinner in the family may mean relief from a crushing, and often impossible, burden. It should be clear that among the poor and the working class of America, women have always worked in very large numbers in order to make ends meet in the family. But in the past, that necessity often was viewed as a man's personal failure by both husband and wife since the fairy tale had it that he would provide for and protect her forever more. Now, as more and more women enter the work force both out of economic necessity and out of a desire to share the intrinsic and extrinsic rewards to be found there, the stigma attached to having or being a working wife is rapidly disappearing.

All the research evidence available shows that we still have a long way to go before equity is achieved between men and women whether inside the family or out. For example, even when women work outside the home, they continue to carry the major responsibility for work inside the home as well. But already there have been significant changes in attitudes if not behavior. And as women continue to take their place beside men in the labor force, we will see more and more behavioral changes as well.

Such shifts in family life will cause conflict, of course. But in the long run, everyone will benefit. As men spend more time with their children, their relationships with them will improve significantly; understanding and the capacity to communicate will surely grow. Similarly, as women spend more time away from the children, we will hear less and less about the problems of maternal overprotection that have engaged professionals who work with families for so long. Child care, of course, will continue to be an enormous problem in a society that talks about the importance of family and children but fails to provide adequate facilities for the care of children whose parents either must or want to work. But for those families who are fortunate enough to solve the problem adequately, all the evidence suggests that the children will benefit in their capacity for independence and self-direction.

In conclusion, while in the present moment, the entry of larger numbers of women than ever before into the work force may cause some conflict and dislocation in family life, in the long run, it will have a salutary effect. As women gain equity outside the home and men take more responsibility in it, the fantasy of marriage as a shared partnership will come closer to reality. When both mothers and fathers work outside the home, children will assume responsibilities consonant with their capacities, thereby developing a greater sense of independence and self-reliance.

Periods of transition are always difficult and often frightening to those of us who must live through them. These are times when the old rules for living have been challenged while the new ones have not yet emerged very clearly. But if we can live with the present ambiguity about roles and rules in the family, we will find, I am certain, that not only will the family survive, but it will grow stronger for the new strengths that women, men and children will find within themselves.

Phyllis Schlafly. The statement is false. The number of working women has not increased at all. Women have always worked and worked very hard. The question reflects the stereotyped bias of persons in paid employment who seem to think that the wife and mother in the home doesn't work. In fact, she works very hard.

Presumably what the statement intended to say is that millions of women have shifted their work environment from the home to paid employment in the factory or office. More precisely, they have shifted twenty to forty-eight hours of their workweek from the environment of the home to the office or factory.

Inflation is the principal reason that millions of wives have moved into the paid labor force. They need the money to pay for the groceries and to meet the mortgage payments.

The biggest effect of this migration has been windfall profits to the tax collectors. Wives who have taken paid employment have flung themselves into the eager arms of the Internal Revenue Service. Wives who move into the labor force pay anywhere from 30 to 50 percent of their earnings directly to the federal government.

The second biggest effect has been increased unemployment. From 1960 to 1977, the number of women in the labor force increased 8.7 million and the number of persons unemployed increased 3 million.

The effect on family life cannot be calculated in dollars and cents, but it is more pervasive and far-reaching. Who can estimate the results of the denial of mothering to millions of children? No one has begun to estimate the harm to children and to society from the phenomenon known in cities as the "key children" (children who wear a door key around their necks because there is no one at home to let them in after school).

Another effect on family life is the increased divorce rate. What is called the independence effect of wives earning as much or more than their husbands is widely recognized as a cause. *Glamour* magazine, which asks women in headlines "Love and Success—Can We Have It All," noted in the fine print in June 1981 that, both Census Bureau figures and those of a recent management study suggest that the more money a wife earns, the more frequently she divorces, and the acceleration curve is very steep.

WHAT SPECIAL ADVANTAGES OR DISADVANTAGES WOULD A WOMAN HAVE SERVING AS PRESIDENT OF THE UNITED STATES?

Dr. Sharon N. Barnartt. It is difficult to predict whether a female president of the United States would bring any special advantages to the job or not, since what would be seen by one voter as an advantage would be seen by another as a disadvantage. It is clear, though, that the first female president would definitely encounter more disadvantages than male presidents do. (Whether these disadvantages would persist past the first female president would depend upon the reaction of the public and the media.) The form this disadvantage would take is that a female president would come under even closer scrutiny than male presidents do now. All innovators—people who are the first of their group in a given position—endure such close scrutiny, which is embodied in two types of questions which are continually asked of such people. One question asks if they are in fact good enough to have been allowed to take on this unusual and important position, and the other asks if characteristics usually imputed to all members of that group are in any way interfering with the person's ability to do the job.

The evaluation of the skill of a female president probably would be even more stringent than it has become for male presidents in recent years, because of the expectation that all innovators should be superior, not ordinary. A female president could make even fewer mistakes than a male president can—and the public and the media permit male presidents to make few enough mistakes these days.

However, it is always difficult to evaluate the job of president objectively or apart from considerations of the personal characteristics of the president, and this is where a female president is likely to find herself even more vulnerable than male presidents do. American society has a well-developed set of expectations about what constitutes appropriate female behavior (which are not changing quickly), including such areas as dress, emotions and style of self-presentation. Since the role of president is quintessentially a male role, a woman would be censured any time she exhibited too much femaleness. For example, if she cried in public—even in a situation in which a male would have been expected to show some emotion—she would be said to be acting like a woman, not a president. Any decision a critic or opposing party disagreed with would be likely to be called irrational, and hesitation in taking action would be attributed to female passivity rather than to discretion or prudence.

On the other hand, she could not err in the direction of being overly masculine in dress or actions. Aggressive actions or actions lacking in compassion would raise questions about her being "female enough." So the first female president would be left treading an extremely narrow tightrope. She would be lacking role models of appropriate behavior which are usually drawn from past presidents, and she would have a great deal of difficulty convincing everyone to evaluate her on her performance and not on sex-role-related characteristics.

Arlene K. Daniels. A woman serving as United States president should have the advantages that appreciation and understanding of the world of women can bring, through firsthand experience. She can see the relations between the support and facilitative functions women manage in the private worlds of home and family and in the service sectors where they cluster in low-pay, low-prestige occupations. At the same time, she would not attain high office without experience in public life and high-prestige, professional circles and governmental groups at local and regional, if not national, levels. Therefore she would understand the worlds of power and status traditionally dominated by males.

This double experience should make her more sensitive to many social policy issues surrounding the integration of work and family that are coming up for increasing discussion. These issues, though still not given priority consideration in our society, will inevitably become more important in the future as more and more women join the labor force outside the home. A woman president is more likely to have the necessary experience and interest to focus upon these issues, take a leadership position in resolving the conflicts and problems they produce, and mediate between opposing traditional and egalitarian (or reformist) interests in this sensitive arena.

I see no particular (or generic) disadvantages attached to a woman's presidency. As our experience so far tells us, the nature of the president is revealed only in the actions taken while in office. The office both constrains and reveals the person, often in unanticipated ways.

Muriel Fox. The main advantages in electing a woman as president of the United States is that we would henceforth double our talent pool for this difficult job. Many Americans feel our choice of presidential candidates has not been adequate in recent years. The task has become increasingly complex and demanding; yet we still have not widened the field of possible nominees to include women, blacks, Hispanics or members of other outsider groups.

The first woman elected president of the United States will be an unusually capable and charismatic person; otherwise she'd never succeed in winning election in the first place. She probably will have the advantages of not being "one of the boys" and not having moved to the top through traditional political clubhouse channels; this will give her greater credibility with an American public that is increasingly skeptical about politics.

If she is a successful leader she will ultimately overcome the disadvantage of not providing the father figure Americans usually seek in the president. Eventually she might even lead Americans to discover they can be equally comfortable with a mother figure—just as the Israelis came to love the motherly and grandmotherly image of Golda Meir.

I don't believe that women have any innate qualities that make them more able or less able to govern this country. But I do believe the programming women have received since birth makes them especially well qualified for the kind of leadership America needs today. Women— especially the powerful and successful ones—have learned how to motivate and inspire, how to encourage teamwork and cooperation, how to evoke idealism and compassion. Our first woman president would also be, in order to win election, tough, quick-thinking and creative. She will also be a consummate artist in conveying her ideas on television. Altogether that could add up to the perfect combination for our nation in the perilous final decade of the twentieth century.

Florence Z. Perman. Long-term there would probably be no difference having a woman serve as president of the United States. In the short run there may be advantages and disadvantages.

Depending on her background a woman president may be more sensitive to issues that impact adversely on women and children. This could appeal to a large segment of the population. However, too much attention to issues solely from a woman's point of view, or even perceived that way by the public, could generate less support for a particular program or position. The few examples of women presidents or prime ministers in other countries provide no reason to assume there would be any other advantages, or that the behavior would be different from that of male presidents.

Short-term there could be skepticism by the White House staff, male and female, about the competence of a woman president. Another disadvantage is the scrutiny that every move would be receiving because the action is by a woman. She would probably be more isolated than men socially, but perhaps by the time we have a woman president attitudes about women will have improved dramatically.

EMPLOYMENT

"I F ANY WOULD NOT WORK, neither should he eat." The early Americans took that biblical adage to heart. For them, the Puritan work ethic was part of the survival ethic. They knew that hard workers might thrive in the new land, but the idle would almost certainly starve in the wilderness.

Even after the wilderness was cleared, Americans continued to emphasize the ideal of hard work. The land of opportunity, they stressed, offered only opportunity. Ambitious immigrants would not find roads paved with gold but they would find jobs—at least at the bottom rungs of the ladder.

What has happened to job opportunities in the land of opportunity? The good news is that more people are working. According to figures from the Bureau of Labor Statistics, the total American labor force swelled from about 64 million workers in 1950 to almost 105 million in 1979. Population increases account for a good part of the change, but growing numbers of women in the labor force also mean that higher percentages of the population hold jobs. The overall percentage of Americans in the work force climbed from 59.9 percent in 1950 to 64.2 percent by 1979. While more people are working, the average nonfarm worker is spending less time at the office or plant. A 1979 study revealed that the average workweek has shrunk from about fifty-three hours in 1900 to slightly more than forty-two hours today.

But while there are more jobs and fewer work hours, job opportunities can be hard to come by—especially in some employment areas and for some workers. High unemployment has plagued the United States since the early 1970s, affecting as much as 8.5 percent of the labor force in 1975. As of April 1981 about 7.7 million Americans, or 7.3 percent of the entire labor force, were out of jobs. Statistics from the Labor Department reveal that some sectors of the economy lost far more jobs than others. The construction industry, for example, suffered a jobless rate as high as 14.4 percent, while government employees reported only 4.9 percent unemployment. Similarly, job prospects varied greatly from state to state. Unemployed auto workers in Michigan helped to boost that state's jobless rate to 11.9 percent, while the overall rate for Texans was only 4.6 percent.

The greatest inequalities appear among the workers themselves. Traditionally, unskilled teen-agers have little luck in the job market, and the problem is especially acute for minority teen-agers. For example, while the nation's overall jobless rate went up only 0.4 percent between April 1980 and April 1981, the teen-ager unemployment rate grew 2.7 percent from 16.4 to 19.1 percent. Minority teen-agers suffered even more as their jobless rate soared more than 4 percent from 31.8 percent in 1980 to a staggering 36.1 percent in 1981. Adult men, on the other hand, maintained a steady unemployment rate of 5.8 percent.

Although statistics can show trends, critics question the accuracy of the government figures on unemployment. They point out that many people claim to be looking for a job in order to collect unemployment insurance while they actually have no intention of working. On the other hand, would-be employees, such as housewives and retired people, might be informally looking for work but not officially in the labor force. Moreover, the figures do not take into account the millions of underemployed: people who work only part-time but would like to work full-time, or workers who, like the taxi driver with a Ph.D., are over-qualified for their jobs.

Whether because of unemployment or job dissatisfaction, millions of Americans look for new jobs every month. As in the past, most of the jobs available are at the bottom of the success ladder. The Bureau of Labor Statistics estimates that more than half of the new openings in the 1980s will be in routine, low-paying jobs. While Ph.D.s in the humanities may pound the pavements for college teaching positions, there will be plenty of openings for clerks, cashiers, clerical workers and janitors.

Most people, however, want the "good jobs." Believing in a blend of the Puritan work ethic and the "challenging career" ethic, they look for jobs that provide food for thought as well as food for the table. Many will spend months, even years looking for their ideal job or for just an acceptable substitute. What careers look the most promising for the future? The following section surveys employment in both the private and the public sectors and suggests where the good jobs for the 1980s might be found. Local, state and federal government, which in recent years has provided jobs for millions of people, is also examined in light of its major role in the employment picture.

CONTRIBUTORS

Lawrence M. Kahn, Associate Professor of Economics and Labor and Industrial Relations, University of Illinois at Urbana-Champaign

Ernest C. Miller, Ph.D., Professor of Human Resources Management, Management Department, School of Business, California Polytechnic State University, San Luis Obispo, California

James M. Peirce, President, National Federation of Federal Employees, Washington, D.C.

Louis T. Rader, Professor, Graduate School of Business Administration, University of Virginia, Charlottesville, Virginia

U.S. Department of Labor, Bureau of Statistics, Washington, D.C.

Betty M. Vetter, Executive Director, Scientific Manpower Commission, Washington, D.C.

Dr. Seymour L. Wolfbein, Temple University, Philadelphia, Pennsylvania

WHAT ARE THE BEST JOBS FOR THE 1980S?

Lawrence M. Kahn. According to United States Bureau of Labor Statistics projections, communications, banking and medical services all will offer rapidly expanding employment opportunities in high-paying jobs over the 1980s. These good prospects are due primarily to technological advances in these sectors.*

In communications, the advances in cable television and teletext (for example, sending news text directly to television sets) will open up many new jobs in advertising and public relations. In banking, the data processing revolution is creating highly skilled jobs. Further, because of the increasing competition in financial markets, there will be more jobs for those skilled in marketing and developing financial services. Finally, our growing demand for and the technological advances in health care will continue to make the medical profession (including health administration) a good field to enter. Nonprofessional jobs in the health field such as dental assistants and nurses' aides will also offer many new opportunities.

In addition to these general areas, the Bureau of Labor Statistics has projected that the following specific jobs will offer good prospects for the 1980s.* Among professional and technical jobs (besides those just mentioned), mining and petroleum engineering will grow rapidly in the 1980s. Further, mathematical technicians, airline pilots, computer systems analysts, architects and social scientists will all have greatly expanded opportunities. Among managerial jobs, purchasing agents and sales managers will be in increased demand. Preparation for these jobs will generally require a bachelor's degree and, with increasing frequency, advanced degrees in these fields. New bachelor's and master's graduates with degrees in engineering and business administration have been

*The figures referred to and occupations mentioned are discussed in *The New York Times*, October 12, 1980.

doing particularly well on the job market, commanding starting salaries in the $20,000–$30,000 per year range.

A final area that the Bureau of Labor Statistics anticipates will offer many new jobs in the 1980s is secretarial work, particularly medical and legal. The current shortage of secretaries is likely to drive their salaries up.

Ernest C. Miller, Ph.D. Any crystal ball attempt to forecast the occupational areas which will produce the opportunities for employment within the immediate, ten-year future would be, at best, only conjectural.

However, some generalizations may be made, based primarily upon the most recent *Occupational Outline Handbook* published by the Bureau of Labor Statistics, United States Department of Labor.

For once, I am in complete agreement with the Department of Labor. In effect, the following forecast represents both its view and mine:

1. Topping the list would be jobs within the energy field; specifically those concerned with research, development and implementation of alternative sources of energy.

2. Closely allied are a wide range of related jobs in engineering with specific emphasis on petroleum engineering and mining engineering.

3. We are experiencing current, almost critical shortages in the health fields. Specific requirements will be apparent for registered nurses, licensed practical nurses, nurses' aides, general medical practitioners (as opposed to specialists, medical technicians and dentists).

4. Rapid and sometimes phenomenal advances are being and will continue to be made in the computer technology area. Considerable demand will be exerted for jobs requiring skills in design, engineering repair, manufacturing, operation programming, general systems, management information systems, robotics and automation.

5. Similar growth is being and will continue to be experienced in electronic communications. This appears to be a fast-growing occupation which will have considerable impact not only on our economy, but also on our social structure . . . our way of life. Jobs in this growth area are many and varied.

6. Since the Industrial Revolution there has been an ever-increasing growth of what has been called the Social Ethic. Throughout the world, the population has placed more and more reliance on services. It is anticipated that jobs in the service sector (including agriculture) will continue to expand.

7. Any job which is environmentally oriented will continue to be in demand. New and innovative skills will increase the demand for positions.

8. Finally, the need for educated and trained managers in every con-
    ceivable occupation is apparent. No longer can managers hope to
    achieve through the "learn it from dad" process.

On the negative side, occupations less susceptible to increased demand
appear to be law, secondary and college teaching, manual farm labor,
low-skill jobs, and those in tax supported agencies.

Louis T. Rader. The best jobs for the 1980s will be as follows: (1) Programming and management of programmers is a major growth area
not recognized by many. Office automation will contribute to the
demand. (2) Engineering, particularly computer science and electrical,
because of large-scale integrated technology. (3) Genetic engineering,
including biologists and chemical engineers. (4) Technicians in every
medical field (X-ray, lab, dental) as well as engineering.

United States Department of Labor. Overall, the computer, business
services, health, engineering and energy-related fields are expected to
provide the best job prospects during the 1980s. Each of these fields
encompasses many different occupations at a variety of skill levels, and
the amount of education, training or technical expertise required varies
from one occupation to another. The health field alone includes hundreds of distinct occupations, each with its own set of training requirements.

To most people, job prospects imply the amount of competition the
job seeker can expect to face. How hard is it to get the job you want or
think you're qualified for? There is no simple answer; in nearly every
occupation, conditions vary by geographic region, by salary level, and by
kind of skill, experience or specialization. Currently, beginning librarians
may have trouble finding a job while experienced librarians with administrative potential are in demand. In health and social services, the
job market is highly competitive in cities like Boston and San Francisco,
but openings in rural areas go unfilled. Among prospective college
faculty, individuals with a Ph.D. in the arts or humanities probably will
continue to experience poor job prospects during the 1980s, while
individuals in such fields as engineering, computer science or law will
find that prospects for college teaching are good. In each of these
situations, the difference lies in the relative availability of qualified
applicants.

There are other perspectives from which to consider job prospects,
however. The rate of employment growth is one. The computer and
health fields, for example, will provide many job openings during the
1980s if the very rapid employment growth of recent years is maintained. The following table reflects the Bureau of Labor Statistics occupational projections. It lists occupations in which employment in 1990 is
projected to be at least 50 percent higher than it was in 1978. The

projected national average growth of all occupations is about 21 percent. Employment growth in white-collar and service occupations, in general, is expected to exceed rates of growth in blue-collar jobs; farm workers are projected to continue to decline in number.

Ultimately, job prospects depend on the number of people looking for the same kind of job. The Bureau of Labor Statistics Occupational Outlook Handbook provides information—to the extent that available data resources will allow—on the degree of competition over the long run, nationally, that job seekers are likely to encounter in certain occupations.

FASTEST GROWING JOBS, 1978–90 (PROJECTED)

Occupation	Percent change in employment	Annual openings
Occupational therapists	100.0	2,500
Computer service technicians	92.5	5,400
Speech pathologists and audiologists	87.5	3,900
Dental hygienists	85.7	6,000
Homemaker-home health aides	70.0	36,000
Industrial machinery repairers	66.0	58,000
Dining room attendants and dishwashers	62.8	37,000
Licensed practical nurses	62.2	60,000
Travel agents	62.2	1,900
Lithographers	61.1	2,300
Health service administrators	57.1	18,000
Flight attendants	56.2	4,800
Business machine repairers	56.0	4,200
Respiratory therapy workers	55.0	5,000
Bank officers and financial managers	54.5	28,000
Podiatrists	53.7	600
City managers	52.0	350
Nursing aides, orderlies and attendants	52.0	94,000
Teacher aides	51.8	26,000
Bank clerks	50.5	45,000
Construction inspectors	50.0	2,200
Dental assistants	50.0	11,000
Guards	50.0	70,000
Occupational therapy assistants	50.0	1,100
Physical therapists	50.0	2,700

U.S. DEPARTMENT OF LABOR
Bureau of Labor Statistics
June 3, 1981

Betty M. Vetter. The best jobs for the 1980s are those dealing with some facet of the computer industry, and particularly those which require at least the educational level of the bachelor's degree in computer science or a related discipline such as electrical engineering.

The growth in computer use will be limited only by the lack of appropriately trained specialists to design, build, install, repair, program and operate the computers. Shortage of software (and persons capable of producing software) already is a bottleneck to some expansion that would be taking place.

The current transition of the United States from an industrial to an information society, currently taking place, is impeded by a severe shortage of computer scientists. Students are flocking into computer courses, but faculty shortages are acute and getting worse, so that universities will be increasingly unable to accommodate all those who seek training in areas of top demand by industry.

Other areas offering excellent employment opportunity include all of the engineering disciplines, geophysics, geology and probably chemistry. Among the skilled crafts in demand will be machinists.

Nonetheless, the best jobs for individuals in the 1980s, as always, will be those jobs which provide to the individual such a sense of satisfaction that she/he would want to work there even if she/he had no need to work anywhere. Such jobs will be found in the arts, the humanities, the business world, in industry, in schools and colleges, in government and in every level and sector of the economy. Unfortunately, fitting the right person to the right job does not happen as often as it should.

Dr. Seymour L. Wolfbein. There are three job sectors where the job outlook is best for the 1980s:

The first is for those with manual talent, for those who can design things, make things and keep things in repair. The jobs involved run the gamut from the various engineering fields to technicians to skilled crafts such as machinists or repair people. Our increasingly technologically based society is demanding more and more of this kind of talent.

The second, and related in important ways to the first, is the whole field of computer and information science. Here, too, there is a wide range of jobs, all the way from designing new machines and how they are powered, to software systems design, to actually programming and operating those machines. Major advances are expected to continue not only in office computer systems, but in industrial robotology (hooking up machines to computers) and even in the home for personal and household use.

The third is the health care and service field which includes, again, a wide range of jobs from doctors to nurses to health technicians as well as other personnel involved in institutional care in hospitals, nursing homes and the like. Increasing levels of living as well as an increasingly older population will continue to buttress the demand for people in these fields.

All of these fields (as well as others with relatively favorable job outlooks) require people with strong reading, writing and number skills. And, no matter what the job outlook may be, the best prognosis for the individual and his or her career is not only to have the talent, but the interest and motivation as well.

HOW MANY LOCAL, STATE AND FEDERAL EMPLOYEES ARE THERE IN THE UNITED STATES? WHAT PERCENTAGE OF THE WORK FORCE DO THEY REPRESENT? WILL THE TIME COME WHEN THERE ARE AS MANY PERSONS ON THE GOVERNMENT PAYROLL AS THERE ARE PERSONS EMPLOYED IN PRIVATE INDUSTRY?

Lawrence M. Kahn. As of March 1981, the United States Bureau of Labor Statistics reports that there were 2,786,000 federal and 13,318,000 state and local government employees in the United States. In the following table, the percentage of total employment represented by government workers for various years is shown.

FEDERAL AND STATE AND LOCAL EMPLOYEES AS A PERCENTAGE OF ALL EMPLOYMENT

	Federal	State and Local	All Government Employees
March 1961	3.930%	11.720%	15.650%
March 1971	3.600%	13.859%	17.459%
March 1976	3.382%	15.206%	18.588%
March 1981	2.967%	14.186%	17.153%

SOURCE: Bureau of Labor Statistics, *Monthly Labor Review*, various issues.

The table shows that just over 17 percent of total U.S. employment was in the government sector (federal plus state and local). In addition, federal employment's share has been steadily coming down since 1961, while the share of state and local employment rose from 1961 to 1976 and began to come down after that. Total government employment as a percentage of total employment peaked in the mid-1970s at about 18.5 percent and has been gradually falling ever since. Although the absolute number of federal and state and local employees has been steadily increasing, the Bureau of Labor Statistics data show that government employment considered as a percentage of total employment is on the way down.

This data and current fiscal trends make it extremely unlikely that there will, in the foreseeable future, be as many government employees as private sector employees. First, the peak figure (18.588 percent) for government's share of employment is well below 50 percent and, as indicated, is falling. Second, given the present trend toward tax cuts— both federal as well as state and local—and fiscal conservatism, the shrinking of the government sector relative to the rest of the economy is likely to continue.

Ernest C. Miller, Ph.D. The United States Department of Commerce reports that some 15,971,000 full- and part-time workers were employed by federal, state and local governments in 1979. It is likely that a slight increase in employment will be indicated in 1980 and 1981. The total full- and part-time work force in 1979 was 106,500,000. Thus, approximately 15 percent of the total work force was employed by government.

The combination of variables such as the current political climate, inflation, reduction of funds at all levels of government, the demand for less government spending, and expanding work force (women, handicapped, senior citizens, etc.) will produce a climate which, in the foreseeable future, will possibly reduce the ratio of government workers to the available full-time and part-time work force.

James M. Peirce. There never will come a time when the number of government employees equals the number of workers in private industry. Indeed, to state otherwise would be to predict that, at some point in the future, all employees in the private sector would have a personal civil servant to look after their affairs. Actually, statistics point to a leveling-off of government employment; in 1970, the percentage of government workers to all employees in the United States was exactly the same as it is today.

United States Department of Labor. According to the Bureau of Labor Statistics establishment survey of employment, hours and earnings, the average number of government employees in 1980 was 16,170,000. This employment figure includes part-time as well as full-time workers and is distributed among the three basic categories of government as follows: local government, 9,728,900; state government, 3,575,100; federal government, 2,866,000.

As a percentage of the total number of employees on nonagricultural payrolls in the United States, government employees represented 17.8 percent in 1980. Local government employment accounted for the largest portion with 10.7 percent of total nonfarm employment, while state and federal government employment represented 3.9 and 3.2 percent, respectively.

Since 1975, government's share of total employment has been declining, both for total government and for each of its components. If this trend continues, obviously the number of persons on the government payroll will not reach the number of persons employed in private industry.

Betty M. Vetter. In 1979, the total number of government employees averaged 15,920,000 and in 1980, the number was 16,170,000. Thus, the total is increasing. However, the increase is not at the federal level; growth is fastest in state and local government.

In addition to the federal civilian employees in the United States, the United States pays for services overseas. Among 125,964 United States civilian employees overseas, 63,943 are United States citizens and 62,021 are civilian employees who are citizens of some other country.

Among civilian employees of the federal government, 90.44 percent are employed full-time and 7.37 percent are employed part-time in regularly scheduled positions. Only 6.22 percent are temporary employees, and 2.19 percent are classified as intermittent employees.

Total federal civilian employment has remained between two and three million in every year since 1951. State and local employment, on the other hand, has risen from 4.1 million in 1951 to 13.6 million in 1981.

The U.S. Armed Forces are also employees of the federal government; while state governments employ state militia members. The numbers in these uniformed populations vary widely, depending on United States relations with other nations. It might be possible that in time of war, the increases in these uniformed populations when added to the numbers of civilian employees of government at all levels might result in having as many persons on the government payroll as on private industry payrolls. However, if only the civilian population is considered, it appears doubtful that government employees will equal or outnumber private industry employees. On the other hand, government employment has increased 153 percent over the past thirty years compared to a 90 percent increase in total employment. If this net increase of 2 percent per year should continue to prevail, half of the civilian labor force would be employed by some level of government by about 1997.

Dr. Seymour L. Wolfbein. In the middle of 1981 there were about 16.5 million civilian personnel on payrolls at all levels of government: federal, state and local. The overwhelming majority of them—about 85 percent—were working for state and local governments where the big increase in government employment has taken place since the end of World War II. These government employees accounted for about one out of every six people employed in America.

There were another 2.1 million people in the armed forces. And on top of all of this, governments—like people and households—also purchase things, from paper clips to bombers. These purchases generate employment in private industry which supplies the goods and services governments buy. An estimated 8.5 million people are employed in the private sector and owe their jobs to these government purchases. A substantial amount of employment also is generated indirectly by government, subsidies to housing, interstate highway programs, farm support programs, etc. No reliable estimate of the number of jobs all this represents is available.

For the foreseeable future, it is doubtful that the number of persons on government payrolls is going to equal the number in the private sector. President Reagan's program of budget cuts, and a variety of state and local laws such as Proposition 13 in California, are all expected to put a damper on the growth of government jobs.

We may, however, get an increase in government-generated employment in private industry if President Reagan's increased military budget expenditures come to pass.

For the longer future, a good deal will depend on our economic situation. If employment holds up reasonably well, that is, if the private sector can afford jobs for most people, then government employment will be held in check. If, however, there is a serious economic overturn (as in the 1930s) we can expect an upturn in the role of government.

LONGEVITY

*T*HERE IS MORE to growing old than sporting gray hair and wrinkles. To be truly old requires a certain chronological age, but it is becoming difficult to define exactly what that age is—or how the old should act when they reach it. Should a woman of sixty-five concentrate on her grandchildren or pursue a graduate degree? Should a man of seventy retire to a "leisure village" or move into the White House?

For many people, the age of "old" is arriving later than ever before. Take the case of the last three generations of a hypothetical American family. When the grandfather was born in 1900, he could have expected to outlive (barely) his midlife crisis; the average lifespan at the turn of the century was only forty-seven years. For the father, born in 1940, the odds were against surviving to enjoy retirement; the average lifespan that year ended at about age sixty-three. Yet his son, born in 1980, can look forward to almost a decade of life after sixty-five, for the average lifespan today stretches to more than seventy-three years.

Of course, recent increases in the average lifespan do not mean that larger numbers of people can expect to celebrate their centennials, although there are an estimated 12,000 people in the United States over 100 years old. What the longer lifespans do reflect is that for the first time in history the majority of Americans live into their seventies and often into their eighties.

On a national level, the graying of America entails widespread changes in the economic and social policies directed toward the aged. Not so long ago, the elderly were a very small proportion of the population. In 1900, for example, only 4 percent of the population was over age sixty-five.

Thanks to the high birthrate and huge influx of immigrants around the turn of the century, combined with today's increased lifespans, people aged sixty-five and over now make up about 10 percent of the population. The proportion is expected to grow in future years and to reach more than 12 percent by the year 2000, according to 1978 estimates by the Bureau of the Census. For social planners, this demographic shift signals the need for revisions in such fields as pension plans, Social Security, medical services, employment and housing.

On a personal level, the aging of America means that a significant minority of the people—a minority to which anyone might someday belong—faces the prospect of ten to twenty years of life after age sixty-five.

What is life like for the elderly? There is a sad stereotype of the aged as frail, often senile, and frequently institutionalized because they need constant care. There are undoubtedly many people over sixty-five who fit this description, but they are by no means the majority any more than delinquents make up the majority of teen-agers. Only about 5 percent of those over sixty-five live in institutions. Women outnumber men at age sixty-five about ten to seven and so, not surprisingly, far more elderly men are married (79 percent) than women (39 percent). More elderly than nonelderly own their own homes, and most people over sixty-five live with their spouses or other relatives.

A house is usually the older person's greatest financial asset. In general, the elderly tend to be poorer than the rest of the population, having incomes about half the size of younger groups. Social Security is the most common source of income. Other incomes, such as pensions, tend to be fixed and therefore diminish rapidly in the face of rising costs of living.

Illness, physical as well as mental, is also a problem: an estimated 86 percent of those over sixty-five have at least one chronic disease, and many older people frequently have several long-term health problems. The elderly themselves, however, do not seem to view their health as much of a drawback. According to a 1975 study by the National Center for Statistics, in which elderly people were asked to assess their health compared to others in their age group, 68 percent considered themselves to be in excellent or good health, 22 percent rated their health as fair, and only 9 percent said they were in poor health.

In fact, a sizable proportion of the over-sixty-five age group not only enjoys fairly good health but also adequate incomes and free time to devote to the projects that most interest it. As some sociologists have noted, the more affluent elderly may be emerging as the nation's new leisure class. Active, involved senior citizens are redefining the concept of *old*; some people now use terms such as *young-old*, *middle-old*, and even *old-old* to describe the phenomenon. As those over sixty-five emerge as a powerful interest group, they are demanding that Americans of all ages recognize the problems and potential of the aging.

CONTRIBUTORS

Fred L. Behling, M.D., orthopedic surgeon, Stanford University, Stanford, California; team physician, San Francisco Forty-niners Football Team

Prof. Jack Botwinick, Department of Psychology, Washington University, St. Louis, Missouri

Walter S. Cartwright, Ph.D., Professor of Sociology and Gerontology, Texas Tech University, Lubbock, Texas

William G. Clancy, M.D., Associate Professor and Head, Section of Sports Medicine, Division of Orthopedic Surgery, and Head Team Physician and Orthopedic Surgeon, University of Wisconsin, Madison, Wisconsin

Pauline E. Council, Ph.D., independent sociologist and gerontologist, Silver Spring, Maryland

Dr. Donald O. Cowgill, Professor Emeritus of Sociology, University of Missouri, Columbia, Missouri

Larry Gibbons, M.D., Director, Cooper Clinic, Dallas, Texas

Barbara Gilchrest, M.D., Harvard University Medical School, Cambridge, Massachusetts

M. Gene Handelsman, Acting Commissioner on Aging, Administration on Aging, Department of Health and Human Services, Washington, D.C.

Martin Katahn, Ph.D., Professor of Psychology and Director, Vanderbilt Weight Management Program, Vanderbilt University, Nashville, Tennessee

Woodrow W. Morris, Ph.D., Professor and Associate Dean, College of Medicine, The University of Iowa, Iowa City, Iowa

Prof. George C. Myers, Director, Center for Demographic Studies, Duke University, Durham, North Carolina

James A. Nicholas, M.D., Chief, Department of Orthopedics, Lenox Hill Hospital; Director, Institute of Sports Medicine and Athletic Trauma, Lenox Hill Hospital, New York, New York

Erdman B. Palmore, Ph.D., Professor, Department of Sociology and Psychiatry, Duke University, Durham, North Carolina

Lawrence Power, M.D., College of Medicine, Wayne State University, Detroit, Michigan

Nathan Pritikin, nutritional scientist and author, Santa Barbara, California

John A. Reinecke, Ph.D., Professor of Marketing and Director, International Marketing Institute, University of New Orleans, New Orleans, Louisiana

Isadore Rossman, M.D., Ph.D., Medical Director, Home Care and Extended Services Department, Montefiore Hospital and Medical Center; Associate Professor of Medicine, Albert Einstein College of Medicine, The Bronx, New York

James H. Schulz, Professor of Welfare Economics, Brandeis University, Waltham, Massachusetts; President, Gerontological Society of America

Richard E. Shepherd, Executive Secretary, National Association of Mature People, Oklahoma City, Oklahoma

Dr. Diana S. Woodruff, Associate Professor of Psychology, Temple University, Philadelphia, Pennsylvania; author of *Can You Live to Be 100?*

WHO (A GROUP OF PEOPLE OR A COUNTRY) ARE THE MOST LONG-LIVED PEOPLE ON EARTH? WHERE IN AMERICA DO PEOPLE LIVE THE LONGEST? WHY DO SOME PEOPLE LIVE LONGER THAN OTHERS?

Professor Jack Botwinick. Good genes, good health, sensible living habits and luck make some people live longer that others.

Pauline E. Council, Ph.D. Before we address this question of longevity there are several considerations that must be taken into account. The first one is that a distinctions must be made between what the terms *life span* and *life expectancy* mean. The first term refers to the biological limit to the length of life of any species. At this point there are few documented cases of persons living past 105 or 110 years, the *life span* for human beings. Almost all populations or groups of people can point to persons who have lived a complete life span.

The second term, *life expectancy*, is a statistical term used when predictions are made about to what age on the average persons will live at birth or some other point in their lives. There is a tendency for us to confuse life expectancy and life span. Whereas life expectancy, in the Western industrialized countries, has been increased due to the control of infectious diseases affecting young people, life span has not changed. We have greater numbers of people who are living more years of the possible life span.

Two population factors affect the development of a population which contains a high proportion of old people. A group may have either a very low birthrate or a high infant and child mortality rate. Also migration of young people out of a group and old people into it can affect the ratio.

There are documented cases of some small populations, such as a group high in the Ecuadorian Andes, with a surprisingly large number of persons about 100 years old. These cases were viewed with some skepticism by the persons who studied the Ecuadorians and went to great lengths to check genealogies and records. They found that many were not as old as they said and that there was a strong tendency for persons who were over the age of seventy to exaggerate their ages.

Despite these cautions, interest continues to motivate people to find populations with large numbers of old people—sort of modern Fountain of Youth quests. However, our more generalized information about populations indicates that greater numbers of people live out higher proportions of the human lifespan in industrialized Western countries, such as the United States, Great Britain, Sweden and Germany. We do know that in almost every part of the world women have greater life expectancies than men and that whites live longer than nonwhites. Although we know some correlates for these differences, we have not learned the causes.

The population of the United States, a country with vast distances, is highly mobile. Thus there is a tendency for people to live out their lives away from the places where they were born. Since so few people stay put, it is difficult to say where people live the longest. Some states such as Iowa have large proportions of old people because younger persons have moved out. On the other hand Florida and California have high proportions because older people have moved into those states.

The life chances of any group of people result from the interaction of a number of factors which affect the make-up of the population. Some obvious examples are that it is better to live in an area that is free of malaria-carrying mosquitoes, or not to be in an area where the climate is changing due to overgrazing with starvation as the consequence. Other populations have been subjected to appalling death tolls from war or other political actions. Still others are so poor they lack the living conditions conducive to longevity. Thus we know that longevity is complex and cannot be understood without knowledge of environmental, political and socioeconomic conditions, and the availability and utilization of medical technology.

Historically we know that improved living conditions such as sanitary environments, clean water, ample food and control of infectious diseases have been most effective in lowering the death rate of a population. Thus it is easy to see on a broad scale why some groups have better life chances in general and longevity in particular.

In recent years the bio-medical researchers have introduced us to the term "population at risk." Their studies of mortality (death) and morbidity (illness) have attempted to identify the correlates of life-threatening conditions. Thus we are just now beginning to understand more about the subgroups in our population that have greater risks of cancer, heart attacks, accidents or some other condition that will affect longevity.

Dr. Donald O. Cowgill. In the genetic sense, no one knows. No people lives its full potential lifespan. Currently the Japanese are rivaling the Dutch and the Scandinavians in expectation of life at birth, but as diets, health conditions, health habits and health care improve other peoples are likely to prove equally long-lived. Whether the Abkhasians of the Caucasus region of the Soviet Union are really any longer-lived than people of other areas is still in debate. The Vilcabamba region of Ecuador which is similarly touted has recently been demonstrated to be a myth—a myth born of the inhabitants' propensity to exaggerate their age. Such cases are difficult to prove or disprove in view of the general lack of documentary evidence, the anecdotal nature of available evidence, the lack of adequate demographic information on the total population of the relevant area. A few centenarians, even with proof of their age, do not make a long-lived people. We need life tables based on valid age-specific death rates for the whole population.

M. Gene Handelsman. Japan and Iceland are the countries with the longest life expectancy (seventy-six years at birth), followed by the United States, Canada, Denmark and Israel (seventy-four years at birth). These estimates appear in the *1981 World Data Sheet*, published by the Population References Bureau, Inc.

Hawaii is the state with the longest life expectancy (seventy-four years at birth), followed by Minnesota and Utah (seventy-three years at birth). These estimates appear in the *1969–1971 Life Tables*, published by the National Institute of Health.

There are many reasons why some people live longer than others. Genetic heritage is the greatest determinant of longevity. However, good health coupled with reasonable living conditions and lifestyle also play an important role.

Woodrow W. Morris, Ph.D. In the 1972 *Demographic Yearbook* of the United Nations, eighty-one of the nations of the world were categorized as follows: thirty-four "aged," thirteen "mature," and thirty-four "young" nations on the basis of the proportions of their populations which were sixty-five years of age and older. The aged countries were those which had more than 7 percent of their populations sixty-five and older. The mature countries had between 4 and 7 percent, and the young nations had under 4 percent.

Most of the aged nations are among the developed countries, and are primarily located in Europe, North America and Oceania. The following examples give the percent of population age sixty-five and over and their rank among the thirty-four aged nations: German Democratic Republic (15.6 percent, ranked first), England and Wales (13.1 percent, ranked seventh), United States (9.9 percent, ranked nineteenth) and New Zealand (8.5 percent, ranked twenty-seventh). Exceptions were the following nations located outside of these three areas: Argentina (7.5 percent, ranked thirty-second), Barbados (7.4 percent, ranked thirty-third) and Japan (7.1 percent, ranked thirty-fourth). In general, it is the northern and western European nations which are the most aged.

It is noteworthy that in these countries the crude birthrates and the crude death rates tend to be relatively low. Thus, in the aged nations the median birthrate was 16.8 per 1,000 population and the death rate was 9.5. It is striking to contrast these data with the comparable figures for the young nations in which the median birthrate was 43.6 and the death rate was 11.7.

But those reported by Dr. Alexander Leaf (though not completely confirmed) as the most long-lived people on earth live in quite different portions of the globe. These very old people lived in three disparate areas of the world: southeastern Russia in the foothills of the Caucasus mountains; in Hunza in the high valleys near the borders of China and Afghanistan; and in Vilcabamba, an Andean village in Ecuador. In these areas it was common to find people who reportedly were well over 100 years old—some, in Abkhasia, Russia were said to be upwards of 140 years of age. A census taken in 1971 showed that Vilcabamba, with a population of only 819, had 9 individuals who reported that they were above the age of 100. The number in Hunza is not known since there are no records, but the largest number of people over 100 years old appears to exist in the Caucasus region. In 1970 a census placed the number of centenarians at 4,500 to 5,000 in the entire region. Of these, 1844 lived in Georgia, or 39 per 100,000 population; 2,500 lived in Azerbaijan, or 63 per 100,000. In the United States, by comparison, the figure is about 3 centenarians per 100,000 population.

A high proportion of the Great Plains farmbelt of the United States (Iowa, Kansas, Missouri, Nebraska, Oklahoma and South Dakota) as well as some northeastern (e.g., Maine, Massachusetts and Pennsylvania) and southern (e.g., Florida and Arkansas) states had high percentages (12.5 percent and more) of elderly persons in 1979. While some of this may be attributed to aging *per se*, it is important to take into account the factors of in- and out-migration and fertility and death rates. In about one-fifth of the counties in the West North Central Division of the United States, over 20 percent of the population in 1976 was over sixty-five years of age.

All of the factors which result in longevity in some groups, and in wasting chronic illness and long-term dependency in others, are not known. What evidence is available suggests that primary factors in successful aging include good, well-balanced nutrition, being and staying active and vigorous, and being able successfully to cope with stress in addition to biological (especially genetic) mechanisms. In truth, however, the research data on factors associated with very old age have not been comprehensively addressed as yet.

Professor George C. Myers. I do not think that there are groups of people, nor countries in which individuals live longer. Of course, life expectancy may vary substantially between groups or countries. There is very little regional difference in the United States in this regard. People live longer because they don't die earlier. Which simply means that they do not become chronically ill, and when they do they avail themselves of superior medical services. As for the greater life expectancy of females compared with males, I think that the factors responsible probably have a genetic basis.

Erdman B. Palmore, Ph.D. The countries with the most long-lived people on earth are Norway, Denmark, the Netherlands, Japan; and Canada and the United States (women only). Most of the stories of long-lived people in some parts of South America and the Georgian region of Russia have been found to be exaggerations and frauds.

In the United States, life expectation at birth is greatest for men in the states of Alaska, Hawaii, Connecticut, Minnesota, South Dakota (all 70.9 years or higher); for women in the states of Alaska, Hawaii, Minnesota, North and South Dakota, Nebraska, Washington, D.C., Florida, Colorado, Arizona, and Utah (all 78 years or over).

Life expectancy at birth is about eight years greater for women than for men. This is because of a combination of sex-linked genetic factors (for example, hormonal differences) and lifestyle differences.

Dr. Diana S. Woodruff. The country with the longest life expectancy is Sweden. This is primarily because health care is extended to everyone in the population and there is little or no poverty. Infant mortality rates in Sweden are the lowest in the world. This suggests that health care is excellent in this country and it helps people to live longer. In the United States, people in the state of Hawaii have the longest life expectancy. One reason for this is that Orientals in America live an average of two years longer than Caucasians, and Hawaii has a large Oriental population. This may be a genetically caused difference, or it may relate to the diet of Orientals and the manner in which they deal with stress. Orientals also treat aging and the aged with more dignity than do most other groups. The next longest lived group in the United States are people living in the Midwest. People living in rural areas live longer than people living in big cities and urban areas. Thus, rural living midwesterners live longer.

There are many reasons why some people live longer than others. I have identified thirty-two factors which differentiate individuals on the basis of longevity. These factors are divided into four major categories. The first major factor in longevity is heredity. Your genes predispose you to live a longer or shorter life and make you more or less susceptible to certain diseases which shorten life. The longer your parents and grandparents have lived, the greater your chances for a long life. Health factors are probably the greatest determinants of long life. More than any other activity, smoking shortens life. Other strong health correlates of longevity are diet and activity. Thin, active people live much longer than those who are overweight or inactive. Education and occupation help some people to live longer than others, and lifestyle is the fourth major category influencing long life. People who are unhappy or who place themselves in a great deal of stress shorten their lives. One of the general characteristics of individuals living to be 100 seems to be a positive outlook and an orientation to people.

WHAT ADVANCES, IF ANY, HAVE BEEN MADE IN THE AREA OF PREVENTING AGING?

Professor Jack Botwinick. There have been no advances made to prevent aging.

Pauline E. Council, Ph.D. First, it is important to conceptualize aging as a lifelong process. Then we realize that as persons age chronologically all aspects of a person's life are affected. Students of gerontology have been challenged to determine just how many of our expectations of people in the later stages of the life cycle are due to cultural values, social status, mental health and physical conditions.

Obviously the physical aspect is the most basic element of persons' lives. The major problem for researchers in biology, physiology, psychology and medicine has been to separate the normal aging processes from pathological conditions. More and more we are learning that some sensory, functional and physical problems previously thought to be caused by old age and therefore, inevitable, are pathological and preventable. A few instances of these findings are in the list below.

1. People do not invariably lose their teeth. Proper care of gums as well as teeth can prevent loss.
2. Not all persons experience declines in visual and auditory acuity. Preventive and corrective techniques disregard age as a factor.
3. Most persons maintain their intellectual abilities and can continue to learn throughout their lives.
4. "Aging" of the skin is due more to exposure to sun and weather than to age.
5. Arthritis is not limited to the elderly and may have causes related to nutrition, stress and allergies.
6. Impotence is not inevitable and old people have no physical reason to discontinue active sex lives.

This brief list shows that progress is being made in understanding the process of aging and what preventions and treatments for aging are being developed.

The next three aspects of people's lives—psychological, social and cultural—are intimately bound up with each other. Clearly one's emotional stability, self-esteem, attitudes and life satisfaction are related to the status and roles one has in society, and the value placed upon people like oneself by the culture. We know that people are more apt to think highly of themselves who hold meaningful positions in groups, and who feel they are valued for the kind of persons they are. Furthermore these people are also likely to be in better physical condition.

Some of the advances being made which attempt to reinforce the positive side of the four aspects (physical, psychological, social, cultural) are indicated by: sheltered and subsidized housing; multipurpose senior citizens centers; a network of services provided through state and area agencies on aging; nutrition programs; elimination of mandatory retirement at age sixty-five; retirement communities; nursing home and other long-term care reforms; continuing education extended to the elderly; and Medicare and Medicaid.

Even if some of these advances appear to foster undemocratic segregation, in our age-graded society they are valuable in counteracting the possibility of isolation with all of its insidious ramifications. Sometimes people resist seeing themselves as senior citizens and participating in programs. Such persons might reflect on the findings of studies which show that involvement in group activities and good health go hand in hand with happiness for older persons.

Dr. Donald O. Cowgill. Genetic engineering may have potential for the distant future, but so far the advances, while real, have not been dramatic. Improved diet, improved sanitation, better health care, exercise, reduced stress—anything which reduces or prevents insults to the organism—will slow the aging process and produce a healthier older population. We have been preventing aging for many decades and as a result the expectation of long life has been steadily rising and our older population is healthier.

Barbara Gilchrest, M.D. There are at present no practical means of preventing normal aging. It has been shown in experimental animals that dietary restrictions greatly increase the lifespan of rats and guppies, with a larger effect noted in males than in females. Studies in mice and cats suggest that castration may also increase life expectancy. Finally, it has been shown convincingly in animals and suggestively in man that healthy long-lived parents have offspring with a longer than average life expectancy and a later onset of aging. That is, to prevent early aging, one should choose his parents wisely.

From a more practical point of view, it is important to note that many of the most problematic aspects of aging are related to degenerative diseases, rather than to aging itself. Medical sciences have not identified numerous risk factors (most of which can be modified by the motivated individual) which predispose to conditions such as atherosclerotic heart disease, cancer, degenerative arthritis, diabetes, stroke, wrinkling and loss of teeth—all of which render old age less pleasant. By "living right" and taking reasonable precautions beginning preferably in childhood or even in adulthood, many persons can completely avoid these health problems in their later years, even if they do not truly alter their rate of aging.

In summary, much can be done to prevent the disease and discomfort associated with old age, although effective measures require that people live their lives in a healthful and reasonable manner from the time they are still young. There is no potion for a fountain of youth which can reverse forty to sixty years of abuse to the human system.

Woodrow W. Morris, Ph.D. Preventing aging really means preventing premature aging and premature death. In this sense of the word there have been some dramatic successes in increasing the life expectancy of both the young and the old.

A child born today may expect to live about 73 years. This may be compared with the 49.2 years of life expectancy for a child born in 1900; this is a gain of more than 23 years. Similarly, a person now 65 years old can expect to live another 16 years, contrasted with a 12-year life expectancy in 1900.

All along the lifespan, females have a greater life expectancy than males, and this difference has increased progressively since 1900. Thus, a girl born today may expect to live to age 76.7, while a boy has a life expectancy of only 69, a difference of 7.7 years. Even at age 65, women will average living about 4.3 years longer than men. At the turn of the century this difference was only 2 years.

Furthermore, white persons have greater life expectancies than black and other racial groups, although the gap has been steadily closing over the past eighty years.

In back of these increases in life expectancy is a lowering of the death rate of infants and children to which medical science has recently added a decline in the death rate of people in the older age ranges. Today the most rapidly growing proportion of the elderly population is among those seventy-five years old and over. The steady increase in longevity has been credited to major public health measures and to the general improvement in the standard of living.

Nowadays the primary causes of death among the elderly are the chronic diseases rather than acute infectious diseases. However, within the chronic diseases the major causes of death are moving in opposite directions; death rates from cancer have been rising and death rates from diseases of the heart have been falling.

No doubt the improvement in death rates due to heart disease may be related causally to increased attention to diet, exercise, nonsmoking and remarkable advances in early diagnosis and medical treatment of, and surgical techniques for dealing with heart problems, especially the widespread use of antihypertensive medications and bypass surgical techniques.

Another giant step forward will come when medical science finally conquers the devastations of malignant neoplasms and cerebrovascular diseases. These two, with heart disease, account for 75 percent of the deaths of people over the age of sixty-five.

In the realm of human behavior, it is important to be aware of the roles played by stress in relation to disease and, hence, to premature death. Many of the changes in various life events which affect us require social readjustment. Events such as the death of a loved one, loss of a job, personal injury or illness, divorce and other marital separations, and financial reverses are examples of stressful life events. While some have laid the blame on stress itself, it may be more meaningful to consider that relatively healthy older people can and do cope successfully with such stressful life events. Thus, while stressful life events are related to a greater likelihood of developing an illness, stress *per se* need not be regarded as detrimental to well-being. In the individual who is able to cope with the demands of life event changes, stress may be associated with growth. As such, the individual may well have prevented premature aging as well as illness. Science still has a long way to go in better understanding these mechanisms, but the case is strong that coping and its precursors may be important in understanding successful aging. The recent emphasis on maintaining an active lifestyle provides cultural rewards and incentives for staying relatively young. This includes such behaviors as continued sexual activities, lifelong learning, participation in vigorous sports activities, and continued interest and involvement in the activities of the work place.

Erdman B. Palmore, Ph.D. Obviously no one can prevent aging in the sense of growing older. But there have been advances in reducing the diseases associated with aging, particularly the cardiovascular diseases. Deaths from cardiovascular and other diseases have dropped so much since 1970 that life expectancy at age sixty-five has increased by over one year (now about 16.4 years). There is also some evidence that mental health and life satisfaction of the aged is improving. These favorable trends may have partly resulted from the many programs to prevent atrophy from inactivity, to prevent senility from isolation and boredom, and to prevent depression from poverty and loss of self-esteem. There are also many possibilities for extending life in the future through transplants, through extending the ability of cells to repair themselves and to reproduce, and through preventing the deterioration of tissues.

Nathan Pritikin. Recent exciting advances in aging research indicate that it may be possible not only to retard the rate at which the aging process occurs, thereby increasing the lifespan, but it may also be possible to enhance the feeling of well-being throughout an individual's lifetime.

One way to increase the odds of living longer is to ensure adequate oxygen nutriture. When body tissues receive less than optimal amounts of oxygen, they age faster. Excessive consumption of fats diminishes the oxygen supply to body tissues. Fats cause the red blood cells to stick together, so their ability to release oxygen to tissue cells is impaired. Free radicals also take a large share of the blame for depriving tissues of oxygen. Free radicals are highly reactive substances that cause damage to the cells, tissues and genetic material of the body. They also alter the collagen which surrounds the tissues, making tissues denser and less elastic. Excessive numbers of free radicals are formed when the amount of polyunsaturated fats in the diet is increased. Decreasing the amount of fats in the diet, especially polyunsaturated fats, would thus help retard the rate at which our tissues age.

Engaging in aerobic exercise also causes more oxygen to be brought to our cells, helping us to stay young. In addition, exercise increases the vital capacity of the lungs, increases blood volume and the amount of hemoglobin in the blood, lowers the amount of fat in the blood, stimulates circulation, increases bone strength, and in many other ways contributes to increased longevity.

Restricting total caloric intake has been found to dramatically increase the lifespan of many forms of life, from the simplest one-celled animals to humans. People who live in areas where exceptional longevity is common consume about half the calories that Americans do.

Aside from diet and exercise, researchers are investigating other methods of slowing the aging process, such as using certain experimental drugs and electrically stimulating parts of the brain. To date, however, the safest, most effective and least expensive way to prolong physical, mental and emotional vigor is to follow those dietary and exercise guidelines which have been shown to be effective.

Isadore Rossman, M.D., Ph.D. According to present conceptions aging is an inevitable consequence of life and living, at least in all forms above the most elementary. It may well be programmed into the basic organization of cells since the lifespan is quite fixed and characteristic for a given species. Of practical importance for the individual is how to achieve the maximum lifespan possible. Of the identified factors, cigarette smoking, which statistically shortens the lifespan by more than four years, is probably the most important. It is an individual tragedy to come from a longevous family (which is hereditary) but to die in one's fifties from either lung cancer or a heart attack, both of which are increased in smokers. Other common and treatable or preventable disorders which may prevent one living to one's genetically decreed lifespan are: high blood pressure, high blood fats, diabetes, certain chronic infections, surgically repairable valvular and other vascular diseases, and environmentally related cancers. There appear to be plenty of human examples of living into the nineties and dying without identifiable pathology or of some essentially terminal infection. These very old individuals may remain quite functional until almost their very last days. Hence our increasing ability to successfully treat and prevent disease is relevant to this question.

Experimentally, the most important demonstration of the prolongation of the lifespan was that by McCay, an American biologist, almost fifty years ago, that the lifespan of the calorically undernourished rodent could be almost doubled. This does not hold for other species or, the prolongation is far less dramatic. The heritability of the lifespan has been shown in a number of species to be modifiable by selective breeding. It is also known that repair processes for damage to the DNA of the nucleus are better in the more long-lived species. This suggests the possibility of prolonging the lifespan by improving repair processes in cells, since one manifestation of aging is cellular loss from important tissues such as muscle and brain. It has also been shown that youthful immunocompetent cells can be withdrawn from a younger animal and reinjected when it becomes old in order to repair the immune deficiency often seen with aging. However, at present, really major breakthroughs in the prolongation of life are not looming on the biomedical horizon.

Dr. Diana S. Woodruff. Human life expectancy in ancient times was about twenty years. As recently as the turn of the century, life expectancy in the United States was forty-nine years. In the twentieth century alone, we have added more than twenty-five years to the average life expectancy. This has been done primarily through advances in medical science and the application of public health measures.

The greatest impact on life expectancy in the twentieth century has been the discovery of "wonder" drugs such as sulfonamides and antibiotics. With these drugs, we have been able to successfully combat infectious diseases. These diseases in the past had shortened life expectancy by killing individuals in their childhood. Thus, life expectancy has been extended not by adding more years to old age but by preventing death early in life and allowing more people to reach adulthood and old age. While over twenty-five years have been added to life expectancy at birth, only about five years have been added to life expectancy at the age of sixty-five. To this point, we have been preventing aging by improving health in the younger years and helping people to reach later life in a better state of health.

For an individual, the single step that can prevent aging most is to stop smoking. Other measures individuals can take to slow the aging process are to maintain their bodies at a low weight and to remain active.

HOW MUCH EXERCISE DOES THE AVERAGE HEALTHY AMERICAN ADULT NEED PER WEEK? WILL REGULAR EXERCISE HELP TO PROLONG LIFE?

Fred L. Behling, M.D. The goals of the American adult's exercise program should be somewhere along the lines of enough exercise to keep him in cardiovascular tone as well as enable him to enjoy vigorous physical activities of one form or another. I expect that a minimum of three hours per week would do the job. Whatever amount of time is devoted to exercise should be in segments of no less than one-half hour spread throughout the week—not all obtained on the weekend.

Regular exercise, as far as can be positively stated, will not prolong life but probably will improve the quality of life.

William G. Clancy, Jr., M.D. This has been a very difficult question to answer. The American College of Sports Medicine over the past two years has made a position statement in which they concluded through an extensive review of the world's scientific literature that a normal adult, to achieve a conditioning effect, must sustain his heart rate at a specific level, for a minimum of fifteen minutes three times per week. They have further stated that there is no evidence to support the view that training more times per week and for longer periods each day lead to any significant cardiovascular effect.

Almost all of the longevity studies that have been published to date, have been unable to justify the statement that exercise will prolong life. There has been only one study (published in *The New England Journal of Medicine*) which seems to indicate that a good exercise program may indeed prolong life. I think it is safe to state that although it has not been conclusively shown that exercise will necessarily prolong life, it is clinically evident to those involved in sports medicine that a regularly performed exercise program will improve the quality of one's life.

Larry Gibbons, M.D. An adequate exercise program for the average healthy adult must be of the proper intensity, duration and frequency. The ideal intensity is approximately 75 percent of the predicted maximum heart rate which for an individual, age thirty-five to forty-five, would be a heart rate of approximately 135 beats per minute. If the intensity is higher than this, then the duration can be shorter. If the intensity is lower, then the duration should be longer. If the intensity is approximately 75 percent of the predicted maximum heart rate, then the proper duration is approximately twenty minutes per day. If the intensity is lower, such as would be the case in an exercise such as walking, then the duration should be longer—up to forty-five minutes a day. The optimal frequency of exercise is five times per week.

There is circumstantial evidence that exercise will prolong life. There is some evidence that regular exercise will: (1) help to delay or protect against heart attack; (2) help to lower blood pressure; (3) help individuals to stay lean and thus reduce risk of diabetes and other diseases associated with overweight; (4) help raise HDL (high density Lipoprotein) cholesterol levels which in turn reduces risk of heart disease; and (5) help increase energy and vigor and sense of well-being which may have a very profound effect on overall health. (The fifth point is probably the most important.) There has been no absolute proof from a major longitudinal study that exercise will add years to one's life. Such a study would require immense expenditure of money and time. The circumstantial evidence mentioned above continues to accumulate, however, and suggests that exercise will lengthen life. It most certainly does increase the quality of life.

Martin Katahn, Ph.D. A person in a sedentary occupation needs to expend about 200 calories a day (over what would otherwise be expended) in any pleasurable activity equivalent to brisk walking. I am not certain that the evidence is conclusive, but by preventing obesity, this level of activity should be associated with longevity. I would recommend about forty-five minutes a day of brisk walking, or five days a week of forty minutes of gentle jogging, or five or six hours of singles tennis per week.

James A. Nicholas, M.D. We support the guidelines established by the American College of Sports Medicine in their position statement on the recommended quantity and quality of exercise for developing and maintaining fitness in healthy adults. In addition, these guidelines have been approved by the Research Consortium of the American Alliance for Health, Physical Education, Recreation and Dance.

1. Frequency: three to five days per week.
2. Intensity of training: 60 percent to 90 percent of maximum heart rate reserve, or 50 percent to 85 percent of maximum oxygen uptake.
3. Duration of training: fifteen to sixty minutes of continuous aerobic activity. Duration is dependent upon the intensity of the activity; thus, lower intensity activity should be conducted over a longer period of time. Because of the importance of the total fitness effect and the fact that it is more readily attained in longer duration programs, and because of the potential hazards and compliance problems associated with high intensity activity, lower to moderate intensity activity of longer duration is recommended for the nonathletic adult.
4. Mode of activity: any activity that uses large muscle groups, that can be maintained continuously and is rhythmical and aerobic in nature. For example, walking, hiking, jogging, running, swimming, skating, bicycling, rope skipping.

Although exercise has not proven to prolong life expectancy, research has indicated that it can improve the quality of life.

Lawrence Power, M.D. Long-term studies of 16,000 college graduates have shown that vigorous physical activity lasting a total of four hours per week reduces the chance of a heart attack by 50 percent, even in the presence of other risk factors such as high blood pressure, cigarette smoking or diabetes. Vigorous physical activity is a fitness activity if it takes your heart rate up to 120 beats a minute and holds it there without discomfort. It could be brisk walking, dancing, calisthenics, cycling, swimming, skating, jogging or a game of some team athletic activity.

Not all physical activity produces fitness. Climbing a flight of stairs is not a fitness activity because it does not last long enough. Desk work is not a fitness activity because it is not sufficiently demanding of muscle action. Golf and bowling are not usually fitness activities because they do not get your heart and lungs sufficiently involved for a long enough period of time. Unaccustomed effort is usually required to obtain fitness, and its risk can be minimized by allowing oneself several months of adjustment and slow progression.

Pain and discomfort during exercise are flashing orange signals. They say that too much is being asked, that fibers are being torn or demands for oxygen are not being met. A weakness has surfaced in the system, so cut back. Always have enough breath left over to talk to a fellow exerciser, or to whistle or to sing to oneself while being active. It's a simple way to be sure that enough oxygen is on board. Listen to your breathing and avoid pain, but do start moving around again.

WHAT PERCENTAGE OF PEOPLE OVER SIXTY-FIVE IS POOR? WHAT IS THE BEST WAY FOR AVERAGE PEOPLE TO AVOID POVERTY IN THEIR OLD AGE?

Pauline E. Council, Ph.D. The poverty line, established each year by the Census Bureau, is defined by the amount of cash income only. Thus, when the figures are used, one must realize that there are programs such as housing supplements and food stamps which are provided to help persons avoid the harshest impact of poverty.

For the second year in a row the percentage of the sixty-five and over age group which is below the poverty line has risen. In 1980 the percent was 15.7 and in 1979 it was 15.2. In the table below, one- and two-person households are used to provide the 1980 Census Bureau definitions of poverty since the elderly live in smaller households.

1980 CENSUS BUREAU POVERTY LEVELS

Nonfarm	
1 person household	$4,184
2 person household	$5,338

Farm

1 person household	$3,539
2 person household	$4,502

The Census Bureau redefines the poverty levels each year to take into account changes in the cost of living. The percentage for 1980 means that one out of seven persons over the age of sixty-five, about 3 million persons in the United States, are in the poverty category.

The increases in the proportion of the aged below the poverty line recently are a reversal of a trend in which the proportion had been declining steadily from a high of 35.2 percent in 1959. At a time when changes in Social Security benefits are under consideration, one is reminded that the reductions over the years in the proportion of poverty are due in large part to increases in Social Security programs.

As many people become older they begin to realize their incomes will drop after retirement or the death of a spouse. Also these people already know that their incomes have not kept pace with inflation. These two factors create a fear of falling into poverty which is supported to some extent by the fact that a higher proportion of people over the age of sixty-five have incomes that fit the Census Bureau definition of poverty than of the population as a whole. However, the news is not all bad; people need to take stock of their status while they are still in middle age and make some attempt to predict what their situations will be in their old age.

First, we need to establish that "average" means persons or spouses of persons who have worked regularly throughout their adult lives in jobs or occupations where they were covered by Social Security and/or retirement plans. Neither of these groups is very likely to fall into poverty. The couples, individuals or surviving spouses who will have two sources of income (Social Security and a pension) or a very liberal pension may expect to maintain former lifestyles if the income is 75 percent of that earned while employed. Those persons who will have only one source will probably avoid poverty though they will have to adjust their styles of living.

The second group, which might still be considered average, includes persons whose incomes overall have been borderline because they have experienced layoffs, and those whose incomes may have been high but have worked for a number of employers. Still others may have worked steadily but have been paid low salaries. Persons in this group may have a greater risk of sliding into the poverty category.

The final group, who have no hope of avoiding poverty, are clearly not average because they have always been poor. Many of these people may have worked but will receive minimum Social Security because their pay was low or, for example, as day workers they received pay in cash and did not contribute toward Social Security benefits.

In sum it can be said that the *average* American has a low probability of falling into poverty. The list below includes some points to consider as persons think about the future.

1. Recognize, if you are a woman, the importance of securing Social Security coverage.
2. Learn, if you are a woman, to handle finances and other business matters. (By the time they reach sixty-five, half of the women who have been married are widows.)
3. Keep informed on the management of existent retirement funds where you are employed.
4. Go to your local Social Security Administration office and learn how to predict what your retirement income will be.
5. Take the maintenance of your health seriously including attention to proper nutrition and exercise.
6. Be wary of doing work for which you are paid in cash and for which no Social Security payments are made.
7. Learn to do as many things for yourself as possible so that you will not have to pay for services, repairs, maintenance, etc.
8. Learn, if you are a man, the basics of housekeeping, laundry and cooking.
9. Keep property that is appreciating for investments. Sell any liabilities.
10. Consider deferring some of your income if your position or employer allows for purchase of tax sheltered annuities.
11. Consider the monetary advantages to which you may be entitled such as food stamps and subsidized housing.

Some people think as we look toward the twenty-first century that we are headed for many changes due to dwindling resources and energy supplies. Despite that observation there is no reason to think that persons who maintain good health, are active in groups and can provide for themselves will not continue to be happy in old age.

Walter S. Cartwright, Ph.D. With the exception of those people with inherited wealth or with large investments, enforced retirement or retirement because of health in old age brings a decline in income! Obviously. Those who have always been poor become even poorer. Those who have just barely gotten by will find they have fallen below the poverty line, however it may be defined. On the other extreme, those who have never had to work may find that their wealth is even increasing so that on the average the elderly are no poorer than younger segments of the population but the internal distributions shift to both extremes in old age, either to get poorer or to get richer!

The best way to avoid poverty in old age is to choose your grandparents carefully so they can leave you well fixed. The advice to the

poor to make wise investments is supercilious and unfeeling. The way
to avoid poverty for the rich is to get regular funds because you are a
member of the family. The best support for the poor is to avoid privation
by a national policy which provides support on the same basis, because
people are a part of a "national family"; that is, they belong to the
society. Obviously neither has earned it on any other basis than that
they belong.

For the people in the middle (who will be considered the average
people) there is an opportunity for some savings and some investments;
although in the face of inflation even this is threatened.

Remember, no one works for a living all his life: only in the most
backward of countries are a five year old and an eighty year old expected
to be self-supporting! In our society we expect that our earnings in our
working lifetime shall support us before it begins and after it is over. All
are treated equally in this respect.

Dr. Donald O. Cowgill. By current standards, about 14 percent of
people over age sixty-five are poor. There is no one way for an individual
to avoid poverty in old age; there are many different ways. Furthermore, the answers are somewhat different depending upon the type of
society one is living in. If you are living in a competitive, dog-eat-dog
society in which each individual entirely on his own has to provide for
his own security in old age, and fortunately such a society has never
really existed, then you had better start with healthy ancestors, preferably rich, work like the devil, save a sizable proportion of what you
make—say one-third—invest it wisely, keep healthy and hope nothing
happens to wipe you out, such as depression or inflation. In other
words, be lucky. If you are fortunate enough to live in a society in which
the government is committed to promoting the general welfare, including the welfare of its elderly, one which is affluent enough and far-
sighted enough to have provided for an adequate Social Security system,
your chances are much better.

M. Gene Handelsman. The Bureau of Census estimates revealed that
15 percent of 3,584,000 persons age sixty-five and over had incomes
below the poverty threshold in 1979.

There are a number of ways an average person can prepare for old
age, in terms of income. For example:

1. Maintain a savings of some kind—U.S. Savings Bond, passbook
    account, money market certificates, etc., or a combination of such
    savings.
2. Invest in property which can be converted into cash when income
    is needed.
3. Purchase an adequate inventory of household goods and furnish-
    ings during younger working years.

4. Try to maintain reasonably good health. This is the key to continued employment after retirement age.

Erdman B. Palmore, Ph.D. About 15 percent of people over sixty-five are poor according to the federal definitions of poverty. This is down from about 30 percent in 1960.

The best ways for average people to avoid poverty in their old age is to: (1) invest in a home or other real estate which will increase in value with the cost of living; (2) invest in a good pension or retirement fund to supplement their Social Security benefits; (3) develop some skill, service or business through which they can work part-time to supplement their retirement benefits; (4) get a good medical insurance policy to supplement Medicare to prevent being wiped out by the costs of illness.

John A. Reinecke, Ph.D. According to the Social Security Administration and Census Bureau definition of poverty about 16 to 17 percent of persons over sixty-five were poor in 1979. This classification may be somewhat suspect in rural areas where income is difficult to measure. There is also room for argument on the whole question of dollar income measures, considering all those things other than income which affect the quality of life.

Changes in the percentage of those with below-poverty-line income levels depend largely on several factors: changes in the way that the Social Security escalator clause works, changes in the allowable earnings provision and the general pattern of work after sixty-five. The latter has been changed and is changing because of the raising of the compulsory retirement age from sixty-five to seventy.

For most people, to avoid poverty in old age requires planning. This includes systematic savings, wise investment, making maximum use of the owned home if any, sharing living expenses with others if possible, and above all, staying healthy. Often older people live alone in a large home, the value of which could be put to better use. Often, large sums are left in 5 to 6 percent savings accounts. Often jewelry, silver and other valuables are held as a safety factor or to leave to heirs, even though, if liquidated wisely, they could relieve the poverty or near-poverty of many. The same is true of insurance policies and other assets, the value of which could be spent in later years to make life easier.

James H. Schulz. Assessing income adequacy necessitates standards that are relative. As observed by a 1976 task force of government experts on measuring poverty, "Poor persons living in the United States in the 1970s are rich in contrast to their counterparts in other times and places." The focus today in retirement planning is to maintain living standards in retirement. Following their departure from the labor force, older persons are faced with the prospect of expenditure needs that do not decrease as much as many would like to believe. Retirees need income equal to 60 to 80 percent of their average, pre-tax income just prior to retirement to avoid a drop in retirement living standards.

A 1979 study by the Social Security Administration found that about 85 percent of couples that began receiving Social Security benefits in 1973–74 received a benefit below the 60 to 80 percent level. For about 30 to 40 percent, Social Security benefits were so low that without other income, living standards would have dropped dramatically. If data were available for more recent years, it is unlikely that the situation would be much different.

One key to adequate retirement income is supplemental income from another pension. The Social Security Administration study found that things were better for couples with additional income from a public employee or private pension benefit. About half of these couples had total pension income high enough to enjoy a living standard close to their preretirement situation.

The most disadvantaged situation in retirement occurs as a result of widowhood. Because of differences in life expectancies between men and women, most women can expect to become widows during their lifetime—especially during later life. Social Security income drops sharply when a spouse dies. Typically, private pension income also drops and sometimes ceases entirely. Thus, income that was barely adequate becomes inadequate when a death occurs.

To avoid serious economic problems in retirement, then, one cannot rely on Social Security alone, one must seek adequate survivor protection. It is helpful to seek additional group coverage under a good private pension plan. But investing deferred wages in a private pension does not guarantee a good return in retirement. Benefits can be lost by frequent job changes or lack of adjustment for inflation. Moreover, private plan benefits are often minimal; plans pay only what is promised, not necessarily what is needed for adequate retirement living.

One should take an active role in planning for retirement, and this should begin many years before leaving regular employment is contemplated. Realistically assessing the probable level of retirement income and developing a savings program to meet retirement income goals may require assistance from retirement planning professionals; such planning is complex and difficult to carry out. Often employers, however, have people in the personnel office who can help or, alternatively, provide formal preretirement education programs.

Whether we like it or not, planning for retirement begins for most of us quite early in life.

Richard E. Shepherd. It is difficult to set a standard for poverty. Only ten years ago, an income of $10,000 could afford an average, comfortable standard of living. Today, that's no longer true.

The President's Commission on Pension Policy concluded in 1980 that

Americans over age sixty-five are doing well because a study showed that four-fifths of those over sixty-five own their own home, and four-fifths of these are mortgage-free. But the study did not reflect how many of these people are "house-poor." Inflation increases the value of their homes (in other words, their assets) but upkeep, utilities and taxes are also rising.

A 1980 study by the National Council on Aging reflects a different picture, which is also mirrored by a study conducted by Research & Forecast, Inc., for Americana Healthcare Corporation.

These studies show that of people who are older than sixty, nearly six persons out of ten feel they live a hand-to-mouth existence and they suffer from economic stress.

The only way to avoid economic stress or even poverty in old age is to start planning for retirement years some twenty years ahead of time, and, in case of married couples, both partners need to take an active interest in financial planning.

INDEX

INDEX